ANDREW BURKE
AUSTIN BUSH

BANGKOK
CITY GUIDE

INTRODUCING BANGKOK

The mesmerising spires of Wat Pho (p69)

Same same, but different. It's Thailish T-shirt philosophy that neatly sums up Bangkok, a city where the tastes of many places are mixed into an exotic, often-spicy dish that is never, ever boring.

It's the contradictions that give the City of Angels its rich, multifaceted personality. Scratch the surface and you'll find a city of climate-controlled megamalls and international brand names just minutes from 200-year-old village homes; of gold-spired Buddhist temples sharing space with neon-lit strips of sleaze; of slow-moving rivers of traffic bypassed by longtail boats plying the royal river; and of streets lined with food carts selling Thai classics for next to nothing, overlooked by restaurants on top of skyscrapers serving exotic cocktails.

If all this sounds dizzying, rest assured that despite its international flavour Bangkok remains resolutely Thai. The capital's cultural underpinnings are evident in virtually all facets of everyday life, and most enjoyably through the Thai sense of *sà·nùk*, loosely translated as 'fun'. In Thailand anything worth doing – even work – should have an element of *sà·nùk*. Whether you're ordering food, changing money or haggling at the vast Chatuchak Weekend Market, it will usually involve a sense of playfulness – a dash of flirtation, perhaps, and a smile.

With so much of life conducted on the street, there are few cities in the world that reward exploration as well as Bangkok. By day, a stroll off the beaten track, led by the flavours of lunch, can wind up in conversation with a monk. And after dark, the local bar and music scene reveals a city much more sophisticated and dynamic than you might expect. Come check it out for yourself.

BANGKOK LIFE

With almost half of Thailand's urban population squeezed into the capital, it's no surprise that city life in Bangkok is a fast-changing affair. Yes, there are old neighbourhoods where you can feel like you're in the 1950s. But even these areas are usually juxtaposed with some icon of Bangkok's dynamic alter-ego – a glass tower or condo rising beside a *klorng* (canal), a raised freeway or Skytrain looming noisily over ageing wooden houses, or a counter-culture bar spilling young hipsters into neighbourhoods that have been virtually unchanged for decades.

Despite all this manic energy, Thai society remains deeply conservative. Ironically, in a city with a worldwide reputation for sleaze, politicians and media are never far from a 'social order' campaign that sees bars closed at midnight and calls for the drinking age to be raised to 25.

Such contrasts have rarely been as evident as in recent years, when the capital has been divided along colour lines and passions have boiled over into violence. In one corner are the so-called yellow shirts, representing Bangkok's old establishment and marketing themselves as protectors of the monarchy. In the other corner are the red shirts, a group originally made up largely of supporters of ex–prime minister Thaksin Shinawatra's side of politics but which has gained broader popularity among those disenchanted with the established status quo.

Red–yellow issues are the basis of much conversation in Bangkok, but even during the most dramatic, violent moments of recent years most Bangkokians just go about their daily routines as if nothing untoward is happening. Few Thais have much faith in politics anymore, and the only institution still widely respected is their beloved king. It is his waning health – and the uncertainty around what will happen when he's gone – that inspires most interest.

Earthbound traffic remains a time-consuming hassle for most Bangkokians. The city has too many cars for the available roads and during peak hours the Thai idea of *jai yen* (cool heart) – remaining unperturbed even in the most trying situations – is tested to the full. Mercifully there are ambitious plans to expand the Metro and Skytrain systems and finally turn Bangkok into the 'world city' its promoters so desperately want it to be. Funding, however, has not only been affected by the global financial crisis but also locked up by the ongoing political instability, so Bangkokians are not holding their breath waiting for free-flowing traffic.

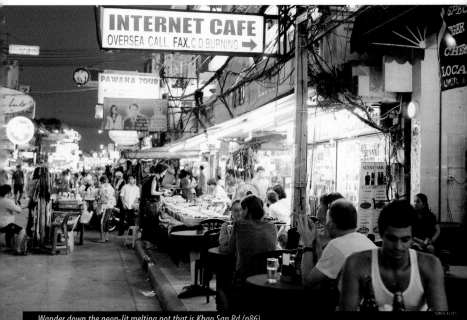

Wander down the neon-lit melting pot that is Khao San Rd (p86)

HIGHLIGHTS

MICK ELMORE

'OLD BANGKOK'

Bangkok's oldest districts, Ko Ratanakosin and Banglamphu, combine must-see sights with a vibrant community of long-time residents and hip new arrivals running counter-culture bars and cool boutiques.

KIMBERLEY COOLE

TOM COCKREM

RICHARD CUMMINS

1 Amulet Market
Invest in some Karmic insurance with an amulet or two (p136)

2 Dusit Park
Admire the sublime combination of Victorian style and Thai sensibilities in this royal enclave (p94)

3 Wat Pho (Reclining Buddha)
Gaze at the 46m-long Reclining Buddha, then submit yourself to an expert massage (p69)

4 Shrines & Spirit Houses
Learn that Thai spirituality is about more than just the Buddha (p107)

5 Phra Sumen Fort
Absorb the history of this original 18th-century fort (p87)

6 Grand Palace
Risk colour overload at Bangkok's original royal palace (p67)

7 Banglamphu
Meander through shophouses and temples as you explore this historic district (p80)

8 Chinatown
Wander through one of the world's last real Chinatowns (p97)

TOM COCKREM

AUSTIN BUSH

RICHARD I'ANSON

THE ROYAL RIVER – MAE NAM CHAO PHRAYA

Winding through Bangkok like a lazy serpent, the royal river is both the city's heart and its soul. The mix of working boats, speeding boats and people fishing, looking and even swimming make it endlessly watchable.

RICHARD I'ANSON

FRANK CARTER

❶ Longtail Boats
Get out on the river and into the fast lane (p278)

❷ Ferry Rides
Sit back and enjoy Bangkok's serene, graceful side (p263)

❸ Royal Barges
Find out how many men and drummers it takes to crew these ornate royal vessels (p78)

❹ River Life
Watch kids leap in; don't be tempted to join them

❺ Riverside Dining
Treat your tastebuds while enjoying river views (p169)

AUSTIN BUSH

GREG ELMS

❶ Siam Paragon
Shop for genuine articles at a mall that's the genuine article (p143)

❷ Chatuchak Weekend Market
Fight off consumer euphoria at one of Asia's biggest flea markets (p148)

❸ Vespa Market
Spend Saturday night shopping for parts with Bangkok's counter-culture kids (p150)

❹ Wet Markets
Animal, vegetable and mineral as you'll never see them sold at home (p146)

AUSTIN BUSH

MARKETS & MALLS

Bangkok is a shopper's paradise with stores to satisfy every desire. The fascinating Asian wet markets remain, and are now complemented by vast outdoor flea markets and plush megamalls.

AUSTIN BUSH

AUSTIN BUSH

ARTS, DESIGN & FASHION

As a regional hub for art, design and fashion, Bangkok supports dozens of galleries and countless artists. Fashionistas should prepare to be pleasantly surprised by what Thai designers have to offer.

AUSTIN BUSH

❶ Bangkok Art & Culture Centre
See what's showing at this impressive multi-purpose art centre (p199)

❷ Galleries
Find something unexpected in Bangkok's eclectic mix of art galleries (p199)

❸ Fashion
Try on the latest fashions in one of the city's chic boutiques (p143)

❹ Design
Appreciate Thai design, whether on display in a gallery or at the market (p129)

AUSTIN BUSH

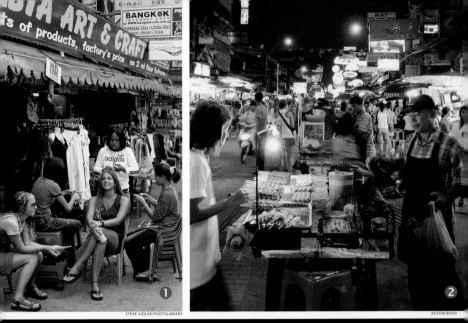

STEVE VIDLER/PHOTOLIBRARY   AUSTIN BUSH

KHAO SAN ROAD

The hub from which a million backpackers have launched themselves into Southeast Asia, Th Khao San (p86) is a unique melting pot of travellers from around the world. And with a bunch of new bars, restaurants and cafes, it now has plenty of Thai spice, too.

PKP/IMAGEBROKER

KEVIN FOY/ALAMY

❶ Beads & Braids
The real Thailand or could it only happen in Thailand?

❷ Khao San at Night
Feel like you're at a festival on the street where every night is a Saturday night

❸ VW Van Bars
Is that a van or a bar, or both?

❹ Songkran
Bring in the new year Thai-style – wet, wet, wet (p21)

❺ Banglamphu Pub Crawl
Do as the Bangkok hipsters do – be seen out in Banglamphu (p186)

1

6

5

2

BANGKOK AFTER DARK

The City of Angels is probably most famous (or infamous) for its after-hours action, but there's more to it than just skin shows. Think sunset cocktails atop skyscrapers, romantic dinners in fine restaurants, cool alternative bars and clubs, and moo·ay tai *fight nights.*

❶ Moon Bar
Drink in the sunset from the roof of a skyscraper (p184)

❷ Moo·ay Tai
Soak up the action and atmosphere of Bangkok's liveliest fight club (p208)

❸ D'Sens
Dining in Bangkok can be very fine indeed – Michelin-star fine (p168)

❹ Live Music
Jazz things up with a night out at a hip live-music venue (p187)

❺ Bed Supperclub
Eat, drink and dance in this space-age club-cum-restaurant (p192)

❻ Clubbing
Step out with the Thai hi-sos at one of Bangkok's super-duper clubs (p191)

❼ Silom Soi 4
Dance the night away in the gay-friendly Soi 4 (p188)

3

4

BILL WASSMAN

EXCURSIONS

Recover from your big city exertions with an excursion. Within three hours of downtown Bangkok are photogenic floating markets, palm-fringed beaches, the old Siamese capital and one of Thailand's best national parks.

PETER PTSCHELINZEW

RICHARD NEBESKY

PAOLO CORDELLI

1 Kanchanaburi
Cross the infamous Death Railway Bridge (p253)

2 Floating Markets
Experience the Bangkok of yore (p245)

3 Ko Samet
Enjoy idyllic beaches just a couple of hours from Bangkok (p241)

4 Ayuthaya
Explore the remains of this ancient capital (p236)

5 Khao Yai National Park
Search the jungle for wildlife and finish with some Thai wine (p257)

BANGKOK'S BEST DISHES

The flavours of Bangkok are a balanced combination of sweet, spicy, salty and sour. Indigenous ingredients such as coconut cream and fish sauce play a strong role, while the cuisines of China and India have also had palpable influences.

AUSTIN BUSH

AUSTIN BUSH

❶ Kà·nǒm bêu·ang
The old-school version of these tacolike snacks comes in two varieties, sweet and savoury. Sample the best of both worlds at Khanom Beuang Phraeng Nara (p163).

❷ Ráhn kôw gaang
'Rice and curry shops' serve a variety of prepared Central Thai–style dishes. Khrua Aroy Aroy (p171) and the stalls at Or Tor Kor Market (p177) are solid examples of the genre.

❸ Mèe gròrp
Crispy noodles made the old-school way are a dying breed. The best place to sample them is the tiny shophouse restaurant Chote Chitr (p163).

❹ Pàt tai
Thin rice noodles fried with egg, shrimp and characteristically Thai seasonings is a dish known far beyond the country's borders. Sample Bangkok's most famous *pàt tai* at Thip Samai (p162).

AUSTIN BUSH

13

KNOW YOUR NOODLE

Noodles are probably the most ubiquitous and diverse dish in Bangkok. A snack or a meal, the city's residents stop for gŏo·ay đĕe·o (noodles) at any time of day or night. To help you out in this jungle of stringy eats, we've put together a basic guide to Bangkok's most common noodles and noodle dishes.

PHOTOGRAPHS BY AUSTIN BUSH

❶ Sên lék These thin rice noodles are the most popular variety of Thai noodle. Served with a huge variety of soup-based noodle dishes, but go particularly well with gŏo·ay đĕe·o reu·a, 'boat noodles' (below).

❷ Sên yài In addition to being served in a variety of noodle soups, these wide rice noodles are also fried with pork, egg and Chinese kale in pat see·éw. They're particularly good with yen đah foh (below).

❸ Kà·nŏm jeen Possibly the only noodle indigenous to Southeast Asia, these fresh rice noodles are made via an extremely labour-intensive and time-consuming process. They are served with several varieties of mild curries and sides of fresh and pickled vegetables and herbs.

❹ Bà·mèe Chinese-style wheat and egg noodles are typically served with slices of barbecued pork, a handful of greens and/or wontons.

❺ Yen đah foh Combining a slightly sweet crimson-colour broth with a variety of meat balls, cubes of blood and crispy greens, yen đah foh is probably both the most intimidating and popular noodle dish in Bangkok.

❻ Gŏo·ay đĕe·o reu·a Known as boat noodles because they were previously served from the canals of central Thailand, these intense pork- or beef-based bowls are among the most full-flavoured of Thai noodle dishes.

❼ Lôok chín Thai-style meat balls, a common ingredient in Thai-style noodle dishes, are predominantly made from pork, but fish and beef are also available.

❽ Bà·mèe hâang A variation on bà·mèe, in this version the wheat noodles are served 'dry,' with just enough broth to keep them moist.

❾ Krêu·ang brung You can recognise a noodle shop simply by the tabletop jars of noodle condiments, which include fish sauce, sugar, dried chilli flakes and, where bà·mèe is served, sliced fresh chillies in vinegar and chopped peanuts.

❶ Kà·nǔn Jackfruit hails from India. The green pod conceals dozens of waxy yellow sections that taste like a blend of pineapple and bananas (it reminds us of Juicy Fruit chewing gum). At its peak from January to May.

❷ Tú·ree·an Due to its intense odour and weaponlike appearance, the durian is possibly Southeast Asia's most infamous fruit, the flesh of which can suggest everything from custard to onions. Available from May to August.

❸ Lín·jèe The pink skin of the lychee conceals an addictive translucent flesh similar in flavour to a grape. Available from April to June.

❹ Ngó Known in English as rambutan, *ngó* has a tough hairy skin (*rambut* is the Malay word for hair) that holds a clear, sweet-tasting flesh and a large pit. Available from May to September.

RICHARD I'ANSON

HAVE A FRUITY TIME

One of the culinary highlights of Thailand is the huge variety of tropical fruit, many of which are still not available at home. You'll most likely come across these fruits in Bangkok's fresh markets and supermarkets.

PHOTOGRAPHS BY AUSTIN BUSH

❺ Lam yai This indigenous fruit, known in English as longan, hides a sweet and fragrant flesh under its brittle shell. Often dried and used in juices or as a snack. Available from June to August.

❻ Má·feuang An import from the Americas, the starfruit or carambola is refreshingly crispy and slightly tart. Available from October to December.

❼ Chom·pôo Resembling a small pear, the indigenous rose apple is a delicate and crispy fruit with a slightly bitter flavour and a mild rose scent. Available from February to June.

❽ Nóy nàh Known in English as custard apple, this native of the Americas has a soft and slightly gritty texture and predominantly sweet flavour. Available from June to September.

❾ Mang·kút Known as mangosteen in English, the thick purple skin of this Queen of Fruit conceals a creamy white flesh that is equal parts rich and tangy. Available from May to October.

❿ Sôm oh The flesh of this indigenous fruit, known in English as pomelo, comes in large sections and is generally sweeter than the grapefruit it resembles. Available August to November.

AUSTIN BUSH

AUSTIN BUSH

STREET FOOD

Bangkok is justifiably renowned for its street food, and it's entirely possible to go several days and several meals without ever setting foot in a proper restaurant. Keep in mind that street vendors take a day off on Monday.

AUSTIN BUSH

❶ Kôw kǎh mǒo
Chinese in origin, braised pork leg served over rice, often with a side of greens and a hard-boiled egg, is the epitome of a one-dish meal. Several vendors in the Banglamphu area (p160) specialise in the dish.

❷ Chinatown & Thanon Silom
Come lunchtime, the best 'hood for street eats is on and around Th Silom (p168). After dark, move over to Th Yaowarat, Bangkok's China-town (p165).

❸ Sà·đé
Grilled skewers of pork or chicken served with a sweet dipping sauce just don't taste the same when eaten indoors. The street stalls of China-town (p165) are a good place to find them.

❹ Sôm·đam
Strips of green papaya bruised in a mortar and pestle hail from Thailand's northeast, but have been fully adopted by the streets of Bangkok. To sample the dish, head to the Th Silom area during lunch (p168).

❺ Roh·đee
This crispy fried pancake, drizzled with con-densed milk and sugar, is the perfect street dessert. Get yours in the Th Silom area (p168).

16

CONTENTS

THE AUTHORS

Andrew Burke

Andrew has been coming to Bangkok for long enough that he can remember Th Khao San with barely any neon and Sukhumvit traffic before the Skytrain (not a good memory). Since then he's spent more than 15 years travelling through, photographing and writing about Asia, the Middle East and Africa, and the last 10 living in Hong Kong, Phnom Penh and the manic megalopolis that is Bangkok. Andrew has written or contributed to more than 20 books for Lonely Planet, and writes and shoots photographs for newspapers and magazines including the *Australian Financial Review, Travel + Leisure Southeast Asia* and *National Geographic Traveller,* and does occasional TV reporting for Channel 4 UK and CNN.

ANDREW'S TOP BANGKOK DAY

My ideal day in the City of Angels would start early. Packing my camera, I'd wander up to the Skytrain (p266) for a treetop view of the city waking as I'm whooshed down to the river. I love the Mae Nam Chao Phraya at any time, but this artery of Bangkok life is at its most seductive at this hour, with barges, ferries and longtails criss-crossing the river as the city's dull thud grows into a roar.

My destination is Chinatown (p97). I'll take the Chao Phraya Express ferry (p263) up to Tha Saphan Phut and start wandering (p101). Chinatown's warren of lanes are an explorer's dream, and reward the 'I-wonder-what's-around-that-corner' attitude. After squeezing through Trok Itsaranuphap (Talat Mai), I'll eat breakfast at whichever street stall takes my fancy, and continue south towards Talat Noi.

I'll enjoy a refreshing river-ferry ride up to Wang Lang, then take the cross-river ferry to Tha Hua Chang, where I'll eat lunch with the navy wives in Rachanawi Samosorn (p160) before getting the camera out and delving into the amulet market (p136). I'll wander south along Th Maharat to Wat Pho and a massage (any ideal day in Bangkok must have a massage; p205). It's late afternoon by now so must be time for a drink at The Deck (p160), where the sunset views over Wat Arun are sublime. Friends will join me for dinner here before we head up to Banglamphu (p160) for a couple more drinks along Th Phra Athit and Th Samsen (p186). A top day indeed.

Austin Bush

After graduating from the University of Oregon with a degree in linguistics, Austin received a scholarship to study Thai at Chiang Mai University and has remained in Thailand ever since. After working several years at a stable job, he made the questionable decision to pursue a career as a freelance photographer/writer. This choice has since taken him as far as northern Pakistan and as near as Bangkok's Or Tor Kor Market. He enjoys writing and taking photos about food most of all because it's delicious. His work can be seen at www.austinbushphotography.com.

The legendary traffic notwithstanding, Bangkok is an easy place to travel and – assuming you avoid protests by people in coloured shirts – one of the safest cities in Asia. Transport is cheap and fairly efficient, enough people speak English to help you out and there are hundreds of hotels (p212) and restaurants (p152) catering to any budget. Bangkok is well wired so it's easy to research most lodgings and events online.

WHEN TO GO

The 'City of Angels' has three distinct seasons: the hot season runs from March to May or June, followed by the rainy season until November, and the cool season from November until the end of February. With its low humidity, relatively low temperatures and clear skies, the cool season is the best time to visit, though regular days of high 20s and low 30s might leave you wondering just who came up with the term 'cool'. The hot season vivifies the famous Noel Coward verse: 'In Bangkok at twelve o'clock they foam at the mouth and run, But mad dogs and Englishmen go out in the midday sun.' The fresh winds from February to April are a relief, but May is deadly. The monsoon season brings rain almost daily, but it's rare that it will rain all day and it's often limited to a short, refreshing afternoon downpour. For more on Bangkok's climate, see p269.

Not surprisingly, Bangkok's peak tourist season is during the cool season, with a secondary peak during July and August. If your main objective is to avoid crowds and to take advantage of discounted rooms and low-season rates, come during April to June and September and October.

FESTIVALS

Thais love little more than a festival full of sà·nùk (fun) and Bangkok is host to an eclectic mix, from Buddhist celebrations to jazz events and festivals of food. Dates and venues often vary from year to year because the festival adheres to the lunar calendar, organisers aren't organised enough or local authorities change festival days. Which means you'll often have to wait until the festival is only months or even weeks away before exact dates and locations are available. That said, wherever dates have been available we have included them here. The Tourism Authority of Thailand (www.tourism thailand.org) features major festivals and events.

On Buddhist holidays it's illegal to sell alcohol so bars stay closed. For a list of public holidays, see p273. For a lunar calendar, see http://kalender-365.de/lunar-calendar.php.

January & February

CHINESE NEW YEAR
3–5 Feb 2011, 23–25 Jan 2012

Some time from late January to late February, Bangkok's large Thai-Chinese population celebrate their lunar new year, called đrùt jeen in Thai, with a week full of house cleaning, lion dances and fireworks. The most impressive festivities, unsurprisingly, take place in Chinatown.

MAKHA BUCHA

Makha Bucha is held on the full moon of the third lunar month (late February to early March) to commemorate the Buddha preaching to 1250 enlightened monks who came to hear him 'without prior summons'. The festival culminates with a candlelit walk around the main chapel at every wát.

March

BANGKOK INTERNATIONAL FASHION WEEK
www.thaicatwalk.com

Thai designers show their work in this trade fair that is busy with catwalk shows and parties, usually in mid-March. If you want a seat but don't have a ticket, be sure to look the part.

KITE FLYING SEASON

During the windy season from the middle of February to early April colourful kites battle it out over the skies of Sanam Luang and Lumphini Park. The Thailand International Kite Festival is held at this time every second year; next in 2012.

WORLD THAI MARTIAL ARTS FESTIVAL
Ayuthaya (p236)
Week-long *moo·ay tai* (also spelt *muay thai*) festival in mid-March with a spiritual aspect, the ancient Waikru Muay Thai ceremony.

April

SONGKRAN
13–15 Apr

Songkran is the celebration of the Thai New Year. Those Bangkokians who don't head home for the holiday observe traditional rites such as Buddha images being 'bathed' and monks and elders receiving the respect of younger Thais through the sprinkling of water over their hands. Travellers tend to become thoroughly immersed in one mega-waterfight or another. The biggest are organised shows at Th Khao San and Patpong, where you can arm yourself with a high-calibre water gun and go beserk. Don't carry anything you don't want to get wet.

May & June

ROYAL PLOUGHING CEREMONY
Sanam Luang (Map p68)

To kick off the official rice-planting season in early May, either the king or the crown prince presides over this ancient Brahman ritual that culminates in sacred white oxen ploughing the earth and priests declaring it a good or bad year for farmers. Thousands of farmers from across Thailand gather to watch.

VISAKHA BUCHA
17 May 2011, 4 Jun 2012

Visakha Bucha, on the full moon of the 6th lunar month, is considered the date of the Buddha's birth, enlightenment and *parinibbana* (passing away). Activities are centred on the local wát, with candlelit processions, chanting and sermonising; a larger festival is held at Sanam Luang.

July & August

ASANHA BUCHA & KHAO PHANSA
15 & 16 Jul 2011, 2 & 3 Aug 2012

This Buddhist festival, on the full moon of the 8th lunar month, commemorates the day the Buddha preached his first sermon after attaining enlightenment and is marked at Theravada Buddhist

temples with a candlelit procession at night. The following day is *kôw pan·säh*, the beginning of the Buddhist rains retreat when young men traditionally enter the monkhood for the rainy season, and all monks sequest themselves in a monastery for three months. It's a good time to observe a Buddhist ordination.

BANGKOK INTERNATIONAL FILM FESTIVAL
www.bangkokfilm.org

Dates and venues are notoriously fickle for Bangkok's two film festivals, but this one usually runs for 10 days and was most recently held in late August. Screenings were primarily at Paragon Cineplex (p199). About 150 films are shown, with an emphasis on Asian cinema. Events end with the awarding of the festival's Golden Kinnaree. For popular films, book ahead.

September

INTERNATIONAL FESTIVAL OF DANCE & MUSIC
www.bangkokfestivals.com

Usually held at the Thailand Cultural Centre (p197), this month-long festival presents international and local orchestral music, jazz, ballet, opera and world music.

THAILAND INTERNATIONAL SWAN BOAT RACES
www.thailandgrandfestival.com

More than 20 international teams race traditional Thai-style long boats in various classes (the largest has 55 paddlers) along Mae Nam Chao Phraya in Ayuthaya.

October

WORLD GOURMET FESTIVAL
www.fourseasons.com/bangkok

The Four Seasons Hotel (p219) hosts Bangkok's premier food event, bringing together international chefs for a 10-day feast.

NAVARATRI HINDU FESTIVAL
Starts 8 Oct 2010, 28 Sep 2011, 16 Oct 2012

Centred on the Sri Mariamman Temple (p119) on Th Silom, this nine-day Hindu festival sees Th Silom pedestrianised as men worship shrines and pierce themselves before smashing coconuts on the sidewalks. Attendees should wear white.

VEGETARIAN FESTIVAL

During the first nine days of the ninth lunar month, this Chinese-Buddhist festival, *têt·sà·gahn gin jair*, sees streetside vendors serving meatless meals to help cleanse the body, all announced with yellow banners and white clothes. Most of the action is in Chinatown.

BANGKOK DESIGN FESTIVAL

www.bangkokdesignfestival.com
Ten days of events, exhibitions, lectures and workshops are held at the Bangkok Art and Culture Centre (p199) and other 'hip places'. Each year has a theme; 2009's was 'Balancing the Future: Innovation, Creativity and Sustainability'.

KING CHULALONGKORN DAY   23 Oct

Rama V is honoured on the anniversary of his death at his revered Royal Plaza statue. Crowds of devotees come to make merit with incense and flower garlands.

WORLD FILM FESTIVAL

www.worldfilmbkk.com
Bangkok's other, less commercial film festival, usually held from late October to early November.

November

LOI KRATHONG   21 Nov 2010, 10 Nov 2011, 28 Nov 2012

www.bangkoktourist.com
On the night of the full moon of the 12th lunar month, small lotus-shaped *grà·tong* (baskets or boats made of a section of banana trunk for flotation, banana leaves, flowers, incense, candles and a coin – don't use the styrofoam versions) are floated on Mae Nam Chao Phraya and other rivers, lakes and canals across Thailand. The ceremony, which originated in Sukhothai, is both an offering to the water spirits and a symbolic cleansing of bad luck.

WAT SAKET FAIR

The grandest of Bangkok's temple fairs *(ngahn wát)* is held at Wat Saket and the Golden Mount (p80) around Loi Krathong. The temple grounds turn into a colourful, noisy fair selling flowers, incense, bells and saffron cloth and tonnes of Thai food. The highlight is a candlelit circumambulation on the mount.

BANGKOK PRIDE WEEK

www.bangkokpride.org
Usually in mid-November, this week-long festival of parades, parties, awards, sequins and feather boas is organised by city businesses and organisations for Bangkok's gay, lesbian, bisexual and transgender community. Don't miss the opening 'Pink in the Park' fair in Lumphini Park (p120).

FAT FESTIVAL

www.fatdegree.com
Sponsored by FAT 104.5FM radio, Bangkok's premier indie music festival has grown to include everything from pop to thrash via hip-hop, plus nonmusic alternative arts. It's usually on the first or second weekend in November, at Muang Thong Thani.

December

KING'S BIRTHDAY   5 Dec

Celebrating King Bhumibol's birthday, the city is festooned with lights and large portraits of the king (especially on Th Ratchadamnoen). In the afternoon, Sanam Luang is packed for a fireworks display that segues appropriately into a noisy concert with popular Thai musicians.

BANGKOK JAZZ FESTIVAL

www.bangkokjazzfestival.com
Started in 2003, this jazz fest kicks off at Sanam Suea Pa at Dusit in commemoration of His Majesty the King's love of jazz. The line-up usually includes internationally known artists and focuses on the lighter side of jazz, per Thai public taste.

HOW MUCH?

Skytrain ride 15–40B

Chao Phraya Express boat ride 10–34B

3km taxi ride 50–100B, depending on traffic

640ml Singha beer from bar 60–120B

1L petrol 34B

500ml/1.5L bottle water 7/15B

Pàt tai 25–40B

Cup of coffee 40–80B

One-hour traditional Thai massage 300–3000B

Souvenir T-shirt 100–250B

CONCERT IN THE PARK
www.bangkoksymphony.org/concertinpark
Free concerts from the Bangkok Symphony Orchestra are performed Sunday evenings (from 5.30pm to 7.30pm) between mid-December and mid-February at Lumphini Park (p120).

PHRA NAKHON SI AYUTHAYA WORLD HERITAGE FAIR
Ayuthaya (p236)
A series of cultural performances and evening sound-and-light shows among the ruins of the World Heritage site in the former Thai capital.

COSTS & MONEY
Bangkok is inexpensive by Western standards but you can still burn through a lot of baht if you choose. On the tightest of budgets you could scrape by on about 700B a day, staying in the simplest guesthouse accommodation, eating mainly street food, seeing a sight or two, taking local transport and drinking horrible Chang beer from 7-Elevens. With closer to 2500B you can creep into the comforts of the midrange and afford a decent meal, and with 3500B you can enjoy a dash of style, a decent restaurant meal and perhaps a rooftop cocktail or two. If you plan on frequenting the city's best hotels, restaurants and clubs you're looking at more than 5000B a day. These numbers are for solo travellers, and per person costs fall if you're travelling as a couple.

Getting your hands on Thai baht is easy enough through the city's thousands of ATMs. Credit cards are widely accepted; see p277.

INTERNET RESOURCES
Take a look at these websites to help plan your trip. For a list of blogs on Bangkok, see p58.

Bangkok Recorder (www.bangkokrecorder.com) For what's on, mainly in bars and clubs.

Bangkok Scams (www.bangkokscams.com) Don't be greedy, don't get scammed.

Bangkok Tourist (www.bangkoktourist.com) City-run site with enough Bangkok sights for a lifetime of sightseeing.

Lonely Planet (www.lonelyplanet.com) Country-specific information as well as reader information-exchange on the Thorn Tree forum.

Real Thai Recipes (www.realthairecipes.com) Get a taste of what you'll find in Bangkok.

Thailand Daily (www.thailanddaily.com) Part of World News Network, offering a thorough digest of Thailand-related news in English.

Top 100 Thai Websites (www.click2thailand.com) What it says on the box – links to all sorts of interesting Thai websites.

Tourism Authority of Thailand (www.tourismthailand.org) Handy planning hints and events guide.

HISTORY

Since the late 18th century, the history of Bangkok has essentially been the history of Thailand. Many of the country's defining events have unfolded here, and today the language, culture and food of the city have come to represent those of the entire country. This role may once have seemed unlikely, given the city's origins as little more than an obscure Chinese trading port, but, today boasting a population of 10 million, Bangkok will certainly be shaping Thailand's history for some time to come.

FROM THE BEGINNING – AYUTHAYA & THONBURI

Before it became the capital of Thailand in 1782, the tiny settlement known as Bang Makok was merely a backwater village opposite the larger Thonburi Si Mahasamut on the banks of Mae Nam Chao Phraya, not far from the Gulf of Siam.

Thonburi Si Mahasamut itself had been founded on the right bank of Mae Nam Chao Phraya by a group of wealthy Thais during the reign of King Chakkaphat (1548–68) as an important relay point for sea- and river-borne trade between the Gulf of Siam and Ayuthaya, 86km upriver. Ayuthaya served as the royal capital of Siam – as Thailand was then known – from 1350 to 1767. Encircled by rivers with access to the gulf, Ayuthaya flourished as a river port courted by Dutch, Portuguese, French, English, Chinese and Japanese merchants. By the end of the 17th century the city's population had reached one million and Ayuthaya was one of the wealthiest and most powerful cities in Asia. Virtually all foreign visitors claimed it was the most illustrious city they had ever seen, beside which London and Paris paled in comparison.

Throughout four centuries of Ayuthaya reign, European powers tried without success to colonise the kingdom of Siam. An Asian power finally subdued the capital when the Burmese sacked Ayuthaya in 1767, destroying most of the great city's Buddhist temples and royal edifices.

Many Siamese were marched off to Pegu (Bago, Myanmar today), where they were forced to serve the Burmese court. However, the remaining Siamese regrouped under Phaya Taksin, a half-Chinese, half-Thai general who decided to move the capital further south along Mae Nam Chao Phraya, closer to the Gulf of Siam. Thonburi Si Mahasamut was a logical choice for the new capital.

Succumbing to mental illness, Taksin came to regard himself as the next Buddha, and his behaviour became increasingly violent and bizarre. Monks who refused to worship him as the Maitreya (the future Buddha) would be punished by flogging, for example. Disapproving of his religious fantasies and fearing the king had lost his mind, in 1782 his ministers deposed Taksin and executed him. His execution was in the custom reserved for royalty – sealing him inside a velvet sack to ensure no royal blood touched the ground, then beating him to death with a scented sandalwood club.

TIMELINE

1548–68	1768	1779
Thonburi Si Mahasamut, at the time little more than a Chinese trading post on the right bank of Mae Nam Chao Phraya, is founded.	King Taksin the Great moves the Thai capital from Ayuthaya to Thonburi Si Mahasamut, a location he regarded as beneficial for both trade and defence.	After a brutal war of territorial expansion, the Emerald Buddha, Thailand's most sacred Buddha image, is brought to Bangkok from Laos, along with hundreds of Lao slaves.

WHAT'S IN A NAME?

Upon completion of the royal district in 1785, at a three-day consecration ceremony attended by tens of thousands of Siamese, the capital of Siam was given a new name: 'Krungthep mahanakhon amonratanakosin mahintara ayuthaya mahadilok popnopparat ratchathani burirom udomratchaniwet mahasathan amonpiman avatansathit sakkathattiya witsanukamprasit'. This lexical gymnastic feat translates roughly as: 'Great City of Angels, the Repository of Divine Gems, the Great Land Unconquerable, the Grand and Prominent Realm, the Royal and Delightful Capital City full of Nine Noble Gems, the Highest Royal Dwelling and Grand Palace, the Divine Shelter and Living Place of Reincarnated Spirits'.

Understandably, foreign traders continued to call the capital Bang Makok, which eventually truncated itself to 'Bangkok', the name most commonly known to the outside world. These days all Thais understand 'Bangkok' but use a shortened version of the official name, Krung Thep (City of Angels). When referring to greater Bangkok, they talk about Krung Thep Mahanakhon (Metropolis of the City of Angels). Expats living in Bangkok have numerous nicknames for their adopted home, with the Big Mango being the most common.

The Chakri Dynasty & the Birth of Bangkok

One of Taksin's key generals, Phraya Chakri, came to power and was crowned in 1782 as Phraphutthayotfa. Fearing Thonburi to be vulnerable to Burmese attack from the west, Chakri moved the Siamese capital across the river to Bang Makok (Olive Plum riverbank), named for the trees that grew there in abundance. As the first monarch of the new Chakri royal dynasty – which continues to this day – Phraya Chakri was posthumously dubbed Rama I.

The first task set before the planners of the new city was to create hallowed ground for royal palaces and Buddhist monasteries. Astrologers divined that construction of the new royal palace should begin on 6 May 1782, and ceremonies consecrated Rama I's transfer to a temporary new residence a month later.

Construction of permanent throne halls, residence halls and palace temples followed.

The plan of the original buildings, their position relative to the river and the royal chapel, and the royal parade and cremation grounds to the north of the palace (today's Sanam Luang) exactly copied the royal compound at Ayuthaya. Master craftsmen who had survived the sacking of Ayuthaya created the designs for several of the more magnificent temples and royal administrative buildings in the new capital.

In time, Ayuthaya's control of tribute states in Laos and western Cambodia (including Angkor, ruled by the Siamese from 1432 to 1859) was transferred to Bangkok, and thousands of prisoners of war were brought to the capital to work. Bangkok also had ample access to free Thai labour via the *prâi lŏoang* (commoner/noble) system, under which all commoners were required to provide labour to the state in lieu of taxes.

Using this immense pool of labour, Rama I augmented Bangkok's natural canal-and-river system with hundreds of artificial waterways feeding into Thailand's hydraulic lifeline, the broad Mae Nam Chao Phraya. Rama I also ordered the construction of 10km of city walls and *klorng rôrp grung* (canals around the city) to create a royal 'island' – Ko Ratanakosin – between Mae Nam Chao Phraya and the canal loop. Sections of the 4.5m-thick walls still stand in Wat Saket and the Golden Mount, and water still flows, albeit sluggishly, in the canals of the original royal district.

1782	1785	1821
Rama I re-establishes the Siamese court across the river from Thonburi, resulting in the creation of both the current Thai capital and the Chakri dynasty.	The majority of the construction of Ko Ratanakosin, Bangkok's royal district, including famous landmarks such as the Grand Palace and Wat Phra Kaew, is finished.	A boatload of opium marks the visit of the first Western trader to Bangkok; the trade of this substance is eventually banned nearly 20 years later.

ALL THE KINGS' WOMEN

Until polygamy was outlawed by Rama VI (King Vajiravudh; r 1910–25), it was expected of Thai monarchs to maintain a harem consisting of numerous 'major' and 'minor' wives and the children of these relationships. This led to some truly 'extended' families: Rama I had 42 children by 28 mothers; Rama II (King Phraphutthaloetla Naphalai; r 1809–24), 73 children by 40 mothers; Rama III, 51 children by 37 mothers (he would eventually accumulate a total of 242 wives and consorts); Rama IV, 82 children by 35 mothers; and Rama V, 77 children by 40 mothers. In the case of Rama V, his seven 'major' wives were all half-sisters or first cousins, a conscious effort to maintain the purity of the bloodline of the Chakri dynasty. Other consorts or 'minor' wives were often the daughters of families wishing to gain greater ties with the royal family.

In contrast to the precedent set by his predecessors, Rama VI had one wife and one child, a girl born only a few hours before his death. As a result, his brother, Prajadhipok, was appointed as his successor. Rama VII also had only one wife and failed to produce any heirs. After abdicating in 1935 he did not exercise his right to appoint a successor, so lines were drawn back to Rama V, and the grandson of one of his remaining 'major' wives, nine-year-old Ananda Mahidol, was chosen to be the next king.

The break with Ayuthaya was ideological as well as temporal. As Rama I shared no bloodline with earlier royalty, he garnered loyalty by modelling himself as a Dhammaraja (dhamma king) supporting Buddhist law rather than a Devaraja (god king) linked to the divine.

Under the second and third reigns of the Chakri dynasty, more temples were built and the system of rivers, streams and natural canals surrounding the capital was augmented by the excavation of additional waterways. Water-borne traffic dominated the city, supplemented by a meagre network of footpaths, well into the middle of the 19th century.

Temple construction remained the highlight of early development in Bangkok until the reign of Rama III (King Phranangklao; r 1824–51), when attention turned to upgrading the port for international sea trade. The city soon became a regional centre for Chinese trading ships, slowly surpassing in importance even the British port at Singapore.

By the mid-19th century Western naval shipping technology had eclipsed the Chinese junk fleets. Bangkok's rulers began to feel threatened as the British and French made colonial inroads into Cambodia, Laos and Burma. This prompted the suspension of a great iron chain across Mae Nam Chao Phraya to guard against the entry of unauthorised ships.

Waterways & Roadways

During the reign of the first five Chakri kings, canal building constituted the lion's share of public-works projects, changing the natural geography of the city, and city planners added two lengthy canals to one of the river's largest natural curves. The canals Khlong Rop Krung (today's Khlong Banglamphu) and Khlong Ong Ang were constructed to create Ko Ratanakosin. The island quickly accumulated an impressive architectural portfolio centred on the Grand Palace, political hub of the new Siamese capital, and the adjacent royal monastery of Wat Phra Kaew.

Throughout the early history of the Chakri dynasty, royal administrations added to the system. Khlong Mahawawat was excavated during the reign of Rama IV (King Mongkut; r 1851–1868) to link Mae Nam Chao Phraya with Mae Nam Tha Chin, thus expanding the canal-and-river system by hundreds of kilometres. Lined with fruit orchards and stilted houses draped with

1851	1855	1868
Rama IV, the fourth king of the Chakri dynasty, comes to power, courts relations with the West and encourages the study of modern science in Thailand.	Bangkok, now Siam's major trading centre, begins to feel pressure from colonial influences; Rama IV signs the Bowring Treaty, which liberalises foreign trade in Thailand.	At the age of 15, Chulalongkorn, the oldest son of Rama IV, becomes the fifth king of the Chakri dynasty upon the death of his father.

fishing nets, Khlong Mahawawat remains one of the most traditional and least visited of the Bangkok canals.

Khlong Saen Saep was built to shorten travel between Mae Nam Chao Phraya and Mae Nam Bang Pakong, and today is heavily used by boat-taxi commuters moving across the city. Likewise, Khlong Sunak Hon and Khlong Damoen Saduak link up Tha Chin and Mae Klong. Khlong Prem Prachakon was dug purely to facilitate travel for Rama V between Bangkok and Ayuthaya, while Khlong Prawet Burirom shortened the distance between Samut Prakan and Chachoengsao provinces.

When Rama IV loosened Thai trade restrictions, many Western powers signed trade agreements with the monarch. He also sponsored Siam's second printing press and instituted educational reforms, developing a school system along European lines. Although the king courted the West, he did so with caution and warned his subjects: 'Whatever they have invented or done which we should know of and do, we can imitate and learn from them, but do not wholeheartedly believe in them.' Rama IV was the first monarch to show his face to the Thai public.

In 1861 Bangkok's European diplomats and merchants delivered a petition to Rama IV requesting roadways so that they could enjoy horse riding for physical fitness and pleasure. The royal government acquiesced, and established a handful of roads suitable for horse-drawn carriages and rickshaws. The first – and the most ambitious road project for nearly a century to come – was Th Charoen Krung (also known by its English name, New Rd), which extended 10km south from Wat Pho along the east bank of Mae Nam Chao Phraya. This swath of hand-laid cobblestone, which took nearly four years to finish, eventually accommodated a tramway as well as early automobiles.

Shortly thereafter, Rama IV ordered the construction of the much shorter Bamrung Meuang (a former elephant path) and Feuang Nakhon roads to provide access to royal temples from Charoen Krung. His successor Rama V (King Chulalongkorn; r 1868–1910) added the much wider Th Ratchadamnoen Klang to provide a suitably royal promenade – modelled after the Champs-Élysées and lined with ornamental gardens – between the Grand Palace and the expanding commercial centre to the east of Ko Ratanakosin.

THE AGE OF POLITICS
European Influence & the 1932 Revolution

Towards the end of the 19th century, Bangkok's city limits encompassed no more than a dozen square kilometres, with a population of about half a million. Despite its modest size, the capital successfully administered the much larger kingdom of Siam – which then extended into modern-day Laos, western Cambodia and northern Malaysia. Even more impressively, Siamese rulers were able to stave off intense pressure from the Portuguese, the Dutch, the French and the English, all of whom at one time or another harboured desires to add Siam to their colonial portfolios. By the end of the century, France and England had established a strong presence in every one of Siam's neighbouring countries – the French in Laos and Cambodia, and the British in Burma and Malaya.

Facing increasing pressure from British colonies in neighbouring Burma and Malaya, Rama IV signed the 1855 Bowring Treaty with Britain. This agreement marked Siam's break from an exclusive economic involvement with China, a relationship that had dominated the previous century.

1893	1910	1917
After a minor territorial dispute, France sends gunboats to threaten Bangkok, forcing Siam to give up most of its territory east of the Mekong River; Siam gains much of its modern boundaries.	Vajiravudh becomes the sixth king of the Chakri dynasty after the death of his older brother; he fails to produce a male heir during his reign.	Founding of Bangkok's Chulalongkorn University, the country's first Western-style institute of higher education; today the university is still regarded as the most prestigious in the country.

The signing of this document, and the subsequent ascension of Rama V led to the largest period of European influence on Thailand. Wishing to head off any potential invasion plans, Rama V ceded Laos and Cambodia to the French and northern Malaya to the British between 1893 and 1910. The two European powers, for their part, were happy to use Thailand as a buffer state between their respective colonial domains.

Rama V gave Bangkok 120 new roads during his reign, inspired by street plans from Batavia (the Dutch colonial centre now known as Jakarta), Calcutta, Penang and Singapore. Germans were hired to design and build railways emanating from the capital, while the Dutch contributed the design of Bangkok's Hualamphong Train Station, today considered a minor masterpiece of civic Art Deco.

In 1893 Bangkok opened its first railway line, extending 22km from Bangkok to Pak Nam, where Mae Nam Chao Phraya enters the Gulf of Thailand; at that time it cost just 1B to travel in 1st class. A 20km electric tramway opened the following year, paralleling the left bank of Mae Nam Chao Phraya. By 1904 three more rail lines out of Bangkok had been added: northeast to Khorat (306km), with a branch line to Lopburi (42km); south-southwest to Phetburi (151km); and south to Tha Chin (34km).

Italian architects, engineers and artists contributed numerous buildings and monuments to the city, from the Old Customs House (p123) and grand Ananda Samakhon Throne Hall (p94) around the turn of the century, to the Democracy Monument (p86) and the city's first fine-arts university (p74), which was set up by and named for Italian sculptor Corrado Feroci (aka Silpa Bhirasi). Americans established Siam's first printing press along with the kingdom's first newspaper in 1864. The first Thai-language newspaper, *Darunovadha,* came along in 1874, and by 1900 Bangkok boasted three daily English-language newspapers: the *Bangkok Times, Siam Observer* and *Siam Free Press.*

As Bangkok prospered, many wealthy merchant families sent their children to study in Europe. Students of humbler socioeconomic status who excelled at school had access to government scholarships for overseas study as well. In 1924 a handful of Thai students in Paris formed the Promoters of Political Change, a group that met to discuss ideas for a future Siamese government modelled on Western democracy.

After finishing their studies and returning to Bangkok, three of the 'Promoters', lawyer Pridi Banomyong and military officers Phibul Songkhram and Prayoon Phamonmontri, organised an underground 'People's Party' dedicated to the overthrow of the Siamese system of government. The People's Party found a willing accomplice in Rama VII (King Prajadhipok; r 1925–35), and a bloodless revolution in 1932 transformed Thailand from an absolute monarchy into a constitutional one. Bangkok thus found itself the nerve centre of a vast new civil service, which, coupled with its growing success as a world port, transformed the city into a Mecca for Thais seeking economic opportunities.

WWII & the Struggle for Democracy

Phibul Songkhram, appointed prime minister by the People's Party in December 1938, changed the country's name from Siam to Thailand and introduced the Western solar calendar. When the Japanese invaded Southeast Asia in 1941, outflanking Allied troops in Malaya and Burma, Phibul allowed Japanese regiments access to the Gulf of Thailand. Japanese troops bombed and briefly occupied parts of Bangkok on their way to the Thai–Burmese border to fight the British in Burma and, as a result of public insecurity, the Thai economy stagnated.

1932	1935–46	1946
A bloodless coup transforms Siam from an absolute to a constitutional monarchy; the deposed king, Rama VII, remained on the throne until his resignation three years later.	Ananda Mahidol, a grandson of one of Rama V's 'major' wives, is appointed king; he spends most of his reign abroad and it ends abruptly when he is found shot dead in his room under mysterious circumstances.	Pridi Phanomyong, one of the architects of the 1932 coup, becomes Thailand's first democratically elected prime minister; after a military coup, Pridi is forced to flee Thailand, returning only briefly one more time.

THE KING

If you see a yellow Rolls Royce flashing by along city avenues, accompanied by a police escort, you've just caught a glimpse of Thailand's longest-reigning monarch – and the longest-reigning living monarch in the world – King Bhumibol Adulyadej. Also known in English as Rama IX (the ninth king of the Chakri dynasty), Bhumibol Adulyadej was born in the USA in 1927, while his father Prince Mahidol was studying medicine at Harvard University.

Fluent in English, French, German and Thai, Bhumibol ascended the throne in 1946 following the death of his brother Rama VIII (King Ananda Mahidol; r 1935–46), who reigned for just over 11 years before dying under mysterious circumstances.

An ardent jazz composer and saxophonist when he was younger, Rama IX has hosted jam sessions with the likes of jazz greats Woody Herman and Benny Goodman. His compositions are often played on Thai radio.

The king administers royal duties from Chitralada Palace in the city's Dusit precinct, north of Ko Ratanakosin. As protector of both nation and religion, he traditionally presides over several important Buddhist and Brahmanist ceremonies during the year.

Rama IX and Queen Sirikit have four children: Princess Ubol Ratana (born 1951), Crown Prince Maha Vajiralongkorn (1952), Princess Mahachakri Sirindhorn (1955) and Princess Chulabhorn (1957).

After more than 60 years in power, and having recently reached his 82nd birthday, Rama IX is preparing for his succession. For the last few years the Crown Prince has performed most of the royal ceremonies the king would normally perform, such as presiding over the Royal Ploughing Ceremony (p21), changing the attire on the Emerald Buddha (p71) and handing out academic degrees at university commencements.

Along with nation and religion, the monarchy is very highly regarded in Thai society – negative comment about the king or any member of the royal family is a social as well as legal taboo.

Phibul resigned in 1944 under pressure from the Thai underground resistance, and after V-J (victory over Japan) Day in 1945 was exiled to Japan. Bangkok resumed its pace towards modernisation, even after Phibul returned to Thailand in 1948 and took over the leadership again via a military coup. Over the next 15 years, bridges were built over Mae Nam Chao Phraya, canals were filled in to provide space for new roads, and multistorey buildings began crowding out traditional teak structures.

Another coup installed Field Marshal Sarit Thanarat in 1957, and Phibul Songkhram once again found himself exiled to Japan, where he died in 1964. From 1964 to 1973 – the peak years of the second Indochina War – Thai army officers Thanom Kittikachorn and Praphat Charusathien ruled Thailand and allowed the US to establish several army bases within Thai borders to support the US campaign in Indochina. During this time Bangkok gained notoriety as a 'rest and recreation' (R&R) spot for foreign troops stationed in Southeast Asia.

In October 1973 the Thai military brutally suppressed a large prodemocracy student demonstration at Thammasat University in Bangkok, but Rama IX and General Krit Sivara, who sympathised with the students, refused to support further bloodshed, forcing Thanom and Praphat to leave Thailand. Oxford-educated Kukrit Pramoj took charge of a 14-party coalition government and steered a leftist agenda past the conservative parliament. Among Kukrit's lasting achievements were a national minimum wage, the repeal of anticommunist laws and the ejection of US military forces from Thailand.

The military regained control in 1976 after right-wing, paramilitary civilian groups assaulted a group of 2000 students holding a sit-in at Thammasat. Officially, 46 people died in the incident,

1951–63	1962	1973
Field Marshal Sarit Thanarat wrests power from Phibul Songkhram, abolishes the constitution and embarks on one of the most repressive and authoritarian regimes in Thai history.	America's involvement in the Indochina War leads to massive economic and infrastructural expansion of Bangkok; dissatisfaction with the authoritarian Thai government leads to a period of Communist insurgency.	Large-scale student protests in Bangkok lead to violent military suppression; 1971 coup leader Thanom Kittikachorn is ordered into exile by Rama IX; Kukrit Pramoj's civilian government takes charge.

although the number may be much higher, and more than a thousand were arrested. Many students fled Bangkok and joined the People's Liberation Army of Thailand (PLAT), an armed communist insurgency based in the hills, which had been active in Thailand since the 1930s.

Bangkok continued to seesaw between civilian and military rule for the next 15 years. Although a general amnesty in 1982 brought an end to the PLAT, and students, workers and farmers returned to their homes, a new era of political tolerance exposed the military once again to civilian fire.

In May 1992 several huge demonstrations demanding the resignation of the next in a long line of military dictators, General Suchinda Kraprayoon, rocked Bangkok and the large provincial capitals. Charismatic Bangkok governor Chamlong Srimuang, winner of the 1992 Magsaysay Award (a humanitarian service award issued in the Philippines) for his role in galvanising the public to reject Suchinda, led the protests. After confrontations between the protesters and the military near the Democracy Monument resulted in nearly 50 deaths and hundreds of injuries, Rama IX summoned both Suchinda and Chamlong for a rare public scolding. Suchinda resigned, having been in power for less than six weeks.

A mere 13 sq km in 1900, Bangkok grew to an astounding metropolitan area of more than 330 sq km by the end of the 20th century. Today the city encompasses not only Bangkok proper, but also the former capital of Thonburi across Mae Nam Chao Phraya to the west, along with the densely populated 'suburb' provinces, Samut Prakan to the east and Nonthaburi to the north. More than half of Thailand's urban population lives in Bangkok.

THE RECENT PAST

The Crisis and the People's Constitution

Bangkok approached the new millennium riding a tide of events that set new ways of governing and living in the capital. The most defining moment occurred in July 1997 when – after several months of warning signs that nearly everyone in Thailand and the international community ignored – the Thai currency fell into a deflationary tailspin and the national economy screeched to a virtual halt. Bangkok, which rode at the forefront of the 1980s double-digit economic boom, suffered more than elsewhere in the country in terms of job losses and massive income erosion.

Two months after the crash, the Thai parliament voted in a new constitution that guaranteed – at least on paper – more human and civil rights than had ever been granted in Thailand previously. The so-called 'people's constitution' fostered great hope in a population left emotionally battered by the 1997 economic crisis.

Prime Minister Chavalit Yongchaiyudh, whose move to float the baht effectively triggered the economic crisis, was forced to resign. Former Prime Minister Chuan Leekpai was then re-elected, and proceeded to implement tough economic reforms suggested by the International Monetary Fund (IMF). During the next few years, Bangkok's economy began to show signs of recovery.

Thaksin Shinawatra: CEO Prime Minister

In January 2001, billionaire and former police colonel Thaksin Shinawatra became prime minister after winning a landslide victory in nationwide elections – the first in Thailand under the strict guidelines established in the 1997 constitution. Thaksin's new party called Thai Rak

1981	1985	1992
General Prem Tinsulanonda is appointed prime minister after a military coup and is largely able to stabilise Thai politics over the next eight years.	Chamlong Srimuang is elected mayor of Bangkok; three years later, after forming his own largely Buddhist-based political group, the Palang Dharma Party, he is elected mayor again.	Street protests led by Chamlong Srimuang against 1991 coup leader Suchinda Kraprayoon lead to violent confrontations; both Chamlong and Suchinda are publicly scolded by Rama IX, leading to Suchinda's resignation.

COBRA SWAMP

If you arrive in Bangkok by air, bear in mind that the sleek glass-and-steel terminal you will most likely pull into was nearly 40 years in the making. Suvarnabhumi (pronounced *sù wanná poom*), Sanskrit for 'Golden Land', could hardly be a more apt name for Thailand's new airport, particularly for the politicians and investors involved.

Thailand's new international airport was originally begun in 1973 and the location chosen was an unremarkable marshy area with the slightly less illustrious working title of Nong Ngu Hao, Thai for 'Cobra Swamp'. Despite the seemingly disadvantageous setting, over the years the flat marshland was eagerly bought and sold by politicians and developers hoping to make a quick profit.

It wasn't until the self-styled CEO administration of Thaksin Shinawatra that work on the airport began in earnest. Thaksin harboured desires to make Bangkok a 'transportation hub' to rival Hong Kong and Singapore, and went on a spending spree, commissioning construction of the world's tallest flight control tower, as well as the world's largest terminal building.

The construction of Suvarnabhumi attracted allegations of corruption, including suggestions that faulty building materials had been used and a substandard runway constructed. Undoubtedly the most embarrassing scandal associated with the airport was the corruption-laden purchase of 20 CTX security scanners from a US company.

On 29 September 2005, Thaksin presided over a much-criticised 'soft' opening. The ceremony was essentially little more than a face-saving measure considering that the airport was still far from operational. Suvarnabhumi eventually began flights a year later, on 28 September 2006. In an ironic twist of fate, Thaksin, the main instigator of the project, was in exile in England, having been ousted in a military coup the week before, the junta citing corruption and shoddy construction of the airport among their justifications for the takeover.

Despite being the largest airport in Southeast Asia, and among the largest in the world, in March 2007 many domestic flights were relocated back to the old Don Muang Airport, officials citing overcrowding of runways and safety concerns as reasons for the move. With little foresight, a train link to the distant airport was only begun after its opening, and wasn't completed until 2010. For details on arriving at Suvarnabhumi, see p264.

Thai (TRT; Thais Love Thailand) swept into power on a populist agenda that seemed at odds with the man's enormous wealth and influence.

The sixth-richest ruler in the world as of late 2003, Thaksin owned the country's only private TV station through his family-owned Shin Corporation, the country's largest telecommunications company. Shin Corporation also owned Asia's first privately owned satellite company, Shin Satellite, and a large stake in Thai AirAsia, a subsidiary of the Malaysia-based airline Air Asia.

Days before he became prime minister, Thaksin transferred his shares in Shin Corp to his siblings, chauffeur and even household servants in an apparent attempt to conceal his true assets. Eventually the country's constitutional court cleared him of all fraud charges connected with the shares transfer in a controversial eight-to-seven vote.

In 2003, Thaksin announced a 'War on drugs' that he claimed would free the country of illicit drug use within 90 days. Lists of alleged drug dealers and users were compiled in every province. The police were given arrest quotas to fulfil, and could lose their jobs if they didn't follow orders. Within two months, more than 2000 Thais on the government blacklist had been killed. The Thaksin administration denied accusations by the UN, the US State Department, Amnesty International and Thailand's own human rights commission that the deaths were extra-judicial killings by Thai police.

1997	1999	2001
Thailand devalues its currency, the baht, triggering the Asian economic crisis; massive unemployment and personal debt, and a significant crash of the Thai stock market, follow.	The BTS Skytrain, Bangkok's first expansive metro system, opens in commemoration of Rama IX's 6th cycle (72nd) birthday; the system is currently in the process of being expanded.	Thaksin Shinawatra, Thailand's richest man, is elected prime minister on a populist platform in what some have called the most open, corruption-free election in Thai history.

Despite this and other controversies, ranging from a bird-flu crisis to early bar-closing and privatisation protests, during the February 2005 general elections the Thaksin administration scored a second four-year mandate in a landslide victory with a record 19 million votes. Armchair observers speculated that the blame lay with the opposition's lack of a positive platform to deal with these same problems. Others, however, believed it was simply that Thaksin and TRT had again been rewarded for appealing directly to the enormous rural vote that exists out of sight of Bangkok, and usually far from the minds of the city elite. An obvious tactic, perhaps, but one that had never previously been employed. Either way, Thaksin became the first Thai leader in history to be re-elected to a consecutive second term.

However, time was running short for Thaksin and party. The final straw came in January 2006, when Thaksin announced that his family had sold off its controlling interest in Shin Corp to a Singaporean investment firm. Since deals made through the Stock Exchange of Thailand (SET) were exempt from capital-gains tax, Thaksin's family paid no tax on the US$1.9 billion sale, which enraged Bangkok's middle class.

Many of the PM's most highly placed supporters had also turned against him. Most prominently, media mogul and former friend, Sondhi Limthongkul organised a series of massive anti-Thaksin rallies in Bangkok, culminating in a rally at Bangkok's Royal Plaza on 4 and 5 February 2006 that drew tens of thousands of protestors. This was an early sign of a growing schism in Thai society between the largely urban middle-class, anti-Thaksin camp and the predominately rural and working-class Thaksin supporters.

Retired major general Chamlong Srimuang, a former Bangkok governor and one of Thaksin's earliest and strongest supporters, also turned against him and joined Sondhi in leading the protests, which strengthened throughout early 2006. Two of Thaksin's ministers resigned from the cabinet and from the TRT, adding to the mounting pressure on the embattled premier.

Thaksin's ministers responded by dissolving the national assembly and scheduling snap elections for 2 April 2006, three years ahead of schedule. The opposition was aghast, claiming Thaskin called the election to whitewash allegations of impropriety over the Shin Corp sale.

During the campaign, which the major opposition parties boycotted, TRT was accused of 'hiring' smaller parties to run in the election to ensure their victory. Thaksin initially claimed victory, but after a conference with the king, announced that he would take a break from politics. Thaksin designated himself caretaker prime minister before another round of elections was scheduled for later that year.

The Coup and the Red/Yellow Divide

On the evening of 19 September 2006, while Thaksin was attending a UN conference in New York, the Thai military led by General Sonthi Boonyaratglin took power in a bloodless coup. Calling themselves the Council for Democratic Reform under the Constitutional Monarch, the junta cited the TRT government's alleged lese-majesty (treason), corruption, interference with state agencies and creation of social divisions as justification for the coup. The general public, particularly those in Bangkok, initially overwhelmingly supported the coup, and scenes of smiling tourists and Thai families posing in front of tanks remain the defining images of the event. Thaksin quickly flew to London, where he remained in exile until his UK visa was revoked in 2008.

In October the junta appointed Surayud Chulanont, a retired army general, as interim prime minister for 12 months, or until elections could be scheduled. The choice of Surayud was seen

2003	3 July 2004	9 June 2006
A three-month crackdown on drugs initiated by the Thaksin government leads to the violent deaths of more than 2,500 people.	The MRT, Bangkok's first underground public transport system is opened; an accident the next year injures 140 and causes the system to shut down for two weeks.	Thailand celebrates the 60th anniversary of its Rama IX's ascension to the throne. The Thai king is currently the longest-serving monarch in the world.

as a strategic one by many, as he was widely respected among both military personnel and civilians. The Surayud administration enjoyed a honeymoon period until late December, when it imposed stringent capital controls and a series of bombings rocked Bangkok during New Year's Eve, killing three people.

In January 2007, an Assets Examination Committee put together by the junta found Thaksin guilty of concealing assets to avoid paying taxes. Two months later, Thaksin's wife and brother-in-law were also charged with conspiracy to evade taxes. In May, a court established by the military government found TRT guilty of breaking election laws. The court dissolved the party and banned its executive members from public service for five years.

In July, growing dissatisfaction with the junta's slow progress towards elections reached a peak when a large group of antigovernment protesters known as the Democratic Alliance Against Dictatorship lay siege to the residence of Privy Councillor and key royal advisor Prem Tinsulanonda, whom they accused of masterminding the coup. Several protesters and police were injured. Nine of the group's leaders were sent to jail, the largest crackdown yet by the junta, which had previously tolerated small-scale protests.

Two months later the Supreme Court issued warrants for Thaksin and his wife, citing 'misconduct of a government official and violation of a ban on state officials being party to transactions involving public interests' in reference to an allegedly unfair land purchase in 2003. Thaksin's assets, some 73 billion baht, were frozen by a graft-busting agency set up after the coup. However, despite his apparent financial troubles, in July 2007 Thaksin fulfilled a long-held dream when he purchased Manchester City Football Club.

In a nationwide referendum held on 19 August, Thais approved a military-drafted constitution. Although the document included a number of undemocratic provisions, including one that mandates a Senate not entirely comprised of elected politicians, its passage was largely regarded as a message that the Thai people wanted to see elections and progress.

Under the new constitution, long-awaited elections were finally held in late 2007. The newly formed People Power Party, for which Thaksin had an advisory role, won a significant number of parliamentary seats, but failed to win an outright majority. After forming a loose coalition with several other parties, parliament chose veteran politician and close Thaksin ally, Samak Sundaravej as prime minister.

Not surprisingly, Samak was regarded as little more than a proxy of Thaksin by his opponents, and shortly after taking office became the target of a series of large-scale protests held by the Peoples' Alliance for Democracy (PAD), the same group of mostly Bangkok-based middle-class royalists who had called for Thaksin's resignation in the lead up to the 2006 coup. By this point, the PAD had already begun wearing their trademark yellow to show their allegiance to the king, and were referred to as the 'yellow shirts' (see boxed text p34).

In August 2008, several thousand yellow-shirted PAD protesters invaded and took over Government House in Bangkok, literally causing the prime minister to flee from his office. The takeover was followed by sporadic violent clashes between the PAD and the United Front for Democracy against Dictatorship (UDD), a loose association of red-shirted Thaksin supporters who had set up camp nearby at Sanam Luang. One incident in early September led to the death of a PAD protester, causing Samak to declare a state of emergency. The event also led to the royal family becoming involved in the long-running conflict when Queen Sirikit chose to attend the protester's funeral, an action that many interpreted as a tacit show of support for the PAD.

19 September 2006	19 August 2007	23 December 2007
A bloodless coup sees the Thai military take power from Thaksin while he is at a UN meeting in New York; he remains in exile.	In a nationwide referendum, voters agree to approve a military-drafted constitution, Thailand's 17th, despite the constitution being regarded by many Thais and international observers as deeply flawed.	A general election sees the Thaksin-allied People's Power Party gain a significant number of seats in parliament. A coalition, led by veteran politician Samak Sundaravej, is formed.

GETTING SHIRTY

Most Thais are aware of the day of the week they were born, and in Thai astrology each day is associated with a particular colour. However in the aftermath of the 2006 coup, these previously benign hues started to take on a much more political meaning.

To show their alleged support for the royal family, the anti-Thaksin Peoples' Alliance for Democracy (PAD) adopted yellow as their uniform. This goes back to 2006, when in an effort to celebrate the 60th anniversary of Rama IX's ascension to the throne, Thais were encouraged to wear yellow, the colour associated with Monday, the king's birthday.

To differentiate themselves, the pro-Thaksin United Front for Democracy Against Dictatorship (UDD) began to wear red, and soon thereafter became known colloquially as the 'red shirts'. To add to the political rainbow, during the riots of April 2009 that disrupted an ASEAN summit in Pattaya, a blue-shirted faction emerged, apparently aligned with a former Thaksin ally and allegedly sponsored by the Ministry of the Interior. And during the subsequent political crisis of 2010, a 'no colour' group of peace activists and a 'black shirt' faction, believed to consist of rogue elements of the Thai military, also emerged.

Because of the potential political associations, many have become wary about sporting the divisive colours, and on Rama IX's birthday in 2009, pink seemingly became the new yellow when Thais wore the colour as a nod to a previous occasion when the king safely emerged from a lengthy hospital visit wearing a bright pink blazer.

Rife with drama, Samak's tenure as prime minister was seemingly over as soon as it began when in September 2008, after fewer than nine months in office, the Thai Supreme Court unanimously ruled that his paid appearances as the host of a TV cookery program constituted a conflict of interest, forcing him to step down. That Samak had allegedly earned only 80,000B (about US$2,400) from hosting the program was an indicator of the partiality of the Supreme Court; in the remaining months of 2008, Samak was succeeded by three prime ministers.

The PAD managed to occupy Government House for nearly four months, yet despite the arrest of its key leader, Chamlong Srimuang, PAD's boldest act was yet to come. On 25 November, hundreds of armed PAD protesters stormed Bangkok's Suvarnabhumi and Don Muang Airports, entering the passenger terminals and seizing control of the control towers. Thousands of additional PAD sympathisers eventually flooded Suvarnabhumi, leading to the cancellation of all flights and leaving as many as 230,000 domestic and international passengers stranded. The stand off lasted until 2 December, when the Supreme Court wielded its muscle yet again in order to ban Samak's successor, Prime Minister Somchai Wongsawat from politics and ordered his political party and two coalition parties dissolved. PAD leader Sondhi Limthongkul declared, 'We have won a victory and achieved our aims.'

If the PAD's aim was to derail Thailand's economy, it succeeded beyond anyone's expectations. The airport seige took place during peak tourist season and the impact wounded the industry profoundly, damaging the country's reputation and leaving many hotels in Bangkok at single-digit occupancy rates. The Bank of Thailand estimates that the incident cost the country 210 billion baht, and in late 2009, Thai Airways sued then Foreign Minister Kasit Piromya and several PAD leaders, claiming that the protests cost the national carrier a loss of 575 million baht.

In addition to financial loss, the events of 2008 also had a significant social cost in that Thailand, a country that had mostly experienced a relatively high level of domestic stability and harmony throughout its modern history, was now effectively polarised between the predominately middle- and upper-class, urban-based PAD and the largely working-class, rural UDD.

November 2008	December 2008	April 2010
Thousands of yellow-shirted anti-Thaksin protesters calling themselves the Peoples' Alliance for Democracy (PAD) take over both of Bangkok's airports.	Abhisit Vejjajiva, leader of the Democrat Party, forms a tenuous parliamentary coalition and becomes Thailand's sixth Prime Minister since the 2006 coup.	Pro-Thaksin supporters clash with troops in central Bangkok, leading to 25 deaths and several hundred injuries.

In December 2008, after a great deal of political wrangling, a tenuous new coalition was formed, led by Oxford-educated Abhisit Vejjajiva, leader of the Democrat Party. Despite being young, photogenic, articulate and allegedly untainted by corruption, Abhisit's perceived association with the PAD did little to placate the UDD.

After 46.37 billion baht (US$1.4 billion) of allegedly illegally gained assets were seized from Thaksin by the Supreme Court in February 2010, another round of protests began. Red Shirts and self-proclaimed prodemocracy activists united to demand that Prime Minister Abhisit Vejjajiva stand down.

In April 2010 there were violent clashes between police and protesters (numbering up to tens of thousands), resulting in 25 deaths. Protesters barricaded themselves into an area stretching from Lumphini Park to the shopping district near Siam Square, effectively shutting down parts of central Bangkok. In May the protesters were dispersed by force, but not before at least 36 buildings were set alight and at least 15 people killed. The death toll from the 2010 conflicts amounted to at least 70 people, making it Thailand's most violent political unrest in 20 years.

At press time, Abhisit clung to power, but divisions within Thailand's military and red-yellow animosity are serious challenges for the prime minister. Meanwhile, seething discontent among UDD supporters over the crackdown and Thaksin's continuing influence from abroad ensure that the Red Shirt movement is anything but defeated.

ARTS

Despite the utterly utilitarian face of the modern city, Bangkok is among Southeast Asia's contemporary art capitals. This tradition stems back to the founding of the city in the late 18th century, when the early Chakri kings weren't satisfied to merely invite artists and artisans from previous Thai royal capitals such as Ayuthaya, Sukhothai and Chiang Mai. Whether via political coercion of neighbouring countries or seductive promises of wealth and position, Bangkok's rulers also had access to the artistic cream of Cambodia, Laos and Myanmar. Mon and Khmer peoples native to the Thai kingdom also contributed much to the visual arts scene. The great artistic traditions of India and China, the subtle renderings of Indo- and Sino-influenced art in neighbouring countries, and the colonial and postcolonial cultural influx from Europe have also played huge roles in the development of art in Bangkok. Likewise, the decades surrounding the two world wars, Thailand's military dictatorships of the '50s, '60s and '70s, followed by the protest-fuelled democracy movement brought a healthy dose of politics and social conscience to the city's art scene. Today, influences from just about every corner of the globe now find free play in the capital.

VISUAL ARTS

Divine Inspiration

The wát served as a locus for the highest expressions of Thai art for roughly 800 years, from the Lanna to Ratanakosin eras. Accordingly, Bangkok's 400-plus Buddhist temples are brimming with the figuratively imaginative if thematically formulaic art of Thailand's foremost muralists. Always instructional in intent, such painted images range from the depiction of the *jataka* (stories of the Buddha's past lives) and scenes from the Indian Hindu epic Ramayana, to elaborate scenes detailing daily life in Thailand. Artists traditionally applied natural pigments to plastered temple walls, creating a fragile medium of which very few examples remain.

Today the study and application of mural painting remain very much alive. Modern temple projects are undertaken somewhere within the capital virtually every day of the year, often using improved techniques and paints that promise to hold fast much longer than the temple murals of old. A privileged

top picks

BANGKOK ART EXPERIENCES

- 100 Tonson (p199)
- Bangkok University Art Gallery (p200)
- Jim Thompson's House (p106)
- National Museum (p72)
- Wat Suthat (p84)

TEMPLE MURALS

Because of the relative wealth of Bangkok, as well as its role as the country's artistic and cultural centre, the artists commissioned to paint the walls of the city's various temples were among the most talented around, and Bangkok's temple paintings are regarded as the finest in Thailand. Details of some particularly exceptional works follow:

Wat Bowonniwet (Map p82) Painted by an artist called In Kong during the reign of Rama II, the murals in the panels of the *ubohsòt* (chapel) of this temple show Thai depictions of Western life during the early 19th century; see p88 for more on Wat Bowonniwet.

Wat Chong Nonsi (Map p132) Dating back to the late Ayuthaya period, Bangkok's earliest surviving temple paintings are faded and missing in parts, but the depictions of everyday Thai life, including bawdy illustrations of a sexual manner, are well-worth visiting.

Phra Thii Nang Phutthaisawan (Buddhaisawan Chapel; Map p68) Although construction of this temple, located in the National Museum, began in 1795, the paintings were probably finished during the reign of Rama III (1824–51). Among other scenes, the murals depict the conception, birth and early life of the Buddha – common topics among Thai temple murals.

Wat Suthat (Map p82) Almost as impressive in their vast scale as in their quality, the murals at Wat Suthat are among the most awe-inspiring in the country. Gory depictions of Buddhist hell can be found on a pillar directly behind the Buddha statue; see p81 for more on Wat Suthat.

Wat Suwannaram (Map p132) These paintings inside a late Ayuthaya-era temple in Thonburi contain skilled and vivid depictions of battle scenes and foreigners, including Chinese and Muslim warriors.

Wat Tritosathep Mahaworawihan (Map p82) Although still a work in progress, Chakrabhand Posayakrit's postmodern murals at this temple in Banglamphu have already been recognised as masterworks of Thai Buddhist art.

few in Bangkok's art community receive handsome sums for painting the interior walls of well-endowed ordination halls.

In sculpture the Thai artists have long been masters, using wood, stone, ivory, clay and metal and a variety of techniques – including carving, modelling, construction and casting – to achieve their designs. Bangkok's most famous sculptural output has been bronze Buddha images, coveted the world over for their originality and grace. Nowadays, historic bronzes have all but disappeared from the art market in Thailand and are zealously protected by temples, museums or private collectors.

The Modern Era

In 1913 the Thai government opened the School of Arts and Crafts in order to train teachers of art and design as well as to codify the teaching of silversmithing, nielloware, lacquerwork and wood carving in traditional Thai styles. It was an effort that was badly timed, as interest in Thai classicism began to weaken in the aftermath of WWI, perhaps the first event in world history to inspire rank-and-file urban Thais to ponder global issues.

The beginnings of Thailand's modern visual-arts movement are usually attributed to Italian artist Corrado Feroci, who was invited to Thailand by Rama VI in 1924. In 1933 Feroci founded the country's first School of Fine Arts (SOFA).

Public monuments sponsored during the Phibun Songkhram government (1938–44) led the government to expand the SOFA's status in 1943 so that it became part of newly founded Silpakorn University (p201), Thailand's premier training ground for artists and art historians. Feroci continued as dean of the university, and in gratitude for his contributions, the government gave Feroci the Thai name Silpa Bhirasri.

In 1944 Bhirasri established the National Art Exhibition, which became an important catalyst for the evolution of Thai contemporary art. The first juried art event in Thai history, the annual exhibition created new standards and formed part of a heretofore nonexistent national art agenda. In the absence of galleries in this era, the competition served as the only venue in Bangkok – in all of Thailand, for that matter – where young artists could display their work publicly. Among the most celebrated artworks of the period were works of realism painted by Chamras Khietkong, Piman Moolpramook, Sweang Songmangmee and Silpa Bhirasri himself.

Other artists involved in this blossoming of modern art, including Jitr Buabusaya, Fua Haripitak, Misiem Yipintsoi, Tawee Nandakhwang and Sawasdi Tantisuk, drew on European movements such as Impressionism, Post-Impressionism, Expressionism and Cubism. For the first time in the Thai modern art movement, there was also a move towards the fusion of indigenous artistic sources with modern modes of expression, as seen in the paintings by Prasong Patamanuj and sculptures of Khien Yimsiri and Chit Rienpracha.

Meanwhile, while writing and lecturing against the iron rule of Field Marshal Sarit Thanarat (1957–59), Thai Marxist academic Jit Phumisak founded the Art for Life (*sĭn·lá· bà pêua chee·wít*) movement, which had many parallels with the famous Mexican School in its belief that only art with social or political content was worth creating. This movement gained considerable ground during the 1973 democracy movement, when students, farmers and workers joined hands with Bangkok urbanites to resist General Thanom Kittikachorn's right-wing military dictatorship. Much of the art (and music) produced at this time carried content commenting on poverty, urban–rural inequities and political repression, and were typically boldly and quickly executed. Painters Sompote Upa-In and Chang Saetang became the most famous Art for Life exponents. The movement even led to a new musical genre called *pleng pêua chee·wít*, literally 'music for life'; see p45.

A contrasting but equally important movement in Thai art later in the same decade eschewed politics and instead updated Buddhist themes and temple art. Initiated by painters Pichai Nirand, Thawan Duchanee and Prateung Emjaroen, the movement combined modern Western schema with Thai motifs, moving from painting to sculpture and then to mixed media. Artists associated with this neo-Thai, neo-Buddhist school include Surasit Saokong, Songdej Thipthong, Monchai Kaosamang, Tawatchai Somkong and the late Montien Boonma. All are frequently exhibited and collected outside Thailand.

Since the 1980s boom years, secular sculpture and painting in Bangkok have enjoyed more international recognition, with Impressionism-inspired Jitr (Prakit) Buabusaya and Sriwan Janehuttakarnkit among the very few to have reached this vaunted status. On Thailand's art stage, famous names include artists of the 'Fireball' school such as Vasan Sitthiket and Manit Sriwanichpoom, who specialise in politically motivated, mixed-media art installations. These artists delight in breaking Thai social codes and means of expression. Even when their purported message is Thai nationalism and self-sufficiency, they are sometimes considered 'anti-Thai'.

In recent years the emphasis is moving away from traditional influences and political commentary and more towards contemporary art. Works such as Yuree Kensaku's cartoon-like paintings, or Porntaweesak Rimsakul's mechanised installations are gaining attention, both in Thailand and abroad.

Modern painting and sculpture are exhibited at dozens of galleries around Bangkok, from the delicately lit darlings of Thai high society to industrially decorated spaces in empty warehouses. Other venues and sources of support for Thai modern art include the rotating displays at Bangkok's luxury hotels, particularly the Grand Hyatt Erawan (p219), the Sukhothai (p226) and the Metropolitan (p227).

FASHION

Unsurprisingly, Bangkok is Thailand's fashion hub, and in fact in all of Southeast Asia only Singapore is a serious rival. Bangkokians not only dabble in the latest American, European and Japanese designer trends, but they have an up-and-coming couture all their own. Shops run by modern Thai designers are particularly easy to find at the Emporium, Gaysorn Plaza, Siam Paragon and Siam Center shopping centres, and in the small lanes of Siam Square. Siam Square focuses on inexpensive 'underground' Thai fashions favoured by university students and young office workers, while Emporium and Siam Center are much more upmarket. Local labels to look for include anr, Good Mixer, Fly Now, Greyhound, Jaspal and Senada Theory. Chatuchak Weekend Market is another place to seek out Bangkok designs at bargain prices.

Take a stroll through Siam Square (p144) or Central World Plaza (p141), especially on a weekend, and the explosion of styles and colours can't fail to impress. On weekends the middle soi (lane) of Siam Square – an area known as Centrepoint – is filled with young Thais wearing the most outrageous clothing experiments they can create. It may not be on par with Tokyo's famous Harajuku district, but in a few years who knows what it may become?

ART, DESIGN & FASHION IN TODAY'S BANGKOK *Steven Pettifor*

As Thai urban living becomes increasingly virtual, fast and disposable, the cultural layering that contributes to the 21st-century megalopolis that is Bangkok becomes more complex and global. Today's cultural currents are as likely to be swayed by Korean soap operas, Japanese Manga comics, Chinese mass merchandising, European fashion and American street culture as traditional Thai life.

These influences are fuelling introspection among artists, with more art being created that pertains to the condition of the self and the societal constraints imposed upon it. Whereas a decade ago, artists seemed to be the defenders of a precious national identity, now themes have become more personal and reflective, as in the gender-explorative art of Pinaree Sanpitak, or young artist Maitree Siriboon's identity-driven work. Though such approaches seem more aligned to the modern Western artist's mindset, there remains an inextricable leaning towards a more spiritual, and ostensibly Buddhist, path.

Names Worth Knowing

In the contemporary scene Thai artists such as Surasri Kusolwong, Navin Rawanchaikul and Nipan Oraniwesna who utilise media, situational and process art, while still infusing elements perceived as Asian, have garnered the most prominent exposure on the international circuit.

Arguably one of the most sought-after artists by domestic collectors, the reclusive Chatchai Puipia creates figurative canvases that testify to the resilience of painting as a medium. His confrontational self-portraits are excavations of the self, yet they also reflect the tension and anxiety of a society uncertain of how to cope with its rapid modernisation.

Jakkai Siributr could be considered one of Thailand's only contemporary fibre artists. With an approach more akin to an expressive painter, his coarsely stitched and dyed tapestries serve in part as a symbol of the futility of nostalgic living within the incessant flux of today's world.

While the inevitability of death is a topic most of us prefer to avoid, Chiang Mai–based female artist Araya Rasdjarm-reansook has made it her trademark. As someone who reads poems to, and plays dress up with actual human corpses, she could be regarded as somewhat maverick.

Fashion shows grace the lobbies of various shopping centres around the city practically every weekend of the year. Since 1999 one of the biggest annual events has been Bangkok Fashion Week, a string of fashion shows in various venues around the city, including the new Fashion Dome, an air dome constructed over the middle of the lake at Benjakitti Park, adjacent to the Queen Sirikit National Convention Center. The Bangkok International Fashion Fair, held in September, is mostly a trade event but weekend days are usually open to the public.

The Thai government's clumsily named Office of the Bangkok Fashion City promotes fashion events and aims to turn Bangkok into a world-class – rather than simply regional – fashion centre by 2012. The office, however, has clashed more than once with Thailand's culture minister, who regularly chastises the organisers of Bangkok Fashion Week for the skimpiness of some of the outfits displayed on the catwalks. Coupled with the conservative night-time entertainment-venue closing times, such puritanism leads many in Bangkok's fashion community to question whether the city can attain world-class status with such government interference.

ARCHITECTURE
Temples, Forts & Shophouses

When Bangkok became the capital of the kingdom of Siam in 1782, the first task set before designers of the new city was to create hallowed ground for royal palaces and Buddhist monasteries. Indian astrologers and high-ranking Buddhist monks conferred to select and consecrate the most auspicious riverside locations, marking them off with small carved stone pillars. Siam's most talented architects and artisans then weighed in, creating majestic and ornate edifices designed to astound all who ventured into the new capital.

The temples and palaces along the riverbanks of Mae Nam Chao Phraya transformed humble Bang Makok into the glitter and glory of Ko Ratanakosin (Ratanakosin Island), and their scale and intricacy continue to make a lasting impression on new arrivals. Whether approaching by river or by road, from a distance your eye is instantly caught by the sunlight refracting off

Best known for his crime-fighting superheroine character in the film *Iron Pussy*, Thai-American multidisciplinary artist Michael Shaowanasai conjures up mockingly camp, open-ended dialogues through outrageous performances, photography, video and installation to express notions of identity and sexual orientation.

A Tradition of Design

As with visual arts, one of the strongest attributes of Thai design is its sensibility of craftsmanship, which stems from its long tradition of skilled artisans. Invigorating ancient crafts with a modern veneer aimed at Western tastes, designers are now moving beyond emulation of pervasive trends as they tune into their own voices. A part of the 2009 Bangkok Design Festival (the third year of the burgeoning festival), product designer Krit Sangvichien's exhibition Thainess was one attempt to define such attributes.

Apart from product design, there is a growing fascination by younger Thais with comics, cartoon art and animation. As with the rest of Asia, Thais are caught up in the recent wave of Japanese- and Korean-led Manga and anime, with Bangkok hosting its first ever Comic Con in early 2010. The trend has inspired artists like Wisut Ponnimit to blur art and animation, or young designer Estrella Montien to create her cartoon character *Estrella – I Believe in Art*.

Fashion Forward

Despite Bangkok slowly edging its way up the fashion rankings, the 2009 Elle Fashion Week, the city's leading annual garment showcase, was more modest than in previous years. This was a reflection of economic belt-tightening rather than lost favour, yet leading designers Stretsis, Kloset, Nagara, Vatit Itthi and Kai were all strutting their stuff, along with sought-after newbie 27Friday and 27Nov.

However, as the West increasingly looks to Asia for economic and cultural inspiration, it's more likely that emigrant fashion designers such as Thakoon Panichgul (who has dressed First Lady Michelle Obama), Disaya Sorakraikitikul (a preferred designer of British crooner Amy Winehouse) or new friend of the Hollywood 'A' List, Nuj Novakhett, will influence the international reputation of Thai fashion.

Artist and writer Steven Pettifor is the author of the book Flavours – Thai Contemporary Art, *and is also the editor of the* Bangkok Art Map (BAM!).

the multitude of gilded spires peeking over the huge walls of Wat Phra Kaew (p67), the Temple of the Emerald Buddha. Inside the brick-and-stucco walls, you can easily lose yourself amid the million-sq-metre grounds, which bring together more than 100 buildings and about two centuries of royal history and architectural experimentation.

Early Bangkok was both a citadel and a city of temples and palaces. Today the massive whitewashed walls of Phra Sumen Fort (p87), punctured by tiny windows and topped with neat crenulations, still loom over the northern end of trendy Th Phra Athit, facing Mae Nam Chao Phraya. On the other side of the battlements, Khlong Banglamphu (Banglamphu Canal) cuts away from the river at a sharp angle, creating the northern tip of Ko Ratanakosin, a man-made 'island' out of the left bank of the river. Erected in 1783 and named for the mythical Mt Meru (Phra Sumen in Thai) of Hindu-Buddhist cosmology, the octagonal brick-and-stucco bunker was one of 14 city fortresses built along Khlong Banglamphu. Of the 4m-high, 3m-thick ramparts that once lined the entire canal, only Phra Sumen and Mahakan have been preserved to show what 18th-century Bangkok was really about – keeping foreign armies at bay.

Open trade with the Portuguese, Dutch, English, French and Chinese made the fortifications obsolete by the mid-19th century, and most of the original city wall was demolished to make way for sealed roadways. By 1900 these roadways were lined with two-storey Sino-Gothic shophouses inspired by Rama V's visits to Singapore and Penang.

Bangkok's oldest residential and business district fans out along the Chao Phraya River between Phra Pin Klao bridge and Hualamphong station. Largely inhabited by the descendants of Chinese residents who moved out of Ko Ratanakosin to make way for royal temples and palaces in the early 19th century, Thais refer to the neighbourhood as Yaowarat (for the major avenue bisecting the neighbourhood) or by the English term 'Chinatown'. One of the most atmospheric streets in this area is Th Plaeng Nam, where several Chinese shophouses, some nearly a century old, can be found.

In the 19th century, Chinese architecture began exerting a strong influence on the city. In Talat Noi (Little Market), a riverside neighbourhood just south of the older Yaowarat, Chinese entrepreneur Chao Sua Son founded a market where larger riverboats could offload wholesale

BANGKOK BUILDINGS WORTH BUILDING

Much of today's Bangkok is faceless concrete, but a handful of structures stand out for their grace, age or uniqueness.

- Bangkok Bank (Map p98; cnr Soi Wanit 1 & Th Mangkon, Chinatown) Thailand was never colonised, but you'd be forgiven for thinking so at the sight of this handsome Thai-European building located deep in Bangkok's Chinatown district.
- Sala Chalermkrung (Map p98; 66 Th Charoen Krung, Chinatown) This theatre, dating back to 1933, is one of the few surviving examples of Thai Art Deco.
- Chao Sua Son's House (Map p98; Talat Noi, Chinatown) Possibly the only remaining, courtyard-style traditional Chinese house in Bangkok; located near San Jao Sien Khong (p100).
- Thai Wah II (Map p122; Th Sathon Tai, Sathon) This 60-storey, wafer-thin tower with a giant hole through the centre is probably better known as the Banyan Tree Hotel (p226). You can see it up close via a drink at the hotel's rooftop Moon Bar (p184).
- Sukhothai Hotel (Map p122; Th Sathon Tai, Sathon) Designed by American architect Edward Tuttle, the Sukhothai's design gracefully straddles 13th-century Thailand and the compory western world.

goods to city merchants. Chao Sua Son's house (Map p98) still stands, a rare example of traditional Chinese architecture in Thailand.

Talat Noi is a cultural and geographic bridge between the almost exclusively Chinese area of Yaowarat to the immediate north and the almost exclusively Western – historically speaking, if not in present-day Bangkok – district of European trading houses and embassies to the immediate south. A portion of Talat Noi was given over to Portuguese residents, who in 1787 built the Holy Rosary Church (Map p98), the capital's oldest place of Christian worship. Originally assembled of wood, after an 1890 fire it was replaced with brick and stucco in the Neo-Gothic stucco style. Today the interior is graced with Romanesque stained-glass windows, gilded ceilings and a very old, life-sized Jesus effigy carried in the streets during Easter processions.

South of Talat Noi at least two or more miles of the Chao Phraya riverside was once given over to such international mercantile enterprises as the East Asiatic Co, Chartered Bank, British Dispensary, Bombay Burmah Trading Co, Banque de l'Indochine, Messrs Howarth Erskine, as well as the Portuguese, French, Russian, British, American, German and Italian embassies. For the era, the well-financed architecture for this area – known then, as today, as Bang Rak – was Bangkok's most flamboyant, a mixture of grand neoclassical fronts, shuttered Victorian windows and Beaux Arts ornamentation. Some of these old buildings have survived to the present. All have been obscured by more modern structures along Charoen Krung Rd, so the best way to appreciate them as a group is from the river itself, by boat.

Thais began mixing traditional Thai architecture with European forms in the late 19th and early 20th centuries, as exemplified by Bangkok's Vimanmek Teak Mansion (p94), the Author's Wing of the Oriental Hotel (Mandarin Oriental; p222), the Chakri Mahaprasat (p69) next to Wat Phra Kaew, and any number of older residences and shophouses in Bangkok. This style is usually referred to as 'old Bangkok' or 'Ratanakosin'. The Old Siam Plaza shopping centre (p165), adjacent to Bangkok's Sala Chalermkrung (p197), is an attempt to revive the old Bangkok school.

Disembark at the Mae Nam Chao Phraya pier of Tha Tien (Map p68), weave your way through the vendor carts selling grilled squid and rice noodles, and you'll find yourself standing between two rows of shophouses of the sort once found along all the streets near the river. Inside, the ground floors display multi-hued tiles of French, Italian or Dutch design, while upper floors are planked with polished teak. Similar shophouses can be found along Th Tanao in Banglamphu.

In the early 20th century, architects left the Victorian era behind, blended European Art Deco with functionalist restraint and created Thai Art Deco. Built just before WWI, an early and outstanding example of this style is Hualamphong Train Station (p100). The station's vaulted iron roof and neoclassical portico are a testament to state-of-the-art engineering, while the patterned, two-toned skylights exemplify Dutch modernism.

Fully realised examples of Thai Deco from the 1920s and '30s can be found along Chinatown's main streets, particularly Th Yaowarat. Whimsical Deco-style sculptures – the Eiffel Tower, a lion, an elephant, a Moorish dome – surmount vertical towers over doorways. Atop one commercial building on Th Songwat perches a rusting model of a WWII Japanese Zero warplane.

Placed there by the Japanese during their brief occupation of Bangkok in 1941, it coordinates perfectly with the surrounding Thai Deco elements. Other examples are the Sala Chalermkrung (p197) and Ratchadamnoen Boxing Stadium (p208).

Office Towers, Hotels & Shopping Centres

During most of the post-WWII era, the trend in modern Thai architecture – inspired by the German Bauhaus movement – was towards a boring International Style functionalism, and the average building looked like a giant egg carton turned on its side. The Thai aesthetic, so vibrant in pre-war eras, almost disappeared in this characterless style of architecture.

The city has been moving skywards almost as quickly as it has expanded outwards. When the Dusit Thani Hotel (p224) opened in 1970 it was the capital's tallest building, and even by the end of that decade fewer than 25 buildings stood taller than six floors. By the year 2000, nearly 1000 buildings could claim that distinction, with at least 20 of them towering higher than 45 floors.

On Th Sathon Tai is the Bank of Asia headquarters (p119), known locally as the 'Robot Building'. Thai architect Sumet Jumsai combined nut-and-bolt motifs at various elevations with a pair of lightning rods on the roof (arranged to resemble sci-fi robot-like antennae) and two metallic-lidded 'eyes' staring out from the upper facade. Another equally whimsical example can be seen in the Elephant Building (Map p132) on Th Phaholyothin in northern Bangkok. Taking influence from Thailand's national symbol, every aspect of the building, from its external shape down to the door handles, is reminiscent of a pachyderm. Both of these buildings represent the last examples of architectural modernism in Bangkok, a trend that had all but concluded by the mid-1980s.

Almost every monumental project constructed in Bangkok now falls squarely in the postmodernist camp, combining rationalism with decorative elements from the past. Proclaiming its monumental verticality like a colossal exclamation point, the 60-storey Thai Wah II building (Map p122), also on Th Sathon Tai, combines rectangles and squares to create a geometric mosaic updating Egyptian Deco. At 305m, the cloud-stabbing Baiyoke Tower II (p112) is currently the second-tallest structure in Southeast Asia after Kuala Lumpur's towering Petronas Twin Towers. Stylistically it shows the inspiration of American post-Deco.

Pure verticality is now giving way to tiered skyscrapers in accordance with the city's setback regulations for allowing light into city streets. The tiered Bangkok City Tower (Map p116) stacks marble, glass and granite around recessed entryways and window lines to create a stunning Mesopotamia-meets–Madison Ave effect. Everything 'neo' is in, including neo-Thai. The Four Seasons (p219), Sukhothai (p226) and Grand Hyatt Erawan (p219) are all examples of hotels that make extensive use of Thai classical motifs in layout and ornamentation.

ARCHITECTURAL ETHICS

Thailand has made numerous admirable efforts to preserve historic religious architecture, from venerable old stupas to ancient temple compounds. The Department of Fine Arts in fact enforces various legislation that makes it a crime to destroy or modify such monuments, and even structures found on private lands are protected.

On the other hand, Thailand has less to be proud of in terms of preserving secular civil architecture such as old government offices and shophouses. Only a few of Bangkok's Ratanakosin and Asian Deco buildings have been preserved, along with a handful of private mansions and shophouses, but typically only because the owners of these buildings took the initiative to do so. Thailand has little legislation in place to protect historic buildings or neighbourhoods, and distinctive early Bangkok architecture is disappearing fast, often to be replaced by plain cement, steel and glass structures of little historic or artistic value. For an illustrated list of buildings in Thailand that have received government protection, seek out the coffee-table book *174 Architectural Heritage in Thailand* (Saowalak Phongsatha Posayanan/ Siam Architect Society, 2004).

Many other countries around the world have regulations that allow the registration of historic homes, and whole neighbourhoods can be designated as national monuments. In neighbouring Laos, Unesco has helped to preserve the charming Lao-French architecture of Luang Prabang by designating the city as a World Heritage Site.

While Bangkok has gone so far in the direction of modern development that it will never recover much of the charm of its 18th- to early 20th-century architecture, if the city or nation doesn't take steps soon to preserve historic secular architecture, there will be nothing left but an internationally homogenous hodge-podge of styles.

LITERATURE
Classical

The written word has a long history in Thailand, dating back to the 11th or 12th centuries when the first Thai script was fashioned from an older Mon alphabet. Sukhothai king Phaya Lithai is thought to have composed the first work of Thai literature in 1345. This was *Traiphum Phra Ruang,* a treatise that described the three realms of existence according to Hindu-Buddhist cosmology. According to contemporary scholars, this work and its symbolism continues to have considerable influence on Thailand's art and culture.

Of all classical Thai literature, however, the Ramakian is the most pervasive and influential. Its Indian precursor – the Ramayana – came to Thailand with the Khmers 900 years ago, first appearing as stone reliefs on Prasat Hin Phimai and other Angkor temples in the northeast. Eventually, Thailand developed its own version of the epic, which was first written during the reign of Rama I. This version contains 60,000 stanzas and is a quarter again longer than the Sanskrit original.

The 30,000-line *Phra Aphaimani,* composed by poet Sunthorn Phu in the late 18th century, is Thailand's most famous classical literary work. Like many of its epic predecessors around the world, it tells the story of an exiled prince who must triumph in an odyssey of love and war before returning to his kingdom.

During the Ayuthaya period, Thailand developed a classical poetic tradition based on five types of verse – *chǎn, gàhp, klong, glorn* and *râi.* Each form uses a complex set of rules to regulate metre, rhyming patterns and number of syllables. During the political upheavals of the 1970s, several Thai newspaper editors, most notably Kukrit Pramoj, composed lightly disguised political commentary in *glorn* verse. Modern Thai poets seldom use the classical forms, preferring to compose in blank verse or with song-style rhyming.

Contemporary

The first Thai-language novel appeared only about 70 years ago, in direct imitation of Western models. Thus far, no more than a handful have been translated into English.

The first Thai novel of substance, *The Circus of Life* (Thai 1929; English 1994) by Arkartdamkeung Rapheephat, follows a young, upper class Thai as he travels to London, Paris, the USA and China in the 1920s. The novel's existentialist tone created quite a stir in Thailand when it was released and became an instant bestseller. The fact that the author, himself a Thai prince, took his own life at the age of 26 only added to the mystique surrounding this work.

The late Kukrit Pramoj, former ambassador and Thai prime minister, novelised Bangkok court life from the late 19th century through to the 1940s in *Four Reigns* (Thai 1953; English 1981), the longest novel ever published in Thai. *The Story of Jan Dara* (Thai 1966; English 1994), by journalist and short-story writer Utsana Phleungtham, traces the sexual obsessions of a Thai aristocrat as they are passed to his son. In 2001, director/producer Nonzee Nimibutr

---

NOVELS

English-language translations of Thai novels are still relatively few, and most foreign-penned novels about Bangkok never make it past the go-go bar door, but the following are quality reads about the city.

- *A Woman of Bangkok*, Jack Reynolds (1956) The precursor of the Bangkok fiction school of writing. (p43), this novel established the city as a setting for countless subsequent exotic crime novels.
- *Bangkok 8*, John Burdett (2003) The first of the popular series of detective novels featuring half-Thai, half-Western detective Sonchai Jitpleecheep.
- *Four Reigns (Si Phaendin),* Kukrit Pramoj (1953; translated 1981) The English translation of a classic of contemporary Thai literature, this novel depicts Thailand's transformation from absolute monarchy to modern society through the eyes of Phloi, a woman working in the Royal Palace.
- *Jasmine Nights*, SP Somtow (1995) Originally released as a series of short stories in the *Bangkok Post,* this semi-autobiographical coming-of-age novel binds American and Thai culture and history.
- *Sightseeing*, Rattawut Lapcharoensap (2004) A Thai voice in contemporary English-language literature.

BANGKOK FICTION

First-time visitors to virtually any of Bangkok's English-language bookstores will notice an abundance of novels with titles such as *The Butterfly Trap, Confessions of a Bangkok Private Eye, Even Thai Girls Cry, Fast Eddie's Lucky 7 A Go Go, Lady of Pattaya, The Go Go Dancer Who Stole My Viagra, My Name Lon You Like Me?, The Pole Dancer,* and *Thai Touch*. Welcome to the Bangkok school of fiction, a genre, as the titles suggest, defined by its obsession with crime, exoticism and Thai women.

The birth of this genre can be traced back to Jack Reynolds' 1956 novel, *A Woman of Bangkok*. Although long out of print, the book is still an acknowledged influence for many Bangkok-based writers, and Reynolds' formula of Western-man-meets-beautiful-but-dangerous-Thai-woman – occasionally spiced up with a dose of crime – is a staple of the modern genre.

Standouts include John Burdett's *Bangkok 8* (2003), a page-turner in which a half-Thai, half-*fà-ràng* (Westerner) police detective investigates the python-and-cobras murder of a US marine in Bangkok. Along the way we're treated to vivid portraits of Bangkok's gritty nightlife scene and insights into Thai Buddhism. A film version of the novel is in the early stages of production, and its sequels, *Bangkok Tattoo* and *Bangkok Haunts*, have sold well in the US.

Christopher G Moore, a Canadian who has lived in Bangkok for the last two decades, has authored 19 mostly Bangkok-based crime novels to positive praise both in Thailand and abroad. His description of Bangkok's sleazy Thermae Coffee House (called 'Zeno' in *A Killing Smile*) is the closest literature comes to evoking the perpetual male adolescence to which such places cater.

Private Dancer, by popular English thriller author Stephen Leather, is another classic example of Bangkok fiction, despite having only been available via download until recently. One of the book's main characters, Big Ron, is based on the real-life owner of Jool's Bar & Restaurant (p184), a Nana-area nightlife staple.

Jake Needham's 1999 thriller *The Big Mango* provides tongue-in-cheek references to the Bangkok bargirl scene and later became the first expat novel to be translated into Thai.

turned the remarkable novel into a rather melodramatic film (see p47). Praphatsorn Seiwikun's rapid-paced *Time in a Bottle* (Thai 1984; English 1996) turned the dilemmas of a fictional middle-class Bangkok family into a bestseller.

Many Thai authors, including the notable Khamphoon Boonthawi *(Luk Isan)* and Chart Kobjitt *(Time)*, have been honoured with the SEA Write Award, an annual prize presented to fiction writers from countries in the Association of South East Asian Nations (Asean). A one-stop collection of fiction thus awarded can be found in *The SEA Write Anthology of Thai Short Stories and Poems* (1996).

When it comes to novels written in English, Thai wunderkind SP Somtow has written and published more titles than any other Thai writer. Born in Bangkok, educated at Eton and Cambridge, and now a commuter between two 'cities of angels' – Los Angeles and Bangkok – Somtow's prodigious output includes a string of well-reviewed science fiction/fantasy/horror stories, including *Moon Dance, Darker Angels* and *The Vampire's Beautiful Daughter*. The Somtow novel most evocative of Thailand and Thai culture is *Jasmine Nights* (1995), which also happens to be one of his most accessible reads. Following a 12-year-old Thai boy's friendship with an African-American boy in Bangkok in the 1960s, this semiautobiographical work blends Thai, Greek and African myths, American Civil War lore and a dollop of magic realism into a seamless whole.

All Soul's Day (1997), by Bill Morris, is a sharp, well-researched historical novel set in Bangkok c 1963. The story, which involves vintage Buicks and the pre-Second Indochina War American military build-up, would do Graham Greene proud.

Thai-American Rattawut Lapcharoensap's *Sightseeing* (2004), a collection of short stories set in present-day Thailand, has been widely lauded for its deft portrayal of the intersection between Thai and foreign cultures, both tourist and expat. Another name worth looking out for is Siriworn Kaewkan, whose novels *The Murder Case of Tok Imam Storpa Karde* and *A Scattered World* have recently been translated into English by Frenchman Marcel Barang. In fact Barang who is also working on an updated translation of *Four Reigns*, is currently the most prodigious translator of Thai fiction into English, and several of his translations, including stories by Chart Korbjitti and two-time SEA Write winner Win Lyovarin, can be downloaded as e-books at www.thaifiction.com.

MUSIC
Classical Thai

Classical central-Thai music *(pleng tai deum)* features a dazzling array of textures and subtleties, hair-raising tempos and pastoral melodies. The classical orchestra or *'bèe-pâht* can include as few as five players or might have more than 20. Leading the band is *'bèe,* a straight-lined woodwind instrument with a reed mouthpiece and an oboe-like tone; you'll hear it most at *moo·ay tai* (Thai boxing; also spelt *muay thai*) matches. The four-stringed *phin,* plucked like a guitar, lends subtle counterpoint, while *ránâht èhk,* a bamboo-keyed percussion instrument resembling the xylophone, carries the main melodies. The slender *sor,* a bowed instrument with a coconut-shell soundbox, provides soaring embellishments, as does the *klùi* or wooden Thai flute.

One of the more noticeable *'bèe pâht* instruments, *kórng wong yài,* consists of tuned gongs arranged in a semicircle and played in simple rhythmic lines to provide the music's underlying fabric. Several types of drums, some played with the hands, some with sticks, carry the beat, often through several tempo changes in a single song. The most important type of drum is the *dà·pohn* (or *tohn*), a double-headed hand-drum that sets the tempo for the entire ensemble. Prior to a performance, the players offer incense and flowers to *dà·pohn,* considered to be the conductor of the music's spiritual content.

The *'bèe pâht* ensemble was originally developed to accompany classical dance-drama and shadow theatre but is also commonly heard in straightforward concert performances. Classical Thai music may sound strange to Western visitors due to the use of the standard Thai scale, which divides the octave into seven full-tone intervals with no semitones. Thai scales were first transcribed by the Thai-German composer Peter Feit (whose Thai name was Phra Chen Duriyanga), who also composed Thailand's national anthem in 1932.

Lôok Tûng & Mŏr Lam

Popular Thai music has borrowed much from Western music, particularly in instrumentation, but retains a distinct flavour of its own. The bestselling of all modern musical genres in Thailand remains *lôok tûng*. Literally 'children of the fields', *lôok tûng* dates back to the 1940s, is comparable to country-and-western in the USA, and is a genre that tends to appeal most to working-class Thais. Subject matter almost always cleaves to tales of lost love, tragic early death and the dire circumstances of farmers who work day in and day out and, at the end of the year, still owe money to the bank.

Lôok tûng song structures tend to be formulaic as well. There are two basic styles: the original Suphanburi style, with lyrics in standard Thai; and an Ubon style sung in Isan (northeastern) dialect. Thailand's most famous *lôok tûng* singer, Pumpuang Duangjan, rated a royally sponsored cremation when she died in 1992, and a major shrine at Suphanburi's Wat Thapkradan, which receives a steady stream of worshippers.

Chai Muang Sing and Siriporn Amphaipong have been the most beloved *lôok tûng* superstars for several years, with lesser lights coming and going. Other more recent stars include God Chakraband (a former soap opera star whose nickname is taken from *The Godfather,* and who is known as the Prince of *Lôok Tûng*) and Mike Piromporn, whose working class ballads have proved enormously popular. One of the more surprising acts of recent years is Jonas-Kristy, a blonde-haired,

top picks

THAI CDS

Most of these CDs are available at domestic chain Mang pong, which has branches at most large malls in town, or at DJ Siam (p144). You can also order online at www.nongtaprachan.com or www.ethaicd.com.

- *Lust for Live* (Bakery Music) Collection of live alt-rock performances by Modern Dog, Chou Chou, Yokee Playboy, POP and Rudklao Amraticha.
- *Made in Thailand* (Carabao) Carabao's classic and internationally popular album.
- *Maw Lam Sa-On 1 – 12* (Jintara Poonlap) Good introduction to *măw lam*.
- *The Best of Loso* (Loso) Thai anthems of teen angst.
- *Best* (Pumpuang Duangjan) Compilation of the late *lôok tûng* diva's most famous tunes.

MADE IN THAILAND

You've undoubtedly seen his lanky frame on billboards, enthusiastically sporting his band's forked-finger salute to promote their eponymous energy drink. You may also have caught him on TV, singing a rallying anthem to sell Chang Beer. And you've probably even heard taxi drivers make passing references to his hit song, 'Made in Thailand'. All these sightings probably have you thinking, who is this guy?

The guy is Yuengyong Ophakun, better known as Aed Carabao, lead singer of Carabao, a Thai band many consider to be the Rolling Stones of Asia.

The name Carabao comes from the Tagalog word for buffalo, and implies diligence and patience (ironically contrasting with the Thai word for buffalo, which is synonymous with stupidity or dim-wittedness). Not unlike the Ramones, the founding members of Carabao, Aed and Khiao (Kirati Promsakha Na Sakon Nakhorn), adopted the word as a surrogate surname after forming the band as students in the Philippines in the early 1980s. Their style of music was inspired by the Thai protest music of the era known as *pleng pêua cheewít*, Filipino music, as well as a healthy dose of Western-style rock and roll. Since their first album, *Chut Khii Mao* (Drunkard's Album), and in the 24 that have followed, Carabao's lyrics have remained political and occasionally controversial. *Ganchaa* (marijuana), a song from their second album, was promptly banned from Thai radio – the first of many. In 2001 Carabao dedicated an album in support of Shan rebels in Myanmar, a source of consternation for the Thai government. When not generating controversy they are almost constantly performing, and have also played in most Southeast Asian countries, as well as Europe and the US.

Through the years, the band has inspired countless copycat acts, but it's unlikely that few acts of any genre will ever equal the influence and popularity of the brothers Carabao.

blue-eyed Swede and his Dutch-English partner, who have been among the hottest-selling *lôok tûng* acts in the country.

Another genre more firmly rooted in northeastern Thailand, and nearly as popular in Bangkok, is *mŏr lam*. Based on the songs played on the Lao-Isan *kaan*, a wind instrument devised of a double row of bamboo-like reeds fitted into a hardwood soundbox, *mŏr lam* features a simple but insistent bass beat and plaintive vocal melodies. If *lôok tûng* is Thailand's country-and-western, then *mŏr lam* is its blues. Jintara Poonlap and Pornsak Songsaeng continue to reign as queen and king of *mŏr lam*. Tune into Bangkok radio station Luk Thung FM (FM 95.0) for large doses of *lôok tûng* and *mŏr lam*.

Songs for Life

The 1970s ushered in a new style inspired by the politically conscious folk rock of the US and Europe, which the Thais dubbed *pleng pêua chee·wít* (literally 'music for life') after Marxist Jit Phumisak's earlier Art for Life movement. Closely identified with the Thai band Caravan – which still performs regularly – the introduction of this style was the most significant musical shift in Thailand since *lôok tûng* arose in the 1940s.

Pleng pêua chee·wít has political and environmental topics rather than the usual love themes. During the authoritarian dictatorships of the '70s many of Caravan's songs were banned. Following the massacre of student demonstrators in 1976, some members of the band fled to the hills to take up with armed communist groups. Another proponent of this style, Carabao, took *pleng pêua chee·wít*, fused it with *lôok tûng*, rock and heavy metal to become one of the biggest bands Thailand has seen (see the boxed text, p45).

T-Pop & Thai Rock

In recent years, Thailand has also developed a thriving teen-pop industry – sometimes referred to as T-Pop – centred on artists who have been chosen for their good looks, and then matched with syrupy song arrangements. Labels GMM Grammy and RS Productions are the heavyweights of this genre, and their rivalry has resulted in a flood of copycat acts. For example, after RS released Parn, an artist meant to appeal to 30-something female listeners, Grammy countered with the nearly identical Beau Sunita. Likewise with Grammy's Golf-Mike and RS's Dan-Beam – two nearly indistinguishable boy bands.

One pop artist seemingly able to subvert genres altogether, not to mention being one of the most popular Thai stars of the last two decades, is Thongchai 'Bird' McIntyre. Born to a half-Scottish father in a musical family, *Pêe Béut* (big-brother Bird), as he is affectionately known, is one of the country's few genuine musical superstars. Many of Bird's songs have become modern Thai pop classics, and in recent years he has expanded his repertoire, working with the likes of *mŏr lam* legend, Jintara Poonlap.

In an effort to bring in more listeners, many of the big labels have also formed smaller imprints. The most influential of these was Bakery Music, a subsidiary of Sony BMG, and a platform for several quasi-alternative, lite-rock and easy listening acts such as Bo, Groove Riders, PRU and Boyd. Many of these artists later went on to form Love Is, currently the 'in' independent label.

In the rock arena, late '90s crowd pleaser Loso (from 'low society') reinvented Carabao's Thai folk melodies and rhythms with indie guitar rock. Grammy responded with a rash of similar Thai headbangers designed to fill stadiums and outsell the indies (independent labels), and popular post-Loso rock acts include Big Ass, Potato and Bodyslam.

Thai Jazz

Yet another movement in modern Thai music has been the fusion of international jazz with Thai classical and folk styles. Fong Nam, a Thai orchestra led by US composer Bruce Gaston, performs a blend of Western and Thai classical motifs, which has become a favourite for movie soundtracks, TV commercials and tourism promotions. Fong Nam plays regularly at Tawan Daeng German Brewhouse (p190). Another leading exponent of this genre is the composer and instrumentalist Tewan Sapsanyakorn (also known as Tong Tewan), who plays soprano and alto sax, violin and *klùi* with equal virtuosity. Other groups fusing international jazz and indigenous Thai music include Kangsadarn and Boy Thai; the latter adds Brazilian samba and reggae to the mix.

Thai Alt/Indie/Hip-Hop

In the 1990s an alternative pop scene – known as *glorng sĕhree* or 'free drum' in Thailand, also *pleng dâi din*, 'underground music' – grew in Bangkok. Modern Dog, a Britpop-inspired band of four Chulalongkorn University graduates, is generally credited with bringing independent Thai music into the mainstream, and their success prompted an explosion of similar bands and indie recording labels. Other major alternative acts in Thailand include Apartmentkunpha, Futon, Chou Chou and Calories Blah Blah. Truly independent labels to look for include Small Room, Panda Records and Spicy Disc.

The indie stuff is almost always reserved for concert performances or one-off club appearances. One spot with regular weekend concerts is the outdoor stage at Centrepoint, Siam Sq. The biggest indie event of the year is Fat Radio-organised, Heineken-sponsored Fat Festival, a three-day outdoor music festival held annually in November. For the latest indie Thai, tune into Fat Radio (www.thisisclick.com/104.5).

Hip-hop is huge in Thailand in terms of radio play and CD sales, but few Thai groups are proficient in performing this genre. Hip-hop/ska artist Joey Boy not only paved the way for others, but released lyrics that the Department of Culture banned. One song, for example, included the Thai euphemism for male masturbation, *chák wôw* (fly a kite). Another hip-hop act that has gained attention is Thaitanium, an all-Thai group that does all its recording in New York and distributes its music independently in Thailand.

ITUNES PLAYLIST

Prepare for your trip by loading up your music player with the following Thai albums, all of which are available at iTunes:

- **GMM Memory Hits Vol 1** The best of modern Thai pop from the country's biggest label, from Bird to Loso.
- **Da Jim Rap Thai** A fun taste of Thai hip hop.
- **Big Ass Begins** Catchy Thai hard rock.
- **Ruam Hit Pleng Thai Amata Lukthong 2** *Lôok tûng* classics from the king of the genre, Chai Muang Sing – look for the influences from Carlos Santana.
- **Palmy** Poppy, but less sappy than most contemporary Thai pop – try not to dance to Yahk Rong Dung Dung.
- **GMM Country Hits Vol 1** A crash course in contemporary *lôok tûng* and *mŏr lam*.
- **Job 2 Do** Ridiculously popular Thai reggae/ska/folk.
- **Silly Fools Mint** The type of Thai-language rock/pop kids in Bangkok grew up with.

CINEMA

Thailand has a lively homespun movie industry and produces nearly 50 comedies, dramas and horror films every year. Cinema is possibly the country's most significant contemporary cultural export, and several Thai films of the last two decades have emerged as international film festival darlings.

Birth of an Industry

Bangkok Film launched Thailand's film industry with the first Thai-directed silent movie, *Chok Sorng Chan*, in 1927. Silent films proved to be more popular than talkies right into the 1960s, and as late as 1969 Thai studios were still producing them from 16mm stock. Perhaps partially influenced by India's famed masala (curry mix) movies – which enjoyed a strong following in post-WWII Bangkok – film companies blended romance, comedy, melodrama and adventure to give Thai audiences a little bit of everything.

The first Thai director to film in the 35mm format was Ratana Pestonji, whose films such as *Rong Raem Narok* (*Country Hotel*; 1957) still influence modern Thai filmmakers. The arrival of 35mm movies in Thailand sparked a proliferation of modern cinema halls and a surge in movie-making, and Thai films attracted more cinema-goers than *năng fà·ràng* (movies from Europe and America). Many today consider the '60s to be a golden age of Thai cinema. More than half of the approximately 75 films produced annually during this period starred the much-admired onscreen duo Mit Chaibancha and Petchara Chaowaraj.

Despite the founding of a government committee in 1970 to promote Thai cinema, Thai film production in the '70s and early '80s was mostly limited to inexpensive action or romance stories. An exception could be found in the films of Prince Chatrichalerm Yukol, in particular *Theptida Rongram* (*The Angel*; 1974) and *Thongpoon Khokpo Rasadorn Temkan* (*The Citizen*; 1977), which introduced substantial doses of dark realism to the Thai film scene. In the same genre was *Luk Isan* (*Child of the North-East*; 1983) which, based on a Thai novel of the same name, follows the ups and downs of a farming family living in drought-ridden Isan. *Luk Isan* became one of the first popular films to offer urban Thais an understanding of the hardships endured by many northeasterners.

Modern Thai Film

The Thai movie industry almost died during the '80s and '90s, swamped by Hollywood extravaganzas and the boom era's taste for anything imported. From a 1970s peak of about 200 releases per year, the Thai output shrank to an average of only 10 films a year by 1997. The Southeast Asian economic crisis that year threatened to further bludgeon the ailing industry, but the lack of funding coupled with foreign competition brought about a new emphasis on quality rather than quantity. The current era boasts a new generation of seriously good Thai directors, several of whom studied film abroad during Thailand's '80s and early '90s boom period.

Recent efforts have been so encouraging that Thai and foreign critics alike speak of a current Thai 'new wave'. Avoiding the soap operatics of the past, the current crop of directors favour gritty realism, artistic innovation and a strengthened Thai identity. Pen-Ek Ratanaruang's *Fun Bar Karaoke* is a 1997 satire of Bangkok life in which the main characters are an ageing Thai playboy and his daughter; the film received critical acclaim for its true-to-life depiction of modern urban living blended with sage humour. It was the first feature-length outing by a young Thai who is fast becoming one of the kingdom's most internationally noted directors. The film played well to international audiences but achieved only limited box-office success at home. Similarly, Nonzee Nimibutr's *2499 Antaphan Krong Meuang* (*Dang Bireley's Young*

top picks

THAI FILMS

Thai cinema has come leaps and bounds in the last 15 years, and the following films, which range from comedy to conceptual, are a good introduction to the genre.

- *Mon Rak Transistor*, Pen-Ek Ratanaruang (2001)
- *Faen Chan (My Girl)*, Komkrit Treewimol et al (2003)
- *Nang Nak*, Nonzee Nimibutr (1998)
- *Ong Bak*, Prachya Pinkaew (2004)
- *Sud Pralad (Tropical Malady)*, Apichatpong Weerasethakul (2004)

BACKGROUND ARTS

GHOSTS & GAGS Kong Rithdee

Thais go to the movies to laugh – and to be frightened. Or at least that's how the stereotype goes.

Comedy and horror films reign supreme at the Thai box office, with audiences fervently embracing every new (or recycled) scare tactic, and film makers diligently ransacking cemeteries for spooky inspirations. The Thai film industry, probably the strongest in Southeast Asia, produces around 45 titles each year, with over half of them relying heavily on clownish gags or stubborn ghosts. And while critics and scholars bemoan the dearth of imagination and the dependence on lowbrow appeal, crowds continue to crave more. So even though Thailand takes pride in its arthouse directors such as Apichatpong Weerasethakul, Pen-ek Ratanaruang and Wisit Sasanatieng, some of whom have made their names known at Cannes, Venice and other top film festivals, it's fair to say that the domestic film industry is oiled – and borne aloft – by the staples of comedy and horror.

Thai films shown in Thai multiplexes usually come with English subtitles, though in most comedy movies the gist of the gags is lost in translation. Most jokes are steeped in witty (and racy) word play, linguistic acrobatics and cultural specificities that are largely untranslatable. In the past five years, the most bankable strategy has been to cast popular TV comedians to play in feature films – these comedians have also become directors themselves – and the mere sight of their faces on a movie poster is a guarantee of box-office profits. Among the masters of the game include Mum Jokmok, Teng Terdterng, Nong Cha Cha Cha and Koh Tee Peenarak. It's easy for people to ridicule the trend, but in watching their fluid wit and straight-faced pranks, it becomes clear that these clowns are extremely talented.

Thai ghost films are famous across Southeast Asia – if not across the world. Films like *Shutter*, in which a photographer captures the presence of a spirit in his pictures, and *4Bia*, an ensemble of four short horror episodes, not only raked in a hundred million baht at home, but were successful exports to various parts of the world, extending as far as Latin America. It's generally believed that Thai ghost movies are more frightening than Hollywood's simply because they are made by people who grew up believing in ghosts – not in a religious sense, but in a spiritual, supernatural and even metaphysical sense. In line with ghost films from other Asian countries, Siamese spirits are often wretched females who were wronged in their lives and return to settle scores. Of these, the most famous is Nang Nak, a legendary figure whose story has been retold at least 30 times on film and TV. Nang Nak (a real person who lived 150 years ago) died while giving birth to her child. Her husband was away with the army at the time, but when he returned home, Nang Nak and her newborn were waiting for him. The family continued to live in bliss – until someone informed the husband that he was living with ghosts.

As horror and comedy are the two most reliable genres, in recent years there's been a Thai trend of combining both into a new breed. Comedy horror, or vice versa, is an indigenous Siamese cinematic creation. A familiar scene in any of these films features a group of people scampering away from a pursuing ghost. In some extreme cases, another potent ingredient is added: homosexuality. The result is a colourful amalgam of camp, horror and comedy, typically involving gay people haunted by ghosts in a movie that's also funny. A weird concoction, yes, just like so many experiences in Thailand.

Kong Rithdee is a film critic for the Bangkok Post.

Gangsters) was hailed abroad – winning first prize at the 1997 Brussels International Film Festival – but was only modestly successful in Thailand.

A harbinger for the Thai film industry was Nonzee Nimibutr's 1998 release of *Nang Nak*, an exquisite retelling of the Mae Nak Phrakhanong legend, in which the spirit of a woman who died during childbirth haunts the home of her husband. This story has had no fewer than 20 previous cinematic renderings. *Nang Nak* not only features excellent acting and period detailing, but manages to transform Nak into a sympathetic character rather than a horrific ghost. The film earned awards for best director, best art director and best sound at the 1999 Asia-Pacific Film Festival.

In 1999 director Pen-Ek Ratanaruang came out with his second feature, a finely crafted thriller set in Bangkok called *Ruang Talok 69 (6ixtynin9)*. Like his first film, it was a critical success that saw relatively little screen time in Thailand.

The 2000 film *Satree Lex (Iron Ladies)* humorously dramatises the real-life exploits of a Lampang volleyball team made up almost entirely of transvestites and transsexuals. At home, this Yongyoot Thongkongtoon–directed film became one of Thai cinema's biggest-grossing films to date, and was the first Thai film ever to reach the art-house cinemas of Europe and the US on general release.

Fah Talai Jone (2000), directed by Wisit Sasanatieng, presents a campy and colourful parody of quasi-cowboy Thai melodramas of the '50s and '60s. The film received an honourable mention at Cannes (where it was quickly dubbed a 'cult hit') and took an award at the Vancouver Film Festival. When Miramax distributed the film in the USA, it was called *Tears of the Black Tiger.*

The next Thai film to garner international attention was 2001's *Suriyothai,* an historic epic directed by Prince Chatrichalerm Yukol. Almost 3½ years and US$20 million in the making, the three-hour film lavishly narrates a well-known episode in Thai history in which an Ayuthaya queen sacrifices herself at the 1548 Battle of Hanthawaddy to save her king's life. *Suriyothai* went on to become the highest-grossing film in Thai history, earning more than 600 million baht, but flopped overseas and was widely criticised for being ponderous and overly long.

In 2001 Nonzee Nimibutr returned with *Jan Dara,* a cinematic rendition of Utsana Pleungtham's controversially erotic 1966 novel of the same name. Filmed almost entirely on sound stages save for outdoor scenes shot in Luang Prabang, Laos, the film was critically compared with Vietnam's famous *Scent of Green Papaya.*

For evidence that Thailand's role in world cinema will continue to expand, you don't need to look any further than Pen-Ek's *Mon Rak Transistor.* This acclaimed film broke ground by seizing a thoroughly Thai theme – the tragicomic odyssey of a young villager who tries to crack the big-time *lôok tûng* music scene in Bangkok – and upgrading production values to international standards. The 2001 release was honoured with a special Directors' Fortnight showing at Cannes 2002, and went on to earn Best Asian Film at the Seattle International Film Festival '02 and the Audience Award at the Vienna International Film Festival '02.

One of Thai cinema's finest moments arrived when the Cannes festival 2002 chose *Sud Sanaeha (Blissfully Yours)* for the coveted Un Certain Regard (Of Special Consideration) screening, an event that showcases notable work by new directors. Directed by 31-year-old Apichatpong Weerasethakul, the film dramatises a budding romance between a Thai woman and an illegal Burmese immigrant, and went on to win a prize in the category.

Another favourite on the 2002 festival circuit, and a blockbuster in Thailand as well, was Jira Malikul's film *15 Kham Deuan 11 (Mekhong Full Moon Party).* The storyline juxtaposes folk beliefs about mysterious 'dragon lights' emanating from the Mekong River with the scepticism of Bangkok scientists and news media, and also with Thai Buddhism. As with *Mon Rak Transistor,* the film affectionately evokes everyday Thai culture for the whole world to enjoy. It's also the first Thai feature film where most of the script is written in the Isan dialect, necessitating Thai subtitles.

The year 2003 saw *Faen Chan (My Girl),* a nostalgic but well-directed-and-acted drama/comedy about childhood friends who become re-acquainted as adults when one of them is about to marry. Directed by a team of six young Thais, the film was hugely successful in Thailand and garnered attention abroad as well.

A further watershed moment occurred when the 2004 Cannes Film Festival awarded Apichatpong's dream-like *Sud Pralad (Tropical Malady)* the Jury Prize. None of the young director's films has generated much interest in Thailand, however, where they are seen as too Western in tone. Much more well received, box office-wise, both in Thailand and abroad, was Prachya Pinkaew's *Ong Bak* (2004), widely hailed around the world as one of the finest 'old-school' martial arts films of all time. The film also set the stage for action star Tony Jaa (Thai name: Panom Yeerum), currently Thailand's hottest big-screen export.

Apichatpong's release, *Syndromes and a Century* (2006), gained somewhat more attention when the director was ordered by the Thai censorship board to cut four seemingly innocuous scenes. This led Apichatpong to cancel the local release of the film in protest, and sparked a subsequent campaign by industry people, critics and audiences to demand that the government do away with the country's antiquated 1930 Film Act and introduce a rating system.

In 2007 Prince Chatrichalerm Yukol followed up 2001's massively popular *Suriyothai* with a duo of historical dramas, *The Legend of King Naresuan,* parts I and II. The epics are a semi-sequel to *Suriyothai,* and tell the story of the 16th-century Thai king who was taken hostage by the Burmese after Ayuthaya was sacked, and who later reclaimed the kingdom's independence. A third part, starring Tony Jaa, began production in 2008.

Today Thailand plays host to two large film festivals, the Bangkok International Film Festival (BKKIFF, p21), and the World Film Festival of Bangkok (p22), further evidence that the country lies at the epicentre of a growing film industry.

HALF CHILD

Leaf through any Thai fashion magazine and you'll come across at least two or three *lôok krêung* faces. Turn on the TV to watch Thai soap operas, commercials or music videos and you're even more likely to see the offspring of *fà·ràng*/ Thai couplings.

Literally 'half child', the *lôok krêung* wasn't always a mainstay of Thai media. In the 1970s and '80s most *lôok krêung* were the children of male American servicemen stationed at one of the seven US military bases scattered around Thailand during the Indochina War. Their mothers may have been Thai women associated only briefly with their fathers; some were *meea chôw* ('rental wives' – a euphemism for prostitute). The resulting Amerasian children of these alliances were typically looked down upon by other Thais.

That perception began to change following Thailand's economic boom in the '80s and '90s, when *lôok krêung* who were schooled abroad or educated at bilingual international schools in Thailand became adults. A new wave of *lôok krêung*, who were the children of expats with more permanent ties to Thailand, were also born during this time, in circumstances deemed more 'respectable' within Thai society.

Coupled with the fading public memory of the Indochina War births, the stigma formerly attached to *lôok krêung* became positive rather than negative almost overnight. Fluency in English and whiter skin tones – apparently a Thai preference long before Europeans arrived in Thailand – lend *lôok krêung* a significant advantage as media figures. Today, a high proportion of models, actors, VJs, beauty queens and pop music stars are *lôok krêung*.

Among the most well-known *lôok krêung* in Thailand are Tata Young (music), Paula Taylor (music/film/VJ), Sonya Couling (modelling), Nat Myria (music), Peter Corp Dyrendal (music), Ananda Everingham (TV/film), Sunny Suwanmethanon (film) and, of course, 'Bird' McIntyre (music/film).

The *lôok krêung* phenomenon has become so topical in Thailand nowadays that a 2006 TV soap opera, *Lady Mahachon*, revolved around a *lôok krêung* pop star (played by real-life *lôok krêung* pop star Paula Taylor) looking for her American father (Erich Fleshman, a bilingual American actor), whom she hadn't seen since early childhood.

THEATRE & DANCE

Traditional Thai theatre consists of five dramatic forms. *Kŏhn* is a formal, masked dance-drama depicting scenes from the Ramakian (the Thai version of India's Ramayana), and originally performed only for the royal court. *Lá·korn* is a general term that covers several types of dance-drama (usually for nonroyal occasions), including *má·noh·rah*, the southern Thai version based on a 2000-year-old Indian story, and Western theatre. *Lí·gair* (likay) is a partly improvised, often bawdy folk play featuring dancing, comedy, melodrama and music. *Lá·korn lék* or *hùn lŏoang* is puppet theatre, and *lá·korn pôot* is modern spoken theatre.

Kŏhn

In all *kŏhn* performances, four types of characters are represented – male humans, female humans, monkeys and demons. Monkey and demon figures are always masked with the elaborate head coverings often seen in tourist promo material. Behind the masks and make-up, all actors are male. Traditional *kŏhn* is very expensive to produce – Ravana's retinue alone (Ravana is the Ramakian's principal villain) consists of more than 100 demons, each with a distinctive mask.

Perhaps because it was once limited to royal venues and never gained a popular following, the *kŏhn* or Ramakian dance-drama tradition nearly died out in Thailand. Bangkok's National Theatre (p196) was once the only place where *kŏhn* was regularly performed for the public; the renovated Sala Chalermkrung (p197) now hosts occasional *kŏhn* performances, enhanced by laser graphics and hi-tech audio.

Scenes performed in traditional *kŏhn* (and *lá·korn* performances – see the following section) come from the 'epic journey' tale of the Ramayana, with parallels in the Greek Odyssey and the myth of Jason and the Argonauts.

Lá·korn

The more formal *lá·korn nai* (inner *lá·korn*, which means that it is performed inside the palace) was originally performed for lower nobility by all-female ensembles. Today it's a dying art, even more so than royal *kŏhn*. In addition to scenes from the Ramakian, *lá·korn nai* performances may include traditional Thai folk tales; whatever the story, text is always sung. *Lá·korn nôrk* (outer *lá·korn*, performed outside the palace) deals exclusively with folk tales and features a mix of sung and spoken text, sometimes with improvisation. Male and female performers are permitted. Like *kŏhn* and *lá·korn nai*, performances of *lá·korn nôrk* are increasingly rare.

Much more common these days is the less refined *lá·korn chah·đree*, a fast-paced, costumed dance-drama usually performed at upcountry temple festivals. *Chah·đree* stories are often influenced by the older *má·noh·rah* theatre of southern Thailand.

A variation on *chah·đree* that has evolved specifically for shrine worship, *lá·korn gâa bon* involves an ensemble of about 20, including musicians. At an important shrine such as Bangkok's Lak Meuang, four *gâa bon* troupes may alternate, each for a week at a time, as each performance lasts from 9am to 3pm and there is usually a long list of worshippers waiting to hire them.

Lí·gair

In outlying working-class neighbourhoods of Bangkok you may be lucky enough to come across the gaudy, raucous *lí·gair*. This theatrical art form is thought to have descended from drama-rituals brought to southern Thailand by Arab and Malay traders. The first native public performance in central Thailand came about when a group of Thai Muslims staged *lí·gair* for Rama V in Bangkok during the funeral commemoration of Queen Sunantha. *Lí·gair* grew very popular under Rama VI, peaked in the early 20th century and has been fading slowly since the 1960s.

Most often performed at Buddhist festivals by troupes of travelling performers, *lí·gair* is a colourful mixture of folk and classical music, outrageous costumes, melodrama, slapstick comedy, sexual innuendo and commentary on Thai politics and society. *Fà·ràng* – even those *fà·ràng* who speak fluent Thai – are often left behind by the highly idiomatic language and gestures. Most *lí·gair* performances begin with the *òrk kàak*, a prelude in which an actor dressed in Malay costume takes the stage to pay homage to the troupe's teacher and to narrate a brief summary of the play to the audience. For true *lí·gair* aficionados, the visit of a renowned troupe is a bigger occasion than the release of an international blockbuster movie at the local cinema.

Lá·korn Lék

Lá·korn lék (little theatre; also known as *hùn lŏoang*, or royal puppets), like *kŏhn*, was once reserved for court performances. Metre-high marionettes made of *kòi* paper and wire, wearing elaborate costumes modelled on those of the *kŏhn*, were used to convey similar themes, music and dance movements.

Two to three puppet masters were required to manipulate each *hùn lŏoang* – including arms, legs, hands, even fingers and eyes – by means of wires attached to long poles. Stories were drawn from Thai folk tales, particularly *Phra Aphaimani* (a classical Thai literary work), and occasionally from the Ramakian. *Hùn lŏoang* is no longer performed, as the performance techniques and puppet-making skills have been lost. The *hùn lŏoang* puppets themselves are highly collectable; the Bangkok National Museum has only one example in its collection. Surviving examples of a smaller, 30cm court version called *hùn lék* (little puppets) are occasionally used in live performances; only one puppeteer is required for each marionette in *hùn lék*.

Another form of Thai puppet theatre, *hùn grà·bòrk* (cylinder puppets), is based on popular Hainanese puppet shows. It uses 30cm hand puppets carved from wood and viewed only from the waist up. *Hùn grà·bòrk* marionettes are still crafted and used in performances today, most notably at the Aksra Theatre (p196).

Lá·korn Pôot

Lá·korn pôot – 'speaking theatre', or live contemporary theatre as known in the West – is enjoyed by a small elite audience in Bangkok. Virtually the entire scene, such as it is, centres on one venue, Patravadi Theatre (p196).

ENVIRONMENT & PLANNING

THE LAND

Located halfway along Thailand's 1860km north–south axis, Bangkok lies approximately 14° north of the equator, putting it on a latitudinal level with Madras, Manila, Guatemala and Khartoum. The rivers and tributaries of northern and central Thailand drain into Mae Nam Chao Phraya, which in turn disgorges into the Gulf of Thailand, a large cul-de-sac of the South China Sea. Bangkok is partly surrounded by a huge, wet, flat and extremely fertile area known as 'the rice bowl of Asia' – more rice is grown here than in any other area of comparable size in all of Asia. Thailand has, in fact, been the world's top exporter of rice for at least the last 30 years.

Metropolitan Bangkok covers 1569 sq km, and may contain as many as 15 million people, making it one of the largest and most densely populated cities in the world. Built on swampland in the midst of one of Southeast Asia's most significant river deltas, the city is only 2m above sea level and sinking 5cm to 10cm a year, which means with rising sea levels it won't be long before the city lies below sea level. Hundreds of kilometres of natural and artificial canals crisscross the region, although many have been filled to create land for new roads and buildings. These canals, or *klorng*, were once Thailand's hydraulic lifeline, but are now seriously degraded by pollution and neglect.

URBAN PLANNING & DEVELOPMENT

When Bangkok became the new royal capital in 1782, the city was originally laid out in a traditional Buddhist mandala (*monton* in Thai) plan, inspired by earlier capitals at Ayuthaya, Sukhothai and Chiang Mai. The Lak Meuang (City Pillar), palaces and royal monasteries stood at the centre, while Khlong Rop Krung was dug around the immediate perimeters to create an island called Ko Ratanakosin. Those nobles and merchants of value to the royal court were encouraged to settle just outside Ko Ratanakosin, and other canals were dug to circumscribe this next layer out from the centre. This rough plan of inner and outer rings – land alternating with water – was a conscious attempt to pay homage to sacred Mt Meru (Phra Sumen in Thai) of Hindu-Buddhist mythology.

GREEN BANGKOK

So extensive are the developments around Bangkok that you'd hardly realise the city is built on one of the world's great river deltas. Even the vast network of canals that once earned Bangkok the nickname 'Venice of the east' are largely lost, and few people remember the vast natural resources and fisheries once submerged by a sea of buildings and pollution. With the world's fastest-growing economy in the 1990s, Thailand in general, and Bangkok in particular, sacrificed environmental concerns in the face of massive profiteering. Bangkok boosts 1000 registered skyscrapers, with hundreds more planned in the ongoing construction boom, leaving little room for unprofitable concepts like city parks, green spaces or healthy ecosystems.

All of the city's canals, as well as the lower reaches of Mae Nam Chao Phraya itself, are considered highly polluted, although plenty of Bangkok residents make daily use of these waterways for bathing, laundry, recreation and even drinking water (after treating it, of course). The worst water quality is found in the black-water canals on the Bangkok side of the river. On average, bacterial contamination of the city's waterways exceeds permissible limits by 75 to 400 times, and contact exposes you to the life-threatening infections that torment the lives of river residents.

The city has undertaken efforts to clean up the canals over the last couple of decades, but with one million cubic metres of liquid waste pouring into the waters each day, there is limited hope for measurable success. It is estimated that 98% of the region's households dump sewage directly into the rivers and canals and this isn't likely to change anytime soon. Efforts to 'clean' the canals includes planting water hyacinths and pumping polluted waters out of canals and pouring it into the river where it flows away into the ocean (out of sight, out of mind).

Roughly 50% of Bangkok's water supply is drawn directly from groundwater siphoned out of significantly depleted aquifers, leaving this water-laden city facing an impending water shortage. Since 1950 the government has constructed about 3000 dams in the Chao Phraya Basin, diverting water for flood control and irrigation, but leaving the lower reaches of the river increasingly contaminated by saltwater that surges upstream as fresh water flows diminish. On a more positive note, Bangkok's notoriously toxic air quality has improved dramatically over the past 15 years. With blue skies now

Early Bangkok was as much a citadel as a city. Today the massive whitewashed walls of Phra Sumen Fort still loom over one end of trendy Th Phra Athit, thrusting out towards Mae Nam Chao Phraya. This brick-and-stucco bunker was one of 14 city *bôrm* (fortresses) built along Khlong Banglamphu, which forms a bow-shaped arc carving an 'island' out of Mae Nam Chao Phraya's left bank.

On the other side of the battlements, Khlong Banglamphu cuts away from the river at a sharp angle, creating the northern tip of Ko Ratanakosin, the royal island that once was the whole of Bangkok. Although often neglected by residents and visitors alike, here stands one of the capital's pivotal points in understanding the city's original plan.

In the other direction, the 7km-long canal curves gently inland towards another wall-and-bunker cluster, Mahakan Fort, marking the southern reach of Ko Ratanakosin. Of the 4m-high, 3m-thick ramparts that once lined the entire canal, only Phra Sumen and Mahakan have been preserved to remind us what 18th-century Bangkok really was about – keeping foreign armies at bay.

Beginning in the early 19th century, Thai kings relinquished the mandala concept and began refashioning the city following European and American models, a process that has continued to this day. Open trade with the Portuguese, Dutch, English, French and Chinese had made the fortifications obsolete by the mid-19th century, and most of the original wall was demolished to make way for sealed roadways. By 1900 these roadways were lined with two-storey, brick-and-stucco Sino-Gothic shophouses inspired by Rama V's visits to Singapore and Penang.

Following WWII, when the Japanese briefly occupied parts of the city, Thai engineers built bridges over Mae Nam Chao Phraya and began filling in canals to provide space for new roads and shophouses. Although many residents continued to occupy stilted houses along the *klorng* and to move about their neighbourhoods by boat, a future of cars and asphalt was inevitable. In the 1960s and '70s the capital's area doubled in size, yet scant attention was paid to managing growth. Well into the 1980s, as adjacent provinces began filling with factories, housing estates, shopping malls, amusement parks and golf courses, urban planning was virtually nonexistent.

Bangkok's first official city plan was issued in 1992, and nowadays the Bangkok Metropolitan Administration (BMA) employs engineers and urban-planning experts to tackle growth and make plans for the future. So far most planning remains confined to paper – noble ideas

the norm, Bangkok has emerged as a role model for other pollution-choked cities in Asia, and placed it on par with air quality found in North America. This is particularly impressive given that traffic has increased 40% in the past decade.

This isn't to say that the city doesn't suffer air quality issues found in other major cities. In 1999, Bangkok introduced the Skytrain, an elevated light-rail system that runs above the city's vehicle-clogged avenues. This public transit system provides welcome relief from the interminable traffic jams and takes cars off the road, but ironically air pollution gets trapped under the train's elevated concrete platforms and creates some of the worst air quality problems in the city.

Bangkok is constructing several new or extended light-rail lines, in a spoke-and-wheel configuration around the city, to persuade more Bangkokians to leave their cars and motorcycles at home. Also in the works are plans for a network of dedicated bus lanes on highways as a way of encouraging more people to use public transport. On a more practical level, every motorcycle sold in Thailand is now required to have a clean-burning four-stroke engine. This is a complete reversal from 10 years ago when all motorcycles were polluting two-stroke models. Air quality in Bangkok is expected to continue improving as old motorcycles and derelict buses are decommissioned and replaced with newer models that adhere to strict European emission standards.

In addition to several large city parks filled with trees and other vegetation, Bangkok relies on immense green areas to the west of the city as a means of detoxifying the air. One of the greatest threats to the environment is continued development, not only in the city centre, but also in outlying areas and neighbouring provinces. Realising the importance of maintaining green 'lungs' for the city, the Thai government attempts to maintain strict control on development in these areas. It has had less success controlling development in the inner city, and almost no success controlling vehicle circulation, one of the most obvious problem areas.

The public rubbish collection system in Bangkok works fairly smoothly, with the city managing to dispose of around 90% of all solid waste produced, an average of 9000 tonnes per day. The piles of street rubbish commonly seen in some South and Southeast Asian capitals are noticeably fewer in Bangkok. Where the rubbish goes is another question altogether. Although some serious attempts to separate and recycle paper, glass and plastic are underway, an estimated 80% of all solid waste ends up at sanitary landfill sites outside Bangkok.

7-ELEVEN FOREVER

Be extremely wary of any appointment that involves the words 'meet me at 7-Eleven'. According to the company's website there are 3912 branches of 7-Eleven in Thailand alone (there will inevitably be several more by the time this has gone to print) – more than half the number found in the entire United States. In Bangkok, 7-Elevens are so ubiquitous that it's not uncommon to see two branches staring at each other from across the street.

The first *sair·wên* (as it's known in Thai) in Thailand was installed at Patpong in Bangkok in 1991. The brand caught on almost immediately and today Thailand ranks behind only Japan and Taiwan in the total number of branches in Asia. The stores are either owned directly by the company or are franchises, owned and managed by private individuals.

Although the company claims its stores carry more than 2000 items, the fresh flavours of Thai cuisine are not reflected in the wares of a typical Bangkok 7-Eleven, whose food selections are even junkier than those of its counterpart in the West. Like all shops in Thailand, alcohol is only available from 11am to 2pm and 5pm to 11pm, and branches of 7-Eleven located near hospitals, temples and schools do not sell alcohol or cigarettes at all (but do continue to sell unhealthy snack food).

7-Eleven and other, less ubiquitous, convenience stores carry a wide selection of drinks, a godsend in sweltering Bangkok. You can conveniently pay most of your bills at the Service Counter, and all manner of phonecards, prophylactics and 'literature' (although, oddly, not most newspapers) are also available. And sometimes the blast of air-conditioning alone is enough reason to stop by. But our single favourite item must be the dirt-cheap chilled scented towels for wiping away the accumulated grime and sweat before your next appointment.

without supporting actions, or with actions thwarted by infighting and profiteering. In theory city authorities have the power to regulate construction by zones, and to monitor land use, but in practice most new developments follow capital, with little thought given to such issues as parking, drainage, or social and environmental impact. For the most part city planners seem preoccupied with the immediate exigencies of maintaining basic city services.

CULTURE & IDENTITY

Whether native or newcomer, virtually every Bangkokian you meet has a story. Although the majority find themselves in Bangkok owing to the simple fact that they were born in the city, a healthy percentage of the population hails from other parts of Thailand and from around the world. Some have followed the promise of work, while others have simply sought out one of the world's most vibrant social climates.

Climb into one of the capital's ubiquitous taxis and the music issuing from your driver's radio or cassette player will often suggest where he's from (virtually all Bangkok taxi drivers are male). If it's *mŏr lam*, with the churning sound of Thai-Lao bamboo panpipes *(kaan)* pounding out zydeco-like chord figures over a strong, simple rhythm, then chances are he moved to Bangkok from one of Thailand's distant northeastern provinces, such as Roi Et or Sakon Nakhon. Switch to *lôok tûng*, a unique hybrid of Thai, Indian and Latin musical influences popular with rural audiences, and the driver almost certainly comes from a province closer to Bangkok, perhaps Suphanburi or Saraburi. And if it's syrupy Thai pop or an older, crooning Bangkok style called *lôok grung*, then you've most likely hitched a ride with a city native.

MAGNET AND MELTING POT

Only a little more than half of the city's inhabitants are in fact true Bangkok Thais, that is, those born of Thai parentage who speak Bangkok Thai as their first language. Although Bangkok Thais are found in all walks of life, they are the backbone of the city's blue-collar workforce in construction, automotive repair and river transport.

Although Chinese Thais live in every quarter of the sprawling city, their presence is most noticeable in a densely populated core of multistorey shophouses along Th Charoen Krung and Th Yaowarat near Mae Nam Chao Phraya, a precinct known as Yaowarat, Sampeng or 'Chinatown'. Chinese in these areas tend to be engaged in all manner of commerce, from wholesale trade in auto parts to the manufacture of high-end kitchen utensils. In other parts of the city they dominate higher education, international trade, banking and white-collar employment in general. Both immigrant and Thailand-born Chinese residents probably enjoy better relations with the majority population here than in any other country in Southeast Asia.

One in 10 Thai citizens lives and works in Bangkok. Roughly 60% of the country's wealth is concentrated here, and per-capita income runs well above the average for the rest of the country – second only to Phuket, an island province in the south. The legal minimum daily wage in Bangkok and the adjacent provinces of Samut Prakan, Samut Sakhon, Pathum Thani, Nonthaburi and Nakhon Pathom amounted to 203B (US$6.12) in 2009, roughly 40B higher than in the rest of Thailand.

A typical civil servant in an entry-level government job earns around 7500B a month, but with promotions and extra job training may earn up to 15,000B. In the private sector an office worker starts at about the same level but will receive pay rises more quickly than those in government positions. Of course Bangkok thrives on private enterprise, from Talat Noi junk auto-parts shops eking out a profit of less than 500B a day, to huge multinational corporations whose upper-level employees drive the latest BMW sedans.

Bangkok women typically control the family finances, and are more likely than men to inherit real estate. Women constitute close to half of the city's workforce, outranking many world capitals. In fields such as economics, academia and health services, women hold a majority of the professional positions – 80% of all Thai dentists, for example, are female.

A CITY OF FAITHS

All of Bangkok's diverse cultures pay respect to the Thai king. The monarchy is considered one of the most important stabilising influences in modern Thai political and cultural life, and on Coronation Day and the King's Birthday the city is festooned with strings of lights and portraits of the king.

Theravada Buddhism

Another cultural constant is Theravada Buddhism, the world's oldest and most traditional Buddhist sect. Around 90% of Bangkokians are Buddhists, who believe that individuals work out their own paths to *nibbana* (nirvana) through a combination of good works, meditation and study of the *dhamma* or Buddhist philosophy. The social and administrative centre for Thai Buddhism is the wát or monastery, a walled compound containing several buildings constructed in the traditional Thai style with steep, swooping roof lines and colourful interior murals; the most important structures contain solemn Buddha statues cast in bronze. The sheer number of wáts scattered around the city – more than 300 – serves as a constant reminder that Buddhism retains a certain dominance, even in increasingly secular Bangkok.

Walk the streets of Bangkok early in the morning and you'll catch the flash of shaved heads bobbing above bright ochre robes, as monks all over the city engage in *bin·tá·bàht,* the daily house-to-house alms food-gathering. Thai men are expected to shave their heads and don monastic robes temporarily at least once in their lives. Some enter the monkhood twice, first as 10-vow novices in their preteen years and again as fully ordained, 227-vow monks sometime after the age of 20. Monks depend on the faithful for their daily meals, permitted only before noon and collected in large, black-lacquered bowls from lay devotees.

Guardian Spirits

Animism predates the arrival of all other religions in Bangkok, and it still plays an important role in the everyday life of most city residents. Believing that *prá poom* or guardian spirits inhabit rivers, canals, trees and other natural features, and that these spirits must be placated whenever humans trespass upon or make use of these features, the Thais build spirit shrines to house the displaced spirits. These dollhouse-like structures perch on wood or cement pillars next to their homes and receive daily offerings of rice, fruit, flowers and water. Peek inside the smaller, more modest spirit homes and you'll typically see a collection of ceramic or plastic figurines representing the property's guardian spirits.

Larger and more elaborate spirit shrines stand alongside hotels and office buildings, and may contain elaborate bronze images of Brahma or Shiva. Undoubtedly Bangkok's most famous example of this is the shrine to Lord Brahma at the Grand Hyatt Erawan Hotel (p107), which has

THE CHINESE INFLUENCE

In many ways Bangkok is a Chinese, as much as a Thai, city. The presence of the Chinese in Bangkok dates back to before the founding of the city, when Thonburi Si Mahasamut was little more than a Chinese trading outpost on the Chao Phraya River. In the 1780s, during the construction of the new capital under Rama I, Hokkien, Teochiew and Hakka Chinese were hired as labourers. The Chinese already living in the area were relocated to the districts of Yaowarat and Sampeng, today known as Bangkok's Chinatown.

During the reign of Rama I, many Chinese began to move up in status and wealth. They controlled many of Bangkok's shops and businesses, and because of increased trading ties with China, were responsible for an immense expansion in Thailand's market economy. Visiting Europeans during the 1820s were astonished by the number of Chinese trading ships in the Chao Phraya River, and some assumed that the Chinese formed the majority of Bangkok's population.

The newfound wealth of certain Chinese trading families created one of Thailand's first elite classes that was not directly related to royalty. Known as *jâo sŭa*, these 'merchant lords' eventually obtained additional status by accepting official posts and royal titles, as well as offering their daughters to the royal family. At one point, Rama V took a Chinese consort. Today it is believed that more than half of the people in Bangkok can claim some Chinese ancestry. The current Thai king is also believed to have partial Chinese ancestry.

During the reign of Rama III, the Thai capital began to absorb many elements of Chinese food, design, fashion and literature. This growing ubiquity of Chinese culture, coupled with the tendency of the Chinese men to marry Thai women and assimilate into Thai culture had, by the beginning of the 20th century, resulted in relatively little difference between the Chinese and their Siamese counterparts.

become a tourist destination in its own right. At virtually all times of the day and night, you'll see Thais kneeling before such shrines to offer stacks of flowers, incense and candles, and to pray for favours from these Indian 'spirit kings'.

The Thais may bestow Thai royal spirits with similar guardian qualities. The spirit of Rama V, who ruled over Siam from 1868 to 1910 and who is particularly venerated for having successfully resisted colonialism, is thought to remain active and powerful in Bangkok today. Every Tuesday evening thousands of Bangkokians throng a bronze equestrian statue of Rama V standing opposite Abhisek Dusit Throne Hall, offering candles, pink roses, incense and liquor to the royal demigod.

Other Religions

Thai royal ceremony remains almost exclusively the domain of one of the most ancient religious traditions still functioning in the kingdom, Brahmanism. White-robed, topknotted priests of Indian descent keep alive an arcane collection of rituals that, it is generally believed, must be performed at regular intervals to sustain the three pillars of Thai nationhood: sovereignty, religion and the monarchy. Such rituals are performed regularly at a complex of shrines near Wat Suthat in the centre of the city. Devasathan (Abode of Gods) contains shrines to Shiva and Ganesha and thus hosts priestly ceremonies in the Shaiva tradition, while the smaller Sathan Phra Narai (Abode of Vishnu) is reserved for Vaishnava ritual.

Green-hued onion domes looming over rooftops and mark the immediate neighbourhood as Muslim, while brightly painted and ornately carved cement spires indicate a Hindu temple. Wander down congested Th Chakraphet in the Phahurat district to find Sri Gurusingh Sabha, a Sikh temple where visitors are very welcome. A handful of steepled Christian churches, including a few historic ones, have been built over the centuries and can be found near the banks of Mae Nam Chao Phraya. In Chinatown large, round doorways topped with heavily inscribed Chinese characters and flanked by red paper lanterns mark the location of *sähn jôw*, Chinese temples dedicated to the worship of Buddhist, Taoist and Confucian deities.

GOVERNMENT & POLITICS

The Bangkok Metropolitan Administration (BMA) administers the capital, which is segmented into 50 districts covering 1569 sq km. Since 1985 metropolitan Bangkok has boasted the country's only elected governors (provincial governors are appointed), and perhaps the most charismatic of these was former army major general, Chamlong Srimuang.

A devout Buddhist, Chamlong is also a self-confessed celibate and a strict vegetarian. In 1985, Chamlong ran for governor as an independent, supported by an organisation calling itself Ruam Phalang (United Force), made up mostly of volunteers from the Santi Asoke Buddhist sect, of which he is a member. Despite facing a much more politically experienced and well-funded competitor, Chamlong won the election by a large margin.

As Governor of Bangkok, Chamlong had a large impact on making the city a more liveable place. He persuaded city street sweepers to sweep streets for the entire day, rather than just during the morning, and encouraged roadside hawkers, technically illegal, to stop selling their wares on Wednesdays. His anti-poverty projects included paving footpaths in squatter communities and establishing thrift stores for the poor. He even established a chain of vegetarian restaurants throughout the city.

In 1988, Chamlong established the Palang Dharma (Moral Force) Party (PDP), a largely Buddhist-based political entity, to contest nationwide parliamentary elections. The party went on to lose these, but Chamlong was able to hold on as Governor of Bangkok. Two years later, Chamlong was again voted governor, and his PDP won 49 out of 55 seats in the election for Bangkok City Council. It was during this term of office that Chamlong became the key opponent and protest leader of the 1991 military government led by army chief Suchinda Kraprayoon. Resigning as governor, Chamlong led massive protests, underwent a hunger strike and was even fired upon by the military before being publicly scolded along with Suchinda by the king on national TV.

Many thought that Chamlong's political career was over after the incidents of 1991. However, in 2006 Chamlong once again gained the political spotlight in Bangkok when he became a key leader of the People's Alliance for Democracy (PAD), a coalition of protesters against the government of Thaksin Shinawatra. Although to Chamlong's chagrin it was the military that eventually took his former protégé out of office, he was instrumental in leading protests in downtown Bangkok that quite possibly led to Thaksin's demise.

In 2004, Bangkok gubernatorial candidate Apirak Kosayothin won a hotly contested race against a candidate backed by the ruling party, Thai Rak Thai. His victory was widely seen as a major loss of face for then prime minister, Thaksin Shinawatra, leader of Thai Rak Thai. Governor Apirak named the reduction of corruption and traffic congestion as his main objectives, and embarked on plans to expand the BTS, the city's mass-transit system. However, some of his policies, including 'smart' taxi and bus stops, flopped, and his proposed Bus Rapid Transit (BRT) project saw little progress.

In March 2008 Apirak voluntarily stepped down as governor so as not to influence an investigation into a fire truck procurement scandal that allegedly involved him and then prime minister, Samak Sundaravej. Subsequent elections led to the landslide election of MR Sukhumbhand Paripatra, a former deputy foreign minister of Thailand and relative of Thailand's king.

MEDIA

Bangkok – and Thailand's – first printed periodical was the *Bangkok Recorder*, a monthly newspaper founded in 1844 by American missionary Dr Dan Beach Bradley. Today Thailand has 38 newspapers, four political weekly magazines, four political monthly magazines, two Chinese newspapers, one newspaper for Muslims, and two English-language newspapers: the *Bangkok Post* and the *Nation*.

In 1955 Thailand became the first country in Southeast Asia to broadcast TV programs. Today there are six free channels and a variety of subscription channels. Thailand also has 523 radio stations, most of which are run by the Public Relations Department, which supervises Radio Thailand, the central government station responsible for broadcasting local and daily news.

The country's previous constitution ensured freedom of the press, although the Royal Police Department reserved the power to suspend publishing licences for national security reasons. Editors generally exercise self-censorship in certain realms, especially with regard to the monarchy.

Thai press freedom reached its high-water mark in the mid-1990s, while Chuan Leekpai's Democrat Party was in power. Following the ascension of Thaksin Shinawatra's Thai Rak Thai

THE INSIDE SCOOP

Several Bangkok residents, both local and foreign, have taken their experiences to the 'small screen' and maintain blogs and websites about living in Bangkok. The following are some of the more informative, entertaining or just weird:

- 2Bangkok (www.2bangkok.com) News sleuth and history buff follows the city headlines from today and yesterday.
- Absolutely Bangkok (www.absolutelybangkok.com) Bangkok news, views and links to several other good blogs and sites.
- Austin Bush Food Blog (www.austinbushphotography.com/category/foodblog) Written by the author of this chapter, the blog focuses on food culture and eating in Bangkok and elsewhere.
- Bangkok Jungle (www.bangkokjungle.com) A blog on the city's live-music scene.
- Bangkok Pundit (www.asiancorrespondent.com/bangkok-pundit-blog) The inside scoop on domestic Thai politics.
- Newley Purnell (www.newley.com) This Bangkok-based American freelance writer comments on everything from local politics to his profound love for pàt grà·prow.
- Gnarly Kitty (www.gnarlykitty.blogspot.org) Written by a female native of Bangkok, a place where 'there are always things worth ranting about.'
- Not The Nation (http://notthenation.com) Thailand's answer to The Onion.
- Stickman (www.stickmanbangkok.com) Formerly associated with naughty Bangkok nightlife, the 'new' Stickman is a more general blog about life, work and love in Bangkok.

Party in 2001, Thailand's domestic media found itself increasingly subject to interference by political and financial interests. The country's international reputation for press freedom took a serious blow in 2002 when two Western journalists were nearly expelled for reporting on a public address presented by the Thai king on his birthday, a portion of which was highly critical of Prime Minister Thaksin. In 2004 Veera Prateepchaikul, editor-in-chief of the *Bangkok Post*, lost his job due to direct pressure from board members with ties to Thaksin and Thai Rak Thai. Allegedly the latter were upset with *Post* criticism of the way in which the PM handled the 2003–04 bird flu crisis.

Observers agree that by 2005 Thai press freedom had reached its lowest ebb since the 1970s era of Thai military dictatorship. However, as popular opinion turned against Thaksin in late 2005 and early 2006, virtually all media (save for military-run TV channel 11) shook off the cloak of self-censorship and joined the public clamour that eventually resulted in Thaksin's deposition from power.

NEIGHBOURHOODS

top picks

Bangkok sprawls across the rice-paddy-flat Chao Phraya plain, hugging both the snaking river itself and a spaghetti-like mess of newer concrete arteries. At first it can be hard to get your head around, with towers spread as far as the eye can see and no discernible centre. But dive into the rivers of flowing metal and sprouting concrete and you'll find a megalopolis that's much more diverse that it first appears, and easier to navigate than you might think.

Along the banks of Mae Nam Chao Phraya (Chao Phraya River) the ancient and skyscraper-free districts of Ko Ratanakosin (Ratanakosin Island, p66) and Thonburi (p77) retain their historic charm. On the east bank – the Bangkok side – stand the monuments to king, country and religion that were once the first shoots of the new capital to grow out of the flood plains. Today these golden spires and fantastic Buddhist temples make it the most visited neighbourhood in the city.

'you'll find a megalopolis that's much more diverse that it first appears, and easier to navigate than you might think'

From Ko Ratanakosin the grand boulevard of Th Ratchadamnoen leads north to Banglamphu (p80), where mansions once housed royal courtiers, and small villages of yellow-and-green shophouses supplied the palace with its many ornate necessities. These days it supplies thousands of travellers with value accommodation, all centred on the intergalactic melting pot that is Th Khao San. Further north the regal enclave of Dusit (p92), fashioned after the capitals of Europe with wide boulevards and palaces set in manicured parks, sits like a crown on the apex of Banglamphu. It is flanked by the contrasting middle-class riverside neighbourhood of Thewet (p92), which has an altogether less pretentious feel.

South of Ko Ratanakosin is the cramped and chaotic district of Chinatown (p97), where deals have been done since the city was founded and continue apace today. Chinatown is Bangkok's most vibrant neighbourhood, and a great place to get lost. Further south the historic riverside (p118) centre of international trade leads east into the business high-rise neighbourhoods of Silom (p119) and Sathon, and the relief and relative sanity of Lumphini Park (p120).

To the north and east of here Bangkok pours forth like an endless concrete spill. Skyscrapers, shopping centres and expressway flyovers dominate the skyline in place of temples. The area around Siam Square (p105) is one giant shopping district and has, thanks largely to the Skytrain interchange here, become the unofficial 'centre' of Bangkok. Immediately to the east is Th Sukhumvit (p126), a busy commercial and residential neighbourhood that is a favourite of expatriates, cosmopolitan Thais and modern midrange hotels.

GREATER BANGKOK
(p131)

THANON SUKHUMVIT
(p125)

SIAM SQUARE, PRATUNAM,
PLOENCHIT & RATCHATHEWI
(p105)

RIVERSIDE,
SILOM & LUMPHINI
(p115)

THEWET & DUSIT
(p92)

BANGLAMPHU
(p80)

CHINATOWN
(p97)

KO RATANAKOSIN
& THONBURI
(p66)

2 km
1 mile
0
0

ITINERARY BUILDER

Bangkok's big-ticket sights are concentrated in the older part of town around Ko Ratanakosin, Thonburi, Dusit and Banglamphu. However, the city's shopping, eating, galleries, bars and spas are widespread. For late-night entertainment, Sukhumvit, Silom and Banglamphu are best.

AREA ACTIVITIES	Sights	Outdoors	Shopping
Ko Ratanakosin & Thonburi	Wat Pho (p69) Wat Phra Kaew and Grand Palace (p67) Museum of Siam (p72)	Wat Arun (p77) Chao Phraya Express Boat (p263) Ko Ratanakosin walking tour (p75)	amulet market (p136) traditional medicine shops (p136)
Banglamphu & Dusit	Wat Suthat (p84) Golden Mount and Wat Saket (p80) Vimanmek Teak Mansion (p94)	Dusit Park (p94) Monk's Bowl Village (p81) Th Khao San (p86)	Th Khao San Market (p137) Taekee Taekon (p137) Nittaya Curry Shop (p137)
Chinatown	Wat Mangkon Kamalawat (p100) Wat Traimit (p99) Hualamphong Train Station (p100)	Talat Noi (p100) Saphan Phut Night Bazaar (p139) Chinatown walking tour (p101)	Saphan Phut Night Bazaar (p139) Pak Khlong Market (p139) Johnny's Gems (p138)
Siam Square & Around	Jim Thompson's House (p106) Siam Ocean World (p107) Wang Suan Phakkat (p112)	Baan Krua (p106) Erawan Shrine (p110) Lingam Shrine (p107)	Siam Center & Siam Discovery Center (p143) Mahboonkrong (MBK, p142) Fly Now (p140)
Riverside, Silom & Lumphini	Queen Saovabha Memorial Institute (p121) Oriental Hotel (Mandarin Oriental, p222) Bangkokian Museum (p118)	Lumphini Park (p120) hotel ferries (p119) Haroon Village (p123)	Thai Home Industries (p145) Suan Lum Night Bazaar (p147) Patpong Night Market (p146)
Th Sukhumvit	Ban Kamthieng (p129)	Benjakiti Park (p128) Soi 38 Night Market (p177) Skytrain (p266)	Th Sukhumvit Market (p150) L'Arcadia (p148) Jim Thompson Factory Outlet (p146)
Greater Bangkok	Ancient City (Muang Boran) (p131)	Ko Kret (p240) Khlong Toey Market (p146) Mahachai Rail Line (p247)	Chatuchak Weekend Market (p148) Vespa Market (p150) Nonthaburi Market (p150)

HOW TO USE THIS TABLE

The table below allows you to plan a day's worth of activities in any area of the city. Simply select which area you wish to explore, and then mix and match from the corresponding listings to build your day. The first item in each cell represents a well-known highlight of the area, while the other items are more off-the-beaten-track gems.

Activities & the Arts	Eating	Drinking & Nightlife
Wat Pho Thai Traditional Massage School (p270) Patravardi Theatre (p196) National Theatre (p196)	The Deck (p160) Rachanawi Samosorn (Navy Club Restaurant; p160) Wang Lang Market (p160)	Amorosa (p181)
Ratchadamnoen Stadium (p208) Khao Cooking School (p155) Queen's Gallery (p201)	Eats Walk: Thanon Tanao (p162) Hemlock (p161) Thip Samai (p162)	Banglamphu pub crawl (p186) Phranakorn Bar (p185) Brick Bar (p187)
Sala Chalermkrung (p197) Co van Kessel bicycle tours (p207)	Tang Jai Yuu (p164) Eats Walk: Chinatown (p165) Royal India (p164)	River View Guest House (218)
100 Tonson Gallery (p199) Calypso Cabaret (p198) Spa 1930 (p205)	Mahboonkrong Food Court (p167) Gianni Ristorante (p166) Sanguan Sri (p167)	Roof (p184) To-Sit (p185) Club Culture (p192)
H Gallery (p200) Lumphini Stadium (p208) Ruen-Nuad Massage (p205)	Ngwan Lee Lang Suan (p172) Somboon Seafood (p170) Khrua Aroy Aroy (p171)	Moon Bar at Vertigo (p184) Tapas Room (p193) DJ Station (p188)
Coran Boutique Spa (p204) Buathip Thai Massage (p204) Thailand Creative & Design Center (p129)	Face (p173) Bo.lan (p174n) Nasir Al-Masri (p174)	Bed Supperclub (p192) Tuba (p186) Bangkok Bar (p182)
Bang Kachao bicycle tour (p207) Bangkok University Art Gallery (BUG; p200) Thailand Cultural Centre (p197)	Or Tor Kor Market (p177) Yusup (p178) Baan Klang Nam 1 (p177)	Parking Toys (p190) Saxophone Pub & Restaurant (p190) Slim/Flix (p193)

CENTRAL BANGKOK

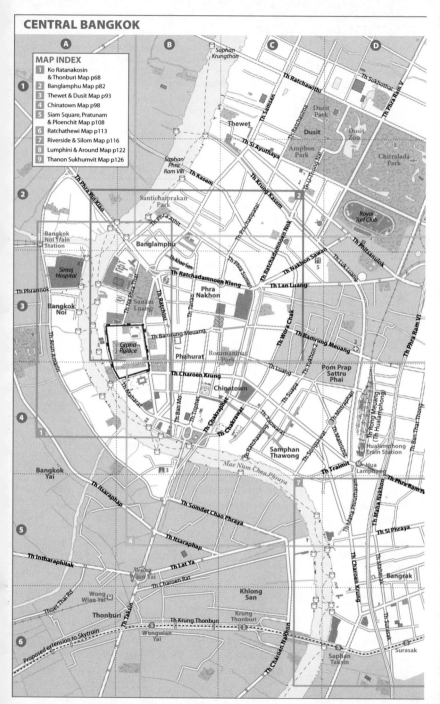

MAP INDEX
1. Ko Ratanakosin & Thonburi Map p68
2. Banglamphu Map p82
3. Thewet & Dusit Map p93
4. Chinatown Map p98
5. Siam Square, Pratunam & Ploenchit Map p108
6. Ratchathewi Map p113
7. Riverside & Silom Map p116
8. Lumphini & Around Map p122
9. Thanon Sukhumvit Map p126

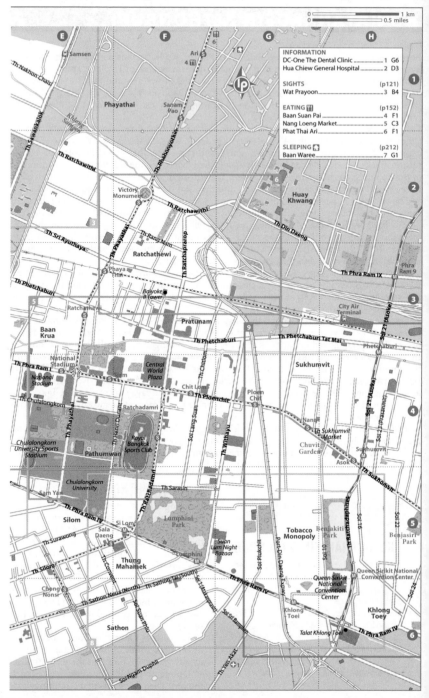

Bordering the eastern bank of Mae Nam Chao Phraya, Ko Ratanakosin is the historic heart of Bangkok and is a veritable Vatican City of Thai Buddhism. Several of Thailand's most honoured and holy sites stand inside burly white walls here, Wat Phra Kaew and the Grand Palace (opposite) and Wat Pho (p69) being the most notable. As it happens, these are also Bangkok's most spectacular tourist attractions – and most obligatory sights – so expect camera-toting crowds rather than exotic eastern mysticism.

Ko Ratanakosin's collection of religious and architectural treasures wasn't accidental. Rama I (Phraphutthayotfa Chulalok; r 1782–1809) intended to re-create the glory of the sacked Siamese capital of Ayuthaya by constructing a new island city – one that would be fortified against future attacks – and to elevate the newly established dynasty in the imagination and adoration of the populace. Both intentions succeeded. The Burmese and other noncommercial invaders never staged an assault on the new capital and the Chakri dynasty survives to the present day.

The ancient city has matured in modern times and is now a lively district of contradictions that only Thailand can juggle. The temples, with their heavenly status, are tethered to earth by nearby food markets shaded by faded green umbrellas sprouting like mouldering mushrooms from the pavement. In the shadows of the whitewashed temple walls are Buddhism's ancient companions – the animistic spirits who govern fortune and fate, neatly packaged into amulets and sold by the thousand in the markets of Thanon Maharat (p71).

While the glimmering golden spires and Buddha images are must-sees, the charm of Ko Ratanakosin is felt just as much – if not more – by wandering on foot, taking in the street life, stopping for lunch at local restaurants or The Deck (p160) and mixing with young Thais in Thammasat (p74) and Silpakorn (p74) universities.

Opposite Ko Ratanakosin, across the busy waters of Mae Nam Chao Phraya, Thonburi (p77) enjoyed a brief 15-year promotion from sleepy port town to royal seat of power immediately before the capital moved to Bangkok. If it weren't for timing, it might otherwise be a footnote in Thai history. Instead it is still revered as a patriotic and divinely inspired step in reuniting the country after the fall of Ayuthaya. The stories of the post-war reunification are filled with poetic symbolism: General Taksin, who expelled the Burmese and subdued rival factions, came across this spot in the river at dawn and pronounced it Ayuthaya's successor. But Taksin was later deposed by a more strategic leader, who decided on a more strategic position across the river for his capital.

Today Thonburi is a rarely visited gem for anyone looking to experience the less commercial, quieter side of Bangkok life. Where Bangkok's *klorng* have largely been concreted over to create traffic-packed roads, in Thonburi they remain an integral part of daily life. To really experience this unique neighbourhood, stay at the Thai House (p232).

top picks

KO RATANAKOSIN & THONBURI

- Amulet market (p136) Traders, monks and collectors trading for countless sacred amulets.
- Wat Arun (p77) Mosaic-decorated stupa on the far bank of the river.
- Wat Phra Kaew and Grand Palace (p67) The Hollywood blockbusters of Thai architecture.
- Wat Pho (p69) One seriously large Reclining Buddha in a rambling complex of hidden sights.
- Amorosa (p181) Unbeatable sunset views over the river and Wat Arun to go with your cocktail.

KO RATANAKOSIN

Forming almost a tear-drop shape, Ko Ratanakosin's boundaries are defined by Mae Nam Chao Phraya on the western side, and the Khlong Banglamphu and Khlong Ong Ang canals to the north and east. The northern part of the island is Banglamphu, and in this book the areas outside Th Somdet Phra Pin Klao to the north of Sanam Luang, and Th Atsadang, which follows Khlong Lawt on the eastern side, are covered in the Banglamphu section (p80).

The district's attractions are concentrated in the area south of Sanam Luang and are ideally visited on foot (see the walking tour, p75), preferably in the morning before it gets too hot. The pavements that circumnavigate the main sights and the temple courtyards are almost completely devoid of shade, so a hat, sunscreen and even an umbrella can be a good idea. Alternatively, túk-túks (pronounced đúk đúk) are a dime a dozen around here (offer half what they ask for).

Four river piers – Tha Phra Chan, Tha Maharat, Tha Chang and Tha Tien – service this district, making transport a scenic, convenient and relaxed experience. It's also a popular area from which to hire longtail boats for tours into Thonburi's canals.

South of Th Na Phra Lan is primarily a tourist zone with a few warehouses abutting the river as reminders that a measure of traditional life still exists. North of the Grand Palace is Sanam Luang (p73), an expansive park where joggers shuffle along in the early morning hours. Alongside Sanam Luang, the National Museum and the National Theatre stand with stoic resolve and people gather to celebrate and protest the kingdom's milestones. On the far eastern side of Wat Phra Kaew are government ministry buildings reflecting a pronounced Western architectural influence – an interesting contrast to the flamboyant Thai architecture across the street.

Rip-off artists prowl the tourist strip, using the country's legendary hospitality to earn a dishonest day's wages. Disregard any strangers who approach you inquiring about where you are from (usually followed by 'oh, my son/daughter is at university there'), where you are going or (the classic opening gambit) telling you the attractions are closed (see p279). Save the one-on-one cultural exchange for genuine people outside the tourist zone.

WAT PHRA KAEW & GRAND PALACE
Map p68

วัดพระแก้ว/พระบรมมหาราชวัง

☎ 0 2222 6889; Th Na Phra Lan; admission to wát, palace & Dusit Park 350B, audio guide for 2hr 200B; ⏰ 8.30am-3.30pm (closes 4pm); 🚌 air-con 503 & 508, ordinary 25, 80 & 91; 🚢 Tha Chang (N9)

Wat Phra Kaew (The Temple of the Emerald Buddha) gleams and glitters with so much colour and glory that its earthly foundations seem barely able to resist the celestial pull. Architecturally fantastic, the temple complex is also the spiritual core of Thai Buddhism and the monarchy, symbolically united in what is the country's most holy image, the Emerald Buddha. Attached to the temple complex is the former royal residence, once a sealed city of intricate ritual and social stratification.

TRANSPORT: KO RATANAKOSIN

Bus Air-con 503, 508 & 511; ordinary 3, 25, 39, 47, 53 & 70

Ferry Tha Rajinee (N7), Tha Tien (N8) & Tha Chang (N9)

There's no Skytrain or Metro to Ko Ratanakosin – yet – so the easiest and most enjoyable ways to get here are by river ferry or on foot. From Banglamphu just walk through Thammasat University or Sanam Luang; from almost anywhere else take either a ferry direct or the Skytrain to Saphan Taksin and a ferry from there. Less fun but faster (unless it's peak hour) are the cheap taxis and expensive túk-túks.

Enter Wat Phra Kaew and the Grand Palace complex through the clearly marked third gate from the river pier. Tickets are purchased inside the complex; anyone telling you it's closed before 3.30pm is a gem tout or con artist.

Past the ticket counters you'll meet the *yaksha,* brawny guardian giants from the Ramakian (the Thai version of the Indian Ramayana epic). Beyond them is a courtyard where the central *bòht* (chapel) houses the Emerald Buddha (see the boxed text, p71). The spectacular ornamentation inside and out does an excellent job of distracting first-time visitors from paying their respects to the image. Here's why: the Emerald Buddha is only 66cm tall and sits so high above worshippers in the main temple building that the gilded shrine is more striking than the small figure it cradles. There are always postcards if you miss it; photos are not allowed.

Outside the main *bòht* is a stone statue of the Chinese goddess of mercy, Kuan Im, and nearby are two cow figures, representing the year of Rama I's birth. In the 2km-long cloister that defines the perimeter of the complex are 178 murals depicting the Ramakian in its entirety, beginning at the north gate and moving clockwise around the compound. If the temple grounds seem overrun by tourists, the mural area is usually mercifully quiet and shady.

Adjoining Wat Phra Kaew is the Grand Palace (Phra Borom Maharatchawang), a former royal residence that is today only used on ceremonial occasions; the current monarch lives in Chitralada Palace. Visitors are allowed to survey the Grand Palace grounds and four of the remaining palace buildings, which are interesting for their royal bombast.

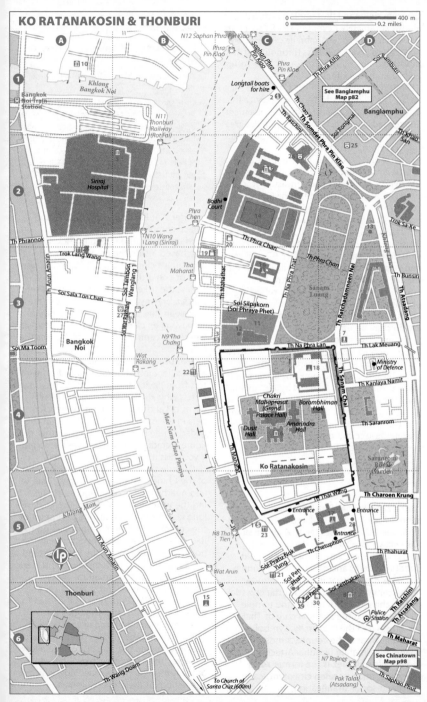

KO RATANAKOSIN & THONBURI

0 — 400 m
0 — 0.2 miles

N12 Saphan Phra Pin Klao

Phra Pin Klao

Saphan Phra Pin Klao

Phra Pin Klao

Longtail boats for hire

Th Phra Athit

Soi Rambutti

Th Chao Fa

Th Somdet Phra Pin Klao

See Banglamphu Map p82

Banglamphu

Th Ratchini

Soi Rongmai

Th Khao San

Khlong Bangkok Noi

Bangkok Noi Train Station

N11 Thonburi Railway (Rot Fai)

Siriraj Hospital

Bodhi Court

Trok Sa-Ke

Phra Chan

Th Phra Chan

Th Phra Chan

Th Bunsiri

Th Phrannok

TN10 Wang Lang (Siriraj)

Trok Lang Wang

Soi Tambon Wanglang 1

Tha Maharat

Th Phra Chan

Th Na Phra That

Th Ratchadamnoen Nai

Th Atsadang

Arun Amarin

Soi Sala Tôn Chan

Th Maharat

Soi Silpakorn (Soi Phraya Phet)

Sanam Luang

Bangkok Noi

Soi Wat Rakang

N9 Tha Chang

Th Na Phra Lan

Th Lak Meuang

Th Sanam Chai

Ministry of Defence

Wat Rakang

Th Kanlaya Namit

Mae Nam Chao Phraya

Chakri Mahaprasat (Grand Palace Hall)

Borombhiman Hall

Amarindra Hall

Dusit Hall

Th Saranrom

Saranrom Royal Garden

Ko Ratanakosin

Th Thai Wang

Th Charoen Krung

Khlong Mon

Arun Amarin

Entrance

Entrance

Entrance

N8 Tha Tien

Th Chetuphon

Th Phahurat

Wat Arun

Soi Pratu Nok Yung

Th Ratchini

Thonburi

Soi Peng Chai

Soi Pratu Nok

Soi Sunthakan

Th Atsadang

Police Station

Th Wang Doem

N7 Rajinee

Pak Talat (Atsadang)

Th Saphan Phut

See Chinatown Map p98

To Church of Santa Cruz (600m)

KO RATANAKOSIN & THONBURI

At the eastern end, Borombhiman Hall is a French-inspired structure that served as a residence for Rama VI (King Vajiravudh; r 1910–25). Today it can only be viewed through its iron gates. But in April 1981 General San Chitpatima used it as the headquarters for an attempted coup. Amarindra Hall, to the west, was originally a hall of justice but is used (very rarely indeed) for coronation ceremonies; the golden, boat-shaped throne looks considerably more ornate than comfortable.

The largest of the palace buildings is the triple-winged Chakri Mahaprasat (Grand Palace Hall). Completed in 1882 following a plan by British architects, the exterior shows a peculiar blend of Italian Renaissance and traditional Thai architecture, a style often referred to as *fà·ràng sài chá-dah* (Westerner wearing a Thai classical dancer's headdress), because each wing is topped by a *mondòp* (a layered, heavily ornamented spire). It is believed the original plan called for the palace to be topped with a dome, but Rama V (King Chulalongkorn; r 1868–1910) was persuaded to go for a Thai-style roof instead. The tallest of the *mondòp,* in the centre, contains the ashes of Chakri kings; the flanking *mondòp* enshrine the ashes of the many Chakri princes who failed to inherit the throne.

The last building to the west is the Ratanakosin-style Dusit Hall, which initially served as a venue for royal audiences and later as a royal funerary hall.

Until Rama VI decided one wife was enough for any man, even a king (see p26), Thai kings housed their huge harems in the inner palace area (not open to the public), which was guarded by combat-trained female sentries. The intrigue and rituals that occurred within the walls of this cloistered community live on in the fictionalised epic *Four Reigns,* by Kukrit Pramoj, which follows a young girl named Ploi growing up within the Royal City.

Remember to hang on to your ticket as it also allows entry to Dusit Park (p94).

WAT PHO Map p68
วัดโพธิ์(วัดพระเชตุพน)

☎ 0 2622 3533; www.watpho.com; Th Sanam Chai; admission 50B; ⏰ 8am-6pm; 🚌 air-con 503 & 508, ordinary 12, 47, 53 & 82; 🚤 Tha Tien (N8)
Of all Bangkok's temples, Wat Pho is arguably the one most worth visiting for both its remarkable Reclining Buddha image and its sprawling, stupa-studded grounds. The temple boasts a long list of credits: the oldest and largest *wát* in Bangkok; the longest Reclining Buddha and the largest collection of Buddha images in Thailand; and the country's first public education institution. For all that, it sees fewer visitors than neighbouring Wat Phra Kaew and feels less commercial.

A temple has stood on this site since the 16th century, but in 1781 Rama I ordered the original Wat Photharam to be completely rebuilt as part of his new capital. Under Rama III (King Phranangklao; r 1824–51), the massive Reclining Buddha was built and Wat Pho became Thailand's first university. Today it maintains that tradition as the national headquarters for the teaching and preservation of traditional Thai medicine, including Thai massage.

Narrow Th Chetuphon divides the grounds in two, and it's well worth entering from either this quiet lane or Th Sanam Chai to avoid the touts and tour groups of the main entrance on Th Thai Wang. You'll come into the northern compound (the southern part is closed to the public), where the main bòht is constructed in Ayuthaya style and is strikingly more subdued than Wat Phra Kaew. Rama I's remains are interred in the base of the presiding Buddha figure in the bòht.

The images on display in the four wíhähn (sanctuaries) surrounding the main bòht are worth investigation. Particularly beautiful are the Phra Jinnarat and Phra Jinachi Buddhas in the western and southern chapels, both rescued from Sukhothai by relatives of Rama I. The galleries extending between the four chapels feature no fewer than 394 gilded Buddha images.

Encircling the main bòht is a low marble wall with 152 bas-reliefs depicting scenes from the Ramakian. You'll recognise some of these figures when you exit the temple past the hawkers with mass-produced rubbings for sale; these are made from cement casts based on Wat Pho's reliefs.

In the northwest corner of the site you'll find Wat Pho's main attraction, the enormous, tremendous Reclining Buddha. The 46m-long and 15m-high supine figure illustrates the passing of the Buddha into nirvana. It is made of plaster around a brick core and finished in gold leaf, which gives it a serene luminescence that keeps you looking, and looking again, from different angles. The 3m-high feet are a highlight, with mother-of-pearl inlay depicting 108 different auspicious láksànà (characteristics of a Buddha).

On the western side of the grounds a collection of four towering tiled stupas commemorates the first four Chakri kings. The surrounding wall was built on the orders of Rama IV (King Mongkut;

r 1851–68), who for reasons we can only speculate about decided he didn't want any future kings joining the memorial. Note the square bell shape with distinct corners, a signature of Ratanakosin style. Wat Pho's 91 smaller stupas include chedi (stupa) clusters containing the ashes of lesser royal descendants.

Small Chinese-style rock gardens and hill islands interrupt the tiled courtyards providing shade, greenery and quirky decorations depicting daily life. Keep an eye out for the distinctive rockery festooned with figures of the hermit Khao Mor, who is credited with inventing yoga, in various healing positions. According to the tradition, a few good arm stretches should cure idleness.

If you're hot and foot sore the air-conditioned massage pavilions (p205) near the east gate could be a welcome way to cool down while experiencing high quality and relatively inexpensive Thai massage.

LAK MEUANG Map p68
ศาลหลักเมือง

☎ 0 2222 9876; cnr Th Sanamchai & Th Lak Meuang; admission free; ⏰ 6.30am-6.30pm; 🚌 air-con 508 & 511, ordinary 15, 47, 53 & 59; 🚢 Tha Chang (N9)

What would otherwise be an uninteresting mileage marker has both religious and historical significance in Thailand. Lak Meuang is the city shrine, a wooden pillar erected by Rama I in 1782 to represent the founding of the new Bangkok capital. From this point, distances are measured to all other city shrines in the country. But its importance doesn't stop there. The pillar is endowed with a spirit, Phra Sayam Thewathirat (Venerable Siam Deity of the State), and is considered the city's guardian. To the east of the main shrine are several other idols added during the reign of Rama V.

Like the sacred banyan trees and the holy temples, Lak Meuang receives daily supplica-

TEMPLE ETIQUETTE

Buddhist monasteries (wáts) and temples are sacred places and should be treated with respect. You must remove your shoes as you enter any building – when you see empty shoes scattered around a doorway or threshold, this is your cue. At some temples, and especially at Wat Phra Kaew and the Grand Palace grounds, dress rules are strictly enforced. If you're wearing shorts or a sleeveless shirt you will not be allowed into the temple grounds – this applies to men and women. Long skirts and three-quarter length pants are not appropriate, either. If you're flashing a bit too much calf or ankle, expect to be shown into a dressing room and issued with a sarong. Once suitably attired, you'll be allowed in. For walking in the courtyard areas you are supposed to wear shoes with closed heels and toes. Officially, sandals and flip-flops are not permitted, though the guards are less zealous in their enforcement of this rule.

THE EMERALD BUDDHA

The lofty perch of the Phra Kaew (Emerald Buddha) in Wat Phra Kaew signifies its high status as the 'talisman' of the Thai kingdom. No one knows exactly where the Buddha comes from or who sculpted it, but it first appeared on record in 15th-century Chiang Rai in northern Thailand. Like so many famous Buddha images around Southeast Asia, legend says it was sculpted in India and brought to Siam by way of Ceylon (Sri Lanka). But stylistically it seems to belong to Thai artistic periods of the 13th to 14th centuries. Despite the name, the sacred sculpture is actually carved from a single piece of nephrite, a type of jade.

Some time in the 15th century, this Buddha is said to have been covered with plaster and gold leaf and placed in Chiang Rai's own Wat Phra Kaew. Many valuable Buddha images were masked in this way to deter potential thieves and marauders during unstable times. Often the true identity of the image was forgotten over the years until a 'divine accident' exposed its precious core. The Emerald Buddha experienced such a divine revelation while it was being transported to a new location. In a fall, the plaster covering broke off, revealing the brilliant green inside. But while his was seen as a divine revelation, the return of the Phra Kaew would prove anything but peaceful for the people of Siam and Laos.

During territorial clashes with Laos, the Emerald Buddha was seized and taken to Vientiane in the mid-16th century. Some 200 years later, after the fall of Ayuthaya and the ascension of the Bangkok-based kingdom, the Thai army marched up to Vientiane, razed the city and hauled off the Emerald Buddha. The return of this revered figure was a great omen for future fortunes of this new leadership. The Buddha was enshrined in the then capital, Thonburi, before the general who led the sacking of Vientiane assumed the throne and had it moved to this location.

A tradition that dates back to this time is the changing of the Buddha's seasonal robes. There are now three royal robes: for the hot, rainy and cool seasons. The three robes are still solemnly changed at the beginning of each season. This duty has traditionally been performed by the king, though in recent years the crown prince has presided over the ceremony.

tions from Thai worshippers, some of whom commission classical Thai dancers to perform *lákon gâa bon* (shrine dancing) as thanks for granted wishes. Offerings also include those cute yet macabre pigs' heads with sticks of incense sprouting from their foreheads.

Lak Meuang is across the street from the eastern wall of Wat Phra Kaew, at the southern end of Sanam Luang.

THANON MAHARAT Map p68
ถนนมหาราช

btwn Th Phra Chan, Th Na Phra Lan & Mae Nam Chao Phraya; 🚌 **air-con 503 & 508, ordinary 32, 53 & 91;** ⛴ **Tha Chang (N9)**
The northern stretch of this street is one of Bangkok's most interesting. On the opposite side of Wat Mahathat's whitewashed walls, the street is monopolised by ancient Thai industries: herbal apothecaries and amulet dealers. In the cool season, medicinal bowls of ginger-infused broth are sold from steaming cauldrons to stave off winter colds (yes, seriously!). Outdoor displays of pill bottles are lined up and dusted daily like prized antiques. Each remedy bears a picture of a stoic healer, a marketing pitch that puts a human face on the medicine. Further along, the amulet market (*ɗalàht prá krêuang; p136*) spills out of its medieval warren into the street, forcing pedestrians

to run zigzag patterns through the plastic mats (the Thai equivalent of blanket stalls) on which the tiny images are displayed.

This is a great place to just wander and watch men (because it's rarely women) looking through magnifying glasses at the tiny amulets, seeking hidden meaning and, if they're lucky, hidden value. The market stretches all the way to the riverside, where a narrow alley leads north to wooden kitchens overhanging the water. Each humble kitchen garners a view of the river; students from nearby Thammasat University congregate here for cheap eats before heading off to class. It's an ideal stop for a lunch of classic Thai comforts and Western adaptations popular with students.

If you continue through the warren all the way to Tha Phra Chan, between 7am and 7pm you'll find a bunch of tarot readers and palmists set up at tables just off the entrance to the pier. Some of them speak English and charge 200B for a 20-minute reading. If experience is anything to go by (my reader told me 'don't go out after 9pm, it is too dangerous' and seemed concerned that I didn't have a *giq* [Thai mistress], though she did accurately predict trouble with my car...), you probably shouldn't make any life-altering decisions based on the wisdom imparted here.

STONE COLD STARE: WAT PHO'S ROCK GIANTS

Aside from monks and sightseers, Wat Pho is filled with an altogether stiffer crowd: dozens of giants and figurines carved from granite. The rock giants first arrived in Thailand as ballast aboard Chinese junks and were put to work in Wat Pho (and other wát, including Wat Suthat), guarding the entrances of temple gates and courtyards.

Look closely and you'll see an array of Chinese characters. The giants with bulging eyes and Chinese opera costumes were inspired by warrior noblemen and are called *Lan Than;* notice their swords tucked behind their ornate robes. The political nobleman wears his hair and moustache below his shoulders and carries a scroll in one hand; his long cloak indicates that he is a member of the aristocracy. The figure in a straw hat is a farmer, forever interrupted during his day's work cultivating the fields. And can you recognise the guy in the fedora-like hat with a trimmed beard and moustache? Marco Polo, of course, who introduced such European styles to the Chinese court.

NEIGHBOURHOODS KO RATANAKOSIN & THONBURI

Unpopular plans to redevelop this area as a cultural theme park with shops catering to tourists have been shelved – for now. But considering Bangkok's love of reinvention, leaving Th Maharat for your next trip is probably not a good idea.

MUSEUM OF SIAM Map p68
สถาบันพิพิธภัณฑ์การเรียนรู้แห่งชาติ
☎ 0 2225 2777; www.ndmi.or.th; 4 Th Sanam Chai; adult 100B, under 15yr free; ☉ 10am-6pm Tue-Sun; 🚌 air-con 503 & 524, ordinary 3, 6, 12, 47, 53 & 82; 🚢 Tha Tien (N8)

This fun new museum employs a variety of media to explore the origins of the Thai people and their culture. Housed in a European-style 19th-century building that was once the Ministry of Commerce, the exhibits are presented in an engaging, interactive fashion not often found in Thailand. They are also refreshingly balanced and entertaining, with galleries dealing with a range of questions about the origins of the nation and its people. Each room has an informative narrated video started by a sensory detector, keeping waiting to a minimum. An Ayuthaya-era battle game, a room full of traditional Thai toys and a street vending cart where you can be photographed pretending to whip up a pan of *pàt tai* will help keep kids interested for at least an hour, adults for longer. Check out the shop and cafe in the grounds for some innovative gift ideas.

NATIONAL MUSEUM Map p68
พิพิธภัณฑสถานแห่งชาติ
☎ 0 2224 1402; www.thailandmuseum.com; Th Na Phra That; admission 50B; ☉ 9am-4pm Wed-Sun; 🚌 air-con 508 & 511, ordinary 12, 47 & 53; 🚢 Tha Chang (N9)

Thailand's National Museum is the largest museum in Southeast Asia and covers a broad range of subjects, from historical

surveys to religious sculpture displays. The buildings were originally constructed in 1782 as the palace of Rama I's viceroy, Prince Wang Na. Rama V turned it into a museum in 1884.

The history wing presents a succinct chronology of events and figures from the prehistoric, Sukhothai, Ayuthaya and Bangkok eras. Despite the corny dioramas, there are some real treasures here: look for King Ramkhamhaeng's inscribed stone pillar (the oldest record of Thai writing), King Taksin's throne and the Rama V section.

The other parts of the museum aren't as well presented, but this might be part of the charm. Dimly lit rooms, ranging in temperature from lukewarm to boiling, offer an attic-like collection of Thai art and handicrafts.

In the central exhibits hall, there are collections of traditional musical instruments from Thailand, Laos, Cambodia and Indonesia, as well as ceramics, clothing and textiles, woodcarving, royal regalia, and Chinese art and weaponry. The art and artefact buildings cover every Southeast Asian art period and style, from Dvaravati to Ratanakosin. The collection is impressive but hard to digest due to poor signage and sheer volume.

The museum grounds also contain the restored Phutthaisawan (Buddhaisawan) Chapel. Inside the chapel (built in 1795) are some well-preserved original murals and one of the country's most revered Buddha images, Phra Phuttha Sihing. Legend claims the image came from Ceylon (legend claims a lot of Buddha images came from Ceylon), but art historians attribute it to the 13th-century Sukhothai period.

While the museum isn't nearly as dynamic as the new Museum of Siam (left), it does run (highly recommended) free tours in English and French on Wednesday and Thursday, Japanese on Wednesday and German on Thursday. All tours start from the ticket pavilion at 9.30am.

SANAM LUANG Map p68
สนามหลวง

bounded by Th Na Phra That, Ratchadamnoen Nai & Na Phra Lan; 🚌 air-con 503, 508 & 511, ordinary 15, 47, 53 & 60; ⚓ Tha Chang (N9)

On a hot day, Sanam Luang (Royal Field) is far from charming – a shadeless expanse of dying grass and concrete pavement ringed by flocks of pigeons and homeless people. Despite its shabby appearance, it has been at the centre of both royal ceremony and political upheaval since Bangkok was founded. Indeed, many of the colour-coded protests you've probably seen on TV in recent years have been held here.

Less dramatic events staged here include the annual Royal Ploughing Ceremony (p21), in which the king (or more recently the crown prince) officially initiates the rice-growing season; an appropriate location given Sanam Luang was used to grow rice for almost 100 years after the royals moved into Ko Ratanakosin. After the rains, the kite-flying season (mid-February to April) sees the air above filled with butterfly-shaped Thai kites. Matches are held between teams flying either a 'male' or 'female' kite in a particular territory; points are won if they can force a competitor into their zone.

Large funeral pyres are constructed here during elaborate, but infrequent, royal cremations, and explain the field's alternate name, Thung Phra Men (Cremation Ground). The most recent cremation was a six-day, 300 million baht ceremony for King Bhumibol Adulyadej's sister, Princess Galyani Vadhana in November 2009; it took 11 months to prepare.

In a way the park is suffering a career crisis, having lost most of its full-time employment to other locales or the whims of fashion. Until 1982 Bangkok's famous Weekend Market was regularly held here (it's now at Chatuchak Park; see p148). Previously the wealthy came here for imported leisure sports; these days they head for the country club. Today the cool mornings and evenings still attract a health-conscious crowd of joggers, walkers and groups playing đà·grôr. If you fancy a big-crowd experience, Sanam Luang draws the masses – and the King – in December for the King's Birthday (5 December), Constitution Day (10 December) and New Year.

Across Th Ratchadamnoen Nai to the east is the statue of Mae Thorani, the earth goddess (borrowed from Hindu mythology's Dharani), which stands in a white pavilion. Erected in the late 19th century by Rama V, the statue was originally attached to a well that provided drinking water to the public.

SARANROM ROYAL GARDEN Map p68
สวนสราญรมย์

bounded by Th Ratchini, Charoen Krung & Sanam Chai; 🕐 5am-9pm; 🚌 air-con 503 & 508, ordinary 1, 2, 12 & 25; ⚓ Tha Tien (N8)

Easily mistaken for a European public garden, this Victorian-era green space was originally designed as a royal residence in the time of Rama IV. After Rama VII (King Prajadhipok; r 1925–35) abdicated in 1935, the palace served as the headquarters of the People's Party, the political organisation that orchestrated the handover of the government. The open space remained and in 1960 was opened to the public.

BANGKOK STREET SMARTS

Keep the following in mind to survive the traffic and avoid joining the list of tourists sucked in by Bangkok's numerous scam artists:

- Good jewellery, gems and tailor shops aren't found through a túk-túk driver.
- Skip the 10B túk-túk ride unless you have the time and will-power to resist a heavy sales pitch in a tailor or gem store.
- Ignore 'helpful' locals who tell you that tourist attractions and public transport are closed for a holiday or cleaning; it's the beginning of a con, most likely a gem scam.
- Don't expect any pedestrian rights; put a Bangkokian between you and any oncoming traffic, and yield to anything with more metal than you.
- Walk outside the tourist strip to hail a taxi that will use the meter – tell the driver 'meter'. If the driver refuses to put the meter on, get out.

Today a wander through the garden reveals a Victorian gazebo, paths lined with frangipani and a moat around a marble monument built in honour of one of Rama V's favourite wives, Queen Sunantha, who died in a boating accident in 1880. The queen was on her way to Bang Pa-In Summer Palace in Ayuthaya when her boat began to sink. The custom at the time was that commoners were forbidden to touch royalty, which prevented her attendants saving her from drowning.

The satellite corners of the park are filled with weightlifting equipment where a túk-túk driver might do some leg crunches in between telling tourists that the sights they are looking for have closed. As the day cools, various aerobics and dance classes practise their synchronisation, and if you're lucky like us you might see a delicate *kun yĭng* – Bangkok matron recognisable for the big perm and generously applied make-up – enjoying a slow-motion workout on the rusty rowing machine.

SILPAKORN UNIVERSITY Map p68
มหาวิทยาลัยศิลปากร
☎ 0 2623 6115; www.su.ac.th; 31 Th Na Phra Lan; 🚌 air-con 503 & 508, ordinary 1, 25 & 82; 🚤 Tha Chang (N9)
Thailand's universities aren't usually repositories for interesting architecture, but Silpakorn, the country's premier art school, breaks the mould. The classical buildings form the charming nucleus of what was an early Thai aristocratic enclave, and the traditional artistic temperament still survives. The building immediately facing the Th Na Phra Lan gate was once part of a palace and now houses the Silpakorn University Art Centre (Map p68; ☎ 0 2218 2965; www.art-centre. su.ac.th; ⏰ 9am-7pm Mon-Fri, 9am-4pm Sat), which

exhibits work by faculty, students and other Thai and international artists. To the right of the building is a shady sculpture garden displaying the work of Corrado Feroci (also known as Silpa Bhirasri), the Italian art professor and sculptor who came to Thailand at royal request in the 1920s and later established the university (which is named after him), sculpted parts of the Democracy Monument (p86) and, much to his own annoyance, the Victory Monument.

Not surprisingly, the campus has an arty, contemporary vibe and is a good place to sit and watch sketchers doing their thing. Stop by the Art Shop beside the gallery for unique postcards and books.

THAMMASAT UNIVERSITY Map p68
มหาวิทยาลัยธรรมศาสตร์
☎ 0 2613 3333; www.tu.ac.th; 2 Th Phra Chan; 🚌 air-con 508 & 511, ordinary 47 & 53; 🚤 Tha Chang (N9)
Much of the drama that followed Thailand's transition from monarchy to democracy has unfolded on this quiet riverside campus. Thammasat University was established in 1934, two years after the bloodless coup that deposed the monarchy. Its remit was to instruct students in law and political economy, considered to be the intellectual necessities for an educated democracy.

The university was founded by Dr Pridi Phanomyong, whose statue stands in Pridi Ct at the centre of the campus. Pridi was the leader of the civilian People's Party that successfully advocated a constitutional monarchy during the 1920s and '30s. He went on to serve in various ministries, organised the Seri Thai movement (a Thai resistance campaign against the Japanese during WWII) and was ultimately forced into exile when the post-war government was seized by a military dictatorship in 1947.

Pridi was unable to counter the dismantling of democratic reforms, but the university he established continued his crusade. Thammasat was the hotbed of pro-democracy activism during the student uprising era of the 1970s. On 14 October 1973 (sìp-sèe dù·lah), 10,000 protesters convened on the parade grounds beside the university's Memorial Building demanding the government reinstate the constitution. From the university the protest grew and moved to the Democracy Monument, where the military and police opened fire on the crowd, killing 77 and wounding 857. The massacre prompted the king to revoke his support of the military rulers and for a brief period a civilian government was reinstated. On 6 October 1976 (hòk đù·lah), Thammasat itself was the scene of a bloody massacre, when at least 46 students were shot dead while rallying against the return from exile of former dictator Field Marshal Than-om Kittikachorn. Near the southern entrance to the university is the Bodhi Court, where a sign beneath the Bodhi tree explains more about the democracy movement that germinated at Thammasat.

Walk south from Th Phra Athit in Banglamphu and you'll go straight through Thammasat, emerging at the south end near Tha Phra Chan pier.

WAT MAHATHAT Map p68
วัดมหาธาตุ

☎ 0 2222 6011; Th Mahathat; admission by donation; ☽ 7am-6pm; 🚌 air-con 503 & 508, ordinary 47 & 53; 🚢 Tha Chang (N9)

While other temples in the area claim all the fame, Wat Mahathat goes about the everyday business of a temple. Saffron-robed monks file in and out of the white-washed gates; grandmas in their best silks come to make merit; and world-weary soi dogs haul themselves out of the shade in search of food, if not nirvana.

Founded in the 1700s, Wat Mahathat is a national centre for the Mahanikai monastic sect and is home to the first of Bangkok's two Buddhist universities, Mahathat Ra-javidyalaya. The university is the most important place of Buddhist learning in mainland Southeast Asia – regional spats notwithstanding, the Lao, Vietnamese and Cambodian governments send selected monks to further their studies here.

Entered through the Thawornwathu Building, Mahathat and the surrounding area have developed into an informal Thai cultural centre. The monastery offers meditation instruction in English (see p270).

KO RATANAKOSIN STROLL
Walking Tour
Bangkok's most famous sites are cradled in Ko Ratanakosin (Ratanakosin Island).

This walk starts at Tha Chang, accessible by Chao Phraya river ferries or, if you're staying in Banglamphu, by an easy walk from Th Phra

Athit through Thammasat University. If you start about 1pm you'll be able to see the palace before it closes at 3.30pm and finish in time for a sundowner by the river before the last ferry leaves from Tha Tien. Alternatively, if you have more energy than time, start early and do this walk and the Chinatown walk (p101) in a single day. Much of the walk is shaded by trees, but it's still worth bringing a hat and sunscreen.

1 Silpakorn University
From the pier, file east past the market towards Th Na Phra Lan. On your left-hand side turn into Silpakorn University (p74), Thailand's first fine-arts university. Drop into the Art Centre, in an old palace, to see the current exhibition.

2 Wat Mahathat
Continue north through the campus and left to get back to Th Maharat (p71). Turn right on Th Maharat and wander past the nylon mats and tables displaying amulets, herbal apothecaries and traditional medicines that, on one recent visit, included the disturbing sight of a full tiger skin. On your right is Wat Mahathat (left), Thailand's most respected Buddhist university.

3 Amulet Market
Turn into the narrow alley immediately after Trok Mahathat to the amulet market (p136), a warren of vendors selling prá krêuang (religious amulets) representing various Hindu and Buddhist deities.

4 Food Vendors
Find the riverside lane within the market and head north (keep the river on your left). This leads past more amulet stalls and stores selling graduation gowns and Buddha images. Several small kitchens with seating overlooking the river are ideal for a cheap, delicious Thai lunch.

5 Tarot Readers
At the northern end of the market you'll emerge at Tha Phra Chan. In a lane just off the entry to the pier are several tarot card readers, some of whom speak English.

6 Sanam Luang
Take Th Phra Chan east past Thammasat University to the vast royal field of Sanam Luang (p73). Turn right along Th Na Phra That and walk to the end.

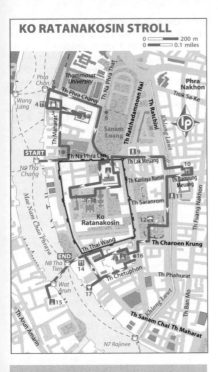

KO RATANAKOSIN STROLL

0   200 m
0   0.1 miles

WALK FACTS

Start Tha Chang (river ferry N9)
End Tha Tien (river ferry N8)
Distance 6km to 7.5km
Duration 3½ to six hours, depending on how much time you spend looking, eating, drinking and getting massaged
Fuel stops Trok Nakhon food vendors, Natthaphorn (p163), Rub Aroon (p160) and The Deck (p160)

7 & 8 Wat Phra Kaew & Grand Palace

Cross Th Na Phra Lan and turn left to the official tourist entrance to Thailand's holiest temple, Wat Phra Kaew (p67), and the formal royal residence, the Grand Palace (p67). See p70 for details on dress restrictions.

9 Lak Meuang

Exiting via the same gate, take a right and cross Th Ratchadamnoen Nai for a quick spin past the Lak Meuang (City Pillar; p70).

10 Natthaphorn

From Lak Meuang walk east along Th Lak Meuang to Khlong Lawt, cross on the foot-bridge, turn right, cross the street and turn left into Th Phraeng Phuthon (there's no English sign; look for the lunchtime kitchen with a dozen dishes on the corner). Turn right at the T-junction and then left and you're now in the village-like setting of Th Phraeng Phuthon. On the corner facing the park is Natthaphorn (p163), Bangkok's most famous coconut ice-cream shop and a great place to cool off.

11 & 12 Pig Shrine & Saranrom Royal Garden

From Natthaphorn, walk south and turn right on Th Bamrung Muang, cross back over the *klorng* and turn left on Th Ratchini. You'll pass the scrappy Queen Patcharinthira shrine, a brass pig built in honour of the queen's 50th birthday in 1913 (she was born in the lunar year of the pig). Continue and enter Saranrom Royal Garden (p73) for a view of Thais exercising and chilling.

13 Wat Pho

Exit the garden on Th Chareon Krung, turn right and cross over to the left and you're at the east entrance to Wat Pho (p69), near the massage studios. Meander through the grounds on your way to the massive Reclining Buddha.

Options, options

OK, so now you have to decide. Depending on the time, and levels of interest, energy, hunger and thirst, you can finish the walk in various ways. Get your timing right and you can do some or all of the following activities and still watch the sun set behind Wat Arun with a cold drink and freshly deknotted body. Remember that the last ferry leaves Tha Tien soon after 7pm, and taxis around here are notorious for refusing to put the meter on – if you need one, insist on the meter.

14 Rub Aroon

Just want to sit with a coffee for a bit? Exit Wat Pho beside the Reclining Buddha, turn left on Th Maharat and settle into Rub Aroon (p160), a friendly cafe serving Thai standards and fresh fruit drinks.

15 Wat Arun

Walk to Tha Tien (N8) and take the regular cross-river ferry to Wat Arun (opposite) to see its striking Hindu-Khmer stupa.

16 Get a massage

Wat Pho is the national repository for traditional massage and offers massages (p205) in the air-conditioned studios near the eastern gate. A thoroughly sensible choice and conveniently open until 6.30pm, which is perfect timing for…

17 Sundowners

Exit Wat Pho beside the Reclining Buddha, turn left on Th Maharat and then right at Th Soi Pratu Nok Yung. Walk past the old Chinese godowns to the end of the soi and The Deck (p160), a restaurant with spectacular views of the river and Wat Arun. The upstairs Amorosa bar (p181), which opens at 6pm, is easily the best place to watch the sun set behind Wat Arun.

THONBURI

Thonburi has lived in the shadow of Bangkok for more than 200 years and is today a not entirely fashionable suburb of the capital. Fashion, of course, is a subjective thing. Particularly in the older area opposite central Bangkok, there aren't that many raised freeways, expensive cars or modern transportation systems. Instead Thonburi retains enough of the traditional transport corridors – the *klorng* that once caused Bangkok to be known as the 'Venice of the East' and Thais to call themselves *jòw nám* (water lords) – to give it a decidedly different feel. A day exploring them is likely to be one of the most memorable of your stay in the Thai capital.

The network of canals and river tributaries still carries a motley fleet of watercraft, from paddled canoes to rice barges via ear-splitting longtails. Homes, trading houses and temples are built on stilts with front doors opening out to the river. According to residents, these waterways protect them from the seasonal flooding that plagues the capital.

Khlong Bangkok Noi is lined with greenery and historic temples, reaching deep into the Bang Yai district, a brief five-minute ride from the concrete entanglements of central Bangkok. Khlong Bangkok Yai was in fact the original course of the river until a canal was built to expedite transits. Today the tributary sees a steady stream of tourists on longtail boat tours en route to floating markets, the Royal Barges Museum (p78) or Wat Intharam, where a *chedi* contains the ashes of Thonburi's King Taksin, ceremonially assassinated in 1782. Fine gold-and-black lacquerwork adorning the main *bòht* doors depicts the mythical *nah·ree·pŏn*

tree, which bears fruit shaped like beautiful maidens.

Most tourists meet only the river-facing part of Thonburi between Khlong Bangkok Noi and Khlong Bangkok Yai, directly across from Ko Ratanakosin, leaving the interior of the community predominantly Thai with hardly an English sign or pestering túk-túk driver in sight. As the river ferries ricochet from stop to stop, a steady stream of commuters is shuttled to and from jobs in downtown Bangkok. There are nine bridges spanning the Chao Phraya, but you will probably end up on a husky cross-river ferry plodding from one side to the other in stress-relieving slow motion.

The giant-sized southern bus station sends services west to Kanchanaburi and south as far as Malaysia. Meanwhile Thonburi has two minor rail terminuses: one departs from Bangkok Noi (near Siriraj Hospital and about 900m from the Thonburi Railway ferry pier) and trundles west to Kanchanaburi; the other is the Mahachai Railway that goes from Wong Wian Yai to the gulf coast suburbs (see p247).

WAT ARUN Map p68
วัดอรุณฯ
☎ 0 2891 1149; www.watarun.org; Th Arun Amarin; admission 50B; ☉ 8am-6pm; 🛳 from Tha Tien (N8) to Tha Wat Arun

The missile-shaped temple that rises from the banks of the Mae Nam Chao Phraya is known as Temple of Dawn and named after the Indian god of dawn, Aruna. It was here that, in the wake of the destruction of Ayuthaya, King Taksin stumbled upon a small local shrine and interpreted the discovery as such an auspicious sign that this should be the site of the new capital

---

TRANSPORT: THONBURI

Bus Air-con 507 & 509, ordinary 21, 42 & 82

Ferry A tour of Thonburi by longtail boat is fun and easy, but for a more local experience consider taking the public ferries. Bang Yai–bound boats from Tha Chang leave every 30 minutes between 6am and 8am, every hour from 8am to 3pm, and depart when the boat is full between 3pm and 9pm. The main Chao Phraya Express ferries stop at a few key Thonburi piers, most notably Wang Lang (Siriraj, N10), Thonburi Railway (N11) and Saphan Phra Pin Klao (N12). Several cross-river ferries also connect to Bangkok piers.

of Siam. King Taksin built a palace beside the shrine, which is now part of Navy Headquarters, and a royal temple that housed the Emerald Buddha for 15 years before Taksin was assassinated (p24) and the capital moved across the royal river to Bangkok.

The central feature is the 82m-high Khmer-style *brahng* (spire), constructed during the first half of the 19th century by Rama II (King Phraphutthaloetla Naphalai; r 1809–24), now immortalised in a riverfront statue with three elephants, and Rama III (King Phranangklao; r 1824–51). From the river it is not apparent that this corn-cob-shaped steeple is adorned with colourful floral murals made of glazed porcelain, a common temple ornamentation in the early Ratanakosin period, when Chinese ships calling at Bangkok used porcelain as ballast.

Also worth a look is the interior of the *bòht*. The main Buddha image is said to have been designed by Rama II, whose ashes are interred beneath. The murals date to the reign of Rama V (King Chulalongkorn; r 1868–1910). Particularly impressive is one depicting Prince Siddhartha (the Buddha) encountering examples of birth, old age, sickness and death outside his palace walls, an experience that led him to abandon the worldly life.

Wat Arun is directly across from Wat Pho, on the Thonburi side of the river. A lot of people visit the wát on expensive river tours, but it's dead easy and more rewarding to just jump on the 3B cross-river ferry from Tha Tien. For our money, visiting Wat Arun in the late afternoon is best, with the sun shining from the west lighting up the *brahng* and the river behind it. If you come earlier, consider taking a stroll away from the river on Th Wang Doem, a quiet tiled street of wooden shophouses.

You must wear appropriate clothing (see p70) to climb on Wat Arun. If you are flashing too much flesh you'll have to rent a sarong for 20B.

CHURCH OF SANTA CRUZ off Map p68
☎ 0 2466 0347; Soi Kuti Jiin, Thonburi; ☽ Sat & Sun; ⛴ from Tha Pak Talat/Atsadang
โบสถ์สั่งตาครูส
Centuries before Sukhumvit became the international district, the Portuguese claimed *fá·ráng* (Western) supremacy and built the Church of Santa Cruz in the 1700s. The land

was a gift from King Taksin in appreciation for the loyalty the Portuguese community had displayed after the fall of Ayuthaya. The surviving church dates to 1913. Very little activity occurs on the grounds itself, but small village streets break off from the main courtyard into the area known as Kuti Jiin, the local name for the church. On Soi Kuti Jiin 3, several houses sell Portuguese-inspired cakes.

ROYAL BARGES NATIONAL MUSEUM
Map p68
เรือพระที่นั่ง
☎ 0 2424 0004; Khlong Bangkok Noi or 80/1 Th Arun Amarin; admission 100B, camera/video 100/200B; ☽ 9.30am-5pm; 🚌 air-con 503, 507, 509 & 511, ordinary 19, 57, 79, 81, 124 & 149; ⛴ Tha Saphan Phra Pin Klao (N12)
Every foreign country has its famous religious monuments and museums, but how many have their own fleet of royal boats on display? The curiously named royal barges were once used daily by the royal family to get about their realm, but are now used only for grand ceremonies. They are not barges like those wide, lumbering vessels you'll see hauling sand and produce up and down Mae Nam Chao Phraya. These barges are slender like their mainstream cousins, the longtail boats, and fantastically ornamented with religious symbolism. The largest is more than 45m long and requires a rowing crew of 50 men, plus seven umbrella bearers, two helmsmen and two navigators, as well as a flag bearer, rhythm keeper and chanter.

Suphannahong, or 'Golden Swan', is the king's personal barge. Built on the orders of Rama I after an earlier version had been destroyed in the sacking of Ayuthaya, *Suphannahong* is made from a single piece of timber, making it the largest dugout in the world. Appropriately, a huge swan's head is carved into the prow. More recent barges feature bows carved into other Hindu-Buddhist mythological shapes, such as the seven-headed naga (sea dragon) and Garuda (Vishnu's bird mount).

To mark auspicious Buddhist calendar years, the royal barges in all their finery set sail during the royal *gà·tǐn*, the ceremony that marks the end of the Buddhist retreat (or *pansǎh*) in October or November. During this ceremony, a barge procession travels to the temples to offer new robes

WORKING FROM HOME: ARTISAN VILLAGES

Long before multinational factories, Bangkok was a town of craftspeople who lived and worked in artisan villages, inheriting their skills and profession from their parents. Many villages made stylised arts and crafts for the palace and minor royalty living along the fashionable avenues of the time. Today most of the villages remain, but the crafts themselves exist only in memories and old photos. You can, however, visit a few villages where the old ways live on.

Soi Ma Toom (Map p68; off Th Arun Amarin) is an example of the old home-and-factory paradigm. This quiet lane, just off a traffic-clogged artery in Thonburi, across from the Naval Department, is where the *màdum* (bael fruit) is peeled, cut into horizontal slices and soaked in palm sugar to make a popular candy.

Surviving primarily on tourist patronage, Ban Baat (Monk's Bowl Village; p81) dates back to the first Bangkok king and continues to create ceremonial pieces used by monks to collect morning alms.

The silk weavers of Baan Krua (p106) no longer weave for Jim Thompson, but a couple of families are still producing high-quality fabrics from looms under their homes.

Near the old timber yards and saw mills, Woodworking Street (Map p132; Soi Pracha Narumit, Th Pracharat, Bang Sue) is still going strong with small Thai-Chinese-owned factories fashioning wooden eaves, furniture and shrines. Shops are open daily, and an annual street fair is celebrated in January.

to the monastic contingent and countless Bangkokians descend on the river to watch.

The museum consists of sheds near the mouth of Khlong Bangkok Noi. To get here take the 3B ferry across the river from Saphan Phra Pin Klao (N12) pier and follow the signs. Most longtail tours will stop here unless you ask them not to.

FORENSIC MEDICINE MUSEUM Map p68
พิพิธภัณฑ์นิติเวชศาสตร์สงกรานต์นิยมเสน

☎ 0 2419 7000, ext 6363; 2nd fl, Forensic Medicine Bldg, Siriraj Hospital; admission 40B; ☻ 9am-4pm Mon-Sat; ☝ Thonburi Railway (Tha Rot Fai, N11) or Tha Wang Lang (Siriraj, N10)

While it's not exactly CSI, pickled body parts, ingenious murder weapons and other crime-scene evidence are on display at this medical museum, intended to educate rather than nauseate. Among the grisly displays is a bloodied T-shirt from a victim stabbed to death with a dildo, and the preserved but rather withered cadaver of Si Ouey, one of Thailand's most prolific and notorious serial killers who murdered – and then ate – more than 30 children in the 1950s. Despite being well and truly dead (he was executed), today his name is still used to scare misbehaving children into submission: 'Behave yourself or Si Ouey will come for you'. There are another five dusty museums on the vast Siriraj Hospital grounds, all with variations on the medical theme.

Given the huge construction project at the northern edge of the hospital grounds, the best way to get here is by express ferry or cross-river ferry to Tha Wang Lang (Tha Siriraj) in Thonburi, turn right (north) into the hospital and follow the signs; or just say 'Si Ouey' and you'll be pointed in the right direction.

BANGLAMPHU

Eating p160; Shopping p137; Sleeping p213
One of Bangkok's oldest neighbourhoods, Banglamphu has more than one personality. In certain streets it's a rundown version of the old aristocratic and artistic enclave of teak houses and tended gardens, with shirtless men sitting in front of ancient shophouses stuffed to the rafters with innumerable goods. In other streets it is brash and new, a cultural melting pot in which Thais are the spice flavouring an ingredients list of backpackers, global nomads, package tourists and anyone else who happened to get off a plane, train or intercity bus in Bangkok.

The reason so many people come to Banglamphu from so many places is Th Khao San. Often referred to simply as 'Khao San', the backpacker enclave of guesthouses and amenities has become the benchmark by which backpacker ghettos are measured the world over. These days 'ghetto' is a little bit harsh, as the lodgings increasingly cater to 'flashpackers', and the lodgings themselves have spread in a 1km radius from the street itself. (For the Khao San story see p86.)

Long before Banglamphu landed on travellers' itineraries, it was the original residential district for farmers and produce merchants from Ayuthaya who followed the transfer of the royal court to Bangkok in the late 18th century. The name means 'Place of Lamphu', a reference to the *lam·poo* tree *(Duabanga grandiflora)* that was once prevalent in the area. By the time of Rama IV, Banglamphu had developed into a thriving commercial district by day and an entertainment spot by night, a role it continues to fulfil today.

Banglamphu spreads from the river north of Th Somdet Phra Pin Klao and eventually melts into Dusit and Thewet beyond Khlong Phadung Krung Kasem. The royal boulevard of Th Ratchadamnoen Klang (royal passage), suitably adorned with billboard-sized pictures of the king, queen and other royal family members, links the Grand Palace in Ko Ratanakosin with newer palaces in Dusit. This central section of the royal road is lined by identical art deco–influenced low-rise buildings, which were built in the early 1940s to house the administration of the new democratic Thailand. Plans to upgrade them and make Th Ratchadamnoen Klang a cultural promenade documenting Thailand's transition to democracy have stalled, with only King Prajadhipok Museum (p87) and the long-established Queen's Gallery (p201) currently welcoming visitors. Running south from Th Ratchadamnoen Klang is Th Tanao, one of Bangkok's most famous food streets; eat your way along it with our Eats Walk (p162).

Despite the numbers of visitors staying in Banglamphu, the neighbourhood rewards those willing to explore away from the neon of KSR itself. Running parallel to the river west of Th Khao San, Th Phra Athit offers a glimpse of the lifestyle of 19th-century Thai nobility via mansions such as the splendidly restored Baan Phra Athit (Map p82; 201/1 Th Phra Athit), which once belonged to Chao Phraya Vorapongpipat, finance minister during the reigns of Rama V, Rama VI and Rama VII. By night it offers more than a glimpse into the lifestyle led by the young hipsters of today. Indeed, Th Phra Athit and Th Samsen boast the best collection of small, cool bars in Bangkok; check them out for yourself with the help of the Banglamphu Pub Crawl (p186).

GOLDEN MOUNT & WAT SAKET
Map p82

วัดสระเกศ

☎ 0 2621 0576; soi off Th Boriphat; admission to summit of Golden Mount 10B; ⏱ 8am-5pm; 🚍 air-con 79, 503 & 511, ordinary 2, 15, 49, 59 & 70; 🛥 klorng boat to Tha Phan Fah

Before glass and steel towers began growing out of the flat monotony of Bangkok's riverine plain, the massive Golden Mount (Phu Khao Thong) was the only structure to make any significant impression on the horizon. At the eastern entrance to Banglamphu, the mount was commissioned by Rama III. He ordered that the earth dug out to create Bangkok's expand-

ing *klorng* network be piled up to build an enormous, 100m-high, 500m-wide *chedi*. As the hill grew, however, the weight became too much for the soft soil beneath and the project was abandoned until Rama IV built a small gilded *chedi* on its crest and added trees to stave off erosion. Rama V later added to the structure and interred a Buddha relic from India (given to him by the British government) in the *chedi*. The concrete walls were added during WWII.

Today serpentine steps wind through gnarled trees, past small tombstones and up to two platforms that afford panoramic views across the city. At the topmost level Thais pray to a central Buddha shrine and test their fortune at a shrine to the Chinese goddess of mercy, Kuan Im. Make a small donation then shake the numbered *seeam see* sticks until one falls to the floor. The piece of paper with the corresponding number gives a no-nonsense appraisal of your future in Thai, English and Chinese. It's a fun diversion, but hopefully you receive a more positive prognosis than we did: 'Lost items could never be recovered. Illness condition unfavourable. No lucks. Should be careful.' We can happily report that the intervening period was not unduly unlucky, we don't recall losing anything more than a USB flash drive, and our health seems fine. But one prediction was correct: 'Forthcoming child shall be baby girl.' When Thais are the subject of such a forecast (ahm, try not to shake out stick number 10) they burn it on the spot (the piece of paper, not the stick), or at least leave it at the temple.

If your fortune is so disturbing you feel the need to seek assistance from a higher power, it's comforting to know that peaceful Wat Saket is just next door. In November there's a festival in the grounds that includes an enchanting candlelight procession up the Golden Mount, and a similar procession is held at Makha Bucha in February.

MAHAKAN FORT Map p82
ป้อมมหากาฬ

Th Ratchadamnoen Klang; ⏰ 8.30am-6pm; 🚌 aircon 79, 503 & 511, ordinary 2, 15, 49, 59, 60 & 70; 🚤 klorng boat to Tha Phan Fah

top picks

BANGLAMPHU

- Th Khao San (p86) More than just freaks in dreadlocks and fisherman pants, this unique cultural melting pot has something for (almost) everyone.
- Golden Mount & Wat Saket (p80) Take in the panoramic views and divine your future on this artificial mount.
- Eating along Th Tanao (p162) Follow our trail of crumbs and stuff yourself silly in this classic Bangkok neighbourhood.
- Banglamphu pub crawl (p186) So many bars, so little time…
- Wat Suthat (p84) Sit and gaze at the huge Buddha and sky-high murals in this peaceful temple.

The area around white-washed Mahakan Fort, one of two surviving citadels that defended the old walled city, has recently been converted into a small park overlooking Khlong Ong Ang. The octagonal fort is a picturesque, if brief and hot, stop en route to Golden Mount, but the neighbouring village is more interesting. This small community of wooden houses has been here for more than 100 years. But since the mid-1990s it has fought the Bangkok municipal government's plan to demolish it and create a 'tourist' park. The community blocked progress and even proposed the development of another tourist attraction: a *li-gair* museum honouring the dance tradition that traces its creation to a school located here in 1897. Some of the homes were eventually demolished, resulting in the park you see today. But behind the fort many others remain (for now). Visitors are welcome. Climb the ramparts (not for children) running away from the fort and walk to the far end, where stairs lead down and into the village.

MONK'S BOWL VILLAGE (BAN BAAT)
Map p82
บ้านบาตร

Soi Ban Baat, Th Boriphat; 🚌 ordinary 12 & 42, 🚤 klorng boat to Tha Phan Fah
Ban Baat is the only remaining village of three established in Bangkok by Rama I for the purpose of handcrafting *bàht* (monk's bowls), the ceremonial bowls used to collect alms from the faithful each morning. As cheaper factory-made bowls are now the norm, the artisanal tradition has shrunk to about half a dozen families. You can usually observe the process of hammering the

NEIGHBOURHOODS **BANGLAMPHU**

BANGLAMPHU

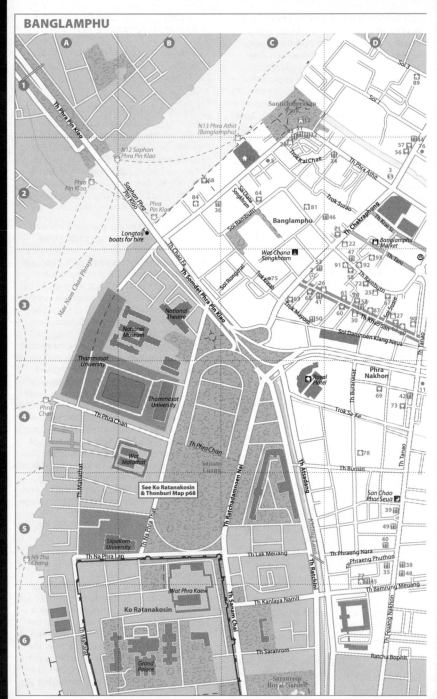

Santichoprakan Park

N13 Phra Athit
(Banglamphu)

N12 Saphan
Phra Pin Klao

Th Phra Pin Klao

Phra
Pin Klao

Saphan Phra Pin Klao

Phra
Pin Klao

Longtail
boats for hire

Th Chao Fa

Th Somdet Phra Pin Klao

Mae Nam Chao Phraya

Th Phra Athit

Trok Mai Chae

Trok Surao

Banglamphu

Soi Chana Songkhram

Soi Rambutri

Soi Rambutri

Wat Chana
Songkhram

Th Chakraphong

Banglamphu
Market

Th Tani

Th Rambutri

Soi Rongmai

Trok Kraisi

Soi Susie

Trok Mayom

Trok Kaichae

Th Khao San

Soi Damnoen Klang Neua

Th Tanao

National
Theatre

National
Museum

Thammasat
University

Thammasat
University

Phra
Chan

Th Phra Chan

Th Phra Chan

Th Phra That

Sanam
Luang

**See Ko Ratanakosin
& Thonburi Map p68**

Royal
Hotel

Phra
Nakhon

Th Buranasat

Th Atsadang

Trok Sa-Ke

Th Tanao

Th Bunsiri

Th Ratchadamnoen Nai

Wat
Mahathat

Silpakorn
University

N9 Tha
Chang

Th Maharat

Th Na Phra Lan

San Chao
Phor Seua

Th Ratchini

Th Atsadang

Th Lak Meuang

Th Phraeng Nara

Phraeng Phuthon

Th Phraeng Nara

Th Bamrung Meuang

Wat Phra Kaew

Ko Ratanakosin

Th Sanam Chai

Th Kanlaya Namit

Th Saranrom

Th Feuang Nakhon

Grand
Palace

Th Saranrom

Saranrom
Royal Garden

Ratcha Bophit

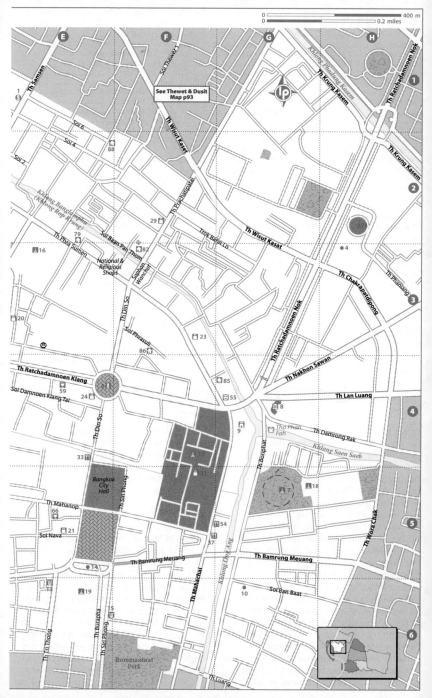

BANGLAMPHU

bowls together from eight separate pieces of steel, said to represent Buddhism's Eightfold Path. The joints are then fused with melted copper wire, and the bowl is beaten, polished and (usually) coated with several layers of black lacquer. A typical *bàht*-smith's output is one large bowl per day; more for smaller bowls.

The alms bowls are sold for between 600B and 2000B and make great souvenirs. But the village itself is just as interesting. When we visited, an elderly woman intercepted us nanoseconds after we'd walked into the soi and quickly ushered us through her living room and out the back door. After leading us down a series of tiny lanes populated with kids, sleeping cats and cockroaches, we were delivered to the artisans at work. Competition is certainly keen for your tourist baht, but you wouldn't call it touristy. More a raw, poor community that is both a window into the

grittier side of Bangkok life and a chance to pick up a souvenir with a story – bypassing the middleman. To find the village, walk south on Th Boriphat, south of Th Bamrung Meuang, then follow the signs into narrow Soi Ban Baat.

WAT SUTHAT Map p82
วัดสุทัศน์

☎ 0 2224 9845; Th Bamrung Meuang; admission 20B; ⏱ 8.30am-4.30pm; 🚌 ordinary 12, 35 & 42; 🚤 klorng boat to Tha Phan Fah

Wat Suthat's truly remarkable Buddha image, acres of colourful murals and – during most of the year – relative tranquillity make it arguably the most appealing of all Bangkok's Buddhist temples. The main attraction is Thailand's biggest *wí·hǎhn* (main chapel) and the imperious yet serene 8m-high Phra Si Sakayamuni that resides within. The image is Thailand's largest surviving Sukhothai-period bronze, a serene-looking gilded masterpiece that was cast in the former capital in the 14th century. In 1808 it was retrieved from the ruins of Sukhothai and floated on a barge down Mae Nam Chao Phraya to be installed in this temple and serve as both the centre of Bangkok and a representation of Mt Meru, the mythical centre of the universe. Today the ashes of Rama VIII (King Ananda Mahidol; r 1935–46) are contained in the base of the image.

Colourful, if now somewhat faded, *Jataka* (murals depicting scenes from the Buddha's life) cover every wall and pillar; see how many crabs (or crab claws) you can find, and not just in the murals. The deep-relief wooden doors are also impressive and were carved by artisans including Rama II himself.

Behind the *wí·hähn*, and accessed via a separate entrance on Th Burapha, the ordination hall is the largest in the country. To add to its list of 'largests', Wat Suthat holds the rank of Rachavoramahavihan, the highest royal temple grade. It maintains a special place in the national religion because of its association with the Brahman priests who perform important ceremonies, such as the Royal Ploughing Ceremony (p21) in May. These priests also perform religious rites at two Hindu shrines near the wát – the Thewa Sathaan (Devi Mandir; Map p82) on Th Siri Phong, and the smaller Saan Jao

Phitsanu (Vishnu Shrine; Map p82) on Th Tri Thong. The former shrine contains images of Shiva and Ganesha while the latter is dedicated to Vishnu.

SAO CHING-CHA Map p82
เสาชิงช้า
Th Botphram, btwn Th Tri Thong & Th Burapha; ordinary 12, 35 & 42; klorng boat to Tha Phan Fah
It is easy to forget the powers of the Brahmans in Thai Buddhism, unless you happen upon the giant red poles of Sao Ching-Cha (the Giant Swing). During the second lunar month (usually in January), Brahman beliefs dictate that Shiva comes down to earth for a 10-day residence and should be welcomed by great ceremonies and, in the past, great degrees of daring. So each year the acrobatic and desperate braved the Great Swing. The ceremony saw these men swing in ever-higher arcs in an effort to reach a bag of gold suspended from a 15m bamboo pole. Whoever grabbed the gold could keep it. But that was no mean feat, and deaths were as common as successes.

The Brahmans enjoyed a mystical position within the royal court, primarily in the coronation rituals. But after the 1932 revolution the Brahmans' waning power was effectively terminated and the festival, including the swinging, was discontinued during the reign of Rama VII.

GET LOST & FIND BANGKOK

Think of the 'sights' described in this chapter not as the only things to see in Bangkok, but rather as an excuse for exploring some of the city's most colourful neighbourhoods. These are your destinations but much of the most interesting travel is what happens in between, who you meet and what you see – especially if you get lost.

Every block will reveal something you've never seen before – blind troubadours with portable karaoke machines, soi dogs wearing T-shirts (who does dress these stray dogs?), vendors selling fresh pineapple, grilled meat, everything plus the kitchen sink. And, let's be honest, there will be some things that are all too familiar – most likely another 7-Eleven store. To add to the excitement, you have to deal with Bangkok's notoriously dodgy pavements, which can be as traffic-clogged as its roads. Look forward to sidestepping a mass of humanity while ducking under huge umbrellas and canvas awnings pitched right at the level of your forehead, before having to squeeze through a bottleneck at a stall selling desserts that look like tacos. It's fun, really, and more so if you take the occasional air-conditioned breather.

Most neighbourhood sections in this book have a walking tour and these are designed to be followed as strictly or loosely as you like. Or just invent your own, remembering that getting lost is the best gift Bangkok gives to visitors.

Bangkok's best neighbourhoods for getting lost in are its oldest districts. The maze of narrow streets, hidden temples and unconstrained commerce in Chinatown (p97) is a good start. Banglamphu (p80) boasts several village-like areas where modest communities live much as they have for decades. Those alongside Khlong Lawt, Khlong Saen Saeb and Khlong Ong Ang are a hive of old-style activity and the *klorng*-side paths are often shaded and usually free of motorised transport. The columns and ornate facades of the warehouses and shops near Tha Tien show off the success of wealthier businesses, while the suburbs along the other side of the river in Thonburi (p77) are perhaps the best of the lot – as local as you like and barely a tourist anywhere. So go on, liberate yourself from the constraints of trying to follow a map, and go forth and wander.

Sao Ching-Cha is two long blocks south of the Democracy Monument and outside Wat Suthat. Despite no longer being used, the Giant Swing was recently replaced with a newer model, made from six giant teak logs. The previous version is kept at the National Museum.

DEMOCRACY MONUMENT Map p82
อนุสาวรีย์ประชาธิปไตย
traffic circle of Th Ratchadamnoen Klang & Th Din So; 🚌 **air-con 79, 503 & 511, ordinary 2, 15, 49, 59, 60 & 70**
The Democracy Monument is the focal point of the grand, European-style boulevard that is Th Ratchadamnoen Klang. As the name suggests, it was erected to commemorate Thailand's momentous

transformation from absolute to constitutional monarchy. It was designed by Thai architect Mew Aphaiwong and the relief sculptures were created by Italian Corrado Feroci who, as Silpa Bhirasri, gives his name to Silpakorn University. Feroci combined the square-jawed 'heroes of socialism' style popular at the time with Mew Aphaiwong's Art Deco influences and keen sense of relevant revolutionary dates.

There were 75 cannonballs around the base, to signify the year BE (Buddhist Era) 2475 (AD 1932); the four wings of the monument stand 24m tall, representing 24 June, the day the constitution was signed; and the central plinth stands 3m high (June was then the third month in the Thai calendar) and supports a chiselled constitution.

WHAT'S SO LONELY ABOUT THE KHAO SAN ROAD?

Thanon Khao San, better known as the Khao San Rd, is genuinely unlike anywhere else on earth. It's an international clearing house of people either entering the liberated state of travelling in Southeast Asia or returning to the coddling bonds of first-world life, all together in a neon-lit melting pot in Banglamphu. Its uniqueness is probably best illustrated by a question: apart from airports, where else could you share space with the citizens of dozens of countries at the same time, people ranging from first-time backpackers scoffing banana pancakes to 75-year-old grandparents ordering G&Ts, via hippies, trendies, squares, style queens, package tourists, global nomads, people on a week's holiday and those taking a gap year, people of every colour and creed looking at you looking at them looking at everyone else?

Th Khao San – pronounced 'cow sarn' and meaning 'uncooked rice' – is perhaps the most high-profile bastard child of the age of independent travel. Of course, it hasn't always been this way. For its first two centuries or so it was just another unremarkable road in old Bangkok. The first guesthouses appeared in 1982 and as more backpackers arrived through the '80s, so one by one the old wooden homes were converted into low-rent dosshouses. By the time Alex Garland's novel *The Beach* was published in 1997, with its opening scenes set in the seedier side of Khao San, staying here had become a rite of passage for backpackers coming to Southeast Asia.

The publicity from Garland's book and the movie that followed pushed Khao San into the mainstream, romanticising the seedy, and stereotyping the backpackers it attracted as unwashed and counter-culturalist. It also brought the long-simmering debate about the relative merits of Th Khao San to the top of backpacker conversations across the region. Was it cool to stay on KSR? Was it uncool? Was this 'real travel' or just an international anywhere surviving on the few baht Western backpackers spent before they headed home to start their high-earning careers? Was it really Thailand at all?

Perhaps one of Garland's characters summed it up most memorably when he said: 'You know, Richard, one of these days I'm going to find one of those Lonely Planet writers and I'm going to ask him, what's so fucking lonely about the Khao San Road?'

Today more than ever the answer would have to be: not that much. With the help of all that publicity Khao San continued to evolve, with bedbug-infested guesthouses replaced by boutique hotels, and downmarket TV bars showing pirated movies transformed into hip design bars peopled by flashpackers in designer threads. But the most interesting change has been in the way Thais see Khao San.

Once written off as home to cheap, dirty *fà-ràng kêe ngók* (stingy foreigners), Banglamphu has become just about the coolest district in Bangkok. Attracted in part by the long-derided independent traveller and their modern ideas, the city's own counter-culture kids have moved in and brought with them a tasty selection of small bars, organic cafes and shops selling a head-spinning array of irreverent T-shirts. Indeed, Bangkok's indie crowd has proved to be the Thai spice this melting pot always lacked. So when you're drinking on Khao San at about 11pm and you start to wonder if you're actually at a major music festival, there are enough Thais around to remind you this is Thailand, not Glastonbury.

Not that Khao San has moved completely away from its backpacker roots. The strip still anticipates every traveller need: meals to soothe homesickness, cafes and bars for swapping travel tales about getting to the Cambodian border, tailors, travel agents, teeth whitening, secondhand books, hair braiding and, of course, the perennial Akha women trying to harass everyone they see into buying wooden frogs. No, not very lonely at all....

Each wing has bas-reliefs depicting soldiers, police and civilians who helped usher in the modern Thai state.

During the era of military dictatorships demonstrators often assembled here to call for a return to democracy, protests that ended in violence and death on 14 October 1973. Such protests, and the resulting loss of life, gave the monument a legitimacy it had previously lacked.

While you're in this area, if you head north from the Democracy Monument on Th Din So you'll see many shophouses that date back to the late 19th and early 20th centuries. As the entire block to the northwest of the Democracy Monument belongs to Wat Bowonniwet (p88), the shop owners pay rent directly to the temple.

OCTOBER 14 MEMORIAL Map p82
อนุสาวรีย์14ตุลาคม

cnr Th Ratchadamnoen Klang & Th Tanao; ☐ aircon 79, 503, 511 & 516, ordinary 2, 15, 49, 59, 60 & 70

A peaceful amphitheatre commemorates the civilian demonstrators who were killed by the military during a pro-democracy rally on 14 October 1973. Over 200,000 people had assembled at the Democracy Monument and along the length of Th Ratchadamnoen to protest against the arrest of political campaigners and continuing military dictatorship. Although some in Thailand continue to deny it, photographs confirm that more than 70 demonstrators were killed when the tanks met the crowd. The complex is an interesting adaptation of Thai temple architecture for a secular and political purpose. A central *chedi* is dedicated to the fallen and a gallery of historic photographs lines the interior wall.

KING PRAJADHIPOK MUSEUM Map p82
พิพิธภัณฑ์พระบาทสมเด็จพระปกเกล้า เจ้าอยู่หัว

☎ 0 2280 3413; kingprajadhipokmuseum.org; 2 Th Lan Luang; admission 40B; ⏱ 9am-4pm Tue-Sun; ☐ air-con 44, 79 & 511, ordinary 2, 15, 59 & 60; ⛴ klorng boat to Tha Phan Fah

A visit to a royal museum might sound like a royal bore, but this collection uses modern techniques to relate the rather dramatic life of Rama VII (King Prajadhipok; r 1925–35), while neatly documenting Thailand's transition from absolute to constitutional monarchy. The museum occupies a grand neocolonial-style building constructed on the orders of Rama V

for his favourite firm of Bond St merchants; it was the only foreign business allowed on the royal road linking Bangkok's two palace districts.

The exhibitions reveal that Prajadhipok did not expect to become king, but once on the throne showed considerable diplomacy in dealing with what was, in effect, a revolution fomented by a new intellectual class of Thais. The first floor deals with the life of Queen Rambhai Barni, while the upper two floors cover the king's own life. It is revealed, for example, that the army officer–turned-king had spent many of his formative years in Europe where he became fond of British democracy. Ironically, those plotting his downfall had themselves learned of democracy during years of European education. A coup, carried out while the king and queen were playing golf, ended Thailand's absolute monarchy in 1932. Prajadhipok's reign eventually ended when he abdicated while in England in 1935; he died there in 1941.

PHRA SUMEN FORT & SANTICHAIPRAKAN PARK Map p82
ป้อมพระสุเมร/สวนสาธารณะสันติชัยปราการ

cnr Th Phra Athit & Th Phra Sumen; ⏱ 5am-10pm; ☐ ordinary 15, 30 & 53; ⛴ Phra Athit (Banglamphu, N13)

Beside Mae Nam Chao Phraya in Banglamphu stands one of Bangkok's original 18th-century forts. Built in 1783 to defend against potential naval invasions and named for the mythical Mt Meru (Phra Sumen in Thai) of Hindu-Buddhist cosmology, the octagonal brick-and-stucco bunker was one of 14 city watchtowers that punctuated the old city wall alongside Khlong Rop Krung (now Khlong Banglamphu but still called Khlong Rop Krung on most signs). Apart from Mahakan Fort (p81), this is the only one still standing.

Alongside the fort and fronting the river is a small, grassy park with an open-air pavilion, river views, cool breezes and a bohemian mix of alternative young Thais and fisherman pants–wearing, fire stick–twirling backpackers. It's an interesting place to sit, people-watch and see what are said to be the last two *lampoo* trees in Banglamphu.

From the park a walkway (⏱ 5am-10pm) built above the river zigzags south from the fort all the way to Saphan Phra Pin Klao. Along the way you can catch glimpses of some of Th Phra Athit's classic

WHAT'S A WÁT?

Bangkok is home to hundreds of wáts, monastery temples that have traditionally been at the centre of community life. Wát literally means 'school' and for centuries formal education was conducted exclusively by Buddhist monks in their wát. These days there are fewer monks and plenty of schools, but the wát remains the focus of numerous Buddhist ceremonies and festivals.

Buildings & Structures

By definition a wát is the whole monastery compound and must have a minimum of three resident monks to be known as such, though in reality a site rarely loses its 'wát' status. Even the smallest wát will usually have a *bóht*, *wí·hǎhn* and monks' living quarters. The larger the wát, the more structures it will have.

Bòht The most-sacred prayer room at a wát, often similar in size and shape to the *wí·hǎhn*. Aside from the fact it does not house the main Buddha image, you'll know the *bóht* because it is usually more ornately decorated and has eight cornerstones to ward off evil.

Chedi (stupa) A large bell-shaped tower usually containing five structural elements symbolising (from bottom to top) earth, water, fire, wind and void; depending on the wát, relics of the Buddha, a Thai king or some other notable are housed inside.

Drum Tower Elevates the ceremonial drum beaten by novices.

Mon·dòp An open-sided, square building with four arches and a pyramidal roof, used to worship religious objects or texts.

Prang A towering phallic spire of Khmer origin serving the same religious purpose as a *chedi*.

Sala A pavilion, often open-sided, for relaxation, lessons or miscellaneous activities.

Wí·hǎhn (vihara) The sanctuary for the temple's main Buddha image and where laypeople come to make their offerings. Classic architecture typically has a three-tiered roof representing the triple gems: the Buddha (the teacher), Dharma (the teaching) and Brotherhood (the followers).

Buddha Images

Elongated earlobes, no evidence of bone or muscle, arms that reach to the knees, a third eye: these are some of the 32 rules, originating from 3rd-century India, that govern the depiction of the Buddha in sculpture and denote his divine nature. Other symbols to be aware of are the various hand positions and 'postures', which depict periods in the life of the Buddha.

Sitting Teaching or meditating. If the right hand is pointed towards the earth, the Buddha is subduing the demons of desire. If the hands are folded in the lap, Buddha is meditating.

Reclining The exact moment of the Buddha's passing into *parinibbana* (postdeath nirvana).

Standing Bestowing blessings or taming evil forces.

Walking The Buddha after his return to earth from heaven.

---

old Ratanakosin-style mansions that are not visible from the street, including those housing parts of the Buddhist Society of Thailand and the UN's Food & Agriculture Organization.

WAT BOWONNIWET Map p82
วัดบวรนิเวศ

☎ 0 2281 2831; www.watbowon.org; Th Phra Sumen; admission free; ⏱ 8.30am-5pm; 🚤 Phra Athit (Banglamphu, N13)

Founded in 1826, Wat Bowonniwet (Wat Bowon) is the national headquarters for the Thammayut monastic sect, a reformed version of Thai Buddhism. Rama IV (King Mongkut; r 1851–68), who set out to be a scholar, not a king, founded the Thammayuts and began the royal tradition of ordination at this temple. In fact, Mongkut was the abbot of Wat Bowon for several years. Rama IX (King Bhumibol Adulyadej; r 1946–present) and Crown Prince Vajiralongkorn, as well as several other males in the royal family, have been ordained as monks here.

Bangkok's second Buddhist university, Mahamakut University, is housed at Wat Bowon. Selected monks are sent from India, Nepal and Sri Lanka to study here. Because of its royal status, visitors should be particularly careful to dress properly for admittance to this wát – shorts and sleeveless clothing are not allowed.

WAT RATCHANATDA Map p82
วัดราชนัดดา

☎ 0 2224 8807; cnr Th Ratchadamnoen Klang & Th Mahachai; admission by donation; ☒ 8am-5pm; 🚌 air-con 511, ordinary 2; 🚤 klorng boat to Tha Phan Fah

Across Th Mahachai from the Golden Mount, this temple is most stunning at night when the 37 spires of the all-metal Loha Prasat (Metal Palace) are lit up like a medieval birthday cake. Displaying Burmese influences, it was built for Rama III in the 1840s in honour of his grand-daughter. The design is said to derive from metal temples built in India and Sri Lanka more than 2000 years ago. The 37 spires represent the 37 virtues that lead to en-lightenment. Recently restored, the interior is relatively unadorned by Thai temple standards, but the hallways and square edges contribute to a symmetry reminis-cent of the much earlier temples at Angkor, in Cambodia.

At the back of the compound, behind the formal gardens, is a well-known market selling Buddhist *prá krêu·ang* in all sizes, shapes and styles. These amulets feature images not only of Buddha, but also fa-mous Thai monks and Indian deities. Full Buddha images are also for sale.

PHRA NAKHON MEANDER
Walking Tour

If the tourist buses and touting túk-túks around the Ko Ratanakosin sights threaten to do your head in, this part of Banglamphu should be more appealing. The area south of Wat Saket combines old wooden and terrace houses, parks, shops selling religious para-phernalia aimed purely at locals and a wát that will leave you wondering why no one else is there. Begin at the Tha Phan Fah *klorng* boat pier. If you don't have much time and don't mind sweating, you could follow this wander with the Chinatown walk (p101) or the Ko Ratanakosin walk (p75) in reverse.

1 King Prajadhipok Museum
Opposite the *klorng* boat pier is this hand-some, modern museum (p87), which details Thailand's turbulent pre-democracy years.

2 Golden Mount
From the museum, cross over Saphan Phan Fah to Golden Mount (p80) for a panoramic view of the city and a chance to have your fortune foreseen: your trip to Bangkok might have you 'discovering a mate who could become a satisfactory match' but, then again, you might also 'like being dumb' and have to 'be careful'. *Chôhk dee!* (Good luck!)

3 Monk's Bowl Village
Leave the Golden Mount and turn left (south) along Th Boriphat, where you'll walk past shops selling carved teak lintels and other decorations for turning your apartment into a Thai restaurant. Cross Th Bamrung Meuang and turn left at Soi Ban Baat to see (actually, it's more of an experience) the artisan village (p81) of beaten steel bowls and life amid at-mospheric, eye-opening alleys.

4 Religious Shops
Backtrack to Th Bamrung Meuang, turn left across the bridge and go straight ahead. The religious shops on this stretch are where Bang-kokians come to buy the sort of goods needed in temples. These are primarily Buddha images of all shapes and sizes (though usually only one colour: gold). Wealthy families make merit by donating these items to their local temples. Of course, you can't actually 'own' a Buddha image so technically these Buddhas are rented, not sold. If you're lucky you'll see a new Bud-dha 'shipment' arrive, the huge figures de-livered aboard pick-ups, all wrapped up like abductees in plastic and monks' robes. Then begins the touch-up process on their golden paint jobs, and the wait for an 'adoption'.

5 Marble Sign
You'll come to a large, paved park with an imposing building at the Th Mahanop end. This is Bangkok's City Hall (BMA building), thoroughly unremarkable except for the mar-ble sign in front spelling out Bangkok's official and unbelievably long Thai name; a quirky photo-op recommended for travellers with very wide-angle lenses.

6 Sao Ching-Cha
Amid the traffic at the other end of the square is the tall, red Sao Ching-Cha (Giant Swing; p85), a spindly gatelike structure that once hosted a (sometimes not) death-defying Brahman spectacle.

7 Wat Suthat

A few metres southeast is the entrance to Wat Suthat (p84), one of the biggest, holiest, most beautiful and undertouristed temples in Thailand.

8 Rommaninat Park & Corrections Museum

Leave Wat Suthat via the east entrance onto Th Burapha and turn right (south). Continue for a few minutes and turn left into Rommaninat Park, a pretty green space of fountains, walking paths, piped music, sleeping people and soi dogs. On the far side of the park is the Corrections Museum (admission by donation; 🕙 9am-4pm Mon-Fri), a rehabilitated colonial building covering the park's former career as a prison in the early 1900s. Most displays are in Thai but the maintenance staff and other hangers-on turn the tour into a social event, giggling at the gruesome displays of torture used in the good old days.

9 Klorng Path

Exit the park at the southwest corner, cross the street and follow the small *klorng* through the neighbourhood on Soi Long Tha, past fruit vendors, drying laundry, the neighbour-

---

WALK FACTS

Start Tha Phan Fah (*klorng* boat)
End Rajinee (N7)
Distance 4km
Duration Two to four hours, depending on how long you spend in the museums
Fuel stops *Klorng*-side noodle shops

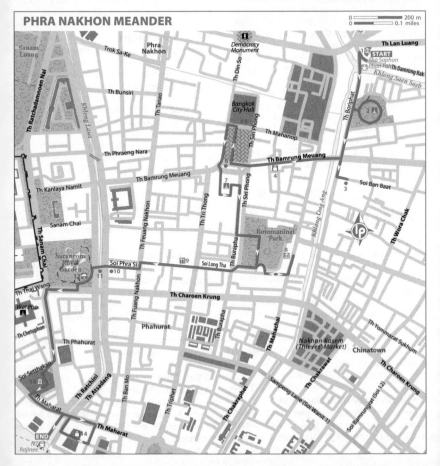

PHRA NAKHON MEANDER

hood shrine, a Chinese temple and noodle and soup vendors. This is what Bangkok looked like when the city's footpaths were riverbanks and, provided the *klorng* isn't having one of its especially stinky days, this is a good place to stop for a real local meal.

10 Sino-Portuguese Shopfronts
At Th Feuang Nakhon turn left and then right on Soi Phra Si past heavily ornamented shopfronts decorated in a style often referred to as Sino-Portuguese. In the early 20th century these buildings were the height of fashion and sold new luxury goods, like motor cars, to the modernising country. Today the fashions have shifted to downtown malls and the old buildings are either warehouses or offer more mundane items – like car parts.

11 Saphan Hok
Cross Th Atsadang to Saphan Hok, a simple lever bridge across Khlong Lawt, the inner-city moat that cut off the royal centre of Ko Ratanakosin from the mere mortals of the outer island. Trading ships from Mon settlements would dock near here on trading missions.

12 Saranrom Royal Garden
The far side of the bridge leads to Saranrom Royal Garden (p73), a park favouring English Victorian gardens with tropical perfumes and earnest exercisers.

13 Museum of Siam
Exit the park south of the fountain, turn right on Th Charoen Krung, then left on Th Sanam Chai and walk south past Wat Pho to Bangkok's newest attraction, the excellent Museum of Siam (p72), where an old ministry has been transformed into a series of interactive and interesting exhibits dealing with Thai history and culture.

14 Pak Khlong Market
Exit on the far side of the museum to Th Maharat, and turn left. Walk 300m to Pak Khlong Market (p139), Bangkok's huge wholesale flower and vegetable market. When you've finished having a look around here, take a walk back up to the canal and turn left to reach Tha Rajinee; this is not one of Bangkok's busiest piers so if you can't wait, take a taxi or túk-túk.

Eating p163; Sleeping p217

Formerly a fruit orchard north of the royal island of Ratanakosin, Dusit was transformed into a mini-European city by Rama V (King Chulalongkorn; r 1868–1910), complete with wide avenues and shady walkways. The area begins east of Th Samsen and follows Th Phitsanulok and Th Si Ayuthaya to the district's most famous sites: the palaces of Dusit Park (p94), Dusit Zoo (p95) and Wat Benchamabophit (p95). Further east is the present monarch's residence of Chitralada Palace, which is open to the public only by appointment and with a good reason.

But for all the elegance of Dusit Park and the European-style grandeur of its buildings and boulevards, the district is hollow in spirit precisely because this is Bangkok, not London or Paris. You can walk for blocks without spotting any of the things that make Bangkok wonderful: street vendors, motorcycle taxis, random stores selling random stuff. Or, as Somerset Maugham put it when driving through Dusit's streets in 1923, 'They seem to await ceremonies and procession. They are like the deserted avenues in the park of a fallen monarch.'

Devotion to the monarchy and particularly to King Chulalongkorn, the man credited with dragging Thailand into the modern world, is the primary purpose of an average Bangkokian's visit to Dusit. Many come to make merit at the bronze equestrian statue of Chulalongkorn, which stands in military garb at the Royal Plaza. Although originally intended as mere historical commemoration, the statue has quite literally become a religious shrine, where every Tuesday evening Bangkok residents come to offer candles, flowers (predominantly pink roses), incense and bottles of whisky.

Rama V is also honoured with an annual festival on 23 October that celebrates his accomplishments in modernising the country, abolishing slavery and maintaining the country's independence when all other Southeast Asian countries were being colonised – avoiding such a fate is a matter of enormous pride to Thais. During this festival thousands of visitors converge on the plaza, accompanied by cacophonous loudspeakers and attendant food vendors, briefly disrupting Dusit's aloofness with Bangkok's engaging chaos. For visitors accustomed to more subdued places, Dusit and its well-maintained green spaces

top picks

THEWET & DUSIT

- Dusit Park (p94) Witness Victorian sense and Thai sensibilities merging in this royal enclave.
- Ratchadamnoen Stadium (p208) Makes Steven Seagal look soft as a pillow.
- Krua Apsorn (p164) Homestyle Thai food good enough for royalty.
- Vimanmek Teak Mansion (p94) How can an all-teak mansion this big have been built without a single nail?
- Wat Benchamabophit (p95) A Thai temple with a difference: Carrara marble, European-style frescoes and red carpet all the way.

will provide a break from Bangkok's incessant noise. Dusit is also home to Thailand's National Assembly (Map p93; Th Ratchawithi), the prime minister's residence at Government House (Map p93; Th Phitsanoluk), several ministries and the UNESCAP complex, the UN's vast Southeast Asian headquarters.

Cradled between Th Samsen and Mae Nam Chao Phraya, the riverside district is referred to as Thewet, after the nearby temple, Wat Ratchathewet. Thewet shelters Thewet Flower Market (Map p93; Th Krung Kasem; ☺ 8am-6pm), a popular flower market beside the *klorng,* and a refreshingly quiet backpacker scene existing cheek-by-jowl with a lively wet market selling vegetables, meat, fish and other sundries – it's a great local breakfast or lunch experience. In spite of the scores of backpackers staying here at any one time, the neighbourhood has resisted the temptation to transform its businesses into the internet cafes, tattoo parlours, bars or souvenir shops that usually pop up where travellers go. Instead vendors prefer the traditional course of business, allowing the foreigners to adjust to local customs. Largely a residential neighbourhood, at rush hour Thewet is packed with uniform-clad residents climbing aboard rickety buses for a sweaty commute to the office districts of Silom or Sukhumvit, while Th Samsen is a near-continuous stream of rattletrap buses and screaming túk-túk.

Street stalls and food markets are most prolific near Thewet, but be sure to be well watered and fed before venturing into food-averse Dusit on foot.

THEWET & DUSIT

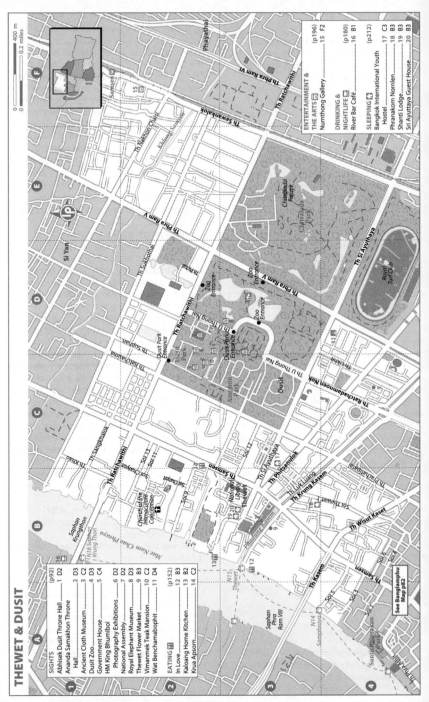

SIGHTS	(p92)
Abhisek Dusit Throne Hall	1 D2
Ananda Samakhon Throne Hall	2 D3
Ancient Cloth Museum	3 C2
Dusit Zoo	4 D3
Government House	5 C4
HM King Bhumibol Photography Exhibitions	6 D2
National Assembly	7 D2
Royal Elephant Museum	8 D3
Thewet Flower Market	9 B3
Vimanmek Teak Mansion	10 C2
Wat Benchamabophit	11 D4

EATING 🍴	(p152)
In Love	12 B3
Kaloang Home Kitchen	13 B2
Krua Apsorn	14 C2

ENTERTAINMENT & THE ARTS 🎭	(p196)
Numthong Gallery	15 F2

DRINKING & NIGHTLIFE 🍸	(p180)
River Bar Café	16 B1

SLEEPING 🛏	(p212)
Bangkok International Youth Hostel	17 C3
Phranakorn Nornlen	18 B3
Shanti Lodge	19 B3
Sri Ayuttaya Guest House	20 B3

See Banglamphu Map p82

0   400 m
0   0.2 miles

93

สวนดุสิต

☎ 0 2628 6300; bounded by Th Ratchawithi, Th U Thong Nai & Th Ratchasima; admission 100B, with Grand Palace ticket free; ⊗ 9.30am-4pm unless otherwise stated; ☒ 510, 70 & 72

A modern country, King Chulalongkorn pronounced, needed a modern seat of government. And so Rama V moved the royal court from the cloistered city of Ko Ratanakosin to the open and manicured lawns of Dusit Park. There he built Beaux Arts institutions and Victorian manor houses. Confectionery buildings of fused Euro-Thai modes housed members of the royal family in a style that must have seemed as futuristic as today's skyscrapers. All of this and the expansive gardens make Dusit Park a worthwhile escape from the chaos of modern Bangkok, with its egg-carton Bauhaus and blue-glass buildings.

Please note: because this is royal property, visitors should wear long pants (no capri pants) or long skirts and sleeved shirts.

Anchoring the Royal Plaza and indeed the whole Dusit precinct is the Ananda Samakhon Throne Hall (admission 150B; ⊗ 9am-5pm). Built in the early 1900s by Italian architect and engineer combination Mario Tamagno and Annibale Rigotti, the great neoclassical dome of the Ananda Samakhon looks out of place in Bangkok but right at home in Dusit. It was designed as a place to host – and impress – foreign dignitaries and on occasion it still serves this purpose, most notably during celebrations of King Bhumibol Aluyadej's 60th year on the throne, when royals from around the world converged here in full regalia. You'll almost certainly see a photo of this during your visit. The elaborate facade of Carrara marble is certainly impressive, but it's the interior that really turns heads.

Standing in the throne hall and looking up into the 40m-high central dome you'll

find a ceiling embellished with frescoes by Italian masters Galileo Chini and Carlo Riguli. This, and six murals dedicated to the most notable achievements of each of the first six Chakri dynasty kings, look at first glance to be European in almost every respect. But look more closely and you'll see subtle Thai identifiers that are enough to remind that you haven't slipped through a sinkhole and landed in Florence.

The first meeting of the Thai parliament was held in this building before being moved to a facility nearby. Today the hall and its exhibition, Arts of the Kingdom (www.artsofthekingdom.com), is open to the public – look particularly for the many uses of emerald-coloured beetle wings. Photos are not allowed.

The highlight of the park is Vimanmek Teak Mansion (⊗ 9.30am-4pm daily, last entry 3.15pm) said to be the world's largest golden teak mansion, built with nary a single nail. For all its finery, grand staircases, octagonal rooms and lattice walls, which are nothing short of magnificent, it is surprisingly serene and intimate. The mansion was originally constructed on Ko Si Chang in 1868 as a retreat for Rama V; the king had it moved to its present site in 1901. For the following few years it served as Rama V's primary residence, with the 81 rooms accommodating his enormous extended family. The interior of the mansion contains various personal effects of the king and a treasure-trove of early Ratanakosin and European art objects and antiques. Compulsory English-language tours of the building start every 30 minutes and last an hour, though it's a lucky dip as to whether your guide will actually speak decent English or not. Try to time your visit to see the Thai classical and folk dances staged in an open-sided säh·lah (often spelt sala) beside the mansion at 10.30am and 2pm.

Immediately behind Vimanmek mansion is Abhisek Dusit Throne Hall. Visions of Moorish palaces and Victorian mansions must have still been spinning around in the king's head when he commissioned this intricate building of porticoes and fretwork fused with a distinctive Thai character. Built as the throne hall for the palace in 1904, it opens onto a big stretch of lawn and flowerbeds, just like any important European building. Inside, the heavy ornamentation of the white main room is quite extraordinary, especially if you've been visiting a lot of

TRANSPORT: THEWET & DUSIT

Bus Air-con 505, 510 & 510; ordinary 3, 16, 18, 32, 53, 70 & 72

Ferry Thewet (N15)

With no Skytrain or Metro connections, peak-hour traffic gets very busy around here. That said, taxi is still a good way to get to Dusit.

overwhelmingly gold temples or traditional wooden buildings. Look up to just below the ceiling to see the line of brightly coloured stained-glass panels in Moorish patterns. The hall displays regional handiwork crafted by members of the Promotion of Supplementary Occupations & Related Techniques (SUPPORT) charity foundation sponsored by Queen Sirikit. Among the exhibits are *mát·mèe*–style (a form of tie-dying) cotton and silk textiles, *má·laang táp* collages (made from metallic, multi-coloured beetle wings), damascene and nielloware, and *yahn lí·pow* basketry (made with a type of vine).

The Dusit grounds are home to several other museums. Beside the Th U Thong Nai gate, the Royal Elephant Museum (p96) showcases two large stables that once housed three white elephants; it's more interesting than it sounds. Near the Th Ratchawithi entrance, two residence halls display the HM King Bhumibol Photography Exhibitions, a collection of photographs and paintings by the present monarch – a man who even today is rarely seen without a Canon SLR camera slung around his neck. Among the many loving photos of his wife and children are pictures of the king playing clarinet with Benny Goodman and Louis Armstrong in 1960. The Ancient Cloth Museum presents a beautiful collection of traditional silks and cottons that make up the royal cloth collection.

DUSIT ZOO Map p93
สวนสัตว์ดุสิต(เขาดิน)

☎ 0 2281 2000; www.zoothailand.org; Th Ratchawithi; adult/child 100/50B; ☽ 8am-6pm; ⊟ aircon 515, ordinary 18 & 28

Originally a private botanic garden for Rama V, Dusit Zoo (Suan Sat Dusit or *kŏw din*) was opened in 1938 and is now one of the premier zoological facilities in Southeast Asia. That, however, doesn't mean all the animal enclosures are up to modern zoological standards, with one endlessly pacing tiger being particularly heart-rending. Squeezed into the 19 hectares are more than 300 mammals, 200 reptiles and 800 birds, including relatively rare indigenous species. The shady grounds feature trees labelled in English plus a lake in the centre with paddle boats for rent. There's also an interesting WWII air raid shelter, a small children's playground and, on the far side of the lake where the exotic birds are kept, a theme-park atmosphere that

top picks

IT'S FREE

The value of the Thai baht in international currencies might turn misers into spendthrifts, but there are still plenty of cheap and even free thrills in Bangkok.

- **Hotel river boats** (p119) Take a free hotel ferry from Central Pier or River City to the plush hotel of your choice; whether you fork out for a drink when you get there is up to you.
- **Markets** (p150) Whether it's the wet-market chaos of Khlong Toey (p146), the flowers of Pak Khlong (p139) or anything you can imagine at Chatuchak (p135), Bangkok's vast outdoor markets are thoroughly memorable and free. And, of course, the more money you do spend, the more you save.
- **Erawan Shrine** (p110) See traditional Thai dancing, paid for by a Bangkokian making merit.
- **Lumphini Park** (p120) Sweat in synchrony at the free evening aerobics classes in Lumphini Park.
- **Victory Monument Skytrain station** (Map p64) Observe breakdancers practising their moves, young couples flirting, fashion trendies exhibiting themselves, and illegal markets on the elevated walkway leading to this station.

assumes said birds enjoy Thai pop and, on the day we visited, the beating drums of a Kenyan dance troupe.

If nothing else, the zoo is a nice place to get away from the noise of the city and observe how Thais amuse themselves – mainly by eating. There are a few lakeside restaurants that serve good, inexpensive Thai food.

WAT BENCHAMABOPHIT Map p93
วัดเบญจมบพิตร (วัดเบญฯ)

☎ 0 2282 7413; cnr Th Si Ayuthaya & Th Phra Ram V; admission 20B; ☽ 8.30am-5pm; ⊟ air con 23, 72, 503 & 509, ordinary 16 & 72

Inside and out, this temple is one of the most unusual, and most extravagent, in the kingdom. Built at the turn of the century on the orders of Rama V, the *bòht* is made of white Carrara marble (hence its alternative name, 'Marble Temple') imported from Italy especially for the job.

The large cruciform *bòht* is a prime example of modern Thai temple architecture. And the interior design is too, melding Thai motifs with European influences. The red carpets, the way the gold-on-white motifs

THE ORIGINAL WHITE ELEPHANTS

Think 'white elephant' and things like Howard Hughes' Spruce Goose wooden plane and the Millennium Dome (02 Arena) in London come to mind. But why is it that these and other supposedly valuable but hugely expensive and basically useless items are known as white elephants? The answer lies in the sacred status given to albino elephants by the kings of Thailand, Cambodia, Laos and Burma.

The tradition derives from the story in which the Buddha's mother is said to have dreamed of a white elephant presenting her with a lotus flower – a symbol of purity and wisdom – just before she gave birth. Extrapolating from this, a monarch possessing a white elephant was regarded as a just and benign ruler. Across the region any genuinely albino elephant automatically became crown property; the physical characteristics used to rank white elephants are outlined in the Royal Elephant Museum (Chang Ton; Map p93; Dusit Park; 9.30am-4pm). Laws prevented sacred white elephants from working, so despite being highly regarded they were of no practical use and cost a fortune to keep.

In modern Thailand the white elephant retains its sacred status, and one is kept at Chitralada Palace, home to the current Thai king. The museum houses a sculptural representation of that elephant. Draped in royal vestments, the statue is more or less treated as a shrine by the visiting Thai public.

are painted repetitively on the walls, the walls painted like stained glass windows and the royal blue wall behind the central Buddha image are strongly reminiscent of a European palace. Which is not all that surprising when you consider how enamoured Rama V (whose ashes are in the base of said Buddha image) was with Europe – just walk across the street to Dusit Park for further evidence.

The courtyard behind the *bòht* has 53 Buddha images (33 originals and 20 copies) representing every *mudra* (gesture) and style from Thai history, making this the ideal place to compare Buddhist iconography. If religious details aren't for you, this temple still offers a pleasant stroll beside landscaped canals filled with blooming lotus and Chinese-style footbridges.

Although many generations removed from the mainland (see the boxed text on p56), Bangkok's Chinatown could be a bosom brother of any Chinese city. The streets are crammed with shark-fin restaurants, gaudy yellow-gold and jade shops and flashing neon signs in Chinese characters. But these are just window dressing for the neighbourhood's relentlessly entrepreneurial soul.

Chinatown fans out along Mae Nam Chao Phraya between Saphan Phra Phuttha Yot Fa (Memorial Bridge) to the west and Hualamphong train station (p100) to the southeast, near the relatively quiet lanes of Talat Noi (p100). Th Yaowarat and Th Charoen Krung are Chinatown's main arteries and they provide the greatest diversity of services, from shopping and eating in the latest mainland Chinese styles to promenading (as much as you can promenade when the pavements are heaving with vendors). The whole district is buzzing from dawn until after dusk, with only the overfed soi dogs splayed out on footpaths seeming in any way relaxed. And where the narrow market soi can be a world of elbows during the day, things are marginally more mellow by night, when banquet dining and dazzling neon contribute to a carnival atmosphere.

Until the 1970s Chinatown was, in effect, the country's most important market, supplying and wholesaling pretty much anything that could be bought in the kingdom. Stores were, and still are, self-segregated by profession – whole streets or blocks are dedicated to sign making, gold and jewellery stores, and machine and tyre shops. However, Bangkok's ongoing affair with consumerism, and its resulting brood of lust children in the form of multistorey megamalls, have seen a steady decline in the area's commercial importance. Much of the middle class has moved out of the cramped district to the villas and condos of Bangkok's new suburbs *(mòo bâhn)*, taking their spending power with them.

Moving through the market is a slow process, though, and after shouldering your way through the claustrophobic commercial chaos of Talat Mai (Trok Itsaranuphap; p101) you'll find it difficult to imagine it could ever have been busier. Chinese remains the district's primary language, and goods, people

top picks

CHINATOWN

- Chinatown walking tour (p101) Immerse yourself in the lanes, the flavours and the chaos of one of the world's last genuine Chinatowns.
- Wat Traimit (p99) Meet the temple's Buddha, made of 5.5 tonnes of gold.
- Talat Noi (p100) Oil-stained machine shops, hidden Chinese temples and twisting lanes leading to a generations-old market: welcome to Talat Noi.
- Talat Mai (p165) Chaos and commerce battle it out in this photogenic, suffocating fresh-food market.
- Delicious street food (p165) Who says you need money – or a roof – to eat well?
- Phahurat (p100) Bollywood-style markets and the city's cheapest and best Indian food.

and services are on a continuous conveyor belt into and out of the area. All of which makes this one of Bangkok's most rewarding areas to simply set out and explore, get lost, and find yourself eating oyster omelettes in a hole-in-the-wall restaurant.

You could follow our Chinatown walking tour (p101), or perhaps fast for a day before embarking on our Chinatown Eats Walk (p165), a mouthwatering meander past some of the world's tastiest street food. Or just make it up as you go along. Whichever option you choose, expect it to be memorable.

But wait, there's more! Just when you thought your senses could be stimulated no more, you arrive at a small but thriving Indian and Islamic district called Phahurat (Little India; p100). Located on the western edge of Chinatown, near the intersection of Th Phahurat and Th Chakraphet, Phahurat shares the dim alleys and affinity for commerce of its neighbour, though their particular expressions provide a fascinating diversity. Th Chakraphet is home to several cheap Indian restaurants where style is secondary to taste; it's undoubtedly the best Indian food in the city.

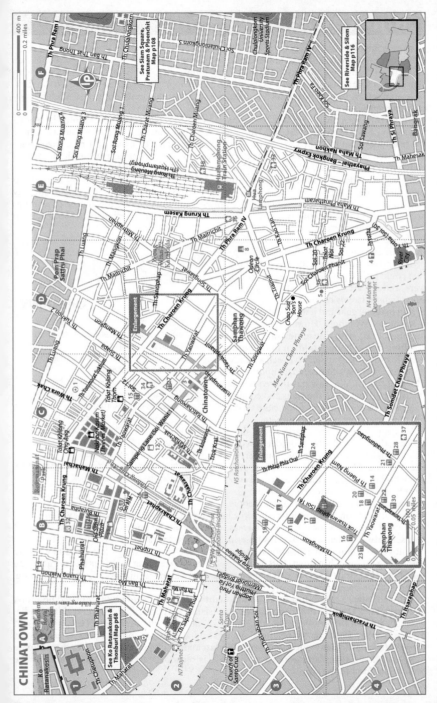

CHINATOWN

98

See Ko Ratanakosin & Thonburi Map p68

See Siam Square, Pratunam & Ploenchit Map p108

See Riverside & Silom p116

Mae Nam Chao Phraya

Samphan Thawong

Chao Sua Son's House

Hualamphong Train Station

Talat Khlong Thom

Nakhon Kasem (Thieves' Market)

Talat Khlong Ong Ang

Church of Santa Cruz

Pom Prap Sattru Phai

Odeon Circle

River City

N4 Marine Department

Phrathai–Bangkok Expwy

Enlargement

Enlargement

CHINATOWN

WAT TRAIMIT (THE GOLDEN BUDDHA) Map p98
วัดไตรมิตร
☎ 0 2225 9775; Th Traimit, near cnr Th Yaowarat & Th Charoen Krung; admission 20B; ☼ 8am-5pm; ⊜ ordinary 25, 35, 40 & 53; ⊕ Tha Ratchawong (N5); Ⓜ Hua Lamphong exit 1

Wat Traimit, also known as the Temple of the Golden Buddha, is home to the world's largest gold statue, a gleaming, 3m-tall, 5.5 tonne Buddha image with a mysterious past and a current value of more than US$40 million in gold alone. Sculpted in the graceful Sukhothai style (notice the hair curls and elongated earlobes), the image is thought to date from the late Sukhothai period. But if it is possible for a Buddha image to lead a double life, then this priceless piece has most certainly done so.

At what is thought to have been a time of great danger to the Siamese kingdom – presumably prior to an invasion from Burma – the Buddha image was rendered with a plaster exterior in an attempt to disguise it from the looting hordes. And it worked. After various assaults the Burmese hauled off vast quantities of Thai treasure, but this most valuable of all Buddha images – indeed the most valuable image in all of Buddhism – remained as shabby-looking and anonymous as intended. It was moved first to Bangkok and later to Wat Traimit, the only temple in the Chinatown area modest enough to take such a world-weary Buddha. And thus it remained, sheltered beneath a tin roof, until the mid-1950s when the temple had collected enough money to build a modest shelter for the image. During the move the Buddha was dropped from a crane, an act of such ill fortune that the workers are said to have downed tools and run. When the abbot inspected the Buddha the following day he found the plaster had cracked and, wouldn't you know it, the golden Buddha's true identity was finally revealed.

The image remained seated in its modest pavilion until 2009, smiling benevolently down upon an underwhelming and seemingly endless procession of tour groups, which seem to have scared off most of the genuine worshippers. But Wat Traimit's days of poverty are long gone. A new, marble hall has been built with a combination of Chinese-style balustrades and a steep, golden Thai-style roof. Surrounding it is a narrow strip of grass watered via mist fountains.

After viewing the image, head to the *wí·hähn* to see fading photos of the 1950s operation to remove the plaster. And drop by the *bòht* to 'play' the mechanical horoscope machines outside, which look like an import from a boardwalk amusement strip. Put a coin in the machine that corresponds to the day of the week you were born; lights flash and then a number appears that corresponds to a printed fortune. Don't worry, these fortunes aren't nearly as confronting as those on Golden Mount (p80).

Keep an eye out for the new Chinatown Museum, which is due to open on the site in 2010.

PHAHURAT Map p98
พาหุรัด

west of Th Chakrawat; 🚌 ordinary 53 & 73; 🚢 Tha Saphan Phut (Memorial Bridge, N6)
Fabric and gem traders set up shop in this small but bustling Little India, where everything from Bollywood movies to bindis is sold by enthusiastic small-time traders. Behind the more obvious storefronts are winding alleys that criss-cross Khlong Ong Ang, where merchants grab a bite to eat or make travel arrangements for trips home – it's a great area to just wander, stopping for masala chai or lassi as you go.

Just off Th Chakraphet is Sri Gurusingh Sabha (Th Phahurat; 🕐 6am-5pm), a gold-domed Sikh temple best viewed from Soi ATM. Basically it's a large hall, somewhat reminiscent of a mosque interior, devoted to the worship of the Guru Granth Sahib, the 17th-century Sikh holy book, which is itself considered the last of the religion's 10 great gurus. *Prasada* (blessed food offered to Hindu or Sikh temple attendees) is distributed among devotees every morning around 9am, and if you arrive on a Sikh festival day you can partake in the *langar* (communal Sikh meal) served in the temple. If you do visit this shrine, be sure to climb to the top for panoramic views of Chinatown. Stores surrounding the temple sell assorted religious paraphernalia.

TRANSPORT: CHINATOWN

Bus Air-con 507 & 508; ordinary 1, 4, 25, 33, 37, 49 & 53

Ferry Tha Marine Department (N4), Tha Ratchawong (N5), Tha Saphan Phut (Memorial Bridge, N6)

Metro Hua Lamphong

While we list bus numbers here, traffic in Chinatown is dire and it's better to arrive by river ferry or take the Metro and walk. Following the walking tour (p101), or just making up your own, is undoubtedly the most interesting (and, ahm, hot) way to get around. If it all gets too much, at weekends a hop-on hop-off red tourist bus (that looks like a tram) loops from opposite Hua Lamphong station up Th Yaowarat and back down Th Charoen Krung.

TALAT NOI Map p98
ตลาดน้อย

bounded by the river, Th Songwat, Th Charoen Krung & Th Yotha; 🚢 Tha Marine Department (N4)
This microcosm of soi life is named after a *noi* (little) market that sets up between Soi 22 and Soi 20, off Th Charoen Krung, selling goods from China. Wandering here you'll find streamlike soi turning in on themselves, weaving through people's living rooms, noodle shops and grease-stained machine shops. Opposite the River View Guesthouse, San Jao Sien Khong (unnamed soi; admission by donation; 🕐 6am-6pm) is one of the city's oldest Chinese shrines, and is guarded by a playful rooftop terracotta dragon. A former owner of the shrine made his fortune collecting taxes on bird-nest delicacies.

WAT MANGKON KAMALAWAT (LENG NOI YEE) Map p98
วัดมังกรกมลาวาส

Th Charoen Krung; 🕐 6am-5.30pm; 🚌 air-con 508, ordinary 16, 73, 75 & 93; 🚢 Tha Ratchawong (N5)
Explore the cryptlike sermon halls of this busy Chinese temple (also known as Leng Noi Yee) to find Buddhist, Taoist and Confucian shrines. During the annual Vegetarian Festival (p22), religious and culinary activities are centred here. But almost any time of day or night this temple is busy with worshippers lighting incense, filling the ever-burning altar lamps with oil and making offerings to their ancestors. Offering oil is believed to provide a smooth journey into the afterlife and to fuel the fire of the present life. Mangkon Kamalawatt means 'Dragon Lotus Temple'. Surrounding the temple are vendors selling food for the gods – steamed lotus-shaped dumplings and oranges – which are used for merit making.

HUALAMPHONG TRAIN STATION Map p98
สถานีรถไฟหัวลำโพง

Th Phra Ram IV; 🚌 air-con 501, ordinary 25 & 75; Ⓜ Hua Lamphong exit 2
At the southeastern edge of Chinatown, Bangkok's main train station was built by Dutch architects and engineers between 1910 and 1916. Above the 14 platforms it was designed in a neoclassical style by Italian architect and engineer combina-

CHINATOWN'S SHOPPING STREETS

Chinatown is the neighbourhood version of a big-box store divided up into categories of consumerables.

Th Charoen Krung (Map p98) Chinatown's primary thoroughfare is a prestigious address. Starting on the western end of the street, near the intersection of Th Mahachai, is a collection of old record stores. Talat Khlong Ong Ang consumes the next block, selling all sorts of used and new electronic gadgets. Nakhon Kasem is the reformed thieves' market where vendors now stock up on nifty gadgets for portable food prep. Further east, near Th Mahachak, is Talat Khlong Thom, a hardware centre. West of Th Ratchawong, everything is geared towards the afterlife and the passing of life.

Th Yaowarat (Map p98) A hundred years ago this was a poultry farm; now it is gold street, the biggest trading centre of the precious metal in the country. Shops are always painted like the interior of a Chinese shrine: blood red and decorated with well-groomed toy dogs that look down on the neighbourhood's fat soi dogs in every way except literally. Near the intersection of Th Ratchawong, stores shift to Chinese and Singaporean tourists' tastes: dried fruit and nuts, chintzy talismans and accoutrements for Chinese festivals. The multistorey buildings around here were some of Bangkok's first skyscrapers and a source of wonder for the local people. Bangkok's skyline has grown and grown, but this area retains a few Chinese apothecaries, smelling of wood bark and ancient secrets.

Th Mittraphan (Map p98) Sign makers branch off Wong Wian 22 Karakada, near Wat Traimit and the Golden Buddha; Thai and Roman letters are typically cut out by a hand-guided lathe placed prominently beside the pavement.

Th Santiphap (Map p98) Car parts and other automotive gear make this the place for kicking tyres.

Sampeng Lane (Map p98; Soi Wanit 1) Plastic cuteness in bulk, from pencil cases to pens, stuffed animals, hair flotsam and enough bling to kit out a rappers convention, all hang out near the eastern end of the alley. Closer to Phahurat, the main merchandise changes to bolts of fabric from India.

Soi 16 (Map p98; Trok Itsaranuphap) This ancient fresh market splays along the cramped alley between Th Yaowarat and Th Charoen Krung. It's fascinating, but anyone who suffers even the mildest form of claustrophobia should not contemplate it. North of Th Charoen Krung funerary items for ritual burnings dominate the open-air stalls.

tion Mario Tamagno and Annibale Rigotti, who were working at the same time on the grand Ananda Samakhom Throne Hall (p94) at Dusit. But it also embraces other influences, such as the patterned, two-toned skylights that exemplify nascent De Stijl Dutch modernism, and through these is known as an early example of the shift towards Thai Art Deco. If you can zone out of the chaos for a moment, look for the vaulted iron roof and neoclassical portico that were a state-of-the-art engineering feat.

HOLY ROSARY CHURCH Map p98
☎ 0 2266 4849; 1318 Th Yotha, near River City; ⏱ Mass Mon-Sat 7.30pm, Sun 8am, 10am & 7.30pm; ⛴ Marine Department (N4)
Portuguese seafarers were among the first Europeans to establish diplomatic ties with Siam and their influence in the kingdom was rewarded with prime riverside real estate. When a Portuguese contingent moved across the river to the present-day Talat Noi district of Chinatown in 1787, they were given this piece of land and built the

Holy Rosary Church, known in Thai as Wat Kalawan, from the Portuguese 'Calvario'. Over the years the Portuguese community dispersed and the church fell into disrepair. However, Vietnamese and Cambodian Catholics displaced by the Indochina wars adopted it and together with Chinese speakers now constitute much of the parish. Of particular note are the splendid Romanesque stained-glass windows, gilded ceilings and a Christ statue that is carried through the streets during Easter celebrations.

CHINATOWN WANDER
Walking Tour
Chinatown is packed – every inch of it is used to make a living. From the fresh-food market festooned with carcasses to alleys full of endless bling, the commerce never rests. This walking tour plunges into the claustrophobic alleys of chaotic dealing for which the district is famous, explores some quiet hidden lanes and visits the touristy but impressive Golden Buddha before finishing

in the relatively peaceful soi of Talat Noi. Be prepared for crowds and smells, and bring your camera. Depending on where you want to go afterwards and what time it is (the ferries stop soon after 7pm), finish either at the Marine Department river ferry, Hua Lamphong Metro (a 10-minute walk back from Talat Noi), or continue wandering south to River City and the hotel ferries.

1 Phahurat (Little India)
Starting from the river ferry at Tha Saphan Phut (Memorial Bridge Pier), walk north along jam-packed Th Chakraphet, past the Constitutional Court and into Phahurat (p100), aka Little India. If it's already lunchtime you could stop for a curry, or plunge straight into the retail madness of Trok Huae Med.

2 Trok Huae Med
There's no sign, but the old stores, street stalls and mass of people reveal you're at the beginning of Trok Huae Med, a largely Indian extension of Sampeng Lane. After 50m cross a *klorng* (or wander right for more informal curry houses) and continue.

3 Sampeng Lane
You'll soon be in Sampeng Lane, signposted (if you can see it) as Soi Wanit 1. This is Chinatown's oldest shopping strip, where the Chinese first set up shop after being moved from Ko Ratanakosin in 1782. Today the sky is completely obscured and bargains lie in ambush – that is, if you really want 500 Hello Kitty pens. This initial stretch is now dominated by Indian fabric merchants.

4 Chinese Shophouses
After a few minutes you'll come to Th Mahachak, where to the right dozens of battered

> **WALK FACTS**
>
> Start Tha Saphan Phut (Memorial Bridge Pier; river ferry N6)
> End Marine Department (river ferry N4) or Hua Lamphong Metro
> Distance 4km
> Duration Three hours
> Fuel stops Hong Kong Noodles (p165) or the streetside kitchens on Th Plaeng Naam

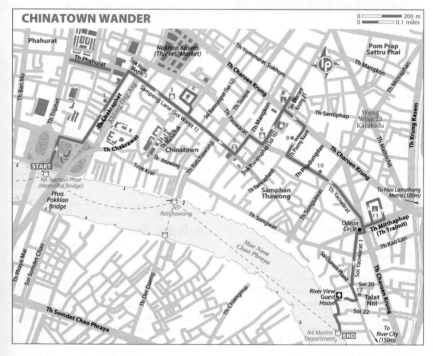

old Vespas wait for their next delivery job (there's no space for trucks around here). Turn left (northeast), walk about 30m and turn left again through a covered passage. On the far side are rows of photogenic, stuccoed yellow Chinese shophouses. It's pretty peaceful here, so a leisurely circuit makes a refreshing intermission in the market tour.

5 Bangkok Bank
Return to Sampeng Lane and continue east. This stretch is dominated by a mind-boggling array of cheap plastic stuff from China; a thousand different varieties of hair-pin, anyone? When you come to Th Mangkon, find somewhere you won't be run over by a trolley full of overstuffed boxes and admire two of Bangkok's oldest commercial buildings, a branch of Bangkok Bank and the venerable Tang To Kang gold shop, both more than 100 years old. The exteriors of the buildings are classic early Ratanakosin, showing lots of European influence; the interiors are heavy with hardwood panelling.

6 Trok Itsaranuphap (Talat Mai)
Turn left (north) on Th Mangkun and walk up to manic Th Yaowarat, Chinatown's main drag. Turn right past the street's famous gold shops (gold is sold by the *bàht*, a unit of weight equal to 15g, and prices are good). After 100m or so, gird your loins and cross Th Yaowarat, then head straight into a tiny lane known variously as Soi Charoen Krung 16, Trok Itsaranuphap and, more commonly, Talat Mai (New Market). There's no sign, but you'll know by the queue of people shuffling into the alley one at a time. If you thought Sampeng Lane was busy, this crush of humanity will have your head spinning like Linda Blair in *The Exorcist*.

7 Talat Leng-Buai-la
A bit over halfway along the lane, look for a turn to the right for Talat Leng-Buai-la. A spry 80 years old, it was once the city's central vegetable market but today sells mainly Chinese ingredients such as fresh cashews, lotus seeds and shiitake mushrooms. The first section is lined with vendors purveying cleaned chickens, plucked ducks, scaled fish, unnaturally coloured vats of pickled food and prepackaged snacks – hungry yet? Hong Kong Noodles (p165), back in the heart of the lane, does a rollick-

ing business catering to appetites aroused by such sights.

8 Wat Mangkon Kamalawat
You will, eventually, pop out the far end onto Th Charoen Krung. Cross over and go a short way down Soi Charoen Krung 21 to Wat Mangkon Kamalawat (p100), one of Chinatown's largest and liveliest temples. Along this stretch of the street, neighbouring shops sell fruit, cakes, incense and ritual burning paper, all for offering at the temple.

9 Thanon Plaeng Naam
Head back to Th Charoen Krung, turn left (east), walk one block and turn right on Th Plaeng Naam. This atmospheric street of shophouses and street food is a more leisurely place for a feed, particularly at the two streetside kitchens at the north end.

10 Thanon Yaowarat
Continue south, then turn left onto hectic Th Yaowarat. This is the neon side of Chinatown, great for photos in the late afternoon and early evening. After passing a couple of old Art Deco buildings that have seen better days, turn left at the Odeon Circle, with its distinctive Chinese gate, onto Th Mitthaphap (aka Th Traimit).

11 Wat Traimit & the Golden Buddha
A couple of minutes along this street of brushes and wicker furniture is Wat Traimit

and its 5.5 tonnes of Golden Buddha (p99). If you've timed your run to get here in the late afternoon (but before it closes at 5pm), it should be free of the usual tour buses and make a welcome respite from all those markets.

12 Talat Noi

If you're knackered, it's a short walk eastwards to Hua Lamphong Metro station. But if it's anywhere near sunset, we strongly recommend heading back to Odeon Circle, braving the traffic and heading down Soi Yaowarat 1. Follow this road of machine shops, then continue onto Soi Charoen Phanit into the local Talat Noi neighbourhood. Follow the signs to the River View Guest House (p218), where the 8th-floor restaurant-bar has cheap beer and amazing sunset views. It's not far from here to the Marine Department ferry pier, but remember the last boats pass a little after 7pm.

SIAM SQUARE, PRATUNAM, PLOENCHIT & RATCHATHEWI

Eating p166; Shopping p139; Sleeping p219

You'll rarely, if ever, see Bangkok described as 'well-organised'. But this central shopping district is surprisingly well connected, and it can be dangerously convenient for unleashing cash. At first glance this neighbourhood is all about shopping, a shrine to modern consumerism where megamalls in two duelling shopping districts cater to every whim.

This is modern Bangkok, where flimsy fashion is no longer a saffron monks' robe but a flouncy skirt and clicky heels. Packs of teenagers shuffle across the concrete pathways, breaking all the social mores their ancestors ever created. Female students wear miniskirts that could easily be mistaken for wide belts, cutesy couples stroll hand in hand, hipsters *(dèk naaou)* assume gangster styles from ghettos they've only heard rapped about. Give Bangkok a few more years of disposable income and the city – which is rightly proud of its creative side – will rival Tokyo and New York for pop power.

The centre of the action is Siam Skytrain station, the interchange for both Skytrain lines, which acts as the heart of the district. Through its network of concrete walkway veins it pumps thousands of passengers into the Siam shopping district, currently *the* place to shop in Bangkok. On the south side of the station is Siam Square (p144), an ageing ground-level mall peopled by baht-flexing students – all in black and white uniforms – who trawl through the closet-sized boutiques that reflect what's hot and what's not. To the north of the station you'll enter the air-conditioned and exclusive atmosphere of Siam Paragon (p143), with its top-end boutiques, European sports cars and world-class oceanarium (p107). On the same side are the more affordable (and more funky) Siam Center (p143) and Siam Discovery Center (p143). A few hundred meters east along Bangkok's miracle mile of shopping centres is the Ratchaprasong shopping district, where the Central World Plaza (p141) towers over hundreds of shops, a clutch of luxury hotels and half a dozen holy deities, including the Erawan Shrine (p107). All the while Mahboonkrong (MBK, p142), to the west of Siam near National Stadium Skytrain station, draws visitors like moths to its discount-everything flame. Wherever you shop, beware of consumer euphoria.

All the action here, coupled with the massive Skytrain stations looming above everything, mean the area is constantly buffeted by a cacophonous din and suffocating exhaust fumes. Mercifully, respite is near at hand. Cinemas (p198) abound, and for something more cerebral the new Bangkok Art & Culture Centre (p199) has regular exhibitions and a counter-culture vibe. There's a chance to step out of the air-conditioned, international city entirely and enter old Bangkok at the famous Jim Thompson's House (p106) or, across Khlong Saen Saeb in Pratunam district, the much less touristed and thoroughly original Muslim village of Baan Krua (p106).

Spreading north of Pratunam is Ratchathewi, an area that attracts few tourists but does have some sights, such as Thailand's tallest skyscraper, the Baiyoke Tower II (p112). The area around Victory Monument is also an interesting place to find bars and restaurants that are very much the staples of the Thai middle class.

South of Th Phra Ram I and west of Th Phayathai, the Pathumwan district is filled with the National Stadium (p207) and the huge campus of Chulalongkorn University (p111), Thailand's most prestigious university. The area extending east along Th Ploenchit includes the tree-lined Soi Lang Suan, with its expensive condos and serviced apartments, and Th Withayu (Wireless Rd), home to embassies and expatriates.

top picks

SIAM SQUARE, PRATUNAM, PLOENCHIT & RATCHATHEWI

- Erawan Shrine (p110) A splash of religion in the midst of all the money.
- Jim Thompson's House (p106) See the teak mansion that put Thai style on the map...before its ex-spy owner disappeared off that map.
- Baan Krua (p106) Explore the Muslim village where Jim Thompson first encountered silk.
- Khlong Saen Saeb Canal Boats (p264) Commute with the locals the old-fashioned way, along this atmospheric (in more ways than one) *klorng*.
- Mahboonkrong (MBK; p142) Indulge in air-con, junk food, a million mobile phones, clothes and plastic stuff.
- Food court frenzy (p167) Like eating on the street, minus the exhaust fumes.

SIAM SQUARE, PRATUNAM & PLOENCHIT

JIM THOMPSON'S HOUSE Map p108
บ้านจิมทอมป์สัน

☎ 0 2216 7368; www.jimthompsonhouse.org; 6 Soi Kasem San 2, Th Phra Ram I; adult/concession (under 25yr with ID) 100/50B; ⏱ 9am-5pm; 🚤 klorng boat to Tha Hua Chang; 🚇 National Stadium exit 1

In 1959, 12 years after he discovered the fine silks being woven across the *klorng* in Baan Krua and single-handedly turned Thai silk into a hugely successful export business, American Jim Thompson bought this piece of land on Khlong Saen Saeb and built himself a house. It wasn't, however, any old house. Thompson's love of all things Thai saw him buy six traditional wooden homes and reconstruct them in this jungle-like garden. Some of the homes were brought from the old royal capital of Ayuthaya; others were pulled down and floated across the *klorng* from Baan Krua – including the first building you enter on the tour.

Thompson became one of the first Westerners to embrace the traditional Thai home as a thing of beauty. Thai homes were multipurpose affairs, with little space for luxuries like separate living and sleeping rooms. Thompson adapted his six build-ings, joining some, to create a larger home in which each room had a more familiar Western function. One room became an air-conditioned study, another a bedroom and the one nearest the *klorng* his dining room.

As well as having good taste in silk, Thompson was an eagle-eyed collector of oriental goods, from Thai residential archi-tecture to Southeast Asian art. Today the house operates as a museum and a tribute to the man. Viewing is by regularly departing English-, French-, Japanese- or Thai-language tour only; pho-tography is not allowed inside the build-ings. New buildings house the excellent Jim Thompson Art Center (p200), a cafe selling drinks and light meals and a vast shop flogging Jim Thompson–branded goods. For a taste of the Bangkok Thompson grew to love (and cheaper drinks and silks), follow your visit here with the Baan Krua walking tour (p114).

Beware well-dressed touts in soi near the Thompson house who will tell you it is closed and then try to haul you off on a dodgy buying spree.

BAAN KRUA Map p108
บ้านครัว

Btwn Khlong Saen Saeb, Th Phayathai & Th Phra Ram VI; 🚤 klorng boat to Tha Hua Chang; 🚇 National Stadium exit 1

Baan Krua literally means 'Muslim Fam-ily Village' and is one of Bangkok's oldest communities. It dates to the turbulent years at the end of the 18th century, when Cham Muslims from Cambodia and Vietnam fought on the side of the new Thai king and were rewarded with this plot of land east of the new capital. The immigrants brought their silk-weaving traditions with them, and the community grew when the residents built Khlong Saen Saeb to better connect to the river.

The 1950s and '60s were boom years for Baan Krua after Jim Thompson (see opposite) hired the weavers and began exporting their silks across the globe. The last 40 years, however, haven't been so good. Silk production was moved elsewhere follow-ing Thompson's disappearance and the community spent 15 years successfully fighting to stop a freeway being built right through it. Through all this many Muslims moved out of the area; today about 30% of the population is Muslim, the rest primarily immigrants from northeast Thailand. How-

---

TRANSPORT: SIAM SQUARE, PRATUNAM & PLOENCHIT

Bus Air-con 141, 183, 204, 501, 508 & 547; ordinary 15, 16, 25, 47 & 73

Klorng boat Tha Hua Chang, Tha Pratunam & Tha Withayu

Skytrain Siam, National Stadium, Chit Lom & Ploen Chit

Even by Bangkok standards, traffic around here is nightmarish. If you're coming from the Silom, Sathon or Sukhumvit areas, or from north towards Chatuchak Weekend Market, take the Skytrain. Coming from Banglamphu and the Th Khao San area, consider the *klorng* boat. The exception is going east along Th Ploenchit and Th Sukhumvit, towards Asoke. Buses have a dedicated lane and come so regularly that they are usually faster than the Skytrain, and only a few baht. Of course, if you just want to dry out, take a taxi and enjoy the air-con.

JIM THOMPSON: INTERNATIONAL MAN OF MYSTERY...& SILK

Born in Delaware in 1906, Jim Thompson was a New York architect who served in the Office of Strategic Services (a forerunner of the CIA) in Thailand during WWII. After the war he found New York too tame compared to his beloved Bangkok. When in 1947 he spotted some silk in a market and was told it was woven in Baan Krua (see p114), he found the only place in Bangkok where silk was still woven by hand.

Thompson thought he could sell the fine silk from Baan Krua to a postwar world with a ravenous appetite for luxury goods. He attracted the interest of fashion houses in New York, Milan, London and Paris, and gradually built a worldwide clientele for a craft that had, just a few years before, been in danger of dying out. They were heady days for the poor Muslim weavers of Baan Krua. Thompson was noted for both his idealism and generosity, and when he set up the Thai Silk Company in 1948 he insisted that his contract weavers became shareholders.

By 1967 Thai Silk had annual sales of almost US$1.5 million. In March that year, when Thompson went missing while out for an afternoon walk in the Cameron Highlands of western Malaysia, his success as a businessman and background as a spy made it an international mystery. Thompson has never been heard from since, but the conspiracy theories – fuelled even further by the murder of his sister in the USA in the same year – have never stopped. Was it communist spies? Business rivals? A man-eating tiger? The most recent theory is that the silk magnate was accidentally run over by a Malaysian truck driver who hid his remains.

The Legendary American: The Remarkable Career & Strange Disappearance of Jim Thompson, written by his long-time friend William Warren, is an excellent account of Thompson's life.

ever, Baan Krua retains its Muslim character, and one of the original families is still weaving silk on old teak looms. The village consists of old, tightly packed homes threaded by tiny paths barely wide enough for two people to pass. It has been described as a slum, but the house-proud residents are keen to point out that they might not live in high-rise condos, but that doesn't make their old community a slum.

The best way to visit Baan Krua is to wander, stopping regularly to eat the delicious Thai Muslim cuisine on offer; see the walking tour, p114, to get started.

SIAM OCEAN WORLD Map p108

☎ 0 2687 2000; www.siamoceanworld.com; basement, Siam Paragon, Th Phra Ram I; adult/child (80-120cm) 850/650B; ⏰ 10am-8pm (last entry 9pm); ☒ Siam exit 5

Southeast Asia's largest oceanarium is also one of its most impressive. More than 400 species of fish, crustaceans and even penguins populate this vast underground facility. The oceanarium is divided into 12 zones accommodating specific species. The main tank is the highlight, with an acrylic tunnel allowing you to walk beneath sharks, rays and all manner of fish. Diving with sharks is also an option if you have your diving licence (for a fee), though you'll have almost as much fun timing your trip to coincide with the shark and penguin feedings; the former are usually at 1pm and 4pm, the latter at 12.30pm and 4.30pm – check the website for details.

LINGAM SHRINE (SAAN JAO MAE THAP THIM) Map p108

ศาลเจ้าแม่ทับทิม

Nai Lert Park Hotel, Th Withayu; ☒ klorng boat to Tha Withayu; ☒ Ploen Chit exit 1

Every village-neighbourhood has a local shrine, either a sacred banyan tree tied up with coloured scarves or a spirit house. But it isn't every day you see a phallus garden like this lingam shrine, tucked back behind the staff quarters of the Nai Lert Park Hotel. Clusters of carved stone and wooden shafts surround a spirit house and shrine built by millionaire businessman Nai Loet to honour Jao Mae Thap Thim, a female deity thought to reside in the old banyan tree on the site. Someone who made an offering shortly after the shrine was built had a baby, and the shrine has received a steady stream of worshippers – mostly young women seeking fertility – ever since.

If facing the entrance of the hotel, follow the small concrete pathway to the right, which winds down into the building beside the car park. The shrine is at the end of the building next to the *klorng*.

RATCHAPRASONG INTERSECTION SHRINES Map p108

cnr Th Ratchadamri & Th Ploenchit; ☒ Chit Lom

A crowd in this part of town usually means a bargain market is nearby. But here the continuous activity revolves around six Hindu shrines credited with making this

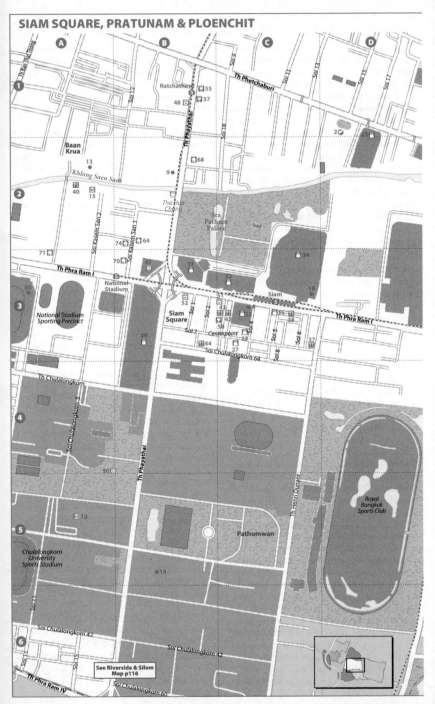

SIAM SQUARE, PRATUNAM & PLOENCHIT

Th Ban Thai Thong

Th Phetchaburi

Ratchathewi

55
57
48

Th Phayathai

Soi 11
Soi 13
Soi 15
Soi 17

2

Baan
Krua

13

68

Khlong Saen Saep

9

40
15

Tha Hua
Chang

Sra
Pathum
Palace

71

74
64

34

Soi Kasem San 2
Soi Kasem San 1

70

Th Phra Ram I

National
Stadium

33

60

National Stadium
Sporting Precinct

51
52

31

Siam

18

Siam
Square

42
43
58

22

35
38

Th Phra Ram I

Soi 2
Soi 5
Soi 6

26

Soi 7
Centerpoint
27
23

Soi 8

37

44

Soi Chulalongkorn 64

Th Chulalongkorn

Soi Chulalongkorn 5

Th Phayathai

Th Henri Dunant

50

Royal
Bangkok
Sports Club

12

Pathumwan

Chulalongkorn
University
Sports Stadium

14

Soi Chulalongkorn 42

Soi Chulalongkorn 42

See Riverside & Silom
Map p116

Th Phra Ram IV

Soi Chulalongkorn 60

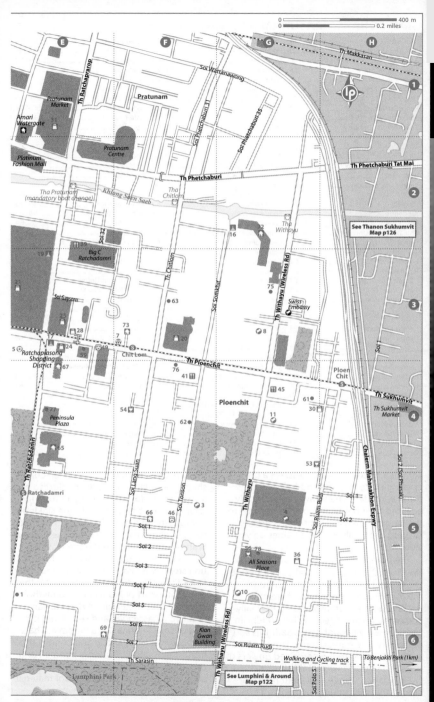

SIAM SQUARE, PRATUNAM & PLOENCHIT

commercial corridor a success. It's a fascinating place to come and just watch the way modern Thais have pragmatically adapted their beliefs – and their hopes – to the perceived reality that success breeds success, especially with the deities on your side.

The primary focus is the Erawan Shrine (San Phra Phrom; 6am-8pm), on the corner beside the Grand Hyatt Erawan Hotel. Brahma, the four-headed Hindu god of creation, holds court here. Brahma would normally command great respect in Thai Buddhism but not nearly enough to warrant this sort of idolatry. The human traffic jam can be directly attributed to the perceived powers of the shrine since it was established in 1956.

Originally a simple Thai spirit house occupied this spot during the construction of

the first Erawan Hotel. This more elaborate shrine was built as a last-ditch effort to end a string of misfortunes – ranging from injured construction workers to the sinking of a ship carrying marble for the hotel – that had delayed the completion of the hotel. A Brahmin priest decided the site was burdened by bad karma because the foundation stone was laid on an inauspicious date. Since the hotel was to be named after the elephant escort of Indra in Hindu mythology, the priest determined that Erawan required a passenger, and suggested it be that of Lord Brahma (Phra Phrom in Thai). A statue was built, and lo and behold, the misfortunes ended, business boomed and eventually the shrine took on a cult of its own, being seen as a harbinger of material success.

After 40 years of largely benign existence, the gilded plaster image was destroyed during a late-night attack in 2006. After smashing the image with a hammer Thanakorn Pakdeepol, a 27-year-old man with a history of mental illness, was immediately set upon by two nearby rubbish collectors and promptly beaten to death. A replacement was cast using parts of the old image, and today devotion is as strong as ever.

There is a constant cycle of worshippers seeking divine assistance for good luck, health, wealth and love. Most people offer marigold garlands or raise a cluster of joss sticks to their foreheads in prayer. The flowers are left on the shrine for a few minutes, before attendants gather them up to be resold. Not everyone goes for that, however – one ex-student told us how, in her university days, a Big Mac would be offered, left for a few minutes and then retrieved; why waste it?

When wishes are granted, the worshippers show their gratitude by commissioning shrine musicians and dancers for a performance. The tinkling tempo, throaty bass and colourful dancers are in marked contrast to the ordinary street corner on which the shrine stands, surrounded by idling cars and self-absorbed shoppers – though most of them will still offer a passing *wâi* (bringing the hands together in a prayer-like manner at chest level).

The businesses posted on the other corners of the intersection have erected their own Hindu shrines in order to counter and/ or copy the power of the Erawan Shrine. This godly one-upmanship sees Lakshmi,

the wife of Vishnu, standing atop Gaysorn Plaza while Vishnu himself is mounted upon Garuda at the Intercontinental Hotel. Another Garuda can be found in the Police Hospital, while Indra is appropriately placed outside the Amarin Plaza, beside the Erawan.

If your head is spinning, you could settle for crossing diagonally from the Erawan Shrine to the square outside Central World for a look at elephant-headed Ganesha – whose presence is no great surprise given his parents are Lakshmi and Vishnu. A little further north on the Central World forecourt is the Trimurthi Shrine (San Trimurthi), most likely included as a cosmic mediator between all these rival deities. This shrine depicts the three supreme Hindu gods (Shiva, Vishnu and Brahma) and symbolises creation, destruction and preservation. Note that 'love' is not mentioned here, but peace and love aren't that far removed and that's enough to have Thai teenagers descending on the shrine on Thursdays to seek romantic success. For details about all six shrines, download the excellent 'Deities@Ratchaprasong' guide from www.heartofbangkok.com.

CHULALONGKORN UNIVERSITY
Map p108

จุฬาลงกรณ์มหาวิทยาลัย

☎ 0 2215 0871; www.chula.ac.th; 254 Th Phayathai; 🚌 air-con 502, ordinary 21; Ⓜ Sam Yan exit 2; 🚈 Siam exit 2 or 6

Thailand's oldest and most prestigious university is nestled in a leafy enclave south of busy Th Phra Ram I. The centrepiece of the campus is the promenade ground on the east side of Th Phayathai where a seated statue of Rama V (King Chulalongkorn) is surrounded by purple bougainvillea and offerings of pink carnations. The showcase buildings display the architectural fusion the monarch favoured, a mix of Italian revival and Thai traditional. The campus has a parklike quality, with noble tropical trees considerately labelled for plant geeks. Of the many species that shade the campus, the rain trees with their delicate leaves are considered symbolic of the university; they are commemorated in a school song, and their deciduous cycle matches the beginning and ending of each school year.

The university has two art galleries, Jamjuree and the Art Centre (☎ 0 2218 2965; www.car.chula.ac.th/art; Centre of Academic Resources Bldg, 7th fl; ⏰ 9am-7pm Mon-Fri, 9am-4pm Sat). The latter shows Chula professors as well as major names in the Thai and international modern art scene; permanent exhibits include Thai art retrospectives.

RATCHATHEWI

VICTORY MONUMENT Map p113
อนุสาวรีย์ชัยสมรภูมิ
Th Ratchawithi & Phayathai; 🚌 ordinary 12 & 62; 🚇 Victory Monument
This obelisk monument is one of the most recognisable, and controversial, in Bangkok. The monument was built by the then military government in 1941 to commemorate a 1940 campaign against the French in Laos. The 'victory' (brokered by Japan) resulted in Cambodian and Lao territory that had earlier been ceded to the French being returned to Thailand. However, by 1945 the monument had become something of an embarrassment, given the territory had to be handed back to the French following the defeat of Japan.

Today the monument is primarily a landmark for observing the social universe of local university students and countless commuters. An elevated walkway circumnavigates the roundabout, funnelling the pedestrian traffic in and out of the Skytrain station as well as providing a gathering spot for breakdancers, flirters and lots of fashion experiments. It's worth fighting your way out of the vendors and pedestrian crush and into the neighbourhood around Victory Monument, which is reminiscent of provincial Thai towns, if not exactly hicksville. Nearby bars and cafes cater to the university crowd – try the rooftop Sky Train Jazz Club (p185) on the corner of Soi Rang Nam. And if you wander down Soi Rang Nam you'll find local lôok tûng and pleng pêu·a chee·wít (songs for life) places with live music most evenings.

BAIYOKE II TOWER Map p113
☎ 0 2656 3000; 22 Th Ratchaprarop; admission 200B, after 6pm 250B; ⏰ 10am-10pm; ⛴ klorng boat to Tha Pratunam
Thailand's tallest tower, if not its most architecturally attractive, the Baiyoke II tower soars to 88 storeys (85 of them above ground), the upper of which are often clad with some truly huge advertising. The main attraction here is the 77th floor observation deck. The views are as impressive as you'd expect (unless it's too smoggy) but only just compensate for the tacky decor, uninspiring restaurant and inconvenient location. If you have a choice, the upstairs rooftop bars and revolving restaurant are better.

WANG SUAN PHAKKAT Map p113
วังสวนผักกาด
☎ 0 2245 4934; Th Si Ayuthaya, btwn Th Phayathai & Th Ratchaprarop; admission 100B; ⏰ 9am-4pm; 🚌 ordinary 72; 🚇 Phaya Thai exit 4
Everyone loves Jim Thompson's House, but few have even heard of Wang Suan Phakkat (Lettuce Farm Palace), another noteworthy traditional Thai house-museum. Once the residence of Princess Chumbon of Nakhon Sawan, the museum is a collection of five traditional wooden Thai houses linked by elevated walkways containing varied displays of art, antiques and furnishings. The landscaped grounds are a peaceful oasis

---

TRANSPORT: RATCHATHEWI

Bus Air-con 503, 513 & 536; ordinary 29, 36, 54, 59 & 112

Klorng boat From Banglamphu and the upper soi of Sukhumvit to Tha Pratunam

Skytrain Ratchathewi, Phaya Thai & Victory Monument

If you're coming from the Silom, Sathon or Sukhumvit areas, or from north towards Chatuchak Weekend Market, take the Skytrain. From Banglamphu and the Th Khao San area, take the klorng boat. If you come by taxi, expect delays – especially during peak hours.

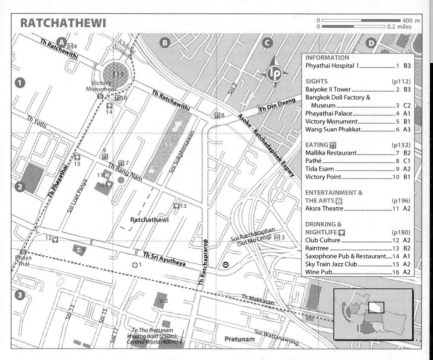

| 0 | 400 m |
| 0 | 0.2 miles |

INFORMATION
Phyathai Hospital 1..................1 B3

SIGHTS (p112)
Baiyoke II Tower..................2 B3
Bangkok Doll Factory &
Museum..................3 C2
Phyathai Palace..................4 A1
Victory Monument..................5 B1
Wang Suan Phakkat..................6 A3

EATING 🍴 (p152)
Mallika Restaurant..................7 B2
Pathé..................8 C1
Tida Esarn..................9 A2
Victory Point..................10 B1

**ENTERTAINMENT &
THE ARTS** 🎭 (p196)
Aksra Theatre..................11 A2

**DRINKING &
NIGHTLIFE** 🍸 (p180)
Club Culture..................12 A2
Raintree..................13 B2
Saxophone Pub & Restaurant....14 A1
Sky Train Jazz Club..................15 A2
Wine Pub..................16 A2

complete with ducks, swans and a semi-enclosed, Japanese-style garden.

The diminutive Lacquer Pavilion at the back of the complex dates from the Ayuthaya period (the building originally sat in a monastery compound on the banks of Mae Nam Chao Phraya, just south of Ayuthaya) and features gold-leaf *Jataka* and Ramayana murals as well as scenes from daily Ayuthaya life. Larger residential structures at the front of the complex contain displays of Khmer, Hindu and Buddhist art, Ban Chiang ceramics and a collection of historic Buddhas, including a beautiful late U Thong–style image. In the noise and confusion of Bangkok, the gardens offer a tranquil retreat.

PHYATHAI PALACE Map p113
☎ 0 2354 7732; King Mongkut Hospital, 315 Th Ratchawithi; admission free; 🕙 9am-4pm Sat; 🚇 Victory Monument exit 3

West of the Victory Monument roundabout, Phayathai Palace was built by Rama V in 1909 as a cottage for retreats into what was then the country. The surviving throne hall, encased in French glass doors and a fanciful tiered roof, is now part of a hospital

complex and is open to the public. Note the limited hours; tours are conducted at 9.30am and 1.30pm on Saturday. The grounds are open at other times. There isn't much in the way of tourist displays, but it's worth a visit to survey the architecture of the buildings and escape the sightseeing masses.

BANGKOK DOLL FACTORY & MUSEUM Map p113
พิพิธภัณฑ์ตุ๊กตาบางกอกดอล
☎ 0 2245 3008; www.bangkokdolls.com; 85 Soi Ratchataphan (Soi Mo Leng), Th Ratchaprarop; admission free; 🕙 8am-5pm Mon-Sat; 🚌 ordinary 62 & 77

It's no exaggeration to say the dolls crafted in this modest workshop have become the template for dolls sold in countless tourist stores across Thailand. The workshop was founded by Khunying Tongkorn Chandevimol in 1956 after she completed a doll-making course while living in Japan. Upon her return to Thailand, she began researching and making dolls, drawing from Thai mythology and historical periods. Her dolls, often in Thai hill-tribe and rural costumes, have won several international awards.

Today her personal collection includes 400 dolls from around the world, plus important pieces from her own workshop, where you can watch the figures being crafted by hand.

The museum is difficult to find: it is best approached via Th Si Ayuthaya heading east. Cross under the expressway past the intersection with Th Ratchaprarop and take the soi to the right of the post office. Follow this windy street until you start seeing signs. Easier, take a taxi and get the driver to call the museum for directions.

DIY BAAN KRUA
Walking Tour

We could tell you to take lefts and rights down little alleys, but exploring this historic Muslim village is more fun if you just venture forth and find your own way. But we will get you into the village… Start this DIY tour when you finish your tour of Jim Thompson's House (p106); head left to the *klorng* and left again. You'll soon come to Garimmin & Sobereen (⏱ 7am-8pm Mon-Sat), a makeshift, *klorng*-side place selling cheap, delicious Muslim curries and noodle dishes plus cold drinks (no beer). It's a great spot to sit and watch the *klorng* boats motor by while observing village life on the other side: men dressed in white dishdashas, exotic caged birds yapping and women selling food

WALK FACTS

Start Jim Thompson's House
End Wherever you like
Distance Not very far
Duration 15 minutes to one hour
Fuel stop Garimmin & Sobereen

and everyday items from tiny stores that are a world away from the nearby megamalls.

Refreshed, cross the footbridge and dive in. Wander around and try to keep a smile on your face; the local people are welcoming and enjoy a bit of banter, but don't enter anyone's house unless you're invited. You can spend as little or long as you like wandering through Baan Krua, but do try to see the silk weavers in action. You'll probably hear the clickety clack of the looms before you see them; if you can't find them, ask for directions (hint: they are in an alley leading off the *klorng*-side path).

Of the two workshops, Phamai Baan Krua (☎ 0 2215 7458 or 0812 439 098) is the easiest in which to watch the weaving and (if he's around) owner Niphon Manuthas speaks English and German; see p111 for an interview with him. The high-quality handwoven silk that originally attracted Jim Thompson is still sold here, and prices are very reasonable compared with the chic store across the *klorng*.

Eating p168; Shopping p144; Sleeping p221

During Bangkok's shipping heyday the city faced the river and welcomed a steady stream of foreign trading ships, European and Chinese envoys and the odd *fà·ràng* chancer. All along Mae Nam Chao Phraya are the remnants of this mercantile era: the ornate French and Portuguese embassies, crumbling Customs House and the elegant Mandarin Oriental (p222) hotel. Narrow, quiet lanes wind through abandoned warehouses, faded facades of historic shipping companies, and the Muslim and Indian communities that have largely replaced the European presence.

Th Charoen Krung, which runs parallel to the river and links Th Silom with Chinatown, was Bangkok's first paved road – built at the behest of European residents who wanted a place for their horses and buggies. How times have changed. The water-based society was so taken by this innovation that, one by one, nearly all the city's canal routes were concreted over to become roads. Today the southern end of Th Charoen Krung is lined with silk and jewellery businesses that sell to wealthy tourists staying at the luxury riverside hotels. But not far away, back behind the commercial facade, are the residential areas where curry shops are more likely to serve Indian-style roti than rice, and silken headdresses distinguish Muslim Thais from their Buddhist sisters.

As industries changed, the financial district migrated inland along Th Silom, which runs from Th Charoen Krung northeast to Lumphini Park and was once the outskirts of the riverside city. Windmills *(silom)* once dotted the landscape, conveying water to the area's rice fields.

Today Silom is known as the Wall St of Thailand and experiences a daily tide of people. Workers flood into the office towers in the morning, are released into the streets for lunch and return home aboard public transport in the evening. Foreigners sweat in their imported suits, maintaining the corporate appearance of New York and London in styles that are ill-suited to the tropics. Thai secretaries prefer polyester suits that are sold off the rack at small markets, alongside bulk toiletries and thick-heeled sandals. Workers returning to the office after lunch are usually loaded down with plastic bags of food for mid-afternoon snacks: in Thailand the snack table is the equivalent of the Western water cooler.

Parallel to Th Silom are Th Surawong to the north and Th Sathon to the south, which is divided into northbound Th Sathon Neua and southbound Th Sathon Tai, running either side of the remains of the *klorng* it has now replaced. None of these streets is especially well blessed with traditional 'sights', but wedged between Silom and Surawong, uncannily convenient to the heart of the business zone, is Bangkok's most infamous attraction, the Patpong strip of go-go bars (p193) and clubs.

Th Sathon is home to several embassies (p271), three of Bangkok's best hotels and endless speeding traffic. One of those hotels hosts the dreamy, decadent Moon Bar at Vertigo (p184), while State Tower on the corner of Th Silom and Th Charoen Krung is crowned with Sirocco (p184). Both host some of the most breathtaking, cocktail-enhanced sunset views on earth.

At the eastern end of this neighbourhood is delightfully, mercifully green Lumphini Park (p120), the city's central green space where kids learn to ride bikes, grandmas stretch out stiff joints, office workers work out and (relatively) fresh air never tasted so good. East of the park is Suan Lum Night Bazaar (p147) and Lumphini Stadium (p208).

top picks

RIVERSIDE, SILOM & LUMPHINI

- Lumphini Park (p120) Relax Bangkok-style among the exercisers and exercise-observers in the 'lungs of the city'.
- Patpong (p120) Ping pong? Well, not exactly…
- Queen Saovabha Memorial Institute (p121) Confront your fear of snakes at this humanitarian snake farm.
- Chao Phraya dinner cruises (p169) End the day (or start the night) with a meal on the river.
- Oriental Hotel (p222) Relive the steamship era of globetrotting authors and aristocrats with tea and crumpets at this legendary establishment.
- Cocktail hour Soak up the sunset views and knock back a cocktail or two at Bangkok's tower-top bar-restaurants, Moon Bar at Vertigo (p184) and Sirocco (p184).

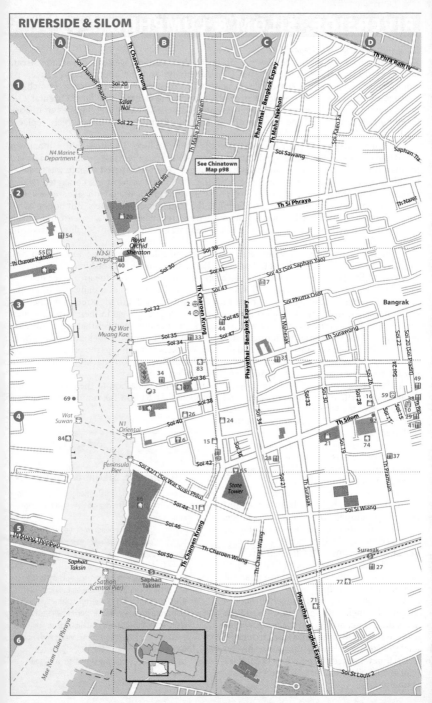

RIVERSIDE & SILOM

See Chinatown Map p98

Bangrak

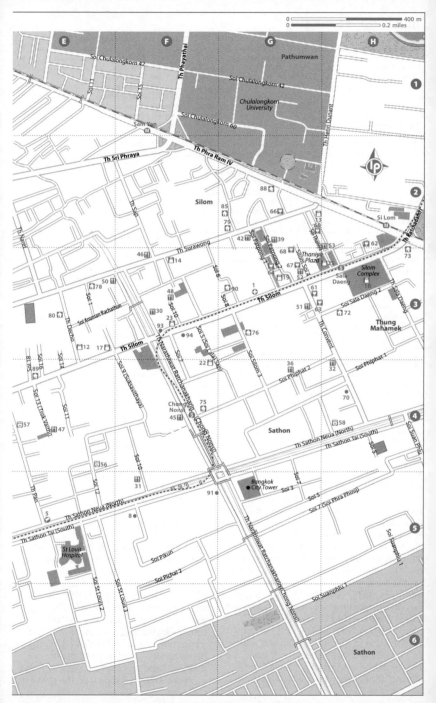

RIVERSIDE & SILOM

RIVERSIDE

BANGKOKIAN MUSEUM Map p116

☎ 0 2233 7027; 273 Soi 43, Th Charoen Krung;
admission free; ☻ 10am-4pm Wed-Sun; ⚓ Tha Si
Phraya (N3)

This collection of three wooden houses illustrates an often-overlooked period of Bangkok's history, the 1950s and '60s. The main building was built in 1937 as a home for the Surawadee family and, as the signs inform us, was finished by Chinese carpenters on time and for less than the budgeted 2400B (which would barely buy a door handle today). This building and the large wooden one to the right, which was added as a boarding house to help cover costs, are filled with the detritus of post-war family life and offer a fascinating window into the period. The third building, at the back of the block, was built in 1929 as a surgery for a British doctor, though he died soon after arriving in Thailand.

OLD CUSTOMS HOUSE Map p116

กรมศุลกากร

Soi 36, Th Charoen Krung; ⚓ Tha Oriental (N1)

Old Customs House was once the gateway to Thailand, levying taxes on traders moving in and out of the kingdom. It was designed by an Italian architect and built in the 1880s; the front door opened onto its source of income (the river) and the grand facade was ceremoniously decorated in columns and transom windows. Today it's a crumbling yet hauntingly beautiful home to the fire brigade, with sagging shutters, peeling yellow paint and laundry flapping on the balconies.

For years the building has been used as a base for the waterborne fire brigade and the firefighters' families, with occasional cameos in films such as Wong Kar Wai's *In the Mood for Love*. Plans to resurrect the building as a luxurious Aman Resort seem to have gone no further than the billboard outside, so anyone with a large wad of spare cash and ambitions as a boutique hotelier should contact the government. It's not open to the public, but it is OK to wander around…as long as you don't get in the way of the volleyball game.

ASSUMPTION CATHEDRAL Map p116

☎ 0 2234 8556; Soi 40 (Soi Oriental), Th Charoen Krung; ⏰ 7am-7pm; 🚢 Tha Oriental (N1); 🚈 Saphan Taksin exit 3

Marking the ascendancy of the French missionary influence in Bangkok during the reign of Rama II, this Romanesque church with its rich golden interior dates from 1910 and hosted a Mass by Pope John Paul II in 1984; his statue now stands outside the main door. The schools associated with the cathedral are considered some of the best in Thailand.

SILOM

SRI MARIAMMAN TEMPLE Map p116

วัดพระศรีมหาอุมาเทวี(วัดแขก)

Wat Phra Si Maha Umathewi; ☎ 0 2238 4007; cnr Th Silom & Th Pan; admission free; ⏰ 6am-8pm; 🚌 air-con 76, 77, 504 & 514, ordinary 77, 162 & 164; 🚢 Tha Oriental (N1); 🚈 Surasak exit 3

TRANSPORT: RIVERSIDE, SILOM & LUMPHINI

Bus Air-con 76, 77, 504 & 514; ordinary 1, 15, 16, 22, 36 & 62

Ferry Tha Si Phraya (N3), Tha Oriental (N1) & Tha Sathon (Central Pier)

Metro Silom & Lumphini

Skytrain Sala Daeng, Chong Nonsi, Surasak & Saphan Taksin

Th Silom is busy at almost every hour and the Skytrain is almost always a better alternative for reaching destinations on this street. Traffic moves more regularly on Th Sathon, though U-turn possibilities are rare.

ON THE RIVER

Getting out on Mae Nam Chao Phraya is a great way to escape the Bangkok traffic and experience the city's maritime past. So it's fortunate that the city's riverside hotels also have some of the most attractive boats shuttling along the river. In most cases these free services run from Tha Sathon (Central Pier) and River City to their mother hotel, departing every 10 or 15 minutes. There's no squeeze, no charge and a uniformed crew to help you on and off. The Millennium Hilton boat has arguably the most polite crew and runs the most useful route. Services usually finish about 10pm.

Arrestingly flamboyant, Sri Mariamman is a Hindu temple that is a wild collision of colours, shapes and deities. Built in the 1860s by Tamil immigrants, the principal temple features a 6m facade of intertwined, full-colour Hindu deities. The main shrine of Sri Mariamman contains three supremes: Jao Mae Maha Umathewi (Uma Devi; also known as Shakti, Shiva's consort) at the centre; her son Phra Khanthakuman (Khanthakumara or Subramaniam) on the right; and her elephant-headed son Phra Phikkhanesawora (Ganesha) on the left. Along the left interior wall sit rows of Shivas, Vishnus and other Hindu deities, as well as a few Buddhas. While most of the people working in the temple hail from the Indian subcontinent, you will likely see plenty of Thai and Chinese devotees praying here as well. This is because the Hindu gods figure just as prominently in their individualistic approach to religion.

The official Thai name of the temple is Wat Phra Si Maha Umathewi, but sometimes it is shortened to its colloquial name Wat Khaek – *kàak* is a common expression for people of Indian descent. The literal translation is 'guest', an obvious euphemism for any group of people not particularly wanted as permanent residents; hence most Indian Thais don't appreciate the term.

BANK OF ASIA (ROBOT BUILDING)
Map p116

ธนาคารเอเชีย

cnr Th Sathon Tai & Soi Pikun; 🚈 Surasak exit 4

During the crazy 1980s, when no building project was too outlandish or expensive,

PUSSY GALORE

Super Pussy! Pussy Collection! The neon signs leave little doubt about the dominant industry in Patpong, the world's most infamous strip of go-go bars and clubs running 'exotic' shows. There is enough skin on show in Patpong to make Hugh Hefner blush, and a trip to the upstairs clubs could mean you'll never look at a ping-pong ball or a dart the same way again.

For years opinion on Patpong has been polarised between those people who see it as an exploitative, immoral place that is the very definition of sleaze, and others for whom a trip to Bangkok is about little more than immersing themselves in planet Patpong. But Patpong has become such a caricature of itself that in recent times a third group has emerged: the curious tourist. Whatever your opinion, what you see in Patpong or in any of Bangkok's other high-profile 'adult entertainment' areas depends as much on your personal outlook on life as on the quality of your vision.

Prostitution is actually illegal in Thailand but there are as many as 2 million sex workers, the vast majority of whom – women and men – cater to Thai men. Many come from poorer regional areas, such as Isaan in the northeast, while others might be students helping themselves through university. Sociologists suggest Thais often view sex through a less moralistic or romantic filter than Westerners. That doesn't mean Thai wives like their husbands using prostitutes, but it's only recently that the gradual empowerment of women through education and employment has led to a more vigorous questioning of this very widespread practice.

Patpong actually occupies two soi that run between Th Silom and Th Surawong (Map p116; G2) in Bangkok's financial district. The two streets are privately owned by – and named for – the Thai-Chinese Patpongpanich family, who bought the land in the 1940s and initially built Patpong Soi 1 and its shophouses; Soi 2 was laid later. During the Vietnam War the first bars and clubs opened to cater to American soldiers on 'R&R'. The scene and its international reputation grew through the '70s and peaked in the '80s, when official Thai tourism campaigns made the sort of 'sights' available on Patpong a pillar of their marketing.

These days Patpong has mellowed considerably, if not matured. Thanks in part to the popular night market that fills the soi after 5pm, it draws so many tourists that it has become a sort of sex theme park. There are still plenty of the stereotypical middle-aged men ogling pole dancers, sitting in dark corners of the so-called 'blow-job bars' and paying 'bar fines' to take girls to hotels that charge by the hour. But you'll also be among other tourists and families who come to see what all the fuss is about.

Most tourists go no further than stolen glances into the ground-floor go-go bars (see p193), where women in bikinis drape themselves around stainless-steel poles, between bouts of haggling in the night market. Others will be lured by men promising sex shows to the dimly lit upstairs clubs. But it should be said that the so-called 'erotic' shows usually feature bored-looking women performing acts that feel not so much erotic as demeaning to everyone involved. Several of these clubs are also infamous for their scams, usually involving the nonperforming (ie clothed, if just barely) staff descending on wide-eyed tourists like vultures on fresh meat. Before you know it you've bought a dozen drinks, racked up a bill for thousands of baht, and followed up with a loud, aggressive argument flanked by menacing-looking bouncers and threats of 'no money, no pussy!'.

Were we saying that Patpong had mellowed? Oh yes, there is a slightly softer side. Several bars have a little more, erm, class, and in restaurants such as the French bistro Le Bouchon (p168) in Patpong 2 you could forget where you are – almost.

architect Sumet Jumsai created his now-famous 'Robot Building' for the Bank of Asia. The whimsical facade does indeed look a bit like a robot (or our idea of what a robot should look like, at least). Needless to say, few architectural purists were keen on it at the time, but now it seems quaint and retro – a real character on Bangkok's often uninspired skyline. The building itself is not open to the public; it is best viewed looking south from the Skytrain between Surasak and Chong Nonsi stations.

LUMPHINI

LUMPHINI PARK Map p122
สวนลุมพินี
bounded by Th Sarasin, Th Phra Ram IV, Th Withayu (Wireless Rd) & Th Ratchadamri; ◷ 5am-8pm; ▣ air-con 505, ordinary 13; Ⓜ Lumphini exit 3; ▣ Sala Daeng exit 3 & Ratchadamri exit 2
Named after Buddha's birthplace in Nepal, this is Bangkok's largest and most popular park. Its 58 hectares are home to an artificial lake surrounded by broad, well-tended lawns, wooded areas, walking paths and the odd scurrying monitor lizard and

ambling turtle to complement the shuffling Bangkokians – it's the best outdoor escape from Bangkok without leaving town.

The park was originally a royal reserve but in 1925 Rama VI declared it a public space. In the years since it has matured and, as the concrete has risen all around, become the city's premier exercise space. One of the best times to visit is early morning, when the air is (relatively) fresh and legions of Chinese are practising t'ai chi, doing their best to mimic the aerobics instructor or doing the half-run half-walk version of jogging that makes a lot of sense in oppressive humidity. Meanwhile, vendors set up tables to dispense fresh snake's blood and bile, considered health tonics by many Thais and Chinese. A weight-lifting area in one section becomes a miniature 'muscle beach' on weekends, when the park takes on a festive atmosphere as the day cools down into evening. Facilities include a snack bar, an asphalt jogging track, a picnic area, toilets and a couple of tables where women serve Chinese tea. Cold drinks are available at the entrances and street food vendors set up tables outside the park's northwest corner from about 5pm.

During the kite-flying season (from mid-February to April), Lumphini is a favoured flight zone, with *wôw* (kites) for sale in the park.

QUEEN SAOVABHA MEMORIAL INSTITUTE (SNAKE FARM) Map p122
สถานเสาวภา

☎ 0 2252 0161; 1871 Th Phra Ram IV; adult/child 200/50B; ☼ 9.30am-3.30pm Mon-Fri, 9.30am-1pm Sat & Sun; ◻ air-con 507, ordinary 4, 47 & 50; Ⓜ Silom exit 1; Ⓡ Sala Daeng exit 3

Venomous snakes such as the formidable cobra, banded krait and pit viper live a peaceful and – though they probably don't know it – altruistic existence at this institute affiliated with the Thai Red Cross. Watching them being milked of their venom (daily at 11am) or, in the case of the python, draped around tourist necks (2.30pm Monday to Friday) is such a tourist draw it has helped pay for a new serpentarium, opened in 2008.

Of course, all the fun isn't just for the amusement of tourists. The institute was founded in 1923, when it was only the second of its kind (the first was in Brazil), and has gone on to become one of the world's leading centres in the study of snakes. The venom collected during the milkings is used to make snake-bite antivenins, which are distributed throughout the country. The institution is named in honour of Queen Saovabha, wife of Rama V, who championed a wide variety of medical causes and education, including a school for midwives and other modern birthing practices.

It's best to arrive 30 minutes before the advertised show time to see a video presentation about the institute and its work (usually in Thai with English subtitles). Outside show times you can stroll the small garden complex where the snakes are kept in escape-proof cages. The snakes tend to

top picks

BANGKOK FOR CHILDREN

Aside from the play centres found on the top floors of several major shopping centres, Bangkok has plenty to keep kids amused (at least until they're exhausted by the heat). For more on bringing children to Bangkok, see p268.

- Tha Thewet (Map p93; Th Krung Kasem; ☼ 7am-7pm) Join the novice monks and Thai children as they throw food (bought on the pier) to thousands of flapping fish.
- Fun-arium (Map p126; ☎ 0 2665 6555; www.funarium.co.th; 111/1 Soi 26, Th Sukhumvit; adult/child under 105cm/child 105cm-13yr 90/180/300B; ☼ 8.30am-8.30pm; ☎) Bangkok's largest indoor playground, with coffee and wi-fi to keep parents happy while the kids play.
- Children's Discovery Museum (p132) Fun...and they might learn something too.
- Queen Saovabha Memorial Institute (Snake Farm; left) Cool snake shows and a chance to touch some cool snake skin.
- Museum of Siam (p72) Modern interactive museum that's a hit with kids from ages four to 15.
- Longtail Boats (p278) A deafening pick-up engine strapped to a surfboard? What kid could resist?
- Wat Prayoon (Map p64; 24 Th Prachathipok, cnr Thetsaban Soi 1; ☼ 8am-6pm; ⛴ Tha Pak Talat/Atsadang) This artificial hill beside the Memorial Bridge is cluttered with miniature shrines and a winding path that encircles a pond full of turtles.
- Theme parks (p260) There are plenty to choose from.

LUMPHINI & AROUND

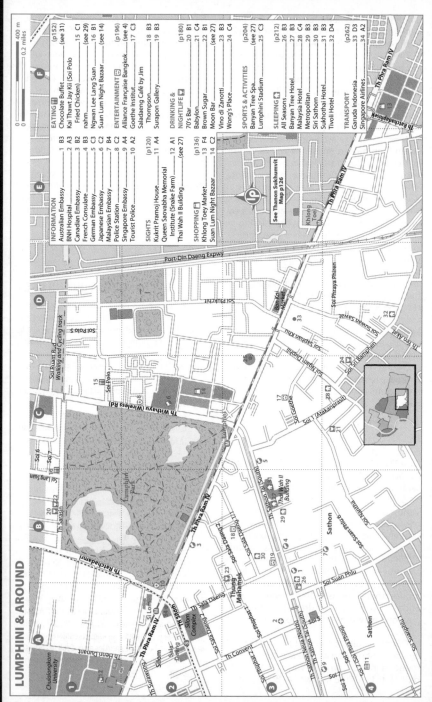

INFORMATION	
Australian Embassy	1 B3
BNH Hospital	2 A3
Canadian Embassy	3 B2
French Consulate	4 B3
German Embassy	5 C3
Japanese Embassy	6 C2
Malaysian Embassy	7 B4
Police Station	8 C2
Singapore Embassy	9 A4
Tourist Police	10 A2

SIGHTS	(p120)
Kukrit Pramoj House	11 A4
Queen Saovabha Memorial Institute (Snake Farm)	12 A1
Thai Wah II Building	(see 27)

SHOPPING	(p136)
Khlong Toey Market	13 F4
Suan Lum Night Bazaar	14 C2

EATING	(p152)
Chocolate Buffet	(see 31)
Kai Thawt Jay Kii (Soi Polo Fried Chicken)	15 C1
nahm	(see 29)
Ngwan Lee Lang Suan	16 B1
Suan Lum Night Bazaar	(see 14)

ENTERTAINMENT	(p196)
Alliance Française Bangkok	(see 4)
Goethe Institut	17 C3
Saladaeng Café by Jim Thompson	18 B3
Surapon Gallery	19 B3

DRINKING & NIGHTLIFE	(p180)
70's Bar	20 B1
Babylon	21 C4
Brown Sugar	22 B1
Moon Bar	(see 27)
Vino di Zanotti	23 B3
Wong's Place	24 C4

SPORTS & ACTIVITIES	(p204)
Banyan Tree Spa	(see 27)
Lumphini Stadium	25 C3

SLEEPING	(p212)
All Seasons	26 B3
Banyan Tree Hotel	27 B3
Malaysia Hotel	28 C4
Metropolitan	29 B3
Siri Sathorn	30 B3
Sukhothai Hotel	31 B3
Tivoli Hotel	32 D4

TRANSPORT	(p262)
Garuda Indonesia	33 D3
Singapore Airlines	34 A2

See Thanon Sukhumvit Map p126

be camera shy during nonperformance times, though you could get lucky and spot a camouflaged king cobra poised to strike. If you opt to 'wear' a python, expect a heavy but remarkably cool and smooth sensation.

KUKRIT PRAMOJ HOUSE Map p122
บ้านหม่อมราชวงศ์คึกฤทธิ์ปราโมช
☎ 0 2286 8185; Soi 7 (Phra Phinij), Th Narathiwat Ratchankharin; adult/child 50/20B; ⏲ 9.30am-5pm Sat & Sun; ⓜ Chong Nonsi exit 2
Author and statesman Mom Ratchawong Kukrit Pramoj (1911–95) once resided in this charming complex now open to the public for tours. Surrounded by a manicured garden famed for its Thai bonsai trees, five teak buildings introduce visitors to traditional Thai architecture, arts and to the former resident, who wrote more than 150 books (including the highly respected *Four Reigns*), served as prime minister of Thailand in 1974 and '75 and spent 20 years decorating this house. The last tour begins at 4.30pm.

RIVERSIDE RAMBLE
Walking Tour
There's more to the riverside district of Bangrak than large luxury hotels. Once Thailand's gateway to the world, its quiet tree-lined soi retain enough of their past character – in the form of old shophouses, embassies and godowns converted into antique stores – for an interesting couple of hours of walking and looking. The starting point is one of the most accessible in Bangkok, at the end of the Skytrain and the main river ferry terminal. If you start after lunch it will be easier to justify regular drink stops in the hotel bars, and you can segue neatly into a rooftop sundowner.

1 Bangrak Market
Walk away from the river and turn left onto Th Charoen Krung. The street is lined with vendors selling all manner of fresh and fried food that make delicious snacks; turn left on Soi 42 to reach Bangrak Market for myriad fresh and dry goods.

2 Assumption Cathedral
Continue along Th Charoen Krung, past the monumentally ugly neoclassical State Tower at the corner of Th Silom. Turn left on Soi Charoen Krung 40 (aka Soi Oriental) and left through a gate to the red-brick Assumption Cathedral (p119).

3 East Asiatic Company Building
Exiting Assumption Cathedral through the front door, walk through the small park and then right, beneath an overhead walkway linking two buildings amid what was once Bangkok's centre of international commerce. Here, in front of Tha Oriental, is the fading, classical Venetian-style facade of the East Asiatic Company, which was built in 1901. Much of Thailand's foreign trade was conducted through this building, with goods coming and going from the surrounding godowns.

4 Mandarin Oriental
Walk east down Soi 40 and turn left into what is now known as the the Mandarin Oriental (p222), Bangkok's oldest and most storied accommodation. Have a wander around, stop for a drink in Lord Jim's, and be sure to check out the Authors' Wing (note that the 'smart, casual' dress code bans open shoes but they usually aren't too strict).

5 Old Customs House
Exit the hotel, head away from the river and turn left past the Oriental Plaza (OP), built as a department store in 1905 and now housing expensive antique shops. Pass the walls of the French embassy and turn left; local Muslim restaurants offer cheap, delicious curry lunches here. Head towards the river and the big, decrepit Old Customs House (p118). Rehabilitation plans seem to have stalled and it remains a fire station, but it's OK to take a look around.

6 Haroon Village
Leave the way you entered and immediately turn left down a narrow lane behind Old Customs House. You're now in Haroon village, a Muslim enclave full of sleeping cats, playing kids, wooden houses and family-run stores selling essentials (including drinks and ice creams). Make your own way through Haroon and you'll eventually come to a larger street running away from the river.

7 Naaz
Follow this road, turn left at Th Charoen Krung and cross the street opposite the imposing art deco General Post Office. Walk down Soi 45 (directly opposite the post office entrance), turn right at the T and just around the bend is tiny Naaz (p172), home to the richest biryanis in town.

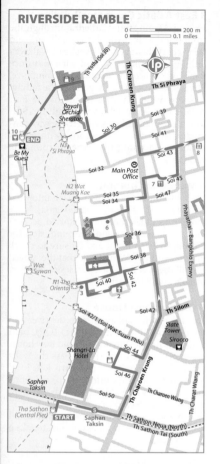

RIVERSIDE RAMBLE

WALK FACTS

Start Tha Sathon (Central Pier) or Skytrain Saphan Taksin
End River City
Distance 4km, extra to post-walk drinking spot
Duration 1½ to two hours
Fuel stops Naaz (p172)

once across turn right. Continue to the next corner and turn left on Soi 30, aka Soi Captain Bush. Follow this road past the tacky 'antique' shops and the walls of the Portuguese embassy, Bangkok's oldest. You could finish your tour here, and take the river express boat from Tha Si Phraya, which is down a lane before the Sheraton Hotel. Alternatively, continue to River City (p146) to view historical artefacts from across Southeast Asia. It's worth noting that anything flagged as being of Cambodian origin might not be strictly kosher, as Cambodian law prohibits the export of most cultural artefacts in an attempt to maintain the cultural heritage of the country. Other countries might have different laws, but the effect of buying is the same. For more information see www.heritagewatch.org.

10 Drinkies

From River City you have several options, depending on your evening plans. This is a departure point for Mae Nam Chao Praya dinner cruises (p169) leaving at 7pm. More appealing are the free shuttle boats to the riverside hotels. If it's after 5pm you could take the Mandarin Oriental boat to the famous hotel for a sundowner there, or walk from the hotel up to State Tower for a rooftop cocktail at Sirocco (p184). Take the Hilton boat just across the river and head to the penthouse jazz bar Three Sixty (p191), which is definitely better if it's raining. For a lesser, but still great, view and much cheaper drinks, take the Hilton boat and walk left from the pier to the riverside Be My Guest and get a table outside the wall.

8 Bangkokian Museum

Continue along Soi 45 and turn left, walk under the expressway and turn right onto Soi 43 to the Bangkokian Museum (p118) for a taste of the Bangkok of a bygone era.

9 River City

Head back to Th Charoen Krung, take your life in your hands crossing the street and

THANON SUKHUMVIT

Eating p173; Shopping p147; Sleeping p228

The Sukhumvit neighbourhood starts at the fleshpots of Nana Entertainment Plaza (p193) in what could be loosely called central Bangkok and tracks its namesake street for 20km all the way to the Gulf of Thailand. Like Bangkok as a whole, it has no real centre and numerous distinct personalities. Apart from the Skytrain, which looms above much of the street, the thing that brings it all together is money. This is Bangkok's most exclusive residential area, one packed with the city's most expensive apartments, villas, restaurants, shops, spas, cars, hospitals and, not surprisingly, its wealthiest residents.

Sukhumvit's two main personality blocks are either side of Soi Asoke (Soi 21). West of Soi Asoke, the soi branching off the main road are dominated by the sleazy sex tourist scene around Nana and Soi Cowboy (p193), which tends to attract the expat (sexpat) and repeat visitor market. On Th Sukhumvit itself the scantily clad bargirls share space with men using battered laminated cards to tout eye-opening shows and a night market flogging fake DVDs, T-shirts and túk-túks made from beer cans to tourists. But it's not all sex and souvenirs. Several chic boutique hotels embellish these soi, and the city's most fashionable nightclubs, including Bed Supperclub (p192) and Q Bar (p193), can be found on Soi 11. Meanwhile, down at Soi 3/1 you can feast on cheap Middle Eastern food in what is known as Little Arabia, where we recommend Nasir Al-Masri (p174).

West of Soi Asoke is where the bulk of the international residents and wealthy Thais live. During the postwar period, the green swathes of rice paddy that once filled the area were initially developed into large, contemporary villas occupying even larger blocks; for a prime example dine at Spring (p175). Over the years these huge blocks have proved prime targets for developers looking to cash in on the Thai infatuation with high-rise apartments. And despite years of economic sluggishness and weak local demand, taller and more extravagent condominiums (think apartments with private balcony pools) continue to go up on almost every soi.

top picks

THANON SUKHUMVIT

- Ban Kamthieng (p129) An informative, well-presented taste of northern Thailand in this pretty teak building.
- Party like it's 1969 Take a trip back in time at trendy retro-themed bars along Th Ekamai and Th Thong Lor, including Happy Monday (p183), Tuba (p186) and Shades of Retro (p185).
- Soi 11 clubs Dance your way down Bangkok's premier clubbing soi, where perennials Bed Supperclub (p192) and Q Bar (p193) compete with the rooftop Nest (p184).
- International restaurants (p173) Pasta, sushi, kim chi, tapas, hommus – sample Th Sukhumvit's huge selection of foreign cuisine.
- Skytrain (p266) Peek into the neighbourhood's many fortressed mansions from this moving vantage point.

Further east the road passes the plush Emporium shopping mall on its way to the Thong Lor (Soi 55) and Ekamai (Soi 63) neighbourhoods. These two areas have their fair share of mansions and a lively, and very trendy, bar and restaurant scene; the Japanese food is exceptional. Ekamai is home to several huge clubs that fill with expensively clad young Thais on weekends.

For all its wealth and foreign faces, Sukhumvit remains resolutely Thai. Walk to the mouth of almost any soi to be reminded you're in a Thai city: street food vendors, motorcycle taxis waiting to cart you home for 10B, soi dogs loitering around vendors selling grilled pork and the ubiquitous 7-Eleven store, known hereabouts as a 'se-vern'. For street food, soi 20, 23, 33 and 38 are particularly good.

Like many modern neighbourhoods, Sukhumvit doesn't boast much in the way of bona fide sights, with temples to Mammon and bacchanalian pleasure more prevalent than those to Buddha.

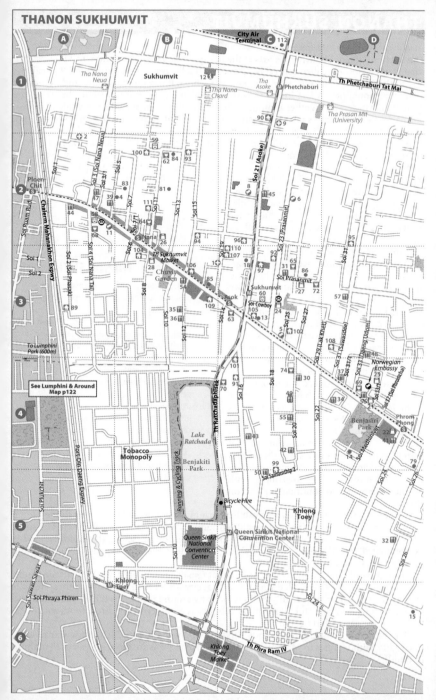

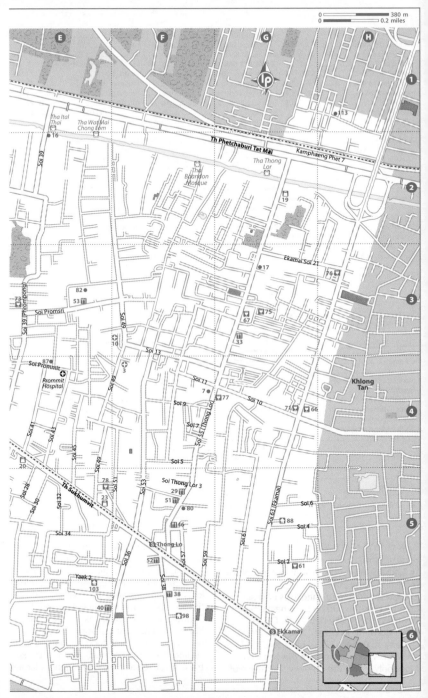

0 ———————— 380 m
0 ———————— 0.2 miles

E   F   G   H   1

● 113

Tha Ital Thai
Tha Wat Mai Chong Lom
● 16

Th Phetchaburi Tat Mai   Kamphaeng Phet 7

Sol 39

Tha Thong Lor

The Brandon Mosque   🏠 19   2

Ekamai Sol 21

● 17   76 🏠

Sol 39 Phrom Phong
73   82 ●
● 53 🍴
Soi Promsri
Sol 49   🏠 75   3
🏠 67
🏠 10   🏠 33

Soi 13   Sol 49
● 87   🏥 3
Soi Prommit
Prommit Hospital   Sol 49
Sol 11
7 ●   🏠 77
Soi 9   Sol 10
Soi 7   Sol 5 Thong Lor   71 🏠 66   4
Khlong Tan

Sol 41   Soi 5
Sol 43   Sol 45
Sol 49
Soi Thong Lor 3
20   🏠 78   Sol 51   Sol 53   29 🍴   Sol 6
🏠 23   51 🍴   Sol 63 (Ekamai)   🏠 88   Sol 4   5
Sol 28   ● 80   Sol 61
Sol 30   Sol 32
Th Sukhumvit   🍴 46
Sol 34   🚆 Thong Lo
Sol 36   52 🍴   Sol 51   Sol 2   🏠 61

Yaek 2
🏠 103   Sol 38
🏠 38
40 🍴
🏠 98
🚆 Ekkamai   6

127

THANON SUKHUMVIT

BENJAKITI PARK Map p126
สวนเบญจกิติ

Th Ratchadaphisek; 🕐 **5am-8pm;** Ⓜ **Queen Sirikit Convention Center exit 3**
The latest addition to Bangkok's emaciated green scene, this 130-rai (20.8-hectare) park encircles a large lake beside the Queen Sirikit Convention Center, and marks the Queen's sixth cycle (72nd birthday). It is built on what was once a part of the Tobacco Monopoly, a vast Crown-owned expanse of low-rise factories and warehouses. Another 300 rai (48 hectares) of buildings is earmarked for transformation into a manmade rainforest. If this ever happens – and Buddha knows Bangkok needs it – it will transform the area into something like New York's Central Park. For now the lake seems too big for the park, but it's much quieter than Lumphini Park (p120) and good for jogging and cycling (bikes can be hired) around the 2km track. If you're still feeling energetic, a largely

TRANSPORT: THANON SUKHUMVIT

Bus Air-con 501, 508, 511 & 513; ordinary 2, 25, 30, 48 & 72

Metro Sirikit Centre, Sukhumvit (joining with Asoke Skytrain) & Phetchaburi (Phetburi)

Skytrain Nana, Asok, Phrom Phong, Thong Lo, Ekkamai, Phra Khanong, On Nut and, due to open in 2010, Bang Chak, Punnawithi, Udorn Suk, Bang Na & Bearing

All odd-numbered soi branching off Th Sukhumvit head north, while even numbers run south. Unfortunately, they don't line up sequentially (eg Soi 11 lies directly opposite Soi 8, Soi 39 is opposite Soi 26). Some larger soi are known by alternative names, such as Soi Nana (Soi 3), Soi Asoke (Soi 21), Soi Phrom Phong (Soi 39), Soi Thong Lor (Soi 55) and Soi Ekamai (Soi 63). Traffic on Th Sukhumvit is notorious; use the Skytrain if you can. The new City Air Terminal at Makkasan links with Phetchaburi Metro station, and is a longish walk or a short, if slow, taxi ride to the Sukhumvit hotels.

elevated walkway near the northern end of the park leads all the way to Lumphini Park. To find it, exit on Th Ratchadaphisek, walk a few metres and turn left down a set of metal steps, painted blue. Walk away from the road along a quiet residential soi, and after 275m turn right, then left before you cross the bridge. You're now on the path beside a *klorng* and can't go wrong. It's 1.5km to the northeast corner of Lumphini Park, and is worth getting off the overhead section to walk alongside the *klorng* and see how many Bangkokians live.

SIAM SOCIETY & BAN KAMTHIENG
Map p126
สยามสมาคม/บ้านคำเที่ยง
☎ 0 2661 6470; www.siam-society.com; 131 Soi Asoke (Soi 21), Th Sukhumvit; admission 100B; ⊗ 9am-5pm Tue-Sat; Ⓜ Sukhumvit exit 1; Ⓡ Asok exit 3 or 6

Stepping off cacophonous Soi Asoke and into the Siam Society's Ban Kamthieng house museum is as close to a northern Thai village as you'll come in Bangkok. Ban Kamthieng is a traditional 19th-century home that was located on the banks of Mae Ping in Chiang Mai. Now relocated to Bangkok, the house presents the daily customs and spiritual beliefs of the Lanna tradition. Communicating all the hard facts as well as any sterile museum (with detailed English signage and engaging video installations), Ban Kamthieng instils in the visitor a sense of place, from the attached rice granary and handmade tools to the wooden loom and woven silks. You can't escape the noise of Bangkok completely, but the houses are refreshingly free of concrete and reflecting glass and make a pleasant, interesting break.

Next door are the headquarters of the prestigious Siam Society, publisher of the renowned *Journal of the Siam Society* and a valiant preserver of traditional Thai culture. Those with a serious interest can use the reference library, which has the answers to almost any question you could have about Thailand (outside the political sphere, since the society is sponsored by the royal family).

THAILAND CREATIVE & DESIGN CENTER Map p126
ศูนย์สร้างสรรค์งานออกแบบ
☎ 0 2664 8448; www.tcdc.or.th; 6th fl, Emporium, Th Sukhumvit btwn Soi 22 & 24; ⊗ 10.30am-9pm Tue-Sun; Ⓡ Phrom Phong exit 3; 🛜

Move over Scandinavian minimalism, this is the dawning of Thai style. The Thailand Creative & Design Center is a government-backed initiative intended to incubate design innovation, which is seen as Thailand's next step in the global marketplace now that labour is no longer competitive. The centre acts as both showroom and shop for Thai design, and is a good place to buy quality (if more expensive) Thai products and souvenirs. Rotating exhibitions feature profiles of international products and retrospectives of regional handicrafts and creativity. The centre includes a permanent library of design-related books and materials and is a good place to meet young Thai designers and students; the adjoining cafe has free wi-fi and good views. The centre is on the top floor of the Emporium shopping mall but is difficult to find – follow signs to the food court, then go up to the cinema and it's opposite the ticket booths.

MARKET, PARK & SPA
Walking Tour

This walk takes in the teeming commerce of Bangkok's largest market, the contrasting quiet of one of the city's newer parks, a bit of northern Thai culture and a massage to help you recover from it all. Klong Toey market is busiest between about 5am and 10am, so if you want to be in the thick of the action start early. It's most easily reached via the Khlong Toei Metro station and a walk.

1 Klong Toey Market

Despite being Bangkok's biggest market, and the distribution point for countless goods going to countless other stores, Klong Toey market sees very few tourists. A photographer's dream.

WALK FACTS

Start Khlong Toei Metro station
End Asok Skytrain station
Distance 4km
Duration Two to four hours
Fuel stops Black Canyon Coffee and Bitter Brown

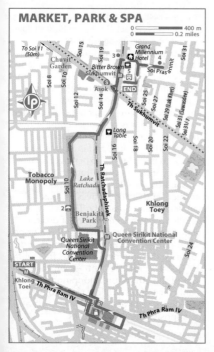

2 Benjakiti Park

Once you've had enough of the market, head out and cross busy Th Phra Ram IV, then west across Th Ratchadaphisek and finally into Benjakiti Park (p128). Head across to the far side of the lake and walk north, stopping for an ice cream or drink en route.

3 Ban Kamthieng

At the far northern end of the park, step back out onto Th Ratchadaphisek and continue north to Th Sukhumvit. Cross over, and continue north on busy Soi Asoke to Ban Kamthieng (p129), the traditional Lanna wooden home relocated to Bangkok. Adjoining is the welcome air-con of Black Canyon Coffee (Soi 21, Th Sukhumvit; meals from 100B; ☺ 8am-8pm), which also serves cheap, tasty light lunches, or cross the street to the classier and quieter Bitter Brown (Soi 21, Th Sukhumvit; meals from 120B; ☺ 10am-9pm Mon-Fri); both have toilets.

4 Massage time

Refreshed enough that you're no longer dripping with sweat, brave the traffic and cross Soi Asoke, then walk through the Grand Millennium Hotel driveway to Soi 23. Turning right, there are a few local restaurants, and you have a choice of massage places. Those on Soi 23 itself are cheap (less than 300B an hour) but the women wear suspiciously short skirts so asking for an 'oil massage' might get you more than you bargained for (foot massages are a safer bet). If you walk along to the T-junction and turn left, just beyond the next corner Mulberry Spa (p205) offers a more spa-like experience, with more professional English-speaking masseuses.

5 Soi Cowboy

Rejuvenated, return to Soi 23, turn left (north) and walk along until you come to neon-filled Soi Cowboy (p193). Depending on the time, you'll find the bars sleepy or just warming up – fun photos if the neon is on. At the far end turn left and after a few metres left again into the Metro station, which connects under Soi 21 (Asoke) to Asok Skytrain.

We apologise for not ending this tour with a drinking spot with a view (the views in Soi Cowboy notwithstanding), but it is supposed to start early. If you've managed to stretch it out to the end of the day, consider walking down to Cheap Charlies (p183) in Soi 11, and be sure to check out the Sukhumvit restaurants (p173).

GREATER BANGKOK

Eating p177; Shopping p150; Sleeping p232

Once rice fields, voracious Bangkok has expanded in every possible direction with few concessions to charm. Surrounding the previously defined neighbourhoods are seemingly endless flat residential suburbs with a small number of scattered attractions. Some of these sights are conveniently located along the Skytrain route, making them easily accessible from downtown. Chatuchak Weekend Market (p135) and the Children's Discovery Museum (p132) are both on the northern branch of the Skytrain, while Rama IX Royal Park (below) is located in the far-eastern part of the city.

The other attractions listed here will require a taxi, a boat, a bike or several forms of public transport (and lots of time and patience).

For details of the fab cycling tours through the 'lungs of Bangkok', the mangroves and plantations of Bang Kachao just across the Chao Phraya from Klong Toey, see p207.

CHILDREN'S DISCOVERY MUSEUM
Map p132

พิพิธภัณฑ์เด็กกรุงเทพมหานคร

☎ 0 2618 6509; Queen Sirikit Park, Th Kamphaeng Phet 4; adult/child 70/50B; ⏰ 9am-5pm Tue-Fri, 10am-6pm Sat & Sun; 🚇 Mo Chit

Through hands-on activities, learning is well-disguised as fun at this museum opposite Chatuchak Weekend Market. Kids can stand inside a bubble, see how an engine works, role-play as a firefighter or jump into the music room to play on traditional instruments. Most activities are geared to primary school age. There is also a toddlers' playground at the back of the main building.

RAMA IX ROYAL PARK Map p132

สวนหลวง ร.๙

Soi 103 (Soi Udom Suk), Th Sukhumvit; admission 10B; ⏰ 5am-6pm; 🚌 ordinary 2, 23 & 25, transfer to green minibus at Soi 103; 🚇 Udom Suk, & taxi

Opened in 1987 to commemorate King Bhumibol's 60th birthday, this green area, about 15km southeast of central Bangkok, covers 81 hectares and includes a water park and botanic garden that is a significant horticultural research centre. There are resident lizards, tortoises and birds, and a flower and plant sale is held here in December. The park's centrepiece is a museum dedicated to the life of the king. In 2009 the water park had yachting facilities added.

SAFARI WORLD Map p132

ซาฟารีเวิลด์

☎ 0 2518 1000; www.safariworld.com; 99 Th Ramindra 1; adult/child 750/450B; ⏰ 9am-5pm

Claiming to be the world's largest 'open zoo', Safari World is divided into two parts, a drive-through Safari Park and a Marine Park. In the Safari Park, visitors take a bus tour (windows remained closed) through an 'oasis for animals' separated into different habitats that are far more livable than the depressingly small old-school enclosures at Dusit Zoo (p95). Hundreds of animals roam through the park, including giraffes, lions, zebras, elephants and orangutans. The Marine Park focuses on stunts by dolphins and other trained animals; if that's not your thing you can go to the Safari Park only. Safari World is 45km northeast of Bangkok, and best reached by taxi.

ANCIENT CITY (MUANG BORAN)
Map p132

เมืองโบราณ

☎ 0 2709 1644; www.ancientcity.com; 296/1 Th Sukhumvit, Samut Prakan; adult/child 300/150B; ⏰ 8am-5pm

Don't have time to see Thailand's most famous historic monuments? Then consider seeing scaled-down versions of them in what claims to be the largest open-air museum in the world. Covering more than 80 hectares of peaceful countryside, Muang Boran is littered with 109 facsimiles of famous Thai monuments. It's an excellent place to explore by bicycle (daily rental 50B) as it is usually quiet and rarely crowded. Ancient City lies outside Samut Prakan, an hour by road east of downtown. To get there, either negotiate with a taxi (about 1200B return) or take air-con bus 511 from the eastern end of Th Sukhumvit. Upon reaching the bus terminal at Pak Nam, board mini-bus 36, which passes the entrance to Ancient City.

GREATER BANGKOK

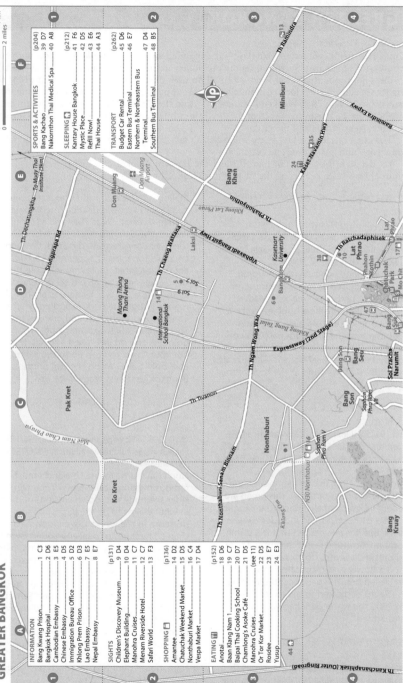

0   2 miles
0   4 km

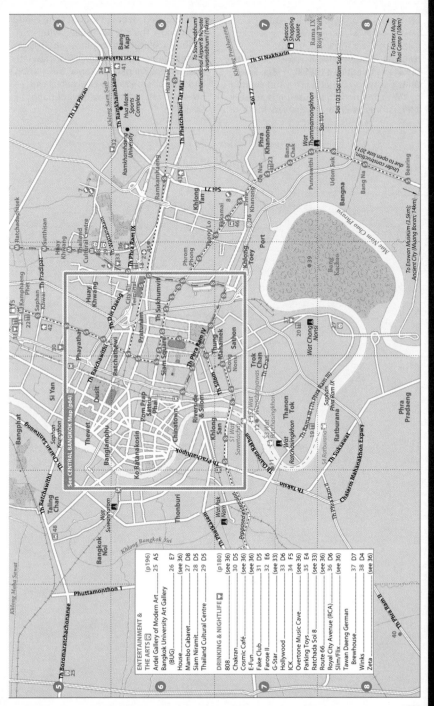

ERAWAN MUSEUM (CHANG SAM SIAN) Map p132
พิพิธภัณฑ์ช้างเอราวัณ(ช้างสามเศียร)

☎ 0 2371 3135; www.erawan-museum.com; Soi 119, Th Sukhumvit; adult/child 150/50B; ⏱ 8am-5pm
On the way to Ancient City (p131) and created by the same man, this museum is actually a five-storey sculpture of Erawan, Indra's three-headed elephant mount from Hindu mythology. The interior is filled with antique sculptures but is most impressive for the stained-glass ceiling. The museum is 8km from Bangkok's Ekamai bus station and any Samut Prakan–bound bus can drop you off; just tell the driver Chang Sam Sian.

top picks

- **Amulet Market** (p136)
- **Chatuchak Weekend Market** (p148)
- **Mahboonkrong** (p142)
- **Nonthaburi Market** (p150)
- **Siam Square** (p144)

SHOPPING

Commerce and shopping are so ubiquitous in Bangkok that they appear to be genetic traits of the city's inhabitants. Hardly a street corner in the city is free from a vendor, hawker or impromptu stall, and Bangkok is also home to one of the world's largest outdoor markets, not to mention Southeast Asia's second-largest mall. There's something here for just about everybody, and often genuine and knock-off items live happily side by side. Although the tourist brochures tend to tout the upmarket malls, Bangkok still lags slightly behind Singapore and Hong Kong in this area, and the open-air markets are where the best deals and most-original items are found.

Bargaining is part of the culture at markets and small family-run shops where prices aren't posted. For tips on engaging in this ancient sport, see the boxed text on p141.

Thais are generally so friendly and laid-back that some visitors are lulled into a false sense of security, forgetting that Bangkok is a big city with untrustworthy characters. While your personal safety is rarely at risk in Thailand, you may be unwittingly charmed out of the contents of your wallet. See p138 for more information about scams.

SHOPPING AREAS

The area around Siam Sq has the greatest concentration of shopping malls for designer and department-store goods. Street markets for souvenirs and pirated goods are on Th Khao San, Th Sukhumvit and Th Silom. Thai-style housewares and handicraft items can be found in the older parts of Bangkok, such as Banglamphu or around Th Charoen Krung.

OPENING HOURS

Most family-run shops are open from 10am to 7pm daily. Street markets are either daytime (from 9am to 5pm) or night-time (from 8pm to midnight). Note that streetside vendors are forbidden by city ordinance to clutter the pavements on Mondays, but do so every other day. Shopping centres are usually open from 10am to 10pm.

KO RATANAKOSIN & THONBURI

Bangkok's oldest district specialises in the ancient arts of health, safety and fortune. Locals come to the leafy lanes to inspect sacred amulets and pick up pellet-sized pills of Thai traditional medicines.

TRADITIONAL MEDICINE SHOPS
Map p68   Health Supplies
Th Maharat from Thammasat University to Wat Pho, Ko Ratanakosin; ⏱ 8am-7pm; 🚌 air-con 503, 508 & 511, ordinary 15 & 53; ⛴ Tha Chang (N9)

Bangkok's commercial medicine cabinet occupies the riverside thoroughfare of Th Maharat. Packaged in plastic pill bottles bearing an unsmiling photo of a trusted authority, commercial formulas combine various herbal ingredients – such as galingale, lemon grass, kaffir lime and other flavourings used in Thai dishes – to target a specific disease or to promote general wellness.

Shops carrying massage supplies cater to practitioners and students at the nearby Wat Pho massage training school. Keep an eye out for the dumpling-shaped herbal compresses that are heated and pressed onto the body during sessions of Thai herbal massage.

AMULET MARKET Map p68   Market
several small soi off Th Maharat, near Wat Mahat-hat, Ko Ratanakosin; ⏱ 8am-6pm; 🚌 air-con 503, 508 & 511, ordinary 15 & 53; ⛴ Tha Chang (N9)
Catholics with their parade of saints and protective medals will recognise a great kinship with this streetside amulet market. Ranging from pendant-sized to

---

SHOPPING GUIDE

The city's intense urban tangle sometimes makes orientation a challenge in finding intimate shops and markets. Like having your own personal guide, *Nancy Chandler's Map of Bangkok* (www.nancychandler.net) tracks all sorts of small, out-of-the-way shopping venues and markets as well as dissecting the innards of the Chatuchak Weekend Market (p148). The colourful map is sold in bookshops throughout the city.

TAX REFUNDS

A 7% Value Added Tax applies to most purchases in Thailand, but if you spend enough and get the paperwork the kindly Revenue Department will refund it at the airport when you leave. To qualify to receive a refund, you must not be a Thai citizen, part of an airline air crew or have spent more than 180 days in Thailand during the previous year. Your purchase must have been made at an approved store; look for the blue and white VAT Refund sticker. Minimum purchases must add up to 2000B per store in a single day, and to at least 5000B total for the whole trip. Before you leave the store get a VAT Refund (PP10) form and tax invoice. Most major malls in Bangkok will direct you to a dedicated VAT Refund desk, which will organise the appropriate paperwork (it takes about five minutes). Note that you won't get a refund on VAT paid in hotels or restaurants.

At the airport, your purchases must be declared at the customs desk in the departure hall, which will give you the appropriate stamp; you can then check them in. Smaller items (such as watches and jewellery) should be hand-carried as they will need to be reinspected once you've passed immigration. You actually get your money at a VAT Refund Tourist Office (☎ 0 2272 8198). At Suvarnabhumi Airport these are on Level 4 in both the east and west wings. For a how-to brochure see www.rd.go.th/vrt.

medallion-sized, *prá krêu·ang* (amulets) come in various classes, from rare objects or relics (like tusks, antlers or the dentures of abbots) to images of Buddha or famous monks embossed in bronze, wood or clay. Itinerant dealers spread their wares on blankets along the broken pavement across from the temple, and more-permanent shops proliferate in the sun-less alleyways along the river. Taxi drivers, monks and average folk squat alongside the displays inspecting novel pieces like practised jewellers. Mixed in with certain amulets are pulverised substances: dirt from a special temple, hair from a monk or powerful herbs.

When the serious collectors aren't perusing the market, they are flipping through amulet magazines that discuss noteworthy specimens. While money changes hands between vendor and customer, both use the euphemism of 'renting' to get around the prohibition of selling Buddhas.

BANGLAMPHU

The spectrum of goods available in this district ranges from backpacker staples along Th Khao San to delicious Thai curry pastes and high-quality handicrafts in the more traditional areas nearby. In recent years the twain have met, and Th Khao San has expanded into the silver business with souvenir-grade baubles sold in bulk to importers.

NITTAYA CURRY SHOP Map p82   Food
☎ 0 2282 8212; 136-40 Th Chakhraphong;
☽ 10am-6pm; 🚌 air-con 3 & 16, ordinary 3, 15 &
16; 🛳 Tha Phra Athit (Banglamphu, N13)

Follow your nose: Nittaya is famous throughout Thailand for her pungent but high-quality curry pastes. Pick up a couple of takeaway canisters for prospective dinner parties or peruse the snack and gift sections, where visitors to Bangkok load up on local specialities for friends back in the provinces.

TAEKEE TAEKON Map p82   Handicrafts
☎ 0 2629 1473/4; 118 Th Phra Athit; ☽ 8.30am-
6pm Mon-Sat; 🚌 air-con 3, ordinary 3 & 15;
🛳 Tha Phra Athit (Banglamphu, N13)

This atmospheric shop has a decent selection of Thai textiles from the country's main silk-producing areas, especially northern Thailand, as well as assorted local knick-knackery and interesting postcards not widely available elsewhere.

THAI NAKORN Map p82   Handicrafts
☎ 0 2281 7867; 79 Th Prachathipathai; ☽ 10am-
6pm Mon-Sat; 🚌 air-con 3 & 16, ordinary 3, 15
& 16

This family-owned enterprise has been in business for 70 years and often fills commissions from the royal family for nielloware and silver ornaments. Silver-moulded cases and clutches, ceremonial bowls and tea sets are also among the offerings. If you can navigate the language, ask to go behind the showroom to witness the aged artisans at work.

THANON KHAO SAN MARKET
Map p82   Market
Th Khao San; ☽ 10am-2am Tue-Sun; 🚌 air-con
44, 59, 157, 503, 509 & 511, ordinary 15, 44, 47, 59,
157 & 159; 🛳 Tha Phra Athit (Banglamphu, N13)

SHOPPING BANGLAMPHU

BUYER BEWARE

The disparity between the Thai baht and foreign currencies often clouds the judgment of otherwise eagle-eyed shoppers. Do your homework and approach each expensive transaction with a healthy amount of scepticism.

Antiques

Real Thai antiques are rare and costly and reserved primarily for serious collectors. Everything else is designed to look old and most shopkeepers are happy to admit it. Reputable antique dealers will issue an authentication certificate. Contact the Department of Fine Arts (☎ 0 2221 4443) to obtain the required licence for exporting religious images and fragments, either antique or reproduction.

Gems & Jewellery

Thailand is one of the world's largest exporters of gems and ornaments, but scams are more prevalent than bargains (for details see p279). Don't buy goods from a shop that claims to have a 'one-day' sale or wants you to deliver uncut gems to your home country for resale.

Reputable dealers don't pay commissions to túk-túk drivers but are known by customer referrals. Most are members of the Jewel Fest Club, established jointly by the Tourism Authority of Thailand (TAT; ☎ 0 2250 5500; www.tourism thailand.org; 🕑 8.30am-4.30pm Mon-Fri) and the Thai Gem Jewellery Traders Association (www.thaigemjewelry. com). When you purchase from a member shop, a certificate detailing your purchase will be issued and a refund is guaranteed (of up to 20%). A list of members offering government guarantees is available from TAT, or visit the association's website for buying information.

The latest trend is to open a gem 'museum', charging a hefty admission price, with an attached jewellery store. Proceed with caution.

Tailor-Made Clothes

Tailors are as prolific as massage parlours in Bangkok and so are the scams. For advice on getting clothes tailored, as well as some reputable shops, see the boxed text, p147.

The main guesthouse strip in Banglamphu is a day and night shopping bazaar, selling all but the baby and the bath water. Cheap T-shirts, trendy purses, wooden frogs, fuzzy puppets, bootleg CDs, hemp clothing, fake student ID cards, knock-off designer wear, souvenirs, corn on the cob, orange juice… You name it, they've got it.

CHAROEN CHAIKARNCHANG SHOP
Map p82   Religious

☎ 0 2222 4800; 87 Soi Nava, Th Bamrung Muang; 🕑 9am-6pm; 🚌 air-con 59, ordinary 42 & 59; 🚤 klorng boat to Tha Phan Fah
Easily the largest and most impressive religious shop in an area of impressive religious shops. The workshop at the back produces gigantic bronze Buddha images for wát all over Thailand. You might be unlikely to buy a life-sized Buddha, but looking is fun and who knows when you might need to do a great deal of merit making.

WAT RATCHANATDA AMULET MARKET Map p82   Market

☎ 0 2224 8807; cnr Th Ratchadamnoen Klang & Th Mahachai; 🕑 9am-5pm; 🚌 air-con 59, ordinary 42 & 59; 🚤 klorng boat to Tha Phan Fah

This Buddhist temple dates from the mid-19th century and today is home to a well-known market selling Buddhist *prá pim* (magical charm amulets) in all sizes, shapes and styles. The amulets not only feature images of the Buddha, but also famous Thai monks and Indian deities. Buddha images are also for, ahm, 'rent'.

CHINATOWN

The Phahurat and Chinatown districts have interconnected markets selling fabrics, clothes and household wares, as well as wholesale shops for every imaginable bulk item. There are a few places selling gems and jewellery.

JOHNNY'S GEMS Map p98   Gems & Jewellery

☎ 0 2224 4065; 199 Th Fuang Nakhon; 🕑 9.30am-6pm Mon-Sat; 🚌 air-con 3, 60, 73 & 512, ordinary 3, 53, 60 & 73
A long-time favourite of Bangkok expats, Johnny's Gems is a reliable name in an unreliable business. The namesake founder has since passed away, but his son carries on the spick-and-span reputation, primarily dealing in rubies and emeralds from fun to serious.

PHAHURAT MARKET
Map p98   Market

Cnr Th Phahurat & Th Triphet; ⏰ 9am-6pm; 🚌 air-con 3, 60, 73 & 512, ordinary 3, 53, 60 & 73; ⛴ Tha Saphan Phut (Memorial Bridge, N6)
If it sparkles, then this market has it. Phahurat proffers boisterous Bollywood-coloured textiles, traditional Thai dance costumes, tiaras, sequins, wigs and other accessories to make you look like a cross-dresser, a *mŏr lam* (Thai country music) performer, or both. This is cloth city, and amid the colour spectacle are also good deals on machine-made Thai textiles and children's clothes.

SAMPENG LANE Map p98   Market

Soi Wanit 1, Th Ratchawong; ⏰ 8am-6pm; 🚌 air-con 4, 21, 25, 507 & MB5, ordinary 4, 25, 29, 53 & 159; ⛴ Tha Ratchawong (N5); Ⓜ Hua Lamphong exit 1 & taxi
Sampeng Lane is a narrow artery running parallel to Th Yaowarat and bisecting the commercial areas of Chinatown and Phahurat. The Chinatown portion of Sampeng is lined with wholesale shops of hair accessories, pens, stickers, household wares and beeping, flashing knick-knacks. Near Th Chakrawat, gem and jewellery shops abound. Weekends are horribly crowded, and it takes a gymnast's flexibility to squeeze past the pushcarts, motorcycles and other roadblocks.

SAPHAN PHUT NIGHT BAZAAR
Map p98   Market

Th Saphan Phut, Chinatown; ⏰ 8pm-midnight Tue-Sun; 🚌 air-con 3, 60, 73 & 512, ordinary 3, 53, 60 & 73; ⛴ Tha Saphan Phut (Memorial Bridge, N6)
On the Bangkok side of Tha Saphan Phut, this night market has bucket-loads of cheap clothes, late-night snacking and a lot of people-watching. As Chatuchak Weekend Market (p148) becomes more design oriented, Saphan Phut has filled the closets of fashion-forward, baht-challenged teenagers.

PAK KHLONG MARKET
Map p98   Plants & Flowers

cnr Th Chakkaphet & Th Atsadang; ⏰ 24hr; 🚌 air-con 3, 60, 73 & 512, ordinary 3, 53, 60 & 73; ⛴ Tha Saphan Phut (Memorial Bridge, N6)
This sprawling wholesale flower market has become a tourist attraction in its own right. The endless piles of delicate orchids, rows of roses and stacks of button carnations

are a sight to be seen, and the shirtless porters wheeling blazing piles of colour set the place in motion. The best time to come is late at night, when the goods arrive from upcountry.

During the morning Pak Khlong Market is also one of the city's largest wholesale vegetable markets.

SIAM SQUARE, PRATUNAM, PLOENCHIT & RATCHATHEWI

If you like your retail upscale and air-conditioned, head directly for the centre of town. Bangkok's ever-expanding repertoire of luxury malls is a major draw for tourists from Asia and the Middle East, and can be found near the intersection of Th Phra Ram I and Th Phayathai, and further east at Th

top picks
LOCAL STUFF WORTH BUYING

- **D&O Shop** (Gaysorn Plaza, p142) This open-air gallery is the first retail venture of an organisation created to encourage awareness of Thai design abroad. The items, which range from furniture to knick-knacks, are modern and funky, and give a new breath of life to the concept of Thai design.
- **Doi Tung-Mae Fah Luang** (Siam Discovery Center, p143) This royally funded project sells beautiful hand-woven carpets, classy ceramics and Thailand's best domestic coffee beans.
- **Harnn & Thann** (Gaysorn Plaza, p142) Smell good enough to eat with these botanical-based spa products. Products are all natural, rooted in Thai traditional medicine, and stylish enough to share space with brand-name beauty.
- **Niwat Cutlery** (Gaysorn Plaza, p142) Born out of the ancient sword-making traditions of Ayuthaya province, the NV Aranyik company, a family-owned business, produces distinctively Thai stainless steel cutlery.
- **Propaganda** (Siam Discovery Center, p143, and Emporium Shopping Centre, p150) Thai designer Chaiyut Plypetch dreamed up this brand's signature character, the devilish Mr P who appears in anatomically correct cartoon lamps and other products.

READING FRENZY

New books and magazines are available at Kinokuniya (www.kinokuniya.com) at Emporium (p150) and Siam Paragon (p143). Asia Books (www.asiabooks.com), Bookazine (www.bookazines.blogspot.com) and B2S (www.b2s.co.th) have outlets at most malls in the city and a few stand-alone branches; check the websites for locations.

Art books can be found at Basheer (Map p126; ☎ 0 2391 9815; www.basheergraphic.com; H1, 998 Soi 55, Th Sukhumvit) and history buffs should visit Orchid Press (p144).

Other than Elite Used Books (Map p126; ☎ 0 2258 0221; 593/5 Soi 33/1, Th Sukhumvit) and Dasa Book Café (Map p126; ☎ 0 2661 2993; btwn Soi 26 & 28, Th Sukhumvit), the Banglamphu area is home to nearly all of Bangkok's secondhand bookstores. You're not going to find any deals here, but the selection is decent.

- Aporia Books (Map p82; 127 Th Tanao; ⏰ 10am-10pm) Stocks both new and used books, including a great selection of guidebooks.
- Moonlight Book Shop (Map p82; Th Khao San; ⏰ 11am-11pm) An alleyway shop featuring used books.
- Passport (Map p82; ☎ 0 2629 0694; 523 Th Phra Sumen; ⏰ 11am-7.30pm) Although the vast majority of the titles here are in Thai, the shop is worth a visit for its artsy atmosphere and tasty drinks.
- Rim Khob Fah Bookstore (Map p82; ☎ 0 2622 3510; 78/1 Th Ratchadamnoen Klang; ⏰ 10am-7pm) Without having to commit loads of your suitcase space, you can sample an array of slim scholarly publications from the Fine Arts Department on Thai art and architecture.
- Saraban (Map p82; ☎ 0 2629 1386; 106/1 Th Rambutri; ⏰ 9.30am-10.30pm) Stocking the largest selection of international newspapers and travel guides, this claustrophobic shop also has a good selection of used yarns.
- Shaman Bookstore (Map p82; ☎ 0 2629 0418; Dang Derm Hotel, 68-70 Th Khao San; ⏰ 9am-9pm) This long-standing shop spans two locations (the second on Soi Susie, off Th Khao San) and has the area's largest selection of used books. Titles can conveniently be searched using a computer program.

Ratchadamri. If you're looking for something a bit more homegrown, designs by Thailand's emerging fashion designers are available at shops in and around Siam Sq.

For penny-pinchers and/or wholesalers the ultimate destination is Pratunam district, where a daily open-air bazaar fuels both locally made and cheap import goods.

Keep an eye out for end-of-season and payday sales, as well as the citywide sales spree in June.

PANTIP PLAZA

Map p108   Computer Equipment

☎ 0 2656 5030; 604 Th Phetchaburi, Pratunam; ⏰ 10am-10pm; 🚇 Ratchathewi exit 4

If you can tolerate the crowds and annoying pornography vendors ('DVD sex? DVD sex?'), Pantip, a multistorey computer and electronics warehouse, might just be your kinda paradise. Shiny new hardware isn't really Pantip's speciality, but grey market goods are. Technorati will find pirated software and music, gear for hobbyists to enhance their machines, flea market–style peripherals and other odds and ends. Up on the 6th floor is IT City (☎ 0 2656 5030), a reliable computer megastore that gives VAT Refund forms for tourists.

FLY NOW   Map p108   Clothing

☎ 0 2656 1359; www.flynowbangkok.com; 2nd fl, Gaysorn Plaza, cnr Th Ploenchit & Th Ratchadamri, Ploenchit; 🚇 Chit Lom exit 9

A long-standing leader in Bangkok's home-grown fashion scene, Fly Now creates feminine couture that has caught the eyes of several international shows. Also available at Siam Center (p143) and Central World Plaza (opposite).

IT'S HAPPENED TO BE A CLOSET

Map p108   Clothing

☎ 0814 037 418; 1st fl, Siam Paragon, 991/1 Th Phra Ram I, Siam Sq; ⏰ 10am-10pm; 🚇 Siam exits 3 & 5

Garbled grammar aside, this domestic brand has gained a reputation for its bright colours and bold patterns. The ever-expanding Closet empire now even features a bakery shop at the basement level of Siam Paragon.

TANGO

Map p108   Clothing

☎ 0 2656 1047; www.tango.co.th; 2nd fl, Gaysorn Plaza, cnr Th Ploenchit & Th Ratchadamri, Ploenchit; 🚇 Chit Lom exit 9

This homegrown brand specialises in funky leather goods, but you may not even recognise the medium under the layers of bright embroidery and chunky jewels. Also available at Siam Center (p143).

UTHAI'S GEMS Map p108 Gems & Jewellery
☎ 0 2253 8582; 28/7 Soi Ruam Rudi, Th Ploenchit, Ploenchit; ⏰ 10am-6pm Mon-Sat; 🚇 Phloen Chit exit 4

With 40 years in the business, Uthai's fixed prices and good service, including a money-back guarantee, make him a popular choice among expats. The showroom boasts a huge stock, and gems can be custom-cut to order.

PRATUNAM MARKET
Map p108 Market

cnr Th Phetchaburi & Th Ratchaprarop, Pratunam; ⏰ 9am-midnight; 🛥 klorng boat to Tha Pratunam; 🚇 Chit Lom exit 9

The emphasis here is on clothes, in particular T-shirts, and the Baiyoke Garment Center, the immense open-air market that comprises much of the area, is the best place in town to buy that black Iron Maiden T-shirt you've had your eye on.

The greater market area occupies the neighbourhood behind the shopfronts on the corner of Th Phetchaburi and Th Ratchaprarop, and also includes several like-minded malls: Indra Square, which carries mostly women's clothing; Pratunam Centre, featuring a decent selection of Thai handicrafts and silver; City Complex and Krung Thong Plaza, two nearly identical wholesale clothing malls; and, across the street, the five-storey Platinum Fashion Mall sports the latest in no-brand couture, including a basement-level Jeans Zone, featuring 100 shops.

CENTRAL CHIDLOM
Map p108 Shopping Centre

☎ 0 2793 7777; www.central.co.th; 1027 Th Ploenchit, Ploenchit; ⏰ 10am-10pm; 🚇 Chit Lom exit 5

Central is a modern Western-style department store with locations throughout the city. This flagship store, Thailand's largest, is the snazziest of all the branches.

The ground floor carries all the big names in cosmetics, with eager perfume spritzers and the token ladyboy sales agent who pulls off blush better than those born with XX chromosomes.

Foreigner-sized clothing is one of the shop's strengths. The helpful sales staff will bluntly steer you to slimming colours and relatively huge sizes to fit your sturdy frame.

A decent selection of English-language books and magazines, not to mention stationery and music, is available at B2S on the 7th floor.

CENTRAL WORLD
Map p108 Shopping Centre

☎ 0 2635 1111; www.centralworld.co.th; cnr Th Ploenchit & Th Ratchadamri, Ploenchit; ⏰ 10am-10pm; 🚇 Chit Lom exits 9 or 6 to Sky Walk

Spanning eight stories of more than 500 shops and 100 restaurants, Central World is one of Southeast Asia's largest shopping centres. But it suffered a huge setback in May 2010 when its centrepiece Zen department store was torched by fleeing protesters (for details on the 2010 political unrest, see p35). Other parts of the complex were largely unaffected, but at press time the specifics of the reconstruction had yet to be announced. We hope that, in addition to a new Zen, the mall's funky F section and Thai Knowledge Park

BARGAINING 101

Many of your purchases in Bangkok will involve an ancient skill that has long been abandoned in the West: bargaining. Contrary to what you'll see on a daily basis on Th Khao San, bargaining (in Thai, *gahn dòr rah-kah*) is not a terse exchange of numbers and animosity. Rather, bargaining Thai style is a generally friendly transaction where two people try to agree on a price that is fair to both of them.

The first rule to bargaining is to have a general idea of the price. Ask around at a few vendors to get a rough notion. When you're ready to buy, it's generally a good strategy to start at 50% of the asking price and work up from there. If you're buying several of an item, you have much more leverage to request and receive a lower price. If the seller immediately agrees to your first price you're probably paying too much, but it's bad form to bargain further at this point. In general, keeping a friendly, flexible demeanour throughout the transaction will almost always work in your favour. And remember: only begin bargaining if you're really planning on buying the item. Most importantly, there's simply no point in getting angry or upset over a few baht. The locals, who inevitably have less money than you, never do this.

(TK Park; ☎ 0 2250 7620; www.tkpark.or.th), a multimedia library meant to cultivate reading and learning habits in children, will be operating as normal by the time you read this.

ERAWAN BANGKOK

Map p108   Shopping Centre

☎ 0 2250 7777; www.erawanbangkok.com; 494 Th Ploenchit, Ploenchit; ☽ 10.30am-8.30pm; ☒ Chit Lom exit 8

Bangkok's chichi crowd has a new stomping ground: the shopping wing of the Erawan Hotel. Luxury matrons occupy the 1st floor, while street-smarts chill on the 2nd floor, fusing the generation gap with a shared closet. The top floor is a dedicated wellness centre, should conspicuous consumption prove hazardous to your health. The ladies who lunch can often be found in the basement-level Urban Kitchen or the 2nd-floor Erawan Tea Room (p166).

GAYSORN PLAZA Map p108 Shopping Centre

☎ 0 2656 1149; www.gaysorn.com; cnr Th Ploenchit & Th Ratchadamri, Ploenchit; ☽ 10am-10pm; ☒ Chit Lom exit 9

A haute couture catwalk, Gaysorn has spiralling staircases, all-white halls and mouthfuls of top-name designers. The 2nd-floor 'Urban Street Chic' zone is a crash course in the local fashion industry. Established Thai labels including Tango, Fly Now and Stretsis have outlets, or you could head over to Myth, an umbrella store for smaller domestic labels.

Stores on the 3rd floor offer the same level of sophistication for your home. Thann Native sells locally inspired soaps and shampoos fragrant enough to eat. The open-air D&O Shop is the first retail venture of an organisation created to encourage awareness of Thai design abroad.

In addition to shops, Gaysorn also offers a Lifestyle Consultant (☎ 0 2656 1177). Available by appointment, but free of charge, the service consists of two 'experts', a local fashion designer and a makeup artist, whose goal is to guide you to that perfect outfit, shade of mascara, or spa treatment.

MAHBOONKRONG (MBK)

Map p108   Shopping Centre

☎ 0 2620 9111; www.mbk-center.com; cnr Th Phra Ram I & Th Phayathai, Siam Sq; ☽ 10am-10pm; ☒ National Stadium exit 4

This unbelievably immense shopping mall is quickly becoming one of Bangkok's top

FAKING IT

One of the most ubiquitous aspects of shopping in Bangkok, not to mention a drawcard for many visitors, is fake merchandise. Counterfeit clothes, watches and bags line sections of Th Sukhumvit and Th Silom, while there are entire malls dedicated to copied DVDs, music CDs and software. Fake IDs are available up and down Th Khao San, and even fake Lonely Planet guides, old editions of which are made over with a new cover and 'publication date' to be resold (often before the new editions have even been written!). Fakes are so prominent in Bangkok that there's even a Museum of Counterfeit Goods (☎ 0 2653 5555; www.tillekeandgibbins.com/museum/museum.htm; Tilleke & Gibbins, Supalai Grand Tower, 1011 Th Phra Ram III; admission free; ☽ 8am-5pm Mon-Fri by appointment only; Ⓜ Khlong Toei & taxi), where all the counterfeit booty that has been collected by the law firm Tilleke and Gibbins over the years is on display.

The brashness with which fake goods are peddled in Bangkok gives the impression black-market goods are fair game, which is and isn't true. Technically, knock-offs are illegal, and periodic crackdowns by the Thai police have led to the frequent closure of shops and the arrest of vendors. But the shops typically open again after a few months, and the purchasers of fake merchandise are rarely the target of such crackdowns.

The tenacity of Bangkok's counterfeit goods trade is largely due to the fact that tourists aren't the only ones buying the stuff. A recent poll conducted by Bangkok University's research centre found that 79.9% of the 1104 people polled in Bangkok admitted to having purchased counterfeit goods (only 48% admitted they felt guilty for having bought fakes).

Before we climb onto the moral high ground, it's worth pointing out that some, including even a few luxury brands, argue that counterfeit goods can be regarded as a net positive. A preponderance of fake items inspires brand awareness and fosters a demand for 'real' luxury items, claim some, while also acting as a useful gauge of what's hot. But the argument against fake goods claims that the industry supports organised crime and potentially exploitive and abusive labour conditions, circumvents taxes and takes jobs away from legitimate companies.

If the legal or moral repercussions aren't enough to convince you, keep in mind that in general, with fake stuff, you're getting exactly what you pay for. Consider yourself lucky if, after arriving home, you can actually watch all of season four of the Simpsons DVD you bought at Pantip Plaza; if the Von Dutch badge on your new hat hasn't peeled off within a week; and if your 'Rolex' is still ticking after the first rain.

attractions. Half of the city filters through the glass doors on weekends, stutter-stepping on the escalators, stuffing themselves with junk food or making stabs at individualism by accessorising their mundane school uniforms with high slits or torturous heels. You can buy everything you need here: mobile phones, accessories, shoes, name brands, wallets, handbags, T-shirts. The middle-class Tokyu department store also sells good-quality kitchenware.

The 4th floor resembles something of a digital produce market. A confusing maze of stalls sell all the components to send you into the land of cellular – a new phone, a new number and a SIM card. Even if you'd rather keep yourself out of reach, do a walk-through to observe the chaos and the mania over phone numbers. Computer print-outs displaying all the available numbers for sale turn the phone numbers game into a commodities market. The luckier the phone number, the higher the price; upwards of thousands of dollars have been paid for numbers composed entirely of nines, considered lucky in honour of the current king, Rama IX, and because the Thai word for 'nine' is similar to the word for 'progress'.

MBK is also one of the more convenient one-stop shopping destinations for photo equipment. Foto File, on the ground floor, has a good selection of used gear, though be sure to inspect the quality closely. The shop's sister venture, Photo Thailand, stocks all manner of new photo-related gear on the 3rd floor. Sunny Camera, also on the 3rd floor, contains shelves of gleaming new Nikon and Mamiya equipment.

SIAM CENTER & SIAM DISCOVERY CENTER Map p108 Shopping Centre
cnr Th Phra Ram I & Th Phayathai, Siam Sq; 10am-10pm; Siam exit 1

These linked shopping malls are surprisingly subdued, almost comatose compared with frenetic Mahboonkrong. Thailand's first shopping centre, Siam Center was built in 1976 but, since a recent nip and tuck, hardly shows its age. Its 3rd floor is one of the best locations to check out local labels such as Fly Now, Senada Theory and Tango.

In the attached Siam Discovery Center, the 4th floor continues to be a primary outpost for the Thai design scene. Panta creates modern furnishings and *objets d'art*

out of uniquely Asian materials, such as water hyacinth and bamboo. Bangkok-based French designer Gilles Caffier and his store, 2 Gilles Caffier, sells hand-beaded vases, palm-wood chopsticks and other Asian-esque decorative objects that have landed his designs in Alain Ducasse's restaurant. Doi Tung-Mae Fah Luang is a royally funded crafts shop selling handmade cotton and linen from villages formerly involved with poppy production. Check out the beautiful handmade rugs. On the same floor is a huge branch of Asia Books, which carries a wide selection of design magazines, Thailand fiction titles, and new guidebooks.

Siam Discovery Center is also, somewhat incongruously, one of the best places in town to stock up on camping gear. Within tent-pitching distance of each other on the 3rd floor are Pro Cam-Fis, Equinox Shop and the North Face.

SIAM PARAGON Map p108 Shopping Centre
0 2690 1000; www.siamparagon.co.th; 991/1 Th Phra Ram I, Siam Sq; 10am-10pm; Siam exits 3 & 5

Paragon epitomises the city's fanaticism for the new, the excessive, and absurd slogans. The 'peerless' venue is the second-largest mall in Southeast Asia, sprawling over 500,000 sq metres, and is a showcase for luxury retailers, like Van Cleef & Arpels and Mikimoto, who had not previously had a pedestal in the country. There's a Lamborghini dealer on the 2nd floor should you need a ride home, and one floor up a True Urban Park 'lifestyle centre' featuring a cafe, internet access and a shop selling books, music and camera equipment. Bookworms will fancy Kinokuniya (3rd floor), the largest bookstore in Thailand, as well as an expansive branch of Asia Books (2nd floor).

Even more audacious than the retail sections are the spectacular aquarium Siam Ocean World (p107) and an IMAX theatre (p199). Whew.

SIAM SQUARE Map p108　　Shopping Centre
Th Phra Ram I, near Th Phayathai, Siam Sq;
⏰ 11am-9pm; 🚇 Siam exits 2, 4 & 6
It doesn't look like much, just an ageing open-air shopping area divided into 12 soi (lanes), but Siam Sq is ground zero for teenage culture. Pop music blares out of tinny speakers, and gangs of hipsters in various costumes ricochet between fast-food restaurants and closet-sized boutiques. Digital Gateway (cnr Th Phra Ram I & Soi 4), a new and imposing mall, stocks everything electronic, from computers to cameras. DJ Siam (Soi 4) carries all the Thai indie (like Modern Dog) and T-pop albums you'll need to speak 'teen'. Small shops peddle pop-hip styles along Soi 2 and Soi 3, but most outfits require a barely-there waist. Centerpoint (Soi 7) plugs in on weekends with concerts from the latest bands, b-boys (breakdancers) and perky models. And intertwined are fast-food joints, sweets, snacks and drinks.

NARAI PHAND Map p108　　Souvenirs
☎ 0 2656 0398; www.naraiphand.com; Ground fl, President Tower, 973 Th Ploenchit; ⏰ 10am-8pm; 🚇 Chit Lom exit 7
Souvenir-quality handicrafts are given fixed prices and comfortable air-conditioning at this government-run facility. You won't find anything here that you haven't already seen at all of the tourist street markets, but it is a good stop if you're pressed for time or spooked by haggling.

RIVERSIDE, SILOM & LUMPHINI

Those looking for a painting by a contemporary Burmese artist, or an Ayuthaya-era Buddhist manuscript cabinet will undoubtedly find something interesting in this part of town. Considering the prices, much of what's on sale in this area is better for browsing than buying. However, if petty issues such as budget or luggage weight restrictions aren't obstacles, you're sure to find a shiny new toy at one of the numerous antique shops and art galleries.

HOUSE OF CHAO
Map p116　　Antiques
☎ 0 2635 7188; 9/1 Th Decho, Silom; ⏰ 9am-7pm; 🚌 air-con 76, 77, 177, 504, 514, 547 & MB12, ordinary 77, 162, 163 & 164; 🚇 Chong Nonsi exit 3
This three-storey antique shop, appropriately housed in an antique house, has everything necessary to deck out your fantasy colonial-era mansion. Particularly interesting are the various weatherworn doors, doorways, gateways and trellises that can be found in the covered area behind the showroom.

ORCHID PRESS Map p116　　Books
☎ 0 2231 3300; www.orchidbooks.com; 4th fl, Silom Complex, 191 Th Silom; ⏰ 11am-7pm Mon-Sat; Ⓜ Si Lom exit 2; 🚇 Sala Daeng exit 4
The venerable Asiana publisher Orchid Press now has a Bangkok showroom. Titles span the region from academic to glossy art books, as well as a few out-of-print or rare titles.

NIKS/NAVA IMPORT EXPORT
Map p116   Camera Equipment
☎ 0 2235 2929; www.niksthailand.co.th; 166 Th Silom; ⏰ 8.30am-5.30pm Mon-Fri; 🚌 air-con 76, 77, 177, 504, 514, 547 & MB12, ordinary 77, 162, 163 & 164; 🚇 Chong Nonsi exit 3
On the northwest corner of Soi 12, Thailand's biggest camera importer sells all types of professional equipment, including Nikon, Mamiya and Rollei. It's also the best place to bring your sick Nikon for a check-up.

SUNNY CAMERA
Map p116   Camera Equipment
☎ 0 2236 8365; 144/23 Th Silom; ⏰ 10am-6pm Mon-Sat; 🚇 Chong Nonsi exit 4
Dedicated Nikon-heads should head directly to Sunny Camera to satisfy their gear addiction. There are other branches on the 3rd floor of Mahboonkrong (Map p108; ☎ 0 2620 9293) and on Th Charoen Krung (Map p116; ☎ 0 2235 2123; 1267 Th Charoen Krung; ⏰ 9.30am-6.30pm Mon-Sat).

MAISON DES ARTS
Map p116   Handicrafts
☎ 0 2233 6297; 1334 Th Charoen Krung; ⏰ 11am-6pm Mon-Sat; 🚌 air-con 504, 544 & 547, ordinary 1, 15, 35 & 163; 🚢 Tha Oriental (N1)
Hand-hammered, stainless steel tableware haphazardly occupies this warehouse retail shop. The bold style of the flatware dates back centuries and the staff applies no pressure to indecisive shoppers.

TAMNAN MINGMUANG
Map p116   Handicrafts
☎ 0 2231 2170; 3rd fl, Thaniya Plaza, Th Silom; ⏰ 11am-8pm; Ⓜ Si Lom exit 2; 🚇 Sala Daeng exit 1
As soon as you step through the doors of this museum-like shop, the earthy smell of dried grass and stained wood rushes to meet you. Rattan, yahn lí·pow (a fern-like vine), water hyacinth woven into silk-like patterns, and coconut shells carved into delicate bowls are among the exquisite pieces that will outlast flashier souvenirs available on the streets.

THAI HOME INDUSTRIES
Map p116   Handicrafts
☎ 0 2234 1736; 35 Soi Oriental, Th Charoen Krung; ⏰ 9am-6.30pm Mon-Sat; 🚌 air-con 504, 544 & 547, ordinary 1, 15, 35 & 163; 🚢 Tha Oriental (N1)
A visit to this temple-like building and former monks' quarters is like discovering an abandoned attic of Asian booty. On a recent visit, the display cases absentmindedly held cotton farmer shirts, handsome stainless steel flatware, and delicate mother-of-pearl spoons. Despite the odd assortment of items and lack of order (not to mention the dust), it's heaps more fun than the typically faceless Bangkok handicraft shop.

CHIANG HENG
Map p116   Homewares
☎ 0 2234 7237; 1466 Th Charoen Krung; ⏰ 10.30am-7pm; 🚢 Saphan Taksin exit 3
In need of a handmade stainless steel wok, old-school enamel-coated crockery, or a manually operated coconut milk strainer? Then we suggest you stop by this third-generation family-run kitchen supply store. Even if your cabinets are already stocked, a visit here is a glance into the type of specialised, cramped but atmospheric shops that have all but disappeared from Bangkok.

CLOTHING SIZES

Women's clothing

Aus/UK	8	10	12	14	16	18
Europe	36	38	40	42	44	46
Japan	5	7	9	11	13	15
USA	6	8	10	12	14	16

Women's shoes

Aus/USA	5	6	7	8	9	10
Europe	35	36	37	38	39	40
France only	35	36	38	39	40	42
Japan	22	23	24	25	26	27
UK	3½	4½	5½	6½	7½	8½

Men's clothing

Aus	92	96	100	104	108	112
Europe	46	48	50	52	54	56
Japan	S		M	M		L
UK/USA	35	36	37	38	39	40

Men's shirts (collar sizes)

Aus/Japan	38	39	40	41	42	43
Europe	38	39	40	41	42	43
UK/USA	15	15½	16	16½	17	17½

Men's shoes

Aus/UK	7	8	9	10	11	12
Europe	41	42	43	44½	46	47
Japan	26	27	27½	28	29	30
USA	7½	8½	9½	10½	11½	12½
Measurements approximate only – try before you buy						

FROM NYMPH TO JUMBO

In your home town you may be considered average or even petite but, based on the Thai measuring stick, you're an extra large, clearly marked in the tag as 'LL' or, worse still, 'XL'. If that batters the body image, then skip the street markets, where you'll bust the seams from the waist up – if you can squirm that far into the openings. Only street vendors on Th Khao San accommodate foreign women's natural endowments in the shoulders, bust and hips. If you're larger than a US size 10 or an Australian size 12, you strike out altogether. Men will find that they exceed Thai clothes in length and shoulder width, as well as shoe sizes. For formal wear, many expats turn to custom orders through tailors. For ready-to-wear, many of the vendors at Pratunam Market (p141) and several stalls on the 7th floor of Mahboonkrong (p142) stock the larger sizes.

PATPONG NIGHT MARKET
Map p116   Market

Soi Patpong 1 & Soi Patpong 2, Th Silom; ☼ 6pm-midnight; Ⓜ Si Lom exit 2; 🚇 Sala Daeng exit 1
You'll be faced with the competing distractions of strip-clubbing and shopping on this infamous street. And true to the area's illicit leanings, pirated goods (in particular watches) make a prominent appearance even amid a wholesome crowd of families and straight-laced couples. Bargain with determination, as first-quoted prices tend to be astronomically high.

SOI LALAI SAP Map p116   Market

Soi 5, Th Silom; ☼ 9am-8pm; Ⓜ Si Lom exit 2; 🚇 Sala Daeng exit 2
The ideal place to buy an authentic Thai secretary's uniform, this 'money-dissolving soi' has mobs of vendors selling insanely cheap but frumpy clothing, as well as heaps of snacks and housewares.

RIVER CITY Map p116   Shopping Centre

☎ 0 2237 0077; www.rivercity.co.th; 23 Th Yotha, Th Charoen Krung; ☼ 10am-10pm, many shops close Sunday; 🚌 air-con 504, 544 & 547, ordinary 1, 15, 35 & 163; 🚢 Tha Si Phraya (N3), Tha Sathon (Central Pier)
Near the Royal Orchid Sheraton, this multistorey centre is an all-in-one stop for old-world Asiana, much of it too large to fit in the bag of most travellers. Several high-quality art and antique shops occupy the 3rd and 4th floors, including the Verandah, which deals in 'tribal' art from Borneo and abroad, and Hong Antiques, with 50 years of experience in decorative pieces. Acala is a gallery of unusual Tibetan and Chinese artefacts. And Old Maps & Prints proffers one of the best selections of one-of-a-kind, rare maps and illustrations. As with many antique stores in Bangkok, the vast majority of pieces at River City appear to come

from Myanmar (Burma), and to a lesser extent Cambodia. It's worth noting that trading in bona fide antiquities might not be either ethical or, in your country, legal. For more on this issue and the campaign to preserve Southeast Asia's cultural heritage, see Heritage Watch (www.heritagewatchinter national.org).

SILOM GALLERIA Map p116   Art

☎ 0 2630 0944; cnr Soi 19 & Th Silom; ☼ 10am-8pm; 🚌 air-con 76, 77, 177, 504, 514, 547 & MB12, ordinary 77, 162, 163 & 164; 🚇 Surasak exit 3
The only reason to visit this spooky half-deserted mall is for the contemporary Asian art exhibitions hosted by the various galleries inside. To avoid disappointment proceed directly to the back or check the posters in the lobby to see what's on display at the better galleries such as Thavibu (p201) or Tang (p201).

JIM THOMPSON Map p116   Handicrafts

☎ 0 2632 8100; www.jimthompson.com; 9 Th Surawong; ☼ 9am-9pm; Ⓜ Si Lom exit 2; 🚇 Sala Daeng exit 3
The surviving business of the international promoter of Thai silk, the largest Jim Thompson shop sells colourful silk handkerchiefs, placemats, wraps and cushions. The styles and motifs appeal to older, somewhat more conservative tastes. There are also branches at Jim Thompson's House museum (p106), the Emporium (p150), and a factory outlet (☎ 0 2235 8931; 149/4-6 Th Surawong; ☼ 9am-6pm) just up the road, which sells discontinued patterns at a significant discount.

KHLONG TOEY MARKET Map p122   Market

cnr Th Ratchadaphisek & Th Phra Ram IV, Lumphini; ☼ 2am-10am; Ⓜ Khlong Toei exit 1
This wholesale wet market, one of the city's largest, is inevitably the origin of many of

the meals you'll eat during your stay in Bangkok. Get there early, and although some corners of the market can't exactly be described as photogenic, be sure to bring a camera to capture the stacks of durians or cheery fishmongers.

SUAN LUM NIGHT BAZAAR

Map p122   Market

cnr Th Withayu & Th Rama IV, Lumphini; ⏱ 7pm-midnight; Ⓜ Lumphini exit 3

Like Chatuchak without the hot weather and crowds, the Night Bazaar specialises in modern Thai souvenirs, clothes and handicrafts. Highlights among the 3700 stalls include handmade jewellery, one-of-a kind designer T-shirts and a unique furniture and home decor section. If you can find it,

Nancy Chandler's map (p136) outlines interesting shopping at the bazaar. If shopping's not your idea of fun, the central outdoor beer garden is the perfect place to nurse an imported beer while the family is hunting for gifts.

There has long been talk that Suan Lum is slotted for the wrecking ball, but until the bulldozers arrive, we're remaining sceptical.

THANON SUKHUMVIT

Supplies for the recently arrived expat can be found in the shops that line never-ending Th Sukhumvit. Furniture, clothes and household knick-knacks hang out on upper Sukhumvit, while tourist souvenirs are centred west of Soi 11.

ONE NIGHT IN BANGKOK…IS NOT ENOUGH TO HAVE A SUIT MADE

Many tourists arrive in Bangkok with the notion of getting clothes custom-tailored at a bargain price. Which is entirely possible. Prices are almost always lower than what you'd pay at home, but common scams ranging from commission-hungry túk-túk drivers to shoddy workmanship and inferior fabrics make bespoke tailoring in Bangkok a potentially disappointing investment. To maximise your chances of walking away feeling (and looking) good, read on…

The golden rule of custom tailoring is that you get what you pay for. If you sign up for a suit, two pants, two shirts and a tie, with silk sarong thrown in for US$169 (a very popular offer in Bangkok), the chances are it will look and fit like a sub-US$200 wardrobe. Although an offer may seem great on the surface, the price may fluctuate significantly depending on the fabric you choose. Supplying your own fabric won't necessarily reduce the price by much, but it should ensure you get exactly the look you're after. If it's silk you fancy, go straight to the Jim Thompson outlet (opposite) for quality at good prices.

Have a good idea of what you want before walking into a shop. If it's a suit you're after, should it be single- or double-breasted? How many buttons? What style trousers? Of course, if you have no idea then the tailor will be more than happy to advise… Alternatively, bring a favourite garment from home and have it copied.

Set aside a week to get clothes tailored. Shirts and trousers can often be turned around in 48 hours or less with only one fitting, but no matter what a tailor may tell you, it takes more than one and often more than two fittings to create a good suit. Most reliable tailors will ask for two to five sittings. Any tailor that can sew your order in less than 24 hours should be treated with caution.

Reputable tailors include the following:

- Forchong (Map p126; ☎ 0 2258 7823; Th Sukhumvit; ⏱ 9am-9pm Mon-Sat, 9am-4pm Sun) Recommended by both locals and expat residents, this long-standing tailor does quality work.
- Manhattan Custom Tailor (Map p126; ☎ 0 2253 0173; 155/9 Soi 11/1, Th Sukhumvit; ⏱ 10am-7pm Mon-Sat) One of an abundance of tailors located around the lower Sukhumvit area, Manhattan gets good reviews.
- Marco Tailors (Map p108; ☎ 0 2251 7633; 430/33 Soi 7, Siam Sq; ⏱ 10am-5pm Mon-Fri) Dealing solely in men's suits, this longstanding and reliable tailor has a wide selection of banker-sensibility wools and cottons.
- Nickermann's Tailor (Map p126; ☎ 0 2252 6682; www.nickermanns.net; basement, Landmark Hotel, 138 Th Sukhumvit; ⏱ 10am-9pm) Corporate ladies rave about Nickermann's tailor-made power suits: pants and jackets that suit curves and busts. Formal ball gowns are another area of expertise.
- Pinky Tailors (Map p108; ☎ 0 2252 9680; www.pinkytailor.com; 888/40 Mahatun Plaza Arcade, Th Ploenchit; ⏱ 10am-7.30pm Mon-Sat) Custom-made suit jackets have been Mr Pinky's speciality for 35 years. Located behind the Mahatun Building.
- Raja's Fashions (Map p126; ☎ 0 2253 8379; 1/6 Soi 4, Th Sukhumvit; ⏱ 10.30am-8.30pm Mon-Sat) One of Bangkok's more famous tailors, Raja's gets a mixed bag of reviews but the majority swear by the service and quality.
- Siam Emporium (Map p126; ☎ 0 2251 9617; www.siamemporium.net; Soi 8, Th Sukhumvit; ⏱ 10am-8.30pm) Another reliable and low-key tailor.

L'ARCADIA
Map p126   Antiques

☎ 0 2259 9595; 12/2 Soi 23, Th Sukhumvit;
🕙 10am-9pm; Ⓜ Sukhumvit exit 2; 🚇 Asok exit 3
The buyer at L'Arcadia has a sharp eye for collectables from Myanmar, Cambodia and Thailand, including cute red-lacquer containers, Khmer-style sandstone figures and carved wooden temple decorations. If you simply can't resist that colonial-era lounge chair, the shop can also arrange to have it shipped home for you.

CHATUCHAK WEEKEND MARKET

Imagine all the city's markets fused together in one great big market-style concentration camp. Now add a little artistic flair, a sauna-like climate and bargaining crowds and you've got a rough sketch of Chatuchak (Th Phahonyothin, Chatuchak; 🕙 9am-6pm Sat & Sun; Ⓜ Chatuchak Park exit 1 & Kamphaeng Phet exits 1 & 2; 🚇 Mo Chit exit 1).

Everything is sold at Chatuchak (also spelled 'Jatujak' or nicknamed 'JJ'), from live snakes to vintage fans and *mŏr lam* CDs. More than 15,000 stalls cater to hundreds of thousands of visitors. Once you're deep in the bowels, it will seem like there is no order and no escape, but Chatuchak is arranged into relatively coherent sections. Our map can only accommodate so much detail; consider using Nancy Chandler's map (p136) as your machete in this jungle of commerce.

Antiques, Handicrafts & Souvenirs

Section 1 is the place to go for Buddha statues, old LPs and random antiques that make the selection not unlike Amulet Market (p136). More secular arts and crafts, like musical instruments and hill-tribe items, can be found in Sections 25 and 26. Baan Sin Thai (Section 24, Stall 130, Soi 1) sells *kŏhn* masks and old-school Thai toys, and Kitcharoen Dountri (Section 8, Stall 464, Soi 15) specialises in Thai musical instruments, including flutes, whistles and drums, and CDs of classical Thai music.

Golden Shop (Section 17, Stall 19, Soi 1) is your bog-standard souvenir shop, and boasts an equal blend of tacky and worthwhile items, ranging from traditionally dressed dolls to commemorative plates.

Other quirky gifts available at Chatuchak include the lifelike plastic Thai fruit and vegetables at Marché (Section 17, Stall 254, Soi 1), or their scaled-down miniature counterparts nearby at Papachu (Section 17, Stall 23, Soi 1).

Section 7 is a virtual open-air gallery; we particularly liked Pariwat A-nantachina's (Section 7, Stall 118, Soi 2) Bangkok-themed murals. Several shops in Section 10, including Tuptim Shop (Section 10, Stall 261, Soi 19), sell Burmese lacquer-ware. Meng (Section 26, Stall 195, Soi 8) features a mish-mash of quirky antiques from Thailand and Myanmar (Burma).

Clothing & Accessories

Clothing dominates Chatuchak, starting in Section 8 and continuing through the even-numbered sections to 24. Sections 5 and 6 deal in used clothing for every Thai youth subculture, from punks to cowboys, while Soi 7, where it transects Sections 12 and 14, is heavy on hip-hop and skate fashions. Tourist-sized clothes and textiles are found in sections 10 and 8.

Sections 2 and 3, particularly the tree-lined Soi 2 of the former, is the Siam Sq of Chatuchak, and is home to heaps of trendy independent labels. Moving north, Soi 4 in Section 4 boasts several shops selling locally designed T-shirts. In fact, Chatuchak as a whole is a particularly good place to pick up quirky T-shirts of all types. The shirts at Real Gold (Section 4, Stall 41, Soi 2) blend modern and traditional Thai designs, Bang! Bang! (Section 20, Stall 288, Soi 2) features custom-designed hand-drawn T-shirts of various celebrities, and there's even a stall selling airline logo T-shirts (Section 23, Stall 280, Soi 4). And if you thought there was a limit to Chatuchak's obscure clothing offerings, Link (Section 7, Stall 146, Soi 4) deals in 'retro underwear for men' and Scout Story (Section 21, Stall 66, Soi 2) specialises in scouting clothing and accessories from around the world.

For something more subdued, Khaki-Nang (Section 8, Stall 267, Soi 17) sells canvas clothing and tote bags, many featuring old-school Thai themes. And if you can't make it up to Chiang Mai, One to Tree (Section 26, Stall 235, Soi 8) or Roi (Section 25, Stall 268, Soi 4) is where you'll find hand-woven cotton scarves, clothes and other accessories from Thailand's north.

For accessories, several shops in Sections 24 and 26, such as Modern Silver (Section 26, Stall 246, Soi 8) specialise in chunky silver jewellery and semiprecious uncut stones.

Eating & Drinking

Lots of Thai-style eating and snacking will stave off Chatuchak rage (cranky behaviour brought on by dehydration or hunger), and numerous food stalls set up shop between Sections 6 and 8. Long-standing standouts include Foon Talop (Section 26, Stall 319, Soi 8), an incredibly popular Isan restaurant; Café Ice (Section 7, Stall 267, Soi 3), a Western-Thai fusion joint that does good *pàt tai* and tasty fruit shakes; and Saman Islam (Section 16, Stall 34, Soi 24), a Thai-Muslim restaurant that serves a tasty chicken biryani. If you need air-con, pop into Toh-Plue (Th Kamphaengphet 2; 🕙 11am-8pm; Ⓜ Kamphaeng Phet exit 1) for all the Thai standards. And as evening draws near, down a beer at Viva's (Section 26, Stall 149, Soi 6), a cafe-bar that features live music and stays open late, or cross Th Kamphaengphet 2 to the cosy whisky bars that keep nocturnal hours.

NANDAKWANG

Map p126   Handicrafts

☎ 0 2259 9607; www.nandakwang.com; 108/2-3 Soi 23, Th Sukhumvit; ☼ 9am-5pm Mon-Thu, 9am-6pm Fri & Sat, 10am-5pm Sun; Ⓜ Sukhumvit exit 2; Ⓡ Asok exit 3

A satellite of a Chiang Mai store, Nandakwang sells a fun and handsome mix of cloth, wood and glass products. The cheery hand-embroidered pillows and bags are particularly attractive. There is also a branch on the 3rd floor of Siam Discovery Center (p143).

Housewares & Decor

The western edge of the market, particularly sections 8 to 26, specialises in all manner of housewares, from cheap plastic buckets to expensive brass woks. This area is a particularly good place to stock up on inexpensive Thai ceramics, ranging from celadon to the traditional rooster-themed bowls from Lampang. N & D Tablewares (Section 25, Stall 185, Soi 4) has a huge variety of stainless steel flatware, and Tan-Ta-Nod (Section 22, Stall 061, Soi 5) deals in coconut and sugar palm–derived plates, bowls and other utensils.

Those looking to spice up the house should stop by Spice Boom (Section 26, Stall 246, Soi 8), where you can find dried herbs and spices for both consumption and decoration. Other notable olfactory indulgences include the handmade soaps, lotions, salts and scrubs at D-narn (Section 19, Stall 204, Soi 1) and the fragrant perfumes and essential oils at Karmakamet (Section 2, Soi 3).

Pets

Possibly the most fun you'll ever have window shopping will be petting puppies and cuddling kittens in sections 13 and 15. Soi 9 of the former features several shops that deal solely in clothing for pets.

Plants & Gardening

The interior perimeter of sections 2 to 4 feature a huge variety of potted plants, flowers, herbs and fruits, and the accessories needed to maintain them. Many of these shops are also open on weekday afternoons.

CHATUCHAK MARKET

0 —————— 200 m
0 —————— 0.1 miles

INFORMATION
Bua Luang 1 B2
Chatuchak Park Office.......2 B2
Kasikorn 3 B2
Krung Thai 4 B2
Thai Commercial Bank......5 B2
Thai Military Bank.............6 B2

SHOPPING 🛍
Airline Logo T-Shirts 7 B3
Baan Sin Thai 8 B3
Bang! Bang! 9 C3
D-narn 10 C2
Golden Shop 11 C2
Karmakamet 12 B3
Khaki-Nang.....................13 C1
Kitcharoen Dountri 14 C1
Link 15 C1
Marché 16 C2
Meng 17 B3
Modern Silver 18 B3
N & D Tablewares............19 B3
One To Tree....................20 B3
Papachu.........................21 C2
Pariwat A-nantachina......22 C1
Real Gold 23 C3
Roi.................................24 B3
Scout Story.....................25 C3
Spice Boom 26 B3
Tan-Ta-Nod 27 B3
Tuptim Shop 28 C2

MAP INDEX
◼ Antiques, Handicrafts & Souvenirs
◼ Housewares & Decor
◼ Clothing & Accessories
◼ Pets
◼ Plants & Gardening

EATING 🍴
Café Ice 29 C1
Foon Talop.....................30 B3
Saman Islam...................31 C2
Toh-Plue.........................32 B3

DRINKING 🍸
Viva's.............................33 B3

149

top picks

BANGKOK'S BEST MARKETS

- **Chatuchak Weekend Market** (p148) Stock up on souvenirs or invest in a vintage tracksuit – they're all here.
- **Nonthaburi Market** (right) The most picturesque fresh market in the area, but get here early, ideally before 8am
- **Pak Khlong Market** (p139) Show up late for the visual poetry that is the nightly flower market.
- **Pratunam Market** (p141) Acres of cheap togs, much of it for less than you'd pay for a pair of socks at home.
- **Vespa Market** (right) Antique vehicles and urban hipsters unite here every Saturday night.

THANON SUKHUMVIT MARKET
Map p126   Market
Th Sukhumvit, btwn Soi 3 & Soi 15; ☽ **11am-11pm;** 🚇 **Nana exits 1 & 3**

Leaving on the first flight out tomorrow morning? Never fear about gifts for those back home; the street vendors will find you with faux Fendi handbags, soccer kits, 'art', sunglasses and jewellery, to name a few. You'll also find stacks of nudie DVDs, Chinese throwing stars, penis-shaped lighters and other questionable gifts for your high-school-aged brother.

EMPORIUM SHOPPING CENTRE
Map p126   Shopping Centre
☎ 0 2269 1000; www.emporiumthailand.com; 622 Th Sukhumvit, cnr Soi 24; ☽ 10am-10pm; 🚇 Phrom Phong exit 2

Once Bangkok's most chichi shopping centre, Emporium is finally starting to show its age in comparison to its hipper and younger siblings, Siam Paragon (p143) and the recently remodelled Central World Plaza (p141).

The ground floor is filled with Euro fashion labels, like Prada, Miu Miu and Chanel. The 2nd floor is more casual, with home-grown contenders, such as Soda, which has snipped punk into haute wear, and image-maker Greyhound. Staid Jim Thompson even gets a facelift with its branch here. On the 3rd floor, indigenous kitschy-cool gifts and home decor can be found at Propaganda.

Even more impressive than the resident fashionistas is the Thailand Creative & Design Centre (TCDC; ☎ 0 2664 8448; www.tcdc.or.th; 6th fl), a design museum, with an attached gift shop selling cool souvenirs related to the various exhibits, and a design library.

GREATER BANGKOK

Markets really capture the hubbub of Bangkok and the real reason to visit the burbs is the world famous Chatuchak Weekend Market (p135).

ÁMANTEE
Map p132   Antiques/Art
☎ 0 2982 8694; www.amantee.com; 131/3 Soi 13, Th Chaeng Wattana, Greater Bangkok; ☽ 9am-8pm; 🚇 Mo Chit exit 3 & then taxi

Although well outside of the city centre, this 'repository of Oriental and Tibetan art and antiques' is well worth the trip. Consisting of several interconnecting wooden Thai houses holding a variety of classy items, the peaceful compound also boasts a cafe (☽ 9am-5pm), accommodation and occasional cultural events.

A Thai-language map for taxi drivers can be downloaded from the website.

NONTHABURI MARKET
Map p132   Market
Tha Nam Non, Nonthaburi; ☽ **5am-9am;** 🚢 **Tha Nonthaburi (N30)**

Located a short walk from Tha Nonthaburi, the northernmost extent of the Chao Phraya Express boats, this is one of the most expansive and atmospheric produce markets in the area. Exotic fruits, towers of dried chillies, smoky grills and the city's few remaining rickshaws form a very un-Bangkok backdrop here. Come early though, as most vendors are gone by 9am.

To get to the market, take any northbound Chao Phraya Express boat and get off at Tha Nonthaburi, the final stop. The market is a two-minute walk along the main road from the pier.

VESPA MARKET
Map p132   Market
cnr Th Rachadaphisek & Th Lat Phrao, Lat Phrao; ☽ **6-11pm Sat;** Ⓜ **Lat Phrao exit 1**

Uniting urban cowboys, hip-hoppers, wannabe mods and pissed-off punks, this expansive outdoor market is a virtual melting pot of Bangkok youth subculture. The original emphasis was on vehicles, and you can still find heaps of vintage Vespas and Lambrettas, Volkswagens and Austin Minis for sale or show betwixt quirky T-shirts, used sneakers and modern antiques.

top picks

- **Bo.lan** (Thai, p174)
- **Krua Apsorn** (Thai, p164)
- **Gianni Ristorante** (Italian, p166)
- **Mahboonkrong Food Court** (Thai & International, p167)
- **Street food in Chinatown** (Thai-Chinese, p165)

EATING

In Thailand, food is culture, and vice versa. Appreciation of the national cuisine is so central to their cultural identity that Thais often assume that foreigners are unable to partake in it unless they have been trained in the difficult art of feeling exhilarated over a bowl of well-prepared *gŏo·ay dĕe·o* (noodle soup). You will not be asked simply whether you like to eat Thai food, but '*Gin ah·hăhn tai ɓen măi*?' ('Do you know how to eat Thai food?').

Nowhere else is this reverence for food more evident than in Bangkok. The city's characteristic odour is a unique blend of noodle stalls and car exhaust, and in certain parts of town, restaurants appear to form the majority of businesses, often flanked by streetside hawker stalls and mobile snack vendors. To the outsider, the life of an average Bangkokian can appear to be little more than a string of meals and snacks punctuated by the odd stab at work, not the other way around. If you can adjust your gutteral clock to fit this schedule, we're confident your stay in Bangkok will be a delicious one indeed.

ETIQUETTE

While Thai table manners would hardly ever be described as 'formal' in the Western sense, there are plenty of subtleties to be mastered, and using the correct utensils and eating gestures will garner much respect from Thais.

Originally Thai food was eaten with the fingers, and it still is in certain regions. In the early 1900s Thais began setting their tables with fork and spoon to affect a 'royal' setting, and it wasn't long before fork-and-spoon dining became the norm in Bangkok and later spread throughout the kingdom. Some foods, such as *kôw nĕe·o* (sticky rice), are eaten by hand naturally.

The *sôrm* (fork) and *chórn* (spoon) are placed to the left of the plate, and usually wrapped in a paper or cloth napkin. In simpler restaurants, these utensils are laid bare on the table or may not arrive until the food is served. Some restaurants place a supply of clean forks and spoons in a steel or glass container on each table.

To use these tools the Thai way, use a spoon to take a single mouthful of food from a central dish, and ladle it over a portion of your rice. Then use the fork to push the portion back onto the spoon, with which you place the food in your mouth.

Đà·gèeap (chopsticks) are reserved for dining in Chinese restaurants or for eating Chinese noodle dishes (see p154). Noodle soups are eaten with a spoon in the left hand (for spooning up the broth) and chopsticks in the right.

Whether at home or in a restaurant, Thai meals are always served 'family style', that is, from common serving platters. Traditionally, the party orders one of each kind of dish, perhaps a curry, a fish, a stir-fry, a *yam* (hot and tangy salad), a vegetable dish and a soup, taking care to balance cool and hot, sour and sweet, salty and plain. One dish is generally large enough for two people. One or two extras may be ordered for a large party.

For the most part, *đôm yam* (chilli and lemon-grass soup) and other soups aren't served in individual bowls except in more elegant restaurants or those aimed at tourists. You serve yourself from the common bowl, spooning broth and ingredients over your rice or into your own spoon. Sometimes serving spoons are provided. If not, you simply dig in with your own spoon.

HOW THAIS EAT

Aside from the occasional indulgence in deep-fried savouries, most Thais sustain themselves on a varied and healthy diet of many fruits, rice and vegetables mixed with smaller amounts of animal protein and fat.

THE RIGHT TOOL FOR THE JOB

If you're not offered chopsticks, don't ask for them. Thai food is eaten with fork and spoon, not chopsticks. When *fà·ràng* (Westerners) ask for chopsticks to eat Thai food, it only puzzles the restaurant proprietors.

Chopsticks are reserved for eating Chinese-style food from bowls or for eating in all-Chinese restaurants. In either case you will be supplied with chopsticks without having to ask. Unlike their counterparts in many Western countries, restaurateurs in Thailand won't assume you don't know how to use them.

Satisfaction seems to come not from eating large amounts of food at any one meal, but rather from nibbling at a variety of dishes with as many different flavours as possible throughout the day.

Nor are certain kinds of food restricted to certain times of day. Practically anything can be eaten first thing in the morning, whether it's sweet, salty or chilli-ridden. *Kôw gaang* (curry over rice) is a very popular morning meal, as are *kôw nĕe·o mŏo tôrt* (deep-fried pork with sticky rice) and *kôw man gài* (sliced chicken cooked in chicken broth and served over rice).

Lighter morning choices, especially for Thais of Chinese descent, include *ʉah·tôrng·gŏh* (deep-fried bits of dough) dipped in warm *nám dôw hôo* (soy milk). Thais also eat noodles, whether fried or in soup, with great gusto in the morning, or as a substantial snack at any time of day or night.

As the staple with which almost all Thai dishes are eaten (noodles are still seen as a Chinese import), *kôw* (rice) is considered an absolutely indispensable part of the daily diet. Most Bangkok families will put on a pot of rice, or start the rice cooker, just after rising in the morning to prepare a base for the day's menu. All other dishes, aside from noodles, are considered *gàp kôw* (side dishes) that supplement this *ah·hăhn làk* (staple).

Finding its way into almost every meal is *ʉlah* (fish), even if it's only in the form of *nám ʉlah* (a thin amber sauce made from fermented anchovies), which is used to salt Thai dishes, much as soy sauce is used in eastern Asia. Pork is undoubtedly the preferred protein, with chicken in second place. Beef is seldom eaten in Bangkok, particularly by Thais of Chinese descent who subscribe to a Buddhist teaching that forbids eating 'large' animals.

Thais are prodigious consumers of fruit. Vendors push glass-and-wood carts filled with a rainbow of fresh sliced papaya, pineapple, watermelon and mango, and a more muted palette of salt-pickled or candied seasonal fruits. These are usually served in a small plastic bag with a thin bamboo stick to use as an eating utensil.

Because many restaurants in Thailand are able to serve dishes at an only slightly higher price than they would cost to make at home, Thais dine out far more often than their Western counterparts. Dining with others is always preferred because it means everyone has a chance to sample several dishes. When forced to fly solo by circumstances – such as during lunch breaks at work – a single diner usually sticks to one-plate dishes such as fried rice or curry over rice.

STAPLES & SPECIALITIES

Bangkok's central position, and more importantly its wealth relative to the rest of the country, means that spices, seasonings and produce hailing from any corner of the kingdom are easily available. Coconuts from the south, bamboo shoots from the north, *maang dah* (water beetle) from the northeast – all find their way into Bangkok markets.

Rice

Bangkok sits right in the middle of the Mae Nam Chao Phraya delta, the country's 'rice bowl'. Although Thailand's role as the largest producer of rice was recently taken over by Vietnam, its product is still considered the best in the world. Thailand's *kôw hŏrm má·lí* (jasmine rice) is so coveted that there is a steady underground business in smuggling bags of the fragrant grain to neighbouring countries.

Rice is so central to Thai food culture that the most common term for 'eat' is *gin kôw* (literally 'consume rice'), and one of the most common greetings is, '*Gin kôw rĕu yang?*' ('Have you eaten rice yet?'). Cooked rice is usually referred to as *kôw sŏo·ay* – literally 'beautiful rice', yet another clue as to how thoroughly Thais esteem this staple. When you order plain rice in a restaurant you may use this term or simply *kôw ʉlòw* ('plain rice'). Restaurants may serve rice by the *jahn* (plate) or you can order a *tŏh* (large bowl) of rice, lidded to keep it warm and moist.

In Chinese-style eateries, *kôw dôm* ('boiled rice'), a watery porridge sometimes involving brown or purple rice, is a common carb.

Noodles

Exactly when the noodle reached Thailand is difficult to say, but it probably arrived along trade routes from China since the preparation styles in contemporary Thailand are similar to those of contemporary southern China.

You'll find four basic kinds of noodle in Bangkok. Hardly surprising, given the Thai fixation on rice, is the overwhelming popularity of *sên gŏo·ay dĕe·o*, noodles made from pure rice flour mixed with water to form a paste, which is then steamed to form wide, flat sheets. The sheets are then folded and sliced into *sên yài* (flat 'wide line' noodles 20mm to 30mm wide), *sên lék* ('small line' noodles about 5mm wide) and *sên mèe* ('noodle line' noodles only 1mm to 2mm wide). *Sên mèe* dry out so quickly that they are sold only in their dried form.

At most restaurants or vendor stands specialising in *gŏo·ay đěe·o*, you are expected to specify which noodles you want when ordering.

The king of Thai noodles, *gŏo·ay đěe·o* comes as part of many dishes. The simplest and most ubiquitous, simply called *gŏo·ay đěe·o mŏo*, takes the form of noodles served in a bowl of pork stock accompanied with balls of ground pork, and perhaps a handful of mung bean sprouts. Season your noodle soup by choosing from a rack of small glass or metal containers on the table (see boxed text, below).

In recent years, one of the most popular types of *gŏoay đěeo* in Bangkok has been *yen đah foh*, an intimidating-looking mixture of assorted fish balls, cubes of blood, water spinach and rice noodles in a bright-red broth. The dish is probably the biggest culinary contribution by the Teo Chew, an ethnic group originally from southern China that comprises the largest group of Chinese in Bangkok. The *yen đah foh* sold next door to the Sri Mariamman Temple (p119), the Hindu temple off Th Silom (known locally as Wát Kàak), is said to be the most authentic.

Chilli-heads must give *gŏo·ay đěe·o pàt kêe mow* ('drunkard's fried noodles') a try. A favourite lunch or late-night snack, this spicy stir-fry consists of wide rice noodles, holy basil leaves, meat (typically seafood, but also chicken or pork), seasonings and an eye-opening dose of fresh sliced chillies and garlic. Jay Fai (p161) makes the most lauded – and most expensive – *pàt kêe mow* in town.

Probably the most well-known *gŏo·ay đěe·o* dish among foreigners is *gŏo·ay đěe·o pàt tai*, usually called *pàt tai* for short. Taking the form of thin rice noodles stir-fried with dried or fresh shrimp, bean sprouts, tofu, egg and seasonings, the dish is traditionally served with lime halves and a few stalks of Chinese chives and a sliced banana flower. Thip Samai (p162), a nondescript shophouse restaurant in Banglamphu, is generally regarded as the best place in Bangkok to try this dish.

Another popular dish using this type of noodle is *gŏo·ay đěe·o râht nâh*, noodles served with marinated pork and slightly slimy gravy. A seafood version of the latter, *gŏo·ay đěe·o râht nâh tá·lair*, is one of the most popular versions in Bangkok. A good version of the dish can be found at Raat Naa Yot Phak (p162), a 40-year-old restaurant in Bangkok's Banglamphu district.

Another kind of noodle, *kà·nŏm jeen*, is produced by pushing a fermented rice-flour paste through a sieve into boiling water, in much the same way as pasta is made. *Kà·nŏm jeen* is eaten topped with various curries. The most standard curry topping, *nám yah* (herbal sauce), contains a strong dose of *grà·chai* (Chinese key), a root of the ginger family used as a traditional remedy for a number of gastrointestinal ailments, along with ground fish.

The third kind of noodle, *bà·mèe*, is made from wheat flour and sometimes egg (depending on the noodle-maker or the brand). It's yellowish in colour and is sold only in fresh

PERK UP YOUR NOODLE

Much as chicken soup is viewed as something of a home remedy for colds in the West, rice-noodle soups in Thailand are often eaten to ward off colds, hangovers or general malaise. When you face a bowl of noodles and the array of condiments available to season them, you must be prepared to become your own pharmacist, mixing up the ingredients to create the right flavour balance.

If you see a steel rack containing four lidded glass bowls or jars on your table, it's proof that the restaurant you're in serves *gŏo·ay đěe·o* (rice noodles). Typically these containers offer four choices: *nám sôm prík* (sliced green chillies in white vinegar), *nám blah* (fish sauce), *prík bon* (dried red chilli, flaked or ground to a near powder) and *nám đahn* (plain white sugar).

In typically Thai fashion, these condiments offer three ways to make the soup hotter – hot and sour, hot and salty, and just plain hot – and one to make it sweet.

The typical noodle eater will add a teaspoonful of each one of these condiments to the noodle soup, except for the sugar, which in sweet-tooth Bangkok usually rates a full tablespoon. Until you're used to these strong seasonings, we recommend adding them a little at a time, tasting the soup along the way to make sure you don't go overboard. Adding sugar to soup may appear strange to some foreign palates, but it does considerably enhance the flavour of *gŏo·ay đěe·o nám*.

EATING STAPLES & SPECIALITIES

NOW YOU'RE COOKING

Having consumed everything Bangkok has to offer is one thing, but imagine the points you'll rack up if you can make the same dishes for your friends back at home. A visit to a Thai cooking school has become a must-do for many Bangkok itineraries, and for some visitors it is a highlight of their trip.

Courses range in price and value: a typical half-day course should include at least a basic introduction to Thai ingredients and flavours and a hands-on chance to both prepare and cook several dishes. Nearly all lessons include a set of printed recipes and end with a communal lunch consisting of your handiwork.

- Baipai Thai Cooking School (Map p132-3; ☎ 0 2294 9029; www.baipai.com; 150/12 Soi Naksuwan, Th Nonsee; per lesson 1800B; ⏱ 9.30am-1.30pm & 1.30-5.30pm Tue-Sun) Housed in an attractive suburban villa and taught by a small army of staff, Baipai offers two daily lessons of four dishes each. Transport is available.
- Blue Elephant Cooking School (Map p116; ☎ 0 2673 9353; www.blueelephant.com; 233 Th Sathon Tai, Silom; per lesson 2800B; ⏱ 8.45am-12.30pm & 1.15-5pm Mon-Sat) Bangkok's most chichi Thai cooking school offers two lessons a day. The morning class squeezes in a visit to a local market, while the afternoon session includes a detailed introduction to Thai ingredients.
- Khao Cooking School (Map p82; ☎ 0 891 110 947; khaocookingschool@gmail.com; D&D Plaza, 68-70 Th Khao San; per lesson 1500B; ⏱ 8.30am-12.30pm & 2.30-6.30pm Mon-Sat) Although located smack dab in the middle of Khao San, this new cooking school was started up by an authority on Thai food and features instruction on a wide variety of authentic dishes. Located directly behind D&D Inn.
- Oriental Hotel Thai Cooking School (Map p116; ☎ 0 2659 9000; www.mandarinoriental.com; 48 Soi 38, Th Charoen Krung; per lesson 4500B; ⏱ 9am-12.30pm Mon-Sat) Located across the river in an antique wooden home, the Oriental's cooking class features a daily revolving menu of four dishes. The lessons are less 'hands-on' than elsewhere, and cooking is done in teams, rather than individually.
- Silom Thai Cooking School (Map p116; ☎ 0 847 265 669; www.bangkokthaicooking.com; 68 Soi 13, Th Silom; per lesson 1000B; ⏱ 9am-1pm & 1.40-6pm Mon-Sat) Although the facilities are basic, Silom crams a visit to a local market and instruction of six dishes into nearly four hours, making it the best bang for your baht. Transport available.

bundles. After being briefly parboiled, the noodles are mixed with broth and meat, typically barbecued pork or crab, to create *bà·mèe nám*. Served in a bowl with a small amount of garlic oil and no broth, it's *bà·mèe hâang*.

Finally there's *wún sên*, an almost clear noodle made from mung-bean starch and water. Sold only in dried bunches, *wún sên* (literally 'jelly thread') is easily prepared by soaking in hot water for 10 to 15 minutes. It's used for only a handful of dishes in Bangkok. The most native, *yam wún sên*, is a hot and tangy salad made with lime juice, fresh sliced *prík kêe nŏo* ('mouse-dropping chilli'), shrimp, ground pork and various seasonings. Bean-thread noodles baked in a lidded clay pot with crab and seasonings is *ɓoo òp wún sên*. Lastly, *wún sên* is a common ingredient in *gaang jèut*, a bland, Chinese-influenced soup containing ground pork, soft tofu and a few vegetables.

Curries

In Thai, *gaang* (pronounced similarly to 'gang') is often translated as 'curry', but it actually describes any dish with a lot of liquid

and can thus refer to soups (such as *gaang jèut*) as well as the classic chilli paste–based curries such as *gaang pèt* (red curry) for which Thai cuisine is famous. The preparation of all chilli-based *gaang* begins with a *krêu·ang gaang*, created by mashing, pounding and grinding an array of fresh ingredients with a stone mortar and pestle to form an aromatic, extremely pungent-tasting and rather thick paste. Typical ingredients in a *krêu·ang gaang* include dried chilli, galingale (also known as Thai ginger), lemon grass, kaffir lime zest, shallots, garlic, *gà·ɓì* (shrimp paste) and salt. Dried spices such as coriander seeds and cumin are added for certain kinds of curries.

Most *gaang* are blended in a heated pan with coconut cream, to which the chef adds the rest of the ingredients (meat, poultry, seafood and/or vegetables), along with diluted coconut milk to further thin and flavour the *gaang*. Some recipes omit coconut milk entirely, such as *gaang ɓàh* (jungle curry), a fiery soup that combines a mixture of vegetables and meat. Another *gaang* that does not use coconut milk is *gaang sôm* (sour curry), made with dried chillies, shallots, garlic and Chinese key ground with salt and *gà·ɓì*. Cooked with

MUITO OBRIGADO

Try to imagine a Thai curry without the chillies, *pàt tai* without the peanuts, or papaya salad without the papaya. Many of the ingredients used on a daily basis by Thais are in fact relatively recent introductions, courtesy of European traders and missionaries. During the early 16th century, while Spanish and Portuguese explorers were first reaching the shores of Southeast Asia, expansion and discovery was taking place in the Americas. The Portuguese in particular were quick to seize the exciting new products coming from the New World and market them in the East, thus introducing modern-day Asian staples such as tomatoes, potatoes, corn, lettuce, cabbage, chillies, papaya, guava, pineapples, pumpkins, sweet potatoes, peanuts and tobacco.

Chillies in particular seem to have struck a chord with Thais, and are thought to have first arrived in Ayuthaya via the Portuguese around 1550. Before their arrival, the natives got their heat from bitter-hot herbs and roots such as ginger and pepper.

And not only did the Portuguese introduce some crucial ingredients, but also some enduring cooking techniques, particularly in the area of sweets. The bright yellow duck egg and syrup-based treats you see at many Thai markets are direct descendants of Portuguese desserts known as *fios de ovos* ('egg threads') and *ovos moles*. And in the area surrounding Bangkok's Church of Santa Cruz (p78), a former Portuguese enclave, you can still find *kà·nŏm fà·ràng*, a bun-like sweet baked over coals.

tamarind juice and green papaya to create an overall tanginess, the result is a soupy, salty, sweet-and-sour ragout that most Westerners would never identify with the word 'curry'.

A few extra seasonings such as *bai má·gròot* (kaffir lime leaves), *bai hŏh·rá·pah* (sweet basil leaves) and *nám 'blah* (fish sauce) may be added to taste just before serving. Bangkok Thais like their curries a bit sweeter than other regions of Thailand.

Most Bangkokians eat curries only for breakfast or lunch, hence the average *ráhn kôw gaang* (rice-curry shop) is only open from 7am to 2pm. It is considered a bit odd to eat curries in the evening, and hence most restaurants (tourist restaurants excepted) don't offer them on the evening menu.

To witness a truly amazing selection of curries, check out the vendors at the Or Tor Kor Market (p177). In general, the best place to find authentic curries is at a *ráhn kôw gaang* such as Khrua Aroy Aroy (p171), rather than a regular restaurant.

Hot & Tangy Salads

Standing right alongside *gaang* in terms of Thainess is the ubiquitous *yam*, a hot and tangy salad containing a blast of lime, chilli, fresh herbs and a choice of seafood, roast vegetables, noodles or meats. Bangkokians prize *yam* dishes so much that they are often eaten on their own, without rice, before the meal has begun.

On Thai menus, the *yam* section will often be the longest. Yet when these same menus are translated into English, most or all of the *yam* are omitted because Thai restaurateurs

harbour the idea that the delicate *fà·ràng* palate cannot handle the heat or pungency. The usual English menu translation is either 'Thai-style salad' or 'hot and sour salad'.

Without a doubt, *yam* are the spiciest of all Thai dishes, and a good *yam* to begin with if you're not so chilli-tolerant is *yam wún sên*, bean-thread noodles tossed with shrimp, ground pork, Chinese celery, lime juice and fresh sliced chilli. Another tame *yam* that tends to be a favourite among Thais and foreigners alike is *yam 'blah dùk foo*, made from fried shredded catfish, chilli and peanuts with a shredded-mango dressing on the side. Because of the city's proximity to the Gulf of Thailand, Bangkok eateries serve a wide variety of seafood *yam*, and at seafood restaurants such as Kaloang Home Kitchen (p164) these are a very good choice. *Yam* may also be made primarily with vegetables, such as the decadent *yam hŏo·a 'blee* (banana blossom salad), at Chote Chitr (p163).

Stir-Fries & Deep-Fries

The simplest dishes in the Thai culinary repertoire are the *pàt* (stir-fries), brought to Thailand by the Chinese, who are of course world famous for being able to stir-fry a whole banquet in a single wok.

The list of *pàt* dishes seems endless. Most are better classified as Chinese, such as *néu·a pàt nám man hŏy* (beef in oyster sauce). Some are clearly Thai-Chinese hybrids, such as *gài pàt prík kĭng*, in which chicken is stir-fried with ginger, garlic and chilli – ingredients shared by both traditions – but seasoned with fish sauce. Also leaning towards Thai – because cashews

EATING STAPLES & SPECIALITIES

are native to Thailand but not to China – is *gài pàt mét má·môo·ang hì·má·pahn* (sliced chicken stir-fried in dried chilli and cashews), a favourite with *fà·ràng* tourists.

Perhaps the most Thai-like *pàt* dish is the famed lunch meal *pàt gà·prow*, a chicken or pork stir-fry with garlic, fresh sliced chilli, soy and fish sauce, and lots of holy basil. Another classic is *pàt pèt* (literally 'hot stir-fry'), in which the main ingredients are quickly stir-fried with red curry paste and tossed with sweet basil leaves before serving. This recipe usually includes seafood or freshwater fish, such as shrimp, squid, catfish or eel.

Stir-fry chicken, pork, beef or shrimp with black pepper and garlic and you have *pàt prík tai grà·tee·am*, a relatively mild recipe often ordered as a 'fill-in' dish during a larger meal. For lovers of fresh vegetables, *pàt pàk ka·náh* (Chinese kale stir-fried with a fermented soy-bean sauce) is worth looking out for, as is *pàt pàk bûng fai daang*, flash-fried morning glory. For above-average fried dishes, the best destination is the street stalls of Chinatown (see p165).

Tôrt (deep-frying in oil) is mainly reserved for snacks such as *glôo·ay tôrt* (fried bananas) or *ʼbò ʼbée·a* (egg rolls). An exception is *ʼblah tôrt* (deep-fried fish), which is the most common way any fish is prepared.

Soups

Thai soups fall into two broad categories, *đôm yam* and *gaang jèut*, that are worlds apart in terms of seasonings. *Đôm yam* is almost always made with seafood, though chicken may also be used. *Đôm yam gûng* (*đôm yam* with shrimp) can be found in nearly all Thai restaurants as well as in many serving non-Thai cuisine. It is often translated on English menus as 'hot and sour Thai soup', although this often misleads non-Thais to think of Chinese hot and sour soup, which is milder and thinner in texture, and includes vinegar.

Lemon grass, kaffir lime leaf and lime juice give *đôm yam* its characteristic tang. Galingale is also added to *đôm yam* and, like its friends, is not meant to be eaten, but rather simply to add flavour. Fuelling the fire beneath *đôm yam*'s often velvety surface are fresh *prík kêe nòo* (tiny spicy chillies) and sometimes half a teaspoonful of *nám prík pŏw* (a paste of dried chilli roasted with *gà·ʼbi*). In addition to the tart-inducing ingredients, coriander leaf is an important garnish for both appearance and fragrance.

Keep in mind that *đôm yam* is meant to be eaten with rice, not sipped alone. The first swallow of this soup often leaves the uninitiated gasping for breath. It's not that the soup is so hot, but the chilli oils that provide the spice tend to float on top.

Of the several variations on *đôm yam* that exist, probably the most popular with Westerners is the milder *đôm kàh gài* (literally 'boiled galingale chicken', but often translated as 'chicken coconut soup'). The chilli is considerably muted in this soup by the addition of coconut milk.

Gaang jèut covers the other end of the spectrum with a soothing broth seasoned with little more than soy or fish sauce. Although the variations on *gaang jèut* are many, common ingredients include *wún sên* (mung-bean starch noodles), *đôw hôo* (tofu), *hŏo·a chai tów* (Chinese radish) and *mŏo sàp* (ground pork). Krua Noppharat (p162) in Banglamphu does a few very tasty *gaang jèut*, and Thai-Chinese eateries such as Ngwan Lee Lang Suan (p172) excel in hot and spicy soups such as *đôm yam*.

Fruit

The omnipresent *pŏn·lá·mái* (literally 'fruit of the tree', a general term for all fruit) testifies to the Thais' great fondness for fruit, which they appear to consume at every opportunity. An evening meal is normally followed by a plate of sliced fresh fruit, not pastries or Western-style desserts – no doubt one reason Thais stay so slim, as a rule.

THE CULT OF SÔM ĐAM

Pounded green papaya salad, known in Thai as *sôm đam*, probably has its origins in Laos but is today one of the most popular dishes in Bangkok. It is made by taking strips of green unripe papaya and bruising them in a clay or wood mortar along with garlic, palm sugar, green beans, tomatoes, lime juice, fish sauce and a typically shock-inducing amount of fresh chillies. *Sôm đam low*, the 'original' version of the dish, employs heartier chunks of papaya, sliced eggplants, salted field crabs, and a thick unpasteurised fish sauce known as *ʼblah ráh*. Far more common in Bangkok is *sôm đam tai*, which includes dried shrimp and peanuts, and is seasoned with bottled fish sauce. Almost always made by women, *sôm đam* is also primarily enjoyed by women, often as a snack rather than an entire meal – the intense spiciness provides a satisfying mental 'full'.

Other common year-rounders include *má·prów* (coconut), *fa·ràng* (guava), *kà·nŭn* (jackfruit), *má·kăhm* (tamarind), *sôm kĕe·o wăhn* (mandarin orange), *má·lá·gor* (papaya), *sôm oh* (pomelo), *đaang moh* (watermelon) and *sàp·bà·rót* (pineapple). All are most commonly eaten fresh, and sometimes dipped in a mixture of salt, sugar and ground chilli. Fruit juices of every kind are popular as beverages. Probably the best, if not the most expensive, place to shop for fruit is Or Tor Kor Market (p177).

Sweets

English-language Thai menus often have a section called 'Desserts', even though the concept doesn't exist in Thai cuisine, nor is there a direct translation for the word. The closest equivalent, *kŏrng wăhn*, simply means 'sweet stuff' and refers to all foods whose primary flavour characteristic is sweetness, although many have a salty element as well. Sweets mostly work their way into the daily Thai diet in the form of between-meal snacks, so you won't find *kŏrng wăhn* in a traditional Thai restaurant at all. Instead, they're prepared and sold by market vendors or, more rarely, by shops specialising in *kŏrng wăhn*.

Prime ingredients for many Thai sweets include grated coconut, coconut milk, rice flour (from white rice or sticky rice), cooked sticky rice (whole grains), tapioca, mung-bean starch, boiled taro and various fruits. For added texture and crunch, some sweets may also contain fresh corn kernels, sugar-palm kernels, lotus seeds, cooked black beans and chopped water chestnuts. Egg yolks are a popular ingredient for *kŏrng wăhn* – including the ubiquitous *fŏy torng* (literally 'golden threads') – probably influenced by Portuguese desserts and pastries introduced during the early Ayuthaya era (see p156).

Thai sweets similar to the European concept of 'sweet pastry' are called *kà·nŏm*. Here again the kitchen-astute Portuguese were influential. Probably the most popular type of *kà·nŏm* in Thailand are the bite-sized items wrapped in banana leaves, especially *kôw gà·tí* and *kôw đôm mát*. Both consist of sticky rice grains steamed with *gà·tí* (coconut milk) inside a banana-leaf wrapper to form a solid, almost toffeelike, mass. *Kôw đôm gà·tí* also contains fresh grated coconut, while *kôw đôm mát* usually contains a few black beans or banana. *Đà·gôh*, a very simple but popular steamed sweet made from tapioca flour and coconut milk over a layer of sweetened seaweed gelatine, comes in small cups made from pandanus leaves. A similar blend, minus the gelatine and steamed in tiny porcelain cups, is called *kà·nŏm tôo·ay* (cup pastry). The best place to try many of these sweets is Bangkok's open-air markets, such as Or Tor Kor Market (p177) or Nang Loeng Market (p177), the latter particularly celebrated for its high-quality central Thai-style sweets.

A WILD CAKE HUNT

Few Westerners, even those who've lived in Thailand for decades, seem to take to the hyper-sweet technicolour world of *kŏrng wăhn* and *kà·nŏm* (traditional Thai sweets and desserts). Luckily, in recent years Bangkok has seen an abundance of high-quality, domestically made Western-style cakes, ice creams and chocolates.

The best place to begin your search for the sweet is undoubtedly the basement of Siam Paragon (p143). Within this expansive temple to indulgence, cake lovers will be delighted to find branches of the Oriental Hotel Shop, Face, Café le Nôtre, Vanilla Brasserie and It's Happened to be a Closet. Gelaté, a gelato stall located in the supermarket, makes excellent Italian-style ice cream served in freshly made waffle cones.

Duc de Praslin (Map p126; ☎ 0 2258 3200; www.gallothai.com; ground fl, Fenix Tower, Soi 31, Th Sukhumvit; ⏲ 8am-9pm), a Belgian-owned chocolatier, has opened several of its classy European cafes at various locations around town. As well as the spot-on bon-bons, try a hot cocoa, made with steaming milk and shards of rich chocolate in front of your eyes. Just up the road, the friendly ladies and GMM scriptwriters at Memay Café (Map p126; ☎ 0 2259 4821; www.memaycafe.com; 44/33-34 Soi 21, Th Sukhumvit; ⏲ 10am-9pm Mon-Fri, 10am-6pm Sat; 🛜) use the best-quality ingredients they can get their hands on to make authentic cakes and pastries, and there's free wi-fi.

Nowadays even the Thais need their tiramisu and tartes. Ka-nom (Map p108; ☎ 0 2252 8520; 266/8 Soi 3, Siam Sq; ⏲ 8.30am-8pm), a self-proclaimed 'fashion bakery', serves delicious *kà·nŏm kài*, a baked sweet similar to Portuguese egg tarts. Several purveyors of Western-style desserts can also be found along Th Phra Athit in Banglamphu. Anshada of Ann's Sweet (Map p82; ☎ 0 868 891 383; 138 Th Phra Athit; ⏲ 10am-10pm) makes some pretty fly cakes, and the decadent desserts at Baan Phra Arthit (p161) leave little to be desired.

Coconut milk also features prominently in several soupier sweets with colourful names. In the enormously popular *glôo·ay bòo·at chee* ('bananas ordaining as nuns'), banana chunks float in a white syrup of sweetened and slightly salted coconut milk. *Boo·a loy* ('floating lotus') consists of boiled sticky rice dumplings in a similar coconut sauce. Substitute red-dyed chunks of fresh water chestnut and you have *táp tim gròrp* ('crispy rubies').

Although foreigners don't seem to immediately take to most Thai sweets, one dish few visitors have trouble with is *ai dim gà·tí*, Thai-style coconut ice cream. At more traditional shops, the ice cream is garnished with toppings such as kidney beans or sticky rice, and is a great snack on a sweltering Bangkok afternoon.

PRACTICALITIES
Opening Hours
Restaurants serving Thai food are generally open from 10am to 8pm or 9pm, although some places are open later. Foreign-cuisine restaurants tend to keep only dinner and lunch hours (ie 11am to 2pm and 6pm to 10pm), although this varies. Thais are consummate eaters and are always within reach of a snack or a light meal, so meal times are quite flexible, although restaurants can get crowded around 8pm.

Bangkok has recently passed a citywide ordinance banning street vendors from setting up shop on Mondays. The footpaths are so uncluttered on these days that a roadside eater might feel both hungry and abandoned.

How Much?
A bowl of noodles or a stir-fry dish bought from a street vendor should cost 25B to 30B, depending on the portion size and ingredients. Climbing up the scale are the canteen shops that have a selection of pre-made dishes, sturdier chairs and a roof. For these luxuries, you'll probably pay 30B to 50B.

Thai restaurants with an army of servers and laminated menus usually offer main dishes for 60B to 120B. Add ambience, air-con and fancy uniforms, and a main jumps to 120B to 200B. Anything above 300B will deliver you into the arms of some of the city's fancier restaurants. An exception is top-end hotel restaurants, which feature prices close to what you'd expect to pay at any flash hotel in the world.

PRICE GUIDE
$$$ more than 500B
$$ 200-500B
$ less than 200B
Price is for a meal for one person, including an appetiser or dessert, a main course and a drink.

In most parts of the city, Western food occupies the high end of the scale, costing from 200B to 350B. One obvious exception is Banglamphu, where *fà·ràng* food comes in under 200B a plate.

Note also that nearly all hotel restaurants include '++' (often referred to as 'plus plus'), which implies an additional 7% for VAT (value added tax) and a 10% 'service charge' on top of your total bill.

Booking Tables
If you have a lot of friends in tow or will be attending a formal restaurant (including hotel restaurants), reservations are recommended. Bookings are also recommended for Sunday brunches and dinner cruises.

Otherwise, you shouldn't have a problem scoring a table at the vast majority of restaurants in the city, especially if you arrive during off-peak hours. Following the European tradition (or because of the wretched evening commute), peak dinner time starts around 8pm. The lunchtime crush typically starts around noon and lasts for close to an hour.

Tipping
You shouldn't be surprised to learn that tipping in Thailand isn't as exact as it is in Europe (tip no one) or the USA (tip everyone). Thailand falls somewhere in between, and some areas are left open to interpretation. Everyone agrees that you don't tip streetside vendors, although some add a little surcharge when tallying up a bill for a foreigner. To avoid getting annoyed about this double-pricing scheme, consider it an implicit tip.

When eating at a restaurant, tipping becomes more a game of finesse. Some people leave behind roughly 10% at any sit-down restaurant where someone fills their glass every time they take a sip. Others don't. Most upmarket restaurants will apply a 10% service charge to the bill. Some patrons leave extra on top of the service charge; others don't. The choice is yours.

KO RATANAKOSIN & THONBURI

Despite the riverfront setting, there are surprisingly few restaurants along this stretch of the Mae Nam Chao Phraya (Chao Phraya River).

THE DECK Map p68   International/Thai $$
☎ 0 2221 9158; www.arunresidence.com; Arun Residence, 36-38 Soi Pratu Nok Yoong; mains 200-690B; ✆ 8am-10pm Wed-Thur, 8am-11pm Fri-Sun; ◻ air-con 503, 508 & 511, ordinary 15 & 53; ⛴ Tha Tien (N8)
The Deck's claim to fame is its commanding views over Wat Arun, but the restaurant's short but diverse menu, ranging from duck confit to Thai-style pomelo salad, sweetens the pot. Consider arriving early for a sunset drink in Amorosa (✆ 5.30pm-1am), the hotel's rooftop bar.

RACHANAWI SAMOSORN (NAVY CLUB RESTAURANT) Map p68   Thai $
☎ 0 2222 0081; 77 Th Maharat; mains 70-150B; ✆ 11am-2pm & 4-10pm Mon-Fri, 4-10pm Sat & Sun; ◻ air-con 503, 508 & 511, ordinary 15 & 53; ⛴ Tha Chang (N9)
Commanding one of the few coveted riverfront locations along this stretch of Chao Phraya, this restaurant has a reputation among locals in the know for cheap and delicious seafood-based Thai nosh.
To find the restaurant, use the entrance near the ATM at Tha Chang.

RUB AROON Map p68   Thai $
☎ 0 2622 2312; 310-312 Th Maharat; mains 60-95B; ✆ 8am-6pm; ◻ air-con 503, 508 & 511, ordinary 15 & 53; ⛴ Tha Tien (N8)
Perfectly situated for a post-temple refresher, this cafe across the street from Wat Pho also throws in great old-word atmosphere and a few simple dishes.

WANG LANG MARKET
Map p68   Thai $
Th Phra Chan & Trok Wang Lang; mains 30-80B; ⛴ cross-river ferry at Tha Tien (N8)
Beside Siriraj Hospital is a busy market that sprawls west from Tha Wang Lang. Many of the vendors prepare fiery southern-style curries and dishes such as *pàt pèt sà·đor* (spicy red-curry stir-fry with stink beans). The theory is that southern Thai food took

top picks

DINING WITH A VIEW

- The Deck (left) The prime position for viewing a sunset over Wat Arun.
- D'Sens (p168) Modern French cuisine and one of Bangkok's greenest views.
- Emporium Food Hall (boxed text p167) The cheapest dining room with a view in town.
- Erawan Tea Room (p166) One of Bangkok's busiest intersections at your feet.
- Kaloang Home Kitchen (p164) Home to an atmospheric deck overlooking Mae Nam Chao Phraya (Chao Phraya River).
- Rang Mahal (boxed text p176) A sea of concrete towers meets the horizon from this rooftop perch.

root here because of the nearby train station that served southern destinations.

BANGLAMPHU

Bangkok's most traditional district is not surprisingly one of the best places to try authentic central Thai and Bangkok-style nosh. To really get an idea of what is on offer, be sure to try our food-based walking tour of the area on p162.

Because of the long-standing backpacker presence, Western and vegetarian food is also plentiful and cheap.

OH MY COD! Map p82   English $$
☎ 0 2282 6553; www.fishandchipsbangkok.com; 95d Soi Rambuttri Village Inn, Soi Rambutri l; mains 40-220B; ✆ 7am-11pm; ◻ air-con 3 & 16, ordinary 3, 15 & 16; ⛴ Tha Phra Athit (Banglamphu, N13)
English cuisine bears the burden of a negative reputation, but is there anything more satisfying than fish and chips? An order here takes the form of a puffy fillet accompanied by thick-cut chips and peas, prepared 'garden' or 'mushy' style. Breakfast is served all day, and parched Anglophiles can enjoy a cuppa in the sunny courtyard dining area.

CAFÉ PRIMAVERA Map p82   Italian $$
☎ 0 2281 4718; 56 Th Phra Athit; mains 95-375B; ✆ 8am-11pm; ◻ air-con 3, ordinary 3 & 15; ⛴ Tha Phra Athit (Banglamphu, N13)
If the coffee was just a tad better, this darkwood and marble-topped table trattoria

is just the kind of place we'd like to make our local cafe. The pizzas and homemade gelati offer more hope, and the friendly and efficient staff seal the deal.

HEMLOCK Map p82 — Thai $$
☎ 0 2282 7507; 56 Th Phra Athit; mains 65-140B; ✹ 4pm-midnight Mon-Sat; 🚌 air-con 3, ordinary 3 & 15; 🛥 Tha Phra Athit (Banglamphu, N13)
Taking full advantage of its cosy shop-house location, this perennial favourite has enough style to feel like a special night out but doesn't skimp on flavour or preparation. The eclectic menu reads like an ancient literary work, reviving old dishes from the aristocratic kitchens across the country. Try the flavourful *mêe·ang kam* (wild tea leaves wrapped around ginger, shallots, peanuts, lime and coconut flakes) or *yam kà·moy* (thieves' salad).

JAY FAI Map p82 — Thai $$
☎ 0 2223 9384; 327 Th Mahachai; mains 200-250B; ✹ 3pm-2am; 🚌 air-con 59, ordinary 42 & 59; 🛥 klorng boat to Tha Phan Fah
You wouldn't think so by looking at her bare-bones dining room, but Jay Fai is known far and wide for serving Bangkok's most expensive *pàt kêe mow* (drunkard's noodles). The price is justified by the co-pious fresh seafood, as well as Jay Fai's

distinct frying style that results in a virtually oil-free finished product.

BAAN PHRA ATHIT (COFFEE & MORE)
Map p82 — Cafe $
☎ 0 2280 7878; 102/1 Th Phra Athit; mains 50-120B; ✹ 10am-9pm Sun-Thu, 10am-10pm Fri & Sat; 🚌 air-con 3 & 15; 🛥 Tha Phra Athit (Banglamphu, N13)
When only air-conditioning will do, why not do it in style? This classy cafe features a few basic Western-Thai fusion dishes, decent coffee, and even better cakes and sweets. And all of this for less than the price of a latte back at home.

SHOSHANA
Map p82 — Israeli $
☎ 0 2282 9948; 86 Th Chakraphong; mains 90-150B; ✹ 8am-midnight; 🚌 air-con 3 & 16, ordinary 3, 15 & 16; 🛥 Tha Phra Athit (Banglamphu, N13)
One of Khao San's longest-running Israeli restaurants, Shoshana resembles your grandparents' living room down to the tacky paintings and perpetual reruns of *Seinfeld*. The 'I heart Shoshana' T-shirts worn by the wait staff may be a hopelessly optimistic description of employee morale, but the gut-filling chips-felafel-and-hummus plates leave nothing to be desired.

VEGGING OUT IN BANGKOK
Vegetarianism is a growing trend among urban Thais, but veggie restaurants are still generally few and far between.

Banglamphu has the greatest concentration of vegetarian-friendly restaurants, thanks to the nonmeat-eating *fà·ràng*; these are typically low-scale stir-fry shops that do something akin to what your hippie roommates have cooking in their kitchens. Examples include the entirely meat-free Arawy Vegetarian Food (Map p82; 152 Th Din So; ✹ 7am-8pm) and May Kaidee's (Map p82; ☎ 0 2281 7699; www.maykaidee.com; 33 Th Samsen; ✹ 9am-10pm), the latter of which also offers a veggie Thai cooking school. Ranee Guesthouse (Map p82; 77 Trok Mayom; ✹ 8am-10pm) and Hemlock (above) are two regular restaurants that have extensive meat-free menus.

In the centre of town, Koko (Map p108; ☎ 0 2658 4094; 262/2 Soi 3, Siam Sq; ✹ 11am-9pm) offers an extensive veggie menu in addition to its usual Thai menu – perfect for a mixed crowd. Ariya Organic Café (Map p108; ☎ 0 2626 0188; 2nd fl, Mahboonkrong, Siam Sq; ✹ 10am-10pm) takes it a step further and offers only raw (not heated above 46°C) snacks. Upstairs, Mahboonkrong's Food Court (p167) has a delicious vegetarian stall (stall C8) that requires mastery of the Asian queue in order to sneak in an order.

North of town, Baan Suan Pai (Map p64; ☎ 0 2617 2090; 17/1 Th Phahonyothin, Central Bangkok; ✹ 7am-3pm) and Chamlong's Asoke Café (Map p132; ☎ 0 2272 4282; 580-592 Th Phahon Yothin, Greater Bangkok; ✹ 6am-2pm Tue-Fri, 6am-3pm Sat & Sun) are two dedicated and expansive vegetarian food centres. And upscale-ish Thai- and Italian-style veggie eats can be found at Anotai (Map p132; ☎ 0 2641 5366; 976/17 Soi Rama 9 Hospital, Greater Bangkok; ✹ 10am-9.30pm Thu-Tue), which also has an organic vegetable market.

Indian restaurants, particularly those featuring southern Indian cuisine such as Chennai Kitchen (p170), are also largely veggie.

During the Vegetarian Festival in October, the whole city goes mad for tofu, and stalls and restaurants indicate their nonmeat menu with yellow banners; Chinatown has the highest concentration of stalls.

KRUA NOPPHARAT Map p82   Thai $

☎ 0 2281 7578; 130-132 Th Phra Athit; mains 40-140B; ☉ 10.30am-2.30pm & 5-9pm Mon-Sat; 🖬 air-con 3, ordinary 3 & 15; 🚢 Tha Phra Athit (Banglamphu, N13)

A few dusty paintings are the only effort at interior design at this family-run standby. Where flavour is concerned, however, Krua Noppharat is willing to expend considerably more energy. Krua Noppharat is as popular among foreigners as it is among Thais, but does not tone down its excellent central- and southern-style Thai fare for the former.

PAN Map p82   Thai $

☎ 0 838 174 227; Th Rambutri; mains 50-90B; ☉ 11.30am-10pm; 🖬 air-con 3 & 16, ordinary 3, 15 & 16; 🚢 Tha Phra Athit (Banglamphu, N13)

If you're looking for authentic Thai but don't want to stray far from the comforts of Th Khao San, this streetside eatery (next to Viengtai Hotel) is your best bet. Simply look for the overflowing tray of raw ingredients, point to what you want and Pan will mix it up for you. The clientele is decidedly international, but the flavours wholly domestic.

THIP SAMAI Map p82   Thai $

☎ 0 2221 6280; www.thipsamai.com; 313 Th Mahachai; mains 25-120B; ☉ 5.30pm-1.30am; 🖬 air-con 59, ordinary 42 & 59; 🚢 klorng boat to Tha Phan Fah

Brace yourself, but you should be aware that the fried noodles sold from carts along Th Khao San have nothing to do with the dish known as *pàt tai*. Luckily, less than a five-minute *túk-túk* ride away lies Thip Samai, also known by locals as *pàt tai bràdoo pĕe*, and home to the most legendary *pàt tai* in town. For something a bit different, try the delicate egg-wrapped version, or the *pàt tai* fried with *man gûng*, decadent shrimp fat. Closed on alternate Wednesdays.

ROTI-MATABA Map p82   Thai-Muslim $

☎ 0 2282 2119; 136 Th Phra Athit; mains 50-90B; ☉ 9am-10pm Tue-Sun; 🖬 air-con 3, ordinary 3 & 15; 🚢 Tha Phra Athit (Banglamphu, N13)

This classic eatery appears to have become a bit too big for its britches in recent years, but still serves tasty Thai-Muslim dishes such as roti, *gaang mát·sà·màn* (Muslim curry), a brilliantly sour fish curry, and *má·tà·bà* (a sort of stuffed Indian pancake).

An upstairs air-con dining area and outdoor tables provide barely enough seating for its loyal fans.

EATS WALK: THANON TANAO Walking Tour

Despite its proximity to the faux *pàt tai* and tame *đôm yam* of Th Khao San, Banglamphu, particularly in the area around Th Tanao, is one of the most legendary eating areas in town. The flavours here are very Bangkok, featuring a balance of tastes with a slight emphasis on the sweet. This is where your Thai friends' parents ate as children, and despite the good reputations, the prices are low.

You'd have to be a competition-class eater to visit every place along this walk, so we recommend stopping in at whatever stall or restaurant most appeals to you. Bringing an eating companion gives you the opportunity to hit up even more places, and it's always fine to order just one dish to share.

Opening times vary, but the best time to do this walk is on a weekday from 11am to approximately 2pm, when the vendors are stocked and ready for the daily lunch barrage. Start at the intersection of Th Ratchadamnoen Klang and Th Tanao (the side opposite Th Khao San).

1 Kim Leng

Walking along Th Tanao on the right side of the road, the first restaurant you'll encounter is this tiny family-run restaurant, Kim Leng (กิม เล้ง; ☎ 0 2622 2062; 158-160 Th Tanao; ☉ 10am-10pm Mon-Sat), specialising in the dishes and flavours of central Thailand. This is a good place to whet your appetite with an authentic *yam* (Thai-style salad) such as *yam blah dùk foo*, a mixture of crispy catfish and mango.

2 Raat Naa Yot Phak

Continuing for about 300m until you pass San Chao Phor Seua, the Chinese temple, you'll come to Raat Naa Yot Phak (ราดหน้ายอดผัก; ☎ 0 2622 1910-0; 512-514 Th Tanao; ☉ 10am-9.30pm), an open-air restaurant that has been selling the eponymous fried noodle dish for 40 years. Don't miss the *pàt see éw*, wide rice noodles flash-fried with marinated pork, egg, Chinese kale and soy sauce. On your way out grab a pork satay or *kôw klúk gà·bì* (rice cooked in shrimp paste) from the vendors who sit directly in front of this restaurant during lunch.

EATS WALK: THANON TANAO

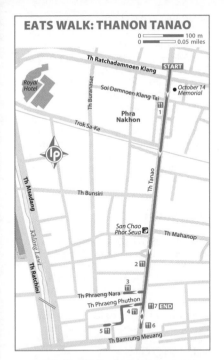

WALK FACTS

Start Cnr Th Ratchadamnoen Klang & Th Tanao
End Th Tanao at Phraeng Phuthon
Distance Approximately 600m
Duration Up to three hours, depending on how many dishes you care to scoff

3 Khanom Beuang Phraeng Nara

Turn right down Th Phraeng Nara, a popular lunchtime destination for the area's ravenous civil servants. Continue 50m on the right-hand side until you reach a woman at two coal burning stoves warming what look like miniature tacos. This is Khanom Beuang Phraeng Nara (ขนมเบื้องแพร่งนรา; ☎ 0 2222 8500; Th Phraeng Nara; ⏰ 11am-3pm), and the eponymous snacks come in two forms, sweet and savoury. Bag a couple and make your way back to Th Tanao.

4 Chote Chitr

Continue along Th Tanao until you reach Th Phraeng Phuthon. At your left just inside the entrance is Chote Chitr (☎ 0 2221 4082; 146 Th Phraeng Phuton; ⏰ 11am-10pm), a Bangkok foodie land-

mark renowned for its delicious *mèe gròrp* (sweet-and-spicy crispy fried noodles). If you require a sit-down meal at this point, this is a good place to do it.

5 Natthaphorn

Continuing into the courtyard area and on your left past the first side street is Natthaphorn (นัฐพร; ☎ 0 2221 3954; 94 Th Phraeng Phuthon; ⏰ 7am-7pm), a crumbling shophouse that for the last 70 years has been churning Bangkok's most famous coconut ice cream (a refreshing palate cleanser after the noodles).

6 Poj Spa Kar

Backtrack to Th Tanao, and cross the street to Poj Spa Kar (โภชนสภาคาร; ☎ 0 2222 2686; 433 Th Tanao; ⏰ 11am-9pm), reputedly Bangkok's oldest restaurant, serving recipes handed down from a former palace cook. This is another good option for a sit-down meal, and be sure to order the simple but tasty lemon-grass omelette.

7 K Phanich

Virtually next door is K Phanich (ก.พานิช; ☎ 0 2221 3554; 431 Th Tanao; ⏰ 10am-3pm), the most famous producer of sweet sticky rice in the city. There are no seats, but grab some rice to go, top it with a ripe mango from the vendors in front of the shop, and you've got yourself one of Thailand's most famous desserts.

Now take a moment to focus on dinner plans – after all, it is only a few hours away.

THEWET & DUSIT

The primary draw to this sleepy neighbourhood is the riverside setting, with restaurants that drink in the cool river breeze and grill whole fish for communal picking.

IN LOVE

Map p93   Thai $$

☎ 0 2281 2900; Th Krung Kasem; mains 150-200B; ⏰ 11am-10pm; 🚌 air-con 3 & 16, ordinary 3, 15 & 16; ⛴ Tha Thewet (N15)

This recently remodelled perch straddling Mae Nam Chao Phraya has undergone a transformation from homey to chic, reflecting much of the change in today's newfangled Bangkok. Slate grey and minimalist decor now define your settings, but the seafood-heavy menu, thankfully, still has its head in the past.

KALOANG HOME KITCHEN

Map p93   Thai $$

☎ 0 2281 9228; 2 Th Si Ayuthaya; mains 80-200B;
🕑 11am-11pm; 🚌 air-con 3 & 16, ordinary 3, 15 &
16; ⚓ Tha Thewet (N15)

Don't be alarmed by the peeling paint and
dilapidated deck. The laid-back atmosphere
and seafood-heavy menu will quickly dispel
any concerns about sinking into Chao
Phraya, and a beer and the breeze will
temporarily erase any scarring memories of
Bangkok traffic.

KRUA APSORN Map p93   Thai $$

☎ 0 2668 8788; 503-505 Th Samsen; mains
40-250B; 🕑 10.30am-7.30pm Mon-Fri, 10.30am-
6pm Sat; 🚌 air-con 3 & 16, ordinary 3, 15 & 16;
⚓ Tha Thewet (N15)

This homey dining room has served members of the Thai royal family and, back in
2006, was recognised as Bangkok's Best
Restaurant by the *Bangkok Post*. Must-eat
dishes include mussels fried with fresh
herbs, the decadent crab fried in yellow
chilli oil and the *tortilla Española*–like crab
omelette. Note the early closing times.

CHINATOWN

Although Chinatown seems to be dominated by restaurants serving shark fin and
bird's nest soup, significantly less ostenta-
tious dishes, usually prepared by the street
vendors that line Th Yaowarat after dark, are
the true Chinatown meal. With this in mind,
we've compiled the area's best street eats in
our food-based walking tour (opposite).

During the annual Vegetarian Festival (see p161)
in October, the neighbourhood embraces
meatless meals with yellow-flagged street
stalls.

Phahurat, Bangkok's Little India, has several inconspicuous Indian restaurants and
an afternoon samosa vendor near Soi ATM.

SHANGARILA RESTAURANT

Map p98   Chinese $$$

☎ 0 2224 5933; 306 Th Yaowarat; mains 220-500B;
🕑 11am-10pm; 🚌 air-con 4, 21, 25, 507 & MB5,
ordinary 4, 25, 29, 53 & 159; ⚓ Tha Ratchawong
(N5); Ⓜ Hua Lamphong exit 1 & taxi

This massive, banquet-style restaurant pre-
pares a variety of banquet-sized Cantonese
dishes for ravenous families. The dim sum
lunches are worth the effort of muscling
your way past the outdoor steam tables.

TANG JAI YUU

Map p98   Thai-Chinese $$$

☎ 0 2224 2167; 85-89 Th Yaowaphanit; mains
220-500B; 🕑 11am-10pm; 🚌 air-con 4, 21, 25,
507 & MB5, ordinary 4, 25, 29, 53 & 159; ⚓ Tha
Ratchawong (N5); Ⓜ Hua Lamphong exit 1 & taxi

In Thailand, policemen and big-haired
women are usually a tip-off for good eats,
not suspicious activity, and Tang Jai Yuu is
no exception. This place specialises in Teo
Chew and Chinese-Thai specialities with
an emphasis on seafood, and you can't go
wrong choosing a fresh fish from the tank
out the front and letting the boys grill it
for you.

HUA SENG HONG

Map p98   Chinese $$

☎ 0 2222 0635; 371-373 Th Yaowarat; mains
100-720B; 🕑 10am-midnight; 🚌 air-con 4, 21, 25,
507 & MB5, ordinary 4, 25, 29, 53 & 159; ⚓ Tha
Ratchawong (N5); Ⓜ Hua Lamphong exit 1 & taxi

Shark-fin soup may draw heaps of Asian
tourists into this place, but Hua Seng
Hong's varied menu, which includes dim
sum, braised goose feet and noodles,
makes it a delicious destination for any-
body craving Chinese.

ROYAL INDIA Map p98   Indian $$

☎ 0 2221 6565; 392/1 Th Chakraphet, Phahurat;
mains 100-250B; 🕑 10am-10pm; 🚌 air-con 3, 60,
73 & 512, ordinary 3, 53, 60 & 73; ⚓ Tha Saphan
Phut (Memorial Bridge, N6)

A windowless dining room of 10 tables
in a creepy alley may not be everybody's
ideal lunch destination, but this legendary
north Indian place continues to draw
foodies despite the lack of aesthetics. Try
any of the delicious breads or saucy curries, and finish with a homemade Punjabi
sweet.

CHIANG KII Map p98   Thai-Chinese $$

54 Soi Bamrungrat (Soi 12), Th Yaowarat; mains
250B; 🕑 5pm-10pm; 🚌 air-con 4, 21, 25, 507 &
MB5, ordinary 4, 25, 29, 53 & 159; ⚓ Tha Ratchawong (N5); Ⓜ Hua Lamphong exit 1 & taxi

At 250B, Chiang Kii's *kôw đôm ʰblah* (rice
soup with fish) is among the most expensive in town. Before baulking at the
price, witness the care that the elderly
Thai-Chinese owners put into every bowl,
not to mention the generous amount of
exceedingly fresh fish, and it begins to
make sense.

HONG KONG NOODLES

Map p98   Chinese $

136 Trok Itsaranuphap (Soi 16), Th Charoen Krung; mains 30B; 🕙 **9am-6pm;** 🚌 **air-con 4, 21, 25, 507 & MB5, ordinary 4, 25, 29, 53 & 159;** 🚢 **Tha Ratchawong (N5);** Ⓜ **Hua Lamphong exit 1 & taxi**
Deep in the heart of the vendor-lined soi also known as Talaat Mai (New Market), this claustrophobic shop does a busy trade in steaming bowls of wheat-and-egg noodles. If you can find a seat, there's a nice vista of the surrounding commerce.

OLD SIAM PLAZA Map p98   Thai $

cnr Th Phahurat & Th Triphet, Phahurat; mains 30-90B; 🕙 **10am-8pm;** 🚌 **air-con 3, 60, 73 & 512, ordinary 3, 53, 60 & 73;** 🚢 **Tha Saphan Phut (Memorial Bridge, N6)**
Wedged between the western edge of Chinatown and the northern edge of Phahurat, this shopping plaza has a decent 3rd-floor food centre serving Thai and Chinese food. Even better yet, the ground floor is a crash course in Thai desserts, with vendors selling streetside sweets in a more sanitary setting.

THAI CHAROEN Map p98   Thai-Chinese $

🕿 **0 2221 2633; 454 Th Charoen Krung; mains 20-30B;** 🕙 **9am-7pm;** 🚌 **air-con 4, 21, 25, 507 & MB5, ordinary 4, 25, 29, 53 & 159;** 🚢 **Tha Ratchawong (N5);** Ⓜ **Hua Lamphong exit 1 & taxi**
Simply look for the table of delicious-looking eats out front. This unassuming restaurant specialises in cheap and delicious Thai-Chinese specialities such as stuffed squid, stir-fried eggplant, and *jàp chài* (a Chinese vegetable 'stew').

EATS WALK: CHINATOWN
Walking Tour

Street food rules in this part of town and many of Chinatown's best kitchens don't require walls or a roof, making the area ideal for a food-based adventure.

Many of the dishes you'll encounter along this walk are noodle-based and thus quite filling, so bringing a friend or three and sharing is a good way to ensure that you can try as many dishes as possible.

Although many vendors stay open until the wee hours, the more popular stalls tend to sell out quickly, and the best time to feast in this area is from 7pm to 9pm. Don't try this walk on a Monday when most of the city's street vendors stay at home.

1 Burapa Birds Nest

Start your walk at the intersection of Th Yaowarat and Th Phadung Dao. Moving west, turn right into Th Plaeng Nam. Immediately on your right you'll see Burapa Birds Nest (🕿 0 2623 0191; Th Plaeng Nam; 🕙 11am-midnight), as good a place as any to try the very Chinatown dish, bird's nest soup.

2 Khrua Phornlamai

Directly across from Burapa you'll see a gentleman on the street working three coal-fired stoves. This stall, Khrua Phornlamai (ครัวพรละมัย; 🕿 0 818 230 397; Th Plaeng Nam; 🕙 7pm-late Tue-Sun), is where you'll find greasy but delicious *pàt kêe mow* (wide rice noodles fried with seafood, chillies and Thai basil).

3 Nay Mong

Continue down Th Plaeng Nam and cross Th Charoen Krung. Go straight, staying on the right-hand side for about 50m, until you reach Nay Mong (นายหมง; 🕿 0 2623 1890; 539 Th Phlap Phla Chai; 🕙 11am-9.30pm), a minuscule restaurant renowned for its delicious *hŏy tôrt* (mussels or oysters fried with egg and a sticky batter).

WALK FACTS

Start/End Cnr Th Yaowarat and Th Phadung Dao
Distance Approximately 1km
Duration Two to three hours, depending on how many dishes you tackle

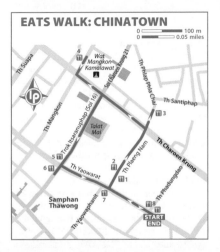

EATS WALK: CHINATOWN

EATING CHINATOWN

4 Jek Pui

Backtrack to Th Charoen Krung and turn right. Upon reaching Th Mangkorn make a right and immediately on your left-hand side you're bound to see a row of people waiting in line, and several more sitting on plastic stools holding plates of food in their hands. This is Jek Pui (เจ๊กปุ้ย; ☎ 0818 509 960; Th Mangkorn; ☾ 5pm-9pm Tue-Sun), a table-less stall known for its Chinese-style Thai curries. Try the *gaang kěe·o wǎhn lôok chín 'blah grai*, a mild green curry with freshwater fish dumplings.

5 Gǒo·ay Đěe·o Kôo·a Gài

Cross Th Charoen Krung again, turn left, and continue east until you reach Soi 16, a narrow alleyway also known as Talat Mai (p101), the area's most famous strip of commerce. At the end of the alley you'll see a gentleman frying noodles with a brass wok and a spoon. He's making gǒo·ay đěe·o kôo·a gài (ก๋วยเตี๋ยวคั่วไก่; Soi 16, Th Charoen Krung; ☾ 6pm-midnight Tue-Sun), a simple but delicious dish of rice noodles fried with chicken, egg and garlic oil.

6 Nay Lek Uan

Upon emerging at Th Yaowarat, cross over to the busy market area directly across the street. The first vendor on the right, Nay Lek Uan (นายเล็ก อ้วน; ☎ 0 2224 3450; Soi 11, Th Yaowarat; ☾ 6pm-1am Tue-Sun), is among the most popular stalls in Bangkok, and sells gǒo·ay jáp nám sǎi, an intensely peppery broth containing noodles and pork offal. If offal doesn't whet your appetite, there are several more stalls here selling everything from *pàt tai* to satay.

7 Mangkorn Khao

Returning back to Th Yaowarat, turn right and continue until the next intersection. On the corner of Th Yaowaphanit and Th Yaowarat you'll see a stall with yellow noodles and barbecued pork. This is Mangkorn Khao (มังกรขาว; ☎ 0 2682 2352; ☾ 7pm-11pm Tues-Sun). Delicious wontons and, if you can manage it, *bà·mèe* (Chinese-style wheat noodles), are the order of the day from this respected vendor.

8 Lek & Rut, T&K

Cross the road and continue east along Th Yaowarat for one block and you're back to where you started. By now the two opposing seafood places, Lek & Rut (☎ 0816 375 039; ☾ 6pm-midnight) and T&K (☎ 0 2223 4519; ☾ 6pm-midnight)

should be buzzing. You could join the tourists for grilled prawns and fried rice, but possibly by this point you've had your fill of what Chinatown really has to offer.

SIAM SQUARE, PRATUNAM, PLOENCHIT & RATCHATHEWI

Welcome to Mall Land. Although the plastic facades of famous franchises seem to prevail, there are some noteworthy independent eats, both with and without amenities such as air-conditioning and shopping families. Soi Lang Suan is a virtual Little Italy of Italian restaurants, and the area around Th Withayu is home to a few longstanding Thai restaurants.

SIAM SQUARE, PRATUNAM & PLOENCHIT

GIANNI RISTORANTE
Map p108   Italian $$$

☎ 0 2252 1619; www.giannibkk.com; 34/1 Soi Tonson, Th Ploenchit; mains 330-990B; ☾ 10am-10pm; 🚇 Chit Lom exit 4

Widely considered among Bangkok's finest Italian restaurants, Gianni also offers more than 250 wines and one of the most generous lunch specials in town. The eponymous and ebullient owner is always on site, and is always willing to recommend a dish or the right bottle to accompany it.

CRYSTAL JADE LA MIAN XIAO
LONG BAO Map p108   Chinese $$

☎ 0 2250 7990; Urban Kitchen, Basement, Erawan Bangkok, 494 Th Ploenchit; mains 160-400B; ☾ 10am-10pm; 🚇 Chit Lom exit 8

The tongue-twistingly long name of this excellent Singaporean chain refers to the restaurant's signature wheat noodles (*la mian*) and the famous Shanghainese steamed dumplings (*xiao long pao*). If you order the hand-pulled noodles (which you should do) allow the staff to cut them with kitchen shears, otherwise you'll end up with ample evidence of your meal on your shirt.

ERAWAN TEA ROOM Map p108   Thai $$

☎ 0 2250 7777; 2nd fl, Erawan Bangkok, 494 Th Ploenchit; mains 170-450B; ☾ 10am-10pm; 🚇 Chit Lom exit 8

The oversized chairs, panoramic windows and variety of hot drinks make this one of Bangkok's best places to catch up with the paper. The lengthy menu, with an emphasis on regional Thai dishes, will likely encourage you to linger longer, and the selection of jams and teas to take away lets you recreate the experience at home.

COCA SUKI

Map p108   Thai-Chinese $$

☎ 0 2251 6337; 416/3-8 Th Henri Dunant, Siam Sq; mains 60-200B; ⏰ 11am-11pm; 🚇 Siam exit 6
Immensely popular with Thai families, sù·gêe takes the form of a bubbling hotpot of broth and the raw ingredients to dip therein. Coca is one of the oldest purveyors of the dish, and the Siam Sq branch reflects the brand's efforts to appear more modern. Fans of spice be sure to request the tangy 'tom yam' broth.

FOOD PLUS

Map p108   Thai $

alleyway btwn Soi 3 & Soi 4, Siam Sq; mains 30-70B; ⏰ 6am-6pm; 🚇 Siam exit 2
This claustrophobic alleyway is bursting with the wares of several ráhn kôw gaang (rice and curry stalls). Everything is made ahead of time, so simply point to what looks tasty: you'll be hard-pressed to spend more than 100B, and the flavours are unanimously authentic and delicious. Try to avoid the heart of the lunch rush (approximately 12.15pm to 12.45pm) when virtually every shopkeeper in the area (and believe us, there are many) seems to descend on the place.

NEW LIGHT COFFEE HOUSE

Map p108   Thai $

☎ 0 2251 9592; 426/1-4 Soi Chulalongkorn 64, Siam Sq; mains 60-200B; ⏰ 8am-11.30pm; 🚇 Siam exit 2
Travel back in time to 1960s-era Bangkok at this vintage diner popular with students from nearby Chulalongkorn University. Try old-school Western dishes, all of which come accompanied by a soft roll and green salad, or choose from the extensive Thai menu.

SANGUAN SRI Map p108   Thai $

☎ 0 2252 7637; 59/1 Th Withayu, Ploenchit; mains 60-150B; ⏰ 10am-3pm Mon-Sat; 🚇 Phloen Chit exit 5
This restaurant, resembling a concrete bunker filled with furniture circa 1973, can afford to remain decidedly cher-i (old-fashioned) simply because of its reputation. Mimic the area's hungry office staff and try the excellent gaang pèt ʔèt yâhng, red curry with grilled duck breast served over snowy white kà·nŏm jeen noodles.

FOOD COURT FRENZY

Every Bangkok mall worth its escalators has some sort of food court. In recent years many have gone upscale, and the setting, cuisine and service have also elevated accordingly. The following are some of the better choices:

- FoodPark (Map p108; ☎ 0 2250 4888; 5th fl, Big C Ratchadamri, 97/11 Th Ratchadamri; ⏰ 9am-10pm) is the proletariat of the genre. The food selections here are not going to inspire you to move east, but they are numerous and cheap, and representative of the kind of 'fast food' Thais enjoy eating. To pay you must first exchange your cash for a temporary credit card at one of several counters; your change is refunded at the same desk.

- Food Loft (Map p108; 6th fl, Central Chidlom, 1027 Th Ploenchit; ⏰ 10am-10pm) at Central Chidlom pioneered the concept of the upscale food court, and mock-ups of the various Indian, Italian, Singaporean and other international dishes aid in the decision making process. Upon entering, you'll be given a temporary credit card and will be led to a table. You have to get up again to order, but the dishes will be brought to you. Paying is done on your way out.

- MBK Food Court (Map p108; 6th fl, Mahboonkhrong, cnr Th Phra Ram I & Th Phayathai, Siam Sq; ⏰ 10am-9pm), the granddaddy of the genre, offers vendors selling food from virtually every corner of Thailand and beyond. Standouts include an excellent vegetarian food stall (stall C8) and a very decent northeastern Thai food vendor (C22).

- Park Food Hall (Map p126; 5th fl, Emporium Shopping Centre, 622 Th Sukhumvit, cnr Soi 24; ⏰ 10am-10pm) brings together some of the city's most well-known international restaurants. Emporium Food Hall, on the same floor, features cheaper, mostly Chinese and Thai food, and what must be the cheapest meal with a view in town. Paying is done by buying coupons at the windows in the entrance. Be sure to leave these in your pocket until the next day when it's too late to get a refund – it's an integral part of the food-court experience.

RATCHATHEWI

MALLIKA RESTAURANT Map p113   Thai $$
☎ 0 2248 0287; 21/36 Soi Rang Nam; mains 30–70B; ☷ 10.15am–10pm Mon–Sat; ☷ Victory Monument exit 2

Visit this corner of northern Bangkok for a taste of Thailand's southern provinces. The menu spans the region with spicy hits such as *kôo-a glîng* (minced meat fried with curry paste), or *gaang sôm* (a turmeric-laden seafood soup). Prices are slightly higher than elsewhere, but you're paying for quality.

TIDA ESARN Map p113   Thai/International $$
☎ 0 2247 2234; 1/2–5 Soi Rang Nam; mains 50–150B; ☷ 10.30am–10.30pm; ☷ Victory Monument exit 2

Tida Esarn sells country-style Thai food in a decidedly urban setting. Foreigners provide the bulk of the restaurant's customers, but to its benefit, the kitchen still insists on serving full-flavoured Isan-style dishes such as *súp nòr mái*, a tart salad of shredded bamboo.

PATHÉ Map p113   Thai $$
☎ 0 2644 4321; 507 Th Ratchawithi; mains 70–140B; ☷ 7am–midnight; ☷ Victory Monument exit 4

The modern Thai equivalent of a 1950s-era American diner, this popular place combines solid Thai food, a fun atmosphere and a jukebox playing scratched records. The menu is equally eclectic, and combines Thai and Western dishes and ingredients – be sure to save room for the deep-fried ice cream.

VICTORY POINT Map p113   Thai $
cnr Th Phayathai & Th Ratchawithi; mains 30–60B; ☷ 6pm–midnight; ☷ Victory Monument exit 4

In Bangkok, the best meals are always in unlikely places. Far from the foreign forces of inner Bangkok, Victory Point can be as provincial as it wants, with a squat village of concrete stalls lit in neon and a mix of super-casual and delicious food vendors.

RIVERSIDE, SILOM & LUMPHINI

Riverside Bangkok is often associated with hotel fine dining, but this is actually one of the city's most diverse eating districts. Those willing to try something different can poke into one of the numerous Thai-Muslim or Indian restaurants near the intersection of Th Silom and Th Charoen Krung. Authentic foreign food can be found at the eastern end of Th Silom, near BTS Sala Daeng, and several old-school eating houses can be found towards the river end. And if you're set on decadent dining, but can't justify the price tag, consider lunch, when many of Bangkok's most famous hotel restaurants offer cut-rate specials to entice diners.

RIVERSIDE & SILOM

D'SENS Map p116   French $$$
☎ 0 2200 9000; www.dusit.com; 22nd fl, Dusit Thani Hotel, 946 Th Rama IV; mains 250–1900B; ☷ 11.30am–2pm Mon–Fri & 6–10pm Mon–Sat; ☷ Si Lom exit 3; ☷ Sala Daeng exit 4

Bangkok's swankiest diners come to D'Sens, located in what looks like a control tower at the top of the Dusit Thani Hotel, for vibrant contemporary French cuisine as designated by the Michelin star–lauded brothers, Jacques and Laurent Pourcel. Gracious service and one of the best views of Bangkok round out the package.

LE BOUCHON Map p116   French $$$
☎ 0 2234 9109; 37/17 Soi Patpong 2, Th Silom; mains 180–830B; ☷ noon–3pm & 7pm–midnight; ☷ Si Lom exit 2; ☷ Sala Daeng exit 1

Cast aside any preconceived notions of pretentious waiters and intimidating menus; this homely bistro in the middle of one of Bangkok's more 'colourful' districts is a capable and fun introduction to French cooking. Choose your dishes from the blackboard menu toted around by cheery waiting staff, but it'd be a shame to miss the garlicky frogs' legs or the savoury foie gras pâté.

LE NORMANDIE Map p116   French $$$
☎ 0 2236 0400; www.mandarinoriental.com; Oriental Hotel, Soi 38, Th Charoen Krung; dishes 750–3900B, 4-course/6-course degustation menu 3800/4400B; ☷ noon–2.30pm & 7–10.30pm Mon–Sat, 7–10.30pm Sun; ☷ air-con 504, 544 & 547, ordinary 1, 15, 35 & 163; ☷ Tha Oriental (N1)

For decades Le Normandie was synonymous with fine dining in the city. And although today's Bangkok boasts a plethora of upmarket choices, Le Normandie has maintained its niche and is still the only place to go for a genuinely old-world 'continental' dining experience. A revolving cast of Michelin-starred guest chefs and some of the world's most decadent ingredients keep up the standard, and appropriately formal attire (including jacket) is required.

EAT ME RESTAURANT
Map p116   International $$$

☎ 0 2238 0931; www.eatmerestaurant.com; Soi Phiphat 2, Th Convent; mains 390-1200B; ☾ 3pm-1am; Ⓜ Si Lom exit 2; Ⓡ Sala Daeng exit 2

A little bit of Sydney has blossomed here off Th Silom, helping to give Bangkok more cosmo cred. Chic, minimalist decor is accessorised by rotating art exhibits supplied by H Gallery (p200), the city's leading contemporary gallery. And lest we forget, the food is creative and modern, spanning the globe from pumpkin risotto to tuna tartare.

BLUE ELEPHANT Map p116   Thai $$$

☎ 0 2673 9353; www.blueelephant.com; 233 Th Sathon Tai; mains 180-880B; ☾ 11.30am-2.30pm & 6.30-10.30pm; Ⓡ Surasak exit 4

The Blue Elephant got its start in Brussels more than two decades ago as an exotic outpost of royal Thai cuisine. After spreading to other cities, the owners boldly chose Bangkok, the cuisine's birth mother, as its ninth location. Set in a stunning Sino-Portuguese colonial building with service fit for royalty, the restaurant also features an impressive cooking school (see boxed text p155).

SOUVLAKI Map p116   Greek $$

☎ 0 2632 9967; 114/4 Soi 4, Th Silom; mains 120-280B; ☾ 11.30am-2.30pm & 6pm-late; Ⓜ Si Lom exit 2; Ⓡ Sala Daeng exit 1

Greek is among Bangkok's most elusive cuisines, and this new eatery has finally brought Hellenic flavours to town. The menu runs the predictable gamut of Greek-style fast food and mezze, but also offers interesting daily specials. Warning: serving sizes are truly Olympian.

INDIAN HUT
Map p116   Indian $$

☎ 0 2635 7876; www.indian-hut.com; 311/2-5 Th Surawong; mains 160-380B; ☾ 11am-10.30pm; 🚌 air-con 504, 544 & 547, ordinary 1, 15, 35 & 163; 🚢 Tha Oriental (N1)

This Indian restaurant, across from the Manorha Hotel, specialises in Nawabi (Lucknow) cuisine. Try the vegetarian samosas, fresh prawns cooked with ginger or the homemade paneer in tomato and onion curry.

SCOOZI Map p116   Italian $$

☎ 0 2267 4344; www.scoozipizza.com; 174 Th Surawong; mains 150-350B; ☾ 10.30am-11pm; Ⓜ Si Lom exit 2; Ⓡ Sala Daeng exit 1

At this chic pizzeria you can witness your pie being skilfully tossed and topped before it's blistered in a wood-burning oven from Italy. Go minimalist and order the tasty napoletana, a pizza topped with little

DINNER CRUISES

Mae Nam Chao Phraya is lovely in the evenings, with the skyscrapers' lights twinkling in the distance and a cool breeze chasing the heat away. A dozen or more companies run regular dinner cruises along the river. Some are mammoth boats so brightly lit inside that you'd never know you were on the water; others are more sedate and intimate, allowing patrons to see the surroundings. Several of the dinner boats cruise under the well-lit Saphan Phra Ram IX, the longest single-span cable-suspension bridge in the world.

- Loy Nava (Map p116; ☎ 0 2437 4932; www.loynava.com; set menu 1766B; ☾ 6-8pm & 8.10-10pm) Two cruises travel from Tha Si Phraya aboard a converted rice barge. Vegetarian menu available.
- Manohra Cruises (Map p132; ☎ 0 2477 0770; www.manohracruises.com; Bangkok Marriott Resort & Spa, Thonburi; cocktail cruise 900B, dinner cruise 1250-1990B; ☾ cocktail cruise 6-7pm, dinner cruise 7.30-10pm) Manohra commands a fleet of converted teak rice barges that part the waters with regal flair. Boats depart from the Marriott Resort, accessible via a free river shuttle that operates between the hotel and Tha Sathon (Central Pier), near Saphan Taksin Skytrain station.
- Wan Fah (Map p116; ☎ 0 2222 8679; www.wanfah.in.th; set menu 1200B; ☾ 7-9pm) Departing from River City Shopping Centre, Wan Fah runs a buxom wooden boat that floats in style with accompanying Thai music and traditional dance. Dinner options include a standard or seafood set menu and hotel transfer is available.
- Yok Yor Restaurant (Map p116; ☎ 0 2439 3477; www.yokyor.co.th; dinner 300-550B, surcharge 140B; ☾ 8-10pm) This long-running floating restaurant on the Thonburi side of the river also runs a daily dinner cruise, as well as several boats that can be hired for private functions.

more than mozzarella, anchovies and olives. The ever-expanding Scoozi empire now boasts branches at Th Khao San (Map p82; ☎ 0 2280 5280; 201 Soi Sunset) and Thonglor (Map p126; ☎ 0 2391 5113; Fenix Thonglor, Soi 1, Soi 55 (Thong Lor), Th Sukhumvit).

SUSHIKO Map p116   Japanese $$

☎ 0 2233 0565; 9/11-12 Soi Thaniya, Th Silom; mains 120-700B; ◷ 11am-midnight; Ⓜ Si Lom exit 2; Ⓡ Sala Daeng exit 1

The strip known as Soi Thaniya is home to dozens of Japanese restaurants ranging in quality from dive to opulent. Sushiko, Japanese run and frequented, is a good middle ground. The restaurant is divided into three levels, with the ground floor specialising in sushi and sashimi, the 2nd floor serving tempura, and the 3rd serving sukiyaki and shabu-shabu. There's no English-language sign here, so simply look for the white corner restaurant.

MIZU'S KITCHEN Map p116   Japanese/Steak $$

☎ 0 2233 6447; 32 Soi Patpong 1, Th Silom; mains 65-200B; ◷ noon-midnight; Ⓜ Si Lom exit 2; Ⓡ Sala Daeng exit 1

This certifiable hole-in-the-wall oozes character, not to mention the beefy essence of thousands of steaks served over the decades. Do order the house Sarika steak, and do take a hint from the regulars and use your chequered tablecloth to protect your clothes from the spray of the hot plate when it arrives.

KALAPAPRUEK Map p116   Thai $

☎ 0 2236 4335; 27 Th Pramuan; dishes 60-120B; ◷ 8am-6pm; 🚌 air-con 76, 77, 177, 504, 514, 547 & MB12, ordinary 77, 162, 163 & 164; Ⓡ Surasak exit 3

This venerable Thai eatery has numerous branches and mall spin-offs around town, but we still fancy the quasi-concealed original branch. The diverse menu spans regional Thai specialities from just about every region, daily specials and occasionally, seasonal treats as well.

SOMBOON SEAFOOD Map p116   Thai $$

☎ 0 2233 3104; www.somboonseafood.com; cnr Th Surawong & Th Narathiwat Ratchanakharin (Chong Nonsi); mains 150-400B; ◷ 4pm-midnight; Ⓡ Chong Nonsi exit 3

Somboon, a classy seafood hall with a reputation far and wide, is known for doing the best curry-powder crab in town. Soy-steamed sea bass (*blah grà·pohng nêung see·éw*) is also a speciality and, like all good Thai seafood, should be enjoyed with an immense platter of *kôw pàt boo* (fried rice with crab) and as many friends as you can gather together.

BOSPHORUS

Map p116   Turkish $$

☎ 0 2237 5168; 1043/4 Soi 21, Th Silom; mains 80-500B; ◷ 10am-8pm; 🚌 air-con 76, 77, 177, 504, 514, 547 & MB12; ordinary 77, 162, 163 & 164; Ⓡ Surasak exit 1

The food of Turkey is a bona fide endangered culinary species here in Bangkok. Savour your discovery by choosing from the variety of predominately vegetarian mezze in the display case, or proceed directly to any of the menu's various grilled meat dishes. There are also several Turkish desserts. Framed portraits of the Thai king and Mustafa Kemal Atatürk provide a regal setting.

RAN NAM TAO HU YONG HER

Map p116   Chinese $

☎ 0 2635 0003; 68 Th Narathiwat Ratchanakharin (Chong Nonsi); mains 40-205B; ◷ 11am-10pm; Ⓡ Chong Nonsi exit 3

Although the name of this blink-and-you'll-miss-it shophouse eatery translates as 'soy milk restaurant', the emphasis here is on northern Chinese cuisine – a rarity in Bangkok. Try the Shanghainese speciality *xiao long bao*, described on the menu as 'small steamed bun', actually steamed dumplings encasing a pork filling and rich hot broth that pours out when you bite into them.

CHENNAI KITCHEN

Map p116   Indian/Vegetarian $

☎ 0 2234 1266; 10 Th Pan, Th Silom; mains 50-150B; ◷ 10am-3pm & 6-9.30pm; 🚌 air-con 76, 77, 177, 504, 514, 547 & MB12, ordinary 77, 162, 163 & 164; Ⓡ Surasak exit 3

This thimble-sized restaurant near the Hindu temple puts out some of the most solid southern Indian vegetarian food around. Yard-long *dosai* (a crispy southern Indian bread) is always a good choice, but if you're feeling indecisive (or exceptionally famished) go for the banana-leaf *thali* that seems to incorporate just about everything in the kitchen.

MASHOOR

Map p116   Indian/Vegetarian $

☎ 0 2234 9305; 38 Th Pan, Th Silom; mains 50-
120B; ⏰ 9am-9pm; 🚌 air-con 76, 77, 177, 504,
514, 547 & MB12, ordinary 77, 162, 163 & 164;
🚇 Surasak exit 3
Indian-Nepali vegetarian cuisine via Myanmar may sound like an entirely new cuisine
altogether, but somehow it tastes just
right. This informal kitchen, operated by a
Burmese cook of Nepali descent, assem-
bles a mean meat-free *thali*. Cap off your
meal with a visit to Kathmandu (p200), the
photography gallery across the street, and
you'll soon forget which part of Asia you're
actually in.

CILI PADI

Map p116   Malaysian $

☎ 0 2634 2839; 160/9 Th Narathiwat Ratchanakharin (Chong Nonsi); mains 30-100B; ⏰ 11am-
10pm Sun-Thu; 🚇 Chong Nonsi exit 4
This culinary outpost from south of the border exudes a casual cafe-like atmosphere,
and authentic *teh tarik* (Malaysian-style
sweet tea) and *roti canai* (a crispy pancake
served with a lentil dip) make it a clever
stop for an air-conditioned break. Lunch
specials and an expansive menu ranging
from noodle dishes to hearty Malaysian-
style curries provide even more excuses to
linger.

CIRCLE OF FRIENDS

Map p116   Thai $

☎ 0 2237 0080; Soi 10, Th Sathon Neua; mains
60-100B; ⏰ 10am-8pm Mon-Fri, 4pm-8pm Sat;
🚇 Surasak exit 3
Somehow remaining cool and shady on
even the hottest days, this leafy cafe shares
space with the adjacent Saeng-Arom
Ashram. With each day of the week comes
two attractive set-menu options, and refreshing herbal and fruit drinks abound.

HARMONIQUE Map p116   Thai $

☎ 0 2237 8175; Soi 34, Th Charoen Krung; mains
65-200B; ⏰ 11am-10pm Mon-Sat; 🚌 air-con
504, 544 & 547, ordinary 1, 15, 35 & 163; 🚢 Tha
Oriental (N1)
A tiny oasis squeezed into a former Chinese
residence, Harmonique is an expat staple
for thrifty romantic dinners. The dishes are
unabashedly designed for folks fearful of
chillies and fish sauce, but the ambience
of fairy lights, a central banyan tree and

DAY OFF

Fans of street food be forewarned that all of Bangkok's stalls close on Monday for compulsory street
cleaning (the results of which are not always entirely
evident come Tuesday morning). If you happen to be
in the city on this day, take advantage of the lull to
visit one of the city's upscale hotel restaurants, which
virtually never close.

marble-topped tables have spared Harmonique from our chopping block.

JAY SO

Map p116   Thai $

☎ 0859 994 225; 146/1 Soi Phiphat 2, Th Convent;
mains 20-50B; ⏰ 10am-5.30pm Mon-Sat; Ⓜ Si
Lom exit 2; 🚇 Sala Daeng exit 2
This bright-red crumbling shack is living
proof that, where authentic Thai food is
concerned, ambience is often considered
more a liability than an asset. Fittingly,
Jay So has no menu as such, but a mortar
and pestle and a huge grill are the telltale
signs of ballistically spicy *sôm đam*, sublime
herb-stuffed grilled catfish and other Isan
specialities.

KHRUA AROY AROY

Map p116   Thai $

☎ 0 2635 2365; Th Pan, Th Silom; mains 30-70B;
⏰ 6am-6pm; 🚌 air-con 76, 77, 177, 504, 514, 547
& MB12, ordinary 77, 162, 163 & 164; 🚇 Surasak
exit 3
Despite being the kind of family-run Thai
restaurant where nobody seems to mind a
cat slumbering on the cash register, Khrua
Aroy Aroy ('Delicious Delicious Kitchen')
lives up to its lofty name. Stop by for some
of the richest curries around, as well as
the interesting daily specials including, on
Thursdays, *kôw klúk gà·bì*, rice cooked in
shrimp paste and served with sweet pork,
shredded green mango and other toppings.

SOI 10 FOOD CENTRES

Map p116   Thai $

Soi 10, Th Silom; mains 20-60B; ⏰ 8am-2pm Mon-
Fri; Ⓜ Si Lom exit 2; 🚇 Sala Daeng exit 1
These two adjacent hangar-like buildings
tucked behind Soi 10 are the main lunchtime fuelling stations for this area's office
staff. Choices range from southern-style
kôw gaang (point-and-choose curries ladled
over rice) to virtually every form of Thai
noodle.

EATING RIVERSIDE, SILOM & LUMPHINI

SOI PRADIT MARKET Map p116　　Thai $

Soi 20, Th Silom; ⏰ 10am-10pm; mains 25-100B; 🚌 air-con 76, 77, 177, 504, 514, 547 & MB12, ordinary 77, 162, 163 & 164; 🚇 Surasak exit 3
This blue-collar street market is a virtual microcosm of Thai cuisine. Muslims deep-fry marinated chicken in front of the mosque, while across the way Chinese vendors chop up stewed pork leg and Isan women pound away at mortars of *sôm đam*. Live on the edge a little and proceed past the stalls with English signs peddling the predictables.

SOMTAM CONVENT Map p116　　Thai $

☎ 0 2634 2839; 2/4-5 Th Convent; mains 30-120B; ⏰ 10.30am-9pm Mon-Fri, 10.30am-5pm Sat & Sun; Ⓜ Si Lom exit 2; 🚇 Sala Daeng exit 2
Northeastern-style Thai food is usually relegated to less-than-hygienic stalls perched by the side of the road with no menu or English-speaking staff in sight. A less intimidating introduction to the wonders of *lâhp*, *sôm đam* and other Isan delights can be had at this popular restaurant.

HOME CUISINE ISLAMIC
RESTAURANT Map p116　　Thai-Muslim $

☎ 0 2234 7911; 196-8 Soi 36, Th Charoen Krung; mains 45-130B; ⏰ 11am-10pm Mon-Sat, 6pm-10pm Sun; 🚌 air-con 504, 544 & 547, ordinary 1, 15, 35 & 163; ⚓ Tha Oriental (N1)
Hidden in a leafy corner mercifully distant from hectic Th Charoen Krung, this bungalow-like restaurant does tasty Thai-Muslim with an endearing Indian accent. Sit out on the breezy patio and try the simultaneously rich and sour fish curry, accompanied ideally by a flaky roti or three.

top picks

OLD-SCOOL BANGKOK DINING

- Chote Chitr (p163) Enjoy the flavours of Olde Bangkok served up in an antique shophouse.
- Mizu's Kitchen (p170) Travel back in time to the R&R days of the 'American' War.
- Muslim Restaurant (right) Pull up a booth and enjoy dishes that haven't changed in nearly a century.
- Ngwan Lee Lang Suan (right) Indulge at this tasty food hall with decades of experience.
- Sanguan Sri (p167) Party like it's 1969; fortunately the food is that of the timeless variety.

MUSLIM RESTAURANT
Map p116　　Thai-Muslim $

☎ 0 2234 1876; 1354-6 Th Charoen Krung; mains 30-90B; ⏰ 10am-8pm; 🚌 air-con 504, 544 & 547, ordinary 1, 15, 35 & 163; ⚓ Tha Oriental (N1)
Plant yourself in any random wooden booth of this ancient eatery for a glimpse into what restaurants in Bangkok used to be like. The menu, much like the interior design, doesn't appear to have changed much in the restaurant's 70-year history, and the biryanis, curries and samosas are still more Indian-influenced than Thai.

NAAZ Map p116　　Thai-Muslim $

☎ 0 2234 4537; 24/9 Soi 45, Th Charoen Krung; mains 35-90B; ⏰ 8.30am-10pm Mon-Sat; 🚌 air-con 504, 544 & 547, ordinary 1, 15, 35 & 163; ⚓ Tha Oriental (N1)
Hidden in a nondescript alleyway is Naaz (pronounced Nát), a tiny living-room kitchen serving some of the city's richest *kôw mòk gài* (chicken biryani). Various daily specials include chicken masala and mutton korma, but we're most curious to visit on Thursday when the restaurant serves something called Karai Ghost.

LUMPHINI

NAHM Map p122　　Thai $$$

☎ 0 2625 3388; www.metropolitan.como.bz; Metropolitan Hotel, 27 Th Sathon Tai; set dinner 1800B; ⏰ noon-2pm & 6.30-10.30pm; Ⓜ Lumphini exit 2
Renowned Australian chef and author David Thompson is bringing his Michelin-starred Thai cuisine home to Bangkok. Diners can expect similar interpretations of the classic dishes available at Thompson's London restaurant, as well as sublime Thai sweets prepared by Thompson's partner, Tanongsak Yordwai.

NGWAN LEE LANG SUAN
Map p122　　Thai-Chinese $$

☎ 0 2250 0936; cnr Soi Lang Suan & Th Sarasin; mains 150-300B; ⏰ 6pm-3am; 🚇 Ratchadamri exit 2
This cavern-like staple of copious consumption is still going strong after all these decades. If you can locate the entrance, squeeze in with the post-clubbing crowd and try some of those dishes you never dare to order elsewhere, such as *jàp chài* (Chinese-style stewed veggies) or *hŏy lai pàt nám prík pŏw* (clams stir-fried with chilli sauce and Thai basil).

KAI THAWT JAY KII (SOI POLO FRIED CHICKEN)

Map p122   Thai $

☎ 0 2655 8489; 137/1-3 Soi Polo, Th Withayu; mains 30-150B; ⏰ 7am-9pm; Ⓜ Lumphini exit 3

This Cinderella of a former street stall has become virtually synonymous with fried chicken. Although the *sôm đam*, sticky rice and *lâhp* (spicy 'salad' of minced meat) give the impression of an Isan eatery, the restaurant's namesake deep-fried bird is none other than a truly Bangkok experience. Regardless, smothered in a thick layer of crispy deep-fried garlic, it is none other than a truly Bangkok experience.

SUAN LUM NIGHT BAZAAR

Map p122   Thai $

cnr Th Withayu & Th Rama IV; mains 50-150B; ⏰ 7pm-midnight; Ⓜ Lumphini exit 3

Find a seat (as far from the stage as possible if you value your eardrums), order a draught *hefeweizen* and a dish of deep-fried soft-shell crabs, and settle down for an evening of typically tasty Thai entertainment. Although the live music performances might not be to everybody's taste, the combo of decent eats and copious beer tends to tip the scales. There has long been talk that Suan Lum is slotted for the wrecking ball, but until the bulldozers arrive, we remain sceptical.

THANON SUKHUMVIT

Th Sukhumvit is Bangkok's international avenue. Running through the immigrant community of Little Arabia at Soi 3/1, past the girlie bars around Nana, and skirting the well-heeled Thai and executive expat neighbourhoods further east, there's hardly a cuisine not represented here. You wouldn't come to Sukhumvit to eat Thai, but you do come for everything else, from hummus to burgers.

GREAT AMERICAN RIB COMPANY

Map p126   American $$$

☎ 0 2661 3801; 32 Soi 36, Th Sukhumvit; mains 165-400B; ⏰ 11am-11pm; ▣ Thong Lo exit 2

The term 'barbecue' often inspires images of grilled meat, but slow-cooking as it's done in the American south is another beast altogether. Avoid the burgers at this blandly named but popular joint and stick to the fall-apart-at-the-touch Memphis-style ribs and rich pulled pork.

top picks

AUTHENTIC IMPORTS

- **Boon Tong Kiat Singapore Hainanese Chicken Rice** (p176) Singapore's unofficial national dish has found a home in Bangkok.
- **Gianni Ristorante** (p166) Not necessarily the way Mama made it; Gianni's Italian cuisine is even better.
- **Le Bouchon** (p168) You'll be the only one speaking English at this Francophile outpost.
- **Mokkori** (p175) Feel like an authentic Japanese *sarariman* as you slurp your noodles.
- **Ran Nam Tao Hu Yong Her** (p170) One of the few places in town to get your northern Chinese on.

CRÊPES & CO

Map p126   French $$$

☎ 0 2653 3990; www.crepes.co.th; 18 Soi 12, Th Sukhumvit; mains 150-540B; ⏰ 9am-midnight; Ⓜ Sukhumvit exit 3; ▣ Asok exit 2; 🛜

Want to pretend you're part of Bangkok's expat community? This cute cottage crêperie, another 50m down the same soi as Cabbages & Condoms (p175), is a good place to start. The homely setting and excellent service, not to mention a menu that offers much more than the restaurant's name suggests, keep the desperate housewives of Bangkok's diplomatic corps coming back again and again.

BEI OTTO Map p126   German $$$

☎ 0 2262 0892; www.beiotto.com; 1 Soi 20, Th Sukhumvit; mains 175-480B; ⏰ 11am-midnight; Ⓜ Sukhumvit exit 2; ▣ Asok exit 4

Claiming a Bangkok residence for nearly 20 years, Bei Otto's major culinary bragging point is its pork knuckles, reputedly the best in town. A good selection of German beers and an attached delicatessen with brilliant breads and super sausages make it even more attractive to go Deutsch.

FACE Map p126   Indian/Thai $$$

☎ 0 2713 6048; www.facebars.com; 29 Soi 38, Th Sukhumvit; mains 280-1750B; ⏰ 6.30-10pm Mon-Fri, to 11pm Sat & Sun; ▣ Thong Lo exit 4

Housed in several interconnected Thai-style wooden structures, this handsome dining complex is essentially three very good restaurants in one. Lan Na Thai does flawless domestic with an emphasis on regional Thai dishes, Misaki handles the Japanese end of things, while Hazara dabbles in exotic-sounding 'North Indian frontier cuisine'.

BED SUPPERCLUB

Map p126   International $$$

☎ 0 2651 3537; www.bedsupperclub.com; 26 Soi 11, Th Sukhuvmit; 3-course set menu Sun-Thu 1450B, 4-course set menu Fri & Sat 1850B; ☺ 8-11pm; Ⓡ Nana exit 3

It's the modern equivalent of breakfast in bed, except that it's not breakfast and your 'bed' is a gigantic white tube that you share with other diners. Regardless, leave your nightclothes at home and come for Aussie chef Cameron Stuart's modern eclectic cuisine, which relies heavily on local Thai ingredients. Friday sees a surprise four-course menu.

KUPPA Map p126   International $$$

☎ 0 2663 0495; 39 Soi 16, Th Sukhumvit; mains 165-695B; ☺ 10am-11pm Tue-Sun; Ⓜ Sukhumvit exit 2; Ⓡ Asok exit 4

For Bangkok's ladies who lunch, Kuppa is something of a second home. Resembling an expansive living room, this place fancies itself as a 'tea and coffee trader' and the coffee is truly among the best in town. Thankfully the eats are just as good, in particular the spot-on Western-style pastries and sweets.

Kuppa is located a long walk down Soi 16; to find it, simply look for the Mercedes-laden car park peopled with loitering chauffeurs.

SUKHUMVIT PLAZA (KOREAN TOWN) Map p126   Korean $$$

cnr Soi 12 & Th Sukhumvit; ☺ 11am-midnight; Ⓜ Sukhumvit exit 3; Ⓡ Asok exit 2

Known around Bangkok as 'Korean Town', this multistorey complex is the city's best destination for authentic 'Seoul' food. Local residents swear by Arirang (☎ 0 2653 0177; ground fl, Sukhumvit Plaza; dishes 120-350B), although there are a few cheaper places in the complex as well.

BO.LAN

Map p126   Thai $$$

☎ 0 2260 2962; www.bolan.co.th; 42 Soi Rongnarong Phichai Songkhram, Soi 26, Th Sukhumvit; set meal 1500B; ☺ 6.30pm-midnight Tues-Fri, 11.30am-3pm & 6.30pm-midnight Sat & Sun; Ⓡ Phrom Phong exit 4

Upscale Thai is usually not worth the bill, but this chic new restaurant, started up by two former chefs of London's Michelin-starred Nahm, is the exception. Bo and Dylan (Bo.lan, a play on words that also means 'ancient') take a scholarly approach to Thai cuisine, and perfectly executed set meals featuring full-flavoured regional Thai dishes are the results of this tuition.

RUEN MALLIKA Map p126   Thai $$$

☎ 0 2663 3211; www.ruenmallika.com; sub-soi off Soi 22, Th Sukhumvit; mains 150-450B; ☺ 11am-11pm; Ⓜ Sukhumvit exit 2; Ⓡ Asok exit 4

Thai restaurateurs have tourists figured out: convert an old teak house into a restaurant and they will come, regardless of the food. Ruen Mallika ups the ante by offering exquisite dishes, like dizzyingly spicy *nám prík* (a thick dipping sauce with vegetables and herbs) and soulful chicken wrapped in banana leaves. The surrounding garden supplies the ingredients for the deep-fried flower dish, a house speciality.

The restaurant is a little tricky to find; approach from Soi 22 off Th Ratchadapisek.

BOURBON ST BAR & RESTAURANT

Map p126   American $$

☎ 0 2259 0328; www.bourbonstbkk.com; 29/4-6 Soi 22, Th Sukhumvit; mains 150-495B; ☺ 7am-1am; Ⓡ Phrom Phong exit 6

Although the 'spicy' reputation of New Orleans cuisine will probably make most Thais chuckle, any restaurant run by a man who owns a crayfish farm, stuffs his own andouille and has written a cookbook on spicy food is obviously serious about eats. Stop by on Monday, when the traditional New Orleans dinner of red beans and rice is served buffet-style.

NASIR AL-MASRI

Map p126   Egyptian $$

☎ 0 2253 5582; 4/6 Soi 3/1, Th Sukhumvit; mains 65-350B; ☺ 8am-5am; Ⓡ Nana exit 1

Part restaurant, part shrine to the glories of stainless-steel furnishings, this popular Egyptian joint simply can't be missed. This is Muslim food, with the emphasis on meat, meat and more meat, but the kitchen also knocks off some brilliant veggie mezze as well. Enhance your post-prandial digestion and catch up on the Arabic-language TV news with a puff on the hookah in the super-casual smoking room upstairs.

SPRING Map p126 International $$

☎ 0 2392 2747; 199 Soi Promsri, Soi 39, Th Sukhumvit; mains 140-350B; 🕙 11.30am-2.30pm & 6-10.30pm; 🚇 Phrom Phong exit 3

The expansive lawn of this smartly reconverted '70s-era house is probably the only chance you'll ever have to witness Bangkok's fair and beautiful willingly exposing themselves to the elements. The pan-Asian cuisine can be hit and miss, but the desserts, with names like Better Than Sex, are as almost good as they sound.

MOKKORI Map p126 Japanese $$

☎ 0 2392 0811; 8/3 Soi 55 (Thong Lor), Th Sukhumvit; mains 70-130B; 🕙 11am-midnight; 🚇 Thong Lo exit 3

You know you're in the right place if, upon entering this restaurant, the staff drop everything they're doing and scream at you. Tiny Mokkori serves Japanese-style ramen in a resoundingly authentic setting, and many agree it does the best bowl in town. In addition to noodles, be sure to order the wonderfully simple snack of cucumber chunks served with a spicy miso dipping sauce.

TAPAS CAFÉ Map p126 Spanish $$

☎ 0 2651 2947; www.tapasiarestaurants. com; 1/25 Soi 11, Th Sukhumvit; mains 90-800B; 🕙 11am-1am; 🚇 Nana exit 3; 🛜

Although it's the least expensive of Bangkok's Spanish joints, a visit to this newcomer is in no way a compromise. Vibrant tapas, refreshing sangria and an open, airy atmosphere make Tapas Café well worth the visit. Come before 7pm, when tapas are buy-two-get-one-free. Tapas Café is located nearly next door to Suk 11 Hostel.

ANA'S GARDEN Map p126 Thai $$

☎ 0 2391 1762; 67 Soi 55, Th Sukhumvit; mains 150-250B; 🕙 5pm-midnight; 🚇 Thong Lo exit 3

Ana's lush garden of broad-leafed palms and purring fountains will almost make you forget about the urban jungle on the other side. The spicy *yam tòo-a ploo* (wing bean salad) and the house speciality grilled chicken, on the other hand, will leave no doubts about which city you're in.

CABBAGES & CONDOMS
Map p126 Thai $$

☎ 0 2229 4611; Soi 12, Th Sukhumvit; mains 100-350B; 🕙 11am-10pm; Ⓜ Sukhumvit exit 3; 🚇 Asok exit 2

'Be fed and be sheathed' is the motto of the restaurant outreach program of the Population & Community Development Association (PDA), a sex education/AIDS prevention organisation. And likewise, for many visitors to Bangkok, this quirky garden restaurant has served as an equally 'safe' introduction to Thai food. Thankfully it's done relatively well. This is a good place to gauge the Thai staples, such as the rich green curry, or the briny *pàt pàk bûng fai daang* (flash-fried water spinach). Instead of after-meal mints, diners receive packaged condoms, and all proceeds go towards PDA educational programs in Thailand.

JE NGOR Map p126 Thai-Chinese $$

☎ 0 2258 8008; www.jengor-seafoods.com; 68/2 Soi 20, Th Sukhumvit; mains 100-500B; 🕙 11am-2pm & 5-11pm; Ⓜ Sukhumvit; 🚇 Asoke

Je Ngor proffers banquet-sized servings of tasty Thai-Chinese dishes in a banquet-like setting. The Sukhumvit branch of this

SUPERMARKETS

Are you an American in need of a peanut butter fix or an Aussie craving Vegemite? Don't fret, as Bangkok is home to an abundance of well-stocked international grocery stores.

- Foodland (Map p126; ☎ 0 2254 2179; ground fl, Nai Lert Building, Soi 5, Th Sukhumvit; 🕙 24hr) Particularly popular with Muslim visitors and residents, this branch of Foodland stocks all manner of international food items.
- Gourmet Market (Map p108; basement, Siam Paragon, 991/1 Th Phra Ram I, Siam Sq; 🕙 10am-10.30pm) The expansive basement-level Gourmet Paradise is as the name describes, and the attached supermarket carries a wide range of Western-style staples. There's also a branch on the 5th floor of Emporium (p150).
- Tops Market (Map p108; basement, Central Chidlom, 1027 Th Ploenchit; 🕙 10am-10pm) This branch of Tops Market has a wide selection of imported foods, particularly deli items from Europe.
- Villa Market (Map p126; ☎ 0 2662 1000; www.villamarket.com; Soi 33, Th Sukhumvit; 🕙 24hr) The main branch of Bangkok's most well stocked international grocery store is the place to pick up necessities from Cheerios to cheddar cheese. There are several branches around town including near Ari and Nana Skytrain stations – check the website for locations.

HOTEL BUFFET BONANZA

Sunday brunch has become something of a Bangkok institution, particularly among resident foreigners, and virtually every large hotel in town puts together decadent buffets on every other day as well. Reservations are generally required, and the following choices will leave you with more than simply a distended stomach.

- Chocolate Buffet (Map p122; ☎ 0 2344 8888; www.sukhothai.com; Sukhothai Hotel, 13/3 Th Sathon Tai; 790B; ☼ 2-6pm Fri-Sun) For those who love the sweet stuff, the Sukhothai Hotel offers a unique entirely cocoa-based high tea.

- Four Seasons Sunday Brunch (Map p108; ☎ 0 2250 1000; Four Seasons Hotel, 155 Th Ratchadamri, Ploenchit; 2340B; ☼ 11.30am-3pm Sun) All of the Four Seasons' highly regarded restaurants, Shintaro, Biscotti and Madison, set up steam tables for their decadent Sunday brunch buffet.

- ISO (Map p108; ☎ 0 2253 0123; www.swissotel.com; Swissotel Nai Lert Park, 2 Th Withayu, Ploenchit; per minute 5B; ☼ 11.30am-2pm Mon-Fri) Bangkok's biggest eaters have been raving about the Swissotel Nai Lert Park's international buffet that costs 5B per minute. Clock in (we're not speaking figuratively here) and enjoy everything from sushi to sweets.

- Lord Jim (Map p116; ☎ 0 2655 9900; Mandarin Oriental, Soi 38, Th Charoen Krung, Riverside; 1500B; ☼ noon-2pm Mon-Sat, 11am-3pm Sun) Even if you can't afford to stay at the Oriental Hotel, you should save up for the hotel's riverside seafood buffet.

- Marriott Café (Map p126; ☎ 0 2656 7700; ground fl, JW Marriott, 4 Soi 2, Th Sukhumvit; ☼ 11am-3pm) American-style abundance fills the buffet tables with fresh oysters, seafood, pasta and international nibbles at its daily buffet. There are also activities for children.

- Rang Mahal (Map p126; ☎ 0 2261 7100; 26th fl, Rembrandt Hotel, 19 Soi 20, Th Sukhumvit; 848B; ☼ 11am-2.30pm Sun) Couple views from this restaurant's 26th floor with an all-Indian buffet, and you have one of the most popular Sunday destinations for Bangkok's South Asian expat community.

- Sunday Jazzy Brunch (Map p126; ☎ 0 2649 8353; 1st fl, Sheraton Grande Sukhumvit, 250 Th Sukhumvit; 1850B; ☼ 11.30am-3pm Sun) If you require more than just victuals, then consider the Sheraton's Sunday brunch, which unites all the hotel's restaurant outlets to a theme of live jazz.

lauded Thai franchise is probably not an ideal choice for a first date, but it would be a great locale for grandma's birthday dinner. The relatively short, seafood-heavy menu features rarities such as *sôm ɗam ɓoo dorng* (papaya salad with preserved crab) and baked rice with preserved olive.

NEW SRI FAH
Map p126   Thai-Chinese $$
☎ 0 2258 2649; www.newsrifa33.com; 12/19-21 Soi 33, Th Sukhumvit; mains 80-450B; ☼ 5pm-3am; 🚇 Phrom Phong exit 5
This former Chinatown shophouse restaurant, originally opened in 1955, has relocated to a tight but classy location in new Bangkok. Just about anything from the Thai-Chinese seafood-heavy menu is bound to satisfy, but we particularly love the stir-fried minced pork with salted black olive, and the stir-fried water mimosa.

IMOYA Map p126   Japanese $
☎ 0 2663 5185; 3rd fl, Terminal Shop Cabin, 2/17-19 Soi 24, Th Sukhumvit; mains 40-150B; ☼ 6pm-midnight; 🚇 Phrom Phong exit 4

Temporarily set aside thoughts of Bangkok and whisk yourself back to 1950s Tokyo. A visit to this well-hidden Japanese restaurant, with its antique ads, wood panelling and wall of sake bottles, is like taking a trip in a time machine. Even the prices of the better-than-decent Eastern-style pub grub haven't caught up with modern times.

BOON TONG KIAT SINGAPORE HAINANESE CHICKEN RICE
Map p126   Singaporean $
☎ 0 2390 2508; 440/5 Soi 55, Th Sukhumvit; mains 60-100B; ☼ 10am-10pm; 🚇 Thong Lo exit 3 & taxi
The unofficial national dish of Singapore is treated with holy reverence at this humble eatery. After taking in the exceedingly detailed and ambitious chicken rice manifesto written on the walls, order a plate of the restaurant's namesake and witness how a dish can be so simple, yet so delicious. And while you're there you'd be daft not to order *rojak*, the spicy/sour fruit 'salad', which is referred to here tongue-in-cheek as 'Singapore Som Tam'.

EATING THANON SUKHUMVIT

BHARANI CUISINE (SANSAB BOAT NOODLE) Map p126   Thai $

☎ 0 2664 4454; Soi 23, Th Sukhumvit; mains 35-200B; ⏰ 10am-10pm; Ⓜ Sukhumvit exit 2; 🚇 Asok exit 3

This cozy Thai restaurant dabbles in a bit of everything, from ox tongue stew to rice fried with shrimp paste, but the real reason to come is for the rich, meaty 'boat noodles' – so called because they used to be sold from boats plying the *klorng* of Ayuthaya.

SOI 38 NIGHT MARKET

Map p126   Thai-Chinese $

Soi 38, Th Sukhumvit; mains 30-60B; ⏰ 8pm-3am; 🚇 Thong Lo exit 4

It's not the best street food in town by a long shot, but after a hard night of clubbing on Sukhumvit, you can be forgiven for believing so. If you're going sober, stick to the knot of 'famous' vendors tucked into an alley on the right-hand side as you enter the street; the flame-fried *pàt tai* and herbal fish ball noodles are musts.

THONGLEE

Map p126   Thai $

☎ 0 2258 1983; Soi 20, Th Sukhumvit; mains 50-100B; ⏰ 9am-8pm, closed 3rd Sun of month; Ⓜ Sukhumvit exit 2; 🚇 Asok exit 4

With the owners' possessions overflowing into the dining room, a heavily laden spirit shrine and tacky synthetic tablecloths, Thonglee is the epitome of a typical Thai restaurant. However, in the sea of foreign food that is Th Sukhumvit, this is exactly what makes it stand out. Thonglee offers a few dishes you won't find elsewhere, like *mŏo pàt gà·bì* (pork fried with shrimp paste) and *mèe gròrp* (sweet-and-spicy crispy fried noodles).

YUY LEE Map p126   Thai $

☎ 0 2258 4600; 25 Soi 31, Th Sukhumvit; mains 25-60B; ⏰ 10am-8pm Mon-Sat; 🚇 Phrom Phong exit 5

This aged but spotless eatery serves a variety of dishes, but most folks come for the northern Thai noodle duo of *kôw soy* (wheat noodles in a curry broth) and *kà·nŏm jeen nám ngée·o* (fresh rice noodles in a tomato and pork broth). The former, although not bad for Bangkok, can't compete with the real deal from Chiang Mai, but the latter is an excellent take on a hard-to-find dish.

GREATER BANGKOK

Although it will involve something of a schlep for most visitors, an excursion to Bangkok's suburbs can be a profoundly tasty experience. The northern reaches of the city in particular are home to heaps of restaurants that wouldn't even consider toning down their food to suit foreigners. The city's outskirts are also a particularly great place to sample regional Thai cuisine.

BAAN KLANG NAM 1

Map p132   Thai $$$

☎ 0 2292 0175; www.baanklangnam.net; 3792/106 Soi 14, Th Phra Ram III, Greater Bangkok; mains 200-400B; ⏰ 11am-midnight; 🚇 Saphan Taksin exit 4 & taxi

Near Khlong Toey Port, this rustic wooden house is a favourite of the Thai matriarchs and guests at nearby Montien Riverside. The cost of seafood here is a little higher than at other riverside restaurants, but reflects the quality. Crab, prawns and whole white fish are among the hits that make people swoon.

NANG LOENG MARKET

Map p64   Thai $

btwn Soi 8-10, Th Nakhon Sawan, Central Bangkok; ⏰ 10am-2pm Mon-Sat; 🚌 air-con 72

Dating back to 1899, this atmospheric fresh market is a wonderful glimpse of old Bangkok, not to mention a great place to grab a bite. Nang Loeng is renowned for its Thai sweets, and at lunchtime is also an excellent place to fill up on savouries. Try a bowl of handmade egg noodles at Rung Rueng (☎ 0 2281 9755; 62/147 Soi 8, Th Nakhon Sawan) or the wonderful curries across the way at Ratana (☎ 0 2281 0237).

OR TOR KOR MARKET

Map p132   Thai $

Th Kampangphet, Greater Bangkok; mains 30-60B; ⏰ 10am-5pm; Ⓜ Kamphaeng Phet exit 3

Or Tor Kor is Bangkok's highest-quality fruit and agricultural market, and sights such as toddler-sized mangoes and dozens of pots full of curries are reason enough to visit. The vast majority of vendors' goods are takeaway only, but a small food court and a few informal restaurants exist, including Rot Det, which does excellent stir-fries and curries, and Sut Jai Kai Yaang, just south of the market, which does sublime Isan.

top picks

REGIONAL VICTUALS

- Jay So (p171) Supreme northeastern Thai – if you can handle the heat.
- Khrua Aroy Aroy (p171) The closest you'll get to an authentic southern Thai curry shack without hopping on a train.
- Mallika Restaurant (p178) Authentic southern Thai flavours in a comfortable setting.
- Nang Loeng Market (p177) A variety of vendors hawking true central Thai flavour.
- Yuy Lee (p177) Northern-style noodles in the heart of Bangkok.

To get here, take the MRT to Kampheng Phet station and exit on the side opposite Chatuchak (the exit says 'Marketing Organization for Farmers').

PHAT THAI ARI
Map p64   Thai $$

☎ 0 2270 1654; Th Phahonyothin, Central Bangkok; mains 70-120B; ◌ 11am-10pm Mon-Sat; ◉ Ari exit 4

One of Bangkok's most famous *pàt tai* restaurants has moved from its namesake soi to a new home across the street. Try the innovative 'noodle-less' version, where long strips of crispy green papaya are substituted for the traditional rice noodles from Chanthaburi. The restaurant is located on the small sub-soi just south of Soi 8 that is labelled 'Phahonyothin Center'.

ROSDEE Map 132   Thai-Chinese $

☎ 0 2331 1375; 2357 Th Sukhumvit, cnr Soi 95/1, Greater Bangkok; mains 40-120B; ◌ 8am-9pm; ◉ On Nut exit 3 & taxi

This stodgy family eating hall is never going to make it on to any international magazine's 'hot list' of places to dine, but the elderly bow-tied staff does give the place a certain element of charm. Instead, Rosdee is known for its consistently tasty, well-executed Thai-Chinese favourites such as the garlicky *aw sùan* (oysters fried with egg and a sticky batter), or the house speciality, braised goose.

YUSUP Map 132   Thai-Muslim $

☎ 0851 362 864; Kaset-Navamin Hwy, Greater Bangkok; mains 30-90B; ◌ 11am-2pm; ◉ Mo Chit exit 3 & taxi

The Thai-language sign in front of this restaurant boldly says *rah·chah kôw mòk* (King of Biryani) and Yusup backs it up with flawless biryani (try the unusual but delicious *kôw mòk ɓlah*; fish biryani), not to mention mouth-puckeringly sour oxtail soup and decadent *gaang mát·sà·màn*. For dessert try *roh·đi wăhn*, a paratha-like crispy pancake topped with sweetened condensed milk and sugar – a dish that will send most carb-paranoid Westerners running away screaming.

To find Yusup, get in a taxi heading north from Mor Chit BTS station and ask the driver to take you to Th Kaset-Navamin (also locally known as the *sên đàt mài*). Turn right at the Kaset intersection and continue about 1km past the first stoplight; Yusup is on the left-hand side.

DRINKING & NIGHTLIFE

top picks

DRINKING & NIGHTLIFE

Disregard the tired cliché of Bangkok's nightlife as a one-trick pony. The infamous girlie-bar scene may still be going just as strong as it has been for the last 30 years but, despite what your uncle told you, having a good time in Bangkok does not necessarily have to involve ping-pong balls or bar fines. Just like in any other big international city, the drinking and partying scene in Bangkok ranges from points classy to trashy, and touches on just about everything in between.

The powers that be, however, take a slightly different view on fun, and would seemingly rather have us watching traditional dance performances and being tucked into bed by 9pm. Since 2004 the vast majority of Bangkok's bars and clubs have been ordered by authorities to close by 1am. A complicated zoning system sees venues in designated 'entertainment areas', including RCA (Royal City Avenue), Th Silom, and parts of Th Sukhumvit, open until 2am, but even these 'later' licenses are subject to police whimsy. Despite the resulting financial losses and negative impact on tourism (not to mention Bangkok's reputation), the policy has been popular among Thais, and there is little chance of seeing any changes to the policy in the near future.

The good news is that everything old is new again. Th Khao San, that former outpost of foreigner frugality, has undergone something of an upscale renaissance and is now more popular with the locals than ever. In addition to the main strip, Th Rambutri and Th Phra Athit also draw drinkers and fun seekers from across the city, and the world. And RCA (Royal City Avenue), a suburban nightclub zone previously associated with gum-snapping Thai teenagers, has finally graduated from high school and is drawing in dancers and drinkers of all ages and races.

DRINKS

Bangkok is justifiably renowned for its food and nightlife, but markedly less so for its beverages. Yet drinks are the glue that fuse these elements, and without them, that market tour or ladyboy cabaret show would be less entertaining. From potable domestic brews to a rainbow of refreshing fruit drinks, hydrating in Bangkok is nearly always a pleasure.

FRUIT DRINKS

With the abundance of fruit growing in Thailand, the variety of juices and shakes available in markets, street stalls and restaurants is extensive. The all-purpose term for fruit juice is *nám pŏn·lá·mái*. When a blender or extractor is used, you've got *nám kán* (squeezed juice), hence *nám sàp·Bà·rót kán* is freshly squeezed pineapple juice. *Nám ôy* (sugar-cane juice) is a Thai favourite and a very refreshing accompaniment to *gaang* dishes. A similar juice from the sugar palm, *nám đahn sòt,* is also very good, and both are full of vitamins and minerals. Mixed fruit blended with ice is *nám Ɓan* (literally 'mixed juice'), as in *nám má·lá·gor Ɓan*, a papaya shake.

BEER

Advertised with such slogans as '*Ɓrà·têht row, bee·a row*' ('our land, our beer'), the Singha label is considered the quintessential Thai beer by *fà·ràng* (Westerners) and locals alike. Pronounced *sǐng*, this pilsner claims about half the domestic market. Singha's original recipe was formulated in 1934 by Thai nobleman Phya Bhirom Bhakdi, the first Thai to earn a brewmaster's diploma in Germany. The barley for Singha is grown in Thailand, while the hops are imported from Germany. The alcohol content for Singha beer is a heady 6%. It is sold in brown glass bottles (330ml and 660ml) with a shiny gold lion on the label, as well as in cans (330ml). It is available on tap as *bee·a sòt* (draught beer) – much tastier than either bottled or canned brew – in many Bangkok pubs and restaurants.

Singha's biggest rival, Beer Chang, pumps the alcohol content up to 7%. Beer Chang has managed to gain an impressive following mainly because it retails at a significantly lower price than Singha and thus offers more bang per baht.

Boon Rawd (the makers of Singha) responded with its own cheaper brand, Leo. Sporting a black-and-red leopard label, Leo

A THAI-PILSNER PRIMER

We relish the look of horror on the faces of Thailand newbies when the waitress casually plunks several cubes of ice into their pilsners. Before you rule out completely this supposed blasphemy, there are a few reasons why we and the Thais actually prefer our beer on the rocks. Firstly, despite all the alleged accolades displayed on most bottles, Thai beer does not possess the most sophisticated bouquet in the world and is best drunk as cold as possible. Also, if you haven't already noticed, the weather in Thailand is often extremely hot, another reason it makes sense to maintain your beer at maximum chill. And lastly, domestic brews are generally quite high in alcohol and the ice helps to dilute this, preventing dehydration and one of those infamous Beer Chang hangovers the next day. Taking these theories to the extreme, some laces in Thailand serve something called *beea wún* (jelly beer), beer that has been semifrozen until it reaches a deliciously slushy and refreshing consistency.

If you tire of the mainstream domestic stuff, try the decent home-brewed German-style beers at Tawan Daeng German Brewhouse (p190) or imported Erdinger, Weihenstephaner and others at the Suan Lum Night Bazaar (p147). Londoner (Map p126; ☎ 0 2261 0238/9; basement, UBC II Bldg, cnr Soi 33 & Th Sukhumvit) brews a passable English-style bitter, and Molly Malone's (p184) has imported Kilkenny and Guinness on tap, not to mention several other imports. And HOBS (p183) specialises in the beers of Belgium, arguably some of the world's greatest. However, a brief warning: it is a painfully obvious sign that you have been in Thailand too long if your preference is to put ice in your draught Hoegaarden.

costs only slightly more than Beer Chang but is similarly high in alcohol.

Dutch-licensed but Thailand-brewed Heineken comes third after Singha and Chang in sales rankings. Similar 'domestic imports' include Asahi and San Miguel. Other Thai-brewed beers, all at the lower end of the price spectrum, include Cheers and Beer Thai. More variation in Thai beer brands is likely in the coming years as manufacturers scramble to command market share by offering a variety of flavours and prices.

RICE WHISKY & RUM

Rice whisky is a favourite of the working class in Bangkok, since it's more affordable than beer. It has a sharp, sweet taste not unlike rum, with an alcohol content of 35%. The most famous brand for many years was Mekong (pronounced '*mâa kŏng*'), but currently the most popular brand is the slightly more expensive rum, Sang Som. Both come in 750ml bottles called *glom* or in 375ml flask-shaped bottles called *baan*. Thais normally drink whisky with ice and plenty of soda water.

Then there are the more-expensive barley-based whiskies produced in Thailand, which appeal to the can't-afford-Johnnie-Walker-yet set. Such whiskies include Blue Eagle, 100 Pipers and Spey Royal, each with a 40% alcohol content. These come dressed up in shiny boxes, much like the expensive imported whiskies they are imitating.

DRINKING

Bangkok's watering holes cover the spectrum from English-style pubs where you can comfortably sit with a pint and the paper, to chic dens where the fair and beautiful go to be seen, not to imbibe. A laundry list of beverages is available, though alcohol prices are relatively more than, say, cab rides or street food.

Because food is so integral to any Thai outing, most bars have tasty dishes that are absent-mindedly nibbled between toasts. Bars don't have cover charges, but they do strictly enforce closing time at 1am, sometimes earlier if they suspect trouble from the cops.

AMOROSA
Map p68   Bar

☎ 0 2221 9158; www.arunresidence.com; Arun Residence, 36-38 Soi Pratu Nok Yoong; ⏰ 6-11pm)

Perched above the Arun Residence, Amorosa takes advantage of a location directly above the river and opposite Wat Arun to make it one of the best places for a sundowner in Bangkok. Watching boats ply their way along the royal river as Wat Arun is lit up behind is richly evocative of traditional ideas of the East. A memorable end to a day or start to an evening.

BACCHUS WINE BAR
Map p108   Wine Bar

☎ 0 2650 8986; 20/6-7 Soi Ruam Rudi, Ploenchit; ⏰ 6pm-midnight; 🚇 Phloen Chit exit 4

THE WHISKY SET

Thai beer is generally more miss than hit, so the next time you're out on the town, why not drink like the Thais do and order a bottle of whisky?

Your first step is to choose a brand. For a particularly decadent night out, the industry standard is a bottle of *bláak* (Johnnie Walker Black Label). Those on a budget can go for the cheaper imported labels such as Red Label or Benmore, and a rock-bottom-priced, but fun, night can be had on domestically produced spirits such as 100 Pipers or Sang Som. And it's not unusual to bring your own bottle to many Thai bars, although some might charge a modest corkage fee.

As any Thai can tell you, your next immediate concern is mixers. These will take the form of several bottles of soda water and a bottle or two of Coke, along with a pail of ice. Most waiters will bring these to you as a matter of course.

Mixing is the easiest step and requires little or no action on your part; your skilled waiter will fill your glass with ice, followed by a shot of whisky, a splash of soda, a top-off of Coke and, finally, a swirl with the ice tongs to bring it all together.

If you can't finish your bottle, shame on you, but don't fret, as it's perfectly normal to keep it at the bar. Simply tell your trusted waiter, who will write your name and the date on the bottle and keep it for your next visit.

Wine bars are still a new and relatively uncommon concept in Bangkok. Bacchus was among the first, and still sets the aesthetic standard with exposed brick walls, floating stairs and sculpture seating. Despite the slightly upscale setting, it's a friendly enough place to down a glass or two of one of the 400 varieties of wine, or cop a nibble from the lengthy menu of tapas and appetisers.

BAGHDAD CAFÉ Map p82   Bar
☎ 0850 400 054; 15 Th Samsen, Banglamphu; ⏰ 8pm-1am; 🚌 air-con 3 & 16, ordinary 3, 15 & 16; 🚤 Tha Phra Athit (Banglamphu, N13)
Roughly the size of a large closet and decorated with a mishmash of vaguely Middle East–related photos and paraphernalia, this is the place to simultaneously suck down a Singha and a *sheesha*. And when you've had your fill it's just a door over to the rocking live tunes at Ad Here the 13th (p187).

BANGKOK BAR Map p126   Bar/Restaurant
☎ 0 2714 3366; Soi 2, Soi 63 (Ekamai), Th Sukhumvit; ⏰ 8pm-1am; 🚉 Ekkamai exit 1
Bounce with Thai indie kids at this fun but astonishingly uncreatively named bar. There's live music, and the eats are strong enough to make Bangkok Bar a dinner destination in itself. And we double-dog dare you to walk a straight line after two Mad Dogs, Bangkok Bar's infamous house drink.

BARBICAN
Map p116   Bar
☎ 0 2234 3590; www.greatbritishpub.com; 9/4-5 Soi Thaniya, Silom; ⏰ 6pm-1am; Ⓜ Si Lom exit 2; 🚉 Sala Daeng exit 1

Decked out in slate-grey and blonde wood, this upscale-ish pub is an oasis of subdued cool in a strip consisting mostly of Japanese-frequented massage parlours. Where else could you suck down a few cocktails with friends from Thailand, Singapore and Norway, and then stumble out to find a line of Thai women dressed like cheap prom dates reciting 'Hello, massage' in faulty Japanese?

BLACK SWAN
Map p126   Bar/Restaurant
☎ 0 2229 4542; www.blackswanbkk.com; 326/8-9 Th Sukhumvit; ⏰ 9-1am; Ⓜ Sukhumvit exit 3; 🚉 Asok exit 4
Liable to bring a tear to the eye of a homesick Brit, the combination of supping mates, dining families and bad decor make the Black Swan the most authentic of Bangkok's numerous English pubs. Come on Friday when you can enjoy your draught bitter with fresh fish flown directly from Scotland.

CAFÉ TRIO
Map p108   Bar
☎ 0 2252 6572; 36/11-12 Soi Lang Suan, Ploenchit; ⏰ 6pm-1am, closed 2nd & 4th Sun of month; 🚉 Chit Lom exit 4
This jazz bar offers live music on an irregular basis – it's best to check ahead. The real highlights are the laid-back local atmosphere and the proprietor, Patti, whose artwork graces the walls and whose laughter and boisterous conversation have the ability to render music redundant.

CHEAP CHARLIE'S
Map p126   Bar
Soi 11, Th Sukhumvit; 6pm-1am Mon-Sat; Nana exit 3

You're bound to have a mighty difficult time convincing your Thai friends to go to Th Sukhumvit only to sit at an outdoor wooden shack decorated with buffalo skulls and wagon wheels. Fittingly, Charlie's draws a staunchly foreign crowd who don't mind a bit of kitsch and sweat with their Singha.

COCO WALK
Map p108   Bar
87/70 Th Phayathai, Siam Sq; 6pm-1am; Ratchathewi exit 2

This covered compound is a smorgasbord of pubs, bars and live music popular with Thai university students. The Tube left its heart in London, and is heavy on Brit Pop, Chilling House Café features a few pool tables and Thai hits played by live acoustic guitar, and 69 sets the pace with cover bands playing Western rock staples and current hits.

COSMIC CAFÉ
Map p132   Bar
0816 059 469; Block C, Royal City Ave (RCA), off Th Phra Ram IX, Greater Bangkok; 7pm-2am; Phra Ram 9 exit 3 & taxi

Decidedly more low-key than most places on RCA, Cosmic calls itself a cafe and looks like a live-music club but in reality is more of a bar… Despite the slight identity crisis, this is a fun place to drink, rock to live music and meet Thai-style.

COYOTE ON CONVENT
Map p116   Bar/Restaurant
0 2631 2325; www.coyoteonconvent.com; 1/2 Th Convent, Silom; 11-1am; Si Lom exit 2; Sala Daeng exit 2

Coyote on Convent serves decent but pricey Mexican nosh with a relatively light dose of kitsch. But what really keeps the people coming, in particular Bangkok's female population, are the 75+ varieties of margaritas. Come Wednesday evening, when from 6pm to 8pm the icy drinks are distributed free to all women who pass through the door. On weekdays the frosty drinks are buy-one-get-one-free from 3pm to 7pm.

DIPLOMAT BAR
Map p108   Bar
0 2690 9999; Conrad Hotel, 87 Th Withayu, Ploenchit; 5pm-1am; Phloen Chit exit 5

Named for its location in the middle of the embassy district, this is one of the few hotel lounges that the locals make a point of visiting. Choose from an expansive list of innovative martinis and sip to live jazz, played gracefully at conversation level.

HAPPY MONDAY
Map p126   Bar/Restaurant
0 2714 3935; Ekkamai Shopping Mall, Soi 10, Soi 63 (Ekkamai), Th Sukhumvit; 7pm-1am Mon-Sat; Ekkamai exit 1 & taxi

This vaguely hidden pub follows the tried and true Ekkamai/Thong Lor formula of retro furniture, a brief menu and some truly bizarre house drinks. The diverse soundtrack, spun by local and visiting DJs, sets it apart.

HOBS (HOUSE OF BEERS)
Map p126   Bar/Restaurant
0 2392 3513; 522/3 Soi 16, Soi 55 (Thong Lor), Th Sukhumvit; 10am-1am; Thong Lo exit 3 & taxi

Arguably the word's best brews, Belgian beers have been fleetingly available around Bangkok for a while now, but have found a permanent home at this new pub. Be sure to accompany your beer with a bowl of crispy *frites*, served here Belgian-style with mayonnaise.

top picks

LITTLE-KNOWN BANGKOK BARS YOU CAN CLAIM TO HAVE 'DISCOVERED'

- **Lollipop** (p184) A rockin' shack in an old Bangkok neighbourhood.
- **Nest** (p184) Sukhumvit Soi 11's most well-concealed nightlife spot.
- **Parking Toys** (p189) Although certainly not a secret any longer, its distant location lends it an undiscovered aura.
- **Bangkok Bar** (p182) Located just far enough off one of Bangkok's main party strips to maintain your street cred.
- **Sky Train Jazz Club** (p185) The hidden rooftop location will surprise even the locals.

DRINKING WITH THE STARS

In recent years we've seen Bangkok become New York's main competitor to the title of rooftop-bar capital of the world. And we mean rooftop in the most literal sense – often it's only a waist-high barrier that separates you from a surreal Bangkok sunset or Chao Phraya River, dozens of floors below. Throw in a stiff drink and a stiff breeze, and you have an experience few other cities can match.

Although many of the places below also offer food, the price tags are typically as lofty as the addresses so we recommend a sunset cocktail or two before heading elsewhere for dinner. Also, keep in mind that most hotel-bound bars vigorously enforce the ubiquitous 'no shorts, no flip-flops' dress code.

- Long Table (Map p126; ☎ 0 2302 2557; 25th fl, 48 Column Bldg, Soi 16, Th Sukhumvit; ☷ 5pm-2am; M Sukhumvit exit 3; ⊠ Asok exit 4) Not exactly a rooftopper, but the open-air section of this 25th-floor upmarket Thai restaurant-bar provides great views of one of Bangkok's busiest central districts. Most easily accessed via Th Ratchadaphisek.
- Moon Bar (Map p122; ☎ 0 2679 1200; www.banyantree.com; 61st fl, Banyan Tree Hotel, 21/100 Th Sathon Tai; ☷ 5pm-1am; M Lumphini exit 2) The Banyan Tree's Moon Bar kick-started the rooftop trend and as Bangkok continues to grow at a mad pace, the view from 61 floors up only gets better. Arrive well before sunset and grab a coveted seat to the right of the bar for the most impressive views.
- Nest (Map p126; ☎ 0 2255 0638; www.nestbangkok.com; 8th fl, Le Fenix Hotel, 33/33 Soi 11, Th Sukhumvit; ☷ 5pm-2am; ⊠ Nana exit 3) Perched eight floors above ground on the roof of Le Fenix Hotel, Nest is a chic maze of cleverly concealed sofas and inviting day-beds. A DJ soundtrack and one of the most interesting pub grub menus in town keep things down to earth.
- RedSky (Map p108; ☎ 0 2100 1234; 55th fl, Centara Grand, Central World Plaza, Siam Sq; ☷ 5pm-1am; ⊠ Chit Lom exit 9 to Sky Walk, Siam exit 6 to Sky Walk) Perched on the 55th floor of a striking new skyscraper, Bangkok's most recent rooftop dining venture is probably the most formal of the lot and boasts an extensive martini menu.
- Roof (Map p108; ☎ 0 2217 3070; Siam@Siam Design Hotel; 25th fl, 865 Th Phra Ram I, Siam Sq; ☷ 5.30pm-12.30am; ⊠ National Stadium exit 1) In addition to views of central Bangkok from 25 floors up, the Roof offers a dedicated personal martini sommelier and an extensive wine and champagne list.
- Sky Bar (Map p116; ☎ 0 2624 9555; 63rd fl, The Dome at State Tower, 1055 Th Silom; ☷ 6pm-1am; ⊠ Saphan Taksin exit 3) Allegedly one of the highest alfresco bars in the world, Sky Bar, located on the 63rd floor of this upmarket restaurant compound, provides heart-stopping views over Chao Phraya River.

JOOL'S BAR & RESTAURANT

Map p126   Bar/Restaurant

☎ 0 2252 6413; Soi 4 (Soi Nana Tai), Th Sukhumvit; ☷ 11am-midnight; ⊠ Nana exit 2

With the walls virtually covered with pictures of the bar's regulars, you'll feel like part of the crowd even if you're drinking alone. When things are buzzing, lots of Nana Plaza girly-bar vets take a breather here for a good-natured romp with beer buddies.

LOLLIPOP

Map p82   Bar/Restaurant

☎ 0 2252 6413; 1 Soi 1, Th Mahanop, Banglamphu; ☷ 5pm-1am Tue-Sun; 🚌 air-con 59, ordinary 42 & 59; 🚤 klorng boat to Tha Phan Fah

Hidden in a residential lane in a quiet corner of old Bangkok, this wooden Thai house refurbished in pastel colours has a small but dedicated following. The Thai indie bands that play here have a reputation for being as intense as the drinks are strong.

MOLLY MALONE'S

Map p116   Pub

☎ 0 2266 7160; www.mollymalonesbangkok.com; 1/5-6 Th Convent, Silom; ☷ 11-1am; M Si Lom exit 2; ⊠ Sala Daeng exit 2

The third and, we hope, final reincarnation of this Bangkok Irish staple has retained much of the faux-shamrock charm of its predecessor. Like most of its countryfolk, Molly's is equal parts game for a quiet pint alone or a rowdy night out with your friends.

OPERA RISERVA WINETHEQUE

Map p126   Wine Bar

☎ 0 2258 5601; www.operariserva.com; 53 Soi 39, Th Sukhumvit; ☷ 5.30pm-1am; ⊠ Phrom Phong exit 3 & taxi

Decked out in leather and wood and sporting a speakeasy feel, Opera's wine bar is more for the discreet conversationalist than the sensationalist. You're more than likely to find something you'll fancy from the week's wine pics, and an attractive and extensive menu of wine-friendly Italian-style meals and snacks is also available.

PHRANAKORN BAR
Map p82   Bar
☎ 0 2282 7507; 58/2 Soi Damnoen Klang Tai, Banglamphu; ☾ 8pm-1am; 🚌 air-con 59, ordinary 42 & 59; 🚤 klorng boat to Tha Phan Fah
It must have taken a true visionary to transform this characterless multilevel building into a warm, fun destination for a night out. Students and arty types make Phranakorn Bar a home away from hovel with eclectic decor and changing gallery exhibits.

RIVER BAR CAFÉ
Map p93   Bar/Restaurant
☎ 0 2879 1747; 405/1 Soi Chao Phraya, Th Racha-withi, Thonburi; ☾ 5pm-midnight; 🚤 klorng boat to Tha Saphan Krung Thon
Sporting a picture-perfect riverside location, good food and live music, River Bar Café combines all the essentials of a perfect Bangkok night out. Grab a table closest to the river to fully take advantage of the breeze, as well as to avoid noise fallout from the sometimes overly enthusiastic bands.

SHADES OF RETRO
Map p126   Bar
☎ 0818 248 011; Soi Thararom 2, Soi 55 (Thong Lor), Th Sukhumvit; ☾ 2pm-1am Mon-Sat; 🚇 Thong Lo exit 3 & taxi
As the name suggests, this eclectic place takes the vintage fad to the max. You'll have to climb around Vespas and Gnaw-gahyde sofas to reach your seat, but will be rewarded with friendly service, an eclectic domestic soundtrack (the people behind Shades also run the domestic indie label Small Room) and a drink menu that includes the elusive Beerlao Dark.

SKY TRAIN JAZZ CLUB
Map p113   Bar
☎ 0898 954 299; cnr Soi Rang Nam & Th Phayat-hai, Ratchathewi; ☾ 6pm-1am; 🚇 Victory Monument exit 2
A visit to this comically misnamed bar is more like chilling on the rooftop of a stoner guy's apartment than any jazz club we've ever been to. But there are indeed views of the Skytrain, jazz on occasion and a likeable speakeasy atmosphere. To find it, look for the sign and proceed up the scary graffiti-strewn stairway until you reach the roof.

SRIPOOM ESPRESSO BAR
Map p82   Bar
☎ 0 2281 4445; 95 Th Chakraphong, Banglamphu; ☾ 10am-1am; 🚌 air-con 3 & 16, ordinary 3, 15 & 16; 🚤 klorng boat to Tha Phra Athit (Banglamphu, N13)
During the day this industrial-themed hole in the wall serves a variety of coffee drinks and homemade baked goods. At night the lights dim and espresso morphs into some of the best mixed drinks in the area. There's a diverse soundtrack, and the room upstairs allows you to challenge your drinking mates to a game of Nintendo Wii.

TAKSURA
Map p82   Bar/Restaurant
☎ 0 2622 0708; 156/1 Th Tanao, Banglamphu; ☾ 6pm-1am; 🚌 air-con 59, ordinary 42 & 59; 🚤 klorng boat to Tha Phan Fah
There are no signs to lead you to this seemingly abandoned 93-year-old mansion in the heart of old Bangkok, which is all the better, according to the cool uni/artsy crowd that frequents the place. Take a seat outside to soak up the breezes and go Thai by ordering some spicy nibbles with your drinks.

TO-SIT
Map p108   Bar
☎ 0 2658 4001; www.tosit.com; Soi 3, Siam Sq; ☾ 6pm-1am; 🚇 Siam exit 2
Live, loud and sappy music, cheap and spicy food, good friends and cold beer: To-Sit epitomises everything a Thai university student could wish for on a night out. There are branches all over town (check the website), but the Siam Sq location has the advantage of being virtually the only option in an area that's buzzing during the day but dead at night.

WINE WHINGE
If you're a frequent imbiber of wine back home, you may feel obligated to temporarily shelve the habit while in Thailand. Import wine is subject to a litany of taxes (import, alcohol and luxury among them), making it among the most expensive anywhere in the world. A bottle of retail wine in Thailand typically costs 400% of its sticker price back home, or up to 600% if you're drinking in an upmarket restaurant. Even domestic wines are subject to many of the same taxes, making them only marginally cheaper than imported wines.

BANGLAMPHU PUB CRAWL

The Th Khao San of today offers Bangkok's greatest number and diversity of watering holes. Rather than be prescriptive, we've put together a do-it-yourself pub-crawl guide that points you in the direction of the neighbourhood's best drinking options.

Start your crawl with dinner and/or sunset drinks along Th Phra Athit. For Chao Phraya views try Old Phra Arthit Pier (Map p82; ☎ 0 2282 9202; 23 Th Phra Athit; ❧ 11am-midnight), an attractive wooden lounge-like bar and an open-air deck with intermittent views of the river, or Aquatini (Map p82; ☎ 0 2280 9955; 45/1 Th Phra Athit; ❧ 6.30am-1am), the riverside restaurant at Navalai River Resort.

From Th Phra Athit, turn into Soi Chana Songkhram where you begin Phase Two of your crawl: people-watching. Gecko Bar (Map p82; cnr Soi Chana Songkhram & Soi Rambutri; ❧ 6pm-1am) is a frugal and fun place to gawk at other patrons and passers by, or you can head over to Th Khao San where Center Khao Sarn (Map p82; ☎ 0 2282 4366; 80-84 Th Khao San; ❧ 24hr) offers front-row views of the human parade. Slightly cheaper are the two draught Singha stalls (Th Khao San; ❧ 4pm-midnight) along Th Khao San. For an entirely different perspective, the views from Roof Bar (Map p82; ☎ 0 2629 2301; 3rd fl, 183-185 Th Khao San; ❧ 7pm-1am) cannot be beaten.

If you'd rather listen than watch, a live acoustic soundtrack sets the pace at the numerous open-air pubs on Th Rambutri such as Molly Bar (Map p82; ☎ 0 2629 4074; 108 Th Rambutri; ❧ 8pm-1am), Suksabai (Map p82; ☎ 0 2629 0298; 96 Th Rambutri; ❧ 24hr) and Barlamphu (Map p82; ☎ 0 2282 2149; Th Rambutri; ❧ 11am-2am).

At this point you're probably going to need a short blast of air-con, and Mulligans (Map p82; ☎ 0 2629 4477; 1st fl, Buddy Lodge, 265 Th Khao San; ❧ 8am-midnight), a tidy Irish-themed bar, hits the spot.

It's now time to plant yourself at a proper bar for a while, and Hippie de Bar (Map p82; ☎ 0 2629 3508; 46 Th Khao San; ❧ 3pm-2am) boasts a great soundtrack and several levels of fun, both indoor and outdoor. If you prefer your music live, you could try Ad Here the 13th (opposite) for blues, or Brick Bar (opposite), for Thai pop and raucous ska. Alternatively, you could escape the Th Khao San scene altogether and cross Th Ratchadamnoen Nai to drink with artsy/indie Thai-types at Taksura (p185), Phranakorn Bar (p185) or Lollipop (p184).

If 1am is too early to call it a night, crawl over to Gazebo (p188), a rooftop lounge and disco that stays open until morning.

TUBA
Map p126   Bar/Restaurant

☎ 0 2622 0708; 30 Soi 21, Soi 63 (Ekamai), Th Sukhumvit; ❧ 6pm-2am; ❂ Ekkamai exit 1 & taxi

Used-furniture shop by day, Italian restaurant-bar by night. Oddly enough, this business formula is not entirely unheard of in Bangkok. Pull up a leatherette lounge and take the plunge and buy a whole bottle for once. And don't miss the delicious chicken wings.

VINO DI ZANOTTI
Map p122   Bar/Restaurant

☎ 0 2636 3811; 41 Soi Yommarat, Lumphini; ❧ 5pm-midnight; Ⓜ Si Lom exit 2; ❂ Sala Daeng exit 4

A branch of the nearby Italian institution of the same name, Vino keeps it casual with a wine cellar–like atmosphere, a huge wine list and lots of delicious nibbles. A jazz quartet keeps diners entertained until midnight.

WINE PUB
Map p113   Bar

☎ 0 2680 9999; www.pullmanbangkokkingpower. com; 2nd fl Pullman Bangkok King Power, 8/2 Soi Rang Nam, Th Phayathai, Ratchathewi; ❧ 6pm-2am; ❂ Victory Monument exit 2

If the upmarket but chilled setting and spinning DJ aren't compelling enough reasons to emerge from your Th Sukhumvit comfort zone, consider that this is probably the least expensive place in town to drink wine. Check the website for revolving nibbles promotions that span everything from imported cheeses and cold cuts to tapas.

WONG'S PLACE
Map p122   Bar

27/3 Soi Sri Bumphen, off Soi Ngam Duphli, Th Phra Ram IV, Lumphini; ❧ 8pm-late; Ⓜ Lumphini exit 1

An odd choice for an institution if there ever was one, this dusty den is a time warp into the backpacker world of the early 1980s. The namesake owner died several years ago, but a relative removed the padlock and picked up where Wong left off. Wong's works equally well as a destination or a last resort, but don't bother knocking until midnight, keeping in mind that it stays open until the last person crawls out.

WTF CAFÉ AND GALLERY
Map p126   Bar/Restaurant
☎ 0 2662 6246; www.wtfbangkok.com; 7 Soi 51, Th Sukhumvit; ⏱ 6pm-12.30am Tue-Sun; 🚇 Thong Lo exit 3

No, not that WTF; Wonderful Thai Friendship is a funky and friendly neighbourhood bar that also has two floors of gallery space. Stop by for fun drinks and a bar-snack menu whose influences range from Macau to Spain, or to check out the latest contemporary-art exhibition.

LIVE MUSIC

Music is a part of almost every Thai social gathering, and as Thailand's media capital, Bangkok is the centre of the Thai music industry, packaging and selling pop, crooners, *lôok tûng* (Thai-style country music) and the recent phenomenon of indie bands. The matriarchs and patriarchs like dinner with an easy-listening soundtrack: typically a Filipino band and a synthesizer. Patrons pass their request (on a napkin) up to the stage. An indigenous rock style, *pleng pêu·a chee·wít* (songs for life), makes appearances at a dying breed of country-and-western bars decorated with buffalo horns and pictures of Native Americans. Several dedicated bars throughout the city feature blues and rock bands, but are quite scant on live indie-scene performances. Up-and-coming garage bands occasionally pop up at free concerts where the kids hang out: Santichaiprakan Park (Th Phra Athit), Th Khao San and Siam Sq. Music festivals like Noise Pop and Fat Festival also feature the new breed.

For more on the ins and outs of the Thai music scene, see p44.

AD HERE THE 13TH
Map p82   Bar
13 Th Samsen, Banglamphu; ⏱ 6pm-midnight; 🚌 air-con 3,16 & ordinary 3, 15 & 16; ⚓ klorng boat to Tha Phra Athit (Banglamphu, N13)

Please don't blame the drummer if you're accidentally smacked by a stray drumstick; things can get a bit tight in here. Featuring a soulful house band that plays at 9.30pm nightly, Ad Here is one of those places that somehow manages to be both raucous and intimate.

BAMBOO BAR
Map p116   Bar
☎ 0 2659 9000; Oriental Hotel, Soi 38 (Oriental), Th Charoen Krung, Riverside; ⏱ 11-1am; 🚌 air-con 504, 544 & 547, ordinary 1, 15, 35 & 163; ⚓ klorng boat to Tha Oriental (N1)

Rubber-plantation barons and colonial mansions are not exactly part of Bangkok's history, but Bamboo Bar, in the historic Oriental Hotel, exudes oodles of bygone charm. Internationally recognized jazz bands hold court within a brush stroke of the audience to set a mellow lounge mood.

BRICK BAR
Map p82   Bar
☎ 0 2629 4477; basement, Buddy Lodge, 265 Th Khao San, Banglamphu; ⏱ 8pm-2am; 🚌 air-con 44, 59, 157, 503, 509 & 511, ordinary 15, 44, 47, 59, 157 & 159; ⚓ Tha Phra Athit (Banglamphu, N13)

Resembling Liverpool's Cavern Club c 1960, Brick Bar is an underground den that hosts a nightly revolving cast of live music for an almost exclusively Thai crowd. Come before midnight, wedge yourself into a table a few inches from the horn section, and lose it to Teddy Ska, one of the most energetic live acts in town.

top picks

CHEAP DATES

- Barbican (p182) Daily specials make this one of the cheaper places in town for an import pint.
- Cheap Charlie's (p183) The name says it all.
- Coyote on Convent (p183) Free margarita nights make this a cheap outing for fans of the cocktail.
- Phranakorn Bar (p185) Any place where Thai uni students hang out will probably also fit your budget.
- Raintree (p190) Order a large Singha and nurse it through as many live songs as you can.
- Wong's Place (opposite) Even if it's self-service you still have to pay, but the prices aren't high.

GAY & LESBIAN BANGKOK Grégoire Glachant

Bangkok has a notoriously pink vibe to it. From kinky male-underwear shops mushrooming at street corners to heaving nightclubs, as a gay man, you could eat, shop and play here for weeks without ever leaving the comfort of gay-friendly venues. Unlike elsewhere in Southeast Asia, homosexuality is not criminalised in Thailand and the general attitude remains extremely laissez-faire. But beneath the party vibe, serious issues remain for Bangkok's vast and visible population of lesbian, gays, bis and transgenders (LGBTs). After the government's initial success slowing the progression of HIV among the general population, there are new signs of an epidemic among young gay men. Transgenders are often treated as outcasts, same-sex couples enjoy no legal rights and lesbians have the added burden of negotiating a patriarchal society. In short, Bangkok's LGBTs may party as they please, sleep with whomever they want or even change sex, but they do so without the protection, respect and rights enjoyed by heterosexuals – particularly heterosexual men.

Issues aside, Bangkok's gay scene is as vast and sprawling as the city itself. Unfortunately, the city's lesbian scene is microscopic. It's currently limited to two establishments on Royal City Ave (RCA): the long-standing Zeta (Map p132; ☎ 0 2211 1060; 29 Royal City Ave (RCA), off Th Phra Ram IX, Greater Bangkok; admission free; 🕐 8pm-2am; Ⓜ Phra Ram 9 exit 3 & taxi) and relative newcomer E-Fun (Map p132; www.efunbangkok.com; 21/135-136 Royal City Ave (RCA), off Th Phra Ram IX, Greater Bangkok; admission free; 🕐 8pm-2am; Ⓜ Phra Ram 9 exit 3 & taxi).

Utopia, the well-known gay-information provider, publishes the Utopia Guide to Thailand, covering gay-friendly businesses in 18 Thai cities, including Bangkok. Its website, www.utopia-asia.com, is also a good, if slightly outdated source of information. More up-to-date listings and events can be found at www.fridae.com. For news on Bangkok's lesbian scene, check out www.bangkoklesbian.com. Both gays and lesbians are well advised to visit Bangkok in mid-November when the city's small but fun Pride Festival (www.bangkokpride.org) is in full swing. Dinners, cruises, clubbing and contests are the order of the week.

Silom

Silom is perhaps the biggest and most diverse 'gaybourhood'. Its offerings range from massage parlours and boy bars with in-your-face sex shows in nearby Soi Pratuchai (also known as Soi Twilight) to the chill terraces of Soi 4 and the booming house beats of Soi 2.

Telephone Pub (Map p116; ☎ 0 2234 3279; www.telephonepub.com; 114/11-13 Soi 4, Th Silom; 🕐 6pm-1am; Ⓜ Si Lom exit 2; 🚇 Sala Daeng exit 1) Telephone is famous for the phones that used to sit on every table, allowing you to ring up that hottie sitting across the room. Its popularity remains even if most of the phones are gone. The clientele is mostly 30-and-above white men with their Thai 'friends'.

DJ Station (Map p116; ☎ 0 2266 4029; www.dj-station.com; 8/6-8 Soi 2, Th Silom; admission 200B; 🕐 10.30pm-late; Ⓜ Si Lom exit 2; 🚇 Sala Daeng exit 3) Soi 2 is a covered alley packed with bars. At the end of the soi you'll find DJ Station, where everyone from freelancing money boys to Australian flight attendants, Singaporean weekenders and expats with rice fever all dance and drink to your typical gay-club house music.

Ratchada

Thais have their own way of partying. Bring friends (three minimum), get a table, order whisky and mixers and get drunk fast – pubs close at 1am. That means you can't stroll into Ratchada, prop yourself up at the counter and order a beer – well, you could, but you'd be the only one. And if you don't look Asian, prepare to stand out from the nearly 100% Thai crowd.

BROWN SUGAR
Map p122   Pub

☎ 0 2250 1825; 231/20 Th Sarasin, Lumphini; 🕐 6pm-1.30am; 🚇 Ratchadamri exit 2

If you're hankering for some typical New Orleans–style informality, head for Brown Sugar – but mind your step upon entering, lest you trip over the bass player. Both Friday and Saturday nights see this perpetually packed pub's house band belting out inspired performances that blend soul, jazz, rock and just about anything else you can think of.

GAZEBO Map p82   Pub

☎ 0 2629 0705; www.gazebobkk.com; 3rd fl, 44 Th Chakrapong, Banglamphu; 🕐 7pm-late; admission 300B after 11pm Sun-Wed & after midnight Thu-Sat; 🚌 air-con 3 & 16, ordinary 3, 15 & 16; 🚤 k-lorng boat to Tha Phra Athit (Banglamphu, N13)

Like an oasis above Th Khao San, this vaguely Middle Eastern–themed pub draws backpackers and locals alike with fun cover bands, a disco and fez-topped sheesha attendants. Its elevated location also appears to lend it some leniency with the city's strict closing times.

Ratchada Soi 8 (Map p132; ☎ 0892 310 996; www.ratchadasoi8.com; 76/4 Soi 8, Th Ratchadaphisek; ☼ 8pm-1am; Ⓜ Phra Ram 9 exit 3) The place is packed. The upper age limit here seems to be 25, and everyone knows the moves to the K-Pop (Korean pop) soundtrack – and sometimes the words. There's the usual show with 'coyote boys' (skinny young guys in Speedos and boots). Enjoy.

G-Star (Map p132; ☎ 0 2643 8792; www.g-starpub.com; Soi 8, Th Ratchadaphisek; ☼ 8pm-1am; Ⓜ Phra Ram 9 exit 3) G-Star appears fairly similar to Ratchada Soi 8, but the fact that it doesn't have a sign and sits behind an empty lot suggests it has something to hide. Inside, you'll find not one but three rather large men's rooms. All the urinals are in cubicles with locking doors and one of the men's rooms has particularly bad lighting. We'll let you figure out what goes on in there.

Or Tor Kor

The famed ICQ has gone but Or Tor Kor, by Chatuchak Weekend Market, remains a popular destination for young gays.

Fake Club (Map p132; ☎ 0894 739 262; Th Kamphaeng Phet, Greater Bangkok; ☼ 8pm-1am; Ⓜ Kamphaeng Phet exit 1) This place has found a niche somewhere between Ratchada and Silom. You'll still find students here, but the crowd is a tad older and more sophisticated, as is the decor and music.

Ramkhamhaeng

Ramkhamhaeng is Bangkok's largest university: that's a lot of young gay guys. Dozens of gay pubs, karaoke bars and saunas have opened in the area near the Lamsalee intersection.

ICK (Map p132; ☎ 0891 130 747; Soi 89/2, Th Ramkhamhaeng, Greater Bangkok; ☼ 8pm-1am; Ⓜ Phra Ram 9 exit 3 & taxi) ICK's scrawny coyote boys and cabaret shows are a cultural experience unto themselves. Off-stage, the makeup and body mass index doesn't change that much.

Saunas

In Bangkok, there's a fine line – often no line at all – between male massage and prostitution. Saunas, on the other hand, don't involve any transaction past the entrance fee. They range from dingy shophouses to beautiful five-star-hotel spa-like compounds. Here are the three most notorious:

Babylon (Map p122; ☎ 0 2679 7984; www.babylonbangkok.com; 34 Soi Nandha, off Soi 1, Th Sathon; admission 260B; ☼ 10.30am-10.30pm; Ⓜ Lumphini exit 2) Bangkok's first luxury sauna remains extremely popular with visitors, many from neighbouring Singapore and Hong Kong.

Chakran (Map p132; ☎ 0 2279 1359; 32 Soi 4, Soi Ari, Th Phaholyothin, Greater Bangkok; admission 250B; ☼ noon-11.30pm; Ⓡ Ari exit 3) Chakran is nearly as clean and as elegant as Babylon but, due to its suburban location, sees mostly Thais frequent its 1001 Nights–like decor.

Farose II (Map p132; ☎ 0 2319 4054; www.farosesaunabkk.com; Soi 21, Th Ramkhamhaeng, Greater Bangkok; admission 250B; ☼ 5pm-6am; Ⓜ Phra Ram 9 exit 3 & taxi) If you want to mingle with a really Thai crowd, trek out to Ramkhamhaeng. At this gritty, labyrinthine villa, you can get drunk on cheap Sang Som in the basement, wet in the large pool or propositioned in the dark upper floors.

Grégoire Glachant is the managing editor of BK Magazine.

LIVING ROOM

Map p126   Lounge Bar

☎ 0 2649 8888; www.sheratongrandesukhumvit.com; Level 1, Sheraton Grande Sukhumvit, 250 Th Sukhumvit; ☼ 9pm-1am; Ⓜ Sukhumvit exit 3; Ⓡ Asok exit 5

Although it's not exactly a smoky den filled with finger-snapping hep cats, every night the Sheraton Grande Sukhumvit's deceptively bland hotel lounge transforms into one of the city's best venues for live jazz. Check ahead of time to see which sax master or hide hitter is currently in town.

OVERTONE MUSIC CAVE Map p132   Bar

☎ 0 2203 0423; www.overtone.tv; 29/70-72 Royal City Ave (RCA), off Th Phra Ram IX, Greater Bangkok; ☼ 8pm-2am Wed-Sun; Ⓜ Phra Ram 9 exit 3 & taxi

One of Bangkok's premier rock venues, this place has hosted the likes of Jimmy Page and the occasional international touring act. Overtone is decorated with Thai and international rock paraphernalia, boasts a great sound system, and on Wednesday and Thursday nights hosts a high-quality open-mic session, and on Sundays, a blues jam.

NIGHTLIFE BIOLOGIST

Like other complicated ecosystems, Bangkok's nightlife can, to the untrained eye, appear wild and utterly lacking in order. Misconceptions, unsubstantiated sightings and anecdotal evidence about the inhabitants of this realm abound. But after years of intense research we're proud to say that we've finally been able to divide these organisms into three distinct species: high-society, dèk naaou (trendy child) and low-society. The following are descriptions of these groups, and recommended places to observe them in their natural environs.

The hi-so types split their time between Bangkok and Europe and have pioneered Bangkok's fascination with wine, London lounge, mid-century minimalism and international cuisine – the usual tastes of the rich and famous. You'll find them perched at Nest (see boxed text, p184) or nodding to live jazz at Diplomat Bar (p183).

Younger and more fashion-fearless are dèk naaou, Bangkok's indie kids. Dèk naaou on a budget gravitate towards cheaper Banglamphu pubs such as Sripoom Espresso Bar (p185) or Lollipop (p184), while those with the means part ways with their baht at downtown bars and clubs such as Nang Len (p192) or Slim/Flix (p193).

At the bottom of the feeding chain are the lo-sos, the ordinary middle class who prefer Thai rock to international electronica and drink whisky sets instead of gin and tonics. Lat Phrao, Victory Monument and other suburban neighbourhoods are where the 'real' Thais live and party. Places like Tawan Daeng German Brewhouse (below), Coco Walk (p183) and Raintree (below) attract regular Thais doing regular Thai things.

Foreigners are somehow exempt from this spectrum and can be found virtually anywhere, from trendy dens such as the Barbican (p182) or Opera Riserva Winetheque (p184), to quirky local boozers such as Shades of Retro (p185) or Happy Monday (p183), and fun dives such as Wong's Place (p186) or Cheap Charlie's (p183).

PARKING TOYS

Map p132   Bar

☎ 0 2907 2228; 17/22 Soi Mayalap, Kaset-Navamin Hwy, Greater Bangkok; ☼ 6pm-1am; ⊕ Mo Chit exit 3 & taxi

If you're willing to make the long schlep north of town, this bizarrely named bar is quite possibly Bangkok's best-kept live-music secret. A rambling hall decked out with vintage furniture, Parking Toys hosts an eclectic revolving cast of fun bands ranging in genre from acoustic/classical ensembles to electro-funk jam acts.

To get here, hop in a taxi from Mo Chit BTS station and ask the driver to take you to Th Kaset-Navamin (also locally known as the sên đàt mài). Turn right at the Kaset intersection and continue until you pass the second stop light. Keep an eye out for the Heineken sign immediately on your left.

RAINTREE

Map p113   Bar/Restaurant

☎ 0 2245 7230; www.raintreepub.com; 116/63-64 Soi Ruam Mit, Th Rang Nam, Ratchathewi; ☼ 6pm-2am; ⊕ Victory Monument exit 2

This atmospheric pub is one of the few remaining places in town to hear pleng pêu·a chee·wít, Thai folk music with roots in the communist insurgency of the 1960s and '70s. Buffalo skulls establish the design theme, and fittingly, soulful country-style Thai food is available.

ROCK PUB
Map p108   Pub

☎ 0 2208 9227; www.therockpub-bangkok.com; 93/26-28 Th Phayathai, Siam Sq; ☼ 9pm-2am; ⊕ Ratchathewi exit 2

If you thought the days of heavy metal and hair rock were over, step back in time at this cave-like pub where posters of Iron Maiden pass for interior design and black jeans and long hair are the unofficial dress code. The weak drinks don't exactly complement the strong rock, but for a quirky night, there's no more appropriate choice.

SAXOPHONE PUB & RESTAURANT
Map p113   Pub/Restaurant

☎ 0 2246 5472; www.saxophonepub.com; 3/8 Th Phayathai, Ratchathewi; ☼ 6pm-1.30am; ⊕ Victory Monument exit 4

Don't leave town without a visit to this venerable music club. Whether you're toasting distance from the band or perched in the 2nd-floor alcove, Saxophone's intimate space draws the crowd into the laps of great jazz and blues musicians. The music changes each night – jazz during the week; rock, blues and beyond on weekends. Reggae-fusion sessions define Friday nights.

TAWAN DAENG GERMAN BREWHOUSE Map p132   Beer Hall/Pub

☎ 0 2678 1114; www.tawandaeng.co.th; 462/61 Th Narathiwat Ratchanakharin (cnr Th Phra Ram III), Greater Bangkok; ☼ 5pm-midnight; ⊕ Chong Nonsi exit 2 & taxi

Despite its hangar-like girth, this Thai version of a Bavarian beer hall manages to pack 'em in just about every night. The Thai-German food is tasty, the house-made brews more than potable, and the nightly stage shows make singing along a necessity. Most people come for the Wednesday performance of Fong Nam (see p46). Music starts at 8.30pm.

THREE SIXTY Map p116   Lounge Bar
☎ 0 2442 2000; 32nd fl, Millennium Hilton, 123 Th Charoen Nakhorn, Thonburi; ☼ 5pm-1am; 🚇 Saphan Taksin exit 2 & hotel ferry
Feeling frustrated with Bangkok? A set or two of live jazz in this elegant glass-encased perch 32 floors above the city will help you forget some of your troubles, or at the very least, give you a whole new perspective on the city.

WINKS Map p132   Pub
☎ 0 2939 5684; cnr Soi 37, Th Phahonyothin, Greater Bangkok; ☼ 7pm-1am; 🚇 Mo Chit exit 3 & taxi
Starting to wonder where the Thai people actually hang out? Join wannabe musicians, Kasetsart University students, the odd dah·rah (star) and any others who can't be bothered with the Sukhumvit scene at this fun local boozer. The live bands aren't quite as good as they are loud, but after a couple of drinks and some new friends, you'll wish you could take the bar home with you.

WITCH'S TAVERN
Map p126   Pub
☎ 0 2391 9791; 306/1 Soi 55 (Thong Lor), Th Sukhumvit; ☼ 6pm-1am; 🚇 Thong Lo exit 3 & taxi
This spacious joint claims to be an English pub, but it's closer to a hotel lobby geared toward down-to-earth Thai professionals. Jazz and folk bands start up around 8.30pm, and at 10.30pm the house cover band takes to the stage, accepting requests from the audience. Ballads get the biggest round of applause.

CLUBBING
Fickleness is the reigning characteristic of the Bangkok club scene and venues that were pulling in thousands a night just last year are often only vague memories today. What used to be a rotating cast of hotspots has slowed to a few standards on the sois off Sukhum-

vit, Silom, Ratchadapisek and RCA (Royal City Ave), the city's 'entertainment zones', which qualify for the 2am closing time. Most places don't begin filling up until midnight and cover charges run as high as 600B and usually include a drink. You'll need ID to prove you're legal (20 years old); they'll card even the grey hairs.

To keep the crowds from growing bored, clubs host weekly theme parties and visiting DJs that ebb and flow in popularity. To get an idea of current happenings around town, check out Dude Sweet (www.dudesweet.org), organisers of hugely popular monthly parties, the online mag Bangkok Recorder (www.bangkokrecorder.com), and local listings rags such as BK and the Bangkok Post's Friday supplement, Guru.

70'S BAR
Map p122   Club
☎ 0 2253 4433; 231/16 Th Sarasin, Lumphini; ☼ 6pm-1am; admission free; 🚇 Ratchadamri exit 2
A tad too small to be a club proper, this retro-themed bar spins all the hits for Gen Y in the ultimate Me city. Like much of the strip, the clientele is mixed, but often verges on the pink side of the fence.

808
Map p132   Club
☎ 0843 239 998; www.808bangkok.com; Block C, Royal City Ave (RCA), off Th Phra Ram IX, Greater Bangkok; admission 160-800B; ☼ 9pm-2am; 🚇 Phra Ram 9 exit 3 & taxi
Named after the infamous beat machine, this club fills the space previously occupied by Astra and follows the tradition of big-name DJs and insanely crowded events. Virtually empty on weeknights.

top picks
BANGKOK'S BEST CLUBS
- 808 (above) The place to be when the big names are in town.
- Club Culture (p192) The Thaiest club in town.
- Glow (p192) As intimate and cosy as a club can be.
- Slim/Flix (p193) The playlist is painfully mainstream but you'll be hard-pressed to find a more consistently packed club.
- Tapas Room (p193) Three floors of fun.

OUT ALL NIGHT

With most pubs and dance clubs closing around 2am, One Night in Bangkok is not quite what it used to be. Thankfully there are a few places around town that have gained sufficient 'permission' to stay open until the morning hours. Wong's Place (p186) is so late night, it's best not to show up before midnight. Vaguely Middle Eastern–themed Gazebo (p188) represents the posh side of Th Khao San, and its elevated setting appears to lend it some leniency with the city's strict closing times. Scratch Dog (Map p126; ☎ 0 2262 1234; Windsor Suites Hotel, 8-10 Soi 20, Th Sukhumvit; 🕑 8pm-late) employs a hip-hop theme to propel partiers to the morning hours.

For something a bit edgier, ask your friendly taxi driver to escort you to any of the following: Spicy, Spice Club, Boss or Bossy. These creatively named late-night clubs are all located in central Bangkok and stay open until well past sunrise. We'd tell you a bit more about them and put them on our maps, but our experience and research suggest that these clubs exist in an alternate late-night reality that only Bangkok taxi drivers can navigate…

BED SUPPERCLUB
Map p126   Club
☎ 0 2651 3537; www.bedsupperclub.com; 26 Soi 11, Th Sukhumvit; admission 500-700B; 🕑 8pm-1am; 🚇 Nana exit 3
Bed has basked in the limelight for quite a few years now, but has yet to lose any of its futuristic charm. Arrive at a decent hour to squeeze in dinner (see p174), or if you've only got dancing on your mind, come on Tuesday for the hugely popular hip-hop night.

CAFÉ DEMOC
Map p82   Club
☎ 0 2622 2572; www.cafe-democ.com; 78 Th Ratchadamnoen, Banglamphu; admission free; 🕑 8pm-1am Tue-Sun; 🚤 klorng boat to Tha Phra Athit (Banglamphu, N13)
Up-and-coming DJs present their turntable dexterity at this narrow unpretentious club in Olde Bangkok. Hip hop, break beat, drum 'n' bass and tribal fill the night roster, but only special events actually fill the floor.

CLUB CULTURE
Map p113   Club
☎ 0894 978 422; www.club-culture-bkk.com; Th Sri Ayuthaya (opposite Siam City Hotel), Ratchathewi; admission 250B; 🕑 9pm-2am Tue-Sun; 🚉 Phaya Thai exit 4
Housed in a unique 40-year-old Thai-style building and hosting heaps of fun local events, Culture is the Thaiest locale on Bangkok's club scene. Internationally recognised DJs and what is allegedly the best sound system in town bring things to a cosmopolitan level.

HOLLYWOOD
Map p132   Club
Soi 8, Th Ratchadaphisek, Greater Bangkok; 🕑 8pm-2am; 🚇 Phra Ram 9 exit 3

Like taking a time machine back to the previous century, Hollywood is a holdover from the days when a night out in Bangkok meant corny live stage shows, wiggling around the whisky-set table and neon, neon, neon.

GLOW
Map p126   Club
☎ 0 2261 3007; www.glowbkk.com; 96/4-5 Soi 23, Th Sukhumvit; admission 100-200B; 🕑 7pm-2am; 🚇 Sukhumvit exit 2; 🚉 Asok exit 3
This self-proclaimed 'boutique' club starts things early in the evenings as a lounge boasting an impressive spectrum of vodkas. As the evening progresses, enjoy the recently upgraded sound system and tunes ranging from hip hop (Friday) to electronica (Saturday) and everything in between.

NANG LEN
Map p126   Club
☎ 0 2711 6564; 217 Soi 63 (Ekamai), Th Sukhumvit; 🕑 6pm-1am; 🚉 Ekkamai exit 1 & taxi
Young, loud and Thai; Nang Len (literally 'Sit and Chill') is a ridiculously popular sardine tin of live music and uni students on popular Th Ekamai. Get in before 10pm or you won't get in at all.

NARZ
Map p126   Club
☎ 0 2664 0373; www.narzbangkok.com; 112 Soi 23, Th Sukhumvit; admission 500B; 🕑 9pm-1am; 🚇 Sukhumvit exit 2; 🚉 Asok exit 3
The former Narcissus has undergone a recent nip and tuck and now consists of three separate zones boasting an equal variety of music. It's largely a domestic scene, but be sure to check the website for upcoming international events.

Q BAR Map p126 Club

☎ 0 2252 3274; www.qbarbangkok.com; 34 Soi 11, Th Sukhumvit; admission 500B; ⏱ 8pm-1am; Ⓜ Nana exit 3

In club years, Q Bar is fast approaching retirement age, but it still rules over Bangkok's club scene with slick industrial style. The dance floor is monopolised by working girls and pot-bellied admirers, but Sunday theme parties and celebrity DJs bring in everybody else in town. Q also boasts perhaps Thailand's largest range of drinks – 27 types of vodka and 41 brands of whisky/bourbon.

ROUTE 66

Map p132 Club

☎ 0 2203 0936; www.route66club.com; 29/33-48 Royal City Ave (RCA), off Th Phra Ram IX, Greater Bangkok; admission 200B; ⏱ 8pm-2am; Ⓜ Phra Ram 9 exit 3 & taxi

This place has been around just about as long as RCA, but a recent facelift has given it a new feel and an impressive following. Hip hop rules here, although there are several different themed 'levels', featuring anything from Thai pop to live music.

SLIM/FLIX Map p132 Club

☎ 0 2203 0504; 29/22-32 Royal City Ave (RCA), off Th Phra Ram IX, Greater Bangkok; admission free; ⏱ 8pm-2am; Ⓜ Phra Ram 9 exit 3 & taxi

Ideal for the indecisive raver, this immense three-in-one complex dominating one end of RCA features chilled house on one side (Flix), while the other (Slim) does the hip hop/R & B soundtrack found across much of the city. Oh, and there's a restaurant thrown in there somewhere as well. Despite its size, this place is packed on weekends.

TAPAS ROOM Map p116 Club

☎ 0 2234 4737; www.tapasroom.net; 114/17-18 Soi 4, Th Silom; admission 100B; ⏱ 9pm-3am; Ⓜ Si Lom exit 2; Ⓡ Sala Daeng exit 1

Although it sits staunchly at the front of Bangkok's pinkest street, this longstanding box manages to bring in just about everybody. Come Thursday to Saturday, when the combination of DJs and live percussion brings the body count to critical level.

GO-GO BARS

Although technically illegal, prostitution is fully 'out' in Bangkok, lucrative kickbacks making it all just too hard for the police to enforce this long-standing law. And like the sex industry in other parts of the world, issues of human trafficking and HIV/AIDS are ever-present, but a visit to any of the establishments listed below is likely confirm that the underlying atmosphere of Bangkok's red-light districts is predominantly one of tackiness and boredom, rather than illicit activity and exploitation.

Nana Entertainment Plaza (Map p126; Soi 4/Nana Tai, Th Sukhumvit; Ⓡ Nana exit 2) is a three-storey complex where the sexpats are separated from the gawking tourists. It's also home to a few ladyboy bars.

Patpong (Map p116; Soi Patpong 1 & 2, Silom; Ⓜ Si Lom exit 2; Ⓡ Sala Daeng exit 1) is possibly one of the most famous red-light districts in the world, however, today any 'charm' that the area used to possess has been eroded by modern tourism; fake Rolexes and Diesel T-shirts are more ubiquitous than flesh. There is, of course, a considerable amount of naughtiness going on, although much of it takes place upstairs and behind closed doors. If you must, before taking a seat at one of Patpong's 'pussy shows', be sure to agree to the price beforehand, otherwise you're likely to receive an astronomical bill.

Soi Cowboy (Map p126; btwn Soi 21 & Soi 23, Th Sukhumvit; Ⓜ Sukhumvit exit 2; Ⓡ Asok exit 3) is a single-lane strip of raunchy bars claims direct lineage from the post–Vietnam War R & R era. A real flesh trade functions amid the flashing neon.

top picks

BEST BARS TO MAKE NEW FRIENDS

- Brick Bar (p187) It's so crowded in here you can't help but meet and greet.
- Cheap Charlie's (p183) The dearth of tables here encourages interaction.
- Club Culture (opposite) Quite possibly Bangkok's least pretentious club.
- Coco Walk (p183) You'll probably be the only foreigner here – a great conversation starter.
- Tapas Room (right) Boasting three floors, all of them full of folks, you'd be hard-pressed not to make a new friend.

Meanwhile, Soi Twilight (Soi Pratuchai; Map p116; Soi Pratuchai, Th Surawong, Silom; Ⓜ Si Lom exit 2; Ⓡ Sala Daeng exit 3) is Patpong's queer little brother, which offers shows ranging in scope from muscle boy to ladyboy.

Asian tourists – primarily Japanese, Taiwanese and Hong Kong men – flock to the Ratchada entertainment strip, part of the Huay Khwang district (Map p132), along wide Th Ratchadaphisek between Th Phra Ram IX and Th Lat Phrao. Lit up like Las Vegas, this stretch of neon boasts huge, male-oriented, massage/snooker/karaoke/go-go complexes with names like Caesar's Sauna and Emmanuelle.

ENTERTAINMENT & THE ARTS

top picks

- 100 Tonson Gallery (p199)
- Ardel Gallery of Modern Art (p199)
- Bangkok Art & Culture Centre (BACC; p199)
- Bangkok University Art Gallery (BUG; p200)
- H Gallery (p200)

Although Bangkok's hyper-urban environment seems to cater to the inner philistine in all of us, the city has a significant but low-key art scene. Encouraged and nurtured largely by the city's expat community, art in today's Bangkok ranges from beautifully benign *objets d'art* to increasingly sophisticated displays of social commentary. The city's galleries are a diverse lot, and include a refurbished wooden house and several chic restaurant-cum-galleries. In recent years, new ones seem to have been opening on a weekly basis. Bangkok also acts as something of a regional art hub, showing many works by emerging artists from places like Myanmar (Burma) and Cambodia.

The performing arts have a long history in Bangkok. Dancing in particular, whether by classically trained performers at a shrine or ladyboys camping about on stage, seems to form a large part of the entertainment options for many visitors to the city.

For profiles of Thai modern artists and movements, pick up a copy of *Flavours: Thai Contemporary Art*, by Steven Pettifor, a leading Bangkok art critic who also authored the boxed text, p38. Rama IX Museum (www.rama9art.org) is an online resource for artists' portfolios and gallery profiles.

THEATRE & DANCE

High-art-wise, Bangkok's heyday passed with the dismantling of the royal court. Today Thai preservationists cling to the classical dance dramas, which attract little government funding or appreciation, as the city races to be more modern than it was the day before.

There is a handful of companies performing Western arts and interesting fusions of Thai-Western traditions, but the number of arts venues is abysmally small compared with more-profitable and less-cultural businesses. The city's daily newspapers and monthly magazines maintain a calendar of cultural events. Performances are typically advertised in the *Bangkok Post* or online at www.bangkokconcerts.org. Reservations are recommended for events, and tickets can be purchased through Thai Ticket Major (www.thaiticketmajor.com).

AKSRA THEATRE Map p113

☎ 0 2677 8888 ext 5604; www.aksratheatre.com; King Power Complex, 8/1 Th Rang Nam, Ratchathewi; tickets 800B; ☼ shows 7pm Tue-Fri, 1pm & 7pm Sat & Sun; ⓡ Victory Monument exit 2
The former Joe Louis Puppet Theatre has moved house and is starting a new life here as the Aksra Hoon Lakorn Lek. A variety of performances are now held at this modern theatre, but the highlight are performances of the Ramakian that use knee-high puppets requiring three puppeteers to manipulate them into humanlike poses.

NATIONAL THEATRE Map p68

☎ 0 2221 0171; Th Ratchini, Ko Ratanakosin; tickets 40-100B; ⌑ air-con 503, 508 & 511, ordinary 15 & 53; ⚓ Tha Chang (N9)
When its seemingly never-ending reconstruction is eventually finished in 2010, the National Theatre will host monthly performances of the royal dance traditions of *lá·kon* and *kŏhn*.

PATRAVADI THEATRE Map p68

☎ 0 2412 7287; www.patravaditheatre.com; 69/1 Soi Wat Rakhang, Thonburi; tickets 500B; ☼ show times vary; ⚓ cross-river ferry from Tha Maharat
Patravadi is Bangkok's sole modern-dance venue. A stylish open-air theatre that also includes a gallery and restaurant, it is the brainchild of Patravadi Mejudhon, a famous Thai actor and playwright. The

SHRINE DANCING

Although scheduled performances are grand, lasting memories are often unscripted and the serendipity of catching a shrine dance is unforgettable, like spotting a rainbow. If you hear the din of drums and percussion from a temple or shrine, follow the sound to see traditional *lá·kon gâa bon* (shrine dancing). At Lak Meuang (p70) and the Erawan Shrine (p107), worshippers commission costumed troupes to perform dance movements that are similar to classical *lá·kon*, but not as refined, as they are specially choreographed for ritual purposes. Free daily performances are also staged in a pavilion on the side of the Vimanmek Teak Mansion (p94) at 10am and 2pm.

dance-troupe performance is a blend of traditional Thai dance and modern choreography, music and costume. The theatre is also the primary venue for the Bangkok International Fringe Festival, held in January and February.

SALA CHALERMKRUNG Map p98
☎ 0 2222 0434; www.salachalermkrung.com; 66 Th Charoen Krung, Chinatown; tickets 1000-1200B; ⏱ shows 7.30pm Fri & Sat; 🚌 air-con 3, 60, 73 & 512, ordinary 3, 53, 60 & 73; ⚓ Tha Saphan Phut (Memorial Bridge, N6)

This art deco Bangkok landmark, a former cinema dating to 1933, is one of the few remaining places *kŏhn* can be witnessed. The traditional Thai dance-drama is enhanced here by laser graphics, hi-tech audio and English subtitles. Concerts and other events are also held – check the website for details.

SIAM NIRAMIT Map p132
☎ 0 2649 9222; www.siamniramit.com; 19 Th Thiam Ruammit, Greater Bangkok; tickets 1500-2000B; ⏱ shows 8pm; Ⓜ Thailand Cultural Centre exit 1 & access by shuttle bus

A cultural theme park, this enchanted kingdom transports visitors to a Disney-fied version of ancient Siam with a techni-coloured stage show depicting the Lanna Kingdom, the Buddhist heaven and Thai festivals. Elaborate costumes and sets are guaranteed to be spectacular both in their grandness and their indigenous interpretation.

The show is predominately popular with tour groups, but if you're visiting independently, a free shuttle-bus service is available at Thailand Cultural Centre Metro station every 15 minutes from 6pm to 7.45pm.

THAILAND CULTURAL CENTRE
Map p132
☎ 0 2247 0028; www.thaiculturalcenter.com; Th Ratchadaphisek btwn Th Thiam Ruammit & Th Din Daeng, Greater Bangkok; Ⓜ Thailand Cultural Centre exit 1 & access by shuttle bus

Bangkok's primary performing-arts facility, the Thailand Cultural Centre is the home of the Bangkok Symphony Orchestra and hosts the International Festival of Dance and Music in September. Classical dance performances, and regional Thai concerts like *lôok tûng* (Thai country music) and Khorat Song also cycle through the yearly calendar.

On performance days a free shuttle bus picks up passengers from the Metro exit 1.

DINNER THEATRE
Another option for viewing Thai classical dance is through dinner theatre. Most dinner theatres in Bangkok are heavily promoted through hotels to an ever-changing clientele, so standards are poor to fair. They can be tolerably worthwhile if you accept them as cultural tourist traps.

SALA RIM NAM Map p116
☎ 0 2437 3080; www.mandarinoriental.com/bangkok; Oriental Hotel, Soi 38, Th Charoen Krung, Riverside; tickets 2650B; ⏱ dinner & show 8-10.30pm; ⚓ Tha Oriental (N1)

The historic Oriental Hotel hosts dinner theatre in a sumptuous Thai pavilion located across the river in Thonburi. Free shuttle boats transfer guests across the river from the hotel's dock. The price is well above average, reflecting the means of the hotel's client base.

SAWASDEE Map p116
☎ 0 2237 6311; www.sawasdeebkk.com; 66 Soi 6, Th Thanon Sathon, Silom; tickets 550B; ⏱ dinner & show 8pm; 🚇 Chong Nonsi exit 2

Sawasdee has been doing the Thai dinner show for 20 years and we reckon it's got it down by now. Shows span five parts and range from Thai martial arts to northeastern Thai dance, and dinner also offers ample options.

SILOM VILLAGE Map p116
☎ 0 2234 4448; www.silomvillage.co.th; 286 Th Silom; mains 150-350B; ⏱ 6-10pm; 🚌 air-con 76, 77, 177, 504, 514, 547 & MB12, ordinary 77, 162, 163 & 164; 🚇 Surasak exit 3

More relaxed than most dinner-show venues, Silom Village delivers comfort, accessibility and decent dinners. Picky eaters swear by the crispy pork and cashew chicken, and witnessing the demonstrations of Thai dance and martial arts (7.30pm and 8.45pm nightly) will strike one 'to do' off the itinerary.

STUDIO 9 Map p68
☎ 0 2866 2144; www.patravaditheatre.com; Patravadi Theatre, 69/1 Soi Wat Rakhang, Thonburi; ⏱ shows 7.30pm-midnight Fri & Sat; ⚓ cross-river ferry from Tha Maharat

Thailand's only modern-dance theatre combines highbrow entertainment and dining in its delightful riverside location. Performances are plucked from a diverse menu of music, dance, puppetry and theatre; check ahead of time to see what's in store.

GÀ·TEU·I CABARET

Joining the sacred temples and longboat tours of Chao Phraya River, *gà·teu·i* (ladyboys) are a recent addition to the itineraries of many visitors to Bangkok. This largely takes the form of *gà·teu·i* cabaret, in which convincing ladyboys take to the stage with elaborate costumes, MTV-style dance routines and rehearsed lip-synching to pop hits. Calypso Cabaret (Map p108; ☎ 0 2653 3960/2; www.calypsocabaret.com; 1st fl, Asia Hotel, 296 Th Phayathai, Siam Sq; tickets 900-1550B; ☯ shows 8.15pm & 9.45pm; ® Ratchathewi exit 1) and Mambo Cabaret (Map p132; ☎ 0 2294 7381; www.mambocabaret.com; 59/28 Th Yannawa Tat Mai, Greater Bangkok; tickets 800-1000B; ☯ shows 7.15pm, 8.30pm & 10pm; ® Chong Nonsi exit 2 & taxi) do family- and tourist-friendly shows of pop and Broadway camp.

CINEMAS

Hollywood movies are released in Bangkok's theatres in a timely fashion. But as homegrown cinema grows bigger, more and more Thai films, often subtitled in English, fill the roster. Foreign films are sometimes altered by Thailand's film censors before distribution; this usually involves obscuring nude sequences. Film buffs may prefer the offerings at Bangkok's foreign cultural centres, listed below, or other private institutions occasionally delving into film, such as Saladaeng Café by Jim Thompson (Map p122; ☎ 0 2266 9167; 120/1 Soi Sala Daeng 1, Lumphini; Ⓜ Si Lom exit 2; ® Sala Daeng exit 4), which has begun screening old Thai and English black-and-white movies nightly from 6pm to 10pm in its outdoor Sala Casa, or Bed Supperclub's (p174) Popcorn Paradiso art-film nights on Mondays from 9.30pm. Tickets (600B) to the latter include two drinks and gourmet popcorn.

The shopping-centre cinemas have plush VIP options (see boxed text opposite), while Lido and Scala (see below for cinema details) are older and artier. House is Bangkok's first 'art house' theatre. Ticket prices range from 120B to 220B for regular seats, and up to 500B for VIP seats. For movie listings and reviews, check the *Nation, Bangkok Post, Metro,* and Movie Seer (www.movieseer.com).

Bangkok also hosts several annual film festivals, including the Bangkok International Film Festival in September.

Alliance Française Bangkok (Map p122; ☎ 0 2670 4200; www.alliance-francaise.or.th; 29 Th Sathon Tai; Ⓜ Lumphini exit 2) French films at the French cultural centre.

EGV (Map p108; ☎ 0 2129 4635-36; www.egv.com; Siam Discovery Centre, 6th fl, Th Phra Ram I, Siam Sq; ® Siam exit 1) Bangkok's poshest venue to view all the mainstream movies.

Goethe Institut (Map p122; ☎ 0 2287 0942; 18/1 Soi Goethe, off Soi 1 (Atakanprasit), Th Sathon Tai; Ⓜ Lumphini exit 2) German films at the German cultural centre.

House (Map p132-3; ☎ 0 2641 5177; www.houserama.com; 3rd fl, UMG Cinema, RCA, Th Phra Ram IX, Greater Bangkok; Ⓜ Phra Ram 9 exit 3 & taxi) Bangkok's first

THE FILM SCENE

'Cinemas in Bangkok aren't generally that much different than those in the West. In fact Thai cineplexes have more comfy seats – and the ticket is certainly much cheaper. My favourite theatres in town are Siam and Scala (opposite). They're the only remaining stand-alone, palace-style cinemas that offer an alternative to the plasticity of modern multiplexes.

In general, Thailand makes a lot of horror and comedy films, though the quality is hardly consistent (see Ghosts & Gags, p48, for more on the Thais' love of horror and comedy). At the same time, we have quite a few art house directors who are well known internationally and who are expanding the horizons of Thai film. I like the films of Apichatpong Weerasethakul, Pen-ek Ratanaruang and Wisit Sasanatieng, and my favourite Thai films are *Black Silk,* by Ratana Pestonji; *Tropical Malady,* by Apichatpong Weerasethakul; and *Monrak Transistor,* by Pen-ek Ratanaruang.

I wouldn't recommend most foreign films shot in Bangkok, as they don't do justice to the city. They tend to exoticise the place and the people, especially films like *The Beach* and *Bangkok Dangerous*.'

Kong Rithdee, aged 36, lives in Bangkok and is a film critic for the Bangkok Post.

CINEMA STRATEGY

Cinemas are a very big deal in Bangkok. Few cities have anything quite like EGV's Gold Class, a ticket that grants you entry into a cinema with fewer than 50 seats, and where you're plied with blankets, pillows, foot-warming stockings and, of course, a valet food-and-drink service. There's also Major Cineplex' Emperor Class seat which, for the price of a sticky stool back home, entitles you to a sofa-like love seat designed for couples. And if you find Paragon Cineplex' 16 screens and 5000 seats a bit plebeian, you can always apply for Enigma, a members-only theatre.

Despite the heat and humidity on the streets, keep in mind that Bangkok's movie theatres pump the air-conditioning with such vigour that a jumper is an absolute necessity – unless you're going Gold Class, that is.

art-house cinema showing lots of foreign flicks of the non-Hollywood type.

Lido Multiplex (Map p108; ☎ 0 2251 1265; Th Phra Ram I, btwn Soi 2 & Soi 3, Siam Sq; 🚇 Siam exit 2) Arty and independent movies.

Major Cineplex (Map p108; ☎ 0 2515 5555; www.major cineplex.com; Central World Plaza, 7th fl, Th Ratchadamri, Ploenchit; 🚇 Chit Lom exit 9 to Sky Walk, Siam exit 6 to Sky Walk) All the amenities and mainstream hits.

Paragon Cineplex (Map p108; ☎ 0 2251 5555; www. paragoncineplex.com; Siam Paragon, Th Phra Ram I, Siam Sq; Ⓜ Siam exits 3 & 5) This cinema offers both quantity (more than a dozen screens) and quality (several classes of viewing).

Scala Multiplex (Map p108; ☎ 0 2251 2861; Soi 1, Th Phra Ram I, Siam Sq; 🚇 Siam exit 2) Last of the old-style theatres, in the heart of Siam Sq.

SF Cinema City (Map p108; ☎ 0 2268 8888; www. sfcinemacity.com; 7th fl, Mahboonkrong, Th Phra Ram I, Siam Sq; 🚇 National Stadium exit 4) Multiplex showing Hollywood blockbusters.

SFV (Map p126; ☎ 0 2260 9333; 6th fl, Emporium Shopping Centre, Th Sukhumvit, cnr Soi 24; 🚇 Phrom Phong exit 2) Creature comforts trimmings and varied screenings.

GALLERIES

In typical Bangkok style, the art scene here lacks a centre – artists and galleries are peppered throughout the city. The more conservative, generally government-sponsored art can be found in the older parts of town, particularly around the Banglamphu area, while the commercial galleries prefer the business districts of Th Silom and Th Sukhumvit.

For maps of the city's art scene, pick up *BAM!* (Bangkok Art Map; www.bangkokartmap.com) or the *Thailand Art & Design Guide*, and check the lifestyle magazines for exhibition opening nights.

100 TONSON GALLERY Map p108
☎ 0 2684 1527; www.100tonsongallery.com; 100 Soi Tonson, Ploenchit; 🕐 11am-7pm Thu-Sun; 🚇 Chit Lom exit 4
Housed in a spacious residential villa, and largely regarded as the city's top commercial gallery, 100 Tonson hosts a variety of contemporary exhibitions of all genres by local and international artists.

ARDEL GALLERY OF MODERN ART
Map p132-3
☎ 0 2422 2092; www.ardelgallery.com; 99/45 Belle Ville, Muu 18, Th Boromaratchatchonanee, Greater Bangkok; 🕐 10am-6.30pm Tue-Sat & 9.30am-5.30pm Sun; 🚇 Wongwian Yai exit 4 & taxi
Despite its distance from the centre of town, Ardel is quickly becoming one of Bangkok's premier galleries. The expansive suburban compound unites two exhibition spaces, a print-making workshop, and a shop and café with a brand new annex that includes an artists' residence and pool. Curated by Ajarn Thavorn Ko-Udomvit, a renowned lecturer at Silpakorn University, the collection often emphasises print and photos, but previous exhibitions have spanned a variety of media.

There are smaller branches of Ardel off Th Sukhumvit and in Bangkok's Chinatown neighbourhood – see the website for details.

BANGKOK ART & CULTURE CENTRE (BACC) Map p108
☎ 0 2214 6630; www.bacc.or.th; cnr Th Phayathai & Th Phra Ram 1, Siam Sq; 🕐 10am-9pm Tue-Sat; 🚇 National Stadium exit 3
This large, modern building in the centre of Bangkok is the most recent and promising addition to the city's arts scene. To date, the compound's three floors and 3000 sq metres of gallery space have played host to several high-quality exhibitions, but bureaucratic setbacks have delayed the library and art-related shops and restaurants slated for the rest of the structure.

BANGKOK UNIVERSITY ART GALLERY (BUG) Map p132

☎ 0 2350 3500; http://fab.bu.ac.th/buggallery; 3rd fl, Bldg 9, City Campus, Th Phra Ram IV, Greater Bangkok; ⏰ 9.30am-7pm Tue-Sat; 🚇 Phra Khanong exit 3 & taxi

This spacious new compound is located at what is currently the country's most cutting-edge art school. Recent exhibitions have encompassed a variety of media by some of the country's top names, as well as the work of internationally recognised artists.

FOREIGN CORRESPONDENTS' CLUB OF THAILAND (FCCT) Map p108

☎ 0 2652 0580; www.fccthai.com; Penthouse, Maneeya Center, 518/5 Th Ploenchit; ⏰ noon-2.30pm & 6pm-midnight; 🚇 Chit Lom exit 2

A bar-restaurant, not to mention gathering place for the city's hacks and photogs, the FCCT also hosts art exhibitions ranging in genre from photojournalism to contemporary painting. Check the website to see what's on.

GALLERY VER Map p116

☎ 0 2861 0933; www.verver.info; 2nd fl, 71/31-35 Klongsarn Plaza, Th Charoen Nakhorn, Thonburi; ⏰ 1-6pm Tue-Sat; 🚢 cross-river ferry from Tha Si Phraya (N3)

Owned by Rirkrit Tiravanija, Thailand's most internationally recognised artist, this gallery on the Thonburi side of the river hosts a rotating display of typically edgy, installation-type conceptual art. The easiest way to reach Ver is to take the cross-river ferry from Tha Si Phraya. The gallery is directly behind the pier on the Thonburi side.

H GALLERY Map p116

☎ 0813 104 428; www.hgallerybkk.com; 201 Soi 12, Th Sathon; ⏰ 10am-6pm Wed-Mon; 🚇 Chong Nonsi exit 1

Housed in a refurbished colonial-era wooden building, H is generally considered among the city's leading private galleries. It is regarded as a jumping-off point for Thai artists with international ambitions, such as Jakkai Siributr and Somboon Hormthienthong.

JAMJUREE ART GALLERY Map p108

☎ 0 2218 3708; Jamjuree Bldg, Chulalongkorn University, Th Phayathai, Siam Sq; ⏰ 10am-7pm Mon-Fri, noon-6pm Sat & Sun; 🚇 Siam exit 2 & taxi

This gallery, part of Chulalongkorn University's Faculty of Arts, emphasises modern spiritual themes and brilliantly coloured abstracts from emerging student artists.

JIM THOMPSON ART CENTER Map p108

☎ 0 2216 7368, 0 2215 0122; www.jimthompsonhouse.com; Jim Thompson House, 6 Soi Kasem San 2, Th Phra Ram I, Siam Sq; ⏰ 9am-5pm; 🚢 klorng boat to Tha Ratchathewi; 🚇 National Stadium exit 1

This popular tourist destination has added an entire new gallery wing with rotating displays ranging from the contemporary to the traditional. Recent exhibitions have included a display of traditional Lao textiles, as well as an interactive work by Pinaree Sanpitak, one of the country's top female artists.

KATHMANDU PHOTO GALLERY Map p116

☎ 0 2234 6700; www.kathmandu-bkk.com; 87 Th Pan, Silom; ⏰ 11am-7pm Tue-Sun; 🚌 air-con 76, 77, 177, 504, 514, 547 & MB12, ordinary 77, 162, 163 & 164; 🚇 Surasak exit 3

Bangkok's only gallery truly dedicated to photography is housed in an attractively restored Sino-Portuguese shophouse. The owner, photographer Manit Sriwanichpoom, wanted Kathmandu to resemble photographers' shops of old, where customers could flip through photographs for sale. Manit's own work is on display on the ground floor, and the small but airy upstairs gallery plays host to changing exhibitions by local and international artists and photographers.

NATIONAL GALLERY Map p68

☎ 0 2282 2639; Th Chao Fa, Ko Ratanakosin; admission 200B; ⏰ 9am-4pm Wed-Sun; 🚌 air-con 508 & 511, ordinary 47 & 53; 🚢 Tha Phra Athit (Banglamphu, N13)

Housed in a weathered colonial building that was the Royal Mint during the reign of Rama V, the National Gallery's permanent exhibition is a rather dusty and dated affair. Secular art is a relatively new concept in Thailand and most of the country's best examples of fine art reside in the temples for which they were created – much as historic Western art was often found in European cathedrals. As such, most of the permanent collection here documents Thailand's homage to modern styles. More interesting are the rotating exhibits held in the spacious rear galleries; take a look at the posters out front to see what's on.

NUMTHONG GALLERY Map p93
☎ 0 2243 4326; www.numthonggallery.com; Room 109, Bangkok Co-op Housing Bldg, 1129/29 Th Toeddamri, Dusit; 🕙 11am-6pm Mon-Sat; 🚇 Ari exit 3 & taxi

A proving ground for Thai contemporary artists, Numthong has featured work by the cream of the crop of Thailand's avant-garde, including Vasan Sitthiket, Michael Shaowanasai and Kamin Lertchaiprasert.

QUEEN'S GALLERY Map p82
☎ 0 2281 5360; www.queengallery.org; 101 Th Ratchadamnoen Klang, Banglamphu; 🕙 10am-7pm Thu-Tue; admission 20B; 🚌 air-con 59, ordinary 42 & 59; ⚓ klorng boat to Tha Phan Fah

This royal-funded museum presents five floors of rotating exhibitions of modern and traditionally influenced art. The building is sleek and contemporary and the artists hail from the upper echelons of the conservative Thai art world. The attached shop is filled with fine-arts books and gifts.

SILPAKORN UNIVERSITY Map p68
☎ 0 2623 6115; www.su.ac.th; 31 Th Na Phra Lan, Ko Ratanakosin; 🚌 air-con 503, 508 & 511, ordinary 15 & 53; ⚓ Tha Chang (N9)

Thailand's universities aren't usually repositories for interesting architecture, but the country's premier art school breaks the mould. Housed in a former palace, the classical buildings form the charming nucleus of an early Thai aristocratic enclave. The building immediately facing the Th Na Phra Lan gate houses the university's art gallery, which showcases faculty and student exhibitions. To the right of the building is a shady sculpture garden displaying the work of Corado Ferroci (aka Silapa Bhirasri), the

Italian art professor who helped establish Silpakorn's fine arts department.

SURAPON GALLERY Map p122
☎ 0 2638 0033-4; www.rama9art.org/gallery/surapon/index.html; 🕙 11am-6pm Mon-Sat; 1st fl, Tisco Tower, 48/3 Th Sathon Neua; 🚇 Lumphini exit 2

Perhaps the most 'Thai' of the city's contemporary galleries, Surapon has featured work by some of the country's most renowned artists such as painters Chatchai Puipia and Muangthai Busamaro.

TANG GALLERY Map p116
☎ 0 2630 1114; basement, Silom Galleria, 919/1 Th Silom; 🕙 11am-7pm Mon-Sat; 🚌 air-con 76, 77, 177, 504, 514, 547 & MB12, ordinary 77, 162, 163 & 164; 🚇 Surasak exit 3

Bangkok's primary venue for modern artists from China has edged its way to become among the city's top contemporary galleries. Check the posters in the lobby of its home, Silom Galleria, to see what's on.

THAVIBU GALLERY Map p116
☎ 0 2266 5454; www.thavibu.com; 3rd fl, Silom Galleria, 919/1 Th Silom; 🕙 11am-7pm Tue-Sat, noon-6pm Sun; 🚌 air-con 76, 77, 177, 504, 514, 547 & MB12, ordinary 77, 162, 163 & 164; 🚇 Surasak exit 3

Thavibu is an amalgam of Thailand, Vietnam and Myanmar. The gallery specialises in contemporary paintings by younger and emerging artists from the three countries.

WHITESPACE Map p108
☎ 0 2252 2900; www.whitespaceasia.com; 2nd fl, Lido Bldg, Soi 3, Siam Sq; 🕙 1-7pm Tue-Fri, 11.30am-8pm Sat & Sun; 🚇 Siam exit 2

An active design studio, Whitespace also includes a small noncommercial gallery that features a diverse array of exhibitions by emerging artists.

top picks

- Wat Pho Massage Pavilions (p205)
- Moo·ay tai (Thai boxing) at Lumphini Stadium (p208)
- Ruen-Nuad Massage & Yoga (p205)
- Bicycle tours (p207)

SPORTS & ACTIVITIES

Although the climate is not conducive to exercise, Bangkokians like to work up a sweat doing more than just climbing the stairs to the Skytrain station. All the popular Thai sports are represented in the capital city, from the top-tier *moo·ay tai* (Thai boxing; also spelt *muay thai*) to a pick-up game of *dà·grôr* (Siamese football).

Thais also consider traditional massage an integral component of health, so you can always pay someone else to do all the work. In tandem with the massage tradition, Bangkok is emerging as one of the world's spa capitals, with facilities to satisfy almost any whim or budget.

HEALTH & FITNESS

Whether you're looking to sweat out the toxins or have them pampered away, Bangkok should be able to satisfy.

SPAS & MASSAGE

According to the teachings of traditional Thai healing, the use of herbs and massage should be part of a regular health-and-beauty regimen, not just an excuse for pampering. You need no excuse to get a massage and it's just as well, because Bangkok could mount a strong claim to being the massage capital of the world. Exactly what type of massage you're after is another question. Variations range from store-front traditional Thai massage to an indulgent spa 'experience' with service and style. And even within the enormous spa category there are choices; there is plenty of pampering going around but some spas now focus more on the medical than the sensory, while plush resort-style spas offer a laundry list of appealing treatments.

The most common variety is traditional Thai massage (*nôo·at păan boh·rahn*). Although it sounds relaxing, at times it can seem more closely related to *moo·ay tai* than to shiatsu. Thai massage is based on yogic techniques for general health involving pulling, stretching, bending and manipulating pressure points. If done well, a traditional massage will leave you sore but revitalised.

Full-body massages usually include camphor-scented balms or herbal compresses, or oil in cheaper establishments. Note that 'oil massage' is sometimes taken as code for 'sexy massage'; see the boxed text, p206, for the low-down. A foot massage is arguably (and it's a strong argument) the best way to treat the legweariness of sightseeing.

Depending on the neighbourhood, prices for massages in small parlours are 200B to 350B for a foot massage and 300B to 500B for a full-body massage. Spa experiences start at about 800B and climb like a Bangkok skyscraper.

BANYAN TREE SPA Map p122
☎ 0 2679 1052; www.banyantreespa.com; 21st fl, Banyan Tree Hotel & Spa, 100 Th Sathon Tai; massage/package from 3300/5800B; Ⓜ Lumphini exit 2
This hotel spa delivers modern elegance and world-class pampering. The womb-like spa rooms look out over a silent and peaceful vision of Bangkok from on high. Thai, Swedish and Balinese massages, body scrubs using aromatic oils and herbs with medicinal properties, and beauty treatments comprise the spa's offerings. 'Spa vacation' packages include accommodation.

BUATHIP THAI MASSAGE
Map p126
☎ 0 2251 2627; 4/13 Soi 5, Th Sukhumvit; 1hr massage 270B, foot 250B; ⏰ 10am-midnight; Ⓡ Nana exit 1
On a small sub-soi (lane) behind the Amari Blvd Hotel, this tidy shopfront is in a decidedly sleazy part of town, but inside is a professional masseur whose focused concentration could melt metal.

CORAN BOUTIQUE SPA
Map p126
☎ 0 2651 1588; www.coranbangkok.com; 27/1-2 Soi 13, Th Sukhumvit; 1hr traditional massage 400B; ⏰ 11am-10pm; Ⓡ Nana exit 3
The Thai massage here is top notch partly because it is performed by graduates of the adjacent Thai Traditional Medical Services Society. It's remarkably well priced,

though the aromatherapy treatments are much more expensive.

METRO MASSAGE Map p126
lower ground fl, Robinsons Department Store, Soi 19, Th Sukhumvit; foot massage 250B; 🚇 Asok exit 5
At the entrance to Tops Supermarket, underneath Robinsons and the Golden Arches, this modest little foot massage place is always busy because staff really know how to rub a foot. Highly recommended if you're in the area.

MULBERRY SPA Map p126
☎ 0 2664 1888; www.mulberryspa.com; 132 Soi 23, Th Sukhumvit; 1hr massage from 600B; 🕙 10am-midnight; 🚇 Asok exit 2
Set in a classic 1960s-era Sukhumvit home, Mulberry finds a fairly priced balance between pampering and quality massage in a soothing and professionally run atmosphere.

NAKORNTHON THAI MEDICAL SPA Map p132
☎ 0 2416 5454; www.nakornthonhospital.com; 12th fl, Nakornthon Hospital, Th Phra Ram II; 90 mins traditional massage 550B, packages from 3600B; 🕙 9am-9pm; access by taxi
The wellness centre of this Bangkok hospital has a traditional Thai medicine wing, combining spa therapy with ancient Thai techniques. The primary practice is *đam·ràp torng*, which uses the application of gold leaf and herbs to rejuvenate skin and restore collagen. Other treatments focus on nutritional evaluations and aromatherapy to ensure the balance of the body's essential elements: earth, wind, water and fire.

ORIENTAL SPA Map p116
☎ 0 2659 0444; www.mandarinoriental.com; Oriental Hotel, 48 Soi 40, Th Charoen Krung; 🕙 10am-10pm; half-day packages from 10,000B; 🚢 from Oriental Hotel; 🚇 Saphan Taksin
The Oriental Spa is one of the original hotel superspas and is considered one of the best in the region. Set in a delightful riverside location opposite the hotel itself (and accessed via private launch), it offers nine different massage techniques and numerous health treatments – perhaps an Urdwangam head massage (3300B for one hour) as hangover cure. Privacy is one of

the spa's main strengths, with individual and couples' suites (shower, massage tables and steam room) keeping camera-shy celebs happy. And the packages, in particular, wear rock-star price tags. Bookings are essential.

RASAYANA RETREAT Map p126
☎ 0 2662 4803; www.rasayanaretreat.com; 41/1 Soi Prommit off Soi 39, Th Sukhumvit; massage/packages from 500/3100B; 🚇 Phrom Phong exit 3
Rasayana combines basic beauty and massage treatments with holistic healing techniques, such as detoxification, colonic irrigation and hypnotherapy, for reasonable prices.

RUEN-NUAD MASSAGE & YOGA Map p116
☎ 0 2632 2662/3; 42 Th Convent, Th Silom; 1hr traditional massage 350B; 🕙 10am-10pm; Ⓜ Si Lom exit 2; 🚇 Sala Daeng exit 2
Just the right mix of old and new, Ruen-Nuad is set in a charming converted wooden house opposite BNH Hospital. It has partitioned massage stations, creating a mood of pampering and privacy typical of spa facilities, but at very reasonable parlour prices.

SPA 1930 Map p108
☎ 0 2254 8606; www.spa1930.com; 42 Soi Tonson, Th Ploenchit; massage/packages from 1200/3800B; 🕙 9.30am-9.30pm; 🚇 Chit Lom exit 4
Largely eschewing the contrived spa ambience of New Age music and ingredients you'd rather see at a dinner party (though we did notice some 'foot butter'), this high-end, high-priced spa on embassy row has a small menu that concentrates on the simple (face, body care and body massage). All scrubs and massage oils are based in traditional Thai herbal remedies.

WAT PHO MASSAGE PAVILIONS Map p68
☎ 0 2221 3686; www.watpomassage.com; Wat Pho, Th Sanam Chai; 1hr Thai massage 360B, foot massage 360B; 🕙 8am-6.30pm; 🚢 Tha Tien (N8)
These two air-conditioned *säh·lah* (pavilions) near the eastern entrance to the temple grounds are run by the school affiliated with Wat Pho, which is the country's primary training centre for Thai traditional massage. The menu is short but the quality is guaranteed, and after a day of temple sightseeing

BANGKOK MASSAGE 101

Bangkok has hundreds of massage options, from tiny shops with a couple of masseuses to resort-style spas that have honed pampering to a fine art, via venerable training institutions such as Wat Pho, where centuries of tradition are maintained and passed on. Parlours offering Thai traditional massage are the most prevalent, typically with massage beds in the front window, colourful reflexology charts on the walls and foot or full-body massages selling for very reasonable rates.

But the world of Bangkok massage parlours can sometimes throw up unexpected scenarios. If you're a woman you can rest easy in the knowledge that in the vast majority of cases you'll get, with varying degrees of quality, the massage you asked for. For men, however, your full-body 'oil massage' might involve techniques you didn't have in mind and which are definitely not on the curriculum at Wat Pho.

The tough part about this is that you never really know when you walk into a studio whether the massage is going to extend further up your inner thigh than is normally considered proper. It's not as if the parlours actually advertise 'happy endings 200B extra'. Indeed, many parlours actively discourage the practice, but masseuses are poorly paid and the opportunity to earn a bigger tip is often too hard to ignore.

So what should you do? Firstly, if you're not actually looking for a 'happy ending' then start by avoiding massage parlours in Bangkok's sleazier neighbourhoods – Nana, Sukhumvit near Soi Cowboy or around Patpong. You can also avoid trouble by walking past the shops with young, attractive women in miniskirts sitting outside and chorusing 'Hello sir, massage?' Look instead for the older, stronger-looking women, who normally give better massage. Parlours off the main path are often a good bet.

Once you've selected your parlour, choosing to not undress completely, which is normal for Thai massage – or wearing the unisex disposable knickers provided – will go some way toward deterring wandering hands. But it's no guarantee. If your masseuse's 'innocent' rubbing goes too far it will deliberately be left open to your interpretation; you'll need to either ignore it both physically and verbally, or deal with it verbally.

it's hard to think of a better way to cool down and chill out. For details of massage courses at the nearby school, see p270.

YOGA & PILATES

You might think Thais don't need any extra relaxation, but the international yoga revolution has found many a believer in Bangkok. Yoga studios – and enormous accompanying billboards of smiling gurus – have popped up faster than mushrooms at a full-moon party. Expect to pay about 650B for a one-off class.

ABSOLUTE YOGA Map p108

☎ 0 2252 4400; www.absoluteyogabangkok.com; 4th fl, Amarin Plaza, Th Ploenchit, Pathumwan; 🚇 Chit Lom exit 6
This is the largest of Bangkok's yoga-studio businesses, teaching Bikram hot yoga plus a host of other styles. Another popular branch is Thong Lor (Map p126; ☎ 0 2381 0697; 2nd fl, 55th Plaza, 55 Soi Thong Lor 2, Th Sukhumvit).

PILATES STUDIO Map p108

☎ 0 2650 7797; www.pilatesbangkok.com; 888/58-9 Mahatun Plaza, Th Ploenchit; 🚇 Ploenchit exit 2
The first choice for those looking for pilates.

YOGA ELEMENTS STUDIO

Map p108

☎ 0 2655 5671; www.yogaelements.com; 23rd fl, Vanissa Bldg, 29 Th Chitlom; 🚇 Chit Lom exit 5
Run by American Adrian Cox, who trained at Om in New York and teaches primarily vinyasa and ashtanga, this is the most respected studio in the entire city. The high-rise location helps you rise above it all, too.

GYMS

Bangkok is well stocked with gyms, ranging in style from long-running open-air affairs in spaces such as Lumphini Park (p120) to ultramodern megagyms complete with high-tech equipment, bars selling exotic vegetable drinks and a roster of stunningly good-looking members and instructors. Most large hotels have gyms and swimming pools, as do a growing number of small hotels. If your hotel doesn't, or you prefer the fashion-gym experience, both California Wow (www.californiawowx. com) and True Fitness (www.truefitness.co.th) have several branches in the Sukhumvit, Silom and Siam Square areas and offer pricey day memberships (about 700B). For something more old-school, the Ambassador Hotel Fitness Centre (Map p126; ☎ 0 2254 0444; www.amtel.co.th; Soi 11, Th Sukhumvit; per day 300B; ⏰ 6am-10pm; 🚇 Nana) isn't bad and has instructors who can give you a game of squash. For a personal trainer who comes to you, check out Bangkok Fitness Anywhere (www.bangkokfitnessanywhere.com; per session 1200B).

ACTIVITIES

If your hotel pool is more like a bathtub than a venue for lapping, the National Stadium (Map p108; ☎ 0 2214 0120; Th Phra Ram I; 🚇 National Stadium) has a public pool plus basketball and volleyball courts and other sports facilities.

GOLF

Bangkok's outer suburbs are well stocked with golf courses with green fees ranging from 250B to 5000B, plus the customary 200B tip for caddies. The website Thai Golfer (www.thaigolfer.com) rates every course in Thailand; click through to 'Course Review'. Rental equipment is available. Some courses are closed on Monday, while others are open at night for cooler tee-off times.

JOGGING & CYCLING

Lumphini Park (p120), Sanam Luang (p73) and Benjakiti Park (p128) all host early-morning and late-evening runners. Benjakiti has less shade and fewer people than the others, and rental bikes that can be ridden around the 1.9km-long circuit.

Several Hash groups meet for weekly runs, including the Bangkok Hash House Harriers (www.bangkokhhh.com; Saturday afternoons; men only), Bangkok Monday Hash (www.bangkokmondayhhh.com; Monday evenings; mixed), the Harriettes (www.bangkokharriettes.wordpress.com; Wednesday evenings; mixed) and the Siam Sunday Hash House Harriers (www.siamsundayhhh.com; 1st and 3rd Sunday afternoons of the month; mixed, children welcome).

Cyclists also have their own hash, with the Bangkok Hash House Bikers (www.bangkokbikehash.org) meeting one Sunday a month for a 40km to 50km mountain-bike ride and post-ride refreshments.

Bicycle Tours

You might be wondering who the hell would want to get on a bike and subject themselves to the notorious traffic jams and sauna-like conditions of Bangkok's streets. But the fact they sound so unlikely is part of what makes these trips so cool. The other part is that you discover a whole side of the city that's virtually off-limits to four-wheeled transport. Routes include unusual ways around Chinatown and Ko Ratanakosin, but the pick are journeys across the river to Thonburi and, in particular, to the 'lungs of Bangkok'. Better known as Bang Kachao (Map p132), this exquisite expanse of mangrove, banana and coconut plantations lies just a stone's throw from the frantic city centre, on the opposite side of Chao Phraya. You cycle to the river, take a boat to Bang Kachao and then follow elevated concrete paths that zigzag through the growth to a local village for lunch. The absence of horns, smog and traffic noise is truly serendipitous.

The following companies run regular, well-received tours starting at about 1000B for a half-day. Note that the Bangkok Green Bike Route, around Banglamphu and Ko Ratanakosin, had shut down at the time of research.

ABC Amazing Bangkok Cyclists (Map p126; ☎ 0 2665 6364; www.realasia.net; 10/5-7 Soi 26, Th Sukhumvit; tours from 1000B) Long-running operation with morning, afternoon and all-day tours.

Bangkok Bike Rides (Map p126; ☎ 0 2712 5305; www.bangkokbikerides.com; 14/1-B Soi Promsri 2, off Soi 39 (Phrompong), Th Sukhumvit; tours from 1000B) A division of tour company Spice Roads offering tours urban and rural, including several overnight routes.

Co van Kessel Bangkok Tours (Map p98; ☎ 0 2688 9933; www.covankessel.com; Mezzanine fl, Grand China Princess Hotel, 215 Th Yaowarat, Chinatown; ⏰ 6am-7pm; tours from 950B) Dutch company, very popular with Dutch travellers. It offers Thonburi and Bang Kachao tours, plus some unusual Chinatown offerings.

Velo Thailand (Map p82; ☎ 0892 017 782; www.velothailand.com; 88 Soi 2, Th Samsen, Banglamphu; ⏰ 10am-9pm; tours from 1000B) Small, personal operation based out of a well-stocked bike shop (sales and repairs available) in Banglamphu. Day and night tours to Thonburi and further afield.

SPECTATOR SPORT

Thais have embraced an increasingly diverse range of sports in recent years – tennis, golf, diving and motor racing, among others – but it's football and home-grown *moo·ay tai* that inspire the most devoted support.

KICKING & SCREAMING

More formally known as Phahuyut (from the Pali-Sanskrit *bhahu* or 'arm' and *yodha* or 'combat'), Thailand's ancient martial art of *moo·ay tai* (Thai boxing) is one of the kingdom's most striking national icons. Overflowing with colour and ceremony as well as exhilarating moments of clenched-teeth action, the best matches serve up a blend of such skill and tenacity that one is tempted to view the spectacle as emblematic of Thailand's centuries-old devotion to independence in a region where most other countries fell under the European colonial yoke.

Many martial-arts aficionados agree that *moo·ay tai* is the most efficient, effective and generally unbeatable form of ring-centred hand-to-hand combat practised today. And according to legend, it has been for a while.

After the Siamese were defeated at Ayuthaya in 1767, several expert *moo·ay boh·rahn* (from which *moo·ay tai* is derived) fighters were among prisoners hauled off to Burma. A few years later a festival was held and one of the Thai fighters, Nai Khanom Tom, was ordered to take on prominent Burmese boxers for the entertainment of the king, and to determine which martial art was most effective. He promptly dispatched nine in a row and, as legend has it, was offered money or beautiful women as a reward; he promptly took two new wives. Today a *moo·ay tai* festival (p21) in Ayuthaya is named after Nai Khanom Tom.

Unlike some martial disciplines, such as kung fu or *qi gong*, *moo·ay tai* doesn't entertain the idea that martial-arts techniques can be passed only from master to disciple in secret. Thus the *moo·ay tai* knowledge base hasn't fossilised and in fact remains ever open to innovation, refinement and revision. Thai champion Dieselnoi, for example, created a new approach to knee strikes that was so difficult to defend that he retired at 23 because no one dared to fight him anymore.

Another famous *moo·ay tai* champion is Parinya Kiatbusaba, aka Nong Thoom, a transvestite from Chiang Mai who arrived for weigh-ins wearing lipstick and rouge. After a 1998 triumph at Lumphini, Parinya used the prize money to pay for sex-change surgery and in 2003 the movie *Beautiful Boxer* was made about her life. While Bangkok has long attracted foreign fighters, it wasn't until 1999 that French fighter Mourad Sari became the first non-Thai fighter to take home a weight-class championship belt from a Bangkok stadium.

Several Thai *nák moo·ay* (fighters) have gone on to triumph in world championships in international-style boxing. Khaosai Galaxy, the greatest Asian boxer of all time, successfully defended his World Boxing Association super flyweight world title 19 times before retiring in 1991.

FOOTBALL

Thais, and particularly Bangkokians, have been caught up in the rapid internationalisation of football in recent years. Thailand has a national league, but apart from celebrating a few stars of the underperforming national team (104th in the FIFA world rankings in April 2010), most Thais will be happier watching Manchester United, Chelsea, Liverpool and Manchester City – the club formerly owned by ex-PM Thaksin Shinawatra – on TV rather than their own league. Still, if you want to see a match, most of the 16 Thai Premier League teams are based in Bangkok; most weekends you'll find a match at the conveniently central Chulalongkorn University Sports Stadium (Map p108).

MOO·AY TAI (THAI BOXING)

Quintessentially Thai, almost anything goes in *moo·ay tai*, the martial art more commonly known elsewhere as Thai boxing or kick boxing. If you don't mind the violence, a Thai boxing match is well worth attending for the pure spectacle – the wild musical accompani-

ment, the ceremonial beginning of each match and the frenzied betting.

The best of the best fight at Bangkok's two boxing stadiums. Built on royal land at the end of WWII, the art deco–style Ratchadamnoen Stadium (Sanam Muay Ratchadamnoen; Map p82; ☎ 0 2281 4205; 1 Th Ratchadamnoen Nok; ☻ bouts 6.30-10.30pm Mon, Wed & Thu, 5-8pm & 8.30-11pm Sun; ☒ air-con bus 503, ordinary 70) is the original and has a relatively formal atmosphere. Lumphini Stadium (Sanam Muay Lumphini; Map p122; ☎ 0 2252 8765; www.muaythailumpini.com; Th Phra Rama IV; ☻ bouts 6.30-10.30pm Tue & Fri, 5-8pm & 8.30pm-midnight Sat; ☒ air-con 4, 14, 45, 74 & 507; Ⓜ Lumphini exit 3) was constructed by the Thai army in 1956 and has a looser and more populist atmosphere than at Ratchadamnoen. Lumphini is also more encouraging of non-Thai boxers.

Admission fees are the same at both stadiums and vary according to seating. Ringside seats (2000B) are the most expensive and will be filled with subdued VIPs; tourists usually opt for the 2nd-class seats (1500B); and diehard *moo·ay tai* fans bet and cheer from 3rd class (1000B). If you're thinking these prices sound a bit steep for your average fight fan (taxi drivers are big fans and they make about 600B a day), then you're right. Foreigners pay more than double what Thais do.

We recommend the 2nd- or 3rd-class seats. Second class is filled with numbers-runners who take bets from fans in rowdy 3rd class, which is fenced off from the rest of the stadium. Akin to being in a stock-exchange pit, hand signals communicating bets and odds fly between the areas. Most fans in 3rd class follow the match (or their bets) too closely to sit down, and we've seen stress levels rise near to boiling point. It's all very entertaining.

Most programs have eight to 10 fights of five rounds each. English-speaking 'staff' outside the stadium, who will practically tackle you upon arrival, hand you a fight roster and steer you to the foreigners' ticket windows; they can also be helpful in telling you which fights are the best match-ups (some say that welterweights, between 61.2kg and 66.7kg, are the best). To keep everyone honest, however, remember to purchase tickets from the ticket window, not from a person outside the stadium. For more on the fighters and upcoming programs, see www.muaythai2000.com.

The Isan restaurants on the north side of Ratchadamnoen stadium are well known for their *gài yâhng* (grilled chicken) and other northeastern dishes; a visit is something of a fight-night tradition.

ĐÀ·GRÔR

Sometimes called 'Siamese football' in old English texts, *đà·grôr* (also spelt takraw) refers to a game in which a woven rattan or plastic ball about 12cm in diameter is kicked around. *Đà·grôr* is also popular in several neighbouring countries and is a hotly contested sport in the Southeast Asian Games.

Traditionally *đà·grôr* is played by men standing in a circle (the size of which depends on the number of players) and trying to keep the ball airborne by kicking it soccer style. Points are scored for style, difficulty and variety of kicking manoeuvres. Like watching someone juggling a football, there is something quite mesmeric about watching the best players stand about 8m apart and volley the *lôok đà·grôr* back and forth, sometimes hitting it with their heel while completely unsighted after it has sailed over their heads. Modern competitive *đà·grôr* (known as Sepak Takraw) is played with a volleyball net, using feet and head instead of hands. At the 2009 Southeast Asian Games, Thailand won in five of the eight categories.

Pick-up games are played throughout the city, most commonly in Lumphini Park (Map p122; Th Phra Ram IV; Ⓜ Lumphini; Ⓡ Ratchadamri, Sala Daeng) and National Stadium (Map p108; ☎ 0 2214 0120; Th Phra Ram I; Ⓡ National Stadium).

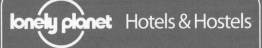

lonely planet | Hotels & Hostels

Want more sleeping recommendations than we could ever pack into this little ol' book? Craving more detail – including extended reviews and photographs? Want to read reviews by other travellers and be able to post your own? Just make your way over to **lonelyplanet.com/hotels** and check out our thorough list of independent reviews, then reserve your room simply and securely.

SLEEPING

top picks

See also our top views (p226) and top romantic lodgings (p215).

- **Sukhothai Hotel** (p226)
- **Peninsula Hotel** (p222)
- **Mandarin Oriental** (p222)
- **The Bhuthorn** (p215)
- **Phranakorn Nornlen** (p217)
- **Mystic Place** (p232)
- **Eugenia** (p228)
- **72 Ekamai** (p229)
- **Refill Now!** (p232)
- **Rose Hotel** (p225)

The last five years have seen Bangkok experience a very welcome hotel-building boom. While the city has long been home to some of the finest luxury hotels in the world, it wasn't so easy to find a decent midrange room. That has all changed, with stylish new midrange properties opening almost every month. Competition is intense and the resulting price war means big discounts are available at almost any time of year (see p224). Of course, the construction activity has extended further than the midrange. Several smaller, quirky luxury properties have emerged to compete with the established big-name dames. And budget lodgings aren't what they once were, either; flashpackers will be right at home in Bangkok's new industrial chic 'hostels'.

Like the city itself, Bangkok's accommodation is spread far and wide. Your choices are modern Sukhumvit, the business centre around Silom, the scenic riverside, the backpacker enclave of Banglamphu, the shopping district around Siam Sq, or boisterous Chinatown. To get a feel for which neighbourhood you might fancy before you book, see p214. And remember, Bangkok traffic can be diabolical...so if you can be near the Skytrain, Metro or river ferry you'll save time.

If money is your main consideration, then there's a good chance you'll end up on or near the famous (or infamous, depending on your experience) Th Khao San backpacking mecca (p86). Th Silom and Th Sukhumvit cater mainly to midrange and top-end budgets. Interesting options in the low end of the midrange can be found in Siam Sq, Ko Ratanakosin and Chinatown.

The best time for discounts is outside Bangkok's peak season, which is November to March and July and August. Discounts can also be had through Thai travel agencies or at Bangkok's airport hotel desks. With few exceptions, Bangkok accommodation wants you to check in at 2pm and check out at noon.

KO RATANAKOSIN & THONBURI

As Bangkok's oldest districts, the royal island of Ko Ratanakosin and Thonburi across the river make an ideal base for exploring the city's major historic sites and experiencing life by Mae Nam Chao Phraya. The sleeping options are suitably charismatic, with these five intimate abodes among the most atmospheric lodgings in the city. The biggest has only 12 rooms, so booking ahead is a good idea.

CHAKRABONGSE VILLAS
Map p68   Boutique Hotel $$$

☎ 0 2222 1290; www.thaivillas.com; 396 Th Maharat, Ko Ratanakosin; villas 4,500-25,000B; 🚇 Tha Tien (N8); 🛰 🛜 🈂

The grounds of Prince Chakrabongse Bhuvanath's 19th-century mansion have been adapted to become one of the city's classiest, most discreet boutique properties. The historic mansion remains a private home; the seven villas are set at either end of the garden. The pick are those nearer to the river, which combine a modern Zen feel with luxuries in Thai and Chinese styles. But the clincher is the delightful riverside din-

ing pavilion with postcard views across to Wat Arun. Meals are cooked to order using the freshest ingredients; the restaurant is open to the public with a day's notice.

AURUM: THE RIVER PLACE
Map p68   Hotel $$

☎ 0 2622 2248; www.aurum-bangkok.com; Soi Pansuk, Th Maharat, Ko Ratanakosin; r 3700-4600B; 🚇 Tha Tien (N8); 🛰 🖳 🛜

At the river end of a row of old Chinese godowns, the Aurum manages to feel at home here despite its faux-Parisian style. The 12 tastefully furnished rooms are by no means big, but the windows are and make the most of the not-wholly-uninterrupted river views. Breakfast is included and there's a riverside cafe right next door.

ARUN RESIDENCE Map p68   Hotel $$

☎ 0 2221 9158/9; www.arunresidence.com; 36-38 Soi Pratu Nok Yoong, Th Maharat, Ko Ratanakosin; d 3500-5500B; 🚇 Tha Tien (N8); 🛰 🖳 🛜

A couple of minutes' walk from Wat Pho along another soi (lane) of godowns, the Arun Residence is a romantic retreat because of its restaurant, The Deck (p160), bar and unrivalled views across to Wat Arun. The six rooms are fitted out with charis-

ROOM RATES – WHAT YOU GET FOR YOUR MONEY

Accommodation in this book is broken down into three categories. We've listed the mid-season rates including the ++, which in Thailand is 10% service and 7% government tax. These are the walk-in rates quoted to us, but where hotels offer online discounts we've included the rates they had available at the time of research. Remember that both the walk-in and online rates change frequently – sometimes hourly. For more on online discounts, see the boxed text on p224.

$$$ more than 4500B a night

$$ 1000B to 4500B a night

$ less than 1000B a night

So what do you get for your money? Bangkok's growing array of top-end hotels start at about 4500B and climb many times higher. In the top tier, rooms start at more than 10,000B, but in most of the luxurious design and boutique hotels, and the vast majority of the international brands, you're looking at 6000B to 9000B, before online discounting.

You can pay up to 4500B for a midrange room, too, though with discounting most are available for between 2000B and 3800B. Of course, more-modest properties have more-modest rates – modesty seemingly defined by the style of the decor. Thus older places are often quite cheap, while trendier new hotels are pricier.

The days of 50B beds in Banglamphu are over, but those on wafer-thin budgets can still get a dorm bed for between 150B and 400B, with a shared bathroom. More comfortable and stylish rooms are available for upwards of 800B, price rising with size, location and facilities.

matic midcentury decor and modern luxuries (including wi-fi), but some have better views and more space than others. Three have private decks, with the Arun Suite being the pick. Wherever you stay, you'll find it hard to drag yourself away from the sunset views from the bar.

IBRIK RESORT Map p68   Boutique Hotel $$
☎ 0 2848 9220; www.ibrikresort.com; 256 Soi Wat Rakhang, Th Arun Amarin, Thonburi; d 4000B; 🚤 Tha Wang Lang (Siriraj, N10); 🖳 🛜
Fancy a room by the river? If you roll out of bed in this three-room resort you could roll right into the river (which, given this is the Chao Phraya, is not recommended). The resort is in a white wooden house and with silks and four-poster beds the rooms are perfect for a romantic getaway that won't feel forced. Note the Moonlight room has no view, but occupants can use the communal riverside terrace. A sister property (Map p116; ☎ 0 2211 3470; 235/16 Th Sathon Tai) is hidden down a lane off Th Sathon, near Surasak BTS. Both have online deals from 3200B.

BANGLAMPHU

To the north of Ko Ratanakosin is Banglamphu (p80), a truly unique backpacker phenomenon and the world's greatest clearing house of international travellers. Centred around Th Khao San – better known simply as 'the Khao San Rd' or 'KSR' – Banglamphu has graduated from the days of spartan, 50B cells with bed

bugs and paper-thin walls (and mattresses) to boast a fast-growing roster of midrange options. Of course, cheap rooms are still available and whether you are flashpacking or counting the pennies, fierce competition means you'll get the best value for your baht in Banglamphu.

Booking ahead is recommended in peak season, particularly in the more expensive places. Still, if you're a bit flexible you should be able to wander around and find something at any time of year.

Banglamphu's popularity has seen lodgings spread out within about a 1km radius of its KSR epicentre. The district can be sliced into three main personalities centred on the following streets: Th Khao San, Soi Rambutri and Th Phra Athit and Th Samsen.

Th Khao San itself has upgraded its image and certainly its prices. Most of the grim shoeboxes have been replaced by comfortable, if not exactly inspiring, mid-rises with air-con and lifts. Prices are more suited to the barely 20s travelling with robust credit cards than the every-baht-is-sacred crowd of yore. Savvy budgeters should shop around for the latest makeover or newcomer luring new business with cut-rate promotions. Or better yet, step off KSR to find better value. For budget travellers who want to stay near KSR and are happy to forfeit cleanliness, privacy and quiet for the sheer thrill of paying close to nothing, a few monastic rooms can still be found along Soi Damnoen Klang and Trok Mayom, alleys running parallel to Khao San where small wooden houses are divided into even smaller rooms.

Along leafy Soi Rambutri and the river-facing Th Phra Athit is a more mature and slightly less crowded scene. Hotels have more creature comforts, there's less techno music to keep you awake and outdoor parties wind up earlier. It's all a short walk from Th Khao San – cut through the little Tel Aviv of the Secret Garden guesthouse – and conveniently near Tha Phra Athit and the express boats to major historical sites along the river.

Heading north across Khlong Rop Krung (aka Khlong Banglamphu), Th Samsen runs parallel to the river heading north to Thewet. Small sois branching off the road shelter a couple of tired no-tell hotels on the east side, and nearer to the river a mix of newer cheap hotels and family-run guesthouses amid a typical village world of thick-hipped mothers, freshly bathed babies and neighbours shuffling off to the nearest shopkeeper to buy sundries. It's a great area to wander.

A final note: we're listing the Banglamphu guesthouses we like most, but there are loads of others that are clean and – possibly – cheaper.

BUDDY LODGE Map p82   Hotel $$

☎ 0 2629 4477; www.buddylodge.com; 265 Th Khao San; r 4000-5000B; 🚌 air-con 511 & 516, ordinary 2 & 82; 🚢 Tha Phra Athit (Banglamphu, N13); ✳ 🖵 🖥

It was when we arrived on Khao San in 2001 and saw a Rolls Royce parked outside the grand new Buddy Lodge that we knew the road had changed forever. With its middle-of-the-action location, rooftop pool and 76 attractive, tropical-manor style rooms, Buddy has been booming ever since – so get up early (or don't go to bed) if you want a sun lounge. The McDonald's in the lobby is cheesier than a cheeseburger and service is patchy, but if you book online (from 2200B) Buddy's is good value. Wi-fi is 60B an hour; non-guests can use the pool for 200B.

OLD BANGKOK INN
Map p82   Boutique Hotel $$

☎ 0 2629 1787; www.oldbangkokinn.com; 609 Th Phra Sumen; d 3190-3990B, ste from 5590B; 🚌 air-con 511 & 516, ordinary 2, 12, 68 & 82; 🚢 klorng boat to Tha Saphan Phan Fah; ✳ 🖵 🖥

Occupying several adjoining shophouses that were once a neighbourhood noodle house, this boutique hotel is now pleasingly decorated in colours that conjure up visions of desserts: crème caramel walls, dark cocoa furnishings, persimmon silk bedspreads and flowing white mosquito nets. The 10 rooms occupy unconventional and sometimes cramped spaces, including mezzanine floors, attics and, in the family-size Lotus room, a walk-through bathroom to a garden bathtub. They all evoke the historic feel of the district, which is what you're here for, while catering to modern needs with internet-ready computer terminals. Service is excellent, and rates include wi-fi and breakfast (with 10% off for cash).

WHERE SHOULD I STAY?

If you don't have time to read through the Neighbourhoods chapter (p60) before booking your hotel, these words and phrases should help give you an idea of what Bangkok's various neighbourhoods (and their soi dogs) have to offer. If your stay inspires other adjectives, by all means share them with us at www.lonelyplanet.com/talk2us.

Ko Ratanakosin & Thonburi (p66) Historic centre, royal palace, temples, golden spires, reclining Buddha, tourist buses, river ferry, sunsets, amulets, students, godowns, lazy soi dogs.

Banglamphu (p80) Old Bangkok, shophouses, village feel, hidden bars, the Khao San Rd, budget beds, intergalactic melting pot, fashion parade, sandals, flip-flops, braids, touts, wooden frogs, neon, traffic, mangy soi dogs.

Thewet & Dusit (p92) Parkland, European palaces, soulless space, village wet market, flowers, few hotels, no trains, royal soi dogs.

Chinatown (p97) Noise, energy, flavours, tiny lanes, neon signs, delicious street food, shophouses, stalls, Chinese characters (both kinds), wholesalers, temples, Golden Buddha, gold shops, túk-túks, battered Vespas, fat soi dogs.

Siam Square, Pratunam & Ploenchit (p105) Shopping, malls, business, air-conditioning, fashion, miniskirts, shopping, students, Jim Thompson, quiet Muslim village, noisy roads, golden gods, traffic, cinemas, harassed and unwelcome soi dogs, shopping.

Riverside, Silom & Lumphini (p116) Diplomatic, professional, establishment, views, river boats, classic hotels, rooftop bars, sleazy clubs, park, kickboxing, night bazaar, aerobics, Patpong.

Thanon Sukhumvit (p126) Modern, frivolous, hi-so, international and frenetic, lots of hotels, fine restaurants, boutique, wannabe-boutique, expats, sports bars, expensive cars, street stalls, T-shirts, sleazy soi, loud, Skytrain, healthy soi dogs with collars (and T-shirts in 'winter').

THE BHUTHORN Map p82   Boutique Hotel $$
☎ 0 2622 2270; thebhuthorn.com; 96-98 Th Phraeng Phuthon, San Chao Phor Seua; d from 2,800B; ⚒ 🖳 🛜
In two century-old shophouses on a peaceful village square five minutes from the royal palace, the Bhuthorn is a delightfully stylish little B&B with wonderfully personal service to match. Its three rooms are the inspiration of Bangkok architects and veteran travellers Chitlada and Direk Senghluang, who spent four years renovating the heritage-listed building and fitting it with four-poster beds, antique cupboards and lamps, old photographs and Arabesque prints. The rooms come with flatscreen TVs, DVD players and free wi-fi. They're not that big, but don't feel so small and are great value… The Bhuthorn room is the pick.

VIENGTAI HOTEL Map p82   Hotel $$
☎ 0 2280 5434; www.viengtai.co.th; 42 Th Rambutri; s/d 2200/2400B; 🚢 Tha Phra Athit (Banglamphu, N13); ⚒ 🖳 🛜 📺
The Viengtai has been a Banglamphu fixture since 1953 – long, long before the first reefer-toting backpackers strung up hammocks on Th Khao San. But as the area has taken off, so the basic Chinese-style hotel has renovated and extended itself firmly into the midrange. The 200 rooms are completely devoid of personality, but peace and comfort are givens. Wi-fi is 100B for 30 minutes.

NAVALAI RIVER RESORT
Map p82   Boutique Hotel $$
☎ 0 2280 9955; www.navalai.com; 45/1 Th Phra Athit; d from 2100B; 🚢 Tha Phra Athit (Banglamphu, N13); ⚒ 🖳 🛜 📺
Navalai is probably the most convincing evidence yet of Banglamphu's rapid emergence as a place as much for midrangers as penny-pinching backpackers. Perched between the banks of Mae Nam Chao Phraya and arty Th Phra Athit, the busy 74-room boutique hotel delivers on location, style and – the ultimate 21st-century luxury – space. The rooms are big, have cheeky peep-show bathrooms and are decorated in an edgy-if-not-wild range of colours and artworks to complement sweeping river views. Then there's the rooftop pool and riverside restaurant. Book ahead, and pay the extra 500B for a River Breeze room; Serene Corner rooms are mostly viewless.

top picks

ROMANTIC STAYS

Money is No Object
- Ma Du Zi (p228) Contemporary luxury, relaxed chic.
- Mandarin Oriental (p222) Conrad, Maugham, Coward…and you.
- Peninsula Hotel (p222) High rise, high style, breathtaking views.
- Eugenia (p228) Explorer-style escapism.
- Chakrabongse Villas (p212) Riverfront royal residence.

Affordable Romance
- Ibrik Resort (p213) Simple west-bank seclusion.
- The Bhuthorn (left) Step back in time without forfeiting modern comforts.
- Arun Residence (p212) Sunsets over Wat Arun.
- Old Bangkok Inn (opposite) Luxury shophouse living, family feel.
- River View Guest House (p218) Million-baht views, pauper's price tag.

LAMPHU TREEHOUSE Map p82   Hotel $$
☎ 0 2282 0991; www.lamphutreehotel.com; Soi Baan Pan Thom, 155 Saphan Wanchat, Th Prachatipatai; s/d 1500/2100B; 🚌 ordinary 9, 12 & 56; ⚒ 🖳 🛜 📺
Accessed via a klorng-side footpath running west from Saphan Wanchat (Wanchat Bridge), the Lamphu is no treehouse, but it is a very good-value hotel. The terracotta-coloured lobby opens onto a modest pool where backpackers loiter and, together with the engaging staff, give the place a pleasantly social ambience. The 40 rooms on four levels (with lift) are colourful, comfortable and now include TVs. Book ahead.

BOONSIRI PLACE Map p82   Hotel $$
☎ 0 2622 1551; www.boonsiriplace.com; 55 Th Buranasat; d 1500-1900B; 🚌 air-con 511 & 516, ordinary 2 & 82; 🚢 Tha Phra Athit (Banglamphu, N13); ⚒ 🖳
In the historic village area south of Th Ratchadamnoen Klang, this modern 48-room hotel is an excellent choice for those looking for style, value and quiet. Over three floors, the brightly coloured rooms are a good size and feature a generous splash of Thai silk. The larger deluxe rooms, in particular, are a bargain at these prices.

NEW SIAM RIVERSIDE Map p82   Hotel $$
☎ 0 2629 3535; www.newsiam.net; 21 Th Phra Athit; d 1390-2490B; ☒ air-con 511 & 516, ordinary 2 & 82; ⛴ Tha Phra Athit (Banglamphu, N13); ❄ ☐

The fortunes of the New Siam guesthouse empire are a metaphor for the rise and rise of Banglamphu itself. With this, the fourth and newest New Siam, they've boldly stepped onto the Chao Phraya riverfront with a 104-room orange behemoth. With a riverside pool, a cafe, well-equipped and vaguely stylish rooms and an attractive location, it's one of the best options in the district – if you pay for view (from 1890B). The nearby New Siams II and III are also very popular. Book ahead.

SLEEP WITHINN Map p82   Hotel $$
☎ 0 2280 3070; www.sleepwithinn.com; 76 Th Rambutri; r 1100-1800B; ⛴ Tha Phra Athit (Banglamphu, N13); ❄ ☐ 🛜 🚲

Reflecting the area's steady move upmarket, Sleep Withinn is the latest place to offer enough global Zen style and comfort to attract the flashpacker baht without pricing themselves out of the budget market. The 50 compact rooms are a step up on those at the Rikka and at the usually discounted rates (1050B to 1300B) are excellent value. The rooftop pool is a bonus, though competition for sunbeds is fierce. Grumpy reception staff do take some of the shine off.

VILLA CHA-CHA Map p82   Hotel $
☎ 0 2280 1025; www.villachacha.com; 36 Th Tanee; r 800-2750B; ⛴ Tha Phra Athit (Banglamphu, N13); ❄ ☐ 🛜 🚲

Tucked away in a cat-filled alley north off Th Rambutri, the popular 74-room Villa Cha-Cha largely lives up to its claim of being 'really a site of calm and tranquillity'. The courtyard pool with overhanging tree, the dim lighting and the island style do most of the work, with staff contributing a laid-back but attentive disposition. Rooms are big but feel like they didn't get quite as much attention (or Balinese statues!) as the public spaces, and can be quite dark.

RIKKA INN Map p82   Hotel $
☎ 0 2282 7511; www.rikkainn.com; 259 Th Khao San; s 600B, d 800-950B; ⛴ Tha Phra Athit (Banglamphu, N13); ❄ ☐ 🚲

If you want a pool but don't want to spend money on rooms with fancy decorations (such as, in many cases, a window), then the Rikka will appeal. The lobby promises

more contemporary style than the 80 small rooms deliver, but credit where it's due – for this price they're fine. The rooftop pool is super.

ROOF VIEW PLACE Map p82   Hotel $
☎ 0 2280 1272; www.roofviewplace.com; Soi 6, Th Samsen; s 580B, d 680-780B, tr 1080B; ⛴ Tha Phra Athit (N13), Tha Thewet (Banglamphu, N15); ❄ ☐ 🛜

The Roof View embraces a sparse but – at this price – relatively stylish minimalism that makes it the pick among an otherwise uninspiring bunch in this quiet village area north of Khao San. Rooms are squeaky clean and very white. The 6th-floor roof does indeed have fine district views, but isn't really set up for hanging out. There's a winch for backpacks but no lift. Guests can use the kitchen in the lobby.

BOWORN BB Map p82   Guesthouse $
☎ 0 2629 1073; www.bowornbb.com; 335 Th Phra Sumen; r 700-800B; ⛴ Tha Phra Athit (Banglamphu, N13); ❄ ☐ 🛜

Cultural chameleons will love this antique neighbourhood of green-and-yellow shophouses and flip-flop-clad families with hardly a sign of tourist incursions. Boworn has bland but clean rooms with wet-all-over bathrooms. But it's the familial atmosphere centred on the cafe-lobby and the garden rooftop that are most attractive – and the *àroy* (delicious) green curries. Wi-fi is 50B per day.

SAM SEN SAM PLACE Map p82   Guesthouse $
☎ 0 2628 7067; www.samsensam.com; 48 Soi 3, Th Samsen; r 500-2100B; ⛴ Tha Phra Athit (Banglamphu, N13); ❄ ☐

Built 90 years ago and once part of a hospital, this welcoming guesthouse is now a palette of pastels with rooms sharing names and colours with grapes, bananas, kiwis, peaches and strawberries, among others. Rooms vary greatly in size but all have polished floorboards and teak furnishings. The smallest rooms share bathrooms. It's in a quiet location opposite a wát, a few minutes' walk from the Khao San action.

LAMPHU HOUSE Map p82   Guesthouse $
☎ 0 2629 5861; www.lamphuhouse.com; 75-77 Soi Rambutri, Th Chakraphong; d 400-740B; ⛴ Tha Phra Athit (Banglamphu, N13); ❄ ☐

A refreshing oasis, Lamphu House creates a mellow mood with its hidden, relatively quiet location and service that is more personal than some of its neighbours. Rooms are clean and some have balconies overlooking the green courtyard; cheaper fan rooms with shared bathrooms are also available. All up, great value – book ahead.

SHAMBARA Map p82 Guesthouse $

☎ 0 2282 7968; www.shambarabangkok.com; 138 Th Khao San; r 300-600B; ⓐ Tha Phra Athit (Banglamphu, N13); ⚇ 🖳 🛜

Just 50m from the noise and neon of Khao San, Shambara feels a world away. The century-old traditional wooden home has nine tiny but appealing rooms that share two clean showers and toilets. You can certainly find more luxurious rooms, but you're buying into the chilled, convivial atmosphere. Price includes coffee and toast; wi-fi is 1B per minute.

PRASURI GUEST HOUSE

Map p82 Guesthouse $

☎ 0 2280 1428; prasuri_gh_bkk@hotmail.com; Soi Phrasuli; s 220-380B, d 280-420B; 🚌 air-con 511 & 516, ordinary 2 & 82; ⓐ Tha Phra Athit (Banglamphu, N13); ⚇ 🖳 🛜

It doesn't get much more everyday Thai than this simple old guesthouse in a leafy soi northeast of Th Khao San. Appropriately in a neighbourhood of family-run shophouses, the Prasuri doubles as a 30B restaurant, A shop for random grocery items and an internet cafe that sees crowds of uniformed Thai schoolchildren battling it out on video games. The rooms are tired but quiet and clean, and all have bathrooms. Wi-fi is 50B a day.

THEWET & DUSIT

Thewet, the district abutting the river north of Banglamphu, has a small backpacker zone that is almost as old as the Khao San scene but remains largely off the radar. The guesthouses on and just off Th Sri Ayuthaya draw budgeters who are generally a little older than their counterparts on Th Khao San, and the vibe is more chilled and convivial and less catwalk. Thewet is a leafy area with a real neighbourhood sensibility, a morning market, a busy temple and easy access to the river ferry. The only drawbacks are that downtown Bangkok is many traffic jams away and the street is prone to flooding at the height of the rainy season (usually September or October).

PHRANAKORN NORNLEN

Map p93 Boutique Hotel $$

☎ 0 2628 8188-90; www.phranakorn-nornlen. com; 46 Soi Thewet 1, Th Krung Kasem, Thewet; s/d 1800/2200B; ⓐ Tha Thewet (N15); ⚇ 🖳 🛜

Everyone seems to love this small, arty boutique hotel where smiles come readily to faces. And there are many parts of it worth loving. The reconditioned wooden building stands in a lush garden, while the 25 rooms possess a rustic charm, have tall showers (with homemade organic soap) and come iPod ready; the wi-fi is free, too. The owners bring their sense of social and environmental responsibility to the hotel, with an organic garden on the roof (and plans for a cafe there, too) and breakfasts that will have the health-conscious drooling with anticipation. Staff also encourage guests to patronise local businesses, and run tours by bicycle and foot to make sure you find the right ones. All up, Phranakorn Nornlen has a real community ambience, fostered by the wonderfully engaging staff. Highly recommended.

SHANTI LODGE Map p93 Hostel $

☎ 0 2281 2497; www.shantilodge.com; 37 Th Si Ayuthaya, Thewet; dm 350B, s 400-850B, d 500-950B; 🚌 ordinary 53 & 30; ⓐ Tha Thewet (N15); ⚇ 🖳 🛜

Shanti Lodge is the sort of place where you might find barefooted backpackers engaging in long, languid conversations about the philosophy of travel and their dislike of Banglamphu, while a fellow backpacker strums a guitar as he waits for fresh coffee. That is, it's a pretty chilled place. Set in a rambling wooden house with a mix of artfully decorated rooms upstairs, it's the blissed-out garden cafe downstairs where you'll spend most of your time. The staff are, and have been for years, prone to a certain ice-queen indifference that annoys some travellers but is ignored by most. That aside, it's a real gem.

SRI AYUTTAYA GUEST HOUSE

Map p93 Hostel $

☎ 0 2282 5942; Th Si Ayuthaya, Thewet; r 650-750B; 🚌 ordinary 53 & 30; ⓐ Tha Thewet (N15); ⚇

Offering a decent alternative to Shanti Lodge, the Sri Ayuttaya has romantic air-con rooms with pretty hardwood floors, exposed brick and other stylish touches. It's not as social as Shanti, and service isn't much more forthcoming, either. But it's still superior to many Khao San–area flophouses charging the same dough.

BANGKOK INTERNATIONAL YOUTH HOSTEL Map p93
Hostel $

☎ 0 2282 0950; www.hihostels.com; 25/2 Th Phitsanulok, Dusit; dm 170B, r 450-1100B; 🚌 ordinary 3, 12, 16, 53, 72, 505 & 516; ⛴ Tha Thewet (N15); 🔀 🖥 📶

In a dull location east of Th Samsen and the Thewet budget abodes, this HI has benefited from almost three years of renovations, with newer rooms boasting silk flourishes. The old rooms and dorms, however, remain cramped and tired. The main reason to stay is the generally enthusiastic nature of the guests and the Thai volunteers who lead free tours for a chance to practise their English. Take 50B off if you're a member. Wi-fi is free.

CHINATOWN

Many visitors venture into this neighbourhood in search of a little more cultural immersion than can be found in the multicultural Disneyland of Khao San. By and large Chinatown's hotels suffer the same sort of total charisma bypass familiar in, well, Chinese cities, though there is one notable exception. The rates and rooms do, however, communicate in the international language for 'value'. The edges of the district and the area around Hualamphong train station have some appealing cheap options among the dross, while the Indian district of Phahurat is less expensive and caters to low-end business travellers from the subcontinent. But do watch your pockets and bags around the Hualamphong area.

SHANGHAI MANSION
Map p98
Boutique Hotel $$

☎ 0 2221 2121; www.shanghaimansion.com; 479 Th Yaowarat; r 3200-6400B; 🚌 air-con 507, ordinary 73; ⛴ Tha Ratchawong (N5); Ⓜ Hua Lamphong exit 3; 🔀 📶

Chinatown is notable for its charisma more than its class, so wandering off manic Th Yaowarat into the boutique Shanghai is serendipity itself – completely unexpected. The hotel (formerly called Shanghai Inn) brings a technicolour, Shanghai Tang–style interpretation of '30s Shanghai to Bangkok, and it has proved so popular that another 20 rooms have recently been added. They remain very good value, kitted out with Chinese-style four-poster beds, brightly painted walls, as many as 10 hanging silk

lights and a free mini-bar (up to a point). Wi-fi is available throughout, and breakfast is included. The best place in Chinatown, by far. Online deals from 2200B.

GRAND CHINA PRINCESS
Map p98
Hotel $$

☎ 0 2224 9977; www.grandchina.com; 215 Th Yaowarat; r 4200-4800B; ste from 8400B; 🚌 air-con 73, ordinary 73; ⛴ Tha Ratchawong (N5); 🔀 🖥 📶 📺

A certifiable monstrosity from the outside, this hotel in the heart of Chinatown is popular with groups and has nondescript but comfortable rooms buoyed by great views. The top floor has a panoramic rotating restaurant to make your dreams of gaudy Asia complete. Service is fairly good and rooms are available online from 2800B.

KRUNG KASEM SRIKUNG HOTEL
Map p98
Hotel $

☎ 0 2225 8900; srikrung_htl@yahoo.com; 1860 Th Krung Kasem; d 700B; 🚌 ordinary 25, 35 & 53; Ⓜ Hua Lamphong exit 3; 🔀

Across the klorng from Hualamphong train station, this institutional-style highrise won't win any design awards but the clean, sizable rooms are fair value. Rear rooms (with even numbers) are better because while the front rooms have train station views, they are buffeted by street noise.

RIVER VIEW GUEST HOUSE
Map p98
Guesthouse $

☎ 0 2234 5429; www.riverviewbkk.com; 768 Soi Phanurangsi, Th Songwat; r 250-950B; 🚌 ordinary 36 & 93; ⛴ Tha Marine Department (N4); Ⓜ Hua Lamphong exit 1; 🔀 🖥

Overlooking a bend in the river, the aptly named River View has an awesome, affordable and refreshingly communal location between Silom and Chinatown, steps from the river. Front rooms on the 5th floor and higher have views you'd pay several times as much for in the nearby top-end hotels, and the rooftop bar-restaurant has one of the best sunset views in town. While renovations have seen fresh paint liberally splashed and a modest spa added downstairs, most rooms remain fan-conditioned; air-con costs more.

River View is hidden among small lanes and can be tough to find, but if you get within about 250m you'll start seeing signs.

TRAIN INN Map p98   Hostel $

☎ 0818 195 544; www.thetraininn.com; 428 Th Rong Muang (Th Hualamphong); r 450-900B; 🚇 ordinary 9 & 36; Ⓜ Hua Lamphong exit 3; ☒ 🖵
In a strip of tired old budget places directly opposite the train station, the clean, secure and relatively funky Train Inn is a breath of fresh air. Owner Jana maintains a young, friendly and helpful atmosphere and her 41 rooms are hostel-style compact; the '1st-class' rooms are best; others can be noisy, so ask to see a few. Cable broadband is included in the 1st-class price and is 200B per day in other rooms.

BAAN HUALAMPONG
Map p98   Guesthouse $
☎ 0 2639 8054; www.baanhualampong.com; 336/20 Chaloen Krung, Th Phra Ram IV; dm/s 220/290B, d 570-900B; Ⓜ Hua Lamphong exit 4; ☒ 🖵

Off a quiet soi a few minutes' walk from the station, this old-style wood-and-concrete guesthouse has developed a loyal following among those seeking a mix of family atmosphere and backpacker self-sufficiency. The tiny rooftop garden is a great place to get to know your baan-mates over a sundowner, and you'll probably spend more time there and in the ground-floor communal space than in the simple rooms. The manager speaks English and German and is a font of knowledge – see the website for the cheapest possible ways of getting here. If you get here and don't fancy it, there's an equally good place directly across the soi.

SIAM SQUARE, PRATUNAM & PLOENCHIT

As central as Bangkok gets, this area is conveniently located on the Skytrain near shopping centres and loads of high-rise chain hotels. In the midrange, a devoted cast of túk-túk and taxi drivers throng the entrances of hotels, zealously pouncing on every map-toting victim. If you're a pedestrian wanderer, you'll be happier at a smaller hotel that is less of a target. Soi Kasem San 1, off Th Phra Ram I, has a cluster of nice guesthouses for the early-to-bed, early-to-rise traveller. For more on the Siam Sq and Pratunam district, see p105.

FOUR SEASONS HOTEL
Map p108   Luxury Hotel $$$
☎ 0 2126 8866; www.fourseasons.com/bangkok; 155 Th Ratchadamri; d from 8000B; 🚇 Ratchadamri exit 4; ☒ 🖵 🛜 🏊
A spectacular mural descending a grand staircase, ceilings adorned with neck-craning artwork and a library-quiet lobby punctuated with muscular columns give the Four Seasons a tone of relaxed opulence that continues into the lauded restaurants – especially Biscotti and Madison. These, and an open-air jungle courtyard, complement the 353 luxurious if not enormous rooms. Wi-fi is extra.

GRAND HYATT ERAWAN
Map p108   Luxury Hotel $$$
☎ 0 2254 1234; bangkok.grand.hyatt.com; 494 Th Ratchadamri; d from 7700B; 🚇 Chit Lom exit 8; 🖵 🖵 🛜 🏊
The Erawan's neoclassical lobby, embellished with mature tropical trees, sets the tone in what is one of Bangkok's most respected hotels. The 320 rooms are relatively big and well designed, with smart use of mirrors and well-positioned desks complementing an attractive modern Asian decor of hardwoods, silks and white marble. Rooms on the west side have the best views, overlooking the prestigious Bangkok Royal Sports Club racetrack.

SIAM@SIAM
Map p108   Boutique Hotel $$$
☎ 0 2217 3000; www.siamatsiam.com; 865 Th Phra Ram I; d from 5700B; 🚇 National Stadium exit 1; ☒ 🖵 🛜 🏊
Siam@Siam has taken the concept of industrial design pretty much as far as it can go. Wire sculptures stand on polished concrete and railway sleepers cover every exposed pylon. And thanks to a thoughtful design and liberal splashes of warm, earthy tones, it works. The 203 rooms occupy the 14th to 25th floors and they are not huge, but all have city views and are well equipped; ask for one overlooking National Stadium. If you're here to party and have money to spend, look no further. The ground-floor Party House One offers nightly live music in themes ranging from Beatles to funk, and the Roof (p184) is a worthy addition to Bangkok's sky-high scene; the dry season full-moon parties are popular. Online deals from 4100B.

SWISSOTEL NAI LERT PARK

Map p108   Luxury Hotel $$$

☎ 0 2253 0123; www.nailertpark.swissotel.com;
2 Th Withayu (Wireless Rd); d from 5600B; 🚇 Tha
Withayu; 🚊 Ploen Chit exit 5, 🔲 🖥 🛜 🅿

This hotel's greatest asset has always been
the jungle-like gardens and shaded pool,
which form a true urban oasis in central
Bangkok. A makeover aimed at the *Wall-
paper** crowd and some rebranding (out
with Hilton, in with Swissotel) has at-
tempted to draw people to the interiors as
well. And while there's only so much you
can do with a classic 1980s atrium (hang
some shiny stuff from the ceiling, appar-
ently), most of the rooms offer more inspi-
ration. We say 'most' because the standard
rooms, with their worn brown floral carpet,
feel more like nanna's parlour; the extra
600B up to the suite is so worth it. The in-
room LAN internet is 749B a day.

HOTEL VIE Map p108   Hotel $$

☎ 0 2309 3939; www.viehotelbangkok.com; 39-40
Th Phayathai; r from 3500B; 🚇 klorng boat to Tha
Hua Chang; 🚊 Ratchathewi exit 2; 🔲 🖥 🛜 🅿

Billed as a 'world class design hotel',
'uniquely stylish' and 'the new benchmark
of the world's hip hotels', this new tower
on the block has a lot to live up to. So how
does it go? Design-wise it is very appealing. The 154 rooms are huge and well laid
out. They come with genuine wooden
floors, voluminous bathtubs, lots of earthy-
coloured silks and a satisfying mix of space,
art and furnishings. It's managed by Accor
and the service is professional. It's not quite
the 'new benchmark', but it is a good hotel
and excellent value for money (except for
the in-room wi-fi: 17B per minute).

LUXX XL Map p108   Boutique Hotel $$

☎ 0 2684 1111; staywithluxx.com; 82/3 Soi Lang
Suan, Th Sarasin; d from 2600B; 🚊 Chit Lom exit 4;
🔲 🖥 🛜 🅿

Luxx XL is extra large compared with the
original 13-room Luxx hotel, but aside from
the 4m-high front door it appeals more for
its style than its size. The 50 rooms range
from 33-sq-metre studios to suites three
times that size. Teak dominates the decor,
with wooden floors, furniture and elegantly
simple corrugated wainscoting accompanied by open bathrooms, flatscreen TVs,
DVD players and free wi-fi. The overall
effect is generally pleasing if you're prepared to overlook some minor details, such
as stickers on the porcelain, which are less
than chic. The rack rates are extra large, too
– be sure to book online.

LUXURY FOR LESS IN EXECUTIVE APARTMENTS

Bangkok is loaded with serviced apartment buildings aimed at the executive market, ranging from midrange comfort
to no-sacrifice-is-too-great luxury. But what few people realise is that most apartments are happy to take short-term
guests as well as longer stayers. And by booking ahead you can get a luxury apartment with much more space than
a hotel room for the same or less money. It's really a great way to stay, especially if you are a family who needs more
room rather than two rooms. During research for this book we were offered apartments for as little as 2900B per day.

Several luxury buildings are on centrally located Soi Lang Suan, between Chit Lom Skytrain station and Lumphini
Park, while others gather on the other side of Lumphini Park in the Silom business district, and along Th Sukhumvit.
The Centrepoint (www.centrepoint.com) group is the biggest manager of serviced apartments, with eight buildings
across Bangkok. Others we like:

- Fraser Place Urbana Langsuan (Map p108; ☎ 0 2250 6666; www.fraserhospitality.com; 55 Th Lang Suan; daily
  from 4400B; 🔲 🖥 🛜 🅿) Architecturally stunning with decor, facilities, service and location to match. Fraser
  has three other properties in Bangkok, with great online deals.
- Siri Sathorn (Map p122; ☎ 0 2266 2345; www.sirisathorn.com; 27 Soi Sala Daeng 1, Th Silom; daily from 4200B;
  🔲 🖥 🛜 🅿) Chic modern apartments starting at 60 sq metres; shuttle bus, spa and satisfying service.
- House by the Pond (Map p126; ☎ 0 2259 3543; www.housebythepond.com; 230/3 Soi Sainumthip 2, Soi 22,
  Th Sukhumvit; daily 1200-2000B, per month 22,000-43,000B; 🔲 🖥 🅿) Older-style apartments and more
  affordable.

For more options try these websites:

- www.sabaai.com Most professional site for apartments.
- www.mrroomfinder.com Wide range, detailed search options.
- www.bangkokapartments.info Cheap places.

VIP GUEST HOUSE/GOLDEN HOUSE

Map p108   Hotel $$

☎ 0 2252 9535; www.goldenhouses.net; 1025/5-9
Th Ploenchit; r from 1650B; ⊠ Chit Lom exit 3;
⊠ ⊙
The 27 clean, quiet and mainly bright
rooms make this a good lower midrange
choice in this otherwise pricey part of
town. Rooms vary so ask to see more than
one.

These next three places are in a quiet soi just
a few minutes' walk west of the Siam shop-
ping extravaganza. If you prefer spending
your baht on shopping rather than sleeping,
look no further.

RENO HOTEL Map p108   Hotel $$

☎ 0 2215 0026; www.renohotel.co.th; 40 Soi
Kasem San 1, Th Phra Ram I; d 1200-1600B;
⊠ klorng boat to Tha Hua Chang; ⊠ National
Stadium exit 3; ⊠ ⊡ ⊠
This Vietnam War veteran has embraced
the new millennium with colour and flair,
making the best of its retro features (check
out the monogrammed pool) and funking
up the foyer and cafe, in particular. The 70
rooms remain fairly simple, the best being
those with a balcony overlooking the pool,
and service can be reluctant. But for the
money (price includes breakfast), the Reno
is a good deal within striking distance of
the shopping.

WENDY HOUSE Map p108   Hostel $$

☎ 0 2214 1149-50; www.wendyguesthouse.
com; Soi Kasem San 1, Th Phra Ram I; s/d/tw
1000/1100/1200B; ⊠ klorng boat to Tha Hua
Chang; ⊠ National Stadium exit 3; ⊠ ⊡ ⊙
Wendy is a cheery backpacker joint with
small but well-scrubbed rooms and tiled
bathrooms. The 38 rooms are all nonsmok-
ing, which is refreshing in this price bracket.
Desk staff are sweet and really try hard,
while the well-lit lobby is the sort of place
you're likely to end up swapping stories
with fellow travellers. Breakfast is included
and the wi-fi is free.

A-ONE INN Map p108   Guesthouse $

☎ 0 2215 3029; www.aoneinn.com; 25/13-15 Soi
Kasem San 1, Th Phra Ram I; d 600-700B; ⊠ klorng
boat to Tha Hua Chang; ⊠ National Stadium exit
3; ⊠ ⊡ ⊙
Family-run A-One has 25 clean if small
rooms (the bathrooms are minuscule) with

hardwood floors. There is an old-school
guesthouse vibe here, and as the cheapest place in the area it lives up to its 'value
in the heart of town' billing. The wi-fi is
charged.

RIVERSIDE, SILOM & LUMPHINI

Bangkok's most established and famous luxury hotels form a necklace along the banks of
Mae Nam Chao Phraya as the royal river flows
out of Bangkok to the south. This is romantic
Bangkok, where colonial-era buildings wilt
under the elements, watched over by towering hotels with priceless views. If the top end
is out of reach, there are a couple of cheapies
that pass the mould-free test. For more on this
part of Bangkok, see p118.

The Silom and Lumphini areas are rather
different to the riverside and bring a different range of accommodation. From stylish
to spinster, Silom's hotels sit in Bangkok's
primary business district and are mainly
popular with business travellers, airline staff
and first-time tourists wanting to be near the
neon of Patpong Market and Suan Lum Night
Bazaar, while remaining within easy reach of
the river and Siam shopping zone. Like the
Sukhumvit area, Silom Rd and its neighbours
have welcomed several new midrange hotels
in recent years, keeping competition fierce
and prices relatively low.

In the Lumphini area, including the east
part of Th Sathon near Lumphini Park, the
trendy Sukhothai and Metropolitan hotels
and the spa-like Banyan Tree make a splash
among the sober embassies and office buildings. Just around the corner, but galaxies
apart in price and comfort, are the survivors
of Bangkok's original backpacker ghetto at
Soi Ngam Duphli.

RIVERSIDE

A combination of the Skytrain to Saphan
Taksin and either a walk or ferry ride is the
way to reach the riverside's top-end hotels.
For our money, it's almost worth booking
into one of the hotels on the far side of the
river just so you can take their complimen-
tary ferries to and from Saphan Taksin and
River City (p146). Even if you choose to stay
in a more modest abode, the hotel ferries are
free to anyone.

MANDARIN ORIENTAL Map p116   Hotel $$$

☎ 0 2659 9000; www.mandarinoriental.com/Bangkok; 48 Soi 38, Th Charoen Krung; r from US$420; ☒ Tha Oriental (N1); ☒ Saphan Taksin exit 3 or exit 2 & hotel ferry; ☒ ☐ ☒

Dating to 1876, the Oriental Hotel is one of Southeast Asia's grand colonial-era hotels and one of the most luxurious and most respected in the region. The hotel's storied history of steamer travel and famous guests (see the boxed text, opposite) lives on in the original Author's Wing, a Victorian-era, gingerbread-style residence with rooms and suites dedicated to the famous writers who bedded and penned here.

The management prides itself on highly personalised service – once you've stayed here the staff will remember your name and what you like to eat for breakfast – though it's more formal and less relaxed than some younger competitors. Most of the 400 rooms are in the ageing River and Tower wings, which have contemporary Thai decorations, spacious bathrooms and river terraces. The establishment feel extends to the famed Le Normandie French restaurant and the bars, though you should find the sublime spa, on the Thonburi side of the river, more relaxing.

PENINSULA HOTEL Map p116   Hotel $$$

☎ 0 2861 2888; www.bangkok.peninsula.com; 333 Th Charoen Nakhon, Khlongsan; d from 13,000B; ☒ Tha Sathon (Central Pier) & private ferry dock near the Oriental Hotel; ☒ Saphan Taksin exit 2 & hotel ferry; ☒ ☐ ☂ ☒

Arguments over which is the best hotel in Bangkok inevitably end up with the Oriental and the Peninsula near the top of the list. And for all the Oriental's history and grandeur, the Peninsula's location, style, classic but unpretentious service and pure class make it very difficult to top. The lobby is poised and polished, an Asian-esque temple of squared black marble hallways and confident power players. Being on the Thonburi side of the river, the Peninsula enjoys views of both the river and the skyline beyond, an incandescent combination so picturesque it can sear a sultry sunset into the mind forever. The 370 tech-filled rooms boast oversized desks and private fax numbers to go with the understated style. All of this is complemented by fine restaurants and one of the city's best spas. World class. Wi-fi is included; online deals from 10,000B.

SHANGRI-LA HOTEL Map p116   Hotel $$$

☎ 0 2236 7777; www.shangri-la.com/bangkok; 89 Soi Wat Suan Phlu, Th Charoen Krung; d from 8000B; ☒ Tha Sathon (Central Pier); ☒ Saphan Taksin exit 1; ☒ ☐ ☂ ☒

The Shangri-La might be more than 20 years old but it has aged gracefully enough that it could be said to have matured. Service is first class and the 799 rooms are done in an understated, New Asia aesthetic. It works particularly well in the main wing, where the curved sides ensure everyone gets a river view (still, it's worth asking for a room close to the river). It's within the luxury sphere, yet families won't feel like bulls in a china shop and compared with its neighbours it's positively cheap. The 'exclusive' Krung Thep wing has lower-rise terraces overlooking the river. Wi-fi is included; online deals from 6000B.

MILLENNIUM HILTON Map p116   Hotel $$$

☎ 0 2442 2000; bangkok.hilton.com; 123 Th Charoen Nakhorn, Klongsan; r from 6500B; ☒ private ferry from River City & Tha Sathon (Central Pier); ☒ ☐ ☂ ☒

After a decade as a 32-storey concrete skeleton on the far bank of Chao Phraya, the Millennium Hilton finally opened in 2006 and now stands proudly, like a sailor in his cap, among the riverside top-end matrons. The modern Asian design creates a more stylish and less formal atmosphere than its neighbours. The buffet cafe, Flow, sets the tone with fresh food and river views. The Beach makes the most of a modest-sized pool by putting the sunbeds in the water, and ThreeSixty bar fills out that sailor's cap with jazz and unrivalled views – nice. The 543 rooms aren't huge but each one has cinemascopic views; the executive-plus suites are the pick. A private ferry connects to River City and Saphan Thaksin Skytrain. There are discounts for longer stays and booking three weeks ahead.

BAAN PRA NOND Map p116   Boutique Hotel $$

☎ 0 2212 2242; www.baanpranond.com; 18/1 Th Charoen Rat, Yannawa, Sathon; d from 3450B; ☒ Surasak exit 2; ☒ ☐ ☂ ☒

Built 70 years ago, and abandoned for most of the last 15, this colonial-style villa has been restored and transformed into a boutique B&B by the original owner's granddaughter. Nine small-but-bright rooms in two yellow-washed colonial-style villas

FROM LITERATI TO GLITTERATI

Now a famous grand dame, the Oriental Hotel started its career as the seafarers' version of a Th Khao San guesthouse. The original owners, two Danish sea captains, traded the nest to Hans Niels Andersen, the founder of the formidable East Asiatic Company. Andersen transformed the hotel into a civilised palace of grand architecture and luxury standards. He hired an Italian architect, S Cardu, to design what is now the Author's Wing, which was the city's most fantastic building not constructed by the king.

The rest of the hotel's history relies on its famous guests. A Polish-born sailor named Joseph Conrad stayed here in 1888. The hotel brought him good luck: he got his first command on the ship *Otago*, from Bangkok to Port Adelaide, which in turn gave him ideas for several early stories. W Somerset Maugham stumbled into the hotel with an advanced case of malaria. In his feverish state, he heard the German manager arguing with the doctor about how a death in the hotel would hurt business. Maugham's overland Southeast Asian journey is recorded in *Gentleman in the Parlour: A Record of a Journey from Rangoon to Haiphong,* which gave literary appeal to the hotel. Other notable guests have included Noel Coward, Graham Greene, John le Carré, James Michener, Gore Vidal and, erm, Barbara Cartland. Some modern-day writers claim that an Oriental stay will overcome writer's block – though we suspect any writer staying these days would need a very generous advance indeed.

feature classic 1930s decor; floor tiles, four-poster beds, overhead fans, wind-up alarm clocks and crisp white linen. The ground floor boasts a communal space that is perfect for chatting with helpful hosts Tasma and Jason, and a pint-sized pool in the courtyard. The only catch is the location between two busy roads; double glazing is not quite enough to muffle all the noise.

SWAN HOTEL Map p116   Hotel $$
☎ 0 2235 9271-73; www.swanhotelbkk.com; 31 Soi 36, Th Charoen Krung, Bangrak; s 800-1200B; d 900-2000B; 🚢 Tha Si Phraya (N3); 🚉 Saphan Taksin exit 3; ❌ 🖳 📶 🏊

Hidden among shade trees and quiet riverside lanes, the Swan Hotel has been around almost long enough (45 years) to have earned its own place in the lore of this historic neighbourhood. The 67 rooms are clean, compact and well equipped, with decor that is tasteful if not extravagent. But the main attractions are the delightful pool and surrounding garden that most rooms look onto, and the excellent value for this area. Wi-fi is 300B a day; rooms are 20% cheaper online.

NEW ROAD GUESTHOUSE
Map p116   Guesthouse $
☎ 0 2630 6994-98; www.jysk-rejsebureau.dk; 1216/1 Th Charoen Krung, Bangrak; dm 130-220B, d 800-1300B, apt 2500B; 🚢 Tha Si Phraya (N3); 🚉 Saphan Taksin exit 3; ❌ 🖳

Despite being far from Banglamphu and just off one of the busiest roads in Bangkok, the New Road is the go-to budget joint in this part of town and one of the more upbeat and enjoyable guesthouses in

all of Bangkok. Run by young Danish guys whose main gig is running budget-priced (and oft-recommended) tours around Thailand, the atmosphere is amiable and the evenings-only bar is a great place to meet other travellers. Rooms range from simple fan dorms to comfortable doubles and a four-room apartment ideal for families.

SILOM

Parts of Silom are well served by the Skytrain, with Sala Daeng and Chong Nonsi stations most useful, which is a relief because traffic crawls day and night. Cars move faster along Sathon's multilane corridor. The east end of Silom is also served by the Metro at Si Lom station.

LE MERIDIEN BANGKOK
Map p116   Hotel $$$
☎ 0 2232 8888; www.lemeridien.com/bangkok surawong; 40/5 Th Surawong; r from 6500B; Ⓜ Sam Yan exit 1; 🚉 Sala Daeng exit 1; ❌ 🖳 📶 🏊

For decades the thought of being right on the doorstep of sleazy Patpong scared high-end hotel chains away from this part of Bangkok. But Starwood Hotels obviously isn't concerned and this ultra-designed, 24-storey glass tower is the result. The look is modern Asian, with bamboo, dark timber and earthy colours delivered in clean lines in the 282 rooms and edgy restaurants. Floor-to-ceiling windows ensure uninterrupted views of the Patpong action and make the rooms seem bigger than they are. Service is excellent. All up, a welcome addition to Bangkok's top tier. Wi-fi is 650B a day; online deals from 5200B.

BOOKING ONLINE: JUST DO IT

'You know,' said the woman as she glanced conspiratorially around the reception of one of Bangkok's top hotels, 'if you book online the rates are much cheaper…about 30% usually.' We have been offered similar surprisingly honest advice several times while researching Bangkok hotels, with the general message being that for midrange and top-end hotels booking ahead gets you discounts you can't even contemplate when you walk in…even during the January peak season.

It doesn't square with the years you may have spent haggling at hotel reception desks, but some hotels offer similar large discounts for phone bookings. In theory, you can call from the guest phone in the lobby, reserve a room at the discount rate, have a drink in the bar and check in 15 minutes later having saved 30%. Even around Th Khao San, that bastion of the backpacker, advance bookings can result in savings, though the cheapest places might still engage in a bit of old-style, person-to-person haggling.

Of course, online booking also has its dangers…read LP author Karla Zimmerman's account of her unwitting encounter with bratwursts and neon bikinis in the boxed text, p227. For independent reviews rather than endless superlatives, Lonely Planet's Hotels & Hostels (www.lonelyplanet.com) features thorough reviews from authors plus traveller feedback, and a booking facility. For an idea of the sort of discounts you're looking at, independent website Travelfish (www.travelfish.org) has a handy list of hotel names and their current online price in its Bangkok pages.

DUSIT THANI Map p116   Hotel $$$
☎ 0 2200 9000; www.dusit.com; 946 Th Phra Ram IV, cnr Th Silom; r from 6500B; Ⓜ Si Lom exit 2; Ⓡ Sala Daeng exit 4; ❌ ▯ 🛜 ▯

The Dusit Thani defined Bangkok glamour in the 1970s when it reigned as the city's tallest skyscraper. From the outside its distinctively '60s look remains, with balconies off every room and a triangular layout. But rather than embracing this with a thoughtful retrovation, the Dusit's attempts at modernisation have left it with an identity crisis. Despite this, the Dusit remains a favourite among Thais and fà·ràng (Westerners) alike, and there is a palpable buzz of excitement as Thais in their finest arrive and depart for wedding banquets or conferences. It also boasts one of Bangkok's best restaurants (and killer views) in D'Sens (p168). Wi-fi is free only in public areas; rooms sell online from about 4800B.

TRIPLE TWO SILOM
Map p116   Boutique Hotel $$
☎ 0 2627 2222; www.tripletwosilom.com; 222 Th Silom; r/ste 6000/7000B; Ⓡ Chong Nonsi exit 2; ❌ ▯ 🛜

How do you take a bland Bangkok shopping mall and turn it into a classy boutique hotel? The answer lies in this four-storey, 75-room hotel in the middle of stylish Th Silom. The 2004 makeover delivered a lot of white marble, dark wood and old-timey photographs, which come together in a pleasing pan-Asian mode. Rooms are large and kitted out with a satisfying amount of comforts and gadgetry, including DVD player and both wi-fi and ADSL internet at the large desk. Guests can use the roof garden, but will have to go next door to the sister Narai Hotel for the swimming pool and fitness centre. Online from 3800B.

THE HERITAGE BAAN SILOM
Map p116   Boutique Hotel $$
☎ 0 2236 8388; www.theheritagebaansilom.com; 659 Soi 19, Th Silom; r 2500-4000B; Ⓡ Chong Nonsi exit 3

One of four new budget boutique hotels from the Heritage Hotels group, this 36-room affair is as eclectic as the marketing promises. The three-storey facade has a classical-cum-Moorish look, while inside it's modern chic littered with classical furnishings – often in white. The rooms are bright if not huge, but are excellent value when booked online (from 1600B). Rooms have cable internet access; wi-fi is free in the lobby. Nearby The Heritage Bangkok (☎ 0 2235 2888; www.theheritagebangkok.com; 198 Soi Phiphat 2, Th Chong Nonsii; r 2200-2500; Ⓡ Chong Nonsi exit 4; ❌ ▯ 🛜 ▯) has a rooftop pool, but the modern rooms are dark and the colours jar. Still, good value online from 1700B.

LA RÉSIDENCE HOTEL
Map p116   Boutique Hotel $$
☎ 0 2233 3301; www.laresidencebangkok.com; 173/8-9 Th Surawong; d/ste 2400/3400B; ▯ aircon 16, ordinary 93; Ⓜ Sam Yan exit 1; Ⓡ Chong Nonsi 2; ❌ 🛜

La Résidence is a charming boutique inn with 26 playfully and individually decorated rooms that, according to the obliging manager, have been continually evolving since it opened in the early 1990s. They're fantastic value. Micro-mini-sized rooms start at 1400B but for 2400B you get a more voluptuous abode, often with richly coloured walls, modern Thai motifs and crystal-clean bathroom. The top-floor studio has its own garden and at 3700B is incredible value. The overall effect is a casual sophistication that will delight anyone who gets twitchy in chain hotels. Wi-fi is 150B a day.

ROSE HOTEL Map p116 — Hotel $$

☎ 0 2266 8268-72; www.rosehotelbkk.com; 118 Th Surawong, Silom; r from 1950B; Ⓜ Sam Yan exit 1; Ⓡ Sala Daeng exit 1; ❌ 🛏 🛜 🛀

Hidden down a lane beside the landmark Montien, the Rose is another Bangkok veteran that has had some much-needed cosmetic surgery. The result is more Halle Berry than Jocelyne Wildenstein, with the 70 spacious rooms sporting a stylish mix of coloured walls, dark tiles and sleek bathrooms. This Rose is a very cheap date, too, considering she comes with an oasis-like pool, a small gym (three machines), a sauna and the delightful Ruen Urai Thai restaurant, set in an old teak house that has been in the owner's family for generations. With breakfast included and wi-fi for 300B a day, it's one of the best deals in town.

LUB*D Map p116 — Hostel $$

☎ 0 2634 7999; www.lubd.com; 4 Th Decho, Th Surawong; dm/d 550/1800B; Ⓡ Chong Nonsi exit 2; ❌ 🛏 🛜

From the owners of Triple Two Silom comes Lub*D (meaning 'sleep well'), a smash hit with flashpackers for its lively social scene. One of Bangkok's new breed of 'boutique hostel', the four storeys of dorms (including a ladies-only wing) and rooms with and without bathrooms are an industrial mix of raw concrete, exposed iron beams, woodchip doors and stencilled signs. The atmosphere is young and hip, with free internet in the streetside bar-cum-

lobby and an attractive young staff to point you in the right direction. Security is tight (even the dorm rooms have key cards). It should be noted that at 1400B for a twin without a bathroom, you can certainly find better-equipped rooms for less elsewhere.

BANGKOK CHRISTIAN GUEST HOUSE

Map p116 — Guesthouse $$

☎ 0 2233 6303; www.bcgh.org; 123 Soi Sala Daeng 2, Th Convent; s/d 1100/1540B; Ⓜ Si Lom exit 2; Ⓡ Sala Daeng exit 2; ❌ 🛏

Located just steps from Patpong's go-go bars, this lower midrange but thoroughly wholesome (no beer, free water) place proves that vice and morality are never far apart. The 58 recently renovated rooms are comfortable and spotlessly clean, with cable TV and air-con standard. The style is more Christian simplicity than global Zen, but at these prices you can't complain. Family-style meals provide fellowship as well as sustenance. A small outdoor playground is available.

TAKE A NAP Map p116 — Hostel $$

☎ 0 2637 0015; www.takeanaphotel.com; 920-926 Th Phra Ram IV; dm 380-750B, s 1000B, d 1300-1500B; Ⓜ Sam Yan exit 1; Ⓡ Sala Daeng exit 3; ❌ 🛏 🛜

At Take a Nap the wall of your tiny guesthouse room is much more than the usual monument to peeling paint and squashed mosquitoes. Instead you'll find Pop Art–style murals of Thai and Bangkok scenes (including Wat Arun and, ahm, cars on elevated highways). The arty visuals feed into an easygoing vibe, with staff and fellow guests seeming more forthcoming because of it. The main drawback is the location on Th Phra Ram IV (Rama IV), near the corner of busy Th Surawong, which means noise is an issue at all hours; light sleepers should bring earplugs. There is wi-fi, but it's patchy.

GREEN HOTELS

Hotels might seem to be gobbling up the landscape, but many are watching what they eat when it comes to world resources. Green Leaf Foundation, a collaborative environmental organisation, has recognised a number of Bangkok hotels for cutting energy and water use and garbage output, and raising awareness of environmental issues among their staff. Among them, green hotels we recommend include Banyan Tree Hotel (p226), Dusit Thani (opposite), Grand China Princess (p218), Grand Hyatt Erawan (p219) and the Malaysia Hotel (p227). See www.greenleafthai. org for specifics of what they have done.

Several smaller hotels have also adopted socially and environmentally responsible practices, notably Phranakorn Nornlen (p217), Baan Pra Nond (p222) and Mystic Place (p232).

top picks

PANORAMAS

If you like to spend time in your room looking out of it, these beanpoles have guaranteed angel's-eye views in the City of Angels. Just remember to ask for a room on an upper floor.

- Millennium Hilton (p222)
- Banyan Tree Hotel (right)
- Peninsula Hotel (p222)
- Dusit Thani (p224)

HQ HOSTEL Map p116   Hostel $$
☎ 0 2233 1598; www.hqhostel.com; 5/3-4 Soi 3, Th Silom; dm 380-750B, d 1500B; Ⓜ Si Lom exit 2; Ⓡ Sala Daeng exit 2; ✕ ▣ 🛜

One of the many things we learned about Bangkok while researching this book was that flashpacker hostels are likely to involve a large amount of polished concrete and other industrial-style themes. HQ Hostel has stuck to the mould, squeezing several four- to 10-bed dorms and a few doubles into a narrow multistorey building just off Silom. It's not quite as good as Lub*D, with doubles being half bed, half bathroom and a mirror proclaiming 'You are awesome'. Yet the vibe is fun and friendly and the communal areas are good for meeting people.

URBAN AGE Map p116   Hostel $
☎ 0 2634 2680; www.guesthouse-bangkok.com; 130/6 Soi 8, Th Silom; dm/d 250/800B; Ⓜ Si Lom exit 2; Ⓡ Sala Daeng exit 1; ✕ ▣ 🛜

The eight-room Urban Age is a sort of New Age version of the classic Bangkok budget haunt, in a quiet soi within crawling distance of the Silom nightspots. Small rooms, all without bathrooms and some without windows, have just enough draped fabric and minor touches to make it more appealing than the prison-cell style competition. The friendly manager is a highlight. The only downside is that the dorms are six storeys up, all stairs. Wi-fi is free but only works in the foyer.

LUMPHINI

Access to Lumphini Park and the business and diplomatic areas of Th Sathon are the main reasons to stay in this part of Bangkok. The other reason is to experience Bangkok's original, pre–Khao San backpacker district. Soi Ngam Duphli and Soi Sri Bamphen have been in the doldrums for quite a while, but the decades-old ultra-budget flophouses so popular with long-term expats have recently been complemented by a couple of newer, smarter guesthouses and hotels taking advantage of the location near to Lumphini Metro station and the fact it's not Banglamphu.

Meanwhile, the leafy area between the east ends of Th Sathon and Th Silom continues to be home to several executive apartment buildings that offer very competitive short-term deals.

SUKHOTHAI HOTEL
Map p122   Hotel $$$
☎ 0 2344 8888; www.sukhothaihotel.com; 13/3 Th Sathon Tai; r from 12,900B; Ⓜ Lumphini exit 2; ✕ ▣ 🛜 🚲

If you're sick of cookie-cutter international hotels where you need to remind yourself what city you're in, stay at the Sukhothai. Architect Ed Tuttle's uniquely Thai modernism embraces both classic Thai features – think winged roofs, hardwood floors and six acres of garden full of brick stupas reminiscent of the ancient capital of Sukhothai – and a modern minimalism that has everything satisfyingly in its right place. The 210 rooms carry the theme and most have views of the extensive gardens and ponds that are far enough back from busy Th Sathorn to be wonderfully quiet. All up, very classy, with restaurants Celadon and La Scala rounding it out. Rooms online from about 8,000B.

BANYAN TREE HOTEL
Map p122   Hotel $$$
☎ 0 2679 1200; www.banyantree.com; Thai Wah II Bldg, 21/100 Th Sathon Tai, Sathon; d from 10,500B; Ⓜ Lumphini exit 2; ✕ ▣ 🛜 🚲

The Banyan Tree is housed in one of Bangkok's most recognisable buildings, a sleek wafer of a skyscraper with a huge circular hole through it and a rooftop fitted out with the dreamy Moon Bar (p184). The mood is more spa than hotel, with the fragrance of gardenias and the sound of splashing water in the foyer and no less than six levels of spa facilities. The views are memorable and the rooms are remarkably smart given the hotel is getting on a bit in years. All up an excellent top-end choice, but with a few too many stairs for families with young kids. Online from 5600B, or third night free.

METROPOLITAN Map p122   Hotel $$$

☎ 0 2625 3322; www.metropolitan.como.bz; 27 Th Sathon Tai, Sathon; d US$290-360, ste US$420-2000; Ⓜ Lumphini exit 2; ✶ ▭ ▦

The very essence of urban cool – with the members- and hotel-guests-only Met Bar to prove it – the Metropolitan was reborn from the ashes of, wait for it, a YMCA. The techno-cool lobby leads to sleek modern rooms with white-on-black contrasts. But the ghost of hostels past is still apparent in the cramped and overpriced City rooms, where minimalist becomes torturous, though the bathrooms remain big enough for rock-star primping. The suites are more humane and the two-storey suites are the ultimate in expansive expensive luxury. The two in-house restaurants are excellent. The Met usually has serious online discounts, with rooms often as cheap as US$119 if you stay two nights.

TIVOLI HOTEL Map p122   Hotel $$

☎ 0 2249 5858; www.thetivolihotelbangkok.com; 71/2-3 Soi Sri Bumphen, Th Yen Akat, Sathon; d 2000-3000B; Ⓜ Khlong Toei, exit 1; ✶ ▭ ≋ ▦

The 133-room Tivoli is a classy new hotel that punches well above its midrange price tag. The contemporary design approaches chic in an orange way, and unlike some in this bracket the Tivoli has few rough edges. Rooms (with DVD players and big flatscreen TVs) and public spaces, including the rooftop pool and bar, are thoughtfully designed. For us, however, the most impressive aspect was the management, with

staff thoroughly professional and only too happy to help out. Wi-fi is free in the lobby but 420B a day in-room.

ALL SEASONS Map p122   Hotel $$

☎ 0 2343 6333; www.allseasons-sathorn.com; 31 Th Sathon Tai; r 2000-2500B; Ⓜ Lumphini exit 2; ✶ ▭ ≋

After a 2008 makeover hauling it into the 21st century, the All Seasons, nee King, offers 78 spacious, mostly high-ceilinged rooms for an attractive price amid the embassies. The ambience is modern Asia, with yellow, red and green on white, and comforts include rain shower, desk with free wi-fi and cable broadband, and flatscreen TV on the wall. Superior and deluxe rooms are best; the rooftop 'exclusive' rooms are small but include a 6pm checkout. Online deals from 1000B.

MALAYSIA HOTEL Map p122   Hotel $

☎ 0 2679 7127; www.malaysiahotelbkk.com; 54 Soi Ngam Duphli, Th Phra Ram IV; d 798-998B; Ⓜ Lumphini exit 1; ✶ ▭ ▦

After almost 40 years the Malaysia's glory days as Bangkok's most famous budget travellers' hotel are long gone, but it remains very busy and good value in an aging, almost-but-not-quite retro-cool way. Its reputation as a gay pick-up scene means that most of the women you will see are on the staff, though the manager assures us that 'anyone is welcome, not only gays'. The 119 rooms are a good size and good value.

THE PERILS OF ONLINE BOOKING Karla Zimmerman

Neon bikinis: that's odd, we thought, as our taxi drove out of the snarled traffic on Th Sukhumvit and up to our hotel. The building across the street was bursting with women clad in glowing skimp-wear. German oompah songs wafted through the air, and advertisements for 'bratwursts' covered menu boards at the surrounding restaurants.

Yes, we were jet-lagged, having just spent 21 hours to reach Bangkok, and it was the middle of the night, when strange things tend to happen. But bratwursts and fluorescent bikinis?

We entered the hotel lobby, where Western men and young Thai women nuzzled on all the available couches. That's when the light bulb popped over our heads, and we realised our situation: the room we'd booked on the internet – a room of 'luxurious comfort' with 'teakwood decorations and cable TV' – was located in a de facto brothel. We'd arrived at the Nana Entertainment Plaza.

A quick amble around the hotel grounds brought us to bars like Hollywood Strip (Pool! Shows! Girls! Darts!), Carnival (GoGo Girls, Girls, Girls!) and G-Spot (250 Girls Upstairs!). The latter's dancers made the neon-bikini group look practically Amish by comparison.

Despite the distraction of drinking one's beer and eating one's *pàt tai* in venues where most of the patrons were getting hand jobs, we appreciated our unplanned bite of this classic slice of Bangkok. Next time, though, we'll be more careful when booking online. While a hotel that touts 'easy access, 24 hours' can't be faulted for false advertising, it's wise to remember that words have multiple meanings.

THANON SUKHUMVIT

Much of Bangkok's recent rush to build condos, offices and hotels has been played out in a sea of cranes and jackhammers along Th Sukhumvit's lower soi. More than 15 new hotels have opened since 2006, mostly falling into the boutique or wannabe boutique categories. As a result Sukhumvit has the city's widest choice of midrange accommodation at the most competitive prices.

Sukhumvit is the most cosmopolitan part of Bangkok, home to thousands of expats and 'hi-so' (high society) Thais whose spending power supports hundreds of restaurants – Italian and Japanese being the most common. Th Sukhumvit itself is dominated by the Skytrain, which runs above it for several kilometres and at points creates a canyon-like sound trap.

Down on the ground the street is divided into two distinct districts. West of Soi Asoke (Soi 21) is the main tourist sector where the 1960s R & R days live on in sois full of girlie bars. It's easy enough to avoid these, though escaping the streetside stalls flogging cheap souvenirs and fake DVDs is impossible. That said, business is so good that the touting is pretty tame. Around Soi 11 and nearby are plenty of lower midrange hotels with rate sheets that often include 'joiner fees'. East of Soi Asoke, the girlie bars are replaced with residential areas, package-tour hotels and a growing number of interesting little abodes, like Eugenia (p228) and Seven (p229).

Sukhumvit traffic is diabolical, but by using the Skytrain you can rise above most of it when heading west to the shopping areas and the riverside. The Metro connects at Asoke and is by far the easiest way to get to the northern bus station, Hualamphong train station and Chinatown.

MA DU ZI Map p126   Boutique Hotel $$$
☎ 0 2615 6400; www.maduzihotel.com; cnr Th Ratchadapisek & Sukhumvit Soi 16; r from 8,900B; Ⓜ Sukhumvit exit 2; Ⓡ Asok exit 6; ❌ 🖳 📶
Ma Du Zi means 'come and see' and those who do come find a masterpiece of design, with every detail thought of and the fittings of the highest order. Each of the 41 rooms has a work desk with fax/copier/printer, an espresso machine, original artwork, and a restrained but stylish luxury in white marble, blonde wood and black furniture – some even have remote-controlled bath tubs. Rooms are huge, starting at 49 sq metres and climbing to 79 sq metres. So too are the

prices, and there is no pool. Still, the service is excellent, it's extremely discreet (no walk-ins), and the French restaurant is top-notch.

SHERATON GRANDE SUKHUMVIT
Map p126   Hotel $$$
☎ 0 2649 8888; www.sheratongrandesukhumvit. com; 250 Th Sukhumvit; r from 7,500B; Ⓜ Sukhumvit exit 3; Ⓡ Asok via dedicated skyway; ❌ 🖳 📶 🛗
The Sheraton is a hit with corporate travellers because it's arguably the most professionally managed hotel in Bangkok. Its 420 large (from 45 sq metres) and meticulously appointed rooms come with handy details like irons, extra-large deposit boxes and big tubs as standard. The sky-high, jungle-fringed pool is an oasis and, if you have a spare 38,000B, the Thai-styled Rama suite can satisfy all your hot-tub fantasies with party-sized indoor and outdoor Jacuzzis. Ask for a lake-view room. Wi-fi is 642B a day; rooms sell online for 20% to 30% less.

DREAM Map p126   Boutique Hotel $$$
☎ 0 2254 8500; www.dreambkk.com; 10 Soi 15, Th Sukhumvit; r from US$250; Ⓜ Sukhumvit exit 1; Ⓡ Asok exit 1; ❌ 🖳 📶 🛗
We must have looked doubtful about the blue neon glow in the bedroom, and the woman showing us around sounded like she'd seen the reaction often enough. 'The blue lights are the Dream signature,' she explained, 'we have some scientific studies that prove it makes you sleep deeper.' The blue-lit rooms are just one of the features that set Dream apart from your average boutique or design hotel. It's totally different. The 195 rooms in two buildings are a rock-star world of cream leather, mirrors, silver and blue motifs and, in the uber-chic Flava lounge-bar-cum-restaurant, a white tiger (yes, blue stripes) and pink leopard. Rooms come with free wi-fi, coffee machines and big flatscreen TVs. The suites, however, are overpriced. Huuuuge discounts online, from 2800B.

EUGENIA Map p126   Boutique Hotel $$$
☎ 0 2259 9017; www.theeugenia.com; 267 Soi 31, Th Sukhumvit; r 6600-8500B; Ⓡ Phrom Phong exit 5 & taxi; ❌ 🖳 📶 🛗
The Eugenia is one unique boutique. Dreamt up by 'Taiwanese Indiana Jones' Eugene Yu-Cheng Yeh, the 12-room residence is modelled on the colonial mansions of Africa and the subcontinent. Think

Livingston/Hemingway/Indian Raj, with the rooms and public spaces packed full of art, books, antique furniture, beaten copper bathtubs and dead animals (we counted zebra, warthog, crocodile, various antelope, peacock and duck). It's not, however, devoid of modern luxuries, with wi-fi internet, VoIP telephony and minibar all included in the rate. Our only criticism is that the rooms aren't huge, especially the tiny Siam suites. Ask about the airport trips in the vintage Mercedes and Jags.

S15 Map p126   Boutique Hotel $$$
☎ 0 2651 2000; www.s15hotel.com; 217 Th Sukhumvit, cnr Soi 15; r 5100-8000B; Ⓜ Sukhumvit exit 3; Ⓡ Asok exit 5; ⌗ 💻 ⌗
Among the better 'boutique' options along Sukhumvit, sleek S15 has at least half an eye on the business market, with free wi-fi and a business centre and meeting room to go with the central location. The reasonably sized rooms are a mix of the browns and whites so preferred by boutique hotels, augmented with modern Asian ornaments. It works pretty well, though better value is available. If you find yourself yearning for something more grungy, the classic little restaurant on the opposite corner of Soi 15 should satisfy. Online from 3750B.

GRAND MILLENNIUM SUKHUMVIT
Map p126   Hotel $$$
☎ 0 2204 4000; www.grandmillenniumskv.com; 30 Soi Asoke, Th Sukhumvit; r from 4600B; Ⓜ Sukhumvit exit 2; Ⓡ Asok exit 2; ⌗ 💻 ⌗ 🏊
Looking like a giant glass zipper opening from the top down, the Grand Millennium is popular with both business and leisure travellers and with good reason. Its 325 bright, spacious (minimum 38 sq metres) and tastefully furnished rooms are set around a triangular atrium fronted by acres of glass. If you don't suffer from vertigo, they're great for business, with decent-sized desks, wi-fi (489B a day) and ADSL internet, and there's even a putting green on top of the carpark. In most respects – the service, restaurants and standard rooms – this hotel is well worth its 'grand' classification; only the tacked-together suites let it down. Online from 3900B (room only).

SEVEN Map p126   Boutique Hotel $$
☎ 0 2662 0951; www.sleepatseven.com; 3/15 Soi 31, Th Sukhumvit; r 3100-6000B; Ⓡ Phrom Phong exit 5; ⌗ 💻 ⌗

This boutique hotel from the designers of London's Ministry of Sound comes with a truly Thai concept. Thais believe each day has its own colour (eg Monday is yellow, and everyone wears a yellow shirt for the king), and each of the seven rooms (including the lobby-cum-bar) is themed in its own colour. Rooms are well appointed with free mobile phones, wi-fi and iPods. They are not, however, very big, ranging from 20 to 26 sq metres, which at the rack rates might have you thinking twice, and then thinking again. Fortunately, at most times booking online brings it down to 3000B to 4000B. Seven will appeal to hip young singles and couples looking for design and informal but well-informed service.

NAPA PLACE BED & BREAKFAST
Map p126   Hotel $$
☎ 0 2661 5525; www.napaplace.com; 11/3 Yaek 2, Soi 36, Th Sukhumvit; d 2750-4800B; Ⓡ Thong Lo exit 2; ⌗ 💻
Tucked away in a quiet soi off Soi 36 and seven minutes' walk to Thong Lo Skytrain, Napa offers a genuinely homey B&B atmosphere. It appeals especially to families because the rooms are huge (36 to 67 sq metres), there is plenty of communal space and solid security, and cable broadband and buffet breakfasts are included in the price. In short, it's superb value.

72 EKAMAI Map p126   Hotel $$
☎ 0 2714 7327; www.72ekamai.com; 72 Soi 63 (Soi Ekamai), Th Sukhumvit; r from 2750B; Ⓡ Ekkamai exit 1; ⌗ 💻 ⌗ 🏊
The Ekamai neighbourhood off Sukhumvit's Soi 63 (Soi Ekamai) is a magnet for young hipsters, so it's no surprise that a stylish, sophisticated, retro-sleek hotel has opened here. The lobby sets the tone with a glowing red counter and '60s-era TV set. Next door a shop sells old vinyl, juke boxes and other pop culture paraphernalia. The rooms maintain the theme with, for example, Fab Four walking dolls striding along a shelf. What is surprising, however, is how big the studios and one-bedroom suites are – from 30 to 62 sq metres. Modern luxuries include flatscreen TVs and free wi-fi standard. Outside a pool is accompanied by a bar-restaurant serving Thai and Italian food, and live music Monday to Saturday. All up, a top choice that's even better with regular online discounts.

THE FUSION SUITES

Map p126   Boutique Hotel $$

☎ 0 2665 2644; www.fusionbangkok.com;
143/61-62 Soi 21, Th Sukhumvit; d 2600-4600B;
Ⓜ Sukhumvit exit 1; Ⓡ Asok exit 1; ✕ 💻 📶

Fusion is the word! It's hard to classify exactly what's going on in this seven-storey, 35-room boutique hotel around the corner from busy Soi Asok. Dark rooms with polished concrete floors are embellished with Persian carpets, Indian wooden furniture, parlour-room buttoned leather couches, Buddhist iconography and a head-spinning array of high-tech gadgetry – think iPod docks, multimedia control panel, free wi-fi, DVD player and big flatscreen TV. It sounds dizzying, but somehow seems to work. Aside from the risk of sensory overload (throw in the flavours of India in the lobby restaurant), the one small downside is that only the standard and deluxe rooms have windows; deluxe rooms are the pick. Note that the motorbike in the foyer is claimed to be from a James Bond film, though (try as we did) we couldn't confirm this.

MIDRANGE MANIA

Bangkok's noughties building boom has seen Th Sukhumvit become a forest of good-value, wannabe-boutique hotels. Most are located near the office towers of Soi Asoke (aka Soi 21), and most have embraced the global Zen style so popular in this range – think faux-wooden floors in smallish rooms, white linens, hanging silks, arty prints, compact bathrooms with rain showers, flatscreen TVs and subtle, earthy colours; all very pleasing if not desperately original. Competition is fierce, and fantastic deals are often available online. Following is a list of those we liked. Note that 'standard' rooms in these hotels are often 'cosy' (aka tiny) windowless gap-fillers. Aside from Bangkok Boutique and Citichic, the others all opened in 2009.

Bangkok Boutique Hotel (Map p126; ☎ 0 2261 2850; www.bangkokboutiquehotel.com; 241 Soi Asoke, Th Sukhumvit; r from 3000B; Ⓜ Phetchaburi exit 2; ✕ 💻 📶) At the north end of noisy Soi Asoke, BB combines a minimalist, polished-concrete mode with high-tech gadgetry (free wi-fi and wireless keyboards to use with the paddock-sized flatscreen). Superior rooms are best; ask for one away from the street.

Citichic (Map p126; ☎ 0 2342 3888; www.citichichotel.com; 34 Soi 13, Th Sukhumvit; r from 2300B; Ⓜ Sukhumvit exit 1; Ⓡ Nana exit 3; ✕ 💻 🏊) Everything (except the TVs) in this 37-room, five-storey place is small, but the space is well used. There's a small rooftop pool, small rooms with small desks and small bathrooms. Fair value.

Citadines Soi 16 (Map p126; ☎ 0 2663 8777; www.citadines.com; 38 Soi 16, Th Sukhumvit; d from 1950B; Ⓜ Sukhumvit exit 2; Ⓡ Asok exit 6 & skyway; ✕ 💻 📶 🏊) Not, perhaps, quite as appealing as the Citidines on Soi 23 (opposite), but still very difficult to argue with the space, service and facilities you get for these prices. Expect bright, well-equipped rooms and one-bed suites, a pool on the roof and efficient service.

On8 (Map p126; ☎ 0 2254 8866; www.on8bangkok.com; 162 Th Sukhumvit; d 2900-3200B; Ⓡ Nana exit 4; ✕ 💻 📶) Literally on the doorstep of Nana Skytrain station, in the heart of the action near the corner of Soi 8, On8 is a highly designed 40-room hotel where space is at a premium. Over four floors, the three categories of room differ only in size and outlook (ie none or an opaque window, which is appropriate given what you'd be looking at). They all have big flatscreen TVs, small desks and appealing decor.

Sacha's Hotel Uno (Map p126; ☎ 0 2651 2180; www.sachas.hotel-uno.com; 28/19 Soi 19, Th Sukhumvit; d from 2500B; Ⓜ Sukhumvit exit 3; Ⓡ Asok exit 1; ✕ 💻 📶) These 56 rooms in adjacent buildings are pretty compact and are neither the 'five-star' promised in the marketing nor quite as impressive as the lobbies suggest. Still, they are very well wired for business and the 'deluxe' rooms in the main building, in particular, won't disappoint at these prices.

Silq (Map p126; ☎ 0 2252 6800; www.silqbkk.com; 54 Soi 19, Th Sukhumvit; d from 2500B; Ⓜ Sukhumvit exit 3; Ⓡ Asok exit 1; ✕ 💻 📶) Just down from Sacha's, the eight-storey, 46-room Silq is a smoother operation with brighter rooms that feel larger than they are thanks to big windows (in most rooms). Service is friendly and the buffet and à la carte breakfast is the clincher.

S Sukhumvit Suites (Map p126; ☎ 0 2661 7252; www.ssukhumvitsuites.com; 403 Th Sukhumvit; d 2600-3600B; Ⓜ Sukhumvit exit 2; Ⓡ Asok exit 6 & skywalk; ✕ 💻 📶) This is a classic of the genre; low-rise with 43 rooms, very near to transport (the Skytrain runs right past the 4th-floor windows; trainspotters ask for rooms 408 or 888), decor in browns and greys, faux-wood floors and desks. Wi-fi is included.

LE FENIX Map p126   Hotel $$

☎ 0 2305 4000; www.lefenix-sukhumvit.com; 33 Soi 11, Th Sukhumvit; r 2500B; 🚇 Nana exit 3; 🅿 💻 🛜

In recent years the big hotel companies have jumped on the 'boutique' bandwagon, with mixed results that sometimes feel more cash and carry than boutique. This 147-room, eight-floor place is one of Accor's attempts. At the end of busy Soi 11, it is aimed at travellers who love the nightlife at least as much as Alicia Bridges. The smooth curves, bright colour palette and lounge-music-filled corridors create a modern feel, though the rooms are small and simple. All have two single mattresses on one base, which means you'll want to get on with your room mate pretty well. That said, the main reason to stay here is the access to nearby clubs, in particular the open-air Nest (p184) on Le Fenix' roof. Rooms have both wi-fi and broadband cable internet, with two hours free per day. Online rates from 2000B.

CITADINES SOI 23 Map p126   Hotel $$

☎ 0 2204 4777; www.citadines.com; 37 Soi 23, Th Sukhumvit; d from 1900B; Ⓜ Sukhumvit exit 2; 🚇 Asok exit 6 & skywalk; 🅿 💻 🛜 🅿

Of the four Citadines 'Apart-Hotels' built by hotel megalith Ascott on this stretch of Sukhumvit, this is our pick. In both the studio (28 sq metres) and one-bedroom (45 sq metres) options the decor is bright with orange and lime flavours, and the design makes the most of the space. Expect a kitchenette you can actually cook in, a living area and bedroom (separated by a partition in the studio). Pasta in the kitchen suggests they might be expecting bachelors, but it's families who'll find the greatest value – where else can you get a separate room, a rooftop pool and a hip cafe-restaurant (the Minibar Royal) downstairs for 2400B?

ATLANTA Map p126   Hotel $

☎ 0 2252 6069, 0 2252 1650; fax 0 2656 8123; 78 Soi 2 (Soi Phasak), Th Sukhumvit; s 642-800B, d 856-1020B; 🚇 Phloen Chit exit 4; 🅿 🅿

The oldest hotel in the Th Sukhumvit area (and proud of it), the Atlanta enjoys cultlike status with return budget travellers who shun the Banglamphu 'tourist' scene. And rightly so. The hotel was started as the Atlanta Club in 1952 by Dr Max Henn, a former secretary to the Maharajah of Bikaner and owner of Bangkok's first international pharmacy. And while it looks thoroughly grim from outside, the perfectly preserved mid-century lobby, complete with old-fashioned writing desks and a grand-entrance staircase sweeping up five floors (there's no lift), makes you want to hang around waiting for Bogart to slip in. The rooms are spacious but more functional than Hollywood; those on the top floor aren't good at all. But the just-kept jungle-landscaped pool is very welcome in this price bracket. Note: 'The Atlanta does not welcome sex tourists and does not try to be polite about it.'

SUK 11 Map p126   Guesthouse $

☎ 0 2253 5927-28; www.suk11.com; sub-soi off Soi 11, Th Sukhumvit; s 500-650B, d 700-900B; 🚇 Nana exit 3; 🅿 💻 🛜

Stepping between the potted plants and into the wooden-fronted oasis of Suk 11, hidden down a small sub-soi off busy Soi 11, is to step into Sukhumvit's primary outpost of backpacker culture, and a definite atmosphere of post-beach chill. Expect a lobby crowded with travellers sitting around, drinking and swapping tales. Upstairs the 80 (yes, 80!) rooms stretch almost the length of the soi, with plank walkways and terracotta accents embellishing otherwise plain rooms with and without bathrooms. Outside is a spa, restaurant and Cheap Charlie's (p183) for the cheapest beers outside 7-Eleven. Wi-fi costs 40B an hour.

NA NA CHART SUKHUMVIT 25
Map p126   Hostel $$

☎ 0 2259 4900; www.thailandhostel.com; Soi 25, Th Sukhumvit; dm/s/d 390/1200/1500B; 🚇 Asok exit 6 & skywalk; 🅿 💻

This HI-affiliated place looks a bit institutional and some staff act like wardens, but it's very convenient to transport and (with membership) good value in this part of town. The large, clean rooms come with cable TV, fridge and air-con – though the dorms need three occupants before the air-con is turned on. Membership costs 200B per person and is granted on the spot, saving 100/300/500B on the dorm/single/double prices quoted above; breakfast is included.

HI SUKHUMVIT Map p126   Hostel $

☎ 0 2391 9338; www.hisukhumvit.com; 23 Soi 38, Th Sukhumvit; dm 330B, s 600B, d 900-1150B; 🚇 Thong Lo exit 4; 🅿 💻

Seemingly lost in a galaxy where budget lodgings usually fear to go, the clean, simple dorms and rooms and welcoming family owners make this budget place a real find. The breezy rooftop is a good place to chill out, wash clothes and watch another Bangkok condo emerge from the ground, and the nearby night market is a great place to eat.

GREATER BANGKOK

If you're staying outside central Bangkok, choose a place near the Skytrain for zippy commutes.

MYSTIC PLACE Map p64 — Hotel $$
☎ 0 2270 3344; www.mysticplacebkk.com; 224/2-18 Th Pradipat btwn Sois 18 & 20; r 2250-3250B; 🚇 Saphan Kwai exit 1; 🍽 🖥 🛜
At Mystic Place, nee Reflections Rooms, your room could be decked out entirely in black-and-white spiral psychedelia, sport portraits of playful puffed-up ladies or be decorated completely in recycled goods. The 36 rooms are each styled by a different artist, designer or celebrity and make Mystic Place the most arty, trippy, kitschy and totally cool hotel in Thailand. A 10-minute walk from Saphan Kwai Skytrain in a refreshingly Thai neighbourhood, rooms are Starbucks-sized: small is really big and large is mega. Each is fitted with a DVD player and free wi-fi. Check out the rooms online to book the one you want; streetside rooms are noisy. In breaking news, the Reflections people have opened a second, slightly cheaper arty hotel called Baan Waree (Map p64; ☎ 0 2272 6300; baanwaree.com; 24 Soi 8 (Soi Sailom 1), Th Paholyothin, Samsennai; d 1290-1490B; 🚇 Ari exit 4; 🍽 🛜) with another 27 individually designed rooms and a restaurant.

THAI HOUSE Map p132 — Guesthouse $$
☎ 0 2903 9611; www.thaihouse.co.th; 32/4 Mu 8, Tambon Bang Meuang, Bang Yai, Nonthaburi; s/d 1500B/1700B
For an experience of traditional Thai life, surrounded by fruit trees and river music and feeling far from Bangkok's urban snarl, it's hard to beat the Thai House. The teak home built with wing-shaped roofs is pure, old-fashioned Siam, with a welcome as warm as you could hope for. Rates include breakfast, and many guests choose to do the cooking courses taught on the premises. By river, take a public boat from Tha Chang to Bang

Yai in Nonthaburi, via Khlong Bangkok Noi. Once you reach the public pier in Bang Yai, charter a boat to Thai House's own pier – all the boat pilots know it. By taxi, get the driver to call for directions.

REFILL NOW! Map p132 — Hostel $$
☎ 0 2713 2044; www.refillnow.co.th; 191 Soi Pridi Banhom Yong 42, Soi 71, Th Sukhumvit; dm/s/d 525/1085/1470B; 🚇 Khlong Tong; 🚇 Phra Kanong or Ramkamhaeng; 🍽 🖥 🛁
From the fertile imaginations of two young Thai architects, Refill promises a 'high-style low-cost' place to 'relax, rejuvenate and replenish'. It delivers with spotless white private rooms and dorms that have flirtatious pull screens between each double-bunk; women-only dorms are also available. Some might baulk at paying this much for rooms with shared bathrooms miles from town. But the hip, unpretentious vibe emanating from the funky bar (called Revive), restaurant (Recommend) and communal areas, and the unflappable, engaging staff, leave a smile on most faces. There is a massage service (Reform) on the top floor. Refill Now! is near trendy Thong Lo and only 20 minutes from the airport by taxi, or 15 minutes by City Link to Ramkamhaeng Station, then a 50B taxi. On the Skytrain, get off at Phra Kanong and take a taxi or moto taxi down Soi 71, turn right on Soi 42 and left; or best of all come by *klorng* taxi to Khlong Tong and walk.

EXCURSIONS

contents

EXCURSIONS

Believe it or not, there is life after Bangkok. The city's central location, not to mention its role as the country's transportation hub, make it a convenient base from which to explore much of what central Thailand has to offer. Destinations range from island beaches to critter-laden jungles, and include day trips and more-relaxed overnighters. Much of the tourism surrounding Bangkok is geared towards locals, and as such there's an emphasis on religious pilgrimages and food – the latter ranging from 'famous' restaurants to buzzing night markets for socialising and dining. Both allow for fascinating insights into Thai culture. Bangkok's outlying areas also have many theme parks and animal attractions that will entertain children who are sick of humouring their parents.

BACK TO NATURE

Going from concrete jungle to real jungle is not as hard as you'd think. A couple of hours on a bus will take you to places so wild you can count elephants and tigers among your neighbours.

To the northeast, the Dangrek Mountains geographically fuse Thailand and Cambodia and break up the fertile central plains around Bangkok. Occupying this wooded landscape is Khao Yai National Park (p257), one of Thailand's biggest and best preserves, where mountainous monsoon forests boast hundreds of resident species. Visitors can take quick dips into nature while staying at a nearby resort, also playing golf and touring start-up wineries. Or immerse yourself completely by staying in a rustic park shelter in the forest. Waterfalls tend to dominate Khao Yai itineraries, but you might also be lucky enough to spot the big game, though don't get your hopes up too high. The wildlife is, erm, wild, and unlikely to just wander up for a quick chat and a beer.

West of Bangkok, limestone hills rise out of the sun-parched land like a great ruined city. Kanchanaburi (p253) is the best base for exploring this area of waterfalls, caves and tropical jungle. Bike rides will take you past shaggy fields of sugar cane being harvested by hand, and lovingly tended spirit houses guarding uninhabited woods. Organised tours take visitors on whirlwind outings by land, water and rail, or you can rent a bike and DIY.

Further south along Thailand's rugged border with Myanmar (Burma), Kaeng Krachan National Park (p249), the country's largest, is a paradise for birdwatchers and others looking to do some camera hunting or just immerse themselves in the steamy jungle.

TIME TRAVEL

Thailand's heroic ancient capital, Ayuthaya (p236), is a Unesco World Heritage site and a major pilgrimage site for anyone interested in Thai history. It is hard to imagine today, but this modern city littered with red-brick temple ruins was once a golden city that bewitched European traders in the heyday of the Asian trade route. Nearby Bang Pa-In, a royal summer palace, survives as testament to the cosmopolitan nature of the Siamese kingdom, embracing architectural styles from far and wide.

More-recent masterpieces of Thai art can be seen in the vivid wall paintings and graceful stucco facades of Phetchaburi's (p249) numerous temples. A day of wandering can provide viewing opportunities of several of the recognised masterpieces of central Thai art, with a glimpse into royal life in the hilltop palace.

Ancient Siam (p260), an architectural museum in Samut Prakan, has reproduced Thailand's great monuments in a tastefully arranged park. Like Ayuthaya, Ancient Siam is best explored by bicycle; the peaceful grounds and impressive structures will inspire excursions throughout the country.

More-recent history is only a train ride away in Kanchanaburi (p253), where vivid museums, themed excursions and touching monuments bring home the area's tragic history as a WWII labour camp.

THAI LIFE

The Mahachai Rail Line (p247), will transport you directly to the rhythms of daily life outside the capital. The destinations, a string of gulfside towns and wáts, are really just excuses to dive into the markets and food stalls that make

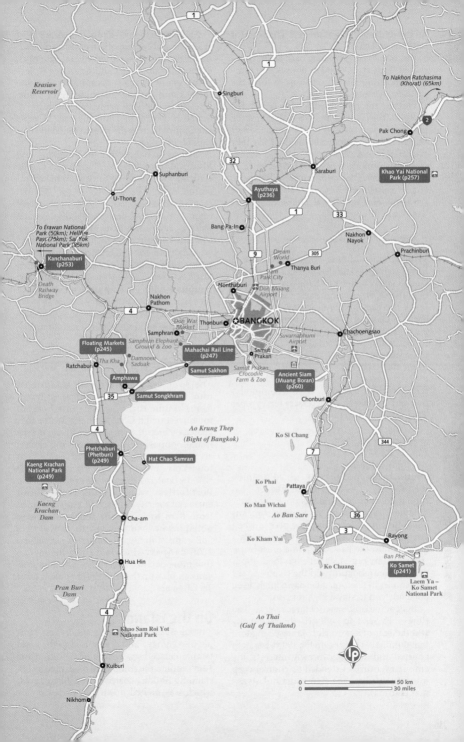

up the journey and are the real Thailand for millions of Thais.

Phetchaburi's (p249) twisting back lanes, peak-roofed Thai-style wooden houses and rambling morning market combine to form the epitome of central Thai life.

Outside the capital, village life is still tied to the *klorng* (canals) and rivers that knit the land to the sea. Amphawa's (p248) canalside setting and ancient wooden houses look like they are straight out of a movie set, and homestays can provide a firsthand experience of this uniquely Thai community. Elsewhere, largely touristy floating markets (p245) are the last remnants of a traditional Thai lifestyle that has all but disappeared.

SAND & SUN

With its emerald seas, languid breezes and blond strips of sand, Ko Samet (p241) is the island getaway nearest to Bangkok. Bungalow operations dot several bays, ranging from break-the-bank luxury to Spartan backpacker shacks. Days are spent in typical island-paradise style; swinging in hammocks, swimming, eating barbecued seafood and other miscellaneous chilling and, if you're up for it, evening partying.

Hat Chao Samran (p252), a short jaunt from Phetburi, provides the sand, cosy accommodation and cheap seafood necessary for a proper Thai-style beach getaway.

AYUTHAYA

พระนครศรีอยุธยา

Drawn by the prospect of ruined temples, the majority of visitors to this former Thai capital do so from a big bus on a tight tour schedule. Which is great, because it means you'll be among relatively few people when you discover that Ayuthaya offers not only a glimpse into the past, but also a great break from city life. Famously delicious food, good-value accommodation and the chance to see the temples in the cool, quiet dawn might even persuade you to stay a night or two.

Built at the confluence of three rivers (Chao Phraya, Pa Sak and Lopburi), this island city was the seat of a powerful Siamese kingdom that dominated the region for 400 years. Both courted and aided by foreign interests, the empire eventually extended its control deep into present-day Laos, Cambodia and Myanmar (Burma).

Ayuthaya remained one of the world's most splendid and cosmopolitan cities until 1767, when the Burmese, after several attempts, eventually conquered and destroyed it, levelling many temples, decapitating Buddha images and carting off anything of value. The surviving Thai army fled south to re-establish control in Thonburi and, 15 years later, moved across the river to found the new capital, Bangkok.

Getting a handle on the religious and historical importance of the temples can be difficult without doing some preliminary research. Ayuthaya Historical Study Centre (☎ 0 3524 5124; Th Rotchana; adult/student 100/50B; ☒ 9am-4.30pm) offers informative, professional displays that paint a very clear picture of the ancient city. The museums in town include Chao Sam Phraya National Museum (☎ 0 3524 1587; cnr Th Rotchana & Th Si Sanphet; admission 30B; ☒ 9am-4pm Wed-Sun), which features a basic round-up of Thai Buddhist sculpture with an emphasis on Ayuthaya pieces, and Chantharakasem National Museum (☎ 0 3525 1586; Th U Thong; admission 100B; ☒ 9am-4pm Wed-Sun), a museum piece in itself, in the northeast corner of town.

AYUTHAYA HISTORICAL PARK

The Ayuthaya Historical Park is separated into two distinct geographical districts. Ruins 'on the island', in the central part of town west of Th Chee Kun, are most easily visited on bicycle or motorbike; those 'off the island', opposite the river from the centre, are best visited by way of an evening boat tour. You can also take a bicycle across the river by boat, starting from the pier near Pom Phet fortress, which is inside the southeast corner of the city centre. The ruins are open from 8am to 6pm daily unless otherwise noted below, and at many there will be a 50B admission fee; alternatively purchase a 220B day pass which will cover the lot. To find more detailed descriptions of the ruins, you can pick up the Ayutthaya booklet from TAT (see p239).

On the Island

Wat Phra Si Sanphet was once the largest temple in Ayuthaya and it was used as the royal temple-palace by several kings. Built in the 14th century, the compound contained a 16m standing Buddha coated with 250kg of gold, which was melted down and carted off by

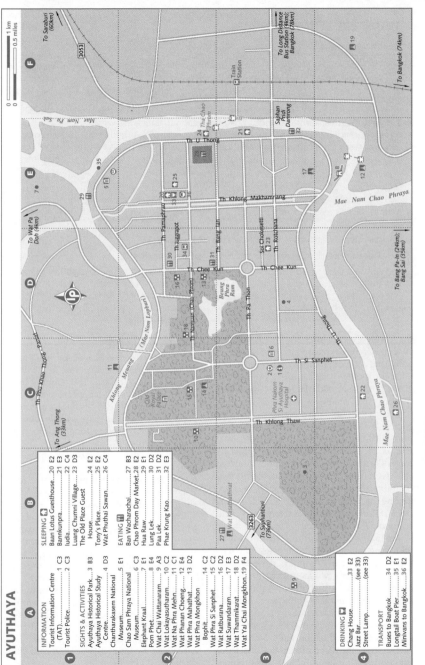

lonelyplanet.com

AYUTHAYA

INFORMATION
Tourist Information Centre
(TAT)..1 C3
Tourist Police...............................2 C3

SIGHTS & ACTIVITIES
Ayutthaya Historical Park..........3 B3
Ayutthaya Historical Study
Centre.......................................4 D3
Chantharakasem National
Museum....................................5 E1
Chao Sam Phraya National
Museum....................................6 C3
Elephant Kraal............................7 E1
Pom Phet....................................8 E4
Wat Chai Wattanaram................9 A3
Wat Lokayasutharam................10 C2
Wat Na Phra Mehn....................11 C1
Wat Phanan Choeng.................12 E4
Wat Phra Mahathat...................13 D2
Wat Phra Mongkhon
Bophit......................................14 C2
Wat Phra Si Sanphet................15 C2
Wat Ratburana..........................16 D2
Wat Suwandaram......................17 E3
Wat Thammikarat......................18 D2
Wat Yai Chai Mongkhon...........19 F4

SLEEPING
Baan Lotus Guesthouse..........20 E2
Bankunpra................................21 E3
Iudia..22 C4
Luang Chumni Village..............23 D3
The Old Place Guest
House.....................................24 E2
Tony's Place............................25 E2
Wat Phuthai Sawan.................26 C4

EATING
Ban Wacharachai.....................27 B3
Chao Phrom Day Market.........28 E2
Hua Raw...................................29 E1
Lung Lek..................................30 D2
Paa Lek....................................31 D2
Phae Krung Kao.......................32 E3

DRINKING
Chang House............................33 E2
Jazz Bar.............................(see 33)
Street Lamp.......................(see 33)

TRANSPORT
Buses to Bangkok....................34 D2
Longtail Boat Pier....................35 E1
Minivans to Bangkok...............36 E2

TRANSPORT: AYUTHAYA

Distance from Bangkok 85km

Direction North

Travel Time Eighty minutes to two hours by bus; 1½ hours by train

Bus 1st-class air-con (72B) and 2nd-class air-con (55B) buses depart Bangkok's Northern and Northeastern Bus Terminal (also called Mo Chit; Map p132) to Th Naresuan in Ayuthaya every 15 minutes between 4.30am and 7.15pm.

Minibus Minibuses hurtle between Bangkok's Victory Monument (Map p64) and Th Naresuan Soi 8, just down from the main concentration of guesthouses, every 30 minutes from 5am to 5pm (60B). This trip took us one terrifying hour, every minute of which we expected to be our last.

Train Northbound trains leave from Bangkok's Hualamphong station (Map p98) roughly every 30 minutes between 6.20am and 9.30am, less frequently until about 4pm, then every 30 minutes or so between 5pm and 9pm. Trains that run only to Ayuthaya are 3rd class and cost 20B; better seats are available on trains running further north. From Ayuthaya's train station, the quickest way to reach the city is to walk straight west to the river, where you can take a short ferry ride (3B) across. Alternatively, a túk-túk to any point in old Ayuthaya should be around 30B to 50B.

Taxi Taxis between Bangkok and Ayuthaya take about 75 minutes and cost 800B.

Boat Boat companies in Bangkok offer scenic boat tours to Ayuthaya; see p278.

Getting Around Guesthouses rent bicycles for 50B per day or motorcycles for 300B; túk-túk tours cost 200B per hour. Guesthouses arrange túk-túk tours starting about 4.30pm at 180B per person for four people. A longtail boat trip (one-hour evening trip 600B) involves a semicircular tour of the island. Arrange at the pier behind Hua Raw Night Market.

the Burmese conquerors. Its three Ayuthaya-style *chedi* (stupas) have come to be identified with Thai art more than any other style. The adjacent Wat Phra Mongkhon Bophit, built in the 1950s, houses one of the largest bronze, seated Buddhas in Thailand.

Wat Phra Mahathat, on the corner of Th Chee Kun and Th Naresuan, has one of the first *prang* (Khmer-style tower) built in the capital and an evocative Buddha head engulfed by fingerlike tree roots – the most photographed site in Ayuthaya. Across the road, Wat Ratburana contains *chedi* and faded murals that are among the oldest in the country. Neighbouring Wat Thammikarat features overgrown *chedi* ruins and lion sculptures.

Wat Lokayasutharam features an impressive 28m-long reclining Buddha, ostensibly dating back to the early Ayuthaya period.

Wat Suwannaram's two main structures boast attractive murals, including a modern-era depiction of a famous Ayuthaya-era battle in the *wí·hähn* (central sanctuary), and classic *jataka* (stories from the Buddha's lives) in the adjacent *bòht* (ordination hall). Nearby Pom Phet served as the island's initial line of defence for centuries. Only crumbling walls remain today, but the spot features breezy views and is also home to a ferry to the mainland.

Off the Island

Southeast of town on Mae Nam Chao Phraya, Wat Phanan Choeng was built before Ayuthaya became a Siamese capital. The temple's builders are unknown, but it appears to have been constructed in the early 14th century, so it's possibly Khmer. The main *wí·hähn* contains a highly revered, 19m sitting Buddha image from which the wát derives its name. The area surrounding the temple was once home to a large Chinese community, and at weekends it is crowded with Buddhist pilgrims from Bangkok who pay for lengths of saffron-coloured cloth to be ritually draped over the image.

The ruined Ayuthaya-style tower and *chedi* of Wat Chai Wattanaram, on the western bank of Mae Nam Chao Phraya, boast the most attractive setting of any of the city's temples. The manicured Thai-style compound across the river belongs to the Thai royal family.

Wat Yai Chai Mongkhon is southeast of town; it can be reached by white-and-green minibus 6. It's a quiet place built in 1357 by King U Thong and was once famous as a meditation centre. The compound contains a large *chedi*, and a community of *mâa chee* (Buddhist nuns) lives here.

North of the city, the Elephant Kraal is a restoration of the wooden stockade once used for the annual roundup of wild elephants. A fence of huge teak logs enclosed the elephants. The king had a raised observation pavilion for the thrilling event.

North of the old royal palace *(wang lŏo·ang)* grounds is a bridge to Wat Na Phra Mehn (8am-5pm). This temple is notable because it escaped destruction when the Burmese overran and sacked the city in 1767. The main *bòht* was built in 1546 and features fortress-like walls and pillars. The *bòht* interior contains an impressive carved wooden ceiling and a splendid 6m-high sitting Buddha in royal attire. Inside a smaller *wí·hähn* behind the *bòht* is a green-stone, European-pose (sitting in a chair) Buddha from Ceylon, said to be 1300 years old. The walls of the *wí·hähn* show traces of 18th- or 19th-century murals.

INFORMATION

Tourist Information Centre (TAT; ☎ 0 3532 2730/1; Th Si Sanphet; 8.30am-4.30pm) Occupying the imposing Old City Hall built in 1941, the helpful ladies at TAT provide maps, bus schedules and information about Loi Krathong festivities (see p22). Ask for a free copy of *Ayutthaya,* the excellent illustrated booklet published by TAT.

Tourist Police (☎ 0 3524 1446 or 1155; Th Si Sanphet; 24h)

EATING

Ban Wacharachai (☎ 0 3532 1333; Wat Kasattrathirat; dishes 60-150B; 10am-midnight) A must for visiting foodies, this gem is legendary among locals and regular visitors alike for its perfectly executed central Thai−style dishes, not to mention a pleasant riverfront location. The smoked snakehead fish is sublime. To get there, cycle or take a túk-túk to Wat Kasattrathirat (known as Wat Kasat); the rambling restaurant is hidden in a thick garden directly north of the temple.

Hua Raw Night Market & Chao Phrom Day Market (Th U Thong) Much of Ayuthaya's best food is prepared in these modest surrounds. Vendors at the open-air night market (5pm-10pm) specialise in Thai-Muslim dishes, while the covered day market (7am-5pm) is more classically central Thai.

Phae Krung Kao (☎ 0 3524 1555; Th U Thong; dishes 60-200B; 9am-9pm) South of the bridge, this floating restaurant is renowned for its carefully prepared seafood dishes and is hugely popular with visiting Thais, though it has a tendency to tone down dishes for *fà·ràng.*

In the past, Ayuthayans got their noodle fix from boat-based vendors who hocked their bowls along the city's canals and rivers. Today the vessels are all landlocked, but the famous *gŏo·ay đĕe·o reu·a* (boat noodles) remain as popular as ever. Lung Lek (Th Chee Kun; dishes 15B; 10am-4pm) serves incredibly intense *gŏo ay·đĕe·o reu·a* with pork or beef that our dining companion euphorically described as 'perhaps the best noodles ever!' Look for the open-air tent-like structure. Slightly more popular but less spicy is Paa Lek (Th Bang lan; dishes 12B; 9am-4pm), a sprawling roadside stall next door to the city's telephone authority; look for the yellow sign in Thai.

Sweet snacks associated with Ayuthaya include *roti săi mài* (thin pancake-like sheets wrapped around candy floss), available from numerous vendors near Phra Nakorn Si Ayuthaya Hospital. *Kà·nŏm bà bin* (tiny pancakes made from sticky rice flour and shredded coconut meat) can be found at the market behind Wat Phra Mongkhon Bophit.

BANG PA-IN
บางปะอิน

This postcard-perfect palace (☎ 0 3526 1044; admission 100B; 8am-5pm) lies 24km south of Ayuthaya. A hodgepodge of international architectural styles reflects the eclectic tastes of Rama IV (King Mongkut; r 1851−68) and his son and heir Rama V (King Chulalongkorn; r 1868−1910), both of whom used the residence as a retreat from the summer rains. The winged-eaved Thai-style pavilion, ornate Chinese-style Wehat Chamrun Palace and Swiss chalet mansion (the preferred residence of Rama V) are all on display. A flamboyant lookout tower (Withun Thatsana) gave the king fine views over the gardens and lakes.

At the nearby Royal Folk Arts & Crafts Centre (☎ 0 3536 6252; admission 100B; 9am-5pm Mon-Fri, 9am-7pm Sat & Sun) at Bang Sai you can see traditional Thai handicrafts and artwork being made.

Bang Pa-In can be reached by blue *sŏrng·tăa·ou* (pick-up truck; 13B, 45 min) or minibus (30B) from Ayuthaya's Chao Phrom Day Market (Map p237) on Th Naresuan. From Bangkok there are buses (50B) every half-hour from the Northern and Northeastern Bus Terminal (Mo Chit; Map p132). You can also reach Bang Pa-In by train from Bangkok; two depart each morning (3rd class, 12B).

DRINKING

Several drinking options are conveniently located along a 50m strip of Soi 8, Th Naresuan, the epicentre of Ayuthaya's traveller scene. When we visited, Street Lamp (7am-midnight) was the pick, with a local one-man-band teeing up the patrons for a remarkably good open jam session. A short stagger along the road are Chang House (6pm-midnight), for nightly beer specials, and Jazz Bar (7pm-midnight), with live jazz at 9pm most nights.

SLEEPING

Ayuthaya has numerous soulless tourist hotels and a few charismatic little guesthouses and midrange places.

Iudia (☎ 0 3532 3208; www.iudia.com; 11-12 Th U Thong; r 1800-4500B;) Opened mid-2009, this delightful little boutique hotel in a removed riverfront locale has raised the standard in this city, and far. The eight luxuriously appointed rooms occupy a modern, highly designed building in Thai and Middle Eastern themes, all overlooking Wat Puthai Sawan. There's a riverside pool, chic coffee shop and good service. Book ahead.

Luang Chumni Village (☎ 0 3532 2990; www.luang chumnivillage.com; Soi Chokesetti; r 640-960B;) On a quiet soi in the centre of town, these old wooden houses have been converted into six rooms while maintaining their classic Thai architectural integrity. That means the modern bathrooms are connected, but are downstairs from the compact all-teak

rooms. It's the real Thai deal, and the setting is lovely.

Bannkunpra (☎ 0 3524 1978; www.bannkunpra.com; 48 Th U Thong; dm/s 250/300B, d 400-800B;) Overlooking the river, this genteel old teak house is one of the most atmospheric, romantic places in town, filled with historic photos, old books, centuries-old swords and a vintage typewriter. The breezy location is ideal and most of the 15 rooms have four-poster beds, though only five have their own bathrooms; we liked room 1 best. Service is just right and it's all amazing value.

Tony's Place (☎ 0 3525 2578; Soi 8, Th Naresuan; d 200-700B;) Long-running Tony's is a sprawling establishment with an energetic party atmosphere and busy patio restaurant and bar. It might not be the 'True Thai Experience', but the 35 rooms in three wooden houses are dependable; ask to see a few. Wi-fi is free.

Baan Lotus Guest House (☎ 0 3525 1988; 20 Th Pamaphrao; r 200-600B;) Around the corner from Soi 8, the tall wooden house and newer building here contain 23 spotless, airy and good-value rooms. The main appeal, however, is the two elderly sisters who run the place – they are great conversationalists and can't do enough for you. Book ahead.

Old Place Guest House (☎ 0 3521 1161; www.theold placeguesthouse.com; 102 Th U Thong; r 350-600B;) There are better rooms in Ayuthaya, but this budget joint has a fantastic location under a tree on the river. Just make sure you get a room away from the road.

KO KRET
เกาะเกร็ด

Bangkok's closest green getaway is this artificial 'island', the result of a canal being dug nearly 300 years ago to shorten an oxbow bend in the Chao Phraya. Today Ko Kret is known for its hand-thrown terracotta pots, which are sold at markets throughout Bangkok, and its food. This island and the pottery tradition date back to one of Thailand's oldest settlements of Mon people, who were a dominant tribe of central Thailand between the 6th and 10th centuries AD. From Wat Paramai Yikawat (Wat Mon), which has an interesting Mon-style marble Buddha, go in either direction to find working pottery centres on the east and north coasts.

Even more prevalent than pottery is food. At weekends droves of Thais flock to Ko Kret to munch on deep-fried savouries, kŏw châa (a Mon dish combining savoury/sweet titbits and chilled rice) and iced coffee.

Baan Dvara Prateep (☎ 0 2373 6457; www.baandvaraprateep.com; 53/3 Moo 5, Ko Kret) offers multiday yoga and meditation retreats in a traditional wooden house on the west coast of the island, but only takes group bookings.

The most convenient way to get to Ko Kret is by taxi or bus (bus 33 from Sanam Luang) to Pak Kret, before boarding the cross-river ferry from Wat Sanam Neua. Going by river is more scenic; on Sundays you can join a busy weekend tour operated by Chao Phraya Express (☎ 0 2623 6001; www.chaophrayaboat.co.th; child/adult 250/300B; 10am-4.45pm Sat & Sun), departing from Tha Sathon and Tha Mahathat; or take a regular express boat to Nonthaburi (N30) and then a taxi to Pak Kret.

KO SAMET
เกาะเสม็ด

The search for sun and sand doesn't have to involve a big trip down south. Only half a day's journey from Bangkok, Ko Samet has famously squeaky sand beaches and a range of accommodation to fit any budget. Plus it is a relatively dry island, making it an excellent place to visit during the rainy season when other tropical paradises might be under water. Of course, all of this makes it very popular with everyone – Thais, foreigners and a remarkable number of stray dogs (not really soi dogs; perhaps they're 'hat' dogs') – especially on weekends or holidays.

Ko Samet earned a permanent place in Thai literature when classical Thai poet Sunthorn Phu set part of his epic Phra Aphaimani on its shores. The story follows the travails of a prince exiled to an undersea kingdom governed by a lovesick female giant. A mermaid assists the prince in his escape to Ko Samet, where he defeats a giant by playing a magic flute. Today the poem is immortalised on the island by a mermaid statue built on the rocky point separating Ao Hin Khok and Hat Sai Kaew.

In the early 1980s, Ko Samet began receiving its first visitors: young Thais in search of a retreat from city life. It was made a national marine park in 1981 and at that time there were only about 40 houses on the island. Rayong and Bangkok speculators saw the sudden interest in Ko Samet as a chance to cash in on an up-and-coming Phuket and began buying up land along the beaches. No one bothered about the fact that it was a national marine park. When fà-ràng (Westerners) soon followed, spurred on by rumours that Ko Samet was similar to Ko Samui '10 years ago' (one always seems to miss it by a decade), the National Parks Division stepped in and built a visitors' office on the island, ordered that all bungalows be moved back behind the tree line and started charging admission to the park.

However, the regulating hand of the National Parks Division is almost invisible beyond its revenue-raising role at the admission gate (Hat Sai Kaew; child/adult 100/200B; ☺ sunrise-sunset). One successful measure, however, is a ban on new accommodation except where it replaces old sites, ensuring that bungalows remain thinly spread over most of the island. Though as one local told us, this suits existing owners just fine and is the least that could be expected in a national park.

BEFORE SAMET MEANT ESCAPE

If marketing minds had been involved, Ko Samet would still be known by its old name: Ko Kaew Phit-sadan (Vast Jewel Isle), a reference to the abundant white sand. But the island's first cash cow, the sà·mèt (cajeput) tree, lent its name to the island as this valuable firewood source grew in abundance here. Locally, the sà·mèt tree has also been used in boat building.

Development is concentrated at the northern end of the island, though compared with Bangkok even this busiest part of Ko Samet seems as sparsely populated as the Australian outback. See Around the Island, below, for more on particular beaches.

Boat trips (per person 400-800B) to the uninhabited islands of Ko Thalu and Ko Kuti, around Ko Samet, or squid fishing after dark can all be easily arranged.

Around the Island

Ko Samet is shaped like a golf tee, with the wide part in the north tapering away along a narrow strip to the south. Most boats from the mainland arrive at Na Dan Pier in the north, which is little more than a transit point for most visitors, though for the many Thais who have come to live and work on Samet, it is home. On the northeastern coast is Hat Sai Kaew (Diamond Beach), the most developed stretch of beaches you'll find on the island and the best place for nightlife. Wealthy Bangkokians file straight into Hat Sai's air-con bungalows with their designer sunglasses and (small) designer dogs.

Scattered south along the eastern shore are a scruffier set of beaches: Ao Hin Khok, Ao Phai and Ao Phutsa, which were once populated solely by backpackers but are increasingly catering to flashpackers and Bangkok expats. A footpath across a rocky headland separates palm-shaded Ao Phutsa from beaches further south. Quiet Ao Nuan and Ao Cho (Chaw) have less-voluptuous beaches that appeal more to romantics than crowds.

Immediately to the south is the prom queen of the bunch: Ao Wong Deuan, whose graceful stretch of sand is home to an entourage of sardine-packed sun-worshippers, screaming jet skis and honky-tonk bars akin to those in Pattaya (with a similar clientele).

Thai college kids claim Ao Thian (Candlelight Beach) for all-night guitar jam sessions

lonelyplanet.com

KO SAMET

0 ____ 1 km
0 ____ 0.5 miles

Laem Noi Na
To Ban Phe (5km)
To Ban Phe (5km)
To Ban Phe (5km)

Laem Phra

27

Ao Noi Na
19

18

Ao Kham

Ao Klang

Na Dan Pier

Na Dan

8
13
11
Ao Phrao

Laem Ya/Ko Samet National Park

1   4
12

Hat Laem Yai

3

14   6
22   20   17
10
Hat Sai Kaew

Laem Yai

28
21
Ao Hin Khok

Ao Phai

Ao Phutsa (Ao Thap Thim)

23

7
Laem Rua Taek

Ao Nuan

25
2
5   26
24
Ao Cho
Ao Wong Deuan

Hat Saeng Thian
9

Ao Thian

Ao Wai

Ao Thai (Gulf of Thailand)

16
Ao Kiu Na Nai

Ao Kiu Na Nok

15
Laem Khut

Ao Karang

EXCURSIONS KO SAMET

and if you're on a tight budget this beach (as well as Naga Bungalows on Ao Hin Khok) are your best bets. Further south is a castaway's dream of near-empty beaches and gentle surf, and the starting point for languid walks to the western side of the island to see fiery sunsets.

The only developed beach on the steeper western side of the island is Ao Phrao (Coconut Beach), which hosts three upmarket resorts and moonlights as 'Paradise Beach' to those escaping winter climates.

Along the oft-overlooked northern shore are Ao Noi Na and Ao Klang, which have several decent midrange resorts and guesthouses.

INFORMATION

There are ATMs near Malibu Garden Resort on Hat Sai Kaew, at the 108 Minimart and near the tourist police on Hat Wong Deuan, and at the 7-Eleven in Na Dan.

Ko Samet Health Centre (☎ 0 3861 2999; btwn Hat Sai Kaew & Na Dan; ☼ 8.30am-8pm Mon-Fri, to 4.30pm Sat & Sun) Small public clinic with English-speaking doctors for minor health problems.

National Park main office (Hat Sai Kaew; admission child/adult 100/200B; ☼ sunrise-sunset) There's another office on Ao Wong Deuan; wherever you arrive a ranger will find you to charge the fee.

Post office (at Naga Bungalows, Ao Hin Khok; ☼ 8.30am-8.30pm daily) Stamps, poste restante and advice in the internet cafe cum information office.

EATING

Every hotel and guesthouse has a restaurant and choosing one is as difficult as a walk along the beach inspecting menus along the way. There are several food stalls along the main drag between Na Dan pier and Hat Sai Kaew, and it's worth looking out for the nightly beach barbecues, particularly along Ao Hin Khok and Ao Phai.

Ao Lung Wan Restaurant (Ao Cho; dishes 80-150B; ☼ 8am-10pm) Low-key without being shabby, this restaurant serves a large menu of tasty, inexpensive Thai dishes in a quiet beachfront location.

Baywatch Bar (☎ 0818 267 834; Ao Wong Deuan; dishes 190-290B; ☼ 8-2am) Pam Anderson is nowhere to be found but the delicious cocktails and international dishes are a decent consolation prize.

Naga Bar (☎ 0 3864 4168; Ao Hin Khok; dishes 100-200B; ☼ 8am-10pm) The bakery-cum-restaurant here serves warm rolls, croissants and donuts in the morning, and sandwiches, pizza and Thai dishes throughout the day. There are plenty of tofu dishes to satisfy vegetarians.

O (☎ 0 3864 4104; Ao Phrao; dishes 80-500B; ☼ 8am-10pm) For a romantic evening it's hard to beat the combination of delicious Italian food and delightful setting at O at Le Vimarn Cottages. Expensive by Thai standards, it's still cheap compared with home.

Panorama Restaurant (Moo Ban Talay Resort, Laem Noi Na; dishes 120-300B; ☼ 11am-11pm) City sensibilities are well served with Asian and Western cuisine instead of guesthouse grub.

DRINKING

Every hotel and guesthouse has a beachside bar, and there are plenty of stand-alone bar-restaurants that occupy the beachfront at Hat Sai Kaew and Ao Wong Deuan. The latter is so packed with bars it's difficult to know where one ends and the next begins – but does it really matter?

Naga Bar (dishes 50-160B; ☺ 8-2am) On Ao Hin Khok at Naga Bungalows, this is a good destination for post-dinner shenanigans and a meeting place for backpackers.

Tok Bar (dishes 40-150B; ☺ 7-2am), nearby to Naga Bar, Tok offers the same thing.

Silver Sand Bar (☎ 0 6530 2417; Ao Phai; ☺ 1pm-2am) As the clock ticks towards the witching hour, the island's night owls congregate under trippy spherical lights to watch the fire twirlers show off, grind to cheesy dance music and knock back more than 35 types of cocktail (all served in buckets, of course).

SLEEPING

Due to the high demand, Ko Samet's prices can seem elevated compared with the amenities on offer, especially on weekends. A ramshackle hut starts at about 300B and with air-con this can climb to 800B. Reservations aren't always honoured, so at peak times (most weekends and especially public-holiday weekends) it is advisable to arrive early, poised for the hunt.

Hat Sai Kaew

Sai Kaew Beach Resort (☎ 0 2438 9771/2; www.samedresorts.com; r 6700-12,100B, bungalows 6700-8,300B; ✖) The original Samet resort has a wide array of rooms scattered across its vast grounds, from blue-and-white bungalows with a Mediterranean feel, to classy zen-style apartments around a pool. It's popular with wealthy Bangkokians, but there are better resorts (and better value) elsewhere.

Lima Bella Resort (☎ 0 2938 1811; www.limabella.com; r 2200-6990B; ✖ 🖳) From the people who gave Lima Coco a younger feel comes Lima Bella, a small, stylish place with a variety of spacious rooms set around a central pool. It's a few minutes walk north of the beach but is in a peaceful, shaded area. Ask about discounts.

Samed Sand Sea (☎ 0 3865 1126, 0875 083 250; www.samedsandsea.com; r 1500-5000B; ✖) Looking more like a Swedish chalet park cum sauna, this bunch of tightly packed bungalows occupies a long, narrow block running back from the beach; ie most have views only of pine bungalow. The rooms are comfortable if not huge, and boast air-con that's borderline cryogenic.

Ao Hin Khok & Ao Phai

Samed Villa Resort (☎ 0 3864 4094; www.samedvilla.com; r incl breakfast 1800-2500B; ✖ 🖳) Hugely popular place with 40 well-maintained, tree-shaded bungalows with verandas, all at fair prices. More stylish places can be found, but the service here is good and the larger bungalows are well-suited to families.

Jep's Bungalows (☎ 0 3864 4112; www.jepbungalow.com; r 300-1500B; ✖ 🖳) Jep's bungalows are a cheery mix of mahogany and magenta that, given the general move upmarket along this stretch of coast, are now reasonably good value. The cheapest rooms share bathrooms, while pricier pads include air-con and breakfast. Mosquito repellent is a must.

Naga Bungalows (☎ 0 3864 4301; r 300-500B; ✖ 🖳) The last real backpacker joint on this stretch, the unadorned but cheap rooms, party atmosphere and smiling service keep it busy.

Tok's Little Hut (bungalows 300-1500B; ✖) One of the island's first bungalow operations is now emblematic of how Samet is moving upmarket. When we visited it had shiny new, excellent-value air-con A-frame bungalows (1500B), a wrecking crew breaking up old bungalows, and at the back a forlorn few, bathroomless shacks that have been housing the baht-challenged for years. They will likely be gone by the time you arrive, and hopefully there will be a phone by then, too.

Ao Phutsa (Ao Thap Thim) & Ao Nuan

Tubtim Resort (☎ 0 3864 4025; www.tubtimresort.com; r 600-3000B; ✖ 🖳 ☜) Tubtim has dozens of bungalows climbing up a rugged hill from the beach. The pick are the modern, stylish bungalows with big windows and balconies that look straight down the beach; mid-priced rooms are thoroughly comfortable, too. The beachfront restaurant isn't bad and is more all-weather prepared than most, but service throughout can be reluctant to the point of rudeness.

Ao Nuan Bungalows (Ao Nuan; bungalows 700-2500B) If you blink you'll miss this beach and the 10 Swiss Family Robinson–style bungalows that give it a real castaway feel. The family running it has recently added bathrooms to some (1500B), and even air-con (2500B). It's a five-minute walk over the headland from Ao Phutsa. There's no phone and it doesn't take reservations.

Ao Wong Deuan & Ao Thian

Baan Thai Sang Thian Samed (☎ 0863 730 774; Ao Thian; r 1700-2500B; ❄) Think of traditional Thai architecture with a tree-house twist and you'll sum up this family-run place. It's the pick of the Ao Thian bunch, but you'll feel better about staying here if you knock the price down a bit.

Vongdeuan Resort (☎ 0 3864 4171; www.vongdeuan. com; Ao Wong Deuan; r 2000-3500B; ❄) This sprawling place occupies much of the southern part of Ao Wong Deuan in its garden-like setting. Bungalows range from teak-style houses to cheaper concrete cottages at the back. Reasonable value.

Other Eastern Beaches

Paradee Resort & Spa (☎ 0 3864 4283; www.paradeeresort. com; villas 17,800-79,200B; ❄ 🖳 🖵) The most luxurious resort on Samet, located on the island's most stunning, secluded beach, is all about four-poster beds in 40 charismatic and self-contained villas. There's gorgeous Thai furniture, a personal plunge pool, DVD player, espresso maker – even your own butler, but is it worth the mega prices? If you laugh in the face of a 6000B speedboat connection to Ban Phe, then maybe. Check online for occasional big discounts.

Nimma Noradee (☎ 0 3864 4271; www.nimmanoradee. com; bungalows 2700-3800B; ❄) On Ao Karang at the very southern end of Samet, this 'eco-resort' will appeal to Robinson Crusoe fans who fancy kayaking, snorkelling and, of course, bright octagonal rooms. Motorbike rental is a steep 600B a day.

Ao Phrao (Paradise Beach)

Ao Prao Resort (☎ 0 2438 9771/2; www.samedresorts. com; chalets 5100-21,200B; ❄ 🖳 🖵) No longer the luxury lodging of choice on Samet, Ao Prao still has all the bells and whistles, excellent service and good prices in quieter times. Ao Prao Divers, at the resort, provides diving, windsurfing, kayaking and boat trips.

Le Vimarn Cottages (☎ 0 3864 4104, Bkk 0 2438 9771/2; www.samedresorts.com; r 8600-21,000B; ❄ 🖳 📶 🖵) Le Vimarn is manicured tranquillity, with 28 elegant cottages and villas where whitewashed walls and thatched roofs open into modern

rooms with teak features. Facilities include the lavish Dhivarin Spa (☎ 0 3864 4104-7). Good choice.

Lima Coco (☎ 0 2938 1811; www.limacoco.com; d 2590-6990B; ❄) Built on the hillside above Ao Phrao beach, Lima Coco's 44 rooms have had numerous makeovers and just manage to hold off the years to appeal to younger, groovier Thais from Bangkok. The resort offers a free ferry from Ban Phe.

The North Shore

In recent years several stylish midrange places have opened along Ao Klang and Ao Noi Na on the north shore. If you're going to stay here, think about renting a motorbike.

Samed Club (☎ 0 3864 4341; www.samedresorts.com; Ao Noi Na; r 3200B; ❄ 🖳 📶 🖵) The 30 rooms at this 'boutique resort' are set on a compact block ranging up a hill. Their colour palette is a mix of terracotta, saffron and polished concrete, and higher rooms reward the steep climb with great views.

Samed Cliff Resort (☎ 0 2635 0800; Ao Noi Na; d 1700-2800B; ❄ 🖳 🖵) These whitewashed bungalows set into the hillside are older and less stylish but cheaper and still perfectly comfortable.

FLOATING MARKETS
ตลาดน้ำ

Pictures of floating markets (đà·làht nám) jammed full of wooden canoes pregnant with colourful exotic fruits have defined the official tourist profile of Thailand for decades. The idyllic scenes are as iconic as the Grand Palace (p67) or the Reclining Buddha (p69), but they are also almost completely contrived for, and dependent upon, tourists. Roads and motorcycles have long moved Bangkokians's daily errands onto dry ground.

The most famous of the breed – the one you've seen photographed hundreds of times – is the Damnoen Saduak Floating Market (Khlong Damnoen Saduak; ☷ 7am–noon daily). You can hire a boat from any pier that lines Th Sukhaphiban 1, which is the land route to the floating market area. The going rate is 150B per person per hour, but you'll need to haggle to get it. The 100-year-old market is now essentially a floating souvenir stand filled with package tourists. This in itself can be a fascinating insight into Thai culture, as the vast majority of tourists here are Thais, and watching the approach to this cultural 'theme park' is instructive. But beyond the market, the

TRANSPORT: FLOATING MARKETS

Damnoen Saduak

Distance from Bangkok 65km

Direction Southwest

Travel Time Two hours

Bus Air-con buses (80B) go direct from Thonburi's Southern Bus Terminal (Map p132) to Damnoen Saduak at least every 40 minutes, beginning at 5.50am. Most buses will drop you off at a pier along the *klorng*, where you can hire a boat directly to the floating market. The regular bus stop is in town just across the bridge. A yellow *sŏrng-tăa-ou* (5B) does a frequent loop between the floating market and the bus stop in town.

Don Wai Market

Distance from Bangkok 50km

Direction Southwest

Travel Time 1½ hours

The easiest way to reach Don Wai Market is to take a minibus (45B, 35 minutes) from beside Central Pinklao (Map p132) in Thonburi.

Amphawa Market

Distance from Bangkok 80km

Direction Southwest

Travel Time 1½ hours

Buses run every 40 minutes from Thonburi's Southern Bus Terminal (Map p132) directly to Amphawa (72B).

Tha Kha Floating Market

Distance from Bangkok 55km

Direction Southwest

Travel Time Two hours

Tours can be organised through Baan Tai Had Resort (p246).

residential canals are quite peaceful and can be explored by hiring a boat for a longer duration. South of the floating market are several small family businesses, including a Thai candy maker, a pomelo (shaddock, a type of citrus) farm and a knife crafter.

Not technically a swimmer, Don Wai Market (Talat Don Wai; 6am-6pm daily) claims a riverbank location in Nakhon Pathom province, having originally started out in the early 20th century as a floating market for pomelo and jackfruit growers and traders. As with many tourist attractions geared towards Thais, the main attraction here is food, including fruit, traditional sweets and *Bèt pah·lóh* (five-spice stewed duck), which can be consumed aboard large boats that cruise Nakhorn Chaisi River (60B, one hour).

The Amphawa Floating Market (ðà-làht nám am-pá-wah; 4-9pm Fri-Sun), about 7km northwest of Samut Songkhram, convenes near Wat Amphawa. If you can get your timing right, several nearby floating markets meet in the mornings on particular lunar days and tend to be mainly tourist-free zones. Tha Kha Floating Market (2nd, 7th & 12th day of waxing & waning moons, & 7am-noon each Sat & Sun) is one notable example, coalescing along an open, breezy *klorng* lined with greenery and old wooden houses.

INFORMATION

Baan Tai Had Resort (0 3476 7220; www.baantaihad.com; 1 Moo 2, Th Tai Had, Samut Songkhram) Rents kayaks and organises trips for exploring the Amphawa and Tha Kha markets.

Bike & Travel (☎ 0 2990 0274; www.cyclingthailand. com) This tour company organises bike trips to Damnoen Saduak and the surrounding villages.

Damnoen Saduak Tourist Information Office (Th Sukha phiban 1; ⊙ 9am-5pm) This office, across from the floating market, can organise transport to outlying canal sites if you want a two- to three-hour tour. It also arranges for homestays and other canal trips.

MAHACHAI RAIL LINE & AMPHAWA

สายรถไฟมหาชัย

If you want to get out of the city but don't know where to go, this might be the perfect trip. The Mahachai Line, a rail spur originally built to link gulfside fishing ports with Thonburi and Bangkok, is a charming trip that sates the wanderlust by introducing you to the sort of Thai life you don't see so much in Bangkok anymore. However, if you are the type that requires a destination, then the quaint canalside village of Amphawa definitely boasts enough atmosphere, accommodation and activities to warrant an overnight stay.

The adventure begins at Wong Wian Yai train station (Map p64; Th Taksin; bus 37; 🚇 Wong Wian Yai). Just past the traffic circle (Wong Wian Yai) is a fairly ordinary food market that camouflages the unspectacular terminus of this commuter line.

After 15 minutes on the rattling train the city density yields to squat villages. From the window you can peek into homes, temples and shops built a carefully considered arm's length from the passing trains. Further on, palm trees, patchwork rice fields and marshes filled with giant elephant ears and canna lilies line the route, punctuated by whistle-stop stations.

Samut Sakhon (Mahachai)

The backwater farms evaporate quickly as you enter Samut Sakhon, popularly known as Mahachai because it straddles the confluence of Mae Nam Tha Chin and Khlong Mahachai. This is a bustling port town, several kilometres upriver from the Gulf of Thailand, and the end of the first rail segment. Before the 17th century it was called Tha Jiin (Chinese Pier) because of the large number of Chinese junks that called here.

After working your way through one of the most hectic fresh markets in the country,

you'll come to a vast harbour clogged with water hyacinths and wooden fishing boats. A few rusty cannons pointing towards the river testify to the existence of the town's crumbling fort, built to protect the kingdom from sea invaders.

Take the ferry across to Baan Laem (3B), jockeying for space with motorcycles that are driven by school teachers and errand-running housewives. From the ferry, take a motorcycle taxi (10B) for the 2km ride to Wat Chawng Lom, home to the Jao Mae Kuan Im Shrine, a 9m-high fountain in the shape of the Mahayana Buddhist Goddess of Mercy that is popular with regional tour groups. The colourful figure, which pours a perpetual stream of water from a vase in the goddess's right hand, rests on an artificial hill into which a passageway is carved, leading to another Kuan Im shrine.

Beside the shrine is Tha Chalong, a train stop with two afternoon departures for Samut Songkhram (see below). The train rambles out of the city on tracks that the surrounding forest threatens to engulf, and this little stretch of line genuinely feels a world away from the big smoke of Bangkok.

Samut Songkhram

The jungle doesn't last long, and any illusion that you've entered a parallel universe free of concrete is shattered as you enter Samut Songkhram. And to complete the seismic shift you'll emerge directly into a hubbub of hectic market stalls. Between train arrivals and departures these stalls set up directly on the tracks, and must be hurriedly cleared away when the train arrives – it's quite an amazing scene.

Commonly known as Mae Klong, Samut Songkhram is a tidier version of Samut Sakhon and offers a great deal more as a destination. Owing to flat topography and abundant water sources, the area surrounding the provincial capital is well suited to the steady irrigation needed to grow guava, lychee and grapes. A string of artificial sea-lakes used in the production of salt fill the space between Mae Klong and Thonburi.

Wat Phet Samut Worawihan, in the centre of town, near the train station and river, contains a renowned Buddha image called Luang Phaw Wat Ban Laem – named after the prá sàk·sìt (holy monk) who dedicated it, thus transferring mystical powers to the image.

TRANSPORT: MAHACHAI RAIL LINE

Distance from Bangkok 28km to Samut Sakhon; 74km to Samut Songkhram

Direction Southwest

Travel Time One hour to Samut Sakhon, 1¾ hours to Samut Songkhram

Train Trains leave Thonburi's Wong Wian Yai station (Map p64) for Samut Sakhon roughly every hour from 5.30am to 8.10pm. You'll need to leave Thonburi before 8.30am in order to do the trip entirely by train. There are four departures from Baan Laem to Samut Songkhram (10B, 3rd class only, 7.30am, 10.10am, 1.30pm and 4.40pm). Returning, trains leave at 6.20am, 9am, 11.30am and 3.30pm. Samut Sakhon has hourly departures to Thonburi until 7pm. Late trains are not unheard of.

Taxi Hire a taxi to/from Bangkok to Samut Sakhon (500B) or Samut Songkram (1200B).

Bus If you get a late start, you can always return to Bangkok by bus. In both Samut Sakhon and Samut Songkhram the train station is a five-minute walk from the bus terminal. Regular buses from Samut Sakhon (45B) and Samut Songkhram (67B) arrive at the Southern Bus Terminal (Map p132) in Thonburi. Both cities have bus services to Damnoen Saduak (p245).

However, it comes as something of a relief that the province's most famous tourist attraction is not a wát. Instead, the honour goes to a bank of fossilised shells known as Don Hoi Lot at the mouth of Mae Nam Mae Klong, not far from town. These shells come from *hŏy lòrt* (clams with a tubelike shell). While nearby seafood restaurants are popular with city folk year-round, the shell bank is best seen during April and May when the river surface has receded to its lowest level. To get there hop into a *sŏrng·tăa·ou* (10B, about 15 minutes) in front of Somdet Phra Phuttalertla Hospital at the intersection of Th Prasitwatthana and Th Thamnimit. Or charter a boat from Mae Klong Market pier *(tâh dà·làht mâa glorng)*, a scenic journey of around 45 minutes (about 1000B).

Wat Satthatham, 500m down the road from Don Hoi Lot, is notable for its *bòht* constructed of golden teak and decorated with 60 million baht' worth of mother-of-pearl inlay. The inlay completely covers the temple's interior and depicts scenes from the *jataka* (stories from the Buddha's lives) above the windows and the Ramakian below.

Amphawa

If you're not ready to turn back yet, charter a boat (1000B) or hop in a *sŏrng·tăa·ou* (9B) near the market for the 10-minute ride to Amphawa. This canalside village has become a popular destination among city folk who seek out what many consider its quintessentially 'Thai' setting. This urban influx has sparked a few signs of gentrification, but the canals, old wooden buildings, atmospheric cafes and

quaint water-borne traffic still retain heaps of charm. At weekends Amphawa puts on a reasonably authentic floating market (p246); visit on a weekday if you want to have the whole town to yourself.

Steps from Amphawa's central footbridge is Wat Amphawan Chetiyaram, a graceful temple thought to be located at the place of the family home of Rama II (King Phraphutthaloetla Naphalai; r 1809–24), and which features accomplished murals. A short walk from the temple is King Buddhalertla (Phuttha Loet La) Naphalai Memorial Park (Km 63, Route 35, Samut Songkhram; admission 20B; ☺ park 9am-6pm daily, museum 9am-6pm Wed-Sun), a museum housed in a collection of traditional central-Thai houses set on four landscaped acres. Dedicated to Rama II, the museum contains rare Thai books and antiques from early 19th-century Siam.

At night longtail boats zip through Amphawa's sleeping waters to watch the star-like dance of the *hìng hôy* (fireflies). Several operators lead tours, including Niphaa (☎ 0814 220 726), an experienced and well-equipped outfit located at the mouth of the canal, near the footbridge. If you take a tour, be aware that people are often sleeping in the homes you'll pass, so insist the driver doesn't make more noise than is absolutely necessary.

EATING

Khrua Chom Ao (☎ 0851 905 677; Samut Sakhon; dishes 60-200B) This open-air seafood restaurant looks over the gulf and has a loyal local following. It is a brief walk from Wat Chawng Lom, down the road running along the side of the temple opposite the statue of Kuan Im.

Tarua Restaurant (☎ 0 3441 1084; Ferry Terminal Bldg, 859 Th Sethakit, Samut Sakhon; dishes 60-200B) Occupying three floors of the imposing ferry building, this busy seafood restaurant offers views over the harbour, an English-language menu and some excellent fish and shellfish dishes.

Amphawa Floating Market (ðà·làht nám am·pá·wah; dishes 20-40B; 4-9pm Fri-Sun) If you're in town on a weekend, plan your meals around this fun market (see p246) where *pàt tai* and other noodle dishes are served directly from boats.

Phu Yai Thawngyib (☎ 0 3473 5073; Amphawa; dishes 20-60B) This community development project and homestay located outside Amphawa includes a restaurant that serves authentic local dishes and sweets. Call ahead to arrange a visit.

SLEEPING

Amphawa is popular with Bangkok's weekend warriors and virtually every other house has opened its door to tourists in the form of homestays. These can range from little more than a mattress and a mosquito net to upscale guesthouse-style accommodation. Baan Song Thai Plai Pong Pang (☎ 0 3475 7333; Amphawa) organises homestays and has been recognised for ecotourism excellence. Most of these places are best reached by boat, though some have road access; call ahead or get your driver to call for directions. Highly recommended.

Reorn Pae Amphawa (☎ 0 3475 1333; 139-145 Rim Khlong, Amphawa; d 800B;) A good upper-budget option is this generations-old wooden home with basic but tidy rooms.

Baan Tai Had Resort (☎ 0 3476 7220; www.baantaihad. com; 1 Moo 2, Th Tai Had, Samut Songkhram; r 1600-5600B;) This riverside resort is more worthy of the description, with bright and comfortable rooms and several activities to choose

from. Staff will organise several half-day boat tours.

Baan Amphawa Resort & Spa (☎ 0 3475 2222; www. baanamphawa.com; 22 Bangkapom-kaewfah, Amphawa; r from 3200B;) At the top of the heap is delightful Baan Amphawa, a traditional Thai-style village with peaking red roofs set among the paddies and klorng, plus luxuries including a spa and some rooms with private pools.

PHETCHABURI (PHETBURI)

เพชรบุรี

Phetchaburi (the 'City of Diamonds', commonly known as Phetburi) has a bit of everything – history, nature, good eats and beaches. Given buses take only a couple of hours some people make a day trip from Bangkok. But this is madness, as Phetburi is one of those chilled Thai towns where the slow pace is half the fun and the food – oh, the food! – means it's worth staying overnight for the dinner alone.

The trip down to Phetburi passes through stereotypically central Thailand – flat plains punctuated by shaggy sugar palms and the occasional unexpected limestone outcroppings. As you get closer to Phetburi you'll see a surprising number of wooden homes, many with the characteristic peaked roof that has all but died out elsewhere in Thailand. The town itself is a repository of traditional central Thai culture, and a walk along the town's twisting back lanes, a peek at the vivid morning market and a tour of the fabled temples provide a glimpse of a lifestyle that has changed little in decades.

Phetburi lives in the shadow of Khao Wang, a looming hill studded with wát and topped by

KAENG KRACHAN NATIONAL PARK

อุทยานแห่งชาติแก่งกระจาน

The largest national park in Thailand and home to the gorgeous Pala-U waterfalls, Kaeng Krachan National Park (☎ 0 3246 7326; child/adult 100/200B) is easily reached from Phetburi. There are caves to explore, mountains, a huge lake and excellent bird-watching opportunities in the evergreen forest blanketing the park. Kaeng Krachan has fantastic trekking, and it is one of the few places to see Asian elephants roaming wild (if you're lucky). Intermittent *sŏrng·tăa·ou* (50B) depart from near Wat Thaw and stop at the park headquarters. To get to some of the higher camp-grounds you'll have to charter a vehicle from the headquarters (900B) or hitch. Tom (☎ 0899 197 446) from Rabieng Rimnum Guest House (p252) has an infectious enthusiasm for the park and arranges fun day trips (2000B per person, minimum four people) and even more enjoyable overnight visits (per person from 2850B, minimum 4 people). The park is usually closed between 1 August and 31 October.

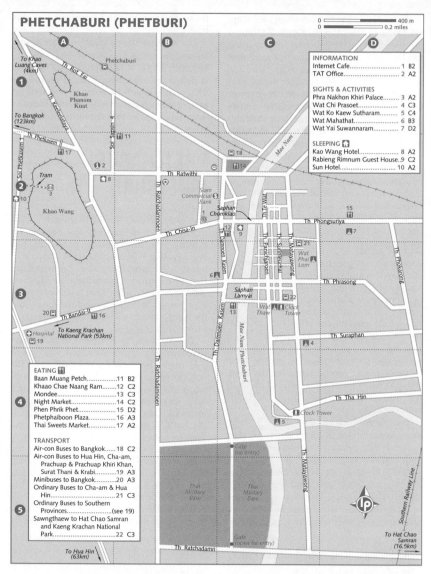

PHETCHABURI (PHETBURI)

INFORMATION
Internet Cafe...........................1 B2
TAT Office.............................2 A2

SIGHTS & ACTIVITIES
Phra Nakhon Khiri Palace.........3 A2
Wat Chi Prasoet....................4 C3
Wat Ko Kaew Sutharam.........5 C4
Wat Mahathat......................6 B3
Wat Yai Suwannaram............7 D2

SLEEPING
Kao Wang Hotel....................8 A2
Rabieng Rimnum Guest House.9 C2
Sun Hotel.............................10 A2

EATING
Baan Muang Petch................11 B2
Khaao Chae Naang Ram........12 C2
Mondee..............................13 C3
Night Market.......................14 C2
Phen Phrik Phet...................15 D2
Phetphaiboon Plaza..............16 A3
Thai Sweets Market..............17 A2

TRANSPORT
Air-con Buses to Bangkok......18 C2
Air-con Buses to Hua Hin, Cha-am,
  Prachuap & Prachuap Khiri Khan,
  Surat Thani & Krabi............19 A3
Minibuses to Bangkok...........20 A3
Ordinary Buses to Cha-am & Hua
  Hin..................................21 C3
Ordinary Buses to Southern
  Provinces.........................(see 19)
Sawngthaew to Hat Chao Samran
  and Kaeng Krachan National
  Park.................................22 C3

various components of King Mongkut's 1860 palace, Phra Nakhon Khiri (☎ 0 3240 1006; admission 150B; ⏰ 8.30am-4.30pm). The mountaintop is divided into three sections; the east peak bears a scaled-down version of Wat Phra Kaew (the Temple of the Emerald Buddha, p67) and an unusual *chedi* made of granite blocks; the middle peak is dominated by a 40m-high *chedi* that affords panoramic views from its upper level, while the western peak is home to Mongkut's

palace, his observatory and other palace essentials built in Thai and Sino-European styles. For more detail ask the information office for its 'map' (3B). To get here, make the strenuous upward climb or head to the west side of the hill and take a funicular straight up to the peak (return child/adult 15/40B). Note that Khao Wang is home to hundreds of cheeky monkeys that are, according to numerous signs, 'not afraid anyone'.

Phetburi is known throughout Thailand for its varied collection of wát. The most prominent is the imposing Wat Mahathat (Th Damnoen Kasem), with its late Ayuthaya–early Ratanakosin adaptation of the *prang* of Lopburi and Phimai. The beautiful murals inside the *wí·hăhn* illustrate the *jataka* (stories from the Buddha's lives) and also show vivid snippets of everyday Thai life during the 19th century. The roof of the adjacent *bòht* holds some fine examples of stucco work, which is characteristic of the Phetburi school of art that can be seen on many of the city's temples.

Wat Yai Suwannaram (Th Phongsuriya) was originally built during the 17th century and renovated during the reign of Rama V (r 1868–1910). Legend has it that the gash in the ornately carved wooden doors of the lengthy wooden *săh·lah* dates to the Burmese attack on Ayuthaya. The faded murals inside the *bòht* date back to the 1730s. Next to the *bòht*, set on a murky pond, is a beautifully designed old *hŏr đrai* (Tripitaka library), though these days it's home only to pigeons.

Wat Ko Kaew Sutharam (Wat Ko; off Th Matayawong) dates back to the Ayuthaya era, and the *bòht* features early 18th-century murals that are among the oldest and the most beautiful in Thailand. One panel depicts what appears to be a Jesuit priest wearing the robes of a Buddhist monk, while another shows other foreigners undergoing Buddhist conversions. You might have to ask the caretaker to open it for you.

Somewhat unusually for a Thai temple, contemporary stucco work portraying the violent political unrest of 1973 can be viewed at Wat Chi Prasoet (Th Suraphan).

About 4km north of town is the cave sanctuary Khao Luang (donation encouraged; 8am-6pm), which has three caverns filled with dozens of Buddha images in various poses – some of them originally placed by Rama IV – and several souvenir stalls. The best time to visit Khao Luang is around 5pm, when the school groups should have gone and the evening light pierces the ceiling, surrounding artefacts below with an ethereal glow. A săhm·lór from town costs about 80B return; a motorcycle taxi is 70B.

INFORMATION

TAT office (☎ 0 3240 2220; cnr Th Ratwithi & Keeleelataya; 8am-noon & 1.15-4pm) Set in a wát-like structure with random baroque chandeliers, this information office doesn't have loads of brochures, but the smiley staff can help with directions and point you in the direction of cheap food and lodgings. There's an internet cafe (Th Chisa-In; per hr 18B; 8am-10pm) in the centre of town, not far from Rabieng Rimnum Guest House.

EATING

Wandering around Phetburi, one of the first things you notice is how good it smells. Even by Thai standards, there are loads of street vendors and small restaurants selling myriad dishes, often with a peculiarly local

---

TRANSPORT: PHETBURI

Distance from Bangkok 166km

Direction South

Travel Time Two to 2½ hours by bus or taxi; 2½ to four hours by train

Bus Air-con buses run to/from Bangkok's Southern bus station (112B; 2½ hours) every 30 minutes between 4am and 8pm. In Phetburi, buses arrive and depart from an office behind the night market. Minibuses (100B, 2½ hours) leave from Th Bandai-It every 30 minutes or so from 5am to 7pm.

Taxi You can charter a Bangkok taxi to Phetburi for about 2000B, but there are no taxis in Phetburi for the return trip.

Train Trains are less convenient than buses, unless you factor in the time taken to get to or from Bangkok's bus terminals. There are frequent services from Bangkok's Hualamphong train station, and fares vary depending on the train and class (3rd/2nd class, 100/200B, three hours; express train 328B). Getting back to Bangkok by train is a bit tougher as there are only two daytime departures: a 3rd-class train at 3pm (four hours, 34B) and an air-con departure at 4.40pm (three hours, 358B).

Getting Around Săhm·lór and motorcycle taxis go anywhere in the town centre for 30B; you can also charter them for the whole day (from 300B). More common are sŏrng·tăa·ou, which cost 20B to 40B around town. Rabieng Rimnum Guest House (p252) rents out motorcycles (per day 250B).

HAT CHAO SAMRAN
หาดเจ้าสำราญ

Lying 18km east of Phetburi, Hat Chao Samran is one of Thailand's oldest beach resorts, dating back to the reign of Rama VI (King Vajiravudh; r 1910–25). While the Thailand of today certainly has more appealing beaches, it's a pleasant enough place to laze your way through a day or two, punctuating your naps with cheap seafood binges. A recent resurgence in popularity has brought with it 'boutique'-style bungalow accommodation. Blue Sky (☎ 0 3244 1399; www.blueskyresort.com; 5 Moo 2, Hat Chao Samran; bungalows 1800-4000B; 🛜 🖳) offers cute bungalows and rooms overlooking the garden or the sea. When you can relax no more, stumble next door to the ramshackle Jaa Piak (☎ 0 3247 8496; dishes 50-280B; 🕙 9am-9pm), which serves all manner of seafood including a mean horseshoe crab–and–egg salad (yam kài maang dah tálair).

To reach Hat Chao Samran, hop on a sŏrng-tăa-ou (35 minutes; 30B) across from the clock tower near Wat Thaw, or ride a rented motorbike.

twist. Phetburi is especially famous for its desserts, many of which can claim a royal pedigree and obtain their sweet taste from the fruit of the sugar palms that dot the countryside around here. Two of the most famous sweets on offer include môr gaang (an egg and coconut-milk custard) and kà·nŏm dahn (bright-yellow steamed buns sweetened with sugar-palm kernels). The best place to sample these and other desserts is along the Thai sweets market (Th Phetkasem) directly north of Khao Wang. We've asked the locals for their tips and below are places with the best reputations in town.

The town features two lively night markets, one at Phetphaiboon Plaza (Th Bandai-It; dishes 20-60B; 🕙 4.30-11pm), and the night market (Th Rot Fai; dishes 20-60B; 🕙 4-11pm) near the Bangkok-bound bus stop.

Baan Muang Petch (☎ 0816 945 031; 20/2-3 Soi Sapsin 4; dishes 25-60B; 🕙 10am-9pm Tue-Sun) This well-situated coffee shop is an excellent place to refill on real coffee, iced or otherwise, and sweets between temple visits. Simple dishes and a great sunset view of Khao Wang are also available.

Khaao Chae Naang Ram (☎ 0848 018 395; Th Damnoen Kasem; dishes 20B; 🕙 8am-5pm) Kôw châa (camphor-scented chilled rice served with sweet/savoury titbits) is a dish associated with Phetburi, and this roadside stall in front of a noodle restaurant is considered one of the best places to try it (it's an odd flavour and icy texture, but worth a go). There's no English sign; look for the cart under the old blue awning).

Mondee (☎ 0816 971 768; Saphan Lamyai; dishes 25-100B; 🕙 10am-midnight) During the day, this cosy wooden shack beside the river serves kà·nŏm jeen (fresh rice noodles served with a variety of curries). At night Mondee takes full advantage of the breezes and river view and serves decent central-Thai fare with an emphasis on seafood.

Phen Phrik Phet (☎ 0 3241 2990; 173/1 Th Phongsuriya; dishes 30B; 🕙 9am-3pm Wed-Mon) Located directly across from the entrance to Wat Yai Suwannaram, this local noodle legend makes delicious gŏoay dĕeo mŏo nám daang (pork noodles in a fragrant dark broth). There's no English sign; look for the umbrellas, pots and potplants.

SLEEPING

There is not much to choose from in the accommodation department, so don't get too excited.

Sun Hotel (☎ 0 3240 0000; www.sunhotelthailand.com; 43/33 Soi Phetkasem 1; r 790-890B, ste 1390B; 🅿 🖳 🛜) Huge, brightly coloured if somewhat sparsely furnished rooms make this the pick of the midrange options.

Kao Wang Hotel (☎ 0 3242 5167; 123 Th Ratwithi; s 250-350B; tw 350-600B; 🅿) Budgeteers seeking relatively quiet nights should stop in this very local place, where there's no English and the rooms are institutional-looking but big and clean enough.

Rabieng Rimnum Guest House (☎ 0 3242 5707; 1 Th Phongsuriya; s/d 120/240B) The cheapest place in town, this wooden house is straight out of the shoestring guides of the '80s, with tiny fan rooms with walls that cut out little of the traffic noise passing across the bridge – it is cheap, though. There is a good vibe here and the restaurant is something of a gathering point for the few travellers in town.

KANCHANABURI

อ.เมือง กาญจนบุรี

Just two hours from Bangkok, Kanchanaburi (pronounced 'gahn-ja-ná-bùree') is a convenient and refreshing retreat from city life. Framed by limestone mountains and fields of sugarcane, the city offers ample riverside accommodation options that specialise in the art of relaxing after a day of sightseeing in the scenic countryside.

But don't be fooled by Kanchanaburi's sleepy daytime demeanour. After the sun sets the river boom-booms its way through the night with disco and karaoke barges packed with Bangkokians looking to let their hair down, especially at weekends. Out-of-tune crooners and shoddy stereo systems disrupt the calm that many travellers are hoping to find in their riverside rooms. If this is you, it won't take long before you're thinking that sometimes Asia needs a mute button. An hour or so later you might be fantasising about bazookas.

The city was originally established by Rama I (King Buddha Yodfa; r 1782–1809) as a first line of defence against the Burmese who, it was commonly believed, might use the old invasion route through the Three Pagodas Pass on the Thai–Burmese border to the west. Crumbling buildings that reflect the town's age can be found on the side streets that run off and parallel to Th Song Khwae.

Despite its unspectacular appearance (it's an iron bridge), the Death Railway Bridge across Mae Nam Khwae is one of Kanchanaburi's most popular attractions (see p255). Indeed, Kanchanaburi can thank director David Lean and his Hollywood epic *The Bridge on the River Kwai* for a good proportion of the city's foreign visitors. The bridge, 2km north of town, was taken from Java by the Japanese and reassembled here with work beginning in 1942. It was bombed repeatedly during WWII, and of what you see today the curved spans are original and the two square sections were rebuilt with Japanese reparation money in 1946. You can walk across the bridge, but keep an ear out for the six trains a day that still use it and the Death Railway en route to the village of Nam Tok; see Kanchanaburi Transport, p256, for details.

Pretty much all of Kanchanaburi town's sights – two cemeteries and three museums – are dedicated to this dark period. It's worth visiting at least one of the museums before

going to a war cemetery. The first two museums are informative, but the third is the real must-see.

The WWII Museum (Th Mae Nam Khwae; admission 40B; 9am-6pm) beside the bridge has a picture-postcard view and a vast and eclectic assortment of war and peace memorabilia – from rusting guns to mural-sized portraits of WWII-era political figures. If you enjoy sifting through junk shops you'll love this place.

The simple JEATH War Museum (Th Pak Phraek; admission 30B; 8.30am-6pm) operates in the grounds of a local temple and has reconstructions of the long bamboo huts used by the POWs as shelter. Inside are various photographs, drawings, maps, weapons, paintings by POWs and other war memorabilia. The acronym JEATH represents the ill-fated meeting of Japan, England, Australia/America, Thailand and Holland at Kanchanaburi during WWII. The war museum is at the end of Th Wisuttharangsi (Visutrangsi). The common Thai name for this museum is *pí·pí·tá·pan sŏng·krahm wát dâi* (Wat Tai War Museum).

The pick of the museums is the Thailand-Burma Railway Centre (0 3451 2721; www.tbrconline.com; 73 Th Jaokannun; child/adult 50/100B; 9am-5pm), where interactive exhibits, short films and clear descriptions provide the context of the Japanese aggression in Southeast Asia, detail their plans for the railway and describe the horrors faced by those prisoners who worked and died constructing it. Give yourself a full hour to read through the museum, and stop for a coffee upstairs for sweeping views across the cemetery. Ex-POWs and their families get special treatment.

The Kanchanaburi Allied War Cemetery (Th Saengchuto; admission free; 7am-6pm) is the final resting place of about 7000 prisoners who died while working on the railway. The cemetery is meticulously maintained by the Commonwealth War Graves Commission (www.cwgc.org), and the rows of

THE RIVER WHAT?

Try as you might, you will find few Thais who have ever heard of the River Kwai. The river over which the Death Railway trundled is pronounced much like 'quack' without the '-ck'. If spelled phonetically, 'Kwai' should be 'Khwae'. In the mispronounced river live *blah yêe·sòk*, the most common edible fish in this area and the model for the city's fish-shaped street signs.

KANCHANABURI

0 — 500 m
0 — 0.3 miles

A   **B**   **C**   **D**

To Wat Pa Luangta Bua
Yannasampanno (Tiger Temple; 45km);
Erawan National Park (50km);
Hellfire Pass Memorial (75km);
Sai Yok National Park (85km);
Sangkhlaburi (203km)

Train
Station

Th Saengchuto

Th Mae Nam Khwae

Mae Nam Khwae

Th Rong Hip Oi

Th Chaokhun

Church

Allied
Cemetery

Chinese
Temple

Wat Neua

Th Teaban Bamrung

Th Kratai Thong

Th Hiran Prasat

Th Bovon

Th U Thong

Bangkok Bank

Th Song Khwae

Market

Th Khu Meuang

Th Pracha

Thai Military Bank

Th Lak Meuang

City Meuang
Gate Shrine

Lak
Meuang

Minibuses to Bangkok

Th Wisuttharangsi

Mae Nam Mae Khlong

Th Pak Praek

Thanakarn
Hospital

Th Chukkadon

CAT
Office

Mae Nam Khwae Noi

To Wat Tham
Khao Pun (700m);
Royal River Kwai
Resort & Spa (5km)

To Jay Tiw (500m);
Kok Kaat (500m);
Bangkok (139km)

Th Safa Klang

INFORMATION	
TAT Office	1 D4

SIGHTS & ACTIVITIES	
Chung Kai Allied War Cemetery	2 B5
Death Railway Bridge	3 A1
JEATH War Museum	4 C4
Kanchanaburi Allied War Cemetery	5 B2
Thailand-Burma Railway Centre	6 B2
WWII Museum	7 A1

SLEEPING	
Blue Star Guest House	8 A2
Kasem Island Resort	9 C5
Ploy Guesthouse	10 A2
Pong Phen Guesthouse	11 A2
River Kwai Bridge Resort	12 A1
Sugar Cane Guest House	13 A2

EATING	
Floating Restaurants	14 B3
Keeree Tara Restaurant	15 A1
Night Market	16 C3
Sitthisang Coffee Shop	17 C3

DRINKING	
Bar Beer	18 C4
Buddha Bar	19 B2
Resort	20 A1
Rest Room	21 B3

TRANSPORT	
Bus Station	22 D4

headstones are identical except for the names and the short, moving epitaphs. It's just around the corner from the riverside guesthouses.

Less visited is the Chung Kai Allied War Cemetery (admission free; 7am-6pm), where about 1700 graves are kept a short and scenic bike ride from central Kanchanaburi. Take the bridge across the river through picturesque corn and sugarcane fields until you reach the cemetery on your left.

Around Kanchanaburi

Viewing the bridge and war museums doesn't quite communicate the immense task of bending the landscape with human muscle that was involved in building the Death Railway. A better understanding comes from a visit to the excellent Hellfire Pass Memorial (Rte 323; 9am-4pm), an Australian–Thai Chamber of Commerce memorial and museum dedicated to the POW labourers, 75km north of Kanchanaburi. A crew of 1000 prisoners worked for 12 weeks to cut a pass through the mountainous area dubbed Hellfire Pass. Nearly 70% of them died in the process. An interactive museum is enhanced by several short films. Below the museum is a walking trail along the track itself and through Hellfire Pass.

Hellfire Pass and the Tiger Temple (below) are accessed via the road running west from Kanchanaburi to Sangkhlaburi and the Myanmar border. It's easy to arrange tours from Kanchanaburi, or take a bus toward Sangkhlaburi (6am, 8.40am, 10.20am and noon) and ask the driver to drop you near your destination. The last return bus leaves Sangkhlaburi at 1.15pm and takes five hours to reach Kanchanaburi. Alternatively, rent a motorbike (per day 150B) or taxi (return to Hellfire Pass, about 1300B; to the Tiger Temple, 600B).

One of Kanchanaburi's more bizarre tourist destinations is Wat Pa Luangta Bua Yannasampanno (www.tigertemple.org; admission 500B; 8.30am-noon & 1.30-5pm), known colloquially as the Tiger Temple. After gaining a reputation as a refuge for wounded animals, the temple received its first tiger cub in 1999 and has accumulated dozens more since. During visiting hours, the cats are led around a quarry and, for a hefty fee, will pose for photos with tourists. Although the efforts are undeniably the result of goodwill, there's something disconcerting (not to mention surreal) about seeing monks leading full-grown tigers around on leashes and tourists posing for pictures (for extra money) with said huge cats lying in their laps. The tigers do look sedated, though the monks deny this. The temple is an oft-debated issue among backpackers and conservationists alike. It is 45km outside town; detailed directions are on the website. To see the tigers close-up, time your visit for around noon.

Northwest of Kanchanaburi town is the area's natural playground. Erawan National Park (0 3457 4222; admission 200B; 8am-4pm) sports a watery mane of waterfalls visited by locals and tourists out for a day trip of photographs, picnics and swimming. Sai Yok National Park (admission 200B) has more variety: waterfalls, limestone caves, hot springs and accommodation. Tour organisers in Kanchanaburi can arrange day outings to these parks on various expeditions: river kayaking, elephant trekking, waterfall spotting and bamboo rafting.

The limestone hills surrounding Kanchanaburi are famous for their temple caves, an underground communion of animistic spirit worship and traditional Buddhism. Winding arteries burrow into the guts of the caves past bulbous calcium deposits and altars for reclining or meditating Buddhas, surrounded by offerings from pilgrims. Wat Tham Khao Pun (admission by donation; 7am-4pm) is one of the closest cave temples, and is best reached by bicycle. The temple is about 4km from the TAT office and 1km southwest of the Chung Kai cemetery across the railroad tracks and midway up the hill.

lonelyplanet.com

THE DEATH RAILWAY

Kanchanaburi's history includes a brutal cameo (later promoted to starring) role in WWII. The town was home to a Japanese-run prisoner of war camp, from which Allied soldiers and many others were used to build the notorious Death Railway, linking Bangkok with Burma (now Myanmar). Carving a rail bed out of the 415km stretch of rugged terrain was a brutally ambitious plan by the Japanese, intended to meet an equally remarkable goal of providing an alternative supply route for the Japanese conquest of Burma and other countries to the west. Japanese engineers estimated that the task would take five years to complete. But the railway was completed in a mere 14 months, entirely by forced labour that had little access to either machines or nutrition. A Japanese brothel train inaugurated the line.

Close to 100,000 labourers died as a result of the hard labour, torture or starvation; 13,000 of them were POWs, mainly from Britain, Australia, the Netherlands, New Zealand and America, while the rest were Asians recruited largely from Burma, Thailand and Malaysia. The POWs' story was chronicled in Pierre Boulle's novel *The Bridge on the River Kwai* and later popularised by the movie of the same name. Many visitors come here specifically to pay their respects to the fallen POWs at the Allied cemeteries.

The original bridge was used by the Japanese for 20 months before it was bombed by Allied planes in 1945. As for the railway itself, only the 130km stretch from Bangkok to Nam Tok remains. The rest was either carted off by Karen and Mon tribespeople for use in the construction of local buildings and bridges, recycled by Thai Railways or reclaimed by the jungle.

TRANSPORT: KANCHANABURI

Distance from Bangkok 130km

Direction West

Travel Time Two to three hours

Bus Regular buses leave from the Southern Bus Terminal (Map p132) in Thonburi (2nd/1st class 80/99B; about two hours; every 30 minutes from 4am until 9pm) to Kanchanaburi's bus station off Th Saengchuto (remember the Kanchanaburi Tourist Information office is right near the bus station). Minibuses do the same trip in as little as 80 minutes for 110B, but your chances of being in a high-speed crash are significantly greater.

Train Kanchanaburi is a stop on the scenic but slow Bangkok Noi–Nam Tok line. Trains leave Bangkok Noi station (Map p68) in Thonburi at 7.45am and 1.55pm (100B), stopping at Kanchanaburi's train station, just off Th Saeng-chuto, at 10.45am and 4.19pm. These two trains, plus a third that leaves Kanchanaburi at 5.57am, run slowly along the scenic Death Railway track to Nam Tok; from Kanchanaburi to Nam Tok takes just over two hours. To return to Bangkok, trains from Nam Tok pass through Kanchanaburi at 7.19am and 2.44pm.

Getting Around Kanchanaburi is very accessible by bicycle; you can hire bikes along Th Mae Nam Khwae (per day 40B). For areas outside town, rent a motorcycle (per day 150B to 250B). Săhm-lór within the city, including to and from the bus and train stations, cost about 35B a trip. Regular sŏrng·tăa·ou (5B) cruise Th Saengchuto, but be careful you don't accidentally charter one all for yourself.

INFORMATION

TAT office (☎ 0 3451 1200; Th Saengchuto; �︎ 8.30am-4.30pm) This office provides a great provincial map with information about trips outside Kanchanaburi, as well as up-to-date bus and train schedules and numerous other brochures. It's near the bus station.

EATING

Keeree Tara Restaurant (☎ 0 3462 4093; Th Rong Hip Oi; dishes 60-180B; ☑ 11am-midnight) With stunning views over the river and bridge, this big, modern place serves delicious Thai food at very reasonable prices. We found the usual suspects – green curry and pàt tai – in excellent form here.

Floating restaurants (Th Song Khwae; dishes 80-200B; ☑ 6-11pm) Down on the river are several large floating restaurants where the quality of the food varies, but it's hard not to enjoy the atmosphere.

Sitthisang Coffee Shop (Th Pak Phraek; coffee from 40B; ☑ 8am-7pm Mon-Fri, 9am-9pm Sat & Sun) In an historic yellow-painted shophouse is this cafe and restaurant with friendly staff and real coffee. The building has been in the family for generations, and the young owner is happy to talk about its history.

Night market (Th Saengchuto; dishes 30-60B; ☑ 6-11pm) An expansive market featuring everything from Thai-Muslim nosh to pàt tai unfolds every night in front of the bus station.

One of the culinary trademarks of Kanchanaburi are the curry restaurants that sell a huge variety of local-style curries, soups and fried dishes – simply check under the lids and choose what looks good. Two that we found particularly good:

Kok Kaat (☎ 0 3451 2481; 211/1 Th Saengchuto; dishes 20-35B; ☑ 7am-3pm) This place stocks an astounding 39 dishes, displayed in rows of stainless-steel pots out front.

Jay Tiw (☎ 0815 264 487; Th Saengchuto; dishes 20-35B; ☑ 7am-3pm) A block away from Kok Kaat towards the city centre, Jay Tiw boasts only 19 dishes, but emphasises quality over quantity. To reach both restaurants, hop on any sŏrng·tăa·ou heading south along Th Saengchuto and ask to get off at săh·lah glahng jang·wàt (City Hall). The restaurants are more or less across the street – just look for the rows of stainless-steel pots.

DRINKING

Much of Th Mae Nam Khwae is filled with bars, cafes and restaurants, and a stroll down the road is the best way to find one you'll like. When we visited, Buddha Bar (Th Mae Nam Khwae; ☑ 5pm-late) was among the best of the small shophouse bars. Resort (☎ 0818 479 227; 318/2 Th Mae Nam Khwae; ☑ 6pm-midnight), a faux-colonial-era veranda bar, is a favourite for visiting Bangkokians and boasts a nightly live band and attractive outdoor seating.

Further south, opposite the floating restaurants, are a couple of bigger, noisier venues, including the imaginatively named Bar Beer and Rest Room (both Th Song Khwae; ☑ 5pm-late).

SLEEPING

The most scenic places to stay are the floating guesthouses, but these are also the loudest, thanks to the nightly disco and karaoke barges. A pair of good earplugs and (quite) a few drinks will help block out the bass. Some places offer to collect guests from the train and bus stations for free.

Royal River Kwai Resort & Spa (☎ 0 3465 3297; www. royalriverkwairesort.com; Th Kanchanaburi-Sai Yok; d from 1850B; ❄ ▯ 🏊) Royal River sports the global zen look and a riverside pool amid landscaped grounds about 3km south of town. The rooms and suites are excellent value.

River Kwai Bridge Resort (☎ 0 3451 4522; www.river kwaibridgeresort.com; Th Mae Nam Khwae; d from 1500B; ❄ ▯ 🏊) You'll need good eyes to see the bridge, but the bungalows here are clean, a bit stylish and more than comfortable for the money.

Kasem Island Resort (☎ 0 3451 3359, Bangkok 0 2255 3604; d 1050-1700B; ❄ 🏊) Sitting on an island in the middle of Mae Nam Mae Khlong, about 200m from Th Chukkadon, Kasem Island Resort has tastefully designed thatched cottages and house rafts. There are facilities for swimming, fishing and rafting, as well as an outdoor bar and restaurant. The resort has an office near Tha Chukkadon where you can arrange a free shuttle boat out to the island.

Ploy Guesthouse (☎ 0 3451 5804; www.ploygh.com; 79/2 Th Mae Nam Khwae; d 650-950B; ❄) The rooms here don't have views, but Ploy makes up for it with a central location, garden atmosphere and peaceful riverfront dining area. Very good value.

Pong Phen Guesthouse (☎ 0 3451 2981; www.pong phen.com; 5 Soi Bangladesh, off Th Mae Nam Khwae; d 400-1300B; ❄ 🏊) Set at the edge of the river, the 50 rooms of mixed heritage range from quite basic to very comfortable, with more creature comforts than most budget options. Very popular.

Blue Star Guest House (☎ 0 3451 2161; www.bluestar -guesthouse.com; 241 Th Mae Nam Khwae; d 150-650B; ❄) Blue Star has the usual eclectic mix of rooms, so ask to see a few. Those in the main building are more comfortable, if not exactly *Wallpaper* stylish. Heading for the river a row of A-frame, stilted wooden houses is divided by a walkway; throw in some furry little creatures, Luke and Princess Leia and you could be in an Ewok village.

Sugar Cane Guest House (☎ 0 3462 4520; www.sugar caneguesthouse.com; 22 Soi Pakistan, Th Mae Nam Khwae; d 200-600B; ❄) Sugar Cane boasts some of the better raft-style accommodation, with rooms on a raft with a wide communal balcony, as well as landlocked bungalows and a social riverside restaurant.

KHAO YAI NATIONAL PARK

อุทยานแห่งชาติเขาใหญ่

Cool and lush, Khao Yai National Park is an easy escape into the primordial jungle. The 2168-sq-km park, part of a Unesco World Heritage site, spans five forest types, from rainforest to monsoon, and is the primary residence of, among many others, shy tigers and elephants, noisy gibbons, colourful tropical birds and countless audible, yet invisible, insects. Like a diligent baker, the jungle wakes up with the dawn, making a different kind of morning noise from the city sounds: chirping insects, hooting monkeys, whooping macaques and anonymous shrieks and trills. Khao Yai is a major birding destination with large flocks of hornbills and several migrators, including the flycatcher from Europe. Caves in the park are the preferred resting place for wrinkle-lipped bats. In the grasslands, batik-printed butterflies dissect flowers with their surgical tongues.

The park has several accessible trails for self-tours, but birders or animal trackers should consider hiring a jungle guide to increase their appreciation of the environment and to spot more than the tree-swinging gibbons and blood-sucking leeches (the rainy season is the worst time for the latter). In total, there are 12 maintained trails criss-crossing the entire park; not ideal if you want to walk end to end. Access to transport is another reason why a tour might be more convenient, although Thai visitors with cars are usually happy to pick up pedestrians.

A two-hour walk from the park headquarters leads to the Nong Pak Chee observation tower, which is a good early-morning spot for seeing insect-feeding birds, occasional thirsty elephants and sambar deer; make reservations at the visitors centre. It's important to understand that spotting the park's reclusive tigers and elephants is considered a bonus, with most people happy just to admire the frothy waterfalls that drain the peaks of Big Mountain. The park's centrepiece is Nam Tok Haew Suwat (Haew Suwat Falls), a 25m-high

EXCURSIONS KHAO YAI NATIONAL PARK

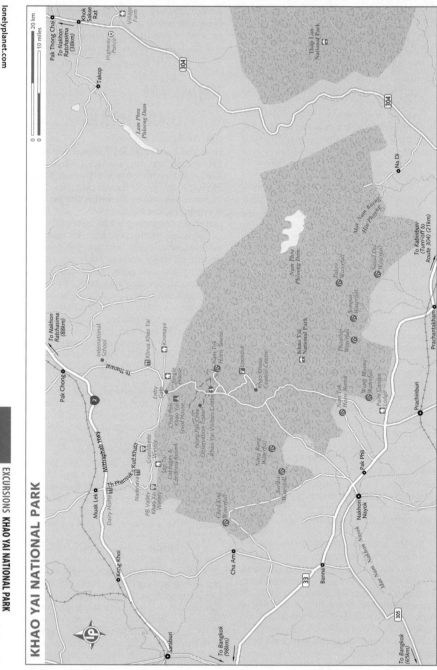

KHAO YAI NATIONAL PARK

cascade that puts on a thundering show in the rainy season. Nam Tok Haew Narok (Haew Narok Falls) is its larger cousin with three pooling tiers and a towering 150m drop.

The cool highlands around Khao Yai are also home to a nascent wine industry. These have been dubbed the 'New Latitude' wines because, at between 14 and 18 degrees north, they fall far outside the traditional wine-grape growing latitudes of between 30 and 50 degrees north or south of the equator. PB Valley Khao Yai Winery (☎ 0 3622 6415; www.khaoyaiwinery.com; 102 Moo 5, Phaya Yen, Pak Chong; tastings 150B, winery day tour incl meal 800B; ☯ 7.30am-4.30pm) and GranMonte (☎ 0819 232 007; www.granmonte.com; 52 Th Phansuk-Kud Khala) are among the wine makers managing to coax shiraz and chenin blanc grapes from the relatively tropical climate. The wines do seem to improve year by year, though they still have a way to go. GranMonte also has some appealing rooms overlooking the vineyards from 3550B.

The best time to visit the park is in the dry season (December to June), but during the rainy season river rafting and waterfall spotting will be more dramatic. Most guesthouses and lodges arrange jungle treks and rafting tours.

INFORMATION

The National Park, Wildlife & Plant Conservation Department website (www.dnp.go.th) has plenty of detail about the park, as does www.thaibirding.com.

Khao Yai Visitors Centre (☎ 0818 773 127 or 0 4429 7406; admission 400B; ☯ 8am-6pm) Pay your entrance fee and get topographical maps, hiking advice, and arrange a jungle guide or wildlife spotlighting tour at this centre within the park.

Sarika Nature Trips (☎ 0816 436 317) This small outfit based in Nakorn Nayok offers nature and wildlife-based tours of the national park and surrounding areas.

TAT Central Region Office 8 (☎ 0 3731 2282; tatnayok@ tat.or.th; 182/88 Moo 1, Th Suwannason, Nakhon Nayok) Information on guides and tours in Khao Yai.

EATING

In recent years, the area surrounding Khao Yai National Park has become a minor culinary destination, with cuisines ranging from upmarket Italian to Thai-Muslim. The towns that surround the park have lively night markets but if you don't have a car, you'll find restaurants within the park.

Dairy Home (☎ 0 4432 2230; Km 144, Th Mitraphab, Muak Lek; mains 50-100B; ☯ 9am-8pm) If a weekend of intense jungle exploring or wine tasting has left you with a need for Western eats, stop by this organic dairy for a country breakfast of homemade sausages, farm-fresh eggs and good coffee.

Khrua Khao Yai (☎ 0 4429 7138; Km 13.5, Th Thanarat, Pak Chong; mains 40-175B; ☯ 9am-8pm Sun-Thu, 9am-10pm Fri & Sat) This informal kitchen is enormously popular with Bangkokians because it serves an inspired repertoire of both Thai and *fà·ràng* dishes, including home-cured ham and marinated mushrooms that are so meat-like you'll find yourself wondering what animal they came from.

Narknava (☎ 0819 247 091; www.narknavafarm.com; Km 8, Th Phansuk-Kud Khala, Pak Chong; mains 50-150B; ☯ 8am-7pm Tue-Sun) Muslim and even Middle Eastern

TRANSPORT: KHAO YAI NATIONAL PARK

Distance from Bangkok 196km

Direction Northeast

Travel Time Three hours

Bus From Bangkok's Northern and Northeastern Bus Terminal (Mo Chit; ☎ 0 2936 2841-8; Map p132), take a bus to Pak Chong (ordinary/air-con 95/165B, three to four hours, every 30 minutes from 5am to 10pm). From Pak Chong, take a *sŏrng·tǎa·ou* (20B, from 6am to 5pm) to the park entrance.

Hire Car For more freedom and a little Thai-driving adventure, rent a car (see p265) and drive; it's totally worth it.

Getting Around From the entrance gate it's possible to charter a vehicle (400B) or flag a passing car for a ride to the visitors centre. Chartered transportation within the park is available via the visitors centre; however, hitchhiking is common.

THEME PARKS

Just outside Bangkok are theme parks for kids and inner kids, delivering everything from dancing elephants to stunt shows. It's worth noting that animals at these parks will often not be treated with the same care they might be in more developed countries. Tour operators service all of these places, but getting your hotel to write the name in Thai and taking a taxi is just as easy and usually cheaper. For further transport options, see the websites listed below.

Ancient Siam (Muang Boran, nee Ancient City; ☎ 0 2709 1644; www.ancientcity.com; 296/1 Th Sukhumvit, Samut Prakan; child/adult 150/350B; ☽ 8am-5pm) Billed as the world's largest open-air museum, Ancient Siam covers more than 80 hectares of peaceful countryside scattered with 109 scaled-down facsimiles of many of the kingdom's most famous monuments. Visions of Las Vegas and its corny replicas of world treasures might spring to mind, but Ancient Siam does have some architectural integrity and is a preservation site for classical buildings and art forms. It's a great place for long, undistracted bicycle rides (rental from the admission office is 50B), as it's usually quiet and never crowded.

Dream World (☎ 0 2533 1152; www.dreamworld-th.com; Km 7 Rangsit-Nakorn Nayok, Thanya Buri; combination ticket 1000B; ☽ 10am-5pm Mon-Fri, 10am-7pm weekends & public holidays) No-excuses fun park with roller coasters, paddle boats, stunt shows, go-carts and an artificial snow world.

Samphran Elephant Ground & Zoo (☎ 0 2295 2938; www.elephantshow.com; Km 30 Th Phetkasem, Nakhorn Pathom; child below 130cm/adult 300/500B; ☽ 8.30am-5.30pm) Samphran is a 9-hectare zoo with elephant round-ups, crocodile shows and an orchid nursery.

Samut Prakan Crocodile Farm & Zoo (☎ 0 2703 4891; Samut Prakan; child/adult 300/200B; ☽ 7am-6pm) More than 30,000 crocs spend their time wallowing in mud, with elephants, monkeys, hippos, snakes and, ahem, camels keeping them company (at a distance). The farm is a monument to trained-animal shows, including croc wrestling and elephant performances. The reptiles get their dinner between 4pm and 5.30pm. It's very popular with tour groups, but won't appeal to animal liberationists.

Siam Park City (Suan Siam; ☎ 0 2919 7200; www.siamparkcity.com; 99 Th Serithai, Khannayao; water park child under 130cm/adult 100/200B, unlimited day pass 900B, kids rides only 100B; ☽ 10am-6pm Mon-Fri, 9am-6pm Sat & Sun) A water park that has grown into a full-blown amusement park with plenty of small and large-scale rides, artificial waves, giant water slides and a flow pool. There is also a small zoo and playground. Probably more fun than Dream World.

fare are unexpected cuisines in this neck of the woods, but Narknava is an established favourite for its infamous chicken biryani – infamous, because at 100B it's superexpensive by Thai standards. Unusually, the food is much better than the website images suggest.

SLEEPING

Golf courses and upmarket resorts ring the perimeter of the national park. Pak Chong is the primary base-camp town, and comes complete with a Tuscan quarter (or eighth, perhaps), but Nakhon Nayok and Prachinburi are beginning to develop some more low-key options. Most accommodation destinations can arrange jungle tours and transport to the park.

Park Lodging (☎ 0 2562 0760; www.dnp.go.th/parkreserve) The Department of National Parks provides a range of clean, simple lodgings scattered through the park, starting at 800B

for two people. Camping is 150B per person with tents and bedding included. It's best to book online, where you can also get more detail on locations and facilities, though bookings are also possible at the information centre.

Jungle House (☎ 0 4429 7183; www.junglehousehotel.com; 21/5 Th Thanarat, Km 19.5, Pak Chong; d 600-1400B; ☒) An old favourite and great budget or lower midrange option, with lots of extras to keep kids entertained. Loft rooms encourage monkey like agility.

Palm Garden Lodge (☎ 0 9989 4470; www.palmgalo.com; Ban Kon Khuang, Moo 10, Dong Keleek, Prachinburi; d 400-600B, ste 1200B; ☒) Woodsy gardens and rustic bungalows keep you in touch with nature. The lodge is 7km south of the park's southern entrance, near Ban Kon Khuang on Highway 33. It arranges park tours and rents motorbikes and vans for 250B/1800B a day.

Sap Tai Cabbages & Condoms Resort (☎ 0 3622 7065; www.pda.or.th/saptai; 98 Moo 6, Th Phaya Yen, Pak Chong; r

2100-11,500B; 💈 🖭) This resort, with its city-hotel ambience, is the sister facility of the Bangkok restaurant (p175) with the same name (and food) and supports a great cause: HIV/Aids education and prevention. It's good value.

Village Farm (☎ 0 4422 8407/8; www.villagefarm.co.th; 103 Moo 7, Tambon Thaisamakee, Wan Nam Kheo, Nakhon Ratchasima; r 2200-11,000B; 💈 🖭) This microwinery is the closest thing Thailand has to a French village. A variety of restored teak villas are cradled in 32 hectares of farmland, and the resort includes a spa and restaurant.

Kirimaya (☎ 0 4442 6000; www.kirimaya.com; 1/3 Moo 6, Th Thanarat, Pak Chong; r 10,500-38,000B; 💈 🛜 🖭) A stunning setting and equally stunning rooms have seen Kirimaya lauded as one of the world's top new hotels. Rooms range from luxurious to vast, lavish tents with their own pools; the spa and Jack Nicklaus–designed golf course round out the experience.

TRANSPORT

Bangkok may seem chaotic and impenetrable at first but, regular traffic jams notwithstanding, its transport system is not nearly as dire as legend would have it. The Skytrain, Metro, river and *klorng* (also spelt Khlong) ferries and more than 70,000 clean and dirt-cheap taxis combine to make getting to most parts of Bangkok reasonably easy. Not surprisingly, the trains and ferries are the fastest options during peak hours, while taxis are handy at other times. And as the urban railways are continually extended the whole system should work better, with faster access to more of the city and fewer cars on the roads (well, that's the theory, at least). Flights, tours and rail tickets can be booked online at www.lonely planet.com/travel_services.

AIR

Bangkok is a major Southeast Asian air hub, and dozens of airlines fly regularly between the Thai capital and the rest of the world. Thailand's national carrier is Thai Airways International (THAI; www.thaiair.com), which also operates a number of domestic air routes.

Airlines
DOMESTIC

Thailand has fewer airlines than it did a few years ago, but competition remains fierce on a large network of domestic routes. Those listed here also fly regional international routes. Nok Air and Thai Air Asia (the local arm of budget behemoth Air Asia) are budget airlines, THAI Airways is full service and Bangkok Airways is somewhere in between. Big

---

discounts are often available online, and most deal only in e-tickets, so there's no reason to schlep out to their distant offices to book a fare; use a travel agent, the internet or the phone. For last-minute fares (which on THAI domestic routes are often cheaper than its online fares), buy at the departures level in the relevant airport.

Bangkok Airways (PG; ☎ 1771; www.bangkokair.com)

Nok Air (OX; ☎ 1318; www.nokair.com)

Thai Air Asia (FD; ☎ 0 2515 9999; www.airasia.com)

THAI Airways International (TG; ☎ 0 2232 8000; www.thaiair.com)

INTERNATIONAL

Some of the airlines flying to Thailand, with offices where they exist:

Air Asia (AK; ☎ 0 2515 9999; www.airasia.com)

Air Canada (AC; Map p116; ☎ 0 2670 0400; www.aircanada.ca; Suite 1708, Empire Tower, River Wing West, 195 Th Sathon Tai, Sathon)

Air France KLM (AF; Map p116; ☎ 0 2635 1191; www.airfrance.com; 20th fl, Vorawat Bldg, 849 Th Silom)

Air New Zealand (NZ; Map p116; ☎ 0 2235 8280; www.airnewzealand.com; 11th fl, ITF Tower, 140/17 Th Silom)

Cathay Pacific Airways (CX; Map p108; ☎ 0 2263 0606; www.cathaypacific.com; 11th fl, Ploenchit Tower, 898 Th Ploenchit)

China Airlines (CI; Map p108; ☎ 0 2250 9898; www.china-airlines.com; 4th fl, Peninsula Plaza, 153 Th Ratchadamri)

Garuda Indonesia (GA; Map p122; ☎ 0 2679 7371-2; www.garuda-indonesia.com; 27th fl, Lumphini Tower, 1168/77 Th Phra Ram IV)

Jetstar (☎ 0 2267 5125; www.jetstar.com)

Malaysia Airlines (MH; Map p108; ☎ 0 2263 0565-71; www.malaysiaairlines.com; 20th fl, Ploenchit Tower, 898 Th Ploenchit)

Qantas Airways (QF; ☎ 0 2627 1701; www.qantas.com.au)

Singapore Airlines (SQ; Map p122; ☎ 0 2353 6000; www.singaporeair.com; 12th fl, Silom Center Bldg, 2 Th Silom)

United Airlines (UA; Map p116; ☎ 0 2353 3900; www.unitedairlines.co.th; 6th fl, TMB Bank Silom Bldg, 393 Th Silom)

THINGS CHANGE...

The information in this chapter is particularly vulnerable to change. Check directly with the airline or a travel agent to make sure you understand how a fare (and ticket you may buy) works and be aware of the security requirements for international travel. Shop carefully. The details given in this chapter should be regarded as pointers and are not a substitute for your own careful, up-to-date research.

CLIMATE CHANGE & TRAVEL

Climate change is a serious threat to the ecosystems that humans rely upon, and air travel is the fastest-growing contributor to the problem. Lonely Planet regards travel, overall, as a global benefit, but believes we all have a responsibility to limit our personal impact on global warming.

Flying & Climate Change

Pretty much every form of motor transport generates CO_2 (the main cause of human-induced climate change) but planes are far and away the worst offenders, not just because of the sheer distances they allow us to travel, but because they release greenhouse gases high into the atmosphere. The statistics are frightening: two people taking a return flight between Europe and the US will contribute as much to climate change as an average household's gas and electricity consumption over a whole year.

Carbon Offset Schemes

Climatecare.org and other websites use 'carbon calculators' that allow jetsetters to offset the greenhouse gases they are responsible for with contributions to energy-saving projects and other climate-friendly initiatives in the developing world – including projects in India, Honduras, Kazakhstan and Uganda.

Lonely Planet, together with Rough Guides and other concerned partners in the travel industry, supports the carbon offset scheme run by climatecare.org. Lonely Planet offsets all of its staff and author travel.

For more information check out our website: www.lonelyplanet.com.

Airports

Bangkok has two airports. The main airport is Suvarnabhumi International Airport (☎ 0 2132 1888; www2.airportthai.co.th), a vast glass-and-concrete construction 30km east of central Bangkok that was opened in 2006. After rather a lot of teething problems, Suvarnabhumi (pronounced su-wan-a-poom) now works fairly efficiently most of the time. The unofficial website www.bangkokairportonline.com has real-time details of airport arrivals and departures. Left-luggage facilities (☺ 24 hr) are available on level 2, beside the helpful TAT office (☎ 0 2134 4077; ☺ 24 hr). For airport hotels, see p232.

Don Muang Airport (Map p132; ☎ 0 2535 1111; www2.airportthai.co.th) is 25km north of the city centre and, after being temporarily retired, now serves domestic routes operated by Nok Air and One Two Go.

Getting to/from Don Muang you can take a taxi or bus. Taking a taxi is the fastest and most comfortable option, and fares at most times will be a very reasonable 200B to 350B depending on the traffic and how far you're going. Taxis depart from outside the arrivals hall, and there is a 50B airport charge added to the meter fare, plus expressway tolls. Air-con buses include the following:

Bus 29 Northern Bus Terminal, Victory Monument, Siam Sq and Hualamphong train station

Bus 510 Victory Monument, Southern Bus Terminal

Bus 513 Th Sukhumvit, Eastern Bus Terminal

BOAT

Although many of Bangkok's *klorng* have been paved over, there is still plenty of transport along and across Chao Phraya River and up adjoining canals.

River Ferries

The Chao Phraya Express Boat Co (☎ 0 2623 6001; www.chaophrayaboat.co.th) operates the main ferry service along Chao Phraya. The central pier is known as Sathorn, Saphan Taksin or sometimes Central Pier, and connects to Skytrain at Saphan Taksin BTS station. Each pier is numbered from Sathorn, and ferries run four stops south to Wat Ratchasingkhon (S4), though tourists rarely use these. Much more useful are the services running to and from Nonthaburi (N30) and Pak Kred (N33) in northern Bangkok; the maps in this book show the piers and their numbers. Fares are cheap and differ by distance and service from 9B to 30B. There are four different services, differentiated by the colour of the flags on their roofs. To avoid an unwanted trip halfway to Nonthaburi be sure to keep an eye on those flags.

Local Line (no flag) The all-stops service, operating every 20 minutes 6.20am to 8.20am and 3pm to 5.30pm.

Orange Express Stops at S3, Sathorn (Central), N1, N3, N4, N5, N6, N8, N9, N10, N12, N13, N15, N18, N21, N22, N24 and N30. The most common service, departs every 10 to 20 minutes from 5.50am until 7pm. All journeys 13B.

GETTING INTO TOWN FROM SUVARNABHUMI AIRPORT

Airport Bus

Airport Express runs four useful routes between Suvarnabhumi and Bangkok city. They operate from 5am to midnight (closer to 7am coming from the city) for a flat 150B fare, meaning a taxi will be a comparable price if there are two people heading to central Bangkok, but more expensive if you're going somewhere further, like Banglamphu. The Airport Express counter is near entrance 8 on level 1. Routes stop at BTS stations, major hotels and other landmarks.

AE-1 to Silom (by expressway) Via Pratunam, Central World, Ratchadamri BTS, Lumphini Park, Sala Daeng BTS, Patpong, Plaza Hotel and others.

AE-2 to Banglamphu (by expressway) Via Th Phetchaburi Soi 30, Amari Watergate Hotel, Democracy Monument, Royal Hotel, Th Phra Athit, Th Phra Sumen, Th Khao San.

AE-3 to Sukhumvit Via Soi 52, Eastern Bus Terminal (Ekamai), Thong Lo BTS, Sukhumvit Sois 38, 34, 24, 20, 18, Asoke BTS/Sukhumvit Metro, Sukhumvit Sois 10 and 6, Central Chidlom, Central World, Soi Nana.

AE-4 to Hualamphong train station Via Victory Monument BTS, Phaya Thai BTS, Siam BTS, Siam Sq, MBK, Chulalongkorn University.

Local Buses

With more time and less money, local buses are the cheapest way into town short of hitching (and no one hitches). Like the intercity buses that run to Pattaya and further, all local buses depart from the Public Transportation Centre (☎ 0 2132 1888), which is about 3km from the terminal at the edge of the airport grounds. Free shuttle buses leave regularly from Level 1 at the terminal 24 hours a day.

Several air-con local buses serve Suvarnabhumi for fares rising to a maximum of 35B. Departures are every 15 or 20 minutes unless stated. Most useful:

Bus 551 Siam Paragon Via Victory Monument. This service operates 24 hours a day and is the cheapest way to Th Khao San and Banglamphu; get off at Victory Monument and take bus 59, 503 or 509 and get out at Democracy Monument.

Bus 552 Klong Toei Via Sukhumvit 101 and On Nut BTS. Services operate 24 hours a day.

Buses 554 & 555 Don Muang Airport Services operate from 5am to midnight.

Bus 556 Southern Bus Terminal Via Democracy Monument (for Th Khao San) and Thammasat University. Services depart hourly from 5am to 10pm.

Yellow Express Stops at S4, Sathorn (Central), N3, N5, N10, N12, N15, N22, N24, N30. Departs every five to 20 minutes depending on the time of day. Service starts at 6am; last boat 8pm.

Green-Yellow Express Nonthaburi express, stops at N3, N5, N10, N12, N15, N22, N24, N30, N32 and N33. Departs every 15 minutes 6.15am to 8.05am, and every 20 minutes 4.05pm to 6.05pm.

Several tourist boat services operate, the most regular being between Phra Athit and Sathorn, with services every 30 minutes between 9.30am and 3pm. A one-day pass for unlimited travel costs 150B. All this is best illustrated in the small, folding maps that detail routes, prices and times and are sometimes available at ferry piers – ask for one – or on boards at the piers.

There are also dozens of cross-river ferries, which charge 3B and run every few minutes until late at night.

Klorng Boats

Canal taxi boats run along Khlong Saen Saep (Banglamphu to Ramkhamhaeng) and are an easy way to get between Banglamphu and Jim Thompson's House, the Siam Sq shopping centres (get off at Th Hua Chang for both), and other points further east along Th Sukhumvit – after a mandatory change of boat at Tha Pratunam. These boats are mostly used by daily commuters and pull into the piers for just a few seconds – jump straight on or you'll be left behind. Fares range from 8B to 18B.

BUS

Bangkok's public buses are a cheap, if not always comfortable, way to get around the city. They are run by the Bangkok Mass Transit Authority (☎ 0 2246 4262; www.bmta.co.th), which has a website with detailed information on bus

Intercity buses to places including Pattaya (106B), Rayong (155B) and Trat (248B) also stop at least six times daily at the Public Transportation Centre. Buses to Laem Ngob (250B), for the Ko Chang ferry, depart between 7.10am and 10am. Some Pattaya buses leave directly from airport level 1.

Minivan

If you are heading to the airport from Banglamphu, the hotels and guesthouses can book you on air-con minivans. These pick up from hotels and guesthouses and cost about 140B per person.

Suvarnabhumi Airport Rail Link (SARL)

After years of delays, the new SARL began operation in 2010 from the bottom floor of the airport to a huge new City Air Terminal (Map p126) in central Bangkok, near Soi Asoke (Sukhumvit Soi 21) and Th Phetchaburi. A 'Skytrain' by any other name, it includes an express service (the Pink Line) that takes 15 minutes and costs 150B one way, and a local service (the Red Line) via five other stations taking about 30 minutes and costing a very reasonable 45B. The express service will travel the 28.6km route at 160km/hour. Both lines connect to the Metro Blue Line at Phetchaburi and the slower Red Line continues to Phaya Thai BTS station.

How useful this service is depends on whether you're travelling alone and how far your hotel is from the City Air Terminal. Except during the worst traffic (hello Friday evenings!), a taxi covers the same trip in about 35 minutes for about 250B.

An extremely useful in-town check-in service, like the one in Hong Kong, is scheduled to start operating during 2010.

Taxi & Limousine

Ignore the annoying touts and all the yellow signs pointing you to 'limousines' (actually cars and 4WDs costing from 600B to 3500B depending on the vehicle and distance), and head outside to the fast-moving public taxi queues outside doors 3 and 10. Cabs booked through this desk should always use their meter, but they often try their luck quoting you an inflated fare; insist by saying 'meter, please'. You must also pay a 50B official airport surcharge and reimburse drivers for any toll charges (up to 60B); drivers will usually ask your permission to use the tollway. Depending on traffic, a taxi to Asoke should cost 200B to 250B, Silom 300B to 350B and Banglamphu 350B to 425B. Fares are per vehicle, not per person. Break big notes before you leave the airport to avoid a 'no change' situation.

Charter taxis also run to Pattaya (1300B), Chonburi (1000B) and Trat (3500B), among many others.

routes. Air-con fares typically start at 10B or 12B and increase depending on distance. Fares for ordinary (fan only) buses start at 7B or 8B. Most of the bus lines run between 5am and 10pm or 11pm, except for the 'all-night' buses, which run from 3am or 4am to midmorning.

Bangkok Bus Map by Roadway, available at Asia Books (www.asiabooks.com) and some 7-Eleven stores, is the most up-to-date route map available.

CAR

Renting a car just to drive around Bangkok is not a good idea. Parking is impossible, traffic is frustrating, road rules can be mysterious and the alternative – taxis – are cheap and ubiquitous. But if you still want to give it a go, all the big car-hire companies have offices in Bangkok and at Suvarnabhumi airport. Rates start at around 1300B per day for a small car. A passport plus a valid licence from your home country (with English translation if necessary) or an International Driving Permit are required for all rentals. Most companies can also provide drivers (from about 600B per day, 8am to 6pm), which gives local drivers a job and means you don't have to navigate, park or deal with overzealous police. Child seats cost an extra 200B a day.

Reliable car-rental companies include the following:

Avis (Map p108; ☎ 0 2251 1131, 0 2255 5300; www.avisthailand.com; 2/12 Th Withayu)

Budget (Map p132; ☎ 0 2203 0225; www.budget.co.th; 19/23 Bldg A, Royal City Ave, Th Phetchaburi Tat Mai)

Hertz (Map p108; ☎ 0 2654 1105; www.hertz.com; M Thai Tower, All Seasons Pl, 87 Th Withayu)

Phetburi Car Rent (Map p126; ☎ 0 2318 8888; 2371 Th Petchaburi)

TAXI

Bangkok's brightly coloured taxis are some of the best-value cabs on earth. Most are new, air-conditioned Toyota Corollas and have working seatbelts in the front seat, though less often in the back. You can flag them down almost anywhere in central Bangkok. The meter charge is 35B for the first 2km, then 4.50B for each of the next 10km, 5B for each kilometre from 12km to 20km and 5.50B per kilometre for any distance greater than 20km, plus a small standing charge in slow traffic. Freeway tolls – 25B to 70B depending on where you start – must be paid by the passenger.

Taxi Radio (☎ 1681; www.taxiradio.co.th) and other 24-hour 'phone-a-cab' services are available for 20B above the metered fare.

During the morning and afternoon rush hours taxis might refuse to go to certain destinations or, in some touristy areas, refuse to use the meter; if this happens, just try another cab. You can hire a taxi all day for 1500B to 2000B, depending on how much driving is involved. Taxis can also be hired for trips to Pattaya (1500B), Ayuthaya (800B), Hua Hin (2300B) and Phetchaburi (1700B), among others; see the Taxi Radio website for fares. If you leave something in a taxi your best chance of getting it back (still pretty slim) is to call ☎ 1644.

Motorcycle Taxi

Motorcycle taxis serve two purposes in Bangkok. Most commonly and popularly they form an integral part of the public transport network, running from the corner of a main thoroughfare, such as Th Sukhumvit, to the far ends of sois that run off that thoroughfare. Riders wear coloured, numbered vests and gather at either end of their soi, usually charging 10B to 20B for the trip (without a helmet unless you ask).

Their other purpose is as a means of beating the traffic. You tell your rider where you want to go, negotiate a price (from 20B for a short trip up to about 150B going across town), strap on the helmet (they will insist for longer trips) and say a prayer to whichever god you're into. Drivers range from responsible to kamikaze, but the average trip involves some time on the wrong side of the road and several near-death experiences. It's the sort of white-knuckle ride you'd pay good money for at Disneyland, but is all in a day's work for these riders. Comfort yourself in the knowledge that there are good hospitals nearby.

TRAIN

Bangkok has three different forms of rail transport. Old-style (and just plain old) trains rattle their way to a few outer suburbs and beyond, but for visitors they are largely useless for getting around the city. In contrast, the underground Metro line and the elevated Skytrain are modern, comfortable and very useful.

Metro

Bangkok's first underground railway line is operated by the Mass Rapid Transit Authority (MRTA; www.mrta.co.th) and is known locally as rót fai đâi din or 'Metro' – no one understands 'subway'. Metro plans see a series of lines running more than 150km, but for now the 20km Blue Line runs from Hualamphong train station north to Bang Sue and features 18 stations. Fares cost from 15B to 40B; child and concession fares can be bought at ticket windows. Trains run every seven minutes from 6am to midnight, more frequently between 6am and 9am and from 4.30pm to 7.30pm.

The Metro is more useful to residents than visitors, unless you're staying in the lower Sukhumvit area. Useful stations (from north to south) include Kamphaeng Phet and Bang Sue for Chatuchak Weekend Market; Thailand Cultural Centre; Sukhumvit, which links to Asok BTS station; Khlong Toei for the market; Lumphini; Si Lom (with access to Sala Daeng BTS station); and Hualamphong train station and Chinatown at its southern end.

Skytrain (BTS)

The BTS Skytrain (☎ tourist information 0 2617 7340; www.bts.co.th) allows you to soar above Bangkok's legendary traffic jams in air-conditioned comfort. Known by locals as 'BTS' or rót fai fáh (literally 'sky train'), services are fast, efficient and relatively cheap, although rush hour can be a squeeze. Fares range from 15B to 40B, and trains run from 6am to midnight. Ticket machines accept coins and notes (when they're working), or you can pick up change at the staffed kiosks. One-day (120B) passes are available, but the rechargeable cards (130B, with 100B travel and 30B card deposit) are more flexible. There are two Skytrain lines, which are well represented on free tourist maps available at most stations.

TAXI ALTARS: INSURANCE ON THE DASHBOARD

As your taxi races into Bangkok from the airport your delight at being able to do the 30km trip for less than US$10 is soon replaced by uneasiness, anxiety and eventually outright fear. Because 150km/h is fast, you're tailgating the car in front and there's no seatbelt. You can rest assured (or not), however, that your driver will share none of these concerns.

All of which makes the humble taxi trip an instructive introduction to Thai culture. Buddhists believe in karma and in turn that their fate is, to a large extent, predestined. Unlike Western ideas, which take a more scientific approach to road safety, many Thais believe factors such as speed, concentration, seatbelts and simple driver quality have no bearing whatsoever on your chances of being in a crash. Put simply, if you die a horrible death on the road, karma says you deserved it. The trouble is that when a passenger gets into a taxi they bring their karma and any bad spirits the passenger might have along for the ride. Which could upset the driver's own fate.

To counteract such bad influences most Bangkok taxi drivers turn the dashboard and ceiling into a sort of life-insurance shrine. The ceiling will have a *yantra* diagram drawn in white powder by a monk as a form of spiritual protection. This will often be accompanied by portraits of notable royals. Below this a red box dangling red tassles, beads and amulets hang from the rear vision mirror, while the dashboard is populated by Buddhist and royal statuettes, and quite possibly banknotes with the King's image prominent and more amulets. With luck (such as it exists in Thailand), the talismans will protect your driver from any bad karma you bring into the cab. Passengers must hope their driver's number is not up. If you feel like it might be, try saying *cháh cháh* soothingly – that is, ask your driver to slow down. For a look inside some of Bangkok's 100,000 or so taxis, check out Still Life in Moving Vehicle (www.lifeinmovingvehicle.blogspot.com).

SI LOM LINE

Starting at National Stadium on Th Phra Ram I in central Bangkok, this line passes the Siam interchange station and bends around via the eastern section of Th Silom and western end of Th Sathon, crosses Chao Phraya River at Saphan Taksin and (since late 2009) finishes at Wongwian Yai. The Saphan Taksin station, on the river near the intersection of Th Charoen Krung and Th Sathon, is superconvenient because it connects to the Chao Phraya river ferries (p263).

SUKHUMVIT LINE

Four new stations are planned to be added to the southern end of the line, which means that by the time you read this the Sukhumvit Line should be running from Bang Na, at distant Soi 105 of Th Sukhumvit, north and then west right along Th Sukhumvit, connecting to the Metro at Asok station. The Sukhumvit line then continues into the shopping and commercial district and the main interchange station at Siam, where it meets the Si Lom BTS Line. From here the line turns north up to Mo Chit, near Chatuchak Weekend Market.

TÚK-TÚK

Bangkok's iconic túk-túk (pronounced đúk dúk; a type of motorised rickshaw) are used by Thais for short hops not worth paying the taxi flag fall for. For foreigners, however, these emphysema-inducing machines are part of the Bangkok experience, so despite the fact they overcharge outrageously and you can't see anything due to the low roof, pretty much everyone takes a túk-túk at least once. It's worth knowing, however, that túk-túk are notorious for taking little 'detours' to commission-paying gem and silk shops and massage parlours. En route to 'special' temples, you'll meet 'helpful' locals who will steer you to even more rip-off opportunities. See p279 for more on these scams, and ignore anyone offering too-good-to-be-true 10B trips.

The vast majority of túk-túk drivers ask too much from tourists (expat *fà·ràng* never use them). Expect to be quoted a 100B fare, if not more, for even the shortest trip. Try bargaining them down to about 40B for a short trip, preferably at night when the pollution (hopefully) won't be quite so bad. Once you've done it, you'll find taxis are cheaper, cleaner, cooler and quieter.

DIRECTORY

BUSINESS HOURS

Most government offices are open from 8.30am to 4.30pm Monday to Friday, but close from noon to 1pm for lunch. In recent years the government has pushed for a 'no lunch closing' policy – you might even see signs posted to this effect – but in reality government employees usually head for lunch at midday precisely and there's a strong chance of disappointment if you expect to get anything done between noon and 1pm.

Regular bank hours in Bangkok are 8.30am to 3.30pm Monday to Friday, but several banks have special foreign-exchange offices that are open longer hours (generally from 8.30am to 8pm), including weekends in touristy areas. Note that all government offices and banks are closed on public holidays (see p273).

Commercial businesses usually operate between 8.30am and 5pm Monday to Friday and sometimes Saturday morning as well. Larger shops usually open from 10am to 6.30pm or 7pm, but the big shopping centres are open later (until 9pm or 10pm). Smaller shops keep more variable hours and often open earlier and close later.

Hours for restaurants and cafes vary greatly. Some local Thai places open as early as 7am, while bigger places usually open around 10am and still others are open in the evenings only. Some close as early as 9pm and others stay open all night. Bars, by law, can't open before 4pm and must close by 1am. This, however, seems to be as typically flexible as many Thai laws, and even moreso since the Democrats took power.

CHILDREN

Thais love children and in many instances will shower attention on your offspring, who will find ready playmates among their Thai counterparts and a temporary nanny service at practically every stop. This means kids are welcome almost anywhere and you'll rarely experience the sort of eye-rolling annoyance often seen in the West.

At a practical level, there are a few things worth knowing before you depart. Many hotels offer family deals, adjoining rooms and – in the midrange and above – cots, so enquire specifically. Car seats, on the other hand, are almost impossible to find, and even if you bring your own most taxis have no seatbelt in the back. Most parents just hold their child, though we always felt more comfortable keeping our daughter in her sling while travelling by taxi. Taxi drivers generally won't temper their speed because you're travelling with a child, so if need be don't hesitate to tell them to *cháh cháh* (slow down). For moving by foot, slings are often more useful than prams as Bangkok sidewalks are rubbish. That said, we often found the sidewalk hassle worth it in order to have a portable bed.

Nappies (diapers), international brands of milk formula and other infant requirements are widely available, and for something more specific you'll find the Central Chidlom department store as well stocked as anywhere on earth (there's an entire floor devoted to kids). In general, Thai women don't breastfeed in public, though in department stores they'll often find a change room.

Not all kids enjoy Thai food, though with the amount of cheap fresh fruit around you should be able to find something to satisfy. Note, though, that for something bland, big hotels usually sell their baked goods for half price after 6pm. Highchairs are rare outside expensive restaurants – an exception is Cabbages & Condoms (p175).

Aside from the usual common sense precautions (drinking lots of water, washing hands etc), parents needn't worry too much about health concerns. The main areas to be aware of are dehydration (bring some rehydration fluids) and warning children specifically to keep their hands off the local soi (lane) dog populace; while rare in Bangkok, rabies is relatively common in Thailand. If you do need a doctor, we found the paediatricians at Samitivej Sukhumvit (p276) excellent.

Kids' clothes can be dirt cheap in Thailand and we know many families who justify their trip by calculating how much they'll save shopping for clothes for the next couple of years (and gifts for all their friends). Department stores have a wide selection, but the real savings are at local markets (usually weekly;

ask your hotel) and centres such as MBK (p142). To target your shopping, try Motif & Maris (Map p116; ☎ 0 2635 9111; 296/7 Th Silom; 🚇 Chong Nonsi), which sells dolls and various other low-tech toys made by charities aiding women. For major brand clothes at discount prices, without the chaos of MBK, try Little Me (Map p126; ☎ 0 2661 4008; Soi 33/1, Th Sukhumvit; ⏰ 10am-8.30pm; 🚇 Phrom Phong).

For a list of places to see and things to do that should keep kids happy, see the boxed text, p121. Check out Lonely Planet's *Travel With Children* for further advice, or visit the following websites:

Thorn Tree Kids To Go forum (www.lonelyplanet.com/thorntree) Questions and answers from other travellers with children, on Lonely Planet's community forum.

Bangkok.com (www.bangkok.com/kids) This broader website lists a dizzying array of things to do for kids.

CLIMATE

At the centre of the flat, humid Mae Nam Chao Phraya delta, Bangkok sits at the same latitude as Khartoum (Sudan) and Guatemala City, and can be as hot as the former and as wet as the latter.

The southwest monsoon arrives between May and July and lasts into November. This is followed by a dry period from around November to May, which begins with lower relative temperatures until mid-February (because of the influence of the northeast monsoon, which bypasses this part of Thailand but results in cool breezes), followed by much higher relative temperatures from March to May. It usually rains most during August and September, though floods in early October may find you in knee-deep water in certain parts of the city. An umbrella can be invaluable – a raincoat will just make you hot.

It's worth remembering that we're talking about the weather here, a temperamental

beast if ever there was one. So all the dates above are flexible. In 2008, for example, Bangkok was flooded by a major storm in normally dry January, and the cool season stretched well into March.

For recommendations on the best times to visit Bangkok see p20; for a handy interactive weather map for Bangkok and the rest of Thailand, see www.travelfish.org/country/thailand.

COURSES

You can learn a lot in Bangkok. In half a day you could learn enough to impress your friends with a firey home-cooked Thai meal; for recommended cooking courses see the boxed text, p155. Taking a course in traditional massage will undoubtedly be well received by your special friends or, if there's someone you don't like, then a week in a *moo·ay tai* (Thai boxing; also spelt *muay thai*) school might help. With more time you could even learn how to talk your way out of trouble.

Language

Tuition at most Thai language schools averages 100B to 200B per hour for group classes, more for private tutoring. We recommend the following:

AAA Thai Language Center (Map p108; ☎ 0 2655 5629; www.aaathai.com; 6th fl, 29 Vanissa Bldg, Th Chitlom, Pathumwan; 🚇 Chit Lom exit 5) Opened by a group of experienced Thai language teachers from other schools, good-value AAA Thai has a loyal following.

American University Alumni Language Center (Map p108; ☎ 0 2252 8170; www.auathai.com; 179 Th Ratchadamri; 🚇 Ratchadamri exit 3) The most intensive language course in Bangkok, with rolling classes for listening only, from 7am to 8pm Monday to Thursday, shorter on Friday and Saturday. The teaching method focuses on listening and comprehension before then advancing to speaking and reading. For long-stayers only.

Thailish Language School (Map p126; ☎ 0 2258 6846; www.thailanguageschool.com; 427 Th Sukhumvit, btwn Sois 21 & 23; Ⓜ Sukhumvit exit 2; 🚇 Asok exit 6) This small, personal school looks like an antique shop and has private or small-group classes concentrating on conversation.

Union Language School (Map p108; ☎ 0 2214 6033; union_lang@yahoo.com; 7th fl, 328 CCT Office Bldg, Th Phayathai; tuition from 7200B; 🚇 Ratchathewi) Generally recognised as having the best and most rigorous courses (many missionaries study here). Union employs a balance of structure- and communication-oriented methodologies in 80-hour, four-week modules.

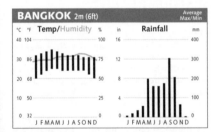

BANGKOK 2m (6ft) — Average Max/Min

Temp/Humidity — Rainfall

Meditation

Although at times Bangkok may seem like the most un-Buddhist place on earth, there are several places where foreigners can practise Theravada Buddhist meditation. Most Buddhist study centres specialise in *vipassana* (insight) meditation. DhammaThai (www.dhammathai. org) has a rundown on several prominent wát and meditation centres, or speak to the World Fellowship of Buddhists (WFB; Map p126; ☎ 0 2661 1284; www.wfb-hq.org; 616 Benjasiri Park, Soi Medhinivet, Soi 24, Th Sukhumvit; 🕙 8.30am-4.30pm Mon-Fri; 🚇 Phrom Phong exit 6), which also hosts occasional meditation classes.

International Buddhist Meditation Center (Map p68; ☎ 0 2623 5881; www.mcu.ac.th/IBMC; Vipassana Section Rm 106, Mahachula Bldg, Wat Mahathat, Th Pra Chan) Holds regular lectures on Buddhist topics in English, and meditation classes.

International Meditation Club (Thailand) (Map p126; ☎ 0 2712 8965; www.intlmedclub.org; 138 Soi 53, Th Sukhumvit; 🚇 Thong Lo exit 6) New, modern centre offering lectures and activities aimed at English speakers. Regular beachside retreats on weekends.

Wat Mahathat Meditation (Map p68; ☎ 0 2222 6011; Section 5, 3 Th Maharat; Ko Ratanakosin; 🕙 7am-9pm; 🚢 Tha Phra Chan or Tha Maharat) Daily meditation sessions every three hours starting at 7am and ending at 9pm. Suitably basic accommodation for long-term meditation is also available; speak with Phra Suphe, the monk who organises visitors.

Massage

Wat Pho Thai Traditional Massage School (Map p68; ☎ 0 2221 3686; www.watpomassage.com; Soi Pen Phat 1, Th Maharat, Ko Ratanakosin) The best place to learn traditional massage. Courses are held at the school headquarters across from Wat Pho on Soi Phenphat, just off Th Maharat. Five-day courses include massage (8500B), foot massage (6500B) and aromatherapy massage (6500B); you must do the basic massage course before starting on aromatherapy. We were told no booking is required, but we recommend you do or drop in first.

Moo·ay Tai

Many foreigners come to Thailand to study *moo·ay tai* (Thai boxing; also spelt *muay thai*). Training regimens can be *extremely* strict. The following camps provide instruction in English and accept men and women. Food and accommodation can be provided for an extra charge. See www.muaythai.com for more information.

Fairtex Muay Thai Camp (off Map p132; ☎ 0 2755 3329; www.muaythaifairtex.com; 99/8 Mu 3, Soi Buthamanuson, Th Thaeparak, Bangpli, Samut Prakan) This long-running, high-profile camp south of Bangkok offers training from 500B a session to 7700B for a week's residence.

Sor. Vorapin Gym (Map p82; ☎ 0 2282 3551; www. thaiboxings.com; 13 Trok Krasab, Th Chakraphong) Just around the corner from Th Khao San; offers daily and weekly training schedules primarily for foreigners of both genders. More serious training is held at a second facility outside the city. A half-day costs 500B, the weekly rate is 2500B and a month is 9000B.

Muay Thai Institute (off Map p132; ☎ 0 2992 0095-99; www.muaythai-institute.net; Rangsit Muay Thai Stadium, 336/932 Th Prahonyothin [after Soi 119], Prachatipat, Pathum Thani; tuition per week from 5800B) Associated with the respected World Muay Thai Council, the institute offers a fundamental course (consisting of three levels of expertise), as well as courses for instructors, referees and judges. If you're interested, make an appointment to visit the facility, which is north of Bangkok, and watch the teachers and students at work.

CUSTOMS REGULATIONS

The white-uniformed officers of Thai customs prohibit the import or export of the usual array of goods – porn, weapons, drugs – and if you're caught with drugs in particular expect life never to be the same again. Otherwise, they're quite reasonable. The usual 200 cigarettes or 250g of tobacco are allowed in without duty, along with 1L of wine or spirits. Ditto for electronic goods as long as you don't look like you're planning to sell them – best to leave your third and fourth laptops at home.

For information on currency import or export, see p276. For details on exporting Buddha images and other antiquities, see p138. For hours of fun reading other customs details (useful if you're planning on moving to Thailand), check out www.customs.go.th/Customs-Eng/indexEng.jsp.

DISCOUNT CARDS

The Th Khao San trade in fake student cards and press passes is still bubbling along 20 years after it began. Not surprisingly, Bangkok institutions don't accept these cards as proof of anything. Which means the only way to get a student discount here is to dress in the black and white uniform of Thai universities…which isn't really worth it.

Most of the major shopping centres around Siam Sq and Emporium offer a standard 5%

off to tourists. To get it, you need a '5% off' card, which usually comes attached to the free tourist maps from the tourist booths around town. If you don't have one, don't fret. If you don't look Thai, in most cases the staff will ask if you are a tourist and, before you can nod, will have whipped out a spare card from under the counter. Once you've paid and had your discount, they'll take you to the VAT Refund office for a bit more saving (see p137 for details).

ELECTRICITY

Electric current is 220V, 50 cycles. Electrical wall outlets are usually of the two-pin type. Some outlets accept plugs with two flat pins, and some will accept either flat or round pins. Any electrical supply shop will carry adaptors for international plugs, as well as voltage converters.

EMBASSIES

Some Bangkok embassies are listed here. For a full and regularly updated list, go to www. mfa.go.th/web/12.php and click through to Thailand and the World, Diplomatic Corps Directory and Diplomatic and Consular List to get to the list under Diplomatic Missions. For Thai missions click Directory and, at the bottom, Thailand's Missions Abroad. In emergency situations after hours, call the relevant number below and listen carefully to the voice prompts for the duty officer's mobile number.

Australia (Map p122; ☎ 0 2344 6300; www.austem bassy.or.th; 37 Th Sathon Tai, Sathon; Ⓜ Lumphini exit 2)

Cambodia (Map p132; ☎ 0 2957 5851; 518/4 Th Pracha Uthit (aka Soi Ramkhamhaeng 39), Wangthonglang)

Canada (Map p122; ☎ 0 2636 0540; geo.international. gc.ca/asia/bangkok; 15th fl, Abdulrahim Bldg, 990 Th Phra Ram IV, Lumphini; Ⓜ Si Lom exit 2; Ⓡ Sala Daeng exit 4)

China (Map p132; ☎ 0 2245 0088, 2245 7044; www. chinaembassy.or.th/eng; 57 Th Ratchadaphisek, Din Daeng; Ⓜ Thailand Cultural Centre exit 3)

France Embassy (Map p116; ☎ 0 2266 8250-56; www. ambafrance-th.org; 35 Soi 36, Th Charoen Krung); Consulate (Map p122; ☎ 0 2287 1592; 29 Th Sathon Tai, Sathon; Ⓜ Lumphini exit 2)

Germany (Map p122; ☎ 0 2287 9000; www.bangkok. diplo.de; 9 Th Sathon Tai, Sathon; Ⓜ Lumphini exit 2)

India Embassy (Map p126; ☎ 0 2258 0300-05; www. indianembassy.in.th; 46 Soi 23, Th Sukhumvit; Ⓡ Asok);

Consulate (Indian Visa Application Center; Map p126; ☎ 0 2665 2968; www.ivac-th.com; 15th fl, Glas Haus Bldg, Soi 25, Th Sukhumvit; Ⓜ Sukhumvit exit 2; Ⓡ Asok exit 6)

Israel (Map p126; ☎ 0 2204 9200; http://bangkok.mfa. gov.il; 25th fl, Ocean Tower II, 75 Soi 19, Th Sukhumvit; Ⓜ Sukhumvit exit 1; Ⓡ Asok exit 3)

Indonesia (Map p108; ☎ 0 2252 3135; 600-602 Th Phetchaburi, Ratchathewi; Ⓡ Ratchathewi exit 4)

Japan (Map p122; ☎ 0 2207 8500; www.the.emb-japan. go.jp; 177 Th Withayu, Lumphini; Ⓜ Lumphini)

Laos (Map p132; ☎ 0 2539 6667; www.bkklaoembassy. com (out of date visa information); 520/1-3 Soi Sahakarn-pramoon, Th Pracha Uthit, Wangthonglong)

Malaysia (Map p122; ☎ 0 2629 6800; 33-35 Th Sathon Tai, Sathon; Ⓜ Lumphini exit 2)

Myanmar (Map p116; ☎ 0 2234 0278; 132 Th Sathon Neua; Ⓡ Surasak exit 3)

Nepal (Map p132; ☎ 0 2390 2280; 189 Soi 71, Th Sukhumvit)

Netherlands (Map p108; ☎ 0 2309 5200; www.nether landsembassy.in.th; 15 Soi Tonson, Ploenchit; Ⓡ Chit Lom exit 4)

New Zealand (Map p108; ☎ 0 2254 2530-33; www. nzembassy.com; 19th fl, M Thai Tower, All Seasons Pl, 87 Th Withayu, Ploenchit; Ⓡ Phloen Chit exit 5)

Singapore (Map p122; ☎ 0 2286 2111; www.mfa.gov. sg/bangkok; 9th & 18th fl, Rajanakam Bldg, 129 Th Sathon Tai; Ⓡ Chong Nonsi & new skywalk)

South Africa (Map p108; ☎ 0 2659 2900; www.saemb bangkok.com; 12th fl, M Thai Tower, All Seasons Pl, 87 Th Witthaya, Ploenchit; Ⓡ Phloen Chit exit 5)

Sweden (Map p126; ☎ 0 2263 7200; www.swedenabroad. com; 20th fl, One Pacific Pl, 140 Th Sukhumvit; Ⓡ Nana exit 2)

UK & Northern Ireland (Map p108; ☎ 0 2305 8333; www.britishembassy.gov.uk; 14 Th Withayu, Ploenchit; Ⓡ Phloen Chit exit 5)

USA (Map p108; ☎ 0 2205 4000; http://bangkok. usembassy.gov; 120/22 Th Withayu, Lumphini; Ⓡ Phloen Chit exit 5)

Vietnam (Map p108; ☎ 0 2251 5836-38; 83/1 Th With-ayu, Ploenchit; Ⓡ Phloen Chit exit 5)

EMERGENCY

The main emergency numbers:

Ambulance (via Police ☎ 191)

Fire (☎ 199)

Police (☎ 191)

Tourist Police (☎ 1155)

You're unlikely to find any English-speaker at the fire number, so it's best to use the default ☎ 191 number. In a medical emergency it's probably best to call the hospital direct, and it will dispatch an ambulance. See p275 for recommended hospitals.

The best way to deal with most problems requiring police, most likely a rip-off or theft, is to contact the tourist police on the 24-hour ☎ 1155 hotline. Unlike the regular Thai police, the tourist police are used to dealing with foreigners and can be very helpful in cases of arrest. Although they typically have no jurisdiction over the kinds of cases handled by regular cops, they should be able to help with translation, contacting your embassy and/or arranging a police report you can take to your insurer.

GAY & LESBIAN TRAVELLERS

Thai culture is very tolerant of homosexuality, both male and female, and notwithstanding the prejudices of some, Bangkok is one of the most gay-friendly cities on earth. Thailand does not have laws that discriminate against homosexuals, and Bangkok's gay scene is way out in the open. For much more information see p190, and take a look at these websites:

Dreaded Ned (www.dreadedned.com) Listings, forums, personal ads.

Fridae (www.fridae.com) Listings of events across Asia; click through Agenda for Thailand.

Gay Guide in Thailand (www.gayguideinthailand.com) Exactly that – a gay tour guide.

Lesbian Guide to Bangkok (www.bangkoklesbian.com) The most active and useful site for lesbians in Bangkok, with helpful forums and news on events and venues.

Long Yang Club (www.longyangclub.org/thailand) A 'multicultural social group for male-oriented men who want to meet outside the gay scene', with branches all over the world. The Thailand chapter hosts occasional events in Bangkok.

Utopia (www.utopia-asia.com) Long-running site with lots of Bangkok information and member reviews.

HEALTH

While urban horror stories can make a trip to Bangkok seem frighteningly dangerous, few travellers experience anything more than an upset stomach and the resulting clenched-cheek waddles to the bathroom. If you do have a problem, Bangkok has some very good hospitals in which you can recover; see p275.

Many medications can be bought over the counter without a doctor's prescription, but it can be difficult to find some newer drugs, particularly antidepressants, blood-pressure medications and contraceptive pills. Bangkok and the surrounding regions of central Thailand are entirely malaria free, so you won't need to worry about taking any antimalarial medication if you don't plan to venture beyond that area. Cases of dengue fever are few but they do occur, so if you come down with flu symptoms do see a doctor.

Food & Water

If a place looks clean and well run and the vendor also looks clean and healthy, then the food is probably safe. In general, the food in busy restaurants is cooked and eaten quite quickly with little standing around, and is probably not reheated. The same applies to street stalls. It's worth remembering that when you first arrive the change in diet might result in a loose stool or two, but that doesn't automatically mean you've got amoebic dysentery, so hold off a bit before rushing to the doc.

Water and ice are the cause of much anxiety among travellers, but follow a couple of simple rules and you should be okay. Don't drink tap water, but do remember that all water served in restaurants or to guests in offices or homes in Bangkok comes from purified sources. It's not necessary to ask for bottled water in these places unless you prefer it. Reputable brands of Thai bottled water or soft drinks are fine. Fruit juices are made with purified water and are safe to drink. Milk in Thailand is always pasteurised.

Ice is generally produced from purified water under hygienic conditions and is therefore theoretically safe. The rule of thumb is that if it's chipped ice, it probably came from an ice block (which may not have been handled well), but if it's ice cubes or tubes, it was delivered from the ice factory in sealed plastic. Almost all ice in Bangkok is the latter.

Medical Problems & Treatment

In Bangkok medicine is generally available over the counter for much less than it costs in the West. However, fake drugs are common so try to use reputable-looking pharmacies, and check storage conditions and expiry dates before buying anything.

AIR POLLUTION

Bangkok has a bad reputation for air pollution, and on bad days the combination of heat, dust and motor fumes can be a powerful brew of potentially toxic air. The good news is that more efficient vehicles, fewer of them thanks to the Skytrain and Metro, and less industrial pollution mean Bangkok's skies are much cleaner than they used to be. To put it into perspective, the air is usually nearer to Singapore standards than diabolical Hong Kong or Shanghai.

FLU

Thailand has seen a number of nasty influenza strains in recent years, most notably the bird (H5N1) and swine (H1N1) varieties. That said, it's no worse than any other country in the region and is probably better prepared than most of the world for any major outbreak because the government has stockpiled tens of millions of Tamiflu doses.

HEAT

By the standards of most visitors Bangkok is somewhere between hot and seriously (expletive) hot all year round. Usually that will mean nothing more than sweat-soaked clothing, discomfort and excessive tiredness. However, heat exhaustion is not uncommon, and dehydration is the main contributor. Symptoms include feeling weak, headache, irritability, nausea or vomiting, sweaty skin, a fast, weak pulse and a normal or slightly elevated body temperature. Treatment involves getting out of the heat and/or sun and cooling the victim down by fanning and applying cool, wet cloths to the skin, laying the victim flat with their legs raised and rehydrating with electrolyte drinks or water containing a quarter teaspoon of salt per litre.

Heatstroke is more serious and requires more urgent action. Symptoms come on suddenly and include weakness, nausea, a hot, dry body with a temperature of more than 41°C, dizziness, confusion, loss of coordination, seizures and, eventually, collapse and loss of consciousness. Seek medical help and begin cooling by getting the victim out of the heat, removing their clothes, fanning them and applying cool, wet cloths or ice to their body, especially to the groin and armpits.

HIV & AIDS

In Thailand around 95% of HIV transmission occurs through sexual activity, and the remainder through natal transmission or through illicit intravenous drug use. HIV/AIDS can also be spread through infected blood transfusions, although this risk is virtually nil in Thailand due to rigorous blood-screening procedures. If you want to be pierced or tattooed, be sure to check that the needles are new.

HOLIDAYS

Chinese New Year (which usually occurs in late February or early March) and Songkran (mid-April) are the two holiday periods that most affect Bangkok. For up to a week before and after these holidays public transport in or out of the city is extremely busy, although during the holidays themselves Bangkok tends to be quiet (except in Chinatown during Chinese New Year and Th Khao San during Songkran). Because it is peak season for foreign tourists visiting Thailand, the months of December and January can also be very tight.

See p20 for detailed information on individual festivals and holidays.

Public Holidays

Government offices and banks close their doors on the following public holidays. For the precise dates of lunar holidays, see the TAT website www.tourismthailand.org/travel-information.

New Year's Day 1 January

Makha Bucha Day January/March (lunar)

Chakri Day 6 April (commemorates the founding of the royal Chakri dynasty)

Songkran 13 to 15 April (Thai New Year)

Labor Day 1 May

Coronation Day 5 May (commemorating the 1950 coronation of the current king and queen)

Visakha Bucha Day May/June (lunar)

Khao Phansa July/August (lunar; beginning of the Buddhist rains retreat, when monks refrain from travelling away from their monasteries)

Queen's Birthday 12 August

King Chulalongkorn Day 23 October

Ok Phansa October/November (lunar; end of Buddhist rains retreat)

King's Birthday 5 December

Constitution Day 10 December

New Year's Eve 31 December

INTERNET ACCESS

Bangkok is a very well-wired town. Internet cafes are scattered throughout the city, charging from about 40B per hour up to 120B. Th Khao San (Map p82) has the highest concentration of internet cafes, with dozens available. Other good areas include Th Silom (Map p116), Th Ploenchit and Siam Sq (Map p108). Additionally, the vast majority of Bangkok guesthouses and hotels offer internet access; look for the 🖳 icon for places with their own net-connected computers, or 🛜 for places with wi-fi.

With so much free internet available, and so many net cafes, paying for a temporary dial-up internet account barely seems worth it. If you think it is, find a 7-Eleven and buy a prepaid card for a couple of hundred baht.

LEGAL MATTERS

Thailand's police don't enjoy a squeaky clean reputation but as a foreigner, and especially a tourist, you probably won't have much to do with them. While some expats will talk of being targeted for fines while driving, most anecdotal evidence suggests the men in tight (we're talking spray-on) brown shirts and dark aviators will usually go out of their way not to arrest a foreigner breaking minor laws.

The big exception is drug laws. Most Thai police view drug-takers as a social scourge and consequently see it as their duty to enforce the letter of the law; for others it's an opportunity to make untaxed income via bribes. Which direction they'll go often depends on drug quantities; small-time offenders are sometimes offered the chance to pay their way out of an arrest, while traffickers usually go to jail.

Smoking is banned in all indoor spaces, including bars and pubs. The ban extends to open-air public spaces, which means lighting

---

up outside a shopping centre, in particular, might earn you a polite request to butt out. If you throw your cigarette butt on the ground, however, you could then be hit with a hefty littering fine. Bangkok has a strong anti-littering law, and police won't hesitate to cite foreigners and collect fines of 2000B.

If you are arrested for any offence, police will allow you to make a phone call to your embassy or consulate in Thailand if you have one, or to a friend or relative. There's a whole set of legal codes governing the length of time and manner in which you can be detained before being charged or put on trial. Police have a lot of discretion and as a foreigner, they are more likely to bend these codes in your favour than the reverse. However, as with police worldwide, if you don't show respect to the men in brown you will only make matters worse, so keep a cool head.

Visiting Prisoners

While the craze for visiting imprisoned foreigners in Bangkok's notorious jails Bang Kwang (Map p132; ☎ 0 2967 3311; www.correct.go.th/brief.htm; Th Nonthaburi, Nonthaburi; 🚢 Nonthaburi) and Khlong Prem (Map p132; ☎ 0 2580 0975; 33/3 Th Ngam Wang Wan, Chatuchak; 🚇 Mo Chit & taxi) has cooled off, some travellers still make the trek. Visiting details are discussed on several websites, notably www.phaseloop.com/foreignprisoners /prisoners-thailand.html and www.khaosan road.com. If you want to see a particular prisoner the best approach is to first contact the prisoner's Bangkok embassy. Consular officials can tell you whether the prisoner, or any other prisoner, wants to be seen; note that they won't give names or details unless the prisoner has authorised them to do so. If so, they can help out and advise on visiting times, usually a couple of days a week. Don't try going directly to the prison without a letter from the prisoner's embassy, as you might be refused entry.

Most foreign prisoners in Thai prisons are from the UK, Australia, Africa and Europe; most American prisoners are repatriated to jails in the US.

MAPS

From the moment you enter Bangkok – literally right after you've passed immigration – you'll see your first free maps. Quality varies between useful and utter rubbish, but the *Official Airport Bangkok Map* and the *City Map of*

WI-FI ACCESS

Wi-fi (wireless fidelity) is not hard to find in Bangkok. Most cafes now offer either free or paid wi-fi access, with free access available at branches of Coffee World and Gloria Jean's; Starbucks charges. Most top-end and midrange hotels have wi-fi, as do quite a few guesthouses, sometimes for free and sometimes available by prepaying for time. Various websites list Bangkok wi-fi spots, including www.bkkpages.com, www.bkkok.com, www.stickmanbangkok.com and www.jiwire.com (see Krung Thep); JI Wire also offers an iPhone app version of its listings.

BANGKOK ADDRESSES Joe Cummings

Any city as large and unplanned as Bangkok can be tough to get around. Street names often seem unpronounceable to begin with, compounded by the inconsistency of romanised Thai spellings. For example, the street often spelt as 'Rajdamri' is actually pronounced 'Ratchadamri' (with the appropriate tones, of course), or in abbreviated form as Rat damri. The 'v' in Sukhumvit should be pronounced like a 'w'... One of the most popular locations for foreign embassies is known both as Wireless Rd and Th Withayu (*wí·tá·yú* is Thai for 'radio').

Many street addresses show a string of numbers divided by slashes and hyphens, for example, 48/3-5 Soi 1, Th Sukhumvit. The reason is that undeveloped property in Bangkok was originally bought and sold in lots. The number before the slash refers to the original lot number. The numbers following the slash indicate buildings (or entrances to buildings) constructed within that lot. The pre-slash numbers appear in the order in which they were added to city plans, while the post-slash numbers are arbitrarily assigned by developers. As a result numbers along a given street don't always run consecutively.

The Thai word *tànŏn* (usually spelt 'thanon') means road, street or avenue. Hence Ratchadamnoen Rd (sometimes referred to as Ratchadamnoen Ave) is always called Thanon (Th) Ratchadamnoen in Thai.

A soi is a small street or lane that runs off a larger street. In our example, the address referred to as 48/3-5 Soi 1, Th Sukhumvit will be located off Th Sukhumvit on Soi 1. Alternative ways of writing the same address include 48/3-5 Th Sukhumvit Soi 1, or even just 48/3-5 Sukhumvit 1. Some Bangkok soi have become so large that they can be referred to both as *tànŏn* and soi, eg Soi Sarasin/Th Sarasin and Soi Asoke/Th Asoke. Smaller than a soi is a *tròrk* (usually spelt 'trok') or alley. Well-known alleys in Bangkok include Chinatown's Trok Itsaranuphap and Banglamphu's Trok Rong Mai.

Bangkok, both usually available at the airport, will get you around the major sights, transport routes and hotels.

Maps for sale in bookshops and some 7-Elevens are better. Shoppers should make sure they pick up a copy of *Nancy Chandler's Map of Bangkok* (www.nancychandler.net), a colourful hand-drawn map with useful inset panels for Chinatown, Th Sukhumvit and Chatuchak Weekend Market; see the website for updates.

To master the city's bus system, purchase Roadway's *Bangkok Bus Map*. For visitors who consider eating to be sightseeing, check out Ideal Map's *Good Eats* series, which has mapped mom-and-pop restaurants in three of Bangkok's noshing neighbourhoods – Chinatown, Ko Ratanakosin and Sukhumvit. Groovy Map's *Groovy Bangkok* combines up-to-date bus and transport routes and sights with a short selection of restaurant and bar reviews. Groovy Map also publishes *Roadway Bangkok*, a GPS-derived 1:40,000 driving map of the city that includes all tollways, expressways, roads and lanes labelled in Thai and English. If travelling to districts outside central Bangkok, Thinknet's *Bangkok City Atlas* is a wise way to spend 250B.

MEDICAL SERVICES

More than Thailand's main health-care hub, Bangkok has become a major destination for medical tourism, with patients flying in for treatment from all over the world. In addi-tion to three university research hospitals, the city is home to an ever-expanding number of public and private hospitals and hundreds of private medical clinics. But it's the hotel-style international hospitals that treat most visitors. Bumrungrad International is the biggest, and though it can feel a bit like a factory it has US accreditation, wi-fi internet, the latest equipment and, in the 'lobby', Starbucks and, erm, McDonalds – would you like a thick shake with that bypass? Many expatriates prefer Samitivej Hospital, which we can personally vouch for.

Whether your stay is to recover from a nasty 'Thai tattoo' (burned inner right calf after a motorcycle mishap), for corrective surgery you couldn't afford or wait for at home, or for something more cosmetic – new nose, lips, breasts, Adam's apple removal – the following hospitals should be able to help. Of course, it's worth checking the websites and searching around online for feedback before booking yourself in for anything. Be aware, too, that hospital doctors will generally lean towards over-prescribing drugs, which then must be bought from the hospital's own dispensary. Doctors will often speak English, but if you need another language contact your embassy for advice (p271).

Bangkok's better private hospitals include the following:

Bangkok Christian Hospital (Map p116; ☎ 0 2235 1000; www.bkkchristianhosp.th.com; 124 Th Silom; 🚇 Sala Daeng exit 1)

Bangkok Hospital (Map p132; ☎ 0 2310 3000; www.bangkokhospital.com; 2 Soi 47, Th Phetburi Tat Mai, Bangkapi)

BNH Hospital (Map p122; ☎ 0 2686 2700; www.bnhhospital.com; 9 Th Convent; Ⓜ Si Lom exit 2; Ⓡ Sala Daeng exit 2)

Bumrungrad International Hospital (Map p126; ☎ 0 2667 1000; www.bumrungrad.com; 33 Soi 3, Th Sukhumvit; Ⓡ Phloen Chit exit 3)

Phyathai Hospital 1 (Map p113; ☎ 0 2617 2444, ext 1711-14; www.phyathai.com; 364/1 Th Si Ayuthaya; Ⓡ Phaya Thai exit 4)

Samitivej Sukhumvit Hospital (Map p126; ☎ 0 2711 8181; www.samitivej.co.th; 133 Soi 49, Th Sukhumvit)

All these hospitals have substantial ophthalmological treatment facilities. The best eye specialist in the city is **Rutnin Eye Hospital** (Map p126; ☎ 0 2639 3399; www.rutnin.com; 80/1 Soi Asoke; Th Sukhumvit; Ⓜ Phetchaburi exit 2; Ⓡ Asok exit 2).

Medical spas mixing alternative therapies, massage and detoxification have taken 'the cure' a step further. See p204 for recommendations.

Chinese Medicine
In the Sampeng-Yaowarat district, along Th Ratchawong, Th Charoen Krung, Th Yaowarat and Th Songwat, are many small Chinese clinics and herbal dispensaries, though not so much English; bring someone to translate. Larger is the **Hua Chiew General Hospital** (Map p64; ☎ 0 2223 1351; www.huachiewhospital.com; 665 Th Bamrung Meuang), a medical facility dedicated to all aspects of traditional Chinese medicine, along with modern international medicine. The team of licensed acupuncturists at Hua Chiew are thought to be Thailand's most skilled, though there isn't much English spoken here.

Dentists
They don't call it the 'land of smiles' for nothing. As you wander around Bangkok it can seem there is a dental clinic on every soi. Business is good in the teeth game, partly because so many *fà·ràng* are combining their holiday with a spot of cheap root canal or some 'personal outlook' care – a sneaky teeth-whitening treatment by any other name. Prices are a bargain compared with Western countries, and the quality of dentistry is generally good. That said, remember that you get what you pay for…Clinics worth considering:

Bangkok Dental Spa (Map p126; ☎ 0 2651 0807; www.bangkokdentalspa.com; 2nd fl, Methawattana Bldg, 27 Soi 19, Th Sukhumvit; Ⓜ Sukhumvit; Ⓡ Asok) This is not a typo. Combines oral hygiene with spa services (foot and body massage).

DC-One the Dental Clinic (Map p64; ☎ 0 2240 2800; www.dc-one.com; 31 Th Yen Akat, Lumphini) Reputation for excellent work and relatively high prices; popular with UN and diplomats.

Dental Hospital (Map p126; ☎ 0 2260 5000-15; www.dentalhospitalbangkok.com; 88/88 Soi 49, Th Sukhumvit; Ⓡ Thong Lo) A private dental clinic with fluent English-speaking dentists.

Siam Family Dental Clinic (Map p108; ☎ 0 2255 6664; www.siamfamilydental.com; 292/6 Soi 4, Siam Sq; Ⓡ Siam) Teeth-whitening is big here.

Pharmacies
Pharmacies are plentiful and in central areas most pharmacists will speak English. If you don't find what you need in a Boots, Watsons or local pharmacy, try one of the hospitals listed above, which stock a wider range of pharmaceuticals but also charge higher prices (and you'll need to see a doctor first). Hospital pharmacies are open 24 hours; smaller pharmacies usually open around 10am and close between 8pm and 10pm. One nonhospital pharmacy that's open 24 hours is **Foodland Pharmacy** (Map p126; ☎ 0 2254 2247; 1413 Soi 5, Th Sukhumvit; Ⓡ Nana).

MONEY
Most travellers rely on credit or debit cards to access cash in Bangkok, where ATMs can be found on almost every corner. The basic unit of Thai currency is the baht. There are 100 satang in one baht – though the only place you'll be able to spend them is in the ubiquitous 7-Elevens. Coins come in denominations of 25 satang, 50 satang, 1B, 5B and 10B. Paper currency comes in denominations of 20B (green), 50B (blue), 100B (red), 500B (purple) and 1000B (beige).

By Thai law, any traveller arriving in Thailand is supposed to carry at least the following amounts of money in either cash, travellers cheques, bank draft or letter of credit, according to visa category: Non-Immigrant Visa, US$500 per person or US$1000 per family; Tourist Visa, US$250 per person or US$500 per family; Transit Visa or no visa, US$125 per person or US$250 per family. In 20 years of flying into Bangkok we have never been asked to show the contents of our wallets. That said, your funds might be checked if you arrive on a one-way ticket or if you look as if you're at 'the end of the road'. There is no limit to the amount of Thai or foreign currency you may bring into Thailand. Upon leaving, you are permitted to take no more than 50,000B per person without special authorisation; exportation of foreign currencies is unrestricted.

Standard banking hours are 8.30am to 3.30pm Monday to Friday, though some banks close at 4pm or 4.30pm on Friday. It's legal to open a foreign-currency account at any commercial bank in Thailand, though fees are relatively high. As long as the funds originate from abroad, there are no restrictions on their maintenance or withdrawal.

ATMs & Credit Cards

You won't need a map to find an ATM in Bangkok – they're everywhere. Bank branches, large hotels, transport hubs and the ubiquitous 7-Elevens are all kitted out with ATMs. Bank ATMs accept major international credit cards and many will also cough up cash (Thai baht only) if your card is affiliated with the Cirrus or Plus networks. You can withdraw up to 20,000B at a time from most ATMs, and 25,000B from some Bangkok Bank ATMs.

Credit cards as well as debit cards can be used for purchases at many shops and pretty much any hotel or restaurant where you might need credit, though you'll have to pay cash for your *pàt tai*. The most commonly accepted cards are Visa and MasterCard, followed by Amex and JCB. To report a lost or stolen card, call the following numbers:

Amex (☎ 0 2273 5544)

MasterCard (☎ 001 800 11 887 0663)

Visa (☎ 001 800 11 535 0660, 0 2256 7324-29)

Changing Money

Banks or legal moneychangers offer the optimum foreign-exchange rates. When buying baht, US dollars and euros are the most readily accepted currencies and travellers cheques receive better rates than cash. British pounds, Australian dollars, Singapore dollars and Hong Kong dollars are also widely accepted. As banks often charge commission and duty for each travellers cheque cashed, you'll save on commissions if you use larger cheque denominations.

Most banks can change foreign currency but it can sometimes take significantly more time than the specialty exchange places. In tourist areas, such as the Siam Sq shopping district and Th Khao San, you'll often find small exchange counters outside banks; these can change cash and cheques in major currencies and are typically open from 8.30am to 8pm daily.

See the inside front cover for exchange rates at the time of research.

Tipping

Tipping is not a traditional part of Thai life and, except in big hotels and posh restaurants, tips are appreciated but not expected. That said, Thais who commonly deal with tourists become increasingly familiar with the practice so expect some hopeful, if not expectant, looks in higher end places. The one place where tipping is considered normal is in taxis, where drivers will usually round the price up to the nearest 10B and most people, including Thais, are happy to let them have the coins.

NEWSPAPERS & MAGAZINES

Bangkok has a well-established English-language media and has possibly the largest concentration of freelance journalists and photographers of any city on earth. The *Bangkok Post* (www.bangkokpost.net) is the major daily broadsheet, with local and international news as well as articles on culture, entertainment, dining and events; the Sunday edition has some good investigative journalism and longer reads, while Friday's paper comes with *Guru*, a magazine for younger readers with entertainment listings and reviews for the weekend. The *Nation* (www.nationmultimedia.com) is now a business paper and comes with a giveaway tabloid called *Daily Xpress*. The *International Herald Tribune* (IHT) is widely available, as are all major international magazines.

For new restaurants, current happy hours, band dates and which DJs are in town, look for the independent, free and irreverent weekly *BK Magazine* (www.bkmagazine.com). For impartial reviews of places to see, eat, drink, dance, view art and sleep pick up a copy of the monthly *Bangkok 101*; it costs 100B in 7-Elevens. The publishers of *Bangkok 101* also produce the excellent *BAM* (Bangkok Art Map), with listings, reviews and directions to galleries and exhibitions.

ORGANISED TOURS

Mastering Bangkok is the urban aficionado's version of conquering Everest. But not everyone enjoys slogging through the sprawl and heat, and for those sensible folk there are many tours available. Almost every hotel and guesthouse can book you on tours of the main historic sights, and a good number of túk-túk (pronounced đúk đúk) drivers will probably try their luck too (don't be tempted). Tours of the river and adjoining *klorng* are the most popular, and bicycle tours (yes, serious) are finding a growing number of happy peddlers; see p207.

River & Canal Tours

The car has long since become Bangkok's conveyance of choice, but there was a time, and there are still places today, where roads are made of water, not asphalt. Taking to these traditional thoroughfares reveals children swimming in the muddy (that's a generous descriptor) waters, huge cargo barges groaning under the weight of sand being shipped to construction sites, and wake-skipping long-tailed boats roaring by. At sunset the famed Wat Arun (p77) and the riverside towers of the luxury hotels are bathed in red and orange hues.

The cheapest and most local way of experiencing riverine Bangkok is by boarding the Chao Phraya Express Boat (☎ 0 2623 6001; www.chaophrayaboat.co.th) at any *tâh* (pier) and taking it in either direction to its final stop; see p263 for details. The company also offers a one-day river pass (150B) for unlimited trips aboard the Chao Phraya Tourist Boat, which stops at 10 major piers from 9.30am to 3pm and has a distracting loudspeaker guide. Even guidebook writers who sightsee at warp speed find this pass poorer value than the average 13B fare. More appealing are the Sunday trips to Ko Kret (p240).

Hiring a longtail boat, sometimes known as a 'James Bond boat' after the chase scene in *The Man with the Golden Gun* that first brought them to the attention of the world, is a popular way of touring the Thonburi *klorng*. Shop around for a tour that doesn't include Wat Arun and the Royal Barge Museum, both of which can be more easily (and more cheaply) visited independently. Longtails can be hired from numerous piers along the river, most notably Tha Si Phraya (N3, Map p116), Tha Chang (N9, Map p64), and Tha Phra Pin Klao

(N12, Map p82); a standard set of fees applies, ranging from 800B for an hour to 1500B for three hours. Bargaining is encouraged. Private tours can be arranged at other piers, including Tha Oriental (N1, Map p116) and Tha Phra Athit (N13, Map p82), at the private pier about 200m south of the express boat pier). You'll need two hours to do it justice and, if you're on a budget, some accomplices to help split the cost.

For dinner cruises, see p169.

The restored wooden rice barges in the Manohra Cruises (Map p132; ☎ 0 2477 0770; www.manohracruises.com) fleet are the grandest of all, having been converted into luxury cruisers with real character. There are several cruising options, all departing the Marriott Resort & Spa (take a hotel boat from Tha Sathon). The dinner cruise (1460B or 2340B depending on menu, 7.30pm to 10pm) is rightly popular for its old-world ambience. If you have both time and money, consider the two- or three-day trips between Bangkok and Ayuthaya, via Ko Kret and Bang Pa-In.

Other Tours

Most Bangkok sights can be visited easily under your own steam, but every travel agent and most hotels can arrange guided tours of important sites. If you want a custom tour with an expert guide, Bangkok Private Tours (www.bangkokprivatetours.com) can cook up an itinerary for just about any interest; their food tours have a particularly good reputation.

POST

Thailand has an efficient postal service, and both domestic and international rates are very reasonable. Bangkok's monolithic, art deco–influenced main post office (Communications Authority of Thailand, CAT; Map p116; ☎ 0 2233 1050; Th Charoen Krung) is open from 8am to 8pm Monday to Friday and from 8am to 1pm Saturday and Sunday and holidays. If you've bought too much at Chatuchak Weekend Market the parcel counter is open from 8am to 5pm Monday to Friday and from 9am to noon on Saturday. If you're a Luddite, or your mum is, you might get to know the helpful guys at the poste restante service; they hold mail for two months.

An international telecommunications service (including telephone, fax and internet) is located in a separate building in the northeast corner of the block; services are paid for with prepaid cards that can also be used at Bangkok airports. The easiest way to reach the main post office is via a Chao Phraya Express Boat to Si Phraya (N3) or Wat Muang Khae (N2), both a short walk away.

Elsewhere, branch post offices are found throughout the city; ask your hotel for the nearest one.

RADIO

Bangkok has around 100 FM and AM stations broadcasting a huge range of music, talk and news. The place you're most likely to hear Thai radio is in a taxi. Given that most Bangkok cabbies are from the northeast Isaan region, expect them to be listening to *lôok tûng* (Thai country music) on Luk Thung 95.0 FM. For Thai Top 40 try Hotwave 91.5 FM; for more alternative Thai tunes try Fat Radio 104.5 FM.

For a taste of what's on offer, listen to live radio online by clicking through to Thailand on www.surfmusic.de.

SAFETY

Bangkok is a safe city and incidents of violence against tourists are rare. Assuming you don't join a political protest on the day they take on the army (an action that is very easy to avoid), it's unlikely you'll experience any physical harm.

On the other hand, scams aimed at separating you and your hard-earned are prevalent. There are numerous methods, with the infamous gem scam being the most common.

The Gem Scam

Bangkok has become synonymous with the term 'gem scam' to the extent that there are several websites dedicated to combatting the scammers. Con artists tend to haunt first-time tourist spots, such as the Grand Palace area, Wat Pho, the Golden Mount and shopping mall forecourts around Siam Sq and Ratchaprasong, and when they strike the average scam is worth more than US$2000.

Most scams begin the same way: a friendly Thai approaches and strikes up a seemingly innocuous conversation. Sometimes the con man says he's a university student or teacher; at other times he might claim to work for the World Bank or a similarly distinguished organisation. If you're on the way to Wat Pho or Jim Thompson's House, for example, he may tell you it's closed for a holiday or repairs. Eventually the conversation works its way around to the subject of the scam – the best fraudsters can actually make it seem as though you initiated the topic. The scammer might spend hours inveigling you into his trust, taking you to an alternative 'special' temple, for example, and linking with other seemingly random people, often túk-túk drivers and foreigners posing as tourists, who seem to independently verify what the scammer is telling you.

The scam itself almost always incorporates gems. The victim is persuaded that they can turn a hefty profit by arranging a gem purchase and reselling the merchandise at home. The jewellery shop can offer these bargains because, they say, the government is running a 'gem sale' that allows students to sell the family jewels tax free to pay for their education. Of course, the government doesn't do gem sales and the whole tale is a load of old bollocks. In reality, the victim buys low-quality sapphires and has them posted home – so they can't change their mind – where they prove to be worth a fraction of the 'bargain' price paid. The Thai police are usually of no help, believing merchants are entitled to whatever price they can get and that tourists are victims of their own greed, which is at least partly true.

Suits & Card Games

At tailor shops the objective is to get you to pay exorbitant prices for poorly made clothes. The tailor shops that do this are adept at delaying delivery until just before you leave Thailand, so you don't have time to object to poor workmanship. For the lowdown on having clothes made in Bangkok, see p147.

The card-playing scam starts out similarly to the gem scenario: a friendly stranger strikes up a conversation and invites the traveller to the house of his relative for a drink or meal. After a bit of socialising, another friend or relative of the con arrives and, lo and behold, a little high-stakes card game is planned for later that day. Like the gem scam, the card-game scam has many variations, but eventually the victim is shown some cheating tactics to use with help from the 'dealer', some practice sessions take place and finally the game gets under way. The mark is allowed to win a few hands first, then somehow loses a few, gets bankrolled by one of the friendly Thais, and then loses the Thai's money. Suddenly your new-found buddies aren't so friendly any more – they want the money you lost. Sooner or later you end up sucking large amounts out of the nearest ATM. Again the police won't take any action – in this case because gambling is illegal in Thailand so you've broken the law, and it's not the job of police to protect those who are cheated in the process of trying to cheat someone else – in other words, you deserve everything you get.

Other minor scams involve túk-túk drivers, hotel employees and bar girls who take new arrivals on city tours; these almost always end in high-pressure sales pushes at silk, jewellery or handicraft shops. In this case greed isn't the ruling motivation – it's simply a matter of weak sales resistance.

The best way to avoid all this is to follow the TAT's number-one suggestion: disregard all offers of free shopping or sightseeing help from strangers. You might also try telling strangers you're on your third trip to Bangkok, even if you only just arrived. Con artists rarely prey on anyone except new arrivals.

You should contact the tourist police if you have any problems with consumer fraud. Call ☎ 1155 from any phone.

TAXES & REFUNDS

Thailand has a 7% value-added tax (VAT) on many goods and services. Midrange and top-end hotels and restaurants might also add a 10% service tax. When the two are combined this becomes the 17% king hit known as 'plus plus', or '++'. You can get a refund on VAT paid on shopping, though not on food or hotels, as you leave the country. For details see p137.

TELEPHONE

The Bangkok telephone system is efficient enough for you to be able to direct-dial most major centres without trouble. Thailand's country code is ☎ 66.

Inside Thailand you must dial the area code no matter where you are. In effect, that means all numbers are nine digits; in Bangkok they begin with ☎ 02, then a seven-digit number. The only time you drop the initial ☎ 0 is when you're calling from outside Thailand. Calling the provinces will usually involve a three-digit code beginning with ☎ 0, then a six-digit number. Mobile phone numbers all have 10 digits, beginning with ☎ 08.

To direct-dial an international number from a private phone, you can first dial ☎ 001 then the country code. However, you wouldn't do that, because ☎ 001 is the most expensive way to call internationally and numerous other prefixes give you cheaper rates. These include ☎ 006, ☎ 007, ☎ 008 and ☎ 009, depending on which phone you're calling from. If you buy a local SIM card (see opposite), which we recommend, the network provider will tell you which prefix to use; read the fine print.

For operator-assisted international calls, dial ☎ 100. For free local directory assistance call ☎ 1133 inside Bangkok.

A useful CAT office (Map p116) stands next to the main post office, and the TOT office (Map p108) on Th Ploenchit is mainly an internet cafe but does have one phone for Home Country Direct calls – buy a phonecard first.

Payphones are common throughout Bangkok, though too often they're beside the thundering traffic of a major thoroughfare. Red phones are for local calls, blue are for local and long-distance calls (within Thailand), and the green phones are for use with phonecards. Calls start at 1B for three minutes; for mobile numbers it's 3B per minute. Local calls from private phones cost 3B, with no time limit.

Internet Phone & Phonecards

The cheapest way to call internationally is via the internet, and many internet cafes in Bangkok are set up for phone calls. Some have Skype loaded and (assuming there's a working headset) you can use that for just the regular per-hour internet fee. Others might have their own VoIP (Voice over Internet Protocol) service at cheap international rates.

CAT offers the PhoneNet card, which comes in denominations of 200B, 300B, 500B and 1000B and allows you to call overseas via VoIP for less than regular rates. You can call from any phone (landline, your mobile etc). Quality is good and rates represent excellent value; refills are available. Cards are available from any CAT office or online at www.thaitelephone.com, from which you get the necessary codes and numbers immediately. See www.thaitelephone.com/EN/RateTable for rates.

That table also displays rates for CAT's standard ThaiCard, a prepaid international calling card selling for 300B and 500B. You can use the ThaiCard codes from either end, eg calling the UK from Thailand or calling Thailand from the UK. These are better value than Lenso cards, which are used from payphones.

Skype aside, these options are all more expensive than the right prepaid SIM card…

Mobile Phones

If you have a GSM phone you will probably be able to use it on roaming in Thailand. If you have endless cash, or you only want to send text messages, you might be happy to do that. Otherwise, think about buying a local SIM card.

Buying a prepaid SIM is as difficult as finding a 7-Eleven. The market is super-competitive and deals vary so check websites first, but expect to get a SIM for as little as 49B. More expensive SIMs might come with pre-loaded talk time; if not then recharge cards are sold at the same stores and range from 100B to 500B. Per-minute rates start at less than 50 satang. Calling internationally the network will have a promotional code (eg ☎ 006 instead of ☎ 001) that affords big discounts on the standard international rates. If you're using an iPhone then the number of open wi-fi connections in Bangkok should keep the costs down. The main networks:

AIS (www.12call.ais.co.th) AIS offers wide coverage across Thailand; One-2-Call is the prepaid option.

DTAC (www.dtac.co.th) Lots of options, including Happy (www.happy.co.th) for prepaid SIM.

True Move (www.truemove.com) Probably the cheapest of the lot, with the Inter SIM offering international calls to many countries for 1B a minute, and cheap local calls too. The network is not as good outside Bangkok.

If your phone is locked, head down to Mahboonkrong (MBK) shopping centre (p142) to get it unlocked, or to shop for a new or cheap used phone (they start at less than 2000B).

TIME

Thailand is seven hours ahead of GMT/UTC. Thus, noon in Bangkok is 9pm the previous day in Los Angeles, midnight the same day in New York, 5am in London, 6am in Paris, 1pm in Perth, and 3pm in Sydney. Times are an hour later in countries or regions that are on Daylight Saving Time (DST). Thailand does not use daylight saving.

The official year in Thailand is reckoned from the Western calendar year 543 BC, the beginning of the Buddhist Era (BE), so that AD 2011 is 2554 BE, AD 2012 is 2555 BE etc. All dates in this book refer to the Western calendar.

TOILETS

If you don't want to pee against a tree like the túk-túk drivers, you can stop in at any shopping centre, hotel or fast-food restaurant for facilities. Shopping centres typically charge 1B to 2B for a visit, and some of the larger shopping centres on Th Silom and Th Ploenchit have toilets for the disabled. Toilet paper is rarely provided, so carry an emergency stash or do as the locals do and use the hose (an acquired skill). In older buildings and wát you'll still find squat toilets, but in modern Bangkok expect to be greeted by a throne.

TOURIST INFORMATION

Bangkok has two organisations that handle tourism matters: the Tourism Authority of Thailand (TAT) for country-wide information, and Bangkok Tourist Division (BTD) for city-specific information. Also be aware that travel agents in the train station and near tourist centres co-opt 'T.A.T.' and 'Information' as part of their name to lure in commissions. These places are not officially sanctioned information services, but just agencies registered with the TAT. So how can you tell the difference? Apparently it's all in the full stops – 'T.A.T.' means agency; 'TAT' is official.

The Bangkok Tourist Division (BTD; Map p68; ☎ 0 2225 7612-14; www.bangkoktourist.com; 17/1 Th Phra Athit; ⏰ 8am-7pm Mon-Fri, 9am-5pm Sat & Sun), operated by the Bangkok Metropolitan Administration (BMA), has this main office near Saphan Phra Pinklao with well-informed staff and a wealth of brochures, maps and event schedules. Kiosks and booths around town, and particularly in major shopping malls, are less useful, but do have maps; look for the green-on-white symbol of a mahout on an elephant.

The larger TAT (☎ 1672 for assistance; www.tourism thailand.org; ⏰ 8am-8pm) Head Office (Map p126; ☎ 0 2250 5500; 1600 Phetchaburi Tat Mai; Makkasan, Ratchathewi; ⏰ 8.30am-4.30pm Mon-Fri); Banglamphu (Map p82; ☎ 0 2283 1555, ext 1556; cnr Th Ratchadamnoen Nok & Th Chakrapatdipong; ⏰ 8.30am-4.30pm); Suvarnabhumi International Airport (☎ 0 2134 4077; International Terminal, 2nd fl, near Exit Door 1 & Exit Door 10; ⏰ 8am-10pm) has well-stocked offices with brochures and maps covering the whole country. The Banglamphu branch is also home to the Tourist Police (Map p82; ☎ 1155; ⏰ 24hr). If you need information over the phone we strongly recommend you call the ☎ 1672 line, not the offices themselves. Questions can be answered online by clicking through the '1672 Tourist Hotline' link from the website.

TAT Offices Abroad

TAT has 20 offices scattered about the globe, mainly in Europe, Asia, North America and Australia. For a full list, with exhaustive contact details, see www.tourismthailand.org/tat-oversea-office.

TRAVELLERS WITH DISABILITIES

Bangkok presents one large, ongoing obstacle course for the mobility-impaired, with its high kerbs, uneven pavements and nonstop traffic. Many of the city's streets must be crossed via pedestrian bridges flanked with steep stairways, while buses and boats don't stop long enough to accommodate even the mildly disabled. Aside from some Skytrain and Metro stations, ramps or other access points for wheelchairs are rare.

A few top-end hotels make consistent design efforts to provide disabled access. Other deluxe hotels with high employee-to-guest ratios are usually good about providing staff help where building design fails. For the rest, you're pretty much left to your own resources. These companies and websites might help:

Asia Pacific Development Centre on Disability (www.apcdfoundation.org)

Society for Accessible Travel & Hospitality (www.sath.org)

Wheelchair Tours to Thailand (www.wheelchairtours.com)

VISAS

Thailand has developed a penchant for changing its immigration laws in recent years, ostensibly to get rid of illegal workers and 'bad influences' such as sex tourists. At the time we went to press the citizens of 42 countries, including most Western European countries, Australia, Canada, Hong Kong, Japan, New Zealand, Singapore and the USA, could still enter Thailand without a visa. If you arrive by air you could stay for up to 30 days, but coming overland you can only stay for 15 days. Either way, citizens of Brazil, Republic of Korea and Peru may enter without a visa for 90 days. For a full list of eligible countries and other visa matters, see the Royal Thai Ministry of Foreign Affairs website: www.mfa.go.th/web/12.php.

Thai authorities love a good crackdown and periodic immigration offensives have meant, in recent years, the once-ignored requirement of an onward ticket is being more strictly enforced, usually by airline staff in the departing city. We've heard of several people who had to buy an onward ticket just to get onto the plane; it can be refunded later, with a penalty. Chances are this won't be a problem, but it's worth remembering that the better dressed you are, the less likely you are to be hassled.

If you're planning to stay longer than 30 days it's best to get a 60-day tourist visa or multiple-entry tourist visa before you arrive. These can then be extended by 30 days at any visa office; see below.

Other Visas

Thai embassies and consulates issue a variety of other visas for people on business, students, retirees or those with employment in Thailand. The Non-Immigrant Visa comes in several classifications and is good for 90 days. To stay longer without needing to constantly renew you need an education visa (minimum requirement four hours a week of Thai classes), an investment visa (minimum requirement 10 million baht – ka-ching!) or a work permit. If you plan to apply for a Thai work permit, you'll need a Non-Immigrant Visa first. Getting a Non-Immigrant Visa with the intention of working in Thailand can be difficult and involves a tedious amount of paperwork. If you get one, usually with the support of an employer, you'll likely end up at the One-Stop Service Centre (☎ 0 2209 1100; www.immigration.go.th; 18th fl, Chamchuree Sq, 319 Th Payathai, cnr Tha Phra Ram IV, Samyan) for several hours of paper pushing.

Note that Transit Visas no longer exist. For information and discussion about all things visa, see www.thaivisa.com.

Visa Extensions & Renewals

The 60-day Tourist Visa can be extended by up to 30 days at the discretion of Thai immigration authorities. Rule changes that limited people on tourist visas staying longer than 90 days in any six-month period are no longer being enforced (though that could change at any time). Which means you can, for now, do a visa run every 90 days and, if you can persuade the Thai officials in Vientiane, Phnom Penh or Penang to give you another 60-day visa, stay quite a while.

In Bangkok, extensions are handled by the Immigration Bureau office (Map p132; ☎ 0 2141 9889, Call Center 1178; Bldg B, Government Center, Soi 7, Th Chaeng Watthana, Thung Hong Song, Laksi; ☺ 8.30am-noon & 1-4.30pm Mon-Fri); elsewhere any immigration office will do. A fee of 1900B will be charged, and you'll need the usual mug shots. Some travel agencies can also organise extensions.

The 15- or 30-day no-visa stay can be extended for a maximum of seven days for 1900B. It's better to get a proper tourist visa. It is, however, possible to plan your itinerary so you leave the country after 15/30 days and get another 15/30 days when you return. Currently this can be done numerous times before officials start asking questions, but this could change at any time.

If you overstay your visa the usual penalty is a fine of 500B for each extra day, with a 20,000B limit (after that, more trouble awaits). Children under 14 travelling with a parent do not have to pay the penalty.

VOLUNTEERING

Volunteering seems to be all the rage at the moment, and Thailand is one of the favourite destinations. Most volunteering positions are in rural Thailand, but there are also plenty of possibilities in Bangkok. Working in some capacity with people who need your help can make a difference and be rewarding both to you and them. But it's not all sweetness and light, and it's important to understand what you're getting yourself into. Unless you know the country, speak the language and have skills needed in a particular field (computing, health and teaching, for example), what you can offer in a short period will largely be limited to manual labour – a commodity not in short supply in Thailand. Having said that, if you can match your skills to a project that needs them, this can be a great way to spend time in Thailand.

There are two main forms of volunteering. For those interested in a long-term commitment, typically two or three years, there are a few long-established organisations that will help you learn the language, place you in a position that will, hopefully, be appropriate to your skills, and pay you (just barely). Such organisations include the following:

Australian Volunteers International (www.australian volunteers.com)

US Peace Corps (www.peacecorps.gov)

Volunteer Service Abroad (www.vsa.org.nz)

Voluntary Service Overseas VSO Canada (www.vso canada.org); VSO UK (www.vso.org.uk)

The more popular form of volunteering, sometimes called 'voluntourism', is something you actually pay to do. This is a fast-growing market, and a quick web search for 'Thailand volunteering' will turn up pages of companies offering to place you in a project in return for your hard-earned. With these companies you can be a volunteer for periods ranging from a week to months or even years. Fees vary, but start at about €500 for four weeks. The projects can be very good, ongoing affairs with a solid chance of success. But some are not. The list below is a starting point and should not be read as a recommendation. Do your own research and check out all the options before making a decision; consider phoning them to ask, among other things, where your money will go.

Locally focused organisations include Volunthai (www.volunthai.com) and Thai Experience (www. thai-experience.org). Other general volunteering sites worth looking at are the Global Volunteer Network (www.volunteer.org.nz), Idealist (www.idealist. org) and Volunteer Abroad (www.volunteerabroad.com), which lists available positions with a variety of companies. Multicountry organisations that sell volunteering trips:

Cross Cultural Solutions (www.crossculturalsolutions.org)

Cultural Embrace (www.culturalembrace.com)

Global Crossroad (www.globalcrossroad.com)

Global Service Corps (www.globalservicecorps.org)

Institute for Field Research Expeditions (www.ifre volunteers.org)

Open Mind Projects (www.openmindprojects.org)

Starfish Ventures (www.starfishventures.co.uk)

Thai Volunteer (www.thaivolunteer.org)

Transitions Abroad (www.transitionsabroad.com)

Travel to Teach (www.travel-to-teach.org)

WOMEN TRAVELLERS

Contrary to popular myth, Thailand doesn't receive a higher percentage of male visitors than most other countries. In fact around 40% of visitors are women, a higher ratio than the worldwide average as measured by the World Tourism Organization. The overall increase for women visitors has climbed faster than that for men in almost every year since the early 1990s.

Everyday incidents of sexual harassment are much less common in Thailand than in India, Indonesia or Malaysia, and this might lull women familiar with those countries into thinking that Thailand is safer than it is. If you're a woman travelling alone it's worth pairing up with other travellers when moving around at night or, at the least, avoiding quiet areas. Make sure hotel and guesthouse rooms are secure at night – if they're not, request another room or move to another hotel or guesthouse.

When women are attacked in Thailand it usually happens in remote beach or mountain areas, and very rarely in Bangkok. So while common-sense precautions are recommended at all times, be especially vigilant if you're on a beach, and even more if you're alone and you've been drinking.

Whether it's tampons or any other women-specific product, you'll have no trouble finding it in Bangkok.

WORK

Bangkok's status as the heart of the Thai economy provides a variety of employment opportunities for foreigners, and tens of thousands live and work here. Having said that, *fà·ràng* are not allowed to work in certain professions (such as medical doctors) and finding a job can be more difficult than it is in more developed countries.

All employment in Thailand requires a Thai work permit. Thai law defines work as 'exerting one's physical energy or employing one's knowledge, whether or not for wages or other benefits', so theoretically even volunteer and missionary work requires a permit. Work permits should be obtained via an employer, who may file for the permit before the employee arrives in-country. The permit itself is not issued until the employee enters Thailand on a valid Non-Immigrant Visa (see p282).

For information about work permits, contact any Thai embassy abroad or check the Ministry of Foreign Affairs website (www.mfa.go.th/web/12.php). No joy? Seek solace and advice on the message boards of www.thaivisa.com.

Busking is illegal in Thailand, where it is legally lumped together with begging.

Teaching English

As in the rest of East and Southeast Asia, there is a high demand for English speakers to provide instruction to Thai citizens. Those with academic credentials such as teaching certificates or degrees in English as a second language will get first crack at the better-paying jobs, such as those at universities and international schools. But there are perhaps hundreds of private language-teaching establishments in Bangkok that hire noncredentialled teachers by the hour. Private tutoring is also a possibility. International oil companies pay the highest salaries for English instructors, but are also quite choosy.

A website maintained by a Bangkok-based English teacher, www.ajarn.com, has tips on finding jobs and pretty much everything else you need to know about getting into the teaching game in Thailand. If you're more dedicated (or desperate) the Yellow Pages (www.yellow.co.th/Bangkok) has contact details for hundreds of schools, universities and language schools.

LANGUAGE

Learning some Thai is a wonderful way to enhance your stay in Bangkok; naturally, the more you pick up, the closer you get to Thailand's culture and people. You'll probably have mixed results with your first attempts to speak the language, but keep trying. Listen closely to the way the Thais themselves use the various tones – you'll catch on quickly. Don't let laughter at your linguistic forays discourage you; this apparent amusement is really an expression of appreciation.

Travellers are particularly urged to make the effort to mix with Thai college and university students. Thai students are usually eager to meet visitors from other countries. They will often know some English, so communication isn't as difficult as it may be with some other locals, and they're generally willing to teach you useful Thai words and phrases.

If you'd like a more comprehensive guide to the language, get a copy of Lonely Planet's compact and user-friendly *Thai* phrasebook.

PRONUNCIATION

Tones

In Thai the meaning of a single syllable may be altered by means of different tones. For example, depending on the tone, the syllable *mai* can mean 'new', 'burn', 'wood', 'not?' or 'not'.

The following chart represents tones to show their relative pitch values:

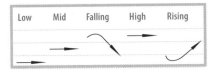

| Low | Mid | Falling | High | Rising |

The tones are explained as follows:

low tone – 'flat' like the mid tone, but pronounced at the relative bottom of one's vocal range; it is low, level and with no inflection, eg *bàht* (baht – the Thai currency)
mid tone – pronounced 'flat', at the relative middle of the speaker's vocal range, eg *dee* (good); no tone mark is used
falling tone – sounds as if you are emphasising a word, or calling someone's name from afar, eg *mâi* (no/not)
high tone – pronounced near the relative top of the vocal range, as level as possible, eg *máh* (horse)
rising tone – sounds like the inflection used by English speakers to imply a question – 'Yes?', eg *săhm* (three)

Consonants

The majority of Thai consonants correspond closely to the English counterparts used to represent them in transliterations. The ones that will be unfamiliar to English speakers are ƀ (pronounced like a cross between 'b' and 'p', as in 'hipbag'), ɖ (pronounced like a cross between a 'd' and a 't', as in 'hardtop') and ng (pronounced as in 'sing', but differing from English in that this consonant can come at the beginning of a word; practise by saying 'singing' and then leave off the 'si-').

Vowels

The many different vowel sounds and combinations in Thai can be tricky at first.

i	as in 'bit'
ee	as in 'feet'
ai	as in 'aisle'
ah	as the 'a' in 'father'
a	as in 'about'; half as long as 'ah'
aa	as the 'a' in 'bat' or 'tab'
e	as in 'hen'
air	as in English, but with no 'r' sound
eu	as the 'er' in 'fern', but with no 'r' sound
u	as in 'put'
oo	as in 'food'
ow	as in 'now'
or	as in 'torn', but with no 'r' sound
o	as in 'hot'
oh	as the 'o' in 'toe'
eu·a	a combination of eu and a
ee·a	as 'ee-ya'
oo·a	as the 'our' in 'tour'
oo·ay	sounds like 'oo-way'
ew	as the 'ew' in 'new'
ee·o	as the 'io' in 'Rio'
aa·ou	as the 'a' in 'cat' followed by a short 'u' as in 'put'
eh·ou	as the 'e' in bed, followed by a short 'u' as in 'put'
oy	as in 'toy'

SOCIAL
Meeting People

Hello.
สวัสดี (ครับ/ค่ะ)   sà·wàt·dee (kráp/kâ) (m/f)
Goodbye.
ลาก่อน   lah gòrn
Please.
กรุณา   gà·rú·nah
Thank you (very much).
ขอบคุณ(มาก)   kòrp kun (mâhk)
Yes.
ใช่   châi
No.
ไม่ใช่   mâi châi

I
ผม/ดิฉัน   pŏm/dì·chăn (m/f)
you
คุณ   kun

Do you speak English?
คุณพูดภาษา   kun pôot pah·săh
อังกฤษได้ไหม   ang·grìt dâi măi
Do you understand?
เข้าใจไหม   kôw jai măi
I (don't) understand.
(ไม่)เข้าใจ   (mâi) kôw jai
My name is …
ผม/ดิฉันชื่อ...   pŏm/dì·chăn chêu … (m/f)

Could you please …?
ขอ...ได้ไหม   kŏr … dâi măi
  repeat that
  พูดอีกที   pôot èek tee
  speak more slowly
  พูดช้าลง   pôot cháh long
  write it down
  เขียนให้   kĕe·an hâi

Going Out

Is there a local entertainment guide?
มีคู่มือสถานบันเทิงบริเวณนี้ไหม
mee kôo meu sà·tăhn ban·teung bor·rí·wairn née măi

Where are the …?
...อยู่ที่ไหน
… yòo têe năi
  clubs
  ไนท์คลับ   nai kláp
  gay venues
  สถานบันเทิงเกย์   sà·tăhn ban·teung gair

  places to eat
  ร้านอาหาร   ráhn ah·hăhn
  pubs
  ผับ   pàp

What's on …?
มีอะไรทำ...
mee à·rai tam …
  locally
  แถวๆนี้   tăa·ou-tăa·ou née
  this weekend
  เสาร์อาทิตย์นี้   sŏw ah·tít née
  today
  วันนี้   wan née
  tonight
  คืนนี้   keun née

PRACTICAL
Question Words

Who?   ใคร   krai
What?   อะไร   à·rai
When?   เมื่อไร   mêu·a rai
Where?   ที่ไหน   têe năi
How?   อย่างไร   yàhng rai

Numbers & Amounts

0	ศูนย์	sŏon
1	หนึ่ง	nèung
2	สอง	sŏrng
3	สาม	săhm
4	สี่	sèe
5	ห้า	hâh
6	หก	hòk
7	เจ็ด	jèt
8	แปด	bàat
9	เก้า	gôw
10	สิบ	sip
11	สิบเอ็ด	sìp·èt
12	สิบสอง	sìp·sŏrng
13	สิบสาม	sìp·săhm
14	สิบสี่	sìp·sèe
15	สิบห้า	sìp·hâh
16	สิบหก	sìp·hòk
17	สิบเจ็ด	sìp·jèt
18	สิบแปด	sìp·bàat
19	สิบเก้า	sìp·gôw
20	ยี่สิบ	yêe·sìp
21	ยี่สิบเอ็ด	yêe·sìp·èt
22	ยี่สิบสอง	yêe·sìp·sŏrng
30	สามสิบ	săhm·sìp
40	สี่สิบ	sèe·sìp
50	ห้าสิบ	hâh·sìp
60	หกสิบ	hòk·sìp
70	เจ็ดสิบ	jèt·sìp

80	แปดสิบ	Ƀàat·sìp
90	เก้าสิบ	gôw·sìp
100	หนึ่งร้อย	nèung róy
1000	หนึ่งพัน	nèung pan
2000	สองพัน	sŏrng pan
10,000	หนึ่งหมื่น	nèung mèun
100,000	หนึ่งแสน	nèung săan
1,000,000	หนึ่งล้าน	nèung láhn

Days

Monday	วันจันทร์	wan jan
Tuesday	วันอังคาร	wan ang·kahn
Wednesday	วันพุธ	wan pút
Thursday	วันพฤหัสฯ	wan pà·réu·hàt
Friday	วันศุกร์	wan sùk
Saturday	วันเสาร์	wan sŏw
Sunday	วันอาทิตย์	wan ah·tít

Banking

I'd like to …
อยากจะ…
yàhk jà …
  change money
  แลกเงิน
  lâak ngeun
  change some travellers cheques
  แลกเช็คเดินทาง
  lâak chék deun tahng

Where's the nearest …?
…ที่ใกล้เคียงอยู่ที่ไหน
… têe glâi kee·ang yòo têe năi
  ATM
  ตู้เอทีเอ็ม
  dôo air·tee·em
  foreign exchange office
  ที่แลกเงินต่างประเทศ
  têe lâak ngeun đàhng Ƀrà·têt

Post

Where's the post office?
ที่ทำการไปรษณีย์อยู่ที่ไหน
têe tam gahn Ƀrai·sà·nee yòo têe năi

I want to send a …
อยากจะส่ง…
yàhk jà sòng …
  fax
  แฝกซ์   fàak
  parcel
  พัสดุ   pát·sà·dù
  postcard
  ไปรษณียบัตร   Ƀrai·sà·nee·yá·bàt

I want to buy …
อยากจะซื้อ…
yàhk jà séu …
  an envelope
  ซองจดหมาย   sorng jòt·măi
  a stamp
  แสตมป์   sà·đaam

Phones & Mobiles

I want to buy a phonecard.
อยากจะซื้อบัตรโทรศัพท์
yàhk jà séu bàt toh·rá·sàp
I want to make a call to …
อยากจะโทรไป…
yàhk jà toh Ƀai …

I'd like a/an …
ต้องการ…
đôrng gahn …
  adaptor plug
  ปลั๊กต่อ
  Ƀlák đòr
  charger for my phone
  เครื่องชาร์จสำหรับโทรศัพท์
  krêu·ang cháht săm·ràp toh·rá·sàp
  mobile/cell phone for hire
  เช่าโทรศัพท์มือถือ
  chôw toh·rá·sàp meu tĕu
  prepaid mobile/cell phone
  โทรศัพท์มือถือแบบจ่ายล่วงหน้า
  toh·rá·sàp meu tĕu bàap jài lôo·ang nâh
  SIM card for the … network
  บัตรซิมสำหรับเครือข่ายของ…
  bàt sim săm·ràp kreua kài kŏrng …

Internet

Where's the local internet cafe?
ร้านอินเตอร์เนตอยู่ที่ไหน
ráhn in·đeu·nét yòo têe năi

I'd like to …
อยากจะ…
yàhk jà …
  check my email
  ตรวจอีเมล   đròo·at ee·mehn
  get online
  ต่ออินเตอร์เนต   đòr in·đeu·nét

Transport

Are you available? (taxi)
ว่างไหม   wâhng măi
Please put the meter on.
เปิดมิเตอร์ด้วย   èut mí·đeu dôo·ay
หน่อย   nòy

How much is it to …?
ไป...เท่าไร   ฿ai … tôw·rai
Please take me to …
ขอพาไป...   kŏr pah ฿ai …

What time does the … leave?
...จะออกกี่โมง
… jà òrk gèe mohng
  bus
  รถเมล์   rót mair
  ferry
  เรือข้ามฟาก   reu·a kâhm fâhk
  train
  รถไฟ   rót fai

What time's the … bus?
รถเมล์...มากี่โมง
rót mair … mah gèe mohng
  first
  คันแรก   kan râak
  last
  คันสุดท้าย   kan sùt tái
  next
  คันต่อไป   kan đòr ฿ai

FOOD

breakfast
อาหารเช้า   ah·hăhn chów
lunch
อาหารเที่ยง   ah·hăhn têe·ang
dinner
อาหารเย็น   ah·hăhn yen
snack
อาหารว่าง   ah·hăhn wâhng

Can you recommend a …
แนะนำ...ได้ไหม
náa·nam … dâi măi
  bar/pub
  บาร์/ผับ   bah/pàp
  café
  ร้านกาแฟ   ráhn gah·faa
  restaurant
  ร้านอาหาร   ráhn ah·hăhn

For more detailed information on food and
dining out, see p152; for drinks, see p180.

EMERGENCIES

It's an emergency!
เป็นเหตุฉุกเฉิน
฿en hèt chùk chĕun

Could you please help me/us?
ช่วยได้ไหม
chôo·ay dâi măi
Call the police/a doctor/an ambulance!
ตามตำรวจ/หมอ/รถพยาบาลด้วย
đahm đam·ròo·at/mŏr/rót pá·yah·bahn
dôo·ay
Where's the police station?
สถานีตำรวจที่ใกล้เคียงอยู่ที่ไหน
sà·tăh·nee đam·ròo·at têe glâi kee·ang yòo
têe năi

HEALTH

Where's the nearest …?
...ที่ใกล้เคียงอยู่ที่ไหน
… têe glâi kee·ang yòo têe năi
  chemist
  ร้านขายยา   ráhn kăi yah
  doctor/dentist
  หมอ/หมอฟัน   mŏr/mŏr fan
  hospital
  โรงพยาบาล   rohng pá·yah·bahn

I need a doctor (who speaks English).
ต้องการหมอ(ที่พูดภาษาอังกฤษได้)
đôrng gahn mŏr (têe pôot pah·săh
ang·grìt dâi)
Could the doctor come here?
หมอมาที่นี่ได้ไหม
mŏr mah têe née dâi măi
I'm sick.
ผม/ดิฉันป่วย
pŏm/dì·chăn ฿òo·ay (m/f)

I have (a) …
ผม/ดิฉัน...
pŏm/dì·chăn … (m/f)
  diarrhoea
  เป็นโรคท้องร่วง   ฿en rôhk tórng
                                 rôo·ang
  fever
  เป็นไข้   ฿en kâi
  headache
  ปวดหัว   ฿òo·at hŏo·a
  pain
  เจ็บปวด   jèp ฿òo·at
  sore throat
  เจ็บคอ   jèp kor

LANGUAGE FOOD

GLOSSARY

baht – *bàht;* Thai currency

BMA – Bangkok Metropolitan Administration

BTS – Bangkok Mass Transit System

CAT – Communications Authority of Thailand

fà ràng – foreigner of European descent

Isan – *isǎan;* general term for northeastern Thailand, from the Sanskrit name for the medieval kingdom Isana, which encompassed parts of Cambodia and northeastern Thailand.

khlong – *klorng;* canal

MRTA – Metropolitan Rapid Transit Authority; agency responsible for the Metro subway.

rai – Thai unit of measurement (area); 1 rai = 1600 sq metres

Ratanakosin – style of architecture present in the late 19th to early 20th century, which combines traditional Thai and European forms; also known as 'old Bangkok'

reua hǎang yao – longtail boat

rót fai fáa – BTS Skytrain

rót fai đâi din – MRTA Metro (subway)

soi – *sawy;* lane or small road

TAT – Tourist Authority of Thailand

tha – pier

THAI – Thai Airways International

thanon – *thanǒn* (abbreviated 'Th' in this guide); road or street

TOT – Telephone Organisation of Thailand

trok – *tràwk;* alleyway

wát – Buddhist temple, monastery

THIS BOOK

The first Lonely Planet guide to Bangkok was published in 1992, researched and written by Joe Cummings. Andrew Burke was the coordinating author for this 9th edition and researched and updated the Introducing Bangkok, Getting Started, Neighbourhoods, Sports & Activities, Sleeping, Excursions, Transport and Directory chapters. Austin Bush researched and updated the Background, Shopping, Eating, Drinking & Nightlife and Entertainment & the Arts chapters. This guidebook was commissioned in Lonely Planet's Melbourne office, and produced by the following:

Commissioning Editors Tashi Wheeler, Shawn Low, Ilaria Walker

Coordinating Editors Erin Richards, Louisa Syme

Coordinating Cartographer David Kemp

Coordinating Layout Designer Paul Iacono

Managing Editor Brigitte Ellemor

Managing Cartographer David Connolly

Managing Layout Designer Celia Wood

Assisting Editors David Carroll, Susie Ashworth, Gabrielle Stefanos

Assisting Cartographers Peter Shields, Jacqueline Nguyen

Cover Research Pepi Bluck, lonelyplanetimages.com

Internal Image Research Jane Hart, lonelyplanetimages.com

Project Managers Chris Girdler, Chris Love

Language Content Laura Crawford, Annelies Mertens

Thanks to Helen Christinis, Daniel Corbett, Bruce Evans, Mark Germanchis, Michelle Glynn, Indra Kilfoyle, Lisa Knights, Rebecca Lalor, John Mazzocchi, Dan Moore, Katie O'Connell, Trent Paton, Kirsten Rawlings, Averil Robertson, Mick Ruff, Fiona Siseman, John Taufa, Nick Thorpe, Angela Tinson, Juan Winata

Cover photographs Wat Arun and Mae Nam Chao Phraya at night, Paolo Cordelli (top); Thai girl in traditional dance costume in Bangkok, Bill Wassman (bottom)

Internal photographs All images are copyright of the photographer unless otherwise indicated. Many of the images in this guide are available for licensing from Lonely Planet Images: www.lonelyplanetimages.com.

THANKS
ANDREW BURKE

I'd like to offer a heartfelt *kòrp kun kráp* to the many people in Bangkok who helped make this book possible. First and foremost it was great to have my wife Anne around for an entire LP job and get her feminine feedback on things Bangkok. Mason Florence and Stuart McDonald were generous with their tips, and May Nekkham, Whan Kullamas, Gun Aramwit and Tui (enjoy the monastery) at MeMay Café helped keep me sane during months of writing. Thanks to my coauthor Austin Bush and at LPHQ in Melbourne a big thank you to my wonderfully patient and good-natured commissioning editors Tashi Wheeler, Shawn Low and Ilaria Walker, and to the editors and cartographers who worked hard to make this a better book.

THE LONELY PLANET STORY

Fresh from an epic journey across Europe, Asia and Australia in 1972, Tony and Maureen Wheeler sat at their kitchen table stapling together notes. The first Lonely Planet guidebook, *Across Asia on the Cheap*, was born.

Travellers snapped up the guides. Inspired by their success, the Wheelers began publishing books to Southeast Asia, India and beyond. Demand was prodigious, and the Wheelers expanded the business rapidly to keep up. Over the years, Lonely Planet extended its coverage to every country and into the virtual world via lonelyplanet.com and the Thorn Tree message board.

As Lonely Planet became a globally loved brand, Tony and Maureen received several offers for the company. But it wasn't until 2007 that they found a partner whom they trusted to remain true to the company's principles of travelling widely, treading lightly and giving sustainably. In October of that year, BBC Worldwide acquired a 75% share in the company, pledging to uphold Lonely Planet's commitment to independent travel, trustworthy advice and editorial independence.

Today, Lonely Planet has offices in Melbourne, London and Oakland, with over 500 staff members and 300 authors. Tony and Maureen are still actively involved with Lonely Planet. They're travelling more often than ever, and they're devoting their spare time to charitable projects. And the company is still driven by the philosophy of *Across Asia on the Cheap*: 'All you've got to do is decide to go and the hardest part is over. So go!'

SEND US YOUR FEEDBACK

We love to hear from travellers — your comments keep us on our toes and help make our books better. Our well-travelled team reads every word on what you loved or loathed about this book. Although we cannot reply individually to postal submissions, we always guarantee that your feedback goes straight to the appropriate authors, in time for the next edition. Each person who sends us information is thanked in the next edition and the most useful submissions are rewarded with a free book.

To send us your updates — and find out about Lonely Planet events, newsletters and travel news — visit our award-winning website: lonelyplanet.com/contact.

Note: We may edit, reproduce and incorporate your comments in Lonely Planet products such as guidebooks, websites and digital products, so let us know if you don't want your comments reproduced or your name acknowledged. For a copy of our privacy policy visit lonelyplanet.com/privacy.

AUSTIN BUSH

I'd like to thank the book's previous authors, China Williams and Joe Cummings, for their excellent work, some of which still survives, my patient and incredibly helpful coordinating author Andrew Burke and commissioning editor Tashi Wheeler, map guru David Connolly and the rest of the LP staff in Melbourne, my local experts Gregoire Glachant, Steven Pettifor and Kong Rithdee, as well as those who introduced me to new places and joined me at the old, including Yuthika Charoenrungruang, Ron Diaz, Nick Grossman, Richard Hermes, Yaowalak Itthichaiwarakom, Wes and Ann Hsu, Paul Hutt and Maylee Thavat.

OUR READERS

Many thanks to the travellers who used the last edition and wrote to us with helpful hints, useful advice and interesting anecdotes:
John Cole, Tony Day, Ca Favier, Daniel Furrer, John Hambleton, Leslaw Kula, Ramamurthi Kunjithapadam, Jason Leis, Alona Lisitsa, Philip Mainwaring, Barbara Mueller, Rickee Ng, Maggie Olson, Soniya P, Stig Bjerregaard Pedersen, Lesueur Romain, Gee Turf, Antoni P Uni, Suresh Viswanathan, Lauren Wistrom

Notes

INDEX

A

Abhisek Dusit Throne Hall 94
accessories, *see* Shopping *subindex*
accommodation 212-32, *see also* Sleeping *subindex*
  Amphawa 249
  Ayuthaya 240
  Banglamphu 213-17
  Chinatown 218-19
  costs 213
  Dusit 217-18
  greater Bangkok 232
  internet resources 220, 224
  Kanchanaburi 257
  Khao Yai National Park 260-1
  Ko Ratanakosin 212-13
  Ko Samet 244-5
  Lumphini 221, 226-7
  Phetchaburi 252
  Ploenchit 219-21
  Pratunam 219-21
  riverside area 221-3
  Siam Square 219-21
  Silom 221, 223-6
  Suvarnabhumi International Airport 232
  Thanon Sukhumvit 228-32
  Thewet 217-18
  Thonburi 212-13

000 map pages
000 photographs

activities 204-10, *see also individual activities,* Sports & Activities *subindex*
addresses 275
Aids 273
air pollution 273
air travel 262-3
ambulance 271-2
Amphawa 236, 247
  accommodation 249
  attractions 248
  food 249
Ananda Mahidol, King 26
Ananda Samakhon Throne Hall 94
animism 55-6
antiques 138, 148, *see also* Shopping *subindex*
Ao Cho 241
Ao Hin Khok 241, 244
Ao Klang 243, 245
Ao Noi Na 243, 245
Ao Nuan 241, 244-5
Ao Phai 241, 244
Ao Phrao 243
Ao Phrao 245
Ao Phutsa 241, 244-5
Ao Thap Thim 241, 244-5
Ao Thian 241-3, 245
Ao Wong Deuan 241, 245
apartments, *see* Sleeping *subindex*
aquariums, *see* Sights *subindex*
architecture 38-41
area codes, *see inside front cover*
art, *see* Shopping *subindex*
art galleries, *see* Entertainment & the Arts *subindex*
arts 35-51, *see also* Entertainment & the Arts *subindex, individual arts*
Asanha Bucha 21
ATMs 277
Ayuthaya 24, 234, 236-40, **237**, **12**
  accommodation 240
  attractions 236-9
  drinking 240

food 239
  information 239
  transport 238
Ayuthaya Historical Park 236-9

B

Baan Baat 81-4, 89
Baan Krua 106-7, 111
  walking tour 114
Baiyoke II tower 112
bamboo rafting 255
Bang Kwang prison 274
Bang Pa-In 239
Bangkok Bank 40, 103
Bangkok Design Festival 22
Bangkok International Fashion Week 20
Bangkok International Film Festival 21
Bangkok Jazz Festival 22
Bangkok Pride Week 22
Banglamphu **82-3**
  accommodation 213-17
  attractions 80-91
  food 160-3
  shopping 137-8
  transport 81
  walking tours 89-91, 162-3, **90**, **163**
Bangrak Market 123
Bank of Asia 119-20
bargaining 141
bars, *see* Drinking & Nightlife *subindex*
bathrooms 281
beaches 241-4
beer 180-1
Benjakiti Park 128-9, 130
Bhumibol, King 22, 29
bicycle travel, *see* cycling
bird-watching 249, 257
boat travel 240, 263-4
  dinner cruises 169
  klorng boats 264
  longtail boats 121
  rafting & kayaking 255
  river ferries 263-4, **6**
  trips 241, 248, 278
books, *see also* Shopping *subindex*
  architecture 41

classical literature 42
contemporary literature 42-3
  fiction 43
  travel literature 223
boxing, *see* moo-ay tai
Brahmanism 56
bridges, *see* Sights *subindex*
Buddha images
  Emerald Buddha 29, 67, 71
  Golden Buddha 99, 103-4
  Reclining Buddha 70, **5**
Buddhism 20, 21, 22, 55
buildings, notable 40, *see also* Sights *subindex*
bus travel 264-5
business hours 268
  bars & clubs 192
  restaurants 159
  street vendors 171

C

cafes, *see* Eating *subindex*
camera equipment 143, 145
camping 260
  equipment 143
car travel 265
cathedrals, *see* Sights *subindex*
cave temples 255
caves 251, 255
cell phones 281
cemeteries 253-4
Chakkaphat, King 24
Chakri Day 273
Chakri dynasty 25-6
Chakri, Phraya 25
Chao Phraya Express 240, 263
Chatuchak Weekend Market 148-9, **149**, **7**
chemists 276
children, travel with 121, 268-9
  internet resources 269
  theme parks 260
Children's Discovery Museum 121, 131
Chinatown **98**, **16**
  accommodation 218-19
  attractions 97-104

INDEX

000 map pages
000 photographs

INDEX

MAP LEGEND

ROUTES

Tollway	Mall/Steps
Freeway	Tunnel
Primary	Pedestrian Overpass
Secondary	Walking Tour
Tertiary	Walking Tour Detour
Lane	*Walking Trail*
Unsealed Road	*Walking Path*

TRANSPORT

Ferry	Rail
Skytrain	Metro

HYDROGRAPHY

River, Creek	Water

BOUNDARIES

Ancient Wall

AREA FEATURES

Building	Land
Campus	Mall
Cemetery, Christian	Market
Cemetery, Other	Park
Forest	Sports

POPULATION

⊙ CAPITAL (NATIONAL)	⊚ CAPITAL (STATE)
● Large City	◉ Medium City
○ Small City	○ Town, Village

SYMBOLS

Information
- Bank, ATM
- Embassy/Consulate
- Hospital, Medical
- Information
- Internet Facilities
- Police Station
- Post Office, GPO
- Telephone

Sights
- Beach
- Buddhist
- Castle, Fortress
- Christian
- Hindu

- Monument
- Museum, Gallery
- Point of Interest
- Pool
- Sikh
- Taoist
- Zoo, Bird Sanctuary

Shopping
- Shopping

Eating
- Eating

Entertainment
- Entertainment

Arts
- Arts

Drinking
- Cafe
- Drinking

Sleeping
- Sleeping
- Camping

Transport
- Airport, Airfield
- Bus Station
- Parking Area
- Petrol Station

Geographic
- Lookout
- National Park
- River Flow
- Waterfall

Published by Lonely Planet Publications Pty Ltd
ABN 36 005 607 983

Australia (Head Office)
Locked Bag 1, Footscray, Victoria 3011,
☎03 8379 8000, fax 03 8379 8111,
talk2us@lonelyplanet.com.au

USA 150 Linden St, Oakland, CA 94607,
☎510 250 6400, toll free 800 275 8555,
fax 510 893 8572, info@lonelyplanet.com

UK 2nd fl, 186 City Rd, London, EC1V 2NT,
☎020 7106 2100, fax 020 7106 2101,
go@lonelyplanet.co.uk

Mixed Sources
Product group from well-managed
forests and other controlled sources
www.fsc.org   Cert no. SGS-COC-005002
© 1996 Forest Stewardship Council
FSC